ARCHAEOLOGICAL INVENTORY OF COUNTY CAVAN

FARDAL SEANDÁLAÍOCHTA CHONTAE AN CHABHÁIN

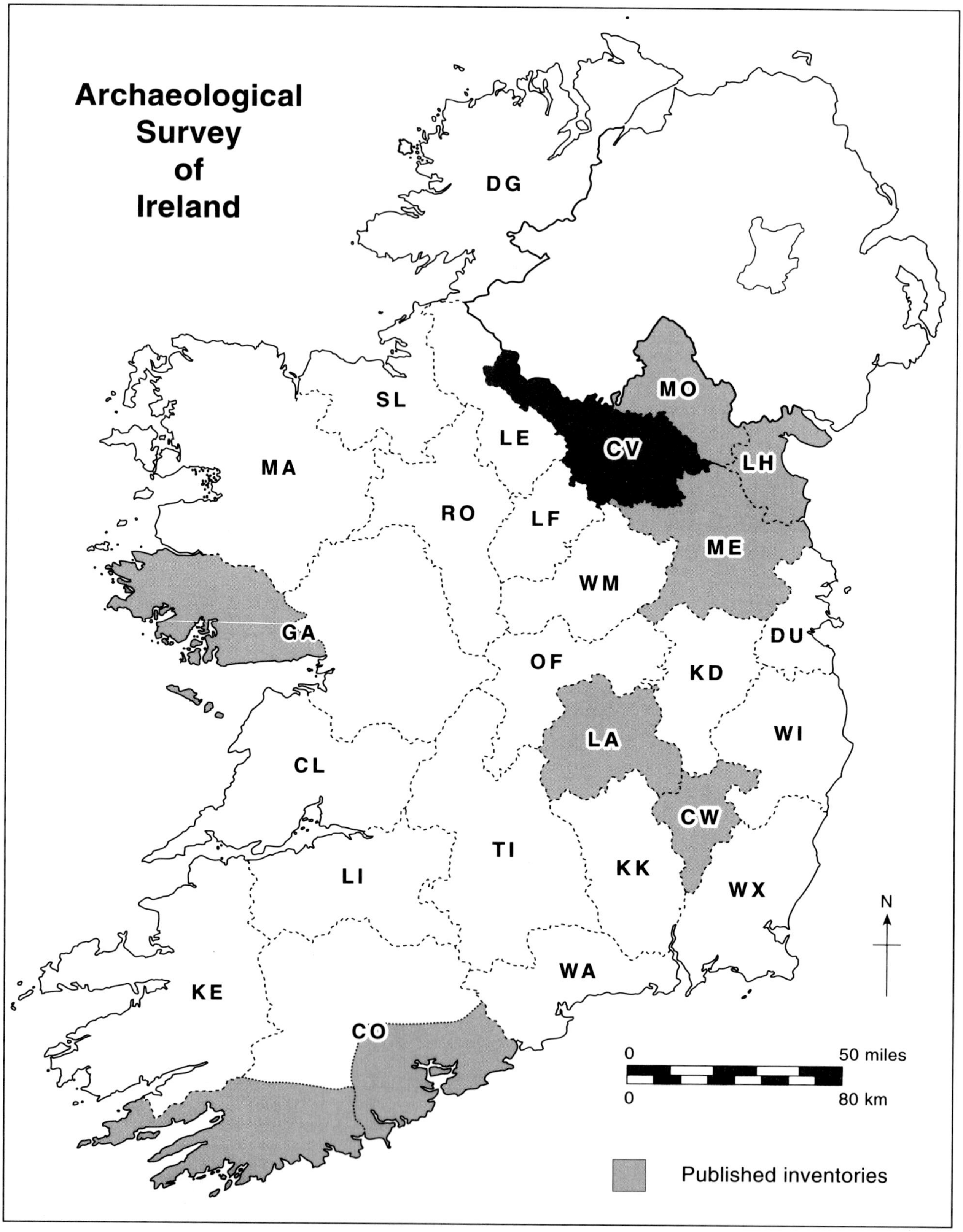
Archaeological Survey of Ireland
DG
MO
SL
LE
CV
LH
MA
RO
LF
ME
WM
GA
DU
OF
KD
LA
WI
CL
CW
TI
LI
KK
WX
N
WA
KE
CO
0
50 miles
0
80 km
Published inventories

Archaeological Inventory of County Cavan

Compiled by

Patrick F. O'Donovan

BAILE ÁTHA CLIATH
ARNA FHOILSIÚ AG OIFIG AN tSOLÁTHAIR
Le ceannach díreach ón
OIFIG DHÍOLTA FOILSEACHÁN RIALTAIS
TEACH SUN ALLIANCE, SRÁID THEACH LAIGHEAN, BAILE ÁTHA CLIATH 2
nó trí aon díoltóir leabhar

DUBLIN
PUBLISHED BY THE STATIONERY OFFICE
To be purchased through any bookseller, or directly from the
GOVERNMENT PUBLICATIONS SALE OFFICE
SUN ALLIANCE HOUSE, MOLESWORTH STREET, DUBLIN 2

PRICE: £23.00

General Editor
P. David Sweetman

Editor
Elizabeth FitzPatrick

Field Archaeologists
Brian Duffy
Vincent Hurley
Helen Lanigan-Wood
Joseph McCabe
Patrick F. O'Donovan
James Reynolds
P. David Sweetman

Photographs
Con Brogan
Peter Crossan

Location Maps
Brian MacDonald

Cover Design
John O'Regan

Archaeological Assistants
Susan Dixon
Patrick O'Donnell
Michael Walker

ACKNOWLEDGEMENTS

The Commissioners of Public Works wish to acknowledge the assistance of the following in the production of this inventory: Eamon Cody of the Archaeological Division, Ordnance Survey, for entries 1–59; Margaret Gowen for entries 169–75; Fionnbarr Moore (OPW) for entries 182–3; Conleth Manning (OPW) for entries 1796 and 1899; the staff of Cavan County Library, especially Brian Connolly; the staff of the Antiquities Division of the National Museum of Ireland; Bridget O'Brien and Ciara Masterson (OPW); Diarmuid C. and Maura O'Donovan and the staff of Jennings O'Donovan (Overseas) Sligo.

ISBN: 07076-1694-8.
Typeset by Wordwell Ltd
Printed in the Republic of Ireland by
Betaprint

OPW

Contents

Black and White Plates

Colour Plates

Introduction

The publication of the **Archaeological Inventory of County Cavan** marks the completion of the second stage of the archaeological survey of the county. The Sites and Monuments Record (SMR) issued in 1991 represented the initial stage and was based primarily on an examination of select documentary sources, including the various editions of the Ordnance Survey maps and other cartographic sources, archaeological, historical and other publications, Office of Public Works field reports and topographical files, National Museum of Ireland and Irish Tourism Association files and Ordnance Survey Letters and Memoirs. In addition the aerial photographic coverage for the county was consulted. The SMR comprises a set of archaeological constraint maps with accompanying manual. It is designed to be used primarily by the planning authorities and those agencies and individuals whose work affects ancient monuments in any way.

The **Archaeological Inventory of County Cavan** was compiled between 1990 and 1994 and is one in an ongoing series of county archaeological inventories published by the Archaeological Survey, Office of Public Works. The inventories are aimed both at the general reader and those engaged in scholarly research. It is hoped that this volume will prove a useful tool in promoting an awareness and appreciation of the unique archaeological heritage of County Cavan.

The archaeological sites identified in the SMR were visited and recorded in some detail. A number of additional sites were identified in the course of fieldwork. Due to limitations of time and personnel, only a few of the county's many crannógs were inspected. The chapter on megalithic tombs was contributed by Eamon Cody, Archaeological Division, Ordnance Survey. The chapter on fulachta fiadh is based on information provided by Margaret Gowen. As a general rule, sites thought to postdate 1700 AD are not included in this volume. Some monument types, for example caldraghs, holy wells and sweathouses, were used over a long period of time and individual examples are often difficult to date closely on the basis of the available evidence.

The entries are divided into thirty-four chapters according to their archaeological classification. Each chapter is prefaced by a brief introduction. Within each chapter the sites are listed in alphabetical order according to the townland in which they occur. Where several townlands have the same name, they are arranged by the Ordnance Survey sheet number. Sites within the same townland and of the same classification are listed in the order of the SMR number. Where a site occurs in more than one townland all of the applicable townlands are listed. Place-names in the text are taken directly from the Ordnance Survey maps, even where current local usage or spelling may differ slightly. Each entry has a unique number for reference purposes and for use with the accompanying location maps.

When looking for a site the reader should consult the townland name index and the location maps. The townland name index refers the reader to the appropriate inventory number. The position of each monument with its accompanying inventory number is marked on the location maps. Single sites are shown as dots and open circles. Multiple sites are marked as ringed dots. Belturbet and Cavan town are shaded indicating the areas of archaeological potential as defined by the Office of Public Works, Urban Archaeological Survey (Bradley and Dunne 1989). The maps are based on the most recent edition of the Ordnance Survey half-inch maps.

The entries are laid out in the following manner:

The first line gives the site's unique inventory number and its townland name.

The second line contains locational information, listed in the following order: Ordnance Survey six-inch Sheet/Plan/Trace, coordinates on the Ordnance Survey six-inch sheet in centimetres (Eastings and Northings), Ordnance Survey designation on the current edition of the six-inch map, the Ordnance Datum (OD) given in feet, and a ten-figure National Grid reference. Monuments or sites which have not been precisely located are marked NPL (not precisely located). In the case of Ordnance Survey designation, italics are used in the instance of words written in Gothic script (i.e. specifically designated as antiquities) on the maps.

The site classification follows this information. Where this is suffixed by the word 'site' it indicates that there were no upstanding remains of the site visible above ground level at the time of the last inspection. This does not imply that the site has been destroyed, as archaeological remains may lie beneath the present ground level. The term 'site of' indicates that the site has been totally destroyed.

There follows a short description of the monument with principal dimensions. Where compass points are given in entries, as in N–W, the meaning is from North to West in a clockwise direction. References are cited where applicable.

The SMR number is given at the bottom left-hand corner of each entry and the last date of visit by survey personnel, where applicable, at the bottom right-hand corner.

Text abbreviations:

Dimensions

av.	average
c.	circa
C	chord
cm	centimetre
D	depth
diam.	diameter
dim.	dimension
dims.	dimensions
est.	estimated
ext.	external
ft	feet
H	height
int.	internal
L	length
m	metre
max.	maximum
min.	minimum
T	thickness
Wth	width

General Abbreviations

By.	Barony
ed.	edition
ED	Electoral District
NPL	not precisely located
OD	Ordnance Datum
Td	townland

Megalithic Tombs

The practice of building megalithic tombs for collective burial was widespread among farming communities in all the lands of Europe's Atlantic coastline during the Neolithic period. Human remains, both cremated and inhumed, accompanied by stone implements and pottery vessels, were placed in these great stone-built structures. Some 1,500 such tombs are known in Ireland where they date from about 4,000 to 2,000 BC or a little later. They are grouped into four main types: court tombs, portal tombs, passage tombs and wedge tombs. Court tombs, usually placed at the broader end of a long mound or cairn, are distinguished by an open area or court of broadly semicircular to circular outline leading to a long rectangular gallery divided by jambs into two or more chambers. Eighteen court tombs are known in County Cavan. Eight and probably ten of these are dual court tombs, a variant of the type where a court and gallery are placed at each end of a cairn. Portal tombs are characterised by two tall portal-stones placed at the entrance to a chamber in which single stones usually form the sides and back and roofing is by means of a large stone. There are twelve examples in the county. Passage tombs normally occur in round mounds or cairns, often on hilltops, and are entered via a passage. A feature of some passage tombs is the presence of distinctive decoration on some of the stones. Such a decorated stone lies prostrate at a damaged site in Banagher (**11**) and it would seem that both it and another disturbed site at Carn (**18**) may be passage tombs. Wedge tombs occur in round or short oval cairns and consist of a narrow gallery which tends to increase in width and height towards its western end. Usually there is a line of stones, constituting an outer wall, around the sides and narrow end of the gallery. Nine wedge tombs are known in County Cavan. In addition, there are six megalithic tombs in the county which cannot be satisfactorily classified in their present state. A further twelve sites, three of them known only from earlier accounts and nine at which there are still some remains, are listed here as possible megalithic tombs. Another six sites, named 'Cromlech' or 'Giant's Grave' on Ordnance Survey six-inch maps, names usually associated with megalithic tombs, are omitted, as the features in question are either other monument types or natural features.

Fig. 1—*Wedge tomb at Aughrim* (**7**), *excavated and re-erected in the grounds of the Slieve Russell Hotel near Ballyconnell in 1992.*

1 AGHADRUMGOWNA OR CALF FIELD
OS 21:12:6 (887,206) *'Giant's Grave'* OD 400–500 25381, 30641

Wedge tomb Situated on sloping ground 3km NE of Laragh village. A gallery some 6m long, aligned W–E, is flanked by straight-sided outer-walling. There are two façade-stones to the N of the gallery entrance and one to the S. A lone orthostat beyond the E end of the gallery may be an outer wall stone. The structure is incorporated in a D-shaped cairn 16.5m long, 13m wide and 1.5m high. A tall septal-stone divides the gallery into a short portico and main chamber. The chamber is hidden in the cairn beneath two large slabs, perhaps originally a single roofstone. Two stones in line with the gallery backstone are of uncertain function. (de Valera and Ó Nualláin 1972, 125–6, No. 25)
21:2 7-9-1990

2 AGHADRUMGOWNA OR CALF FIELD
OS 21:12:6 (872,206) *'Giants Grave* (Site of)' OD 300–400 25363, 30641

Megalithic tomb (possible) The OS 25-inch Name Book of 1908 refers to a small mound here. According to the OS Memoirs for County Cavan there was a 'giant's grave' of the 'common oblong form' measuring 40 links (*c.* 8m) long and 12 links (*c.* 2.5m) in maximum width at this place in the 1850s. There is no trace of it now. This may have been a megalithic tomb. (de Valera and Ó Nualláin 1972, 138, No. 8; OS Memoir, Laragh parish, County Cavan)
21:1 12-9-1990

3 AGHAGASHLAN
OS 18:9:5 (123,203) *'Giant's Grave'* OD 500–600 26524, 31277

Court tomb This dual court tomb is sited on a low ridge. The structure is incorporated in an oval mound, aligned E–W, 23m long, 17.5m wide and 1.5m high. At W two façade-stones articulate with the S arm of a court of semicircular outline. The court at the E end of the cairn seems to have been of a more elongated design. Longitudinally-set jambs mark the entries to both galleries. The eastern gallery, represented by two sidestones at the S and a backstone, is 5m long. The western gallery, represented by a single sidestone at the S, was at least 5m long. It is not clear if both galleries shared a common backstone. The lengths of the galleries would suggest each was of two chambers. (de Valera and Ó Nualláin 1972, 123–4, No. 23)
18:1 14-7-1990

4 AGHAWAY
OS 21:8:6 (875,377) *'Giant's Grave'* OD 300–400 25367, 30824

Megalithic tomb (possible) This is a grassy mound 15m long NW–SE, 5m wide NE–SW and 0.75m high. A block of stone, 1.5m in maximum dimension, lies at the SE corner of the mound and the tops of a number of stones protrude above its surface. The nature of the feature is uncertain. (de Valera and Ó Nualláin 1972, 138, No. 7)
21:4 16-19-90

5 AGHAWEE
OS 31:16:3 (860,141) Not marked OD 300–400 24371, 29291

Portal tomb Situated in rolling pasture 400m S of the River Erne. This E-facing chamber is 2m in overall length and narrows towards the back. Two portal-stones, 0.4m apart, each about 1.5m high, form the entrance. Single stones form each side and overlap the portal-stones. Both sidestones are about 1.2m high. The inward-leaning backstone is 0.7m high. The roofstone is broken. There are some traces of a cairn around the W end of the chamber. (de Valera and Ó Nualláin 1972, 132, No. 33)
31:3 4-6-1992

6 AGHNACALLY
OS 7:16:1 (749,132) *'Giant's Grave'* OD 700–800 22289, 32455

Wedge tomb Situated in an open space in a plantation on the NW flank of Slieve Rushen. The gallery, 4m long, is slightly higher and wider at its open SW end. Two orthostats form the N side and three the S side. The backstone is set beyond the ends of the gallery sides. A massive slab, split in two, covers all but the SW end of the gallery. A tree rooted in peat on top of the roofstone may have caused the break. There are four outer wall stones to the N of the gallery and two lines of outer-walling, the inner of four stones and the outer of three, at the S. The structure is incorporated in a mound measuring 9m E–W and 7.5m N–S. (de Valera and Ó Nualláin 1972, 114–5, No. 13)
7:1 2-9-1988

7 AUGHRIM
OS 10:6:1 (256,412) *'Giant's Grave'* OD 600–700 22745, 32117

Wedge tomb (original location) Originally sited on Church Hill at the SE flank of Slieve Rushen, the position described in the heading, this tomb was excavated in 1992 in advance of quarrying operations and re-erected in the grounds of the Slieve Russell Hotel near Ballyconnell. It consists of a ruined gallery, some 6m long, aligned WSW–ENE, set in a low, round cairn, retained by a kerb. A tall stone at W, splits the entry to the gallery which seems to have been divided into a short portico and main chamber. There are buttress stones along both sides of the gallery. During the excavation both inhumed and cremated bone, in association with beaker and food-vessel pottery, were recovered from below the cairn and inside the gallery under a rough paving. Three cist burials were found at the inner edge of the kerb. (de Valera and Ó Nualláin

1972, 115–6, No. 14; Channing 1992, 4)
10:5 16-5-1993

8 BALLAGHANEA
OS 39:16:2 (779,137) *'Giant's Grave'* OD 300–400 26245, 28644

Portal tomb Situated in rolling land 300m NE of Lough Ramor. In the mid-1960s, when the published plan was made (de Valera and Ó Nualláin 1972), this tomb, incorporated in a field fence, was quite ruined. It consisted of the remains of a gallery, 2.2m long, aligned SSE–NNW. A stone 1.3m high, seemed to mark the N end of the gallery. Three orthostats formed its more easterly side, the tallest 0.8m high. Opposite these a displaced slab protruded from the fence. The remains appeared to be those of a portal tomb. Some fifteen years ago the tomb was considerably damaged, however some structure still remains. (de Valera and Ó Nualláin 1972, 135–6, No. 39)
39:12 4-6-1987

9 BALLYHUGH
OS 14:7:1 (490,420) Not marked OD 200–300 22995, 31488

Court tomb Situated just S of Dungummin Lough in pasture. The monument, a dual court tomb, is well preserved but overgrown. It is aligned roughly N–S and consists of two galleries, each divided by jambs into two chambers, set 1.1m apart in a long oval mound. A single façade-stone is visible at the N end of the mound. A broad open court gives entry to the northern gallery. The front chamber here is 4m long and 1.5m to 1.7m wide. The rear chamber is 3.5m long and narrows towards the backstone. Only two stones, which also serve as entrance jambs, remain of the southern court. The front chamber here was about 4m long but its outer end is now missing. The rear chamber is 3.5m long and also narrows towards the back. (de Valera and Ó Nualláin 1972, 117–8, No. 17)
14:6 22-7-1989

10 BANAGHER
OS 26:10:4 (241,178) *'Giant's Grave'* OD 600–700 24699, 29960

Court tomb (site) This tomb, extant in 1965 when the published plan was made (de Valera and Ó Nualláin 1972) has since been destroyed. It stood alongside a fence on the side of a ridge 200m W of a portal tomb (**12**). A ruined gallery entered from the NNE stood here. A tall stone and low stone E of it, possibly a sill, seemed to mark the gallery entrance. A possible courtstone stood in front of the tall stone. About 1.2m S of the entrance, three stones formed the inner end of the W side of the gallery and two remained on the opposite side. A gable-shaped stone closed the gallery. A set stone stood 2m S of the gallery. (de Valera and Ó Nualláin 1972, 127–8, No. 27)
26:5 4-3-1992

11 BANAGHER
OS 26:9:6 (220,185) Not marked OD 700–800 24667, 29974

Passage tomb One of a complex of burial and ritual sites which occupy an area 150m by 130m on a patch of uneven elevated pasture overlooked from the NW by Slieve Glah (**60, 61, 65, 97, 98**). It consists of a large stone circle within which there is a ruined chambered cairn. The stone circle, 40m E–W by 35m N–S, is represented by twelve stones, five now upright measuring 0.65m to 1.3m high, and the others prostrate. The largely grass-grown cairn is round in outline, 22m in diameter and 1m high. Surviving kerbstones indicate an original diameter of some 15m. A number of set stones near the E side of the cairn represent some form of chamber structure. One of a number of prostrate stones here is decorated with passage tomb art. A number of cists and several pots have been found in the cairn (Waddell 1990, 55), possibly secondary burials in what may have been a small passage tomb (Ó Nualláin 1989, 127).
26:4(04) 16-5-1993

12 BANAGHER
OS 26:10:4 (260,184) *'Giant's Grave'* OD 600–700 24710, 29964

Portal tomb Sited 200m E of the site of destroyed court tomb (**10**). A small chamber, 1.6m long and 1m wide, open to the SE, stands towards the S end of a low mound. The more southerly portal-stone survives. Single stones form each side of the chamber which is closed by a backstone set between their ends. A prostrate slab just S of the chamber may be a displaced roofstone. There are two stones at right angles to each other among a group of stones towards the N end of the mound. These seem to be set and could perhaps indicate a subsidiary structure. (de Valera and Ó Nualláin 1972, 128–9, No. 28.)
26:6 4-3-1992

13 BURNEW
OS 39:3:3 (637,540) *'The Big Man's Grave* (Site of)' OD 400–500 26091, 29089

Megalithic tomb (possible) Sited on the E shoulder of a ridge in pasture. This is an irregular mound of stones, 10m by 8m and 1.5m high at its northern end, which is now largely grass-grown. Bedrock protrudes above its lower southern end. Considerable deposits of field-clearance stones have been dumped here. There is no trace of any structural feature but according to an account in the OS 25-inch Name Book of 1908 the 'stones of this antiquity' were removed some eighteen years earlier. The nature of the site is uncertain. (OS Name Book, County Cavan, Sheet 39, 1908)
39:14 31-3-1987

14 BURREN (ED Tuam)
OS 4:1:3 (229,553) *'Giant's Grave'* OD 800–900 20755, 33538

Wedge tomb Situated in a forest on a hill overlooking Lough Macnean Upper. This ruined gallery, 7.5m long and 1.5m in average width, is aligned roughly SW–NE. Outer-walling, largely collapsed, is visible along both sides. There are vague traces of a mound around the structure. Five orthostats and three fallen sidestones remain on the S side of the gallery and five orthostats and one fallen example on the N side. At the W a tall orthostat to the N and two opposite it at the S may have formed the sides of a portico. Three partly displaced roofstones cover the E end of the gallery. There are two outer wall stones *in situ*. One is outside the middle of the N side of the gallery and the other beyond its E end at the S. Some 10m to the SW there is a small, round, kerbed cairn (**128**). (de Valera and Ó Nualláin 1972, 105, No. 3)

4:3 23-2-1993

15 BURREN (ED Tuam)

OS 4:2:1 (271,551) *'Giant's Grave'* OD 800–900
20800, 33514

Wedge tomb Situated on a hilltop and is surrounded by trees. It is well preserved and consists of a roofed gallery, about 7.5m long, opening to the WSW. A tall septal-stone divides it into a long portico and main chamber. An outer wall surrounds the gallery. Two slabs 0.6m apart, form the entrance to the portico which is 2.4m long and 1.1m wide. It is covered by two roofstones. A stone standing in the portico is of uncertain function. The main chamber, 4.5m long, narrows from 1.3m wide at the septal-stone to 1m at the E. A set stone continues the line of the N side of the gallery beyond the backstone. Three horizontally laid slabs roof the main chamber. Five outer wall stones remain in place. Some are now leaning and the westernmost at the N is broken in two. (de Valera and Ó Nualláin 1972, 106–8, No. 5)

4:5 23-3-1993

16 BURREN (ED Tuam)

OS 4:1:6 (214,486) Not marked OD 800–900
20731, 33458

Portal tomb Situated in a forest overlooking Lough Macnean Upper. This roofed chamber is exposed in a hole in a peat-grown cairn of oval outline, measuring 20m by 16.5m by 2m high. The chamber, in the western half of the cairn, is rectangular in plan and measures about 2m long and 0.65m wide. Entry to it is

Fig. 2—*Roofed gallery of wedge tomb at Burren* (**15**).

at the W between two tall portal-stones, 0.65m apart. Behind each is a low sidestone. A backstone is set between the ends of the sidestones. A corbel rests on the southern sidestone and there are two superimposed examples on the northern one. Two overlapping roofstones cover the chamber. A small slab has been jammed between the roofstones. 'A fine urn' is said to have been found in the chamber. (de Valera and Ó Nualláin 1972, 106, No. 4)
4:1 23-2-1993

17 BURREN (ED Tuam)
OS 4:2:1 (238,540) *'Druidical Altar'* OD 800–900
20767, 33512
Portal tomb This monument lies in a forest and is incorporated in a field fence. Greatly ruined, it consists of four large orthostats and a large displaced slab leaning over them. The structure has been converted for use as a shed by the addition of masonry walling. Although difficult to interpret, the remains appear to be those of a portal tomb. Two tall orthostats, both about 2m high, stand roughly in line and 0.55m apart at the W. Running to the NE from the middle of each is another stone. These two are about half as high as the tall orthostats. The leaning slab, a displaced roofstone, rests with one side against the northern of the two tall stones and another side on the ground at the E. (de Valera and Ó Nualláin 1972, 108–9, No. 6)
4:4 23-2-1993

18 CARN (Tullyhunco By.)
OS 14:7:4 (471,323) *'Carn'* OD 300–400
22971, 31381
Passage tomb Situated on the summit of a ridge and with commanding views in all directions. A large, round cairn, some 3m high, is much denuded and greatly disturbed by field fences. Richardson, writing *c.* 1739, (quoted by Paterson, Gaffikin and Davies 1938), recorded the name of the site as 'Carn Dallan' and claimed that a passage was discovered in the cairn 'about twenty-five years ago' and that 'severall urns, 5 large skulls and a great deal of burnt bones' were found in one of three 'apartments' there. This account would suggest that the cairn may have covered a passage tomb. Richardson also noted, just S of the cairn, a square enclosure about twenty yards across bounded by 'large stones set deep in the ground', and 'in the circuit of the hill . . . four small plots of ground of a circular figure inclosed with large stones, all of which are old burial places.' These have not been located. (Paterson, Gaffikin and Davies 1938, 143–5)
14:8 22-7-1989

19 CARRICKACROY
OS 32:13:5 (139,16) *'Cromlech'* OD 500–600
24598, 29152
Portal tomb Situated near the top of a ridge. This small chamber, 1.2m long and not more than 0.8m wide, is entered from the N. The entrance was formed by two portal-stones with a sill, 0.6m high, between them. The W portal-stone is 1.3m high and the other, now prostrate, would have been of similar height. Single stones form the sides and back of the chamber. All three are about 0.5m lower than the portal-stone. The backstone is gable-shaped and leans inwards. A displaced roofstone lies prostrate to the E of the chamber. (de Valera and Ó Nualláin 1972, 133, No. 35)
32:4 5-7-1989

20 CARRICKAVEE
OS 39:5:4 (32,304) Not marked OD 500–600
25458, 28825
Megalithic tomb (unclassified) Sited close to the base of a slope in rolling country. The tomb is largely concealed in a subcircular mound, 14m across, 0.5m high at the N and 2m at the downslope southern side. A number of set stones visible at the top of the mound indicate a gallery at least 3.3m long, aligned ENE–WSW. Two stones, 1.1m apart and 0.6m high, mark its WSW end. Only the tops of four other stones, two at each side are visible. North of the presumed gallery there is a possible line of outer-walling. (Ó Nualláin 1989, 141 Cv. 43)
39:18 12-9-1986

21 CARRICKBRANNAN/CASHEL (Tullyhaw By.)
OS 5:2:6 (435,518) Not marked OD 200–300
19999, 32845
Court tomb Sited on a small knoll 450m W of the River Shannon. This dual court tomb, aligned NNE–SSW, has been denuded of its cairn this century. Two ruined galleries stand 15m apart. The northern, some 7m long, is divided by jambs into two chambers. A displaced lintel lies in front of the entrance jambs. There are one or possibly two courtstones beyond a fence to the NW. The sides of the front chamber are missing but the second chamber is largely intact. The remains of the southern gallery consist of two jambs marking a division between a northern chamber represented by two sidestones at the W and a southern chamber represented by two at the E. (de Valera and Ó Nualláin 1972, 112–4, No. 12)
5:1 12-8-1988

22 CARRICKCLEVAN
OS 31:1:4 (16,474) Not marked OD 100–200
23484, 29635
Portal tomb Situated in a valley 100m SE of the River Erne. The chamber, approximately 2m long, is incorporated in a stone fence. The entrance, at the E, consists of two portal-stones about 1.1m high at either side of a low stone, possibly a sill. The sides are of single slabs, the southern now pitched inwards. Both are about 1m high. There is no backstone visible. The roofstone is now broken in two parts, the larger of which covers the chamber. (de Valera and Ó Nualláin

1972, 130–1, No. 31)
31:10 3-6-1992

23 CLARAGH (ED Drumcarn)
OS 16:2:4 (276,520) *'Cloghard'* OD 400–500
24711, 31606

Megalithic tomb (possible) Sited on a flat hilltop and 7m SE of the perimeter of a round cairn (**136**). Between two set stones, 2.7m apart, and leaning against one of them is a great block of stone. The set stone to the SW measures 0.8m by 0.6m by 1.1m high and the other 1m by 0.5m by 0.8m high. The intervening block, now split, leans against the latter. It measures 2.1m by 1.5m by 1.1m in size. Two prostrate slabs, the larger 1m in maximum dimension, lie at the E end of the structure. A slight grassy mound around the remains may not be original. The nature of the monument is not now clear.
16:15(02) 9-11-1989

24 COHAW
OS 18:9:4 (58,165) *'Giant's Grave'* OD 400–500
26446, 31255

Court tomb This dual court tomb, sited on the side of a ridge, was excavated by Kilbride-Jones in 1949. Aligned N–S, it was incorporated in a cairn some 24.5m long and an estimated 13.5m wide. The court at N is U-shaped while the perimeter of the southern court describes two-thirds of a circle. Each gallery is divided by jambs and a low sill into two chambers, the outer in each case longer and wider than the inner. A closed central chamber links the ends of both galleries. Cremated and uncremated bones and a few teeth found during the excavation represent at least three individuals. Part of a neolithic pottery bowl was also recovered. (Kilbride-Jones 1951, 75–88; de Valera and Ó Nualláin 1972, 122–3, No. 22)
18:5 14-7-1989

25 COHAW
OS 17:16:3 (919,128) *'Giant's Grave'*
OD 300–400 26375, 31201

Megalithic tomb (unclassified) Situated near the top of a ridge in undulating pasture. Poorly preserved, the remains appear to be those of a gallery, at least 4.2m long, aligned SW–NE. Two orthostats, 1.4m apart at the SW, may mark the gallery entrance. A third

Fig. 3—*Dual court tomb at Cohaw* (**24**), *excavated in 1949.*

orthostat alongside the southern of these may have formed part of a flat facade. A sidestone stands 1.7m E of the northern entrance stone. A number of displaced stones lie close to the structure which is surrounded by a small, low mound. The tomb must remain unclassified though there are indications that it may be a wedge tomb. (de Valera and Ó Nualláin 1972, 121, No 20)
17:13 21-11-1989

26 CORDUFF OR CORMORE
OS 30:3:4 (480,469) Not marked OD 400–500
22996, 29614
Megalithic tomb (possible) According to an account in the National Museum (NMI files, 1932) this monument comprised '20 large boulders of local greenstone 32 feet long by 28 feet wide' (*c.* 9.75m x 8.5m). The stones were 3 to 4 feet (*c.* 0.9m to 1.2m) in height, 3 feet wide and up to 3 feet in the ground. At the W end there was an entrance to a passage 20 feet (*c.* 6.1m) long. A lintel above the entrance measured 7 feet (*c.* 2.1m) by 7 feet by 4 feet. There was paving on the floor of the inner end of the passage with some trace of burning. No finds were reported. The site was levelled in the 1940s or 1950s and the stones used in road construction. There are now no surface remains. The landowner remembers the structure as consisting of three particularly massive boulders upon which rested a fourth stone. Formerly situated in fertile pasture sloping quite steeply from NW to SE. There is a substantial pond adjacent to the site at the NE. This site may have been some form of megalithic monument but its nature is uncertain.
30:8 3-10-1991

27 CORNASEER
OS 25:16:1 (713,142) Not marked OD 400–500
24205, 29921
Megalithic tomb (possible) A site briefly described by Richardson *c.* 1739 has been identified by Paterson, Gaffikin and Davies (1938). Today a scatter of largely prostrate slabs lie alongside the wall of a ruined building. Two at NW are said to have stood opposite each other until 1991. A little to the SE a stone protruding from the wall of the building may be a set stone. Alongside this is a slab, 2m in maximum dimension, now overlying another, said to have been supported by four low stones. Further slabs lie prostrate to the SE. This would seem to have been some form of a megalithic monument but its nature is not now clear. (Paterson, Gaffikin and Davies 1938, 143)
25:27 1-10-1991

28 COSKEMDUFF
OS 23:1:6 (224,519) Not marked OD 300–400
26617, 30985
Megalithic tomb (possible) Sited on a low ridge. This consists of an irregularly shaped boulder, 1.7m by 1.4m by 0.85m thick, supported on four blocks of stone. It is incorporated in and partly obscured by a stone field fence. A stone under the N side of the boulder is not set and the status of three others, one to the W and two to the S is unclear. The nature of the site remains to be determined. (de Valera and Ó Nualláin 1972, xxii, 'at Caskeanduff')
23:14 26-5-1992

29 DERRYRAGH
OS 13:7:3 (671,377) *'Cromlech'* OD 300–400
22219, 31144
Megalithic tomb (possible) Situated at the base of a slope. A large slab, 1.6m long and 1.15m high, leans against an upright stone, 1.35m long and 0.85m high, at right angles to its southern end. A third slab rests against the leaning stone and to the N of the group there is a prostrate stone. Site may be largely natural in origin. (de Valera and Ó Nualláin 1972, 138, No. 5)
13:68 11-8-1989

30 DOOCASSAN
OS 21:3:2 (560,590) Not marked OD 300–400
25021, 31045
Megalithic tomb (unclassified) Sited on a low ridge. A ruined gallery stands towards the SSE end of a mound, 14.5m long, 7m in greatest width and 0.75m high. The gallery, now 3.5m long, is closed by a backstone at the SSE. Three sidestones remain at its more westerly side and four at the E. It narrows from 1.9m wide at the open NNW end to 1.1m near the backstone. The status of a number of low stones beyond the gallery sides is uncertain as is the function of a large set stone 1m SE of the backstone.
21:24 25-9-1990

31 DOON (ED Ballyconnell)
OS 10:10:1 (257,228) Not marked OD 200–300
22741, 31934
Court tomb Situated in rolling countryside just N of Ballyconnell. This is a dual court tomb set in a long cairn. It is somewhat overgrown by trees and bushes. Two galleries, set back to back, are both 9m long, and each is divided by jambs into three chambers. They are likely to have shared a backstone but this is lacking. Eleven stones remain along the combined N sides of the galleries and seven along the S sides. There is a single courtstone just beyond the southern entrance jamb of the SW gallery and another about 2.5m from the S side of the entrance to the NE gallery. (O'Reilly 1988, 575–8; Ó Nualláin 1989, 116 Cv. 41)
10:13 25-5-1993

32 DRUMAVRACK
OS 16:2:2 (348,552) Not marked OD 300–400
24797, 31640

Court tomb This monument, a dual court tomb, sited on a low, rocky ridge, is almost completely overgrown. The two galleries, both 9.5m long, are each preceded by the remains of a court and stand at the NW and SE ends of a cairn 37m long, 17m wide and 2.5m high. The opposed ends of the galleries are 2m apart. The court at the NW is semicircular in outline but only three orthostats remain of the SE court. Both galleries are divided by jambs into three chambers. A lintel rests on the entrance jambs of the SE gallery and on the inner pair of segmenting jambs of the NW gallery. (de Valera and Ó Nualláin 1972, 119–21, No. 19)
16:43 21-9-1989

33 DRUMEAGUE
OS 28:2:4 (267,459) '*Giant's Grave*' OD 500–600
26687, 30281
Wedge tomb Situated on a low hillock. This is a well-preserved gallery, aligned roughly SSW–NNE. There are two outer wall stones to N and S and a facade-stone stands forward of the N side of the gallery. The structure stands in a mound 9.5m by 7m by 1m high. The main chamber, 5.5m long, is closed by a tall, transverse slab at the W. In front of this a small stone, on which rests a displaced slab, may form the S side of a portico. Six stones form the N side of the main chamber, five remain at the S, and it is closed by a low backstone. The eastern pair of stones on both sides are stepped in from the line of the others and are markedly lower than them. (de Valera and Ó Nualláin 1972, 129–30, No. 29; CUCAP BGL 76)
28:19 6-9-1988

34 DRUMERKILLEW
OS 22:2:4 (279,476) '*Giant's Grave* (Site of)'
OD 400–500 25706, 30940
Megalithic tomb (possible) There is no trace of a structure at the site now. According to the OS Memoirs for County Cavan there was a 'Giant's Grave' 40 feet (*c.* 12.2m) long and 12 feet (*c.* 3.65m) wide narrowing to 4 feet (*c.* 1.2m) here in the 1830s. This may have been a megalithic tomb. (de Valera and Ó Nualláin 1972, 138, No. 10; OS Memoir, Kildrumsherdan parish, County Cavan)
22:17 21-10-1990

35 DRUMHART
OS 24:2:4 (276,479) Not marked OD 100–200
22773, 30253
Court tomb Situated near a stream on a flat patch of ground close to a rocky hillock. The remains of a dual court tomb are incorporated in a mound 28.5m long, 13.5m wide and about 0.5m high. At W, a court, perhaps originally of semicircular outline, leads to a gallery, 9m long, divided by jambs into three chambers. The front chamber, the biggest of the three, is built with larger orthostats than the other two and its long axis is out of line with that of the rest of the gallery. The remains of the eastern gallery consist now of a single chamber. About 2m W of this there are a number of low set stones of uncertain function. (de Valera and Ó Nualláin 1972, 126–7, No. 26)
24:40 27-9-1991

36 DRUMHAWNAGH
OS 31:13:1 (35,117) '*Druid's Altar*' OD 200–300
23512, 29250
Portal tomb Situated close to the roadside in rolling grassland. This well-preserved polygonal chamber is formed by two portal-stones, two sidestones and a backstone, covered by a single roofstone. It is 2.3m long and 2m wide inside the portal-stones, narrowing to 1.1m at the backstone. The portal-stones, at the NNW, stand 0.75m apart and both are 1.55m high. Both sidestones lean inwards against the portal-stones and backstone. The inward-leaning backstone is 1.25m high. The roofstone measures 1.9m by 1.8m by 0.2m thick. (de Valera and Ó Nualláin 1972, 131, No. 32)
31:26 23-7-1993

37 DRUMHURT
OS 22:2:3 (442,565) '*Giant's Grave*' OD 200–300
25868, 31030
Megalithic tomb (possible) This consists of an upright stone, 1.3m long, 0.65m thick and 1.3m high, and two prostrate stones close by. (de Valera and Ó Nualláin 1972, 138, No. 9)
22:21(01) 19-10-1990

38 DRUMMANY (Upper Loughtee By.)
OS 15:15:5 (572,8) '*Giants Grave*' OD 100–200
24052, 31060
Megalithic tomb (unclassified) Sited on a slight rise close to the village of Butler's Bridge. A gallery, open at both ends and orientated NNW–SSE, is 6m long and 1.6m wide. Five contiguous stones form the E side but only one orthostat remains on the opposite side. The northern stone at E, 1.95m high, is 0.5m or more taller than the other stones. The southern stone at E is skewed inward suggesting that the gallery may have ended here. There are three prostrate stones at the site. (de Valera and Ó Nualláin 1972, 118–9, No. 18)
15:40 16-9-1989

39 DRUMSALLAGH
OS 35:2:1 (300,599) '*Giant's Grave*' OD 400–500
27671, 29808
Megalithic tomb (unclassified) A rectangular structure, measuring 6.5m by 2m, depicted on the OS 25-inch field trace of 1908, is represented by a number of slabs incorporated in a field fence. Two of the stones are set. One, 1.2m long, 0.45m thick, and 1.65m high, exposed in the S face of the fence, is aligned NW–SE. The other, 3.5m to the W, protrudes from the opposite side of the fence which is about 2m thick.

Fig. 4—*A well-preserved portal tomb with polygonal chamber at Drumhawnagh* (**36**).

This measures 1m long, 0.4m thick and 1.4m high. Between the set stones two partially concealed slabs are embedded in the fence. (de Valera and Ó Nualláin 1972, 134–5, No. 37)

35:38 14-6-1988

40 DUFFCASTLE

OS 32:14:4 (287,69) Not marked OD 500–600
24744, 29204

Portal tomb Situated on the side of a ridge. This E–facing chamber is 2m long. The southern of two large stones at the entrance is a portal-stone, 1.8m high. The other, 1.4m high, appears to be a doorstone. The northern portal-stone is missing. Single stones form the sides of the chamber. The northern is 1m high and the southern, now collapsed inwards, was of like height. The backstone, 1.5m high, leans inwards. The front end of a great roofstone rests on the portal-stone but its opposite end has tilted into the chamber. Two stones at the inner end of the collapsed sidestone are of uncertain origin. (de Valera and Ó Nualláin 1972, 134, No. 36)

32:21 11-7-1989

41 GARTNANOUL

OS 19:12:2 (812,270) Not marked OD 100–200
23337, 30689

Court tomb Situated in a clearing in a forest on land jutting into Lough Oughter. This dual court tomb consists of two galleries, each of two chambers, preceded by a court. Both galleries are about 5m in overall length and they stand 7.5m apart. Two jambs and an intervening sill mark the entry to both. A single jamb marks the segmentation of the NNW gallery and a sillstone divides the SSE gallery. The NNW court is 4m long and 3.5m broad and the other 3.3m by 3.5m. A drop in ground level SE of the more southerly gallery may represent the edge of a mound. (Ó Nualláin 1989, 116, Cv.40)

19:35 18-7-1990

42 GARVAGH

OS 4:6:4 (245,337) Not marked OD 500–600
20767, 33298

Court tomb Situated about 230m S of Garvagh Lough on poor, rocky land. A polygonal chamber stands at the W end of an overgrown cairn. It measures 3.4m long by 2.5m in maximum width. The opposed stones at its

open NE end function as imbricated segmenting jambs. In front of the polygonal chamber two orthostats represent the NW side of a second chamber, 3m long. These have become visible in recent years and are not on the published plan of the site (de Valera and Ó Nualláin 1972). Towards the NE a number of large slabs rise from the surface of the cairn. Their relationship to the gallery is unclear. (de Valera and Ó Nualláin 1972, 112, No. 11)
4:7 10-8-1988

43 GORTAQUILL
OS 1:12:5 (841,225) *'Giant's Grave'* OD 300–400
20420, 33837
Court tomb Situated on elevated ground S of Lough Macnean Upper. The remains of a court and gallery stand at the NE end of an overgrown mound about 25m long. A courtstone adjoins the S side of the gallery and 3.5m E of this, beyond a fence, are two possible examples. The gallery, 5m long, is divided into two chambers of equal length. The northern entrance jamb survives and behind it two stones form the N side of the front chamber. The opposite side consists of a single slab. A segmenting jamb at the N marks the division between the chambers. Four stones form the N side of the rear chamber but only a single stone remains on the S side. The gallery lacks a backstone. (de Valera and Ó Nualláin 1972, 103, No. 1)
1:2 3-7-1988

44 KILLETER
OS 40:10:6 (423,170) Not marked OD 400–500
26842, 28698
Court tomb This monument, situated on a flat patch of ground on a W-facing slope, is overgrown and greatly ruined but would appear to be the remains of a dual court tomb. At the NW end of a cairn, 24m long and 1m or so high, there is an upright stone 1.15m high and alongside it a prostrate slab, both apparently entrance jambs of a gallery of which no other trace is visible. Three stones NW of the upright stone represent a court. On the main axis of the cairn and at its SE end, a line of three low orthostats are partly exposed, and at right angles to the southern of these there is another larger example. The latter may be a jamb and the others part of the side of a gallery.
40:32 18-5-93

45 KILLYCARNEY
OS 2:13:1 (2,139) *'Giant's Grave'* OD 200–300
20523, 33749
Court tomb Situated near the top of a low ridge overlooking the SE end of Lough Macnean Upper. The inner end of a court, to the E, leads to a ruined gallery, now open at the back. The tomb stands at the E end of a long cairn overgrown by thorn bushes. One or possibly two courtstones adjoin the N side of the gallery which consists of an antechamber and two main chambers. The antechamber is 1.4m long and 1.4m wide. A pair of jambs, 0.6m apart, divide it from the first main chamber. This chamber is 2.6m long and 1.6m in greatest width. A sill set between the inner ends of a pair of imbricated jambs separate it from the second chamber which was at least 2m long. (de Valera and Ó Nualláin 1972, 103–4, No. 2)
2:4 6-7-1988

46 KILLYCLUGGIN
OS 13:4:6 (850, 513) Not marked OD 200–300
22238, 31158
Megalithic tomb (possible) There are three set stones here. A large stone, 1.8m by 0.25m by 1m high, is aligned E–W. To the S and at right angles to its W end is a second stone, 1.25m by 0.25m by 0.4m in exposed height. The third stone, 0.7m W of the S end of the last, is aligned E–W and measures 0.6m by 0.4m by 0.6m high. This configuration of stones may represent the remains of some form of megalithic monument. Field-clearance debris has been heaped around it. (Davies, ITA Survey, Co. Cavan 1941)
13:65 25-5-1993

47 KILLYMORIARTY
OS 13:7:3 (618,414) *'Giant's Grave'* OD 200–300
22148, 31471
Court tomb Situated on a hillock in undulating countryside. The monument, greatly ruined, consists of a mound 26m long, 7m wide and 0.75m high incorporating two lengths of gallery structure 7m apart. The mound has been extensively dug in the gap between both. In the western half of the mound the surviving gallery is 5.5m long and almost 2m wide. Two chambers can be recognised here, one to the W, 3.5m long, and the other largely destroyed. At the E end of the mound only two contiguous stones, apparently the N side of a gallery, remain. The overall length of the orthostatic structure would suggest that this was a dual court tomb. (de Valera and Ó Nualláin 1972, 117, No. 16)
13:31 12-6-1989

48 KILNAVERT
OS 13:4:5 (777,492) *'Giant's Grave'* OD 200–300
22316, 31547
Wedge tomb Sited on a slight rise in undulating land. This monument, surrounded by a tree-ring, consists of a ruined gallery flanked by outer-walling around which there are traces of a mound measuring 11m by 10m. A gallery, now 3.5m long, narrows from 1.5m wide at SW to 1.35m at NE. A single slab covers all but its NE end. About 2m W of its more northerly side there is a single façade-stone. Just beyond the S side of the gallery there are three outer wall stones and another 2.5m W of these. There are two outer wall stones, 5m apart, at N. (de Valera and Ó Nualláin 1972, 116, No. 15)
13:37(01) 19-6-1989

49 KNOCKATUDOR
OS 21:12:2 (808,228) *'Giant's Grave'* OD 300–400 25304, 30679
Megalithic tomb (unclassified) Situated on a level tract of pasture in rolling drumlin country. The monument is very ruined. It consists of seven orthostats and a number of large displaced stones. A line of three orthostats seem to represent the N side of a gallery, about 6m long, aligned W–E. Immediately to the N two orthostats may indicate a doubling of the gallery wall. An orthostat with a gable-shaped top stands at right angles to the E end of the presumed side of the gallery and might be a backstone. A stone parallel to this and 2m to the W may be a sill or segmenting stone. (de Valera and Ó Nualláin 1972, 124–5, No. 24)
21:49 11-9-1989

50 LEGALOUGH
OS 4:2:5 (308,529) *'Druidical Altar'* OD 800–900 20840, 33508
Wedge tomb This is 30m E of the court tomb in the same townland (**51**). It consists of the remains of a SW-facing gallery flanked at either side by outer-walling. A single façade-stone survives to the S of the gallery entrance. The gallery is some 6m long and 1.5m to 1.7m wide narrowing to 1.25m at the backstone. A stone partly closes the front of the gallery. Seven sidestones are visible at the S and four at the N. Two stones, one to the N and the other to the S, continue the line of the gallery sides beyond the backstone. Five outer wall stones survive at the N and five more at the S. There appears to be some cairn material between the gallery sides and the outer wall. (de Valera and Ó Nualláin 1972, 109–10, No. 8)
4:10 10-8-1988

51 LEGALOUGH
OS 4:2:1 (305,531) Indicated as small circular enclosure OD 800–900 20837, 33513
Court tomb Situated on a hill-ridge and close to the wedge tomb in the same townland (**50**). The scant remains here are of a W-facing court tomb the gallery of which has been destroyed. Only the inner end of the court, consisting of an entrance flanked at S by three courtstones, now survives. The entrance consists of two well-matched jambs, 0.8m apart, at either side of a low sill. The northern jamb is split in two. The surviving structure stands at the western edge of a circular enclosure, 8.5m by 7.5m, formed by a low, grass-grown stony bank. (de Valera and Ó Nualláin 1972, 109, No. 7)
4:9 10-8-1988

52 MAYO
OS 18:9:1 (64,239) Not marked OD 500–600 26459, 31335
Portal tomb Sited on a ridge in pasture. The chamber, incorporated in a field fence, is quite damaged. It faces NW and is about 3m long and 1.5m wide. At its more northerly side, a portal-stone 1.55m high, rises 0.85m above the adjoining sidestone. Beyond this a low backstone is set skew to the main axis of the chamber. At S a sidestone is in place but the portal-stone has fallen. An outward-leaning sillstone marks the front of the chamber. A displaced slab in the chamber may be part of a roofstone. Another displaced slab lies to the N of the fallen portal-stone. (de Valera and Ó Nualláin 1972, 121–2, No. 21)
18:12 14-7-1990

53 MIDDLETOWN
OS 30:16:3 (893,117) *'Druid's Altar'* OD 200–300 23443, 29244
Portal tomb Situated 350m E of White Lough on undulating ground. This small chamber, about 2m long, lacks a backstone. There are two portal-stones 0.8m apart at SSE, each about 1.7m high. The chamber sides are of single stones, that at E 1.5m high and the other somewhat lower. Just N of the western one there is a small set stone of uncertain function. A roofstone rests in a sloping position on the western portal-stone and both sidestones. (de Valera and Ó Nualláin 1972, 130, No. 30)
30:31 7-9-1991

54 MONEYGASHEL
OS 4:5:2 (99,437) Not marked OD 600–700 20619, 33402
Portal tomb Situated at the head of a valley, the monument consists of a ruined chamber incorporated in the NNE end of a long cairn. The cairn, distorted by fences and partly rebuilt, is 11m long and 5m in average width. A portal-stone at W, 1.85m high, and a low sillstone at its inner end mark the chamber entrance. The eastern portal-stone is missing as is the W side of the chamber. The eastern side is represented by a long, inward-leaning slab, 1.7m high. The chamber is closed by a modern wall of rough stones in which the edges of two slabs are exposed. A massive displaced roofstone, split into two pieces, overlies the chamber. (de Valera and Ó Nualláin 1972, 110–1, No. 9)
4:17 10-10-1992

55 MOYDRISTAN
OS 37:15:6 (677,7) Not marked OD 300–400 24176, 28504
Court tomb The monument stands immediately N of a rath (**1003**) on a broad ridge in rolling grassland. Largely destroyed, it consists of a S-facing court, roughly semicircular in outline, formed by seven substantial stones, three to the W and four to the E, the tallest 1.45m high. Behind the inner stone at W, which also served as an entrance jamb, a stone 0.8m high is all that now remains of the gallery. A considerable

number of prostrate stones of varying size lie in and around what was the gallery area. (Ó Nualláin 1989, 116, Cv. 42)
37:49 30-7-1986

56 MULLACASTLE
OS 32:13:1 (67,80) '*Cromlech*' OD 400–500 24502, 29218
Court tomb Situated on a gentle slope in rolling country. The more easterly side of a chamber, 2.5m long, is represented by three orthostats, a tall jamb at the NNW and, 1m to the S, two adjoining sidestones which in turn articulate with a backstone at the SSE. A large displaced slab leans against the jamb. Another orthostat beside the jamb seems to continue the line of the gallery to the NNW. A set stone about 1m S of the backstone suggests a continuation of the gallery in the opposite direction. There is a displaced slab alongside this. (de Valera and Ó Nualláin 1972, 132–3, No. 34)
32:42 4-7-1989

57 MULLAGHBOY (Tullyhaw By.)
OS 4:5:6 (172,326) '*White Carn* (Ancient Burying Place)' OD 500–600 20697, 33296
Court tomb This monument, situated about 0.7km SW of Garvagh Lough, consists of a court and gallery at the NW end of a substantial trapezoidal cairn, some 19m in length. Kerbstones are visible at its SE end and more westerly side. Some heavy blocks at the front of the cairn may represent a façade. A single courtstone flanks each side of the gallery entrance which is formed by two jambs, 0.9m apart. A sidestone and beyond this a corbel indicate the W side of the gallery. At the E side of the gallery there are two adjoining sidestones 2.5m from the entrance jamb. Outside the first of these there is a set stone angled away from the gallery and 0.7m W of the same sidestone there is a set stone standing in the gallery area. Two slabs lying in the gallery may be displaced roofstones. A loosely set upright stone outside the W side of the gallery may not be an original feature. (de Valera and Ó Nualláin 1972, 111–2, No. 10)
4:20 11-8-1988

58 POLLAREAGH (Castlerahan By.)
OS 31:8:6 (909,359) '*Giant's Grave*' OD 400–500 24426, 29513
Megalithic tomb (possible) This is a long grassy mound, 25m NW–SE by 10m NE–SW and 0.5m high. To the SE of the mound there is a prostrate stone. (de Valera and Ó Nualláin 1972, 139, No. 12)
31:54 3-4-1974

59 RAFFONY
OS 39:8:2 (834,387) Not marked OD 400–500 26297, 28932
Wedge tomb Situated on a ridge 150m W of Raffony Lough. A gallery, aligned WSW–ENE, is divided by a septal-stone into a portico, 1.5m long, and main chamber at least 4.3m long. To the N of the gallery there are four outer wall stones and two to the S. The northern of two façade-stones links the outer wall at the N to the gallery side. The portico is represented by two stones of its N side and the main chamber by two stones to the N and four to the S. Within the chamber a stone 0.7m E of the septal-stone may be displaced. An irregular mound, 13m N–S by 12m E–W, encloses the structure. (de Valera and Ó Nualláin 1972, 135, No. 38)
39:73 9-6-1987

Stone Circles and Embanked Enclosure

In essence a stone circle comprises a circular, oval or D-shaped area defined by a series of upright stones. Archaeological excavation has revealed cremated burials within some stone circles, although this tends to be the exception rather than the rule. They are generally interpreted as being ritual sites - perhaps the focus of ritual or ceremonial practices. Their most dense concentrations are in the south Munster and mid-Ulster areas. As a general rule the Ulster examples are smaller in scale than their Munster counterparts. This is not however the case with the County Cavan examples. Stone circles are generally assigned to the Late Neolithic/Early Bronze periods. Also included in this chapter is a circular embanked enclosure at Banagher (**65**), which is located in close proximity to two stone circles in the same townland (**60, 61**) and is presumably an associated monument of henge type.

60 BANAGHER
OS 26:9:6 (221,188) Not marked OD 700–800
24668, 29975
Stone circle One of a complex of burial and ritual sites which occupy an area 150m by 130m on a patch of uneven elevated pasture overlooked from the NW by Slieve Glah (**11, 61, 65, 97, 98**). Stone circle (int. diam. *c.* 16m). The W half survives and is represented by seven set stones rising at intervals from a low grassy bank (Wth 3.5m; H 0.5m).
26:4(01) 16-5-1993

61 BANAGHER
OS 26:9:6 (220,187) Not marked OD 700–800
24667, 29974
Stone circle A component of the aforementioned complex of ritual sites (**11, 60, 65, 97, 98**). Large stone circle (int. dims. 40m E–W x 35m N–S) comprising twelve stones, five now upright measuring between 0.65m and 1.3m high, and the others prostrate. Within the circle is a ruined chambered cairn which housed a possible passage tomb (**11**) (Ó Nualláin 1989, 127).
26:4(03) 16-5-1993

62 KILLYCLUGGIN
OS 13:4:6 (860,513) Not marked OD 200–300
22402, 31578
Stone circle Situated 10m WNW of the site of the celebrated Killycluggin Stone (**93**). Much disturbed. Subcircular raised area (int. dims. 22m E–W; 18.6m N–S) enclosed by a total of eighteen stones, all but five of which have fallen. The site is divided into two unequal portions by a field boundary running N–S. The smaller portion, W of this, is defined by four orthostats still in position. The largest stone (now fallen) is at NNE (L 3.93m; dims. 1.45m x 0.68m). (Ó Ríordáin 1979, 155; Killanin and Duignan 1989, 61)
13:26(02) 22-6-1989

63 KILNAVERT
OS 13:4:5 (812,501) '*Stone circle*' OD 200–300
22352, 31565
Stone circle Not marked on OS 1836 or 1876 eds. This monument is situated on a ridge which has been planted with coniferous trees. Slightly raised circular area (int. dims. 11.8m NE–SW; 10.9m NW–SE) defined by sixteen squat irregularly shaped boulders. There is a large break in the circle from NE–E–ESE and a smaller one from W–WNW–NW. There is an isolated boulder *c.* 2m SSW of the circle and a second stone within the perimeter at E.
13:41 19-6-1989

64 LISSANOVER
OS 13:4:4 (760,524) '*Stone circle*' OD 200–300
22296, 31589
Stone circle Not marked on OS 1836 or 1876 eds. Situated on the NNW shoulder of a low rise. All that remains of the site is a heap of small stones containing one large partly buried recumbent stone (H 0.9m; dims 2.25m x 0.7m) with two smaller heaps of small stones 11.3m to SSE.
13:42 22-6-1989

65 BANAGHER
OS 26:9:6 (220,187) Not marked OD 700–800
24667, 29974
Embanked enclosure An element of the above-mentioned complex (**11, 60, 61, 97, 98**). A large circular area (int. diam. 42m) enclosed by a wide, low earthen bank with internal fosse. Fosse now identifiable only at N. Breaks in the bank at NNE, NNW and SSE. Cultivation ridges cross the interior.
26:4(06) 16-5-1993

Stone Rows

A stone row comprises two or more standing stones with a shared axis. The two main concentrations of this monument type in Ireland are in the south Munster area and in the Ulster counties of Fermanagh, Derry and Tyrone. In many cases stone rows are located in close proximity to stone circles and it is logical to assume that like the former they served as the focus of ritual or ceremonial practices. They have been variously assigned to the Early Bronze Age by Ó Nualláin (1975, 83–131) and to the Late Bronze Age by Lynch (1981, 73).

Fig. 5— *A possible stone row with NW–SE alignment at Lissanover* (**69**).

66 GARTAQUILL
OS 14:3:6 (654,468) Not marked OD 200–300
23160, 31537

Stone row (possible) Sited on a level patch of ground at the base of a S-facing slope. Two stones aligned ENE–WSW, that to the W (H 1.65m; dims. 1.5m x 0.4m) leaning slightly northwards and the other 1.6m inclining to ENE (H 1.7m; dims. 1.9m x 0.3m). Together they form a row 5m in overall length.
14:33 16-5-1993

67 KILLYMORIARTY
OS 13:7:2 (598,409) *'Standing Stones'*
OD 200–300 22127, 31466

Stone row (possible) Not marked on OS 1836 or 1876 eds. Two large slabs orientated ENE–WSW lying against a field boundary. The outer slab (H 1.12m; dims. 1.1m x 0.22m) now overlies the inner one (H 1.15m; dims. 1.4m x 0.13m). An earlier report (OPW 1969) noted a third similar slab incorporated into the field boundary 4.5m to ENE. This was not located.
13:30 12-6-1989

68 LISSANOVER
OS 13:4:2 (798,550) *'Standing Stones'*
OD 200–300 22336, 31616

Stone row (possible) Not marked on OS 1836 or 1876 eds. Situated at the E extent of a low flat-topped ridge. Only one of the two stones depicted on the OS 1912 ed. is still identifiable. Low slab (H 0.94m; dims. 1.1m x 0.18m) aligned WNW–ESE.
13:44 22-6-1989

69 LISSANOVER
OS 13:4:2 (823,559) *'Standing Stones'*
OD 200–300 22363, 31626

Stone row (possible) Sited on the SE slope of a drumlin ridge. Apparent NW–SE alignment comprising three standing stones, one at SE (H 2.1m; dims. 1.2m x 0.64m) and the other at NW (H 1.55m; dims. 0.95m x 0.7m), and a third fallen stone (H 1.95m; dims. 1.55m x 0.43m) which lies against the NW member. The discolouration of the fallen stone suggests that at least half of its height was formerly beneath ground level.
13:47 22-6-1989

70 SHANTEMON
OS 21:5:6 (211,346) *'Fin Mc Cool's Fingers'*
OD 600–700 24650, 30782

Stone row (possible) Five stones orientated NW–SE. Situated in a clearing within a modern plantation of coniferous trees, on the E shoulder of a high ridge in mountainous terrain. The stones are graded in height. The lowest (H *c.* 0.5m) is at the NW end with the tallest (H *c.* 2m) at the SE end.
21:73 27-9-1990

Standing Stones

Standing stones can be defined as single upright stones. In the Irish language, terms such as *dallán*, *gallán*, and *liagán* are used to refer to this monument type. Archaeological excavation has revealed that some standing stones mark prehistoric burials. Others, such as the *Lia Fáil* stone at Tara, County Meath, undoubtedly had some ritual or ceremonial function. Still others served as ancient boundary markers. In some cases they may represent the last surface remains of a megalithic tomb, stone row or other monument. It must also be noted, however, that for centuries farmers have erected standing stones as scratching posts for their cattle. In almost all cases it is impossible to tell which, if any, of the above suggested functions any individual standing stone served. Standing stones therefore have a very long date span, ranging from the Late Neolithic period up until relatively recent times.

Fig. 6—*Standing stone at Camagh* (**74**).

71 AGHAKNOCK
OS 24:16:1 (718,120) *'Fin McCool's Finger Stone'* OD 400–500 23243, 29890

Standing stone (original location) An earlier report (OPW 1968) recorded that this standing stone had been moved from the location marked on the OS eds. to a point 6m to E. Original position was just SSE of the summit of a high drumlin ridge. It comprised an irregular, hard, composite boulder (H 1.15m; dims. 0.85m x 0.62m) noteworthy for the numerous streaks of quartzite in its composition. The stone has been removed from the second position in recent years and is now unlocated.
24:1 3-9-1991

72 ARDLENY
OS 37:3:3 (626,564) Not marked OD 300–400 24129, 29086

Standing stone Not marked on any OS ed. Sited on a natural knoll in dry pasture. Round-topped standing stone (H *c.* 1.5m; max. dim. at base *c.* 0.7m). Much worn as a consequence of its utilisation as a scratching post by cattle.
37:7 14-7-1986

73 BRUSE (Tullyhunco By.)
OS 24:16:4 (738,23) *'Cloghmore'* OD 300–400 23266, 29788

Standing stone Situated on precipitous ground ESE of Bruse Hill. It has recently been knocked over and broken and now lies flat in the field. Roughly rectangular in plan (H 1.57m; dims 0.85m x 0.28m). Known locally as 'an cloch óir', rather than 'an cloch mór'.
24:13 3-9-1991

74 CAMAGH
OS 13:7:3 (669,409) *'Standing Stone'* OD 200–300 22202, 31466

Standing stone Not marked on OS 1836 or 1876 eds. Situated just N of the summit of a prominent hillock. Irregularly-shaped boulder (H 1.58m; dims. 1.02m x 0.57m) aligned NNE–SSW.
13:7 12-6-1989

75 CLONKEIFFY
OS 42:4:3 (908,572) Not marked OD 300–400 25408, 28467

Standing stone (possible) Not marked on any OS ed. Sited on the W slope of a low drumlin ridge. Small standing stone, approximately triangular in profile (Wth at base *c.* 2m; H *c.* 1.5m). Some small loose stones at its base. May be a scratching post for cattle rather than an antiquity.
42:7 15-6-1987

76 CLONKEIFFY
OS 42:4:3 (917,573) Not marked OD 300–400 25417, 28468

Standing stone Not marked on any OS ed. Sited on level ground in fertile pasture. Small, squat, upright stone (H 1.3m; Wth at base *c.* 1.5m). May be a scratching stone for cattle rather than an antiquity.
42:9 15-6-1987

77 COPPANAGH (Clankee By.)
OS 34:11:3 (647,291) Not marked OD 600–700 27074, 29466

Standing stone Not marked on any OS ed. Sited on the SW shoulder of a high drumlin hill. Standing stone (H 1.4m; max. dim. at base 1.5m) tapering to a point at the top.
34:14 27-5-1988

78 CORNABASTE
OS 16:16:5 (785,64) *'Giants Grave'* OD 200–300 25253, 31129

Standing stone Marked 'Giant's Grave' on all OS eds. Situated on the highest point of a low drumlin ridge. Large irregularly shaped pillar (H 1.9m; dims. 1.1m x 1m). (de Valera and Ó Nualláin 1972, 138, No. 6)
16:26(01) 29-10-1989

79 DRUMBRAWN
OS 15:8:5 (771,336) Not marked OD 200–300 24260, 31408

Standing stone Not marked on any OS ed. Sited in a hollow surrounded on all sides by high ground. Large irregularly shaped block (H 1.03m; dims. 1.05m x 0.28m). Regarded in the locality as an antiquity.
15:27 21-9-1989

80 DRUMHURT
OS 22:1:6 (205,525) *'Giant's Grave'* OD 400–500 25618, 30980

Standing stone A squat upright stone (H 1.3m; dims. 1.3m x 0.65m) associated with two large prostrate stones, one lying 4m N and the other 2m E of the standing stone.
22:21(02) 19-10-1990

81 DRUMLIFF (ED Ballyhaise)
OS 15:12:2 (825,252) *'Standing Stone'* OD 300–400 24319, 31319

Standing stone Not marked on OS 1836 ed. Sited on the highest point of a prominent drumlin ridge. Irregularly shaped slab aligned WNW–ESE (H 1.4m; dims. 0.87m x 0.42m). Lying against it at NE is a buttress stone (H 0.1m; dims. 0.87m x 0.42m).
15:35 15-9-1989

82 GORTNASHANGAN LOWER or BINGFIELD
OS 25 NPL Not marked OD 200–300
Standing stone According to Davies (ITA Survey 1946), this was situated on a slight rise in good pasture with a restricted view. A very weathered block of local granite (H 1.2m; dims. 1m x 0.74m). Socket packed with several small stones. Not located.
25:130

83 KILNAVERT
OS 13:4:4 (756,469) *'Standing Stone'* OD 250
22293, 31530
Standing stone Marked on all OS eds. Large irregular boulder (H 1.1m; dims. 1.15m x 0.76m) orientated E–W. A hole has been cut into the top of the stone to hold a wooden post which forms part of the field boundary. The stone was used as an altar during the Penal times and two apparently natural depressions in its upper surface were used to hold the water and wine (local information). Also on top of the stone is an OS bench-mark.
13:35 19-6-1989

84 KILNAVERT
OS 13:4:5 (778,494) *'Standing Stone'* OD 200–300
22316, 31557
Standing stone Not marked on OS 1836 ed. Situated 4.5m N of Kilnavert wedge tomb (**49**). Large irregularly shaped stone (H 1.76m; dims. 0.8m x 0.35m) aligned ENE–WSW.
13:37(02) 19-6-1989

85 KILNAVERT
OS 13:4:5 (782,483) *'Standing Stone'* OD 200–300
22320, 31545
Standing stone Not marked on OS 1836 or 1876 eds. Sited on the NW slope of a low drumlin ridge. Large irregular boulder (H 2.1m; dims. 0.97m x 0.78m) aligned E–W.
13:38 19-6-1989

86 MAYO
OS 18:9:1 (24,259) Not marked OD 600–700
26399, 31346
Standing stone Not marked on any OS ed. Situated a short distance SE of the highest point of a steep drumlin. An irregularly shaped upright stone slab (H 0.95m; dims. 0.86m x 0.23m).
18:11 16-5-1993

87 MOHER (ED Denn)
OS 26:3:6 (660,480) Not marked OD 600–700
25129, 30287
Standing stone Situated on a small level ridge overlooked by Slieve Glah. Irregularly shaped stone tapering to a point (H 1.55m; dims 1.34m x 0.55m). It contains many cupmark-type depressions which are almost certainly natural in origin.
26:56 25-10-1992

88 MULLAGHBOY (Tullyhaw By.)
OS 4:5:6 (159,323) Indicated OD 500–600
20671, 33282
Standing stone (possible) Not marked on OS 1836 or 1876 eds. Sited on the NE slope of a hillock in rough mountainous terrain. Low irregularly shaped boulder (H 0.47m; dims. 0.5m x 0.47m) aligned NW–SE.
4:19 12-8-1988

89 POLLAMORE NEAR
OS 25:4:3 (867,542) Not marked OD 300–400
24372, 30346
Standing stone An irregularly shaped boulder tapering to a point (H 1.1m; Wth 0.82m). Situated a short distance SSW of a levelled rath (**1046**) and just S of the summit of a high hill.
25:102 13-9-1991

90 TOBERLYAN
OS 13:8:5 (811,367) Not marked OD 200–300
22352, 31423
Standing stone (original location) Formerly sited on the W slope of a drumlin ridge. Original location of a large irregular boulder said to have been in a recumbent position (local information). At the time of this field report it was lying in a quarry *c.* 120m to S.
13:58 24-10-1969

91 TOBERLYAN
OS 13:8:5 (826,346) Not marked OD 200–300
22368, 31401
Standing stone (original location) Formerly sited on the SE slope of a drumlin ridge. Original location of a large irregular boulder said to have been in a recumbent position (local information) and when last visited was lying in a quarry *c.* 80m to NW.
13:60 24-10-1969

92 TULLYBUCK
OS 15:15:5 (587,25) Not marked OD 200–300
24070, 31077
Standing stones (site) Not marked on any OS ed. Situated on the SE shoulder of a low hill. Davies (NMI survey 1942) recorded this as the site of three standing stones. Not visible at ground level.
15:72 12-8-1989

Decorated Prehistoric Stone

The corpus of Irish standing stones decorated with incised motifs of the characteristic La Tène art style comprises the Turoe Stone from County Galway, the Castlestrange Stone from County Roscommon, the Derrykeighan Stone from County Antrim and the Killycluggin Stone described below. The La Tène art form is thought to have been developed in the middle of the last millenium BC by the Celtic peoples of Central Europe. It incorporates and adapts elements of Classical Greek, Etruscan, Roman and even Far Eastern motifs into a unique art style that is immediately recognisable as 'Celtic'. The decoration of the Irish examples cited above belongs to a variation of the La Tène art form known as the Waldalgesheim style dating from the third or second centuries BC.

Fig. 7—*The Killycluggin stone (**93**), decorated in characteristic La Tène style (Reproduced courtesy of National Museum of Ireland).*

93 KILLYCLUGGIN
OS 13:4:6 (860,513) Not marked OD 200–300
22402, 31578

Decorated stone (site) Originally situated 10m ESE of a stone circle (**62**). Two panels of a monolith decorated with intricate La Tène motifs now housed in the National Museum. There were probably at least two other panels but these have been destroyed. Excavation by Raftery (1978, 49–54) revealed that 'the stone stood in a flat-bottomed pit which had been deliberately sunk 80cm into the subsoil to receive it'. Immediately E of the stone he found the remains of a cist burial (**165**). (Macalister 1922, 113–16; Ó Ríordáin 1952, 68; Herity and Eogan 1977, 245; Ó Ríordáin 1979, 114, 155; Harbison 1988, 160; Killanin and Duignan 1989, 12, 61; Flanagan 1992, 130)
13:26(01) 22-6-1989

Barrows

A common feature of Irish prehistoric funerary practice was the construction of a mound of stone or earth over burials. Barrows are generally identifiable as earthen mounds. The purpose of such a mound was twofold; firstly, to mark the position of the burial or burials, and secondly, to protect same from the ravages of nature and human and animal predators. Archaeological excavation has revealed that the practice of covering burials with earthen mounds dates from the Middle Neolithic period up until relatively recent times. However, most are thought to date from the Bronze and Iron Ages. The most common type of barrow in County Cavan is the ring-barrow. These generally survive as small, circular, earthen mounds enclosed by a low earthen bank with an internal fosse. In County Cavan, barrows generally occur in isolation. Nonetheless conjoined barrows are known from Ardlow (**96**) and there would appear to have been cemeteries at Cargagh (**100**) comprising at least six barrows, another at Cornasuas (**104**) comprising at least eight, and perhaps another at Banagher (**97, 98**). The most common funerary rite appears to have been cremation, but inhumations in cists have also been identified. However, archaeological excavation at a number of sites yielded no burial evidence (Ó Ríordáin 1979, 138–42), and consequently their function remains unclear.

Fig. 8—*Ring-barrow at Banagher* (**98**).

94 AGHAVOHER/CLIFTON
OS 14:6:3 (399,397) Hachured OD 300–400
22892, 31460

Ring-barrow Marked 'Fort' on OS 1836 and 1876 eds. Sited on the S slope of a steep hill. Raised circular area (int. diam. 11.8m) enclosed by a low earthen bank with a wide, deep internal fosse. The internal area is greatly disturbed by a modern field boundary running NNW–SSE which divides the site into two roughly equal portions. Original entrance not recognisable.
14:3 19-7-1989

95 ARDLOW
OS 39:8:3 (847,452) Indicated OD 400–500
26314, 28989

Barrow (possible) Marked 'Fort' on OS 1836 and 1876 eds. Situated within a plantation of deciduous and coniferous trees. A poorly preserved low circular mound (diam *c.* 20m N–S; H *c.* 0.4m) defined by a low scarp. This is clearly identifiable from NE–S–W; elsewhere it is largely levelled. Immediately NNW of centre is a roughly circular shallow depression (diam *c.* 9m).
39:4 10-6-1987

96 ARDLOW
OS 39:4:3 (856,590) Hachured OD 400–500 26322, 29134
Barrows (conjoined) Situated on the summit of a low drumlin hill. The NW site is very poorly preserved. It comprises an ill-defined low circular earthen mound (int. diam. *c.* 10.5m) enclosed by vague traces of a bank with internal fosse. Original entrance may have been at E. From ESE–S–SSW its bank merges with that of the SE barrow. The SE site comprises a low circular earthen platform (int. diam. 6.6m; H 0.5m) enclosed by a low but well-defined earthen bank with internal narrow fosse. Break in bank with accompanying causeway at E represents original entrance.
39:6 10-6-1987

97 BANAGHER
OS 26:9:6 (220,187) Not marked OD 700–800 24667, 29974
Ring-barrow One of a complex of burial and ritual sites which occupy an area 150m by 130m on a patch of uneven elevated pasture overlooked from the NW by Slieve Glah (**11, 60, 61, 65, 98**). A largely levelled low circular mound (int. diam. 6.2m; H 0.27m) enclosed by a much-defaced low earthen bank with vague traces of an internal fosse. Original entrance not recognisable.
26:4(02) 16-5-1993

98 BANAGHER
OS 26:9:6 (220,187) Not marked OD 700–800 24667, 29974
Ring-barrow An element of the above mentioned complex of burial and ritual sites (**11, 60, 61, 65, 97**). Low flat-topped mound (diam. 12m; H 0.4m) enclosed by an earthen bank (H 0.3m; Wth 2m) with internal fosse. A field boundary traverses the site in a NW–SE direction.
26:4(05) 16-5-1993

99 BLACKHILLS LOWER
OS 34:11:4 (497,180) Not marked OD 400–500 26916, 29347
Ring-barrow Marked 'Fort' on OS 1836 and 1876 eds. Sited at the foot of a high drumlin hill. Circular area (int. diam. 9m N–S) enclosed by a low earthen bank. Traces of a possible external fosse at NW and SW. Original entrance may have been at NW.
34:3 20-4-1988

100 CARGAGH (Upper Loughtee By.)
OS 26:10:2 (348,249) *'Cromwell's Camp'* OD 500–600 26764, 28778
Barrow cemetery (possible) Sited on the SW shoulder of a high drumlin hill. Low circular earthen mound (diam. 5m; H 0.5m) enclosed by a low earthen bank with shallow internal fosse. One of six small circular enclosures noted on OS 1836 and 1876 eds. under the collective designation 'Cromwell's Camp' — presumably a barrow cemetery. This is the only upstanding barrow of the former complex. It is known locally as the site of 'Cromwell's tent'.
26:9 28-7-1989

101 CARRAMOREEN
OS 12:13:4 (1,41) Hachured OD 200–300 24420, 31738
Ring-barrow Marked 'Fort' on OS 1836 and 1876 eds. Sited on the summit of a prominent drumlin hill. Raised circular area (int. diam. 11.3m) enclosed by a berm (Wth 4.4m), a poorly defined shallow fosse (Wth 2.3m) and a low earthen bank. Original entrance not recognisable. Overgrown with vegetation.
12:1 10-5-1993

102 CARRICKABOY GLEBE
OS 26:10:3 (445,255) *'The Saints Grave or Flags of Denn'* OD 700–800 24904, 30048
Barrow Sited immediately E of the summit of a prominent drumlin hill. Small circular raised area (int. dims. 14.7m N–W; 13m E–W) enclosed by a low bank of earth and stone. No fosse. Narrow break in bank at NE. Internal area uneven. At centre is a low irregular grass-covered mound of stones of unknown significance.
26:13 24-10-1991

103 CLOGHBALLYBEG
OS 40:14:1 (271,96) Indicated OD 300–400 26685, 28616
Barrow (possible) Marked 'Fort' on OS 1836 and 1876 eds. Sited on the NE shoulder of a drumlin ridge. Depicted as a tree-ring on the 1913 ed. Small circular area (int. diam. *c.* 14m N–S) enclosed by a low bank of earth and stone. The enclosed area rises from the perimeter to the centre where there is a large irregularly shaped boulder. The site has been planted with coniferous trees.
40:3 16-7-1987

104 CORNASAUS (Tullygarvey By.)
OS 22:15:1 (487,124) Not marked OD 700–800 25920, 30558

Barrow cemetery (possible, site) Eight very small 'Forts' marked on OS 1836 ed. Marked 'Site of' on 1876 ed. Situated on the SE slope of a high drumlin hill. Probably a barrow cemetery. Not visible at ground level.
22:6(01) 17-10-1990

105 CORRAN (Tullyhaw By.)
OS 13:4:5 (822,473) Not marked OD 200–300
22363, 31535
Ring-barrow Marked 'Fort' on OS 1836 and 1876 eds. Sited on the NE slope of a low drumlin ridge. Low flat-topped circular mound (diam. 5.3m E–W) enclosed by a low earthen bank with wide, shallow, internal fosse. From NE–E–SSE the bank has been greatly disturbed by the construction of a field boundary. Original entrance not recognisable. An earlier report (OPW 1969) recorded a shallow circular depression immediately E of the centre of the mound.
13:16 19-6-1989

106 CORRAN (Tullyhaw By.)
OS 13:4:6 (858,493) Not marked OD 200–300
22400, 31557
Ring-barrow Marked 'Fort' on OS 1836 and 1876 eds. Sited on the NNE slope of a prominent drumlin ridge. Low circular earthen mound (diam. 9.4m) enclosed by a low earthen bank with wide, shallow, internal fosse. Bank identifiable from WSW–N–E. Original entrance not recognisable.
13:17 19-6-1989

107 DOON (ED Ballyconnell)
OS 10:10:1 (265,233) Not marked OD 200–300
22746, 31925
Ring-barrow Not marked on any OS ed. Largely levelled. Remains comprise a low earthen mound (diam. 1.55m; H 0.2m) enclosed by a low earthen bank (Wth 1.35m) with internal fosse (Wth 1.35m). Situated *c.* 75m NE of a court tomb (**31**).
10:14 26-5-1993

108 DRUMAD
OS 28:7:2 (547,395) Hachured OD 500–600
26962, 30214
Ring-barrow This barrow is located in the NW quadrant of a large circular enclosure (**1328**). Raised circular area (H 0.5m; diam. *c.* 13m) surrounded by a shallow fosse (Wth *c.* 3m) which is almost completely infilled at N.
28:12(02) 14-9-1988

109 DUNGUMMIN LOWER
OS 42:3:6 (634,495) Hachured OD 200–300
25119, 28383
Barrow Not marked on OS 1836 or 1876 eds. Sited on the summit of a low hillock. Small circular mound (diam. *c.* 8.5m; H 1.5m) enclosed by a low but well-defined earthen bank. Original entrance not recognisable.
42:13(01) 11-9-1986

110 EDENBURT
OS 44:5:4 (71,315) Indicated OD 300–400
26477, 28205
Ring-barrow (site) Sited on the NW shoulder of a high drumlin ridge. Almost completely levelled. An earlier report (OPW 1969) described a low circular mound (diam. 4.5m) enclosed by a low bank of earth and stone with a narrow, shallow, internal fosse.
44:7 21-8-1987

111 KILL DEMESNE
OS 37:4:1 (729,599) Hachured OD 300–400
24237, 29125
Barrow Sited on the W shoulder of a prominent drumlin hill. Raised circular area (int. diam. 18m) enclosed by a low earthen bank. Break in bank at ENE probably represents original entrance.
37:37 16-7-1986

112 KILNAVERT
OS 13:4:4 (756,459) Hachured OD 200–300
22293, 31519
Ring-barrow Sited immediately S of the highest point of a drumlin ridge. Raised circular area (int. diam. 12.7m N–S) enclosed by a substantial earthen bank with wide, shallow, internal fosse. Original entrance not recognisable.
13:34 19-6-1989

113 KILNAVERT
OS 13:4:4 (761,466) Indicated OD 200–300
22298, 31527
Ring-barrow Sited immediately E of the highest point of a drumlin hill. Marked 'Fort' on OS 1836 and 1876 eds. Roughly circular raised area (int. dims. 29.6m NE–SW; 27.6m NW–SE) enclosed by a low earthen bank with a very wide, shallow, internal fosse. The greater part of the bank has been modified and incorporated into the field boundary. Slight traces are identifiable from ENE–NNE. Original entrance not recognisable.
13:36 19-6-1989

114 KILNAVERT
OS 13:4:5 (813,514) *'Grave'* OD 200–300
22352, 31578
Ring-barrow Sited immediately S of the highest point of a prominent drumlin hill. Small, circular, flat-topped mound of earth and stone (int. diam. 7.5m NNW–SSE) with the remains of a kerb of low stones about the

perimeter of the summit. The mound is enclosed by a narrow, well-defined bank of earth and stone with narrow, deep, internal fosse. The bank has been removed from SW–W probably in relatively modern times. Of the kerbstones, fifteen remain in position; four at SSE and the remaining ten from SW–NNW.
13:40 19-6-1989

115 LISSANOVER
OS 13:4:4 (763,519) Indicated OD 200–300
22300, 31584

Ring-barrow Marked 'Fort' on OS 1836 and 1876 eds. Sited on the highest point of a low natural rise. Raised circular area (int. dims 15.7m N–S; 15.3m E–W) enclosed by a low but well-defined earthen bank with a wide, shallow, internal fosse. Original entrance not recognisable.
13:43 22-6-1989

116 MANRAGH UPPER
OS 4:6:1 (294,431) Hachured OD 500–600
20812, 33397

Ring-barrow Marked 'Fort' on OS 1836 and 1876 eds. Sited on the SE slope of a mountain. Circular mound of earth and stone (diam. 11.9m; H 0.65m) encircled by a wide, shallow, external fosse which has been infilled from WNW–N–NE where a modern stone field boundary skirts the site. The mound is largely flat-topped except for a low irregularly shaped rise in the centre.
4:13 10-8-1988

117 RAHEG
OS 16:13:5 (100,48) Hachured OD 200–300
24530, 31106

Barrow Sited on the summit of a prominent drumlin hill. Raised circular area (int. diam. 8.2m) enclosed by an external bank and two scarps with outer berms. Outside of the outer bank is a shallow depression which may represent a fosse. Both outer fosse and bank are incorporated into the field boundary. Original entrance not recognisable. The site was formerly planted with trees.
16:108 19-10-1989

118 TOBERLYAN
OS 13:8:5 (826,361) Hachured OD 200–300
22368, 31417

Barrow (site) Marked 'Fort' on OS 1836 and 1876 eds. Sited on the WSW slope of a prominent drumlin ridge. Levelled in the early 1960s. The outline of the site was still identifiable in 1969 (OPW 1969). It apparently comprised a small raised subcircular area (int. dims. 8.7m E–W; 7.1m N–S) enclosed by a low earthen bank with possible traces of a shallow external fosse. There was a break in the bank at NNE (local information). Not visible at ground level.
13:61 10-6-1989

Cairns and Mounds

A cairn can be defined as a mound of loose stones. Cairns are a characteristic feature of the morphology of megalithic tombs which are generally assigned to the Neolithic and Early Bronze Ages, while others such as Killarah (**151**) and Killycarney (**152**) cover cist and pit burials which date from the Early Bronze Age. However, not all cairns were constructed as coverings for burials. Some, such as the example at Eshveagh (**146**), appear to have been constructed as boundary markers. Others may have been erected as commemorative monuments. Field-clearance heaps of stones are often difficult to distinguish from genuine prehistoric cairns on the basis of surface remains. Also included in this chapter are a series of earthen mounds which appear to have been constructed as boundary markers, and four other earthen mounds which cannot be more definitively classified on the basis of present evidence.

119 AGHNACALLY
OS 7:12:5 (782,183) Not marked OD 700–800
22311, 32509

Cairn Marked on the OS 1836 and 1876 eds. as the 'Black Carn'. It is depicted as an oval enclosure (dims. *c.* 80m NW–SE; *c.* 55m ENE–WSW) on the 1836 ed. Situated within a dense modern plantation of coniferous trees. Not located.
7:3

120 ALTCROCK/GOWLAN (ED Benbrack)
OS 8:4:4 (695,488) 'Pile of Stones' OD 900–1000
21247, 32181

Cairn (possible) Not marked on the OS 1836 or 1876 eds. Situated in precipitous mountain terrain on the border between the townlands of Altcrock and Gowlan. The site may represent a prehistoric cairn reused as a boundary marker during the introduction of townland divisions, or it may be contemporaneous with this development. Not visited.
8:1

121 ALTEEN
OS 7:1:1 (38,538) 'Mound' OD 1200–1300
21523, 32876

Mound In rough mountainous terrain. One of a series of mounds and cairns which mark the boundary between counties Cavan and Fermanagh. Remains comprise a low, roughly circular, poorly preserved mound (diam. *c.* 8m; H. *c.* 0.6m) mainly composed of peat.
7:5 21-8-1989

122 ALTEEN
OS 7:1:1 (54,538) 'Mound' OD 1200–1300
21539, 32876

Mound In rough mountainous terrain. One of a series of mounds and cairns which mark the border between counties Cavan and Fermanagh. Remains comprise a low, roughly circular, ill-defined, poorly preserved mound (diam. *c.* 15.5m; H. *c.* 0.3m) composed mainly of peat.
7:6 21-8-1989

123 ALTEEN/COMMAS/DUNMAKEEVER
OS 6:3:6 (688,471) Not marked OD 2188
21233, 32803

Cairn An almost circular cairn (diam. *c.* 16m; H 3.2m). The NE half of the site is enclosed by the remains of a substantial drystone wall. Situated on the summit of Cuilcagh Mountain on the border between counties Cavan and Fermanagh. The site was known as 'hacht a mhac a whoole' commemorating McEnhill, chief of a clan driven out of Tyrone by the O'Neills. According to tradition the cairn was used as an inauguration site by the Maguires. In the late forties of this century workers tossed some stones and built a triangulation station on top of the monument (Glangevlin Guild ICA 1983, 42). There are three hut sites a short distance to SE (**1268, 1269, 1270**).
6:1 23-8-1989

124 BELLVILLE
OS 25:10:5 (365,166) Not marked OD 200–300
23845, 29944

Cairn (site) Recorded by Davies (ITA Survey 1942) and given an approximate location close to the highest point of a long, narrow drumlin ridge. A modern pathway now occupies portion of the site. Not visible at ground level.
25:5 19-9-1991

125 BRUSE (Tullyhunco By.)
OS 24:14:4 (253,65) Not marked OD 800–856
22752, 29827

Cairn Site is situated *c.* 100m SW of the summit of Bruse Hill and is heavily overgrown with heather. Oval-shaped cairn (H 0.6m; dims. *c.* 10.4m NE–SW; *c.* 8.4m NW–SE) comprising small and medium-sized stones. Enclosed by at least eight large kerbstones; six are on edge, two have fallen.
24:9 3-9-1991

126 BRUSE (Tullyhunco By.)
OS 24:15:6 (644,39) Not marked OD 800–850
23165, 29804

Cairn An almost circular cairn of small to medium-sized stones (H 0.6m; dims. 6.2m NW–SE; 5.9m NE–SW). Situated close to the summit of Bruse Hill and heavily overgrown with heather.
24:10 3-9-1991

127 BRUSE (Tullyhunco By.)
OS 24:15:6 (645,26) *'Carn'* OD 856 23166, 29791
Cairn Situated on the summit of Bruse Hill. A roughly circular cairn (H 1.2m; dims. 21.5 N–S; 19m E–W) with large stones placed about the perimeter at SE and ENE. Greatly disturbed by modern digging. A triangulation point has been erected on top of the cairn.
24:11 3-9-1991

128 BURREN (ED Tuam)
OS 4:1:3 (75,353) Not marked OD 800–900
Cairn Situated 10m SW of a wedge tomb (**14**). The cairn has been disturbed by tree-planting. It is round in outline, 5.5m in diameter and up to 1m high. Inward-leaning kerbstones survive along its southern half. These are generally 0.5m x 0.8m high with the exception of two at SE and one at W which are each 1.2m high. (Lowry-Corry and Richardson 1937, 168)
4:21 11-5-1993

129 CARN (Upper Loughtee By.)
OS 26:10:3 (442,268) Hachured OD 500–600 24900, 30062
Cairn (site, possible) Marked 'Carn' on the OS 1836 ed. Not marked on OS 1876 ed. Situated on the summit of a steep limestone hill with much rock outcrop protruding. Not visible at ground level.
26:12 23-3-1992

130 CARNAGARVE
OS 34:10:4 (235,153) Not marked OD 644 26640, 29316
Cairn (site, possible) Marked 'Carnagarvie' on OS Fair Plan and 'Carnagarve' on 1836 ed. Not marked on subsequent eds. Situated on the summit of a drumlin hill. Not visible at ground level.
34:6 16-5-1988

131 CARNAGARVE
OS 34:10:4 (238,203) Not marked OD 600–700 26643, 29369
Cairn (site, possible) Marked 'Carn' and depicted as a small circular enclosure on OS 1836 and 1876 eds. Situated on the E shoulder of a drumlin ridge. Not visible at ground level.
34:7 16-5-1988

132 CARNAGARVE
OS 34:10:5 (330,159) Not marked OD 400–500 26740, 29323
Cairn (site) Marked 'Old Carn' on OS Fair Plan. Not marked on subsequent eds. Situated on the SE slope of a drumlin ridge. Not visible at ground level.
34:11 16-5-1988

133 CARNALYNCH
OS 34:9:2 (142,288) *'Carn'* OD 755 26541, 29458
Cairn Sited on the summit of a prominent hill. Circular area (int. diam. *c.* 26m E–W) defined by a low bank composed mainly of stone. From SW–NW it is defined by a low stone embankment. It has been largely levelled from NE–SE. The interior is divided into four roughly equal portions by modern field boundaries. There are low mounds of stone in the S and W quadrants.
34:12 26-3-1974

134 CARNALYNCH
OS 34:9:3 (190,236) Not marked OD 715 26592, 29403
Cairn (site, possible) Marked 'Carnlinh(s)' on OS Fair Plan and 'Carnalynch' on 1836 ed. Not marked on subsequent eds. Situated on the E shoulder of a drumlin hill. Not visible at ground level.
34:13 25-5-1988

135 CARRICKBRANNAN
OS 5:15:1 (491,522) Not marked OD 200–300 20060, 31744
Cairn Not marked on any OS ed. Sited at the foot of a hill in close proximity to a stream. Small irregular cairn of large stones (max. dim. 1.3m; H 0.6m). This feature may be associated with a gravel pit, marked on OS 1836 ed. a short distance to SW.
5:2 12-8-1988

136 CLARAGH (ED Drumcarn)
OS 16:2:4 (276,521) Not marked OD 400–500 24711, 31607
Cairn Sited on the summit of a drumlin hill. An approximately rectangular cairn (dims. 9.1m N–S; 7.1m E–W). Much denuded (max. H. 1.1m). The remains of a megalithic structure called 'Cloghard' (**23**) lies 15m to E.
16:15(01) 9-11-1989

137 COPPANAGHMORE
OS 5:13:3 (163,209) 'Pile of Stones' OD 1200–1800 19711, 32071
Cairn Not marked on OS 1836 or 1876 eds. Situated on the border between counties Cavan and Leitrim. Probably a boundary cairn. Not visited.
5:11

138 COPPANAGHMORE
OS 5:13:3 (159,202) 'Pile of Stones' OD 1200–1800 19706, 32079
Cairn Not marked on OS 1836 or 1876 eds. Situated on the border between counties Cavan and Leitrim. Probably a boundary cairn. Not visited.
5:12

139 COPPANAGHMORE
OS 5:13:3 (180,238) 'Mound' OD 1200–1800 19729, 32041

Mound Not marked on OS 1836 or 1876 eds. Situated on the border between counties Cavan and Leitrim. Most likely a boundary mound. Not visited.
5:10

140 COPPANAGHMORE/TULLANTINTIN
OS 5:13:3 (242,736) 'Mound' OD 1200–1300 19736, 32034

Mound Not marked on OS 1836 or 1876 eds. Situated on the border between the townlands of Coppanaghmore and Tullantintin (both in County Cavan) and between counties Cavan and Leitrim. Most likely a boundary mound. Not visited.
5:9

141 CORCASHEL (Tullyhaw By.)/ MONEENTERRIFF
OS 5:13:3 (230,244) 'Pile of Stones' OD 1200–1800 19782, 32035

Cairn Not marked on OS 1836 or 1876 eds. Situated on the border between the townlands of Corcashel and Moneenterriff (both in County Cavan) and between counties Cavan and Leitrim. Probably a boundary cairn. Not visited.
5:18

142 CORCASHEL (Tullyhaw By.)/SRUHANAGH
OS 5:14:1 (241,677) 'Mound' OD 1200–1800 19793, 32035

Mound Not marked on OS 1836 or 1876 eds. Situated on the border between the townlands of Corcashel and Sruhanagh (both in County Cavan) and between counties Cavan and Leitrim. Probably a boundary mound. Not visited.
5:17

143 CORLECKAGH UPPER/ MONEENTERRIFF
OS 5:13:3 (211,244) 'Pile of Stones' OD 1200–1800 19762, 32035

Cairn Not marked on OS 1836 or 1876 eds. Situated on the border between the townlands of Corleckagh Upper and Moneenterriff (both in County Cavan) and between counties Cavan and Leitrim. Probably a boundary cairn. Not visited.
5:20

144 CORNADIMPAN GLEBE
OS 21 NPL Not marked

Cairn Not marked on any OS ed. An earlier report (NMI 1938) recorded a cairn known as 'The Druid's Cairn' in this townland. During ploughing at the edge of the cairn, two cists containing human bones were uncovered (**160**). Not located.
21:75(01)

145 DOON (ED Benbrack)/Moneensauran
OS 8:6:1 (262,488) '*Cloghnacommerky*' OD 1365 20790, 32135

Cairn (possible) Marked on the OS 1836 and 1876 eds. Situated in steep mountainous terrain on the border between the townlands of Doon and Moneensauran. The term 'clogh' in the site name indicates a stone structure. It may represent a prehistoric cairn which was utilised as a marker during the introduction of townland divisions or it may be contemporaneous with this development. Not visited.
8:2

146 ESHVEAGH
OS 4:14:6 (411,25) 'Pile of Stones' OD 1900–2000 20940, 32969

Cairn Not marked on OS 1836 or 1876 eds. Situated on the border between counties Cavan and Fermanagh. Small, low, circular cairn of stones (diam. *c.* 15m; H 0.6m). Rising from the cairn are four piles of stones, two of which are narrow, steep-sided and tapering to a point (Wth 0.6m; H 1.3m) and apparently constructed from original cairn material. The other two are lower, wider and less well defined. The authors of *The Kingdom of Glan* (Glangevlin Guild ICA 1983, 42) refer to the site as 'Lacht an Phelim' from Phelim O'Dolan who was an ancient proprietor of Gleann Gaibhle, and stated that 'it was erected some centuries ago'.
4:6 14-8-1989

147 GARVESK/SRUHANAGH
OS 5:14:1 (250,240) 'Pile of Stones' OD 1200–1800 19803, 32039

Cairn Not marked on OS 1836 or 1876 eds. Situated on the border between Garvesk and Sruhanagh (both in County Cavan) and between counties Cavan and Leitrim. Probably a boundary cairn. Not visited.
5:33 15-8-1988

148 GORTNALEG (ED Tuam)
OS 4:1:6 (161,519) Not marked OD 700–800 20671, 33489

Cairn (site) Marked 'Carn' on OS 1836 and 1876 eds. At the location indicated, there is a scatter of *c.* forty small and medium-sized stones which may formerly have belonged to a cairn.
4:8 18-5-1993

149 KILLARAH
OS 14:1:4 (38,479) Not marked OD 200–300 22510, 31542

Cairn First noted by Richardson in the early 18th

Fig. 9—*A large cairn at Killarah* (**151**), *close to the summit of Ballyheady Mountain.*

century (Paterson, Gaffikin and Davies 1938, 147). Marked 'Fort' on OS 1836 and 1876 eds. Situated on the summit of a low hill. A much-denuded circular cairn of small stones (diam. 20.7m ENE–WSW; H 0.4m). The site is divided into two unequal portions by a field boundary aligned ENE–WSW. Only the outline of the perimeter is identifiable on the SSE side of the boundary.

14:40 18-7-1989

150 KILLARAH

OS 14:1:4 (52,475) *'Carn'* OD 200–300

22525, 31539

Cairn First noted by Richardson in the early 18th century (Paterson, Gaffikin and Davies 1938, 147). Marked on all OS eds. Situated on the summit of a low hill. It would appear from its depiction on the OS to have been originally oval in plan (dims. *c.* 37m NE–SW; *c.* 22m NW–SE). The site is thickly overgrown with vegetation. Nonetheless a much-denuded apparently circular cairn of small stones (diam. 14m; H 0.8m) is identifiable. A modern field boundary aligned NNE–SSW divides the site into two roughly equal portions. A second bank of earth and stone runs from WNW–SSW and its outline can also be traced from ENE–SE.

14:41 18-7-1989

151 KILLARAH

OS 14:1:5 (100,459) *'Carn'* OD 200–300

22575, 31522

Cairn First noted by Richardson in the early 18th century (Paterson, Gaffikin and Davies 1938, 147). Marked on all OS eds. Situated on a natural terrace, a short distance NE of the summit of Ballyheady Mountain, surrounded by a plantation of coniferous trees. A much-denuded, large, circular, now almost flat-topped cairn of large and small stones (dims. 28m NW–SE; 27.2m NE–SW; H 3.2m). A large slab is visible within a hole which has been dug into the lower edge of the cairn at ENE. It apparently formed part of the cist burial (**163**) investigated by Ó Ríordáin in 1932 (Ó Ríordáin 1933, 167–71).

14:43(01) 18-7-1989

152 KILLYCARNEY

OS 2 NPL Not marked OD 200–400

Cairn (site) Recorded by Wakeman (1879, 183–200)

as a circular 'tumulus' of which the 'circumference was twenty-seven yards; the height, as measured by railway authorities, fifteen feet and a-half'. He described it as a natural mound upon which was laid a stratum of soil covered by a layer of stones. Two stone-lined cists (**164**) containing artifacts were found within the mound. Not located. (Lowry-Corry and Richardon 1937, 160–1)
2:30(01)

153 MARAHILL (Upper Loughtee By.)
OS 25:1:4 (37,472) Indicated OD 100–200
23496, 30264

Cairn Depicted as a circular enclosure on OS 1836 and 1876 eds. Situated in wet marshy ground adjacent to what is apparently an extinct lake. Low cairn of small and medium-sized stones (H 0.3m; dims. 16.1m E–W; 12.2m N–S).
25:95 24-9-1991

154 MONESK
OS 3:6:6 (444,370) Not marked OD 1300–1400
19997, 33325

Cairn Not marked on any OS ed. Situated in rough mountainous terrain *c.* 150m N of Tents Lough. Small circular cairn of large and small loose stones (diam. 2.25m; H 0.9m) tapering to a point.
3:24 12-9-1989

155 MOYER
OS 34:8:2 (786,414) '*Carn*' OD 1119
27220, 29596

Cairn Low circular cairn of stones (diam. 22m; H 2m) surmounted by a triangulation station.
34:41 28-3-1974

156 TEEBANE
OS 3:6:5 (358,316) '*Carn*' OD 1200–1300
19906, 33268

Cairn Marked on all OS eds. Situated on the S shore of Lough Naweelion in rough mountainous terrain. Small subcircular cairn of small loose stones (dims. 3.3m NE–SW; 2.7m NW–SE; H 0.8m) tapering to a point.
3:28 12-9-1989

157 TERMON (Tullyhaw By.)
OS 2:13:1 (50,92) Not marked OD 200–300
20552, 33677

Cairn (site) Not marked on any OS ed. Identified in 1955 by workmen quarrying for road-building material. Examined by Ó Ríordáin (1957, 53–9) in the same year. He found that the cairn was originally circular in plan (diam. *c.* 18m; H *c.* 2.5m) and had contained at least four cists, three of which had been destroyed before he had a chance to record them (**167**). Ó Ríordáin discovered two inverted food vessels at the N end of the surviving cist and three other food vessels from what was believed to have been the largest of the destroyed cists. Not visible at ground level.
2:15(01) 27-8-1988

158 TRINITY ISLAND
OS 20:13:1 (24,88) Not marked OD 100–200
23480, 30499

Cairn Davies (ITA Survey 1942) recorded 'a circular cairn of small stones 40 ft. across and rising 5 ft. above the marsh; clearly artificial. Much overgrown.' If the site location co-ordinates given by Davies are correct, the site is situated on the E shore of 'Scotch Island' in Lough Oughter, a small island in the marshy bay of the much larger Trinity Island. Not visited.
20:59

159 TUAM
OS 2 NPL Not marked OD 100–300

Cairn (site) Not marked on any OS ed. Recorded by Wakeman (1879, 183-200). He described the site as presenting 'the appearance of an ordinary tumulus, the base of which was surrounded by a low rampart'. This was cut into two equal portions in 1879 during the construction of the Sligo-Enniskillen railway. A 'considerable number' of the skeletons of men, women and children were thus exposed. The mound was largely natural but contained 'soil dug and stone-covered kists' in which were found 'deposits of wood-charcoal, containing minute fragments of bone, apparently human' of which only one survived intact (**168**). Other finds from the mound included two well-baked earthen vessels, one of which was decorated, and animal bones. Close to the surface of the mound 'a silver penny of King John, struck in Dublin ... was unearthed'. Not located. (Lowry-Corry and Richardson 1937, 161–2)
2:31(01)

Cists, Pit Burials and Flat Cemetery

A cist comprises a box-like, stone-lined grave found either buried in the earth or within a cairn. In most cases the grave is covered by a single capstone or a number of stones. Short and polygonal cists, containing crouched inhumations or cremations, often accompanied by a food vessel or other grave-goods, are generally believed to be the most common burial-type of the Bronze Age. Because of their extra length, long cists are often covered by more than one lintel. Cists are usually found in isolation. However, this is not the case in County Cavan where the majority have been discovered within cairns. It is possible that in general terms cists were constructed to hold the remains of the social elite whereas simple pit-graves may represent the burial form of those of lower status within the social hierarchy. A flat cemetery at Gortnacargy (**162**), excavated in 1957, is also included in this chapter. Its dating is problematic. The artifacts and burials appeared contemporaneous suggesting an Early Bronze Age date, but the same artifactual evidence could also be attributed to a Bronze Age occupation, with the site possibly being reused as a cemetery in the Early Iron Age (Ó Ríordáin 1967, 73).

160 CORNADIMPAN GLEBE
OS 21 NPL Not marked

Cists An earlier report (NMI 1938) recorded two cists containing human bones which were revealed at the edge of a cairn (**144**) during ploughing. Both were aligned NW–SE. The first (dims; 2.75m x 1m) was 'protected by three large stones, besides one huge upright at the end. There was also an inner lining of flagstones about *c.* 0.45m x 0.15m standing upright. At the NW of the second, (dims. 3.35m x 1.37m) there was 'a huge stone of about ten cwt weight and close to it another of the same weight protecting the N and E sides'. Not located.
21:75(02)

161 CORNASEER
OS 25:16:1 (695,119) Not marked OD 300–400
24195, 29898

Cist (site) Davies (ITA Survey, 1942) recorded that a 'stone-lined cist with capstone' was found at this location. Bones were also found, and what looked like a 'soldiers helmet' (possibly a food vessel). Not visible at ground level.
25:25 1-11-1991

162 GORTNACARGY
OS 9:10:6 (428,226) Not marked OD 200–300
21943, 31910

Flat cemetery Prior to excavation, the site comprised a low, grass-covered natural knoll of limestone (dims. 11m E–W x 10m N–S; H 0.5m). Three separate graves which reputedly contained extended skeletons, one of which was accompanied by a rimsherd of pottery of food vessel type, were discovered when the cemetery was disturbed during the course of construction of an underground water storage tank in 1956. The site was subsequently excavated by Ó Ríordáin in 1957 yielding a further seven burials, several animal teeth and bones, numerous potsherds and other artifacts, among them a small blue glass bead and chert scrapers. All but one of the skeletons were orientated NW–SE with the skull at NW, and placed individually in their own grave extended on their backs. (Ó Ríordáin 1967, 61–73)
9:11

163 KILLARAH
OS 14:1:5 (100,459) *'Carn'* OD 200–300
22575, 31522

Cist Discovered at the E end of Killarah cairn (**151**). Investigated by Ó Ríordáin (1933, 167–71) in 1932. The grave comprised a limestone slab *c.* 2.14m x 1.21m 'which rested in a sloping position on a stone placed beneath it. The front or eastern end of the grave was closed by a low, roughly built, dry-stone wall which formed the arc of a circle of which the eastern end of the slab was the chord. The space between the wall and the slab was closed by flat stones, some of which had collapsed into the grave'. Within the cist he found both inhumed and cremated human remains but no grave-goods. He believed that the cist represented a secondary burial 'built at some time after the cairn and somewhat outside its periphery' and suggested a tentative Middle Bronze Age date for it. A large slab is visible within a hole which has been dug into the lower edge of the cairn at ENE, which is possibly the covering stone of the cist noted above.
14:43(02) 18-7-1989

164 KILLYCARNEY
OS 2 NPL Not marked OD 100–300

Cists (site) Wakeman (1879, 183–200) discovered two cists within Killycarney cairn (**152**). The first, *c.* 1m by 0.74m internally and was divided into two compartments, and although destroyed before it was fully recorded, Wakeman noted an urn, stone chisel and worked bone at the site. A second cist (dims. 0.55m x 0.5m; H *c.* 0.12m) was discovered 7.3m from the latter and on the S slope of the cairn. Two flint objects and an urn were found within it.
2:30(02)

165 KILLYCLUGGIN
OS 13:4:6 (860,513) Not Marked OD 200–300
22402, 31578

Cist (site) In the course of his excavation of the area around the Killycluggin stone (**93**) Raftery (1978, 49–54) discovered a small oval pit (dims. 1.4m x 1.1m; D 0.65m), immediately E of the site of the stone, which yielded flecks of charcoal, tiny fragments of

burnt bone and a flint scraper. Macalister (1922, 116) recorded that treasure hunters had 'dug all round the monument' [the Killycluggin stone] and had ... discovered a small burial-cist, which they proceeded to destroy'. The cist was 'just beside the stone, sunk about 3 feet in the ground, on the E side'. Both writers were apparently referring to the same site.
13:26(03)

166 PORTANURE
OS 36:4:4 (738,511) Not marked OD 200–300
23272, 29023
Cist (site) Identified by Davies (ITA Survey 1941) on a dry ridge on sandy soil overlooking Lough Gowna to the W. Two 'buttons' were found within the cist and slightly to the S in the same field some bronze implements were discovered. Not visible at ground level.
36:11 15-10-1991

167 TERMON (Tullyhaw By.)
OS 2:13:1 (52,92) Not marked OD 200–300
20552, 33677
Cist (site) Ó Ríordáin (1957, 53–9) discovered at least four cists within Termon cairn (**157**), three of which had been destroyed before he had a chance to record them. However, three food vessels were recovered from what was apparently the largest of the destroyed cists. These contained flecks of cremated bone. The fourth was subrectangular in plan (dims. 0.68m N–S; 0.43m E–W) and contained two inverted food vessels covering cremated remains. 'Further scraps of cremated bone were later found at the S end of the cist, some of them lying in the space between the S end slab and the floor slab'. Not visible at ground level.
2:15(02) 27-8-1988

168 TUAM
OS 2 NPL Not marked OD 200–400
Cists (site) Found within Tuam cairn (**159**). Wakeman (1879, 183–200) recorded that the cairn contained 'soil dug and stone covered kists' in which were found 'deposits of wood charcoal, containing minute fragments of bone, apparently human'. Only one of the cists remained intact. This 'was covered very closely by a red sandstone block 1 ft. 8ins long by 1 ft. wide, by 5.5 inches thick,' upon which Wakeman noted much-disturbed inscribed markings which he interpreted as presenting 'a very Ogamic appearance'. (Lowry-Corry and Richardson 1937, 161–2)
2:31(02)

Fulachta Fiadh

Fulachta fiadh are traditionally held to be the ancient cooking places of the legendary Fionn MacCumhail and the Fianna. They are recognisable as small, low, grass-covered, horseshoe-shaped mounds composed of fragments of burnt stone and earth and are generally found close to streams or in low-lying marshy ground. Archaeological excavations and experiments by O'Kelly (1954, 105-55) and others, have revealed that these represent the remains of Bronze Age cooking places, and have provided a unique insight into their operation and applications. The cooking was done in a water-filled rectangular pit the sides and floor of which were lined with wooden planks or stone slabs. A fire was lit nearby and stones placed in it until they reached the appropriate temperature. These were then placed in the pit to heat the water and subsequently to cook the food. After cooking, the burnt and shattered stones were removed from the pit, and piled up around it, forming the characteristic horseshoe-shaped mound. Fulachta fiadh are among the most common of prehistoric monument types. The majority of the 4500 identified to date are located in Munster and south Leinster, with about 2000 known from County Cork (Power et.al., 1992, 79). The County Cavan examples were uncovered during archaeological monitoring for the Gas Pipeline operation.

169 BALLYNAMONA
OS 34:6:6 (465,314) Not marked OD 400–500
26881, 29488
Fulacht fiadh This site was located on firm ground above wet black bog 40m from a stream. The spread of charcoal and sandstone which formed the fulacht fiadh was badly damaged by stripping machines. It had maximum dimensions of 4m by 6m, was *c.* 0.08m deep and appeared to have been overlain by a layer of white clay which was *c.* 0.04m deep.
34:55

170 CLOGHBALLY LOWER
OS 40:13:6 (199,23) Not marked OD 300–400
26609, 28538
Fulacht fiadh The site lay on the side of a hill which slopes down to boggy ground and *c.* 45m NE of a stream. It comprised a semicircular spread of burnt sandstone and charcoal, the outer limits of which are visible. The spread lay 0.1m below sod and was 0.1m–0.15m deep. The stones had average measurements of *c.* 0.05m.
40:52

171 COGHBALLYBEG
OS 40:14:4 (232,22) Not marked OD 300–400
26644, 28538
Fulacht fiadh This site, which had been levelled, lay mostly in the land outside the pipeline corridor, being 9m in maximum length with only 1m of its width visible. The spread lay 0.05m below the sod and consisted of lots of heat-shattered stones, all apparently of sandstone and measuring 0.03m by 0.02m by 0.01m. The spread was *c.* 0.04m deep and there were no associated features.
40:51

172 CLOGHBALLYBEG
OS 44:2:2 (342,584) Not marked OD 300–400
26356, 28729
Fulacht fiadh This site was situated on rising ground above a very boggy area to N and E and *c.* 250m due S of Mullagh Lough. A drain or stream was located *c.* 60m to the E. The site comprised a circular spread of charcoal and burnt stone *c.* 0.13m in diameter, *c.* 0.06m thick. There appeared to be a circular trough (diam. *c.* 1m) associated with the spread which itself lay approximately 0.1m below sod-line. The burnt stones were all sandstone. The site was excavated.
44:22

173 LISLEA (Castlerahan By.)
OS 39:16:3 (906,78) Not marked OD 300–400
26380, 28594
Fulacht fiadh This site, an obvious fulacht fiadh, was located on rising ground 5m from a stream. It comprised an irregular spread of charcoal and burnt sandstone and measured 7m by 15m. A smaller, isolated spread (2m x 3m) was located 2m to the S and may be part of the same site.
39:87

174 LISLEA (Castlerahan By.)
OS 40:13:4 (34,66) Not marked OD 300–400
26435, 28582
Fulacht fiadh This site lay on rising ground, 6m from a stream with bogland to the W. It comprised a circular spread of charcoal (18m x 4m) and fist-sized pieces of sandstone which ran underneath the baulk and outside the corridor. The loam was stained dark by the charcoal and appeared to contain a stone setting or trough (1m x 0.7m) with a gap of *c.* 0.3–0.4m between the stones. Both charcoal and stone lay 0.2m below the sod layer and had a depth of 0.1m, with an underlying layer of grey/black ash which was visible around the stone setting.
40:53

175 LISLEA (Castlerahan By.)
OS 40:13:4 (65,66) Not marked OD 300–400
26467, 28582
Fulacht fiadh Irregular spread of loose burnt

sandstone and dark charcoal-flecked loam. This site has been levelled. It underlay a field ditch. The site differed from other fulachta fiadh in that it was located on dry level ground and was some distance from water. The spread had approximate dimensions of 12m by 6m, was *c*. 0.08m below sod and *c*. 0.1m deep.
40:5

Toghers and Roadway

Toghers can be defined as artificially constructed trackways or causeways traversing areas of bog or marshland. The term derives from the Irish *tóchar*. Toghers vary considerably in morphology. Probably the most common method of construction was to lay down a series of planks or beams, which were held in place by vertical stakes, upon a bed of brushwood or on runners. However, others were composed of gravel and boulder clay with planks placed intermittently. Some toghers are wide enough to have carried carts and can be up to several kilometres in length. They are usually discovered in or under raised bogs. The legendary preservative qualities of peat generally ensure that the organic evidence thus uncovered is of a much higher standard of preservation than is usually encountered in non-wetland sites. As might be expected, the most dense concentrations of these monuments are in the Midlands where there are extensive areas of raised bogland. Excavation and ancillary research has revealed that this monument type has a very long date span — from the Neolithic to the Late Medieval period. Also included in this chapter is a description of a roadway which is traditionally believed to be of 17th-century date.

176 CLONCOLLOW/MULLYNAGOLMAN
OS 14:2:5 (309,463) '*The Togher*' OD 100–200 22796, 31529

Togher (site) Marked 'Togher Br.' on OS 1836 and 1876 eds. A modern concrete bridge now spans 'The Rag River' at this location.
14:11 5-8-1989

177 DERRIES LOWER/KINKEEL
OS 19:12:5 (722,171) '*The Togher*' OD 100–200 23294, 30585

Togher (site) A linear routeway (L *c.* 240m) is shown on all OS eds. running WSW–ENE through low-lying wet marshy ground at this location. Today the site is occupied by a narrow tarmacadamed road which is very susceptible to flooding during wet weather.
19:14 6-7-1990

178 DRUMARD (Upper Loughtee By.)/ GARTBRATTAN (Upper Loughtee By.)
OS 20:9:6 (211,196) Not marked OD 100–200 23676, 30615

Togher Davies (ITA Survey 1942) recorded that 'a long time ago' a causeway of logs was found at this location. It was *c.* 3.65m long and lay *c.* 2.75m beneath the surface of the bog. A modern pathway now overlies the site.
20:23 12-8-1990

179 CORRACANVY/INISHCONNELL
OS 20:9:2 (144,273) '*Cromwell's Road*' OD 100–200 23605, 30695

Road Marked on all OS eds. A modern narrow stretch of tarred roadway (L 960m) aligned approximately NNW–SSE. It is thought that the trackway originally commenced at the 'Castle Offices' (**1852**) in Inniscconnell Td, which are believed to date to the 17th century, and ran roughly NNW–SSE through Corracanvy Td to the summit of a hill in Gartbrattan Td. From there it continued to Cavan Town *c.* 5.5 km to ESE. (local information). Davies (ITA Survey 1942) did not consider the roadway to be contemporaneous with the 17th-century sites noted above.
20:6 17-8-1990

Linear Earthworks

A linear earthwork can be defined as a stretch of earthen bank with an accompanying ditch extending discontinuously for a considerable distance. The most celebrated is *The Black Pig's Dyke*, also variously known as *The Black Pig's Race*, *The Worm Ditch* and *The Dane's Cast,* which is traditionally believed to have formed parts of an ancient boundary of Ulster. This is thought to have run from the vicinity of the Drowes River in County Leitrim, in the west, through the north Midlands, terminating at an extensive series of earthworks known as *The Dorsey* in County Armagh, in the east (de Vismes Kane 1908-9, 301-28; 1916-17, 539-63). However, there is no evidence to suggest that it ran continuously between these points. Rather perhaps, it augmented where necessary, naturally occurring physical obstacles such as mountains, drumlin hills, rivers, tracts of bogland and forests. Excavation of portion of the monument in County Monaghan revealed evidence for a timber palisade alongside the earthwork. Recent dating evidence from stretches of this monument in counties Monaghan and Armagh yielded dates in the last few centuries BC (Walsh 1987, 5-11; Baillie 1988, 37-40).

Fig. 10—*The 'Worm Ditch or Black Pig's Race' traversing the townlands of Ardkill More/Drumavaddy/Drumbarry/Largan* (**180**) *(Reproduced courtesy of Cambridge University Committee for Aerial Photography).*

180 ARDKILL MORE/DRUMAVADDY (Lower Loughtee By.) DRUMBARRY/LARGAN

OS 31:4:6 (856,506) *'Worm Ditch or Black Pig's Race'* OD 400–880 24366, 29668

Linear earthwork This portion of the 'Worm Ditch or Black Pig's Race' as marked on OS 1912 ed. commences at a stream at the base of a high, steep-sided hill in Ardkill More Td. It runs for *c.* 1150m approximately NW–SE along the W and S of the hillside. At the base of the hill in Largan Td it changes direction and runs approximately E–W for *c.* 750m terminating at the E side of a N–S orientated stream in Drumbarry Td. No definite surface remains of the site was identifiable in Ardkill Td. At the W side of the hill in this Td there is a natural ravine at the location indicated on the OS. In Largan Td the site is marked by stretches of a much-denuded earthen rampart (max. Wth 7m; max. H 0.9m) with remains of a fosse at its NNE foot. The rampart and fosse are much disturbed by modern field drains. A rath is built against the S face of the rampart in Largan Td (**833**). For the final *c.* 75m the site is marked by a narrow, modern tarred road (CUCAP ALJ 79, ALJ 80, AYS 29, AYS 31)

31:4/32:12* 17-5-1992

181 DOWRA/KILDUFF LOWER/KILDUFF MIDDLE

OS 5:15:3 (662,361) *'Worm Ditch or Black Pigs Race'* OD 100–200 20239, 31915

Linear earthwork (site) Not marked on OS 1836 or 1876 eds. Depicted on the OS 1911 ed. as an earthwork on the N bank of the River Shannon as it winds its way between Dowra and the Leitrim border at New Bridge, a distance of over 3km. No visible remains and no local knowledge of any antiquity at the location indicated.

5:32 15-8-1988

Ogham Stones

The inscriptions found on ogham stones represent the earliest form of writing in the Irish language. The characters were probably based on the Latin alphabet and the main series of letters were formed by combinations of between one and five parallel lines for the consonants and shorter strokes or notches for the vowels. The letters could be arranged either vertically or obliquely, on either side of or crossing through a stem line, which was usually formed by the angle on the left side of one of the broad faces of the stone. The inscription is usually a short genealogical extract comprising the name of an individual and his/her immediate or tribal ancestor. The key to the script is contained in the late 14th-century *Book of Ballymote*. Approximately 360 ogham stones have been identified in Ireland to date, the most dense concentrations being in counties Cork and Kerry. It is generally accepted that the earliest inscriptions date from the late 4th or early 5th centuries AD and that the custom of inscribing memorial stones in this manner died out in the 7th–8th centuries AD. However, a later version of the script, 'Scholastic ogham' survived until relatively recent times.

Fig. 11—*Ogham stone at Mullagh* (**182**), *bearing the inscription OSBAR.*

182 MULLAGH
OS 40:14:6 (452,13) Not marked OD 300–400
26877, 28530

Ogham stone (present location) Believed to have originated from an early church site at Rantavan (**1697**). Subsequently removed to the graveyard of 'Templekerry' at Mullagh (**1688**), and ultimately reused as a headstone positioned just W of the ruined church of Mullagh (Ferguson 1875, 303). A pillar stone with ogham inscription which reads OSBBAR. A possible second R noted by Ferguson (*ibid.*) was dismissed by Macalister (1916, 185–6).
40:47 16-7-1987

183 OMARD
OS 37:8:5 (798,349) Not marked OD 300–400
24312, 28862

Ogham stone (site, tradition) Tradition of an ogham stone found during the digging of a drain in the 1930s (local information). Its subsequent fate is unknown. Situated on the W shoulder of a high drumlin ridge. Not visible at ground level.
37:65 17-7-1986

Promontory Forts

A promontory fort comprises a natural promontory cut off from the adjoining land by a rampart or ramparts of earth or stone, the exposed sides of which are protected by naturally occurring features such as cliffs, or the waters of a sea or lake. The area thus enclosed varies considerably in size. Some such as 'Caherconree' in County Kerry are very large while others are similar in size to the average rath or cashel. Most are thought to have been used as temporary refuges during times of warfare rather than permanent places of habitation. They are generally assigned to the Iron Age. The three examples from County Cavan are small in size and may well have a similar function and date span to the much more numerous raths and cashels.

184 BALLYHUGH
OS 14:7:1 (486,431) Hachured OD 200–300
22983, 31497

Promontory fort Oval-shaped promontory (dims. 71.1m N–S; 62.5m E–W) surrounded by Dungummin Lough from SSW–N–SE and elsewhere enclosed by a wide, deep, partly waterlogged fosse and substantial earthen bank. Break in bank with accompanying causeway at SSW represents original entrance. Within the enclosed area at NE is a small approximately circular depression (D 0.88m; dims. 4.6m ENE–WSW; 4.2m NNW–SSE) which may be the remains of a hut site, although Davies (ITA Survey 1942) suggested that it might represent the remains of a limekiln.
14:5 12-5-1993

185 GLASLECK
OS 28:3:3 (660,549) Not marked OD 300–400
27079, 30378

Promontory fort (possible) Depicted on OS 1836 and 1876 eds. as a large subrectangular enclosure at the NW end of a long, low promontory, jutting into Milltown Lough. Subrectangular area (int. dims *c.* 42m NW–SE; 37m NE–SW) cut off from the mainland by fragmentary traces of a scarp with wide, shallow, external fosse (Wth *c.* 4m). Scarp is identifiable only from SE–S–SW. Davies (ITA Survey 1942) recorded 'a rather sunken causeway' at S which he believed probably represented the original entrance. A large rectangular enclosure lies *c.* 30m to SE (**1785**).
28:21 2-9-1988

186 MULLAGH
OS 40:14:5 (365,51) 'Green Island' OD 400
26784, 28569

Promontory fort A large irregularly shaped former island close to the N shore of Mullagh Lough. Water-levels in the lake have dropped and the island is now joined to the mainland. Davies (1947, 98) recorded that the island is 'cut off from the mainland by a bank and fosse to form a promontory rath'. He speculated that 'this work might have been the predecessor of Cloghballybeg castle (**1808**), or it may be much older'.
40:42 13-8-1987

Ringforts

Ringforts are the most common and widely distributed of Irish monument types. They are known by a variety of names including *rath, caiseal, lios, cathair, dún* — terms which are incorporated into a great number of Irish place-names. In essence a ringfort comprises a circular, oval or D-shaped raised area, usually measuring between 20m and 50m in diameter, enclosed by one or more banks constructed of earth and stone excavated from a concentric external fosse or fosses (a rath), or by a wall or walls of drystone masonry (a cashel). Cashels are generally situated in coastal or mountainous regions where soil cover is poor and supplies of stone are readily available. Their walls can be as much as 5.5m thick in the lower courses. Although called ringforts, they were not in general, forts in the military sense. Rather they should be regarded as defended farmsteads — affording both inhabitants and their livestock a certain amount of protection from wild animals and cattle raiders. Within the enclosed area archaeological excavation has revealed evidence of circular or rectangular house sites and outbuildings which presumably represent animal shelters and centres for domestic industries including pottery and metalworking. In the case of raths, the enclosed houses and outbuildings were primarily constructed of wood and earth and in most cases no remains survive above ground level. In the case of cashels, the structures were constructed of stone and in many cases the wall-footings are still identifiable. Despite the fact that ringforts are the most numerous Irish field monument type, a comparatively very small number have been archaeologically excavated. The available evidence suggests that most date to the Early Christian period (*c.* 500 – *c.* 1200 AD). However, some such as the Rath of Feerwore Co. Galway, which was excavated by Raftery (1944, 23–52), have been shown to date to the Early Iron Age (*c.* 100 BC – *c.* 100 AD) while others are thought to date to the Late Medieval period. Souterrains are often found within or in close proximity to ringforts. Most of the ringforts in County Cavan are situated on, or close to, the highest point of a drumlin hill or ridge. For ease of use, this chapter is divided into two parts, the first dealing with the more numerous raths, and a subsection detailing the cashels.

187 AGHACASHEL
OS 39:5:3 (176,425) Hachured OD 500–600
25605, 28954
Rath Raised circular area (int. diam. *c.* 60m) enclosed by a bank of earth and stone which survives only from ENE–E–S and is replaced elsewhere by modern stone walls. Faced internally with drystone masonry. Original entrance not recognisable. An earlier report (OPW 1969) noted a long, shallow depression of unknown significance inside the bank at ENE. The upper portion of a rotary quern found at the site was presented by the landowner to the National Museum of Ireland.
39:1(01) 24-3-1987

188 AGHACONNY
OS 31:3:6 (624,484) Hachured OD 400–500
24121, 29642
Rath Raised circular area (int. diam. *c.* 40m) enclosed by two very substantial earthen banks with outer fosses. Berm between outer bank and inner fosse. Corresponding breaks in banks with remains of accompanying causeway at S represents original entrance.
31:1 8-6-1992

189 AGHACONNY
OS 31:3:6 (624,526) Hachured OD 400–500
24120, 29687
Rath (site) Levelled in the late 1970s. An earlier report (OPW 1974) described a raised circular area (int. diam. *c.* 38m) enclosed by a substantial earthen bank and a wide, deep fosse. Break in bank at NE with accompanying causeway represented original entrance. At that time, possible traces of a souterrain were noticed within the internal area (**1220**). The outline of the perimeter of the rath may still be traced, albeit with difficulty.
31:2(01) 8-6-1992

190 AGHACREEVY
OS 37:12:5 (781,180) Not marked OD 200–300
24296, 28683
Rath (site) Marked 'Fort' on OS 1836 and 1876 eds. Situated on the W shoulder of a drumlin ridge. Formerly enclosed by a low earthen bank and a shallow fosse. From SE–S–W the perimeter has been modified and incorporated into the field boundary. Otherwise nothing visible at ground level.
37:1 31-7-1986

191 AGHACREEVY
OS 37:16:2 (797,133) Not marked OD 200–300
24314, 28633
Rath (site) Marked 'Fort' on OS 1836 and 1876 eds. Situated on a low natural hillock in otherwise level ground *c.* 10m E of a second rath (**192**). Not visible at ground level.
37:2 1-8-1986

192 AGHACREEVY
OS 37:16:2 (806,136) Hachured OD 200–300
24323, 28637

Rath Raised circular area (int. diam. *c.* 35m) enclosed by a low earthen bank and slight traces of a fosse. Original entrance may have been at SE. The site of a second rath lies *c.* 10m to W (**191**).
37:3 1-8-1986

193 AGHAGOLRICK
OS 21:15:5 (613,11) Hachured OD 300–400
25078, 30432
Rath Raised circular area (int. diam. 28.1m) enclosed by an earthen bank. An earlier description (OPW 1969) noted the presence of a wide, shallow, external fosse which has since been largely infilled or replaced by modern field drains. From NE–SSE the original curve of the bank has been straightened and incorporated into the field boundary. Original entrance may have been at NE.
21:3 11-9-1990

194 AGHAGOLRICK
OS 26:3:2 (596,560) Hachured OD 200–300
25060, 30371
Rath Raised oval area (int. diam. 48.2m ENE–WSW; 39.2m NNW–SSE) enclosed by the remains of an earthen bank and fosse. Break in bank at SE probably represents original entrance.
26:1 22-10-1991

195 AGHAKNOCK
OS 24:16:1 (724,99) Hachured OD 400–500
23249, 29868
Rath Raised circular area (int. diam. 46m NNE–SSW) enclosed by a substantial earthen bank and fosse. At ESE fosse has become extremely waterlogged. Break in bank at E probably represents original entrance. Overlooked by Bruse Hill to SW.
24:2 3-9-1991

196 AGHALATTAFRAAL/DERRYLURGAN
OS 32:15:3 (656,96) Hachured OD 450
25134, 29242
Rath Raised circular area (int. diam. 39.6m) enclosed by two substantial earthen banks with a wide, deep, waterlogged intermediate fosse. Break in inner bank at E with slight remains of accompanying causeway represents original entrance. Outer bank disturbed here. Two shallow depressions in the interior probably mark the site of a souterrain (**1221**).
32:1(01) 18-5-1977

197 AGHALION
OS 39:5:5 (98,311) Hachured OD 500–600
25525, 28832
Rath Raised circular area (int. diam. 34m) enclosed by a substantial earthen bank. From WSW–WNW and from NNE–ESE the bank has been levelled but its outline is still identifiable. Drystone masonry has been applied to the external face of bank from ESE–S–SW. Original entrance not recognisable.
39:2 23-3-1987

198 AGHALOORY
OS 37:7:1 (524,446) Indicated OD 200–300
24022, 28961
Rath Raised circular area (int. diam. *c.* 45m) enclosed by a substantial earthen bank. An earlier report (OPW 1970) noted a modern trench at the external foot of the bank but no evidence of a fosse. Original entrance not recognisable. Internal area is divided into two roughly equal portions by a field boundary aligned NE–SW.
37:4 11-7-1986

199 AGHALOORY
OS 37:7:3 (689,397) Hachured OD 200–300
24197, 28911
Rath Not marked on OS 1836 or 1876 eds. Situated in low-lying ground adjacent to a stream which is an unusual siting for a rath. Raised circular area (int. diam. *c.* 19m N–S) on a low natural mound. An earlier report (OPW 1970) noted a low counterscarp bank and shallow, partly waterlogged fosse enclosing the site from N–S–WNW. A stream skirts the site from WNW–N. Original entrance may have been at S.
37:5 14-7-1986

200 AGHARAH
OS 28:2:6 (426,507) Hachured OD 600
26833, 30332
Rath Raised D-shaped area (int. diam. 32m N–S; L of straight side 30m) enclosed by a substantial earthen bank and the remains of a fosse. Break in bank at SE, now partially blocked by a modern field boundary, may represent original entrance.
28:1 23-3-1977

201 AGHARASKILLY
OS 14:2:1 (282,594) Hachured OD 200–300
22767, 31667
Rath Raised circular area (int. dims. 29.1m NNE–SSW; 26.4m WNW–ESE) enclosed by an earthen bank. From SSW–NNW bank has been modified and incorporated into the field boundary. Elsewhere it has been levelled but its outline is still identifiable. An earlier report (OPW 1969) recorded traces of an outer fosse and suggested that the original entrance may have been at SE.
14:2 19-7-1988

202 AGHATEGGAL OR RYEFORT
OS 26:13:2 (131,86) Hachured OD 500–600
24574, 29866
Rath Raised oval area (int. dims. 41m E–W; 32.4m

N–S) enclosed by a low earthen bank and traces of a fosse. From NNW–N–ESE there is a trench outside the bank, through which a stream flows from N–E–ESE. No trace of fosse from S–W–NNW. Present entrance to site at E may be original.
26:2 25-10-1991

203 AGHATOTAN
OS 17:13:6 (195,69) Indicated OD 200–300
25673, 30948
Rath Raised circular area (int. diam. 27.2m) enclosed by a substantial earthen bank and vague traces of a fosse identifiable only from NW–N–E. Bank appears to have been modified and has been incorporated into the field boundary. From WSW–WNW the site is skirted by a modern roadway and drainage trench. Break in bank at ESE may represent original entrance.
17:1 11-11-1989

204 AGHATOTAN
OS 17:13:6 (215,32) Hachured OD 300–400
25658, 30889
Rath Raised circular area (int. diam. 25.3m) enclosed by a substantial earthen bank and a wide, deep fosse. A low, poorly preserved counterscarp bank runs outside the fosse from SE–S–SW and at NW. Break in bank with accompanying causeway at NE represents original entrance.
17:2 11-11-1989

205 AGHAVADDY
OS 32:2:4 (237,496) Hachured OD 300–400
24687, 29660
Rath Raised circular area (int. diam. *c.* 38m) enclosed by a substantial earthen bank. Break in bank at SE may represent original entrance. Iron slag found at the site in early 1980s (local information).
32:2 28-6-1989

206 AGHAVADDY
OS 32:2:4 (296,458) Hachured OD 300–400
24750, 29621
Rath (site) An earlier report (OPW 1974) described a raised circular area (int. diam. *c.* 38m) enclosed by a substantial earthen bank and a fosse. Since then the site has been levelled. The perimeter has been modified and incorporated into the field boundary from SW–NW. From E–SE–S it is identifiable as a low scarp.
32:3 26-6-1989

207 AGHAWAY
OS 21:8:3 (907,380) Hachured OD 400
25385, 30824
Rath (site) An earlier report (OPW 1970) described a raised circular area (int. dims. 44.5m NE–SW; 44m NW–SE) enclosed by an earthen bank and fosse. Original entrance was probably at N. Site has been levelled. Not visible at ground level.
21:5 22-9-1990

208 AGHNAGLOGH (Tullygarvey By.)
OS 25:12:3 (850,291) Hachured OD 400
24356, 30081
Rath Raised oval area (int. dims. 44m N–S; 38m E–W) enclosed by a partially denuded earthen bank and slight remains of a fosse. Perimeter has been modified and incorporated into the field boundary. Original entrance not recognisable. The site has been planted with coniferous trees. A spring well lies a short distance to WSW.
25:1 19-9-1991

209 AGHNAGLOGH (Upper Loughtee By.)
OS 22:6:4 (255,364) Hachured OD 500–600
25672, 30810
Rath Raised circular area (int. diam. 25.6m) enclosed by a substantial earthen bank and vague traces of a fosse. Wide break in bank at SSE presumably represents original entrance.
22:1 19-8-1988

210 AGHNAHEDERNY
OS 38:5:3 (230,410) Hachured OD 400–500
24688, 28930
Rath (site) Situated in level pasture-land. An earlier report (OPW 1970) described a raised circular area (int. diam. *c.* 28m) enclosed by a low earthen bank. Original entrance was not then recognisable. Site has been levelled. Nothing visible at ground level.
38:4 11-8-1988

211 AGHNASKEAGH
OS 42:2:3 (412,564) Indicated OD 200–300
24884, 28454
Rath Raised almost circular area (int. diam. *c.* 28m) enclosed by a much-denuded low earthen bank. An earlier report (OPW 1974) recorded traces of a shallow fosse at S and W. Original entrance not recognisable. Interior rises from the perimeter to the centre.
42:2 3-9-1986

212 AGHOUTEREERY
OS 38:6:4 (238,351) Hachured OD 431
24696, 28867
Rath Raised circular area (int. diam. *c.* 34m) enclosed by a substantial earthen bank and a wide, deep, partly waterlogged fosse. From ENE–E–ESE the fosse has been infilled and replaced by a modern laneway. Wide break in bank at S may represent original entrance. Internal area densely overgrown with vegetation.
38:2 11-8-1986

Fig. 12—*Rath at Aghnaglogh* (**208**).

213 AGHOUTEREERY
OS 38:10:1 (252,283) Hachured OD 300–400
24711, 28795

Rath Raised circular area (int. diam. *c*. 31m) enclosed by a much-denuded low earthen bank. From SSE–WNW the bank has been modified and incorporated into the field boundary. Original entrance not recognisable.
38:3 11-8-1986

214 ALTBEAGH
OS 26:8:3 (896,416) Hachured OD 400–500
25379, 30222

Rath Raised circular area (int. diam. 24.4m) enclosed by two earthen banks with intermediate fosse. Outer bank survives only for a short stretch at N. Fosse is almost completely infilled. Break in bank with remains of a causeway at E represents original entrance. Indications of a possible souterrain in the internal area of rath (**1222**).
26:3(01) 22-10-1991

215 ANNAGH (Upper Loughtee By.)
OS 24:8:6 (915,354) Not marked OD 200–300
23449, 30139

Rath (site) Marked 'Fort' on OS 1836 and 1876 eds. Although levelled, the outline of the perimeter of this site enclosing a circular area (int. diam. *c*. 36.4m) is still identifiable. An infilled well lies immediately outside the site at SE.
24:4 21-8-1991

216 ANNAGHARNET
OS 39:4:2 (775,570) Hachured OD 508
26236, 29113

Rath Raised circular area (int. diam. *c*. 35m) enclosed by a substantial earthen bank and a wide, shallow fosse identifiable only from ESE–NNW. From ENE–E–ESE bank has been levelled. Original entrance not recognisable.
39:3 11-6-1987

217 ANNAGHLEE
OS 17:11:4 (477,195) Hachured OD 300–400
26092, 30809

Rath Raised circular area (diam. 20.4m) enclosed by a low, steep scarp and vague traces of a wide fosse identifiable only from N–E–S. An earlier report (OPW 1969) noted slight remains of an earthen bank on the

upper edge of the scarp. Original entrance not recognisable.
17:4 8-11-1990

218 ARDARRAGH
OS 19:15:6 (660,74) Hachured OD 370
23177, 30481
Rath Raised circular area (int. dims. 40m NW–SE; 39m NNE–SSW) enclosed by two substantial earthen banks with outer fosses. External fosse and bank have been much modified and incorporated into the field boundary. Inner bank is exceptionally wide (Wth 8.4m). Original entrance at E.
19:5 12-7-1990

219 ARDERRY
OS 9:10:4 (235,217) Hachured OD 200–300
21739, 31899
Rath Marked 'Fort' on OS 1836 and 1876 eds. Situated in low-lying ground close to a stream. Densely overgrown with vegetation rendering inspection impossible.
9:1 19-9-1988

220 ARDGLUSHIN
OS 16:11:2 (560,278) Hachured OD 300–400
25014, 31353
Rath Raised oval area (int. dims. 35.2m NW–SE; *c.* 30m NNE–SSW) enclosed by a much-denuded, low earthen bank and a wide, deep fosse. Causeway across fosse at SSW presumably represents original entrance. Densely overgrown with vegetation.
16:4 22-11-1968

221 ARDLENY
OS 37:3:2 (611,563) Hachured OD 300–400
24113, 29086
Rath Raised circular area (int. diam. *c.* 38m) enclosed by a substantial earthen bank and a wide, deep fosse identifiable only from NE–E–SE. From SSE–S–W a laneway skirts the site. The outer face of the bank has been modified here and is accompanied by an external trench. Bank has been levelled from W–NW–N and from SE–SSE. Original entrance not recognisable.
37:6 14-7-1986

222 ARDLENY
OS 37:3:6 (688,486) Hachured OD 300–400
24194, 29005
Rath Raised circular area (int. diam. *c.* 45m E–W) enclosed by an earthen bank and a fosse identifiable only from W–WNW. A modern laneway skirts the external foot of the bank from W–N–SE. Break in bank at E may represent original entrance.
37:8 14-7-1986

223 ARDLENY
OS 37:4:4 (701,513) Hachured OD 200–300
24209, 29034
Rath Raised circular area (int. diam. *c.* 29m) enclosed by a low earthen bank and a wide, shallow fosse identifiable only from SW–W–N. The area outside the bank at S has been much disturbed by modern farm buildings. Break in bank at S may represent original entrance.
37:9 14-7-1986

224 ARDLOUGHER (Clanmahon By.)
OS 25:15:6 (685,19) Hachured OD 500
24185, 29792
Rath Raised circular area (int. diam. *c.* 42m) enclosed by a substantial earthen bank and a shallow fosse. Site is divided into two roughly equal portions by a field boundary running NNW–SSE and has been levelled to SSW of field fence. Original entrance not recognisable.
25:2 2-10-1991

225 ARDLOUGHER (Clanmahon By.)
OS 31:3:3 (678,574) Hachured OD 400
24178, 29738
Rath Raised circular area (int. diam. 32.6m) enclosed by a substantial earthen bank and a wide, deep, partly waterlogged fosse largely infilled from N–E–ESE. Break in bank at ENE with remains of accompanying causeway may represent original entrance.
31:5 8-6-1992

226 ARDLOW
OS 39:8:3 (909,437) Hachured OD 400–500
26379, 28973
Rath Raised circular area (int. diam. *c.* 33m) enclosed by a much-disturbed, low earthen bank. Original entrance not recognisable.
39:7 10-6-1987

227 ARDMONE EAST
OS 22:15:6 (682,19) Indicated OD 500–600
26126, 30449
Rath Marked 'Fort' on OS 1836 and 1876 eds. Raised circular area (int. diam. 31.7m) enclosed by a low earthen bank which has been substantially modified and incorporated into the field boundary. Original entrance may have been at W.
22:2 27-8-1990

228 ARDONAN
OS 15:13:3 (172,99) Hachured OD 100–200
23630, 31152
Rath Raised subrectangular area (int. dims. *c.* 46m NNW–SSE; *c.* 38m ENE–WSW) enclosed by a substantial, although partly levelled, earthen bank and

a fosse. Only the outline of the perimeter can be traced from NE–E–SE. Break in bank with accompanying causeway at NNW probably represents original entrance. A large D-shaped annex (int. dims. *c.* 41m ENE–WSW; *c.* 23m NNW–SSE), defined by a low scarp, is separated from the main body of the rath by a wide, deep fosse.
15:3 12-9-1989

229 ARDRA
OS 24:11:1 (501,244) Hachured OD 300–400
23013, 30019
Rath Raised circular area (int. diam. 42.2m) enclosed by two earthen banks with wide, deep, waterlogged intermediate fosse. Outer bank identifiable only from SSW–SW. Fosse has been infilled from SW–W. Break in inner bank with accompanying causeway at SE represents original entrance.
24:7 22-8-1991

230 ARDUE
OS 10:15:4 (531,73) Hachured OD 200–300
23028, 31759
Rath Marked 'Fort' on OS 1836 and 1876 eds. Raised circular area (int. diam. 43.6m) enclosed by a low earthen bank and a fosse identifiable only from ESE–SSE. Perimeter has been levelled from SSW–N–ESE but its outline is still clearly identifiable. Original entrance not recognisable. Internal area greatly disturbed.
10:3 30-3-1993

231 ARDUE
OS 10:15:5 (589,68) Hachured OD 100–200
23090, 31754
Rath Raised D-shaped area (int. dims. *c.* 72m NNW–SSE; *c.* 53m ENE–WSW) enclosed from SE–W–NNE by a substantial earthen bank and a wide, shallow fosse, and elsewhere by Tomkinroad Lough. Traces of a possible counterscarp bank at the external lip of the fosse. An earlier report (OPW 1974) suggested that the original entrance may have been at SSW. Densely overgrown with vegetation.
10:4 15-4-1982

232 ARDVARNY
OS 25:16:4 (756,70) Hachured OD 400–500
24259, 29847
Rath Raised circular area (int. dims. 32.6m ENE–WSW; 31.5m NNW–SSE) enclosed by a substantial earthen bank and a fosse which is wide, deep and partially waterlogged from WNW–N–SE. Original entrance not recognisable.
25:3 1-10-1991

233 ARDVARNY
OS 25:16:4 (758,56) Hachured OD 400–500
24262, 29832
Rath Raised circular area (int. dims. 33m N–S; 30.5m E–W) enclosed by a low earthen bank and the remains of a fosse. Break in bank at S may represent original entrance. Within the internal area is a low earthen mound which may represent a hut site.
25:4 1-10-1991

234 ASHGROVE
OS 15:10:4 (264,180) Hachured OD 200–300
23726, 31238
Rath Raised circular area (int. diam. 34.5m) enclosed by a much-denuded low earthen bank and a wide, shallow fosse identifiable in its original form only from WNW–N–NNE. Elsewhere it has been largely infilled or replaced by modern field boundaries. Break in bank at SSW probably represents original entrance. Internal area densely overgrown with vegetation.
15:5 12-8-1989

235 BALLAGHANEA
OS 39:12:4 (738,169) Not marked OD 300–400
26201, 28688
Rath Marked 'Fort' on OS 1876 ed. Not marked on 1836 ed. Raised circular area (int. diam. *c.* 32m) enclosed by a low earthen bank which has been incorporated into the field boundary from SSW–W–NE. Elsewhere it has been levelled, however, from NE–ESE its outline is still identifiable. Original entrance not recognisable.
39:10 5-6-1987

236 BALLAGHANEA
OS 39:16:2 (837,136) Indicated OD 300–400
26306, 28655
Rath Raised circular area (int. diam. 31.7m) enclosed by a much-denuded, low earthen bank. An earlier report (OPW 1969) suggested that the original entrance was probably at SE. At the centre of the enclosed area is a low, roughly circular platform of earth and stone (diam. *c.* 8.5m) which presumably represents a hut site.
39:13 23-3-1987

237 BALLINTEMPLE
OS 31:3:4 (494,477) Hachured OD 300–400
23985, 29634
Rath (site) An earlier report (OPW 1974) described a raised circular area (int. diam. *c.* 34m) enclosed by a substantial earthen bank and a wide, deep fosse. Break in bank with accompanying causeway at N probably represented original entrance. Site has been levelled. Not visible at ground level.
31:6 5-6-1992

238 BALLINTEMPLE
OS 31:7:1 (508,410) Hachured OD 300–400
24000, 29563

Rath Raised circular area (int. diam. *c.* 38m) enclosed by two earthen banks with wide, deep, intermediate fosse. Outer face of outer bank has been modified and incorporated into the field boundary. Inner bank is very substantial. Break in inner bank at NE with remains of accompanying causeway probably represents original entrance. Densely overgrown with vegetation.
31:8 6-6-1992

239 BALLOUGHLY
OS 35:9:5 (108,176) Hachured OD 500–600
27481, 29347
Rath Raised circular area (int. diam. *c.* 40m) enclosed by a broad, low earthen bank and a wide, shallow fosse identifiable only from NE–E–SE. Bank partly levelled at E. Original entrance not recognisable.
35:1 14-3-1974

240 BALLOUGHLY
OS 35:9:5 (144,155) Hachured OD 500–600
27520, 29326
Rath Raised circular area (int. diam. *c.* 42m) enclosed by two earthen banks with intermediate wide, deep fosse. Outer bank has been levelled and replaced by a modern field wall from SE–S–SSW. Inner bank is quite substantial although it has been partly levelled at N. Original entrance at SE.
35:2 14-3-1974

241 BALLYHALLY
OS 16:12:1 (750,260) Hachured OD 300–400
25214, 31336
Rath (site) Much disturbed. Of the complete circular enclosure marked 'Fort' on the OS 1836 ed. all that remains is a steep scarp running from NNE–E–S. Modern farm buildings occupy the remainder of the site. Situated on the summit of a drumlin hill.
16:5 21-10-1989

242 BALLYHUGH
OS 14:7:2 (579,437) Hachured OD 200
23082, 31504
Rath (site) Marked 'Fort' and depicted as a large oval enclosure on OS 1836 and 1876 eds. An earlier report (OPW 1969) described a raised circular area (int. dims. 30.5m NE–SW; 29m NW–SE) enclosed by a low earthen bank and a shallow fosse. Original entrance may have been at ENE. Site has been levelled.
14:7 22-7-1989

243 BALLYMAGAURAN
OS 13:7:5 (567,323) Hachured OD 200–300
22094, 31374
Rath Raised circular area (int. diam. 18.2m) enclosed by a very low earthen bank and vague traces of a fosse identifiable only from SW–W–N. An earlier report (OPW 1969) suggested that the original entrance may have been at SSE.
13:1 12-6-1989

244 BALLYNAMONA
OS 34:7:4 (483,304) Hachured OD 500–600
26900, 29477
Rath Raised circular area (int. diam. *c.* 25m) enclosed by two earthen banks with intermediate fosse. From E–S–SSW outer bank has been incorporated into the field boundary and fosse is absent. Original entrance may have been either at NE or SW.
34:1 10-5-1988

245 BARCONNY (Nugent)
OS 42:4:5 (808,498) Hachured OD 300–400
25303, 28388
Rath Raised circular area (int. dims. 41.5m NNE–SSW; 39m WNW–ESE) enclosed by a low earthen bank and slight traces of a fosse identifiable only from S–SSW–SW. Break in bank with accompanying causeway at S may represent original entrance.
42:3 8-9-1970

246 BARRAN
OS 1:16:6 (853,30) Hachured OD 300
20426, 33610
Rath Raised circular area (int. diam. *c.* 30m) enclosed by two earthen banks with intermediate fosse. Outer bank identifiable from S–SW–W. From N–E–SSE it has been incorporated into the field boundary. Original entrance not recognisable.
1:1 2-7-1988

247 BEAGHY (ED Cavan Rural)
OS 20:12:3 (902,269) Hachured OD 400–500
24405, 30698
Rath Raised circular area (int. diam. 27m) enclosed by a substantial earthen bank. External fosse has been infilled but its outline may still be traced. Bank has been slightly modified and incorporated into the field boundary. Original entrance not recognisable. A large portion of the interior is occupied by an oval area (int. dims. 9.9m N–S; 7.8m E–W) enclosed by a low but well-defined earthen bank which presumably represents the remains of a house site. A modern trench extends E from the interior of the house site to the perimeter.
20:2 9-8-1990

248 BEAGHY (ED Stradone)
OS 26:9:6 (220,187) Hachured OD 600–700
24667, 29974
Rath Raised subcircular area (int. diam. *c.* 22.4m) enclosed by a substantial earthen bank and a fosse

which although infilled is nonetheless identifiable. Original entrance not recognisable.
26:7 23-10-1991

249 BELLAHEADY OR ROSSBRESSAL
OS 13:4:6 (898,457) Hachured OD 200–300
22443, 31519
Rath (site) Marked 'Fort' on OS 1836 and 1876 eds. Situated close to the summit of a drumlin hill. Not visible at ground level.
13:4 7-8-1989

250 BELLANACARGY
OS 16:14:6 (390,12) Hachured OD 200–300
24837, 31071
Rath Raised circular area (int. diam. 26.8m) enclosed by a substantial earthen bank and a wide, deep fosse. Perimeter has been destroyed from NE–E–SE as a result of the construction of a dwelling-house known as 'Fort House' and its associated farm buildings. Original entrance may have been either at ENE or N.
16:7 19-4-1989

251 BELLSGROVE
OS 37:16:3 (866,143) Hachured OD 200–300
24387, 28645
Rath (site) Marked 'Fort' on OS 1836 and 1876 eds. Apparently originally circular (int. diam. *c.* 38m) enclosed by an earthen bank and a fosse. From E–S–SW the perimeter has been much modified and incorporated into the field boundary. Otherwise, nothing visible at ground level.
37:12 5-8-1986

252 BELLSGROVE/LAVAGH
OS 37:12:6 (868,160) Indicated OD 200–300
24388, 28663
Rath Marked on all OS eds. Large oval area (int. dims. *c.* 80m NNW–SSE; *c.* 50m ENE–WSW) enclosed by a much-denuded low earthen bank. The site is divided into two unequal portions by a field boundary running NNW–SSW. The larger portion, ENE of the boundary, has been levelled. Original entrance not recognisable.
37:13 1-8-1986

253 BELLVILLE
OS 25:10:5 (383,167) Hachured OD 300–400
23864, 29946
Rath Raised oval area (int. dims. 46.8m NNW–SSE; 41.4m ENE–WSW) enclosed by a slight outer earthen bank, intermediate fosse and substantial inner earthen bank. Original entrance may have been at ENE. Adapted for use as a tree-ring in modern times. An earthen bank with a shallow outer trench is built against the external face of the outer bank. In the interior, a small six-sided stone building, now in ruins, is most likely the remains of a summer-house. Both these features are almost certainly modern.
25:7 19-9-1991

254 BELLVILLE
OS 25:14:3 (395,136) Hachured OD 300–400
23877, 29913
Rath Raised oval area (int. dims. 36.4m N–S; 30.7m E–W) enclosed by an earthen bank, remains of a fosse, a narrow berm and a shallow trench. Fosse identifiable only at NNW. The berm and trench probably date to the period when the site was adapted for use as a tree-ring. Original entrance(s) may have been at ENE and/or ESE.
25:8 18-9-1991

255 BELLVILLE
OS 25:10:6 (458,153) Hachured OD 400–500
23943, 29931
Rath Raised circular area (int. diam. 40.9m) enclosed by a substantial earthen bank and a well-defined fosse. Break in bank at SE with accompanying causeway represents original entrance.
25:10 18-9-1991

256 BILLIS (Upper Loughtee By.)
OS 20:12:5 (836,197) Hachured OD 400–500
24336, 30622
Rath Raised circular area (int. diam. 28.5m) enclosed by a substantial earthen bank and a wide, deep fosse infilled from E–SE and from W–NW. From SE–SSE it is replaced by a modern roadway. Original entrance not recognisable. Modern sunken trackway extends through the site slightly S of centre.
20:3 9-8-1990

257 BILLIS (Upper Loughtee By.)
OS 20:12:5 (846,227) Hachured OD 466
24347, 30653
Rath Raised circular area (int. diam. *c.* 38.5m) enclosed by a slight earthen bank and vague traces of a fosse (Wth *c.* 2.3m). Original entrance not recognisable. Modern field bank and trench extends in a NNE–SE direction, dividing the internal area into unequal portions. The smaller portion, ENE of this, has been partially ploughed out.
20:4 9-8-1990

258 BINDOO
OS 22:10:3 (416,252) Hachured OD 700–800
25843, 30693
Rath Raised circular area (int. diam. 31.9m) enclosed by a substantial earthen bank and a shallow fosse. From NNE–S–SW an apparently later deposit of earth has been piled up against the outer face of the bank,

and the fosse considerably narrowed at this point. Original entrance not recognisable.
22:3 10-10-1990

259 BIRRAGH
OS 35:9:6 (166,214) Hachured OD 500 27541, 29389
Rath Raised circular area (int. diam *c.* 35m) enclosed by a substantial earthen bank and a shallow fosse. Original entrance at SE.
35:3 14-3-1974

260 BIRRAGH
OS 35:9:6 (194,170) Hachured OD 400–500 27571, 29342
Rath Raised circular area (int. diam. *c.* 35m) enclosed by an earthen bank, the exterior of which has been faced with stone and incorporated into the field boundary. It is poorly preserved from ESE–S–SW. Original entrance not recognisable.
35:4 14-3-1974

261 BLACKHILLS LOWER
OS 34:11:4 (494,200) Hachured OD 500–600 26913, 29368
Rath Raised circular area (int. dims. *c.* 19m N–S; *c.* 18m E–W) enclosed by a low earthen bank and a wide fosse. From NE–S–WSW fosse has been recut and has a modern external bank. Original entrance not recognisable. Inside the bank at N are the remains of what appears to be a small rectangular house site.
34:2 26-4-1974

262 BOAGH
OS 18:13:5 (115,32) Hachured OD 506 26497, 31107
Rath Raised oval area (int. dims. 40.1m NW–SE; *c.* 37m NE–SW) enclosed by a substantial earthen bank and a wide, shallow, partly waterlogged fosse. Break in bank at W presumably represents original entrance.
18:3 15-7-1990

263 BOAGH
OS 18:13:6 (171,67) Hachured OD 400–500 26555, 31144
Rath Raised circular area (int. diam. 38.5m) enclosed by a substantial earthen bank and a wide, deep fosse. An earlier report (OPW 1969) suggested that the original entrance may have been at SE.
18:4 15-7-1990

264 BRACKLEY
OS 9:7:2 (596,397) Hachured OD 500 22119, 32093
Rath Marked 'Fort' on OS 1836 and 1876 eds. Site is said to have comprised a raised circular area enclosed by two massive earthen banks with an intervening fosse (local information). Situated in mountainous land, adjacent to a stream. The site lies within a dense modern plantation of coniferous trees. Not located.
9:5 11-9-1988

265 BRANKILL
OS 24:11:1 (534,272) Hachured OD 300–400 23047, 30049
Rath Raised circular area (int. diam. 31.5m) enclosed by a substantial earthen bank and a wide, deep fosse accompanied by a low counterscarp bank at its outer lip. Fosse identifiable only from NW–N–NE. Internal area has been planted with deciduous trees.
24:8 21-8-1991

266 BRUSE (Tullyhunco By.)
OS 30:3:3 (642,588) Hachured OD 600–700 23166, 29741
Rath Raised circular area (int. diam. 30.2m) enclosed by a substantial earthen bank and a wide, deep fosse. The fosse has been infilled and a modern laneway runs outside the bank from S–SSW–SW. Bank best preserved from W–N–SE. Elsewhere denuded to level of interior. Break in bank with remains of causeway at SSE represents original entrance.
30:1 4-10-1991

267 BRUSE (Tullyhunco By.)
OS 30:3:3 (661,584) Hachured OD 500–600 23187, 29737
Rath Raised subcircular area (int. diam. *c.* 31.7m) enclosed by very slight remains of an earthen bank and the remains of a fosse, outside of which is a wide, well-defined, berm-like feature. Outer embankment has been modified in recent times. Original entrance may have been at SE.
30:2 4-10-1991

268 BRUSKY
OS 31:10:6 (390,162) Hachured OD 300–400 23878, 29300
Rath Raised circular area (int. diam. *c.* 38m) enclosed by a much-disturbed low earthen bank. The site is divided into two unequal portions by a modern roadway running NW–SE. The larger portion, NE of this, has been levelled. From SSE–W–WNW the perimeter has been modified and incorporated into the field boundary. Original entrance not recognisable.
31:9 9-4-1974

269 BUNNOE
OS 16:11:6 (630,217) Hachured OD 200–300 25088, 31289
Rath Raised subtriangular area (int. dims. *c.* 36m

N–S; *c.* 22m E–W) enclosed by a substantial earthen bank and a wide, deep fosse. From SSW–W–NW there are traces of an external bank which is probably a later feature. The fosse has been largely infilled from NE–S–SSW. From NE–E–SE both faces of the bank have been modified and a modern trench dug at the foot of the internal face. Original entrance not recognisable. The interior slopes appreciably from W–E.
16:10 17-10-1989

270 BUNNOE
OS 16:11:3 (668,289) Hachured OD 300–400
25128, 31366
Rath Raised circular area (int. diam 24.7m) enclosed by a substantial earthen bank and a deep, narrow fosse. Break in bank at ESE probably represents original entrance.
16:11 17-10-1989

271 BUNNOE
OS 16:11:3 (671,280) Hachured OD 300–400
25131, 31357
Rath (site) Situated on a drumlin hilltop. An earlier report (OPW 1968) described a raised circular area (int. diam. *c.* 32m) enclosed by a slight earthen bank and a wide, deep fosse. Original entrance was probably at W. Site has been levelled.
16:12 17-10-1989

272 BURREN (ED Lissanover)
OS 13:16:3 (884,82) Hachured OD 200–300
22431, 31122
Rath Raised circular area (int. dims. 50m WNW–ESE; 48.3m NNE–SSW) enclosed by a substantial earthen bank and a wide, deep, partly waterlogged fosse. From WNW–E–SSW the fosse has been infilled and survives only as a slight depression. Original entrance not recognisable.
13:5 15-5-1993

273 BURREN (ED Lissanover)
OS 13:16:6 (898,10) Hachured OD 200–300
22447, 31047
Rath Raised oval area (int. dims. 54m NE–SW; 45.2m NW–SE) enclosed by a low, wide earthen bank and a fosse. An earlier report (OPW 1969) recorded that there was formerly a limekiln built into the bank at N. Break in bank with accompanying causeway at SE may represent original entrance. Tradition of a spa well within the internal area (local information).
13:6 21-6-1989

274 CABRA
OS 35:3:4 (474,514) Hachured OD 400
27864, 29708
Rath Raised circular area (int. diam. *c.* 30m) enclosed by a much-denuded wide, low, earthen bank. Break in bank at NE may represent original entrance.
35:5 11-3-1989

275 CABRA
OS 35:3:4 (491,476) Hachured OD 300–400
27882, 29668
Rath (site) Marked 'Fort' and depicted on OS 1836 and 1876 eds. as a roughly circular enclosure divided into unequal portions by a roadway aligned NE–SW. On the 1913 OS ed. only the larger portion of the site, WNW of the roadway is depicted. This has since been levelled. The smaller area ESE of the roadway is now occupied by modern farm buildings. Situated on the SW shoulder of a high drumlin ridge. Not visible at ground level.
35:6 20-6-1988

276 CABRA
OS 35:3:4 (500,504) Hachured OD 300–400
27891, 29698
Rath Raised circular area (int. diam. *c.* 35m) enclosed by two earthen banks with intermediate wide, deep fosse. Possible traces of an external fosse at W. Original entrance not recognisable.
35:9 11-3-1974

277 CABRA
OS 35:7:1 (518,436) Hachured OD 300–400
27911, 29626
Rath Marked 'Fort' on OS 1836 and 1876 eds. and depicted as a large oval enclosure. Raised circular area (int. diam. *c.* 48m) enclosed by a substantial earthen bank and traces of a fosse. The site is bisected by a field boundary running NNE–SSW, the area ESE of which has been levelled. Original entrance not recognisable.
35:10 20-6-1988

278 CABRA
OS 35:3:4 (520,484) Hachured OD 420
27913, 29677
Rath Raised circular area (int. diam. *c.* 34m) enclosed by two substantial earthen banks with intermediate wide fosse. A modern drain which runs outside the outer bank from E–SE–S may have replaced an earlier fosse. Intermediate fosse has been infilled and is now utilised as a laneway. Break in inner bank at SE may represent original entrance. The ruins of a small circular building (int. diam. *c.* 2m), enclosed by a stone wall (max. H *c.* 2m), with a collapsed doorway at S, lies at the centre of the interior. This was probably a late-18th or early 19th-century folly.
35:12 20-6-1988

279 CABRAGH, (ED Tullyvin East)
OS 17:10:3 (410,239) Hachured OD 382
26064, 30919

Rath Raised circular area (int. diam. *c.* 46m) enclosed by a partly denuded earthen bank and a wide, deep fosse identifiable only from S–W–N. An apparently modern counterscarp bank occurs at the outer foot of the fosse from S–W. Break in bank with accompanying causeway at SSE represents original entrance.
17:5 19-9-1990

280 CALLANAGH MIDDLE
OS 37:6:5 (345,361) '*Callanagh Fort*' OD 382
23834, 28870

Rath Raised circular area (int. diam. *c.* 49m) enclosed by a substantial earthen bank and a wide, deep, partly waterlogged fosse. Slight traces of an apparently modern counterscarp bank at the outer lip of the fosse from NE–E–S. Original entrance may have been at S.
37:14 28-7-1986

281 CALLANAGH UPPER
OS 37:6:5 (320,362) Hachured OD 300–400
23807, 28871

Rath Levelled in the early 1980s. An earlier report (OPW 1970) described an unusually large circular area (int. diam. *c.* 50m) enclosed by a substantial earthen bank and a wide, deep fosse. Original entrance may have been at SE. Not visible at ground level.
37:15 9-7-1986

282 CAMAGH
OS 13:8:1 (708,400) Hachured OD 200–300
22242, 31457

Rath Raised circular area (int. diam 33.4m) enclosed by a substantial, although partly denuded, earthen bank and a wide, deep, partly waterlogged fosse. At ESE a deep circular hole has been dug into the inner face of the bank. An earlier report (OPW 1969) suggested that the original entrance may have been at SE.
13:8 12-6-1989

283 CAMPSTOWN
OS 17:15:2 (593,93) Hachured OD 200–300
26116, 30590

Rath Raised circular area (int. diam. *c.* 38m E–W) enclosed by a much-denuded low earthen bank and a wide, shallow fosse identifiable only from W–NW–N. From S–SW–W a low modern bank has been built against the natural slope outside the rath, which gives the impression of a berm at the foot of the scarp. Wide break in bank at ENE probably represents original entrance.
17:7 12-9-1990

284 CAMPSTOWN
OS 17:15:3 (669,134) Not marked OD 300–400
26236, 30559

Rath Not marked on any OS ed. Situated on the summit of a drumlin hill. Raised circular area (int. diam. *c.* 29.2m) enclosed by a substantial earthen bank and a fosse. From E–S–WSW the perimeter has been greatly modified and incorporated into the field boundary. Elsewhere it has been levelled but its outline may still be traced.
17:9 12-9-1990

285 CAPPOG
OS 28:1:1 (69,545) Hachured OD 500–600
26455, 30368

Rath Raised circular area (int. diam. *c.* 31m) enclosed by a substantial earthen bank and a wide, deep, partly waterlogged fosse. Original entrance not recognisable. Internal area densely overgrown with vegetation.
28:2 18-8-1988

286 CARGAGH (Castlerahan By.)
OS 33:11:2 (611,255) '*Cargagh Cross*'
OD 400–500 26061, 29418

Rath Marked 'Fort' on OS 1836 and 1876 eds. Raised circular area (int. diam. 31m) enclosed from SE–S–NW by a low earthen bank. Site is divided into two roughly equal portions by a roadway aligned NW–SE. ENE of this, the site has been levelled. On the OS Fair Plan the site is designated the 'Remarkable Stone' while the OS 1836 ed. names it 'Cargagh Cross'. Davies (1948, 98) recorded that the cross (**1719**) had been moved to the priest's garden about a mile away.
33:10(01) 12-9-1988

287 CARGAGH (Upper Loughtee By.)
OS 26:11:6 (677,210) Hachured OD 500–600
25150, 30002

Rath Raised circular area (int. diam. 31.5m) enclosed by a substantial earthen bank and a wide, deep, waterlogged fosse which has been infilled from WSW–W–NNW. Modern building against outer face of bank at N. Original entrance at SE represented by a substantial break in bank with accompanying causeway.
26:8 20-3-1992

288 CARGAGH (Upper Loughtee By.)
OS 26:14:3 (423,101) Hachured OD 400–500
24883, 29885

Rath Raised circular area (int. diam. *c.* 25m) enclosed by a substantial earthen bank and a wide, shallow fosse which has been infilled throughout most of its course and replaced by a laneway from N–E–SSE. An earlier report (OPW 1974) recorded vague traces of a possible outer bank at the outer lip of the fosse from N–NE–E. Original entrance not recognisable.
26:10 23-3-1992

289 CARGAGH (Upper Loughtee By.)
OS 26:10:3 (441,268) Hachured OD 400–500
24900, 30062

Rath Raised circular area (int. diam. *c.* 30m) enclosed by two earthen banks with intermediate fosse. The outer bank and fosse survive only from ENE–E–SSE. Elsewhere, outer bank is incorporated into the field boundary. Original entrance was probably at E.
26:11 23-3-1992

290 CARN (Tullyhunco By.)
OS 14:11:1 (475,295) Hachured OD 300–400
22973, 31353

Rath Raised circular area (int. diam. 49m) enclosed by two substantial earthen banks with wide, deep intermediate fosse. Outer bank has been levelled from ESE–S–W and has been replaced by a low modern field boundary. Break in bank with accompanying causeway at ESE represents original entrance. Corresponding breaks in the banks with accompanying causeway at NW may represent a second original entrance.
14:9 22-7-1989

291 CARNAGARVE
OS 34:9:6 (174,176) Not marked OD 500–600
26575, 29339

Rath (site) Marked 'Fort' on OS 1836 ed. and 'Site of' on 1876 ed. Situated on the SE shoulder of a drumlin ridge. Not visible at ground level.
34:4 16-5-1988

292 CARNAGARVE
OS 34:9:6 (200,164) Hachured OD 500–600
26603, 29327

Rath Raised circular area (int. diam. *c.* 33m) enclosed by a substantial earthen bank and a wide fosse. From WSW–NW fosse has been replaced by a narrow modern drain and field bank. Original entrance not recognisable.
34:5 26-4-1974

293 CARNAGARVE
OS 34:10:1 (246,228) Hachured OD 600–700
26651, 29396

Rath Raised circular area (int. diam. 24m) defined by a low earthen bank from S–W–NE and by a low scarp from SE–S. Perimeter levelled from NE–E–SE. An external, narrow, waterlogged drain running from S–W–NE presumably follows the line of the fosse. Original entrance not recognisable.
34:8 16-5-1988

294 CARNAGARVE
OS 34:10:4 (289,168) Not marked OD 500–600
26696, 29332

Rath (site) Marked 'Fort' on OS 1836 ed. and 'Site of' on 1876 ed. Situated on a drumlin ridge. Not visible at ground level.
34:9 27-3-1974

295 CARNAGARVE
OS 34:14:1 (300,121) Not marked OD 500
26709, 29282

Rath (site) Marked 'Fort on OS 1836 ed. and 'Site of' on 1876 ed. Situated a short distance NE of the highest point of a steep drumlin hill. Not visible at ground level.
34:10 26-5-1993

296 CARNAGH LOWER
OS 37:1:4 (27,472) Hachured OD 200–300
23497, 28984

Rath Raised circular area (int. diam. *c.* 32m) enclosed by a substantial earthen bank. An earlier report (OPW 1970) noted traces of a fosse from SW–WNW. A modern laneway skirts the external foot of the bank from NW–N–NE. Original entrance not recognisable.
37:16 10-7-1986

297 CARNAGH UPPER
OS 37:5:2 (109,402) Hachured OD 300–400
23584, 28911

Rath Raised circular area (int. diam. *c.* 30m E–W) enclosed by a substantial earthen bank. An earlier report (OPW 1970) noted traces of a fosse from N–E–S. From SW–W–N the outer face of the bank has been modified and incorporated into the field boundary and has a modern external trench. Break in bank at E presumably represents original entrance. A large flat stone (H 0.5m; dims. 1m x 1m) lies in the interior at S.
37:18 10-7-1986

298 CARNAGH UPPER
OS 37:5:2 (124,421) Hachured OD 300–400
23600, 28931

Rath Raised oval area (int. dims. 64m E–W; 52m N–S) enclosed by an earthen bank. An earlier report (OPW 1970) noted traces of a fosse from SSW–W–N. The outer face of the bank has been modified and incorporated into the field boundary. It has a modern stone facing in places. Original entrance not recognisable.
37:19 10-7-1986

299 CARNIN
OS 38:8:4 (762,306) Hachured OD 300–400
25250, 28825

Rath Raised circular area (int. diam. *c.* 64m) enclosed by a substantial earthen bank and a wide, shallow fosse. An earlier report (OPW 1970) suggested that the counterscarp bank which is identifiable at the outer lip

of the fosse from WSW–WNW may be a relatively modern feature. Modern laneway runs outside of the fosse from S–WSW. Break in bank at ESE may represent original entrance.
38:6 28-8-1986

300 CARNIN
OS 38:12:6 (872,199) Hachured OD 400–500 25367, 28713
Rath Raised circular area (int. diam. *c.* 38m) enclosed by a substantial earthen bank and the remains of a shallow fosse which is identifiable from SSE–W–NW. Elsewhere it has been infilled or replaced by modern drains. Break in bank with accompanying causeway at S represents original entrance.
38:7 27-8-1986

301 CARRICK WEST
OS 6:5:5 (95,315) Hachured OD 500–600 20609, 32633
Rath Raised subrectangular area (int. dims. 24.8m NW–SE; 21m NE–SE) enclosed by two substantial earthen banks with intermediate wide, deep, waterlogged fosse. Corresponding breaks in banks at NW with accompanying causeway represents original entrance.
6:2 28-8-1988

302 CARRICKACROMAN
OS 27:6:5 (334,352) Hachured OD 600–700 25761, 30158
Rath Raised circular area (int. diam. *c.* 33m) enclosed by two earthen banks with intermediate fosse. Outer bank is best preserved at E and absent at W. Fosse is shallow and densely overgrown with scrub. Original entrance not recognisable.
27:2 17-7-1989

303 CARRICKAKILLEW
OS 41:2:6 (428,529) Hachured OD 300–400 23926, 28408
Rath Raised circular area (int. diam. *c.* 29m) enclosed by a low earthen bank and very slight traces of a fosse identifiable only at N. From ENE–S–SSW bank has been modified and incorporated into the field boundary. Original entrance not recognisable.
41:8 21-6-1974

304 CARRICKALLEN
OS 27:2:2 (330,568) Hachured OD 500–600 25755, 30386
Rath Raised circular area (int. diam. 22.6m) enclosed by a low earthen bank and a fosse identifiable only from SSW–N–E. Break in bank at SE may represent original entrance.
27:3 26-7-1989

305 CARRICKANE
OS 20:11:2 (616,267) Hachured OD 100–200 24103, 30693
Rath Raised oval area (int. dims. 50m N–S; *c.* 43.5m E–W) enclosed by a wide, low earthen bank (Wth 7.7m) and slight remains of a fosse (Wth 3.5m; D 0.3m). Break in bank with traces of possible accompanying causeway at NNW represents original entrance. From N–E–ESE the perimeter of the site has been destroyed as a result of the construction of a now disused railway line.
20:5 19-8-1990

306 CARRICKAVEE
OS 39:5:4 (41,326) Hachured OD 600–700 25464, 28848
Rath Raised circular area (int. diam. *c.* 24m) enclosed by a much-denuded low earthen bank. From N–E–SE this has been modified and incorporated into the field boundary. Original entrance not recognisable.
39:19 12-9-1986

307 CARRICKCREENY
OS 23:12:4 (756,203) Indicated OD 300–400 27177, 30653
Rath (site) Marked 'Fort' on OS 1836 ed. and 'Site of' on 1876 ed. Site is divided into two roughly equal portions by a field boundary aligned NE–SW. NW of this the site has been levelled while the SE portion has been transformed into a small field. It is enclosed by a low bank of earth and stone similar in morphology to other field boundaries in the vicinity and presumably follows the original plan of the perimeter. Original int. diam. of rath *c.* 22.5m.
23:4 4-4-1992

308 CARRICKMORE
OS 16:9:4 (75,206) Hachured OD 300–400 24502, 31273
Rath Raised circular area (int. diam. *c.* 42m) enclosed by a slight earthen bank best defined from NW–N–NE. A modern bank of earth and stone has been piled up against it and a modern ditch dug outside. Original entrance may have been either at E or S. Densely overgrown with vegetation.
16:14 17-09-1989

309 CARRICKNASHOKE
OS 27:1:5 (111,499) Hachured OD 500–600 25525, 30312
Rath Raised circular area (int. diam. 47m) enclosed by a low earthen bank and a shallow fosse. From SE–S–SSW the perimeter has been incorporated into the field boundary. The W half of the site has been levelled, leaving only the outline of the perimeter discernible. Original entrance not recognisable.
27:4 27-7-1989

310 CARRIGAN (ED Kilconny)
OS 15:5:1 (6,423) Hachured OD 200–300
23452, 31493
Rath Raised oval area (dims. *c.* 27m E–W; *c.* 18m N–S) defined by a scarp and a wide, shallow fosse. Original entrance not recognisable.
15:9 2-9-1989

311 CARTRONFREE
OS 37:13:4 (42,17) Hachured OD 300–400
23517, 28503
Rath (site) Levelled in the early 1980s (local information). An earlier report (OPW 1970) described a much-disturbed raised circular area (diam. *c.* 40m). All that survives to indicate the presence of the site is a curve in the field boundary at E. Otherwise, nothing visible at ground level.
37:20 4-7-1986

312 CARTRONFREE
OS 37:13:5 (84,14) Hachured OD 347
23562, 28500
Rath Raised circular area (int. diam. *c.* 28m) enclosed by a substantial earthen bank and a shallow fosse. The fosse has been modified and incorporated into the field boundary from ESE–S–W and has a low, apparently modern, counterscarp bank at its outer lip. Wide break in bank at E presumably represents original entrance. A large pond occupies the northern area of the interior.
37:21 4-7-1986

313 CASHEL (Clankee By.)
OS 23:2:1 (267,540) Hachured OD 400–500
26658, 31005
Rath Raised circular area (int. diam. 21.7m) enclosed by two substantial earthen banks with wide, deep intermediate fosse. The stone facing on the exterior of the outer bank can probably be assigned to the modern period. A wide drainage trench has been dug through the outer bank at SW in recent years. Corresponding breaks in banks with accompanying causeway at SSW represents original entrance. The W half of the interior is occupied by the remains of a rectangular featureless stone building (int. dims. 16.6m NW–SE; 4.9m NE–SW), probably the remains of a house. Its entrance is not recognisable. Possible souterrain in the centre of the rath (**1225**).
23:5(01) 26-5-1992

314 CASTLEPOLES
OS 30:3:5 (547,513) Hachured OD 500–600
23066, 29661
Rath Raised almost circular area (int. dims. 28.3m N–S; 31.6m E–W) enclosed by a substantial earthen bank and vague traces of a fosse. At the outer lip of the fosse at W there is a short stretch of counterscarp bank. From WNW–N a modern field bank has been erected along the outer lip of the fosse. Original entrance at SSE represented by a break in the bank with accompanying causeway.
30:5 4-10-1991

315 CASTLESAUNDERSON DEMESNE
OS 11:11:6 (674,194) Indicated OD 200–300
24153, 31897
Rath Marked 'Fort' on OS 1836 and 1876 eds. and known as same in the locality. Raised circular area (int. diam. *c.* 48m) enclosed by a substantial earthen bank and traces of a fosse. Perimeter has been largely levelled at N. Original entrance not recognisable. Densely overgrown with vegetation.
11:3 16-6-1989

316 CASTLETERRA
OS 21:6:1 (242,422) Hachured OD 400–500
24683, 30863
Rath (possible) Situated just E of the summit of a high drumlin hill. Raised oval area (int. dims. 47.3m N–S; 39.5m E–W) defined by a scarp faced with a wall of drystone masonry. From N–E and from S–SW there is a modern trench at the external foot of the scarp. The interior is used as a graveyard (**1623**). Original entrance, now marked by a modern gate and pillars, was at ESE. The site, from the surface remains, would appear to be a rath later utilised as a burial ground.
21:6(01) 24-9-1990

317 CAUHOO
OS 25:10:3 (412,261) Hachured OD 400–500
23894, 30045
Rath Raised circular area (int. diam. 26m) enclosed by two earthen banks with intermediate wide, deep, waterlogged fosse. Outer bank absent in E quadrant. Original entrance may have been at E where there is a break in the inner bank with accompanying causeway.
25:11 18-9-1991

318 CAUHOO
OS 25:6:6 (427,338) Hachured OD 300
23909, 30127
Rath (site) An earlier report (OPW 1968) recorded that it comprised a raised circular area (int. dims. 30.4m N–S; 31.5m E–W) enclosed by a low earthen bank. Original entrance may have been at SSW. Site has been levelled leaving nothing visible at ground level.
25:12 18-9-1991

319 CAVANAQUILL
OS 9:16:6 (873,61) Hachured OD 300–400
22415, 31741
Rath (site) Marked 'Fort' on OS 1836 and 1876 eds. Situated on slightly elevated ground on the slope of a

drumlin hill. Levelled in the early 1960s as part of a land reclamation scheme. Not visible at ground level.
9:7 19-9-1988

320 CLARAGH (ED Ashfield)
OS 17:6:6 (420,336) Hachured OD 384
26168, 31013
Rath Raised circular area (int. diam. *c*. 47m) enclosed by a substantial earthen bank and a wide, deep, partly waterlogged fosse. From ESE–SSE the site is bordered by a modern roadway and elsewhere is enclosed by field boundaries. Break in bank with accompanying causeway at ESE represents original entrance.
17:12 10-11-1990

321 CLARAGH (ED Drumcarn)
OS 16:6:1 (295,428) Hachured OD 300–400
24733, 31509
Rath Raised circular area (int. diam. 29.4m) enclosed by a low bank of earth and stone from NNE–S–W. From W–N–NNE the perimeter is obscured by a modern field boundary. Original entrance not recognisable. Projecting from the inner face of the bank at S is a small subrectangular area (int. dims. 5.6m NE–SW; 4.2m NW–SE) enclosed by a low, broad bank of earth and stone. Entrance to this may have been either through a wide break in the bank at E or through a smaller break at NNE. Running 2.6m from the NE of this enclosure is a low, much-ruined, linear drystone wall.
16:16 9-11-1989

322 CLARE
OS 38:3:1 (488,591) Indicated OD 300–400
24958, 29123
Rath Marked 'Fort' on the OS 1836 ed. and 'Site of' on 1876 ed. Depicted as a triangular tree plantation on the OS current ed. Within the tree plantation is a raised circular area (int. diam. *c*. 25m) enclosed by a low earthen bank identifiable from W–N–E, and a fosse. Original entrance not recognisable. Densely overgrown with vegetation.
38:9 25-8-1986

323 CLAREBOY
OS 31:8:5 (811,359) Hachured OD 30–400
24320, 29512

Fig. 13—*A well-preserved rath at Claragh* (**320**).

Rath Raised circular area (int. diam. *c*. 29.6m) enclosed by a substantial earthen bank and vague traces of a fosse. Bank has been replaced by a linear field boundary from N–NE–E. Elsewhere it has been modified and incorporated into the field boundary. Original entrance not recognisable.
31:11 2-4-1974

324 CLIFFERNA
OS 27:9:1 (71,272) Hachured OD 600–700
25484, 30071
Rath Raised circular area (int. diam. *c*. 23m) enclosed by an earthen bank and vague traces of a fosse. A later field boundary has been superimposed on the bank at N rendering it square in plan on this side. Original entrance may be represented by a break in bank at NE.
27:6 20-7-1989

325 CLOGGAGH
OS 38:7:3 (676,444) Hachured OD 300–400
25158, 28970
Rath Raised circular area (int. diam. *c*. 31m) enclosed by a low earthen bank and vague traces of a fosse identifiable only from SE–S–W. Elsewhere the fosse has been replaced by a modern trench. An earlier report (OPW 1970) suggested that the original entrance may have been at SSW.
38:10 27-8-1986

326 CLOGHBALLY UPPER
OS 44:2:1 (269,538) Hachured OD 400–500
26684, 28443
Rath Raised circular area (int diam. *c*. 28m) enclosed by a low earthen bank and traces of a possible fosse. Break in bank at SE may represent original entrance. A slight earth and stone bank with a short segment of scarp set at a right angle to its SW side, runs through the interior in a NW–SE direction. At NNE a broad ramp-like feature leads up to the top of the bank from the internal area.
44:4 20-8-1987

327 CLOGHBALLYBEG
OS 40:13:3 (199,107) Hachured OD 300–400
26608, 28627
Rath Raised circular area (int. diam. *c*. 28m) enclosed by a low, much-denuded bank of earth and stone. An earlier report (OPW 1969) recorded traces of an external fosse from SE–S–SW. Original entrance not recognisable.
40:1 12-8-1987

328 CLOGHERGOOLE
OS 40:13:1 (70,127) Hachured OD 300–400
26472, 28646
Rath Raised circular area (int. diam. *c*. 34m) enclosed by slight traces of an earthen bank from W–N–S. Elsewhere the perimeter has been removed. Original entrance not recognisable. The interior is divided into two unequal portions by a field boundary running NNW–SSW. A raised roughly circular platform (diam. *c*. 8m N–S) which may represent a hut site, lies N of centre.
40:6 14-8-1987

329 CLONAGONNELL
OS 25:7:1 (503,452) Hachured OD 300–400
23988, 30248
Rath Raised almost circular area (int. dims. 30m ENE–WSW; 32m NNW–SSE) enclosed by a partly denuded earthen bank and a wide, deep fosse. Original entrance may have been at ENE where there is a break in the bank with accompanying causeway.
25:14 17-9-1991

330 CLONAGONNELL
OS 25:7:1 (510,425) Not marked OD 300–400
23996, 30219
Rath (site) Marked 'Fort' on OS 1836 ed. and 'Site of' on 1876 ed. Situated on the summit of a high drumlin hill. Although levelled, the outline of the perimeter (diam. *c*. 26m) is still identifiable, albeit with difficulty.
25:15 17-9-1991

331 CLONAGONNELL
OS 25:3:4 (533,471) Hachured OD 300–400
24019, 30268
Rath (site) An earlier report (OPW 1970) recorded that it comprised a raised circular area (int. dims. 26.8m E–W; 26m N–S) enclosed by two earthen banks with external fosses. Original entrance was probably at E. Site has been levelled. Not visible at ground level.
25:18 17-9-1991

332 CLONANDRA
OS 11:12:5 (836,164) Hachured OD 200
24325, 31867
Rath Raised circular area (int. diam. *c*. 29m) enclosed by a wide, deep fosse and substantial earthen bank. Break in bank with accompanying causeway at ESE represents original entrance. Densely overgrown with vegetation.
11:8 16-6-1989

333 CLONANDRA
OS 11:12:6 (876,158) Hachured OD 200–300
24367, 31861
Rath (site) Marked 'Fort' on OS 1836 and 1876 eds. An earlier report (OPW 1974) described a raised circular area (int. dims. *c*. 60m N–S; *c*. 50m E–W) enclosed by a low, wide earthen bank. Original entrance was not recognisable. Site has been levelled.

Not visible at ground level.
11:9 16-6-1989

334 CLONARNEY
OS 40:6:5 (320,322) Hachured OD 400–500
26734, 28855
Rath Raised circular area (int. dims. 35.4m NNW–SSE; 35m ENE–WSW) enclosed by a low earthen bank and vague traces of a fosse identifiable only from SE–S. Exterior of bank has been faced with drystone masonry. Modern farm buildings abut the site from NW–N–NE. Original entrance not recognisable. Internal area is divided into three unequal portions by modern field boundaries.
40:7 11-9-1970

335 CLONBOCKOGE
OS 42:3:5 (611,496) Hachured OD 200–300
25094, 28384
Rath Raised circular area (int. diam. *c.* 40m) enclosed by a low bank of earth and stone. An earlier description (OPW 1974) noted traces of an external fosse. The perimeter has been largely destroyed from NNW–N–ENE and at S where modern farm buildings abut the site. Original entrance not recognisable. A raised circular platform (diam. *c.* 12m) in the E quadrant of the interior presumably represents a house platform. A circular mound (H 2m) in a central position in the interior appears to be a natural feature. At the base of this mound, on its N side, foundations of a rectangular house (int. dims. *c.* 10m E–W; *c.* 5m N–S) are visible. Possible remains of souterrain at centre of internal area (**1226**).
42:5(01) 10-4-1986

336 CLONCOSE (ED Killashandra)
OS 14:16:4 (735,66) '*Cloncose Fort*' OD 200–300
23250, 31113
Rath Raised circular area (int. diam. 38.4m) enclosed by two substantial earthen banks with outer fosses. The external fosse has been modified and incorporated into the field drainage system. Corresponding breaks in banks with accompanying causeway at NE represents original entrance. Possible collapsed souterrain running W from the entrance to the centre of the internal area (**1227**).
14:12(01) 17-7-1989

337 CLONCOVET
OS 37:5:1 (26,386) Hachured OD 200–300
23496, 28893
Rath (site) Levelled in the 1980s (local information). An earlier report (OPW 1970) described a raised oval area (int. dims. *c.* 35m WNW–ESE; *c.* 28m NNE–SSW) enclosed by a substantial earthen bank and a wide, shallow fosse. Original entrance was not recognisable. Not visible at ground level.
37:22 10-7-1986

338 CLONCOVET
OS 37:9:5 (136,158) Hachured OD 300–400
23615, 28653
Rath Raised circular area (int. diam. *c.* 31m) enclosed by a low, narrow earthen bank and a wide, shallow, waterlogged fosse identifiable only from E–S–SSW. Original entrance not recognisable.
37:23 4-7-1986

339 CLONEARY
OS 13:3:3 (686,536) Hachured OD 200–300
22218, 31600
Rath Raised circular area (int. diam. 43m ENE–WSW) enclosed by a low earthen bank and a wide, deep, partly waterlogged fosse. From E–S–WSW fosse has been largely infilled. Original entrance not recognisable. An earlier report (OPW 1969) recorded a possible souterrain at the centre of the internal area (**1228**). Densely overgrown with vegetation.
13:9(01) 8-6-1989

340 CLONERVY
OS 21:6:4 (302,318) Hachured OD 400–500
24747, 30753
Rath Raised circular area (int. diam. 31.7m) enclosed by an earthen bank and a fosse which is poorly preserved at E half of site. Break in bank with accompanying causeway at S probably represents original entrance.
21:9 22-9-1990

341 CLONKEIFFY
OS 43:5:1 (62,448) Hachured OD 300–400
25491, 28337
Rath Raised circular area (int. dims. 26.2m E–W; 24.7m N–S) enclosed by a low earthen bank and vague traces of a fosse. Break in bank at SE with remains of accompanying causeway represents original entrance. An earlier report (OPW 1969) recorded a small, low, subrectangular platform of unknown significance adjacent to the inner face of bank at WSW.
43:7 2-9-1970

342 CLONLOSKAN
OS 25:9:1 (59,268) Hachured OD 100–200
23521, 30049
Rath Raised circular area (int. dims. 32.5m E–W; 34.3m N–S) enclosed by a partially denuded low earthen bank and a partly waterlogged fosse. Original entrance may have been at ESE.
25:19 5-9-1991

343 CLONLOSKAN
OS 25:9:1 (60,242) Hachured OD 100–200
23522, 30022

Plate 5a—*The abbey church, round tower and graveyard at Drumlane* (**1647**).

Plate 5b—*A multiple bullaun stone at Termon* (**1703**) *containing St Brigid's cursing stones.*

Plate 6—*A Romanesque doorway at Kilmore Upper* (**1668**), *originally from Trinity Island, Lough Oughter.*

Rath Situated adjacent to the N bank of the River Erne. Raised circular area (int. dims. 33.2m NE–SW; 32.6m NW–SE) enclosed by a very poorly preserved earthen bank and slight remains of a fosse identifiable only from SE–S. Break in bank at NE may represent original entrance.
25:20 5-9-1991

344 CLONOOSE BIG
OS 37:2:6 (438,460) Hachured OD 200–300
23932, 28976
Rath Raised circular area (int. diam *c.* 37m) enclosed by two substantial earthen banks with intermediate wide, deep, partly waterlogged fosse. Outer bank and fosse identifiable from NNW–N–E. Fosse also identifiable at WSW. Break in bank with accompanying causeway at SE represents original entrance.
37:24 11-7-1986

345 CLONOOSE BIG
OS 37:7:1 (472,390) *'Muckram Fort'* OD 300–400
23967, 28902
Rath Raised circular area (int. diam. *c.* 42m) enclosed by a substantial earthen bank and a wide, deep fosse. Break in bank with accompanying causeway at SE represents original entrance. Possible remains of a souterrain in the interior at WNW (**1229**).
37:25(01) 11-7-1986

346 CLONOOSE LITTLE
OS 37:6:3 (396,400) Hachured OD 300–400
23887, 28912
Rath (site) Levelled in the early 1980s (local information). An earlier report (OPW 1970) described a raised circular area (int. diam. *c.* 29m) enclosed by a low earthen bank. Original entrance was not identifiable. Not visible at ground level.
37:26 11-7-1986

347 CLONRAW
OS 22:8:3 (884,406) Hachured OD 400–500
26336, 30860
Rath Raised oval area (int. dims. 36.4m NNE–SSW; *c.* 31m WNW–ESE) enclosed by a low earthen bank. Bank survives only from NE–E–S. Modern laneway and trench extend NNE–SSW across the site. Original entrance not recognisable.
22:4 19-10-1990

348 CLONRAW
OS 23:5:1 (30,434) Hachured OD 400
26409, 30890
Rath (site) Situated on the summit of a drumlin hill. An earlier report (OPW 1977) described a raised almost circular area (int. diam. 37m) enclosed by the remains of a substantial earthen bank and a deep, wide fosse. Original entrance was not recognisable. Site has been levelled.
23:6 26-5-1992

349 CLONTURKAN
OS 35:9:4 (42,155) Hachured OD 500–600
27412, 29325
Rath Raised circular area (int. diam. *c.* 31m N–S) enclosed by a partially denuded earthen bank and vague traces of a fosse. Break in bank at SE may represent original entrance.
35:14 9-6-1988

350 CLONTYDUFFY (Nugent)
OS 42:7:4 (508,327) Hachured OD 200–300
24987, 28205
Rath (site) Marked 'Fort' on OS 1836 and 1876 eds. An earlier report (OPW 1974) described a large subrectangular-shaped raised area (int. diam. 34m E–W) enclosed by a wide, low earthen bank. Original entrance was not recognisable. Site has since been levelled. Not visible at ground level.
42:10 8-9-1986

351 CLONTYDUFFY (Nugent)
OS 42:7:4 (517,317) Hachured OD 200–300
24997, 28194
Rath Remains of a slightly raised, originally circular area (int. diam. *c.* 35m) defined by a low scarp. From NW–N–ENE the perimeter has been destroyed and replaced by a modern roadway. Original entrance not recognisable.
42:11 8-9-1986

352 CLOVERHILL DEMESNE
OS 15:7:2 (613,441) Hachured OD 265
24093, 31517
Rath Raised circular area (int. diam. 42.5m) enclosed by a low earthen bank and a wide, shallow fosse. Fosse and bank have been modified and incorporated into the field boundary. Original entrance not recognisable. The centre of the enclosed area is occupied by a large circular platform (diam. 24.3m; H 0.6m) with slight traces of an enclosing low earthen bank about its perimeter.
15:12 19-9-1989

353 CLOWNEY
OS 14:3:3 (629,580) Indicated OD 200–300
23133, 31655
Rath (site) The site is now occupied by a modern farmyard and farm buildings. It formerly comprised (OPW 1969) a raised circular area (int. dims. 46.3m E–W; 43.2m N–S) enclosed by a substantial earthen bank and traces of a fosse. Original entrance was

probably at SE. All that survives of the perimeter is a short stretch of fosse and bank at NW.
14:14 29-7-1989

354 CLOWNEY
OS 14:3:3 (669,570) Indicated OD 200–300
23175, 31645
Rath Raised circular area (int. diam. 52.6m) enclosed by a low earthen bank and a narrow, shallow fosse, both of which have been incorporated into the field boundary. Perimeter has been levelled from S–SW–W but its outline is nonetheless identifiable. Original entrance not recognisable.
14:16 29-7-1989

355 COOLCANADAS
OS 16:10:3 (391,236) Hachured OD 200–300
24836, 31308
Rath Raised circular area (int. diam. *c.* 32m) enclosed by a substantial earthen bank and a wide, deep, partly waterlogged fosse. Break in bank with accompanying causeway at SE represents original entrance. Outer part of causeway destroyed by modern field boundary.
16:17 17-10-1989

356 COOLCANADAS
OS 16:10:6 (404,196) Hachured OD 300
24850, 31266
Rath Raised circular area (int. diam. *c.* 38m) enclosed by two substantial earthen banks with outer fosses. External fosse is wide and deep from W–NW–N, elsewhere remains are slight. A modern deposit of earth has been piled up against the inner face of the outer bank from ENE–W–N giving the impression of a slight berm between this bank and the inner fosse. Corresponding breaks in banks, with causeway across inner fosse at SSE, represents original entrance. Internal area overgrown with vegetation.
16:18 17-10-1989

357 COOLKILL
OS 38:1:5 (144,504) Indicated OD 516
24596, 29028
Rath Raised circular area (int. diam. *c.* 39m) enclosed by a substantial earthen bank which has been considerably modified and incorporated into the field boundary. Original entrance not recognisable. The site was formerly planted with trees.
38:12 8-8-1986

358 COOLNACARRICK
OS 25:14:1 (288,120) Hachured OD 200–300
23764, 29895
Rath Raised circular area (int. dims. 43.2m NE–SW; 41m NW–SE) enclosed by a substantial earthen bank and the remains of a fosse. Large break in bank from E–SE may represent original entrance.
25:21 10-9-1991

359 COOLNACOLA
OS 33:7:1 (474,388) Hachured OD 400–500
25915, 29558
Rath Raised circular area (int. diam. *c.* 42m) enclosed by a low earthen bank and a wide, deep fosse. Original entrance not recognisable. A modern laneway aligned ENE–WSW divides the internal area into two roughly equal portions.
33:12 4-5-1974

360 COOLNALITTERAGH
OS 15:3:3 (675,541) Hachured OD 200–300
24158, 31623
Rath Very large raised sub-oval area (int. dims. *c.* 109m N–S; *c.* 69m E–W) enclosed by a much-denuded low, narrow earthen bank and the remains of a fosse. Break in bank with accompanying causeway at SSW probably represents original entrance. An earlier report (OPW 1968) noted a small crescent-shaped area demarcated by a low scarp in the interior at N.
15:13 19-9-1989

361 COOLOGE
OS 13:12:3 (851,295) Hachured OD 181
22394, 31348
Rath Raised circular area (int. diam. 50.6m) enclosed by a low, much-denuded earthen bank and a fosse. The site is divided into two unequal portions by a roadway and field boundary running NW–SE. The smaller portion, SW of this, has been levelled and there are no surface remains. Original entrance not recognisable.
13:11 17-6-1989

362 COPPANAGH (Clankee By.)
OS 34:11:3 (650,277) Hachured OD 500–600
27077, 29450
Rath Raised circular area (int. diam. *c.* 29m) enclosed by a substantial earthen bank and traces of a fosse. Perimeter levelled from SE–S–SW. Fosse re-dug as field drain from NW–N–ENE. Break in bank at NW may represent original entrance.
34:15 27-5-1988

363 COPPANAGH (Clankee By.)
OS 34:12:6 (866,159) Indicated OD 600–700
27307, 29328
Rath Raised circular area (int. diam. *c.* 37m) enclosed by a low earthen bank and a field drain which was probably dug on the site of a fosse. Site is divided into two roughly equal portions by a field boundary running NNE–SSW, ESE of which there are no surface indications of the rath. Original entrance not recognisable.
34:16 15-3-1974

364 COR
OS 9:16:4 (731,11) Hachured OD 200–300
22265, 31687
Rath Raised circular area (int. diam. 24.9m) enclosed by an earthen bank and a fosse which is well preserved from N–ENE, and infilled or incorporated into the field boundary elsewhere. Bank absent from SSE–SSW and incorporated into the field boundary from SSW–NNW. Break in bank at E may represent original entrance.
9:8 21-9-1988

365 CORAGH (Lower Loughtee By.)
OS 11:5:5 (117,310) Indicated OD 200–300
23564, 32014
Rath (site) Marked 'Fort' on OS 1836 and 1876 eds. An earlier report (OPW 1974) described a raised circular area (int. diam. *c.* 28m) enclosed by a substantial earthen bank and a fosse, with no recognisable entrance. Although now levelled, the outline of perimeter may still be traced.
11:12 10-6-1989

366 CORBALLYQUILL
OS 17:6:5 (315,373) Hachured OD 300–400
26093, 31153
Rath (site) Situated on the summit of a high drumlin hill within what was formerly a tree plantation. Described by Davies (ITA Survey 1946). It comprised a raised subcircular area (diam. *c.* 40m NE–SW) enclosed by a substantial earthen bank and a fosse. From ENE–E–SW the perimeter had been much modified and formed part of the boundary of the plantation. Both the rath and the plantation have been levelled. (CUCAP ALJ 87, ALJ 90).
17:14(02) 17-11-1989

367 CORBEAGH (Clankee By.)
OS 23:12:2 (828,257) Hachured OD 500–600
27253, 30711
Rath Raised circular area (int. diam. 24.6m) enclosed by an earthen bank and fosse which is virtually levelled except from SSE–S–W where it features as a narrow, very deep, waterlogged trench. Break in bank at SE may represent original entrance. A large stone lies on the surface within the internal area. Break in bank at WNW opens into a shallow, circular depression of unknown significance, just inside the line of the bank.
23:7 30-3-1992

368 CORBEAGH (Clankee By.)
OS 23:12:2 (830,237) Hachured OD 400–500
27255, 30690
Rath Raised circular area (int. diam. 31.3m) enclosed by a substantial earthen bank and faint traces of a fosse. Exterior of bank has been faced with stone from WSW–NW. Original entrance not recognisable. Within the internal area at SE are the remains of an undivided rectangular house represented by a slight grass-covered bank of earth and stone (int. dims. 8m NE–SW; 4.2m NW–SE).
23:8 30-3-1992

369 CORBEAGH (Tullygarvey By.)
OS 17:6:2 (382,444) Hachured OD 300–400
26231, 31164
Rath (site) Situated on the summit of a high drumlin hill. An earlier report (OPW 1969) described a raised circular area (int. diam. *c.* 35m) enclosed by two substantial earthen banks with wide, deep, partly waterlogged outer fosses. Original entrance was at SSE. Site has since been levelled.
17:16 22-9-1990

370 CORCASHEL (Tullyhaw By.)
OS 5:14:2 (367,422) Hachured OD 300–400
19928, 31847
Rath Situated on a terrace, on the N shoulder of a high hill and within a modern plantation of coniferous trees. An earlier report (OPW 1974) described a small raised circular area (int. diam. *c.* 25m) enclosed by a low earthen bank and slight traces of a fosse. At that time the site was already much disturbed by forestry drainage. Not located.
5:14 29-8-1988

371 CORCASHEL (Tullyhaw By.)
OS 5:14:2 (342,391) Hachured OD 400–500
19901, 31880
Rath Situated on a natural hillock, on the N shoulder of a mountain and within a plantation of coniferous trees. An earlier report (OPW 1974) described a raised circular area (int. diam. *c.* 26m) enclosed by two low earthen banks with wide, deep intermediate fosse. Not located.
5:15 29-8-1988

372 CORCASHEL (Tullyhaw By.)
OS 5:14:1 (300,385) Hachured OD 600–700
19857, 31886
Rath Situated on a terrace, on the NW shoulder of a mountainous hill and within a plantation of coniferous trees. An earlier report (OPW 1974) described a raised circular area (int. diam. *c.* 31m) enclosed by a substantial earthen bank and a wide, shallow fosse. Original entrance not recognisable. The site was much disturbed as a result of tree planting. Not located.
5:16 29-8-1988

373 CORCOVETY
OS 16:15:4 (514,36) Hachured OD 300–400
24968, 31097

Rath Raised circular area (int. diam. 25.3m) enclosed by a slight earthen bank and vague traces of a fosse. The bank has been partly refaced with stone in modern times. An earlier report (OPW 1968) noted suggestions of a ploughed-out external bank from N–E–S. Break in bank at S represents original entrance.
16:19 17-10-1989

374 CORCRAFF (ED Drumcarn)
OS 16:11:1 (498,291) Hachured OD 300–400
24948, 31367
Rath Raised circular area (int. diam. *c.* 38m) enclosed by a slight earthen bank and a wide, deep, waterlogged fosse. Break in bank with remains of accompanying causeway at SE represents original entrance. Densely overgrown with vegetation.
16:20 9-9-1989

375 CORCRAFF (ED Rakenny)
OS 16:7:2 (614,397) Hachured OD 300–400
25070, 31480
Rath Raised oval area (int. dims. *c.* 39m NNE–SSW; *c.* 30m WSW–ENE) enclosed by a slight outer bank identifiable from NNW–S–SSW, a substantial inner earthen bank and a wide, shallow fosse. Original entrance not recognisable. Very overgrown with vegetation.
16:21 28-10-1990

376 CORCRAFF (ED Rakenny)
OS 16:7:3 (620,380) Hachured OD 300–400
25076, 31461
Rath (site) Levelled in the early 1950s. It formerly comprised a raised circular area enclosed by a substantial earthen bank and a fosse (local information). Situated just S of the summit of a ridge. Nothing visible at ground level.
16:22 28-10-1990

377 CORDEVLIS
OS 21:8:1 (747,429) '*Cordevlis Fort*' OD 300–400
25216, 30875
Rath Raised circular area (int. diam. *c.* 38m) enclosed by an earthen bank and a fosse. Perimeter is encircled by a modern field boundary. Slight depression in bank with accompanying causeway at SE represents original entrance. Densely overgrown with vegetation.
21:10 25-9-1990

378 CORDOAGH GLEBE UPPER
OS 17:14:3 (385,89) Hachured OD 300–400
25893, 30786
Rath Raised circular area (int. diam. *c.* 28m) enclosed by a substantial earthen bank and a wide, deep fosse. The perimeter has been levelled from NNE–S–WSW. Elsewhere it has been modified and incorporated into the field boundary. Original entrance not recognisable.
17:17 27-9-1990

379 CORFAD (Castlerahan By.)
OS 40:13:2 (100,147) Hachured OD 400–500
26503, 28668
Rath Raised circular area (int. diam. *c.* 25m) enclosed by a substantial earthen bank from S–W–ENE. Elsewhere the perimeter has been replaced by modern field boundaries. An earlier report (OPW 1969) noted traces of an external fosse and that the exterior of the bank had been faced with drystone masonry from N–E–ENE. Original entrance may have been at SW. Internal area densely overgrown with vegetation.
40:8 12-8-1987

380 CORFEEHONE
OS 21:10:3 (388,300) Hachured OD 435
24838, 30735
Rath Raised circular area (int. diam. 26m) enclosed by an earthen bank which has been substantially modified and incorporated into the field boundary. This is particularly the case from NW–N–ESE where its original curve has been altered and is now linear in plan. Original entrance not recognisable.
21:11 19-9-1990

381 CORFREE
OS 30:15:1 (469,91) Hachured OD 200–300
22986, 29216
Rath Situated on a hillock on the shores of Lough Gowna. Raised D-shaped area (int. dims. 28.8m NE–SW; *c.* 29m NW–SE) enclosed by a substantial earthen bank and a fosse. Site is divided into two apparently equal portions by a modern field wall running NW–SE. There are no surface remains NE of this. Slight depression in the bank accompanied by suggestions of a causeway at NNE may represent original entrance.
30:11 10-10-1991

382 CORFREE
OS 30:11:4 (469,208) Hachured OD 300–400
22986, 29338
Rath (site) An earlier report (OPW 1974) recorded a raised circular area (int. diam. *c.* 35m) enclosed by two substantial earthen banks with deep, wide intermediate fosse. Entrance was at SSE represented by corresponding breaks in banks with an accompanying causeway. Although site has been levelled, the outline of the perimeter is still clearly visible.
30:12 10-10-1991

383 CORFREE
OS 30:15:4 (498,69) Hachured OD 300–400
23017, 29192

Rath An almost circular raised area (int. diam. *c.* 28m) enclosed by a substantial earthen bank and a wide, deep fosse. Break in bank at SSE with accompanying causeway represents original entrance.
30:13 28-3-1974

384 CORGARVE
OS 16:14:4 (231,55) Hachured OD 290 24668, 31115
Rath Raised oval area (int. dims. 45m NE–SW; 31m NW–SE) enclosed from N–E–ESE by slight remains of an earthen bank in the form of a steep scarp and a wide, shallow fosse. The remainder of the area is defined by relatively modern field boundaries. Original entrance not recognisable.
16:23 25-9-1989

385 CORGARVE
OS 21:1:3 (208,586) Hachured OD 200–300 24645, 31035
Rath Raised circular area (int. diam. 31.9m) enclosed by a low earthen bank. Outside of this in the SE half of the site is a modern field drain which has presumably replaced the original fosse. From SW–N–E bank has been scarped and incorporated into the field boundary. Narrow break in bank at SE may represent original entrance.
21:12 19-9-1990

386 CORGLASS (Clanmahon By.)
OS 31:15:3 (680,105) Hachured 24184, 29243
Rath Raised circular area (int. diam. *c.* 41.2m) enclosed by a low earthen bank and the remains of a fosse. Modern field boundaries occur at the outer foot of the bank from NW–N and from SSE–SSW. Original entrance may have been at SSE.
31:12 13-11-1970

387 CORGLASS (ED Lisagoan)
OS 35:1:3 (217,599) Hachured OD 500–600 27592, 29795
Rath Raised circular area (int. diam. *c.* 26m) enclosed by two earthen banks with a very wide and deep, partly waterlogged intermediate fosse. Outer bank may be partly modern. Inner bank is quite massive (max. ext. H *c.* 6m). Original entrance at S.
35:17 19-3-1974

388 CORGLASS (Lower Loughtee By.)
OS 19:4:6 (920,520) Hachured OD 200–300 23446, 30954
Rath Raised circular area (diam. *c.* 50.4m) enclosed by a low earthen bank and a wide, deep fosse which is absent from NNW–N–E. Poorly defined entrance at E. Internal area is divided into two roughly equal portions by a trackway which is flanked by modern earthen banks running NW–SE. Modern entrances have been cut through the perimeter at NW and SE. Bank and fosse are densely overgrown with vegetation.
19:11 19-7-1990

389 CORGLASS (Tullgarvey By.)
OS 22:1:4 (6,484) Hachured OD 300–400 25408, 30934
Rath Raised circular area (int. diam. *c.* 30m) enclosed by two earthen banks with intermediate fosse. Outer bank is identifiable only from WNW–E–SE. Partially blocked break in inner bank with accompanying causeway at SSE probably represents original entrance.
22:5 17-10-1990

390 CORGREAGH (Lower Loughtee By.)
OS 10:12:6 (910,213) Hachured OD 200–300 23427, 31911
Rath Raised circular area (int. diam. 35.2m) enclosed by a wide, deep fosse and substantial earthen bank. Although both bank and fosse have been levelled from E–S–SW and partially replaced by a field boundary from E–SE–S, the outline of the perimeter is still identifiable from S–SW. Original entrance may have been at N. 'Castle Bagshaw' (**1811**) was situated either within or in close proximity to the site.
10:7 10-10-1988

391 CORGREAGH (Upper Loughtee By.)
OS 21:14:3 (392,93) Hachured OD 400–500 24844, 30516
Rath Raised circular area (int. dims. 29m N–S; 31m E–W) enclosed by two earthen banks with external fosses. A wide berm separates the outer bank from the inner fosse. Outer fosse identifiable only from NNE–E–SSE. Outer bank has been modified and incorporated into the field boundary. Original entrance at ESE.
21:13 19-9-1990

392 CORICK
OS 17:9:6 (209,178) Hachured OD 200–300 25793, 31049
Rath Situated within a large modern plantation of coniferous trees. An earlier report (OPW 1969) described a raised circular area (int. diam. *c.* 45m) enclosed by a low earthen bank and a wide, shallow fosse which was identifiable only from NNW–N–NNE and from SW–S–SSE. Modern laneway skirted the site from W–NW. Original entrance was not recognisable. Internal area was divided into two unequal portions by a modern field boundary running N–S. Not located subsequently.
17:18

393 CORLATTYLANNAN
OS 28:2:3 (459,555) Indicated OD 500–600 26867, 30383

Rath Raised circular area (int. diam. *c.* 32m) enclosed by two low earthen banks with a narrow intervening fosse. Outer bank is probably relatively modern. Inner bank has been faced with drystone walling in recent times. Original entrance not recognisable. Site has been reused as a tree-ring.
28:5 29-4-1974

394 CORLECKAGH LOWER
OS 5:13:3 (165,528) Hachured OD 300–400
19716, 31734
Rath Raised circular area (int. diam. 32.8m) enclosed by a low earthen bank with low, partly waterlogged internal fosse. Original entrance not recognisable.
5:19 14-8-1988

395 CORLIS
OS 24:4:5 (772,458) Hachured OD 200–300
23297, 30247
Rath Unusually large, almost circular raised area (int. diam. 70.5m) enclosed by a slight earthen bank and a fosse. Bank has been removed at N and fosse has been incorporated into the field drainage system. Internal area occupied by hen-houses and other farm buildings. Original entrance not recognisable.
24:15 21-8-1991

396 CORLISALEE
OS 25:8:5 (803,308) Hachured OD 300–400
24307, 30099
Rath An almost circular raised area (int. diam. *c.* 33m) enclosed by a substantial earthen bank and traces of a fosse. From ESE–W–WSW a modern embankment has been built against the outer face of the bank, and the fosse incorporated into the field drainage system. Narrow break in bank at NE probably represents original entrance.
25:29 2-10-1991

397 CORLISBANNAN
OS 5:14:1 (304,495) Hachured OD 300–400
19863, 31771
Rath Raised circular area (int. diam. *c.* 30m) enclosed by a substantial, although partly denuded, earthen bank and a wide, shallow fosse which has been largely infilled. Break in bank at NE with accompanying causeway, represents original entrance. Possible souterrain within internal area (**1230**).
5:21(01) 24-8-1988

398 CORLISBANNAN
OS 5:14:1 (293,464) Hachured OD 300–400
19850, 31803
Rath Raised circular area (int. diam. 26.6m) enclosed by two earthen banks with wide, deep, partly waterlogged intervening fosse. From W–NW the outer bank has been destroyed and replaced by a modern stone field boundary. It has also been levelled for a short stretch at NW. Break in inner bank with accompanying causeway at NE represents original entrance.
5:22 24-8-1988

399 CORLISBRATTAN
OS 24:9:6 (200,186) Hachured OD 444
22695, 29955
Rath Raised circular area (int. diam. 44.8m) enclosed by two very substantial earthen banks with a wide, deep intermediate fosse. Corresponding breaks in banks at SE with traces of accompanying causeway, represents original entrance. Densely overgrown with vegetation.
24:16 21-8-1991

400 CORLISLEA
OS 31:8:4 (732,318) Hachured OD 400–500
24238, 29468
Rath Raised subcircular area (int. dims. 29.4m NW–SE; 25.8m NE–SW) enclosed by a substantial earthen bank and the remains of a fosse. Bank has been modified and incorporated into the field boundary. Fosse has been infilled but its outline may still be traced. Wide break in bank at NE may represent original entrance.
31:14 8-6-1992

401 CORLISLEA
OS 31:8:4 (737,314) Hachured OD 400–500
24243, 29464
Rath Raised circular area (int. diam. *c.* 30m) enclosed by a substantial earthen bank and vague remains of a fosse. Bank has been modified and incorporated into the field boundary. Break in bank at ESE may represent original entrance. Internal area overgrown with vegetation.
31:15 8-6-1992

402 CORLISLEA
OS 31:8:4 (756,325) Hachured OD 400–500
24263, 29476
Rath Raised circular area (int. diam. 32.4m) enclosed by a substantial earthen bank and a fosse which is wide and deep from E–SSE. Elsewhere it has been infilled but its outline can be traced from WNW–N–E. Bank has been levelled from SSE–S–WNW. From N–ENE it has been incorporated into the field boundary. Original entrance not recognisable. Tradition suggests that the rath was originally bivallate and that the outer bank was levelled *c.* 100 years ago (local information).
31:16 8-6-1992

403 CORLURGAN (Clankee By.)
OS 34:5:3 (178,384) Hachured OD 600–700
26577, 29559

Rath Raised oval area (int. dims. *c.* 30m N–S; *c.* 19m E–W) enclosed by a low earthen bank and traces of a shallow fosse. From NNW–N–E the perimeter has been destroyed and replaced by a modern field boundary. Original entrance not recognisable.
34:18 26-3-1974

404 CORMEEN (Tullyhunco By.)
OS 14:1:2 (81,576) Hachured OD 200–300
22554, 31645
Rath (site) Situated on the NNE slope of a drumlin ridge. It formerly comprised (OPW 1969) a raised circular area (int. dims. 33.4m NNW–SSE; 33m ENE–WSW) enclosed by a low earthen bank. Original entrance not recognisable. Site has been levelled. Not visible at ground level.
14:17 18-7-1989

405 CORMEEN (Tullyhunco By.)
OS 14:1:2 (117,544) Hachured OD 200–300
22593, 31613
Rath Raised circular area (int. diam. 42m) enclosed by slight remains of a low earthen bank. An earlier report (OPW 1969) suggested that the original entrance may have been at ESE or WNW.
14:18 18-7-1989

406 CORMEY
OS 35:3:6 (663,494) Hachured OD 200–300
28064, 29689
Rath Raised circular area (int. diam. *c.* 25m) enclosed by the remains of a substantial earthen bank and a wide, deep fosse. Slight traces of a low counterscarp bank at outer lip of fosse. At S, bank has been destroyed and a modern concrete building erected within the internal area. Original entrance not recognisable.
35:18 12-3-1974

407 CORMEY
OS 35:3:3 (660,537) Hachured OD 200–300
28061, 29734
Rath Raised circular area (int. diam. *c.* 48m N–S) enclosed by a substantial earthen bank and a wide, deep, partly waterlogged fosse. Slight remains of a low counterscarp bank at the outer lip of fosse at S. Original entrance not recognisable.
35:20 12-3-1974

408 CORNABASTE
OS 16:16:4 (762,15) Hachured OD 300–400
25229, 31078
Rath Raised circular area (int. diam. 36.2m) enclosed by a substantial earthen bank and a wide, deep fosse which is absent from E–SE–S. Original entrance not recognisable.
16:24 29-10-1989

409 CORNACARROW (ED Cootehill Rural)
OS 17:6:6 (444,362) Hachured OD 300–400
26219, 31018
Rath Raised circular area (int. diam. 31.1m) enclosed by a substantial earthen bank and a wide, largely infilled fosse. A modern earthen bank with external trench lies outside the fosse. Break in bank at ENE with remains of accompanying causeway represents original entrance.
17:20 22-9-1990

410 CORNACARROW (ED Cootehill Rural)
OS 17:7:4 (488,333) Hachured OD 300–400
26236, 30944
Rath Raised circular area (int. diam. 22.9m) enclosed by a substantial earthen bank and a wide, shallow fosse. Bank identifiable from NNW–N–E. Elsewhere it has been levelled but its outline is still clearly identifiable. An earlier report (OPW 1969) suggested that the original entrance may have been at SSE.
17:21 22-9-1990

411 CORNAFEAN
OS 24:12:6 (881,180) Hachured OD 100–200
23415, 29955
Rath Raised circular area (int. diam. 39.5m) enclosed by two earthen banks with a wide, deep intermediate fosse. Outer bank and external fosse absent from NE–E–S. Corresponding breaks in banks with accompanying causeway at N represents original entrance.
24:18 19-8-1991

412 CORNAGALL
OS 21:7:1 (515,408) Indicated OD 400–500
24971, 30851
Rath Marked 'Fort' on OS 1836 and 1876 eds. Slightly raised circular area (int. diam. 31.7m) enclosed by a steep, narrow earthen bank extending in an arc from NW–S–SE. From SE it straightens and extends for a short distance to NNW. Not present from NW–N–NNE. This bank is similar in morphology to other field boundaries in the vicinity. Original entrance not recognisable. At the centre of the enclosed area is a small oval-shaped earthen mound (max. dims. 3.5m E–W; 2.5m N–S; max. H 0.25m) of unknown significance.
21:15 22-9-1990

413 CORNAGARROW
OS 16:12:4 (708,211) Hachured OD 200–300
25171, 31284
Rath Raised circular area (int. diam. c. 35m) enclosed by a substantial earthen bank and a wide, deep, partly waterlogged fosse. Break in the bank with remains of a possible causeway at E presumably represents original entrance.
16:28 19-9-1989

414 CORNAGEE (Clankee By.)
OS 35:2:5 (345,496) Hachured OD 400–500
27728, 29688

Rath Raised circular area (int. diam. *c.* 28m) enclosed by a substantial earthen bank and a wide, deep fosse. Modern farm buildings encroach on the site at S, and the perimeter of the rath has been levelled as a result. Original entrance not recognisable.
35:22 24-6-1988

415 CORNAGEE (Clankee By.)
OS 35:2:5 (374,516) Hachured OD 400–500
27758, 29710

Rath Raised circular area (int. diam. *c.* 27m) enclosed by a substantial earthen bank and a well-preserved fosse. Original entrance may have been at SE. Modern roadway skirts the site from ESE–S.
35:23 19-3-1974

416 CORNAGLARE OR PALMIRA
OS 40:5:3 (228,406) Hachured OD 500–600
26636, 28942

Rath Raised circular area (int. dims. 46.3m NE–SW; 43m NW–SE) enclosed by a substantial, although partly denuded, earthen bank and traces of a fosse identifiable from S–SW–W. Original entrance not recognisable.
40:10 8-7-1970

417 CORNAGLARE OR PALMIRA
OS 40:6:1 (236,398) Hachured OD 500–600
26645, 28935

Rath Raised circular area (int. diam. 34m) enclosed by a substantial, although partly denuded, earthen bank which has been modified and incorporated into the field boundary. Modern trenches occur at the external foot of the bank. Original entrance not recognisable.
40:11 8-7-1987

418 CORNAGLERAGH OR OLDTOWN
OS 25:4:4 (769,473) Hachured OD 396
24269, 30272

Rath Raised roughly circular area (int. diam. *c.* 32m) enclosed by traces of a substantial earthen bank and indications of a fosse which has been partially incorporated into the field-drainage system. Break in bank at W with traces of accompanying causeway may represent original entrance. Large irregularly shaped depression inside the bank at W appears to be relatively modern.
25:30 15-9-1991

419 CORNAGRAN (Tullyhunco By.)
OS 36:3:2 (575,589) Hachured OD 300
23099, 29104

Rath An earlier report (OPW 1974) recorded that it comprised a raised almost circular area (int. diam. *c.* 38m) enclosed by a substantial earthen bank and a wide, deep fosse. Original entrance was not then recognisable. Site has since been levelled.
36:3 20-5-1974

420 CORNAGROW (Upper Loughtee By.)
OS 32:11:3 (639,265) Not marked OD 300–400
25115, 29420

Rath (site) Marked 'Fort' on OS 1836 and 1876 eds. The outline of the perimeter is marked by a curve in the field boundary from SW–W–NW and by a low scarp from E–SE. Field and map evidence indicates that the area enclosed was *c.* 30m in diameter. Known as the 'fort field' (local information). Site has been levelled.
32:6 18-4-1989

421 CORNAGUNLEOG
OS 13:6:1 (294,454) Hachured OD 200–300
21805, 31509

Rath Raised circular area (int. diam. *c.* 37m WNW–ESE; *c.* 35m NNE–SSW) enclosed by a substantial earthen bank and a wide, deep fosse. An earlier report (OPW 1969) noted a break in the bank at SE with accompanying causeway which presumably represents the original entrance. From SE–S–W the site is skirted by a stream which forms part of the border between counties Cavan and Leitrim. Densely overgrown with vegetation.
13:12 4-7-1989

422 CORNAGUNLEOG
OS 13:2:2 (314,545) Hachured OD 200–300
21825, 31606

Rath Raised circular area (int. diam. 30.8m) enclosed by vague traces of a fosse, identifiable only from S–W–NW. An earlier report recorded a low earthen bank at the upper edge of the scarp from WNW–NW and suggested that the original entrance may have been at SE.
13:13 4-7-1989

423 CORNAKILL (Clankee By.)
OS 35:6:1 (282,427) Hachured OD 400–500
27662, 29614

Rath Raised circular area (int. diam. *c.* 33m) enclosed by a low, partly denuded earthen bank. Original entrance not recognisable.
35:24 12-3-1974

424 CORNAKILL (Clankee By.)
OS 35:6:2 (326,454) Hachured OD 400–500
27709, 29644

Rath Raised circular area (int. diam. *c.* 37m) enclosed by a low earthen bank which is largely denuded at S.

Break in bank at SE may represent original entrance.
35:25 16-6-1988

425 CORNAKILL (Clankee By.)
OS 35:6:2 (334,391) Hachured OD 500–600
27718, 29577
Rath Raised oval area (int. dims. *c.* 72m WNW–ESE; *c.* 61m NNE–SSW) enclosed by a low earthen bank and slight traces of a fosse identifiable only at W. Exterior of bank has been faced with stone and incorporated into the field boundary at W and N. The site is divided into two roughly equal portions by a field boundary running WNW–ESE, the area SSW of which has been largely levelled. Original entrance not recognisable.
35:26 12-3-1974

426 CORNAKILL (Tullygarvey By.)
OS 21:8:2 (838,447) Hachured OD 300–400
25312, 30895
Rath Remains comprise a substantial earthen bank with modern-looking external trench extending from SSW–NNW. The site is divided into two portions by a field boundary running N–S, E of which there are no surface remains. The visible remains suggest that the rath was formerly broad and oval in plan. Original entrance not recognisable.
21:16 25-9-1990

427 CORNAKILL (Tullygarvey By.)
OS 21:4:6 (864,455) Hachured OD 200–300
25339, 30904
Rath Raised circular area (int. diam. 25.6m) enclosed by a substantial earthen bank and an infilled fosse. Outline of fosse (Wth 2.8m) may still be traced. Outer face of bank has been scarped and incorporated into the field boundary. Original entrance not recognisable.
21:17 22-9-1990

428 CORNAKILLY
OS 39:13:2 (128,123) Hachured OD 300–400
25558, 28634
Rath Raised oval area (int. dims. 26m NW–SE; 21m NE–SW) enclosed by a low bank of earth and stone, the exterior of which has been faced with partly collapsed drystone masonry. Original entrance not recognisable.
39:22 17-8-1970

429 CORNAMAHAN
OS 25:16:2 (802,126) Hachured OD 500–600
24307, 29906
Rath Raised circular area (int. dims. 28m N–S; 26.2m E–W) enclosed by the remains of a substantial earthen bank and a fosse. Original entrance was probably at ESE.
25:23 20-9-1991

430 CORNASHESK
OS 39:12:2 (787,260) Hachured OD 400–500
26253, 28785
Rath Much disturbed. Slightly raised circular area (int. diam. *c.* 31m) enclosed by rudimentary remains of two low earthen banks with a wide, shallow intermediate fosse. An earlier report (OPW 1969) suggested that the original entrance was probably at E.
39:23 5-6-1987

431 CORNASLIEVE
OS 39:3:4 (519,500) Hachured OD 300–400
25967, 29036
Rath Raised oval area (int. dims. 30m E–W; 25m N–S) enclosed by two substantial earthen banks with outer fosses. The site is bordered by a river from WNW–N–SE. From WNW–N–NE both fosses and the external bank are absent. Intermediate fosse very wide and liable to flooding. Original entrance not recognisable.
39:25 1-11-1990

432 CORRADARREN
OS 24:2:5 (334,462) Hachured OD 300–400
22834, 30247
Rath Raised circular area (int. diam. 42.25m) enclosed by two substantial earthen banks with a wide, deep intermediate fosse. Outer bank is absent at ESE. Break in inner bank at E accompanied by causeway, represents original entrance.
24:21 21-8-1991

433 CORRADOWNAN
OS 24:15:1 (472,115) Hachured OD 300–400
22983, 29883
Rath Raised circular area (int. diam. 37m) enclosed by a substantial earthen bank and the outline of a fosse. An earlier report (OPW 1977) described the fosse as being wide and deep. Original entrance represented by a break in bank with accompanying causeway at NNE. Between the entrance and the centre of the internal area is a slight irregular depression of unknown significance.
24:22 14-8-1991

434 CORRAGARRY
OS 22:8:4 (693,365) Hachured OD 400–500
26134, 30816
Rath Raised oval area (int. dims. 44.3m E–W; 32.2m N–S) enclosed by a substantial earthen bank and a wide, shallow fosse. Modern field boundary encircles the site. Break in bank with accompanying causeway at SE represents original entrance. Outer extent of

causeway crossed by the field boundary noted above.
22:7 15-10-1990

435 CORRAGARRY
OS 22:8:1 (762,412) Hachured OD 400–500
26206, 30865
Rath Raised circular area (int. diam. 26.2m) enclosed by a wide, low, much-denuded earthen bank and a wide, shallow, partly waterlogged fosse. The site is encircled by a modern field boundary from ESE–W–NW. Break in bank with accompanying causeway at NE represents original entrance.
22:8 15-10-1990

436 CORRALEEHANBEG
OS 8:15:5 (587,36) Hachured OD 400–500
21137, 31703
Rath Raised circular area (int. diam. 30m) enclosed by a much-denuded earthen bank and slight remains of a fosse. Break in bank at NE represents original entrance. Planted with coniferous trees in 1988.
8:3 19-10-1988

437 CORRAN (Tullyhaw By.)
OS 13:8:2 (793,443) Hachured OD 200–300
22332, 31503
Rath Raised circular area (int. diam. 32.8m) enclosed by a low earthen bank. From SSW–N–NNE bank has been modified and incorporated into the field boundary. Elsewhere it has been largely levelled but its outline is still identifiable. There are modern trenches at the external foot of the bank from NNE–ESE and from SSW–W. Original entrance not recognisable.
13:14 19-6-1989

438 CORRANEA GLEBE
OS 24:11:6 (649,152) Hachured OD 300–400
23170, 29923
Rath Raised circular area (int. diam. *c.* 34.5m) enclosed by a very substantial earthen bank and a deep, waterlogged fosse. Break in bank accompanied by slight causeway at SE probably represents original entrance.
24:25 3-9-1991

439 CORRANEARY (Tullyhunco By.)
OS 24:10:6 (394,207) Hachured OD 300–400
22900, 29979
Rath Raised circular area (int. diam. 39m) enclosed by two earthen banks with wide, deep, waterlogged intermediate fosse. The external bank is slight; the inner much more substantial. Original entrance at SSE represented by corresponding breaks in banks accompanied by causeway. Break in outer bank has been narrowed in relatively recent times.
24:26 21-8-1991

440 CORRANEDEN
OS 33:10:6 (386,201) Hachured OD 400–500
25824, 29359
Rath Raised circular area (int. diam. 35m) enclosed by a substantial earthen bank and a shallow fosse. Original entrance not recognisable.
33:14 23-9-1988

441 CORRANEDEN
OS 33:14:3 (422,146) Hachured OD 400–500
25862, 29302
Rath Raised circular area (int. diam. *c.* 24m) enclosed by two substantial earthen banks with outer fosses. External fosse is absent from N–E–S. Elsewhere it is narrow and deep and surrounded by a counterscarp bank suggesting that it may be just a field drain. Both interior and exterior of bank has been faced with stone in places. Original entrance not recognisable. Internal area has been planted with coniferous trees.
33:15 3-5-1974

442 CORRANURE
OS 21:5:4 (21,308) Hachured OD 400–500
24450, 30740
Rath Raised circular area (int. dims. 33m NNW–SSE; 32m NNE–SSW) enclosed by a substantial earthen bank and the remains of an almost completely infilled fosse. Outline of fosse, however, can still be traced. Original entrance at ESE now blocked by a modern field boundary. Internal area overgrown with scrub.
21:18 10-9-1990

443 CORRATINNER
OS 33:15:3 (674,117) Hachured OD 300–400
26129, 29273
Rath Raised circular area (int. diam. *c.* 27m) enclosed by an earthen bank. Original entrance not recognisable. Site was formed by scarping a natural knoll. Bordering the site from SSW–W–NW is a much overgrown, wide, shallow ditch — apparently the remains of a disused laneway.
33:19 20-9-1988

444 CORRATOBER (Tullyhunco By.)
OS 30:6:6 (421,350) Not marked OD 300–400
22934, 29488
Rath (site, possible) Marked 'Gravel Pit' on OS 1836 ed. and 'Fort' on the OS 1876 ed. Situated on the summit of a high drumlin hill. Site has been levelled and the only surface remains at the location indicated is a low kidney-shaped mound of earth and stone.
30:14 10-10-1991

445 CORRATOBER UPPER
OS 5:14:1 (282,538) Hachured OD 300–400
19840, 31725

Rath Raised circular area (int. diam. *c.* 27m) enclosed by a peat-covered bank and slight traces of a fosse. From ESE–SSE there is a modern stone wall at the outer foot of the fosse. Bank has been destroyed from SW–WNW, and from SW–W it has been replaced by a modern stone field wall. Original entrance not recognisable. Internal area is divided into two roughly equal portions by a field boundary running NW–SE.
5:27 16-8-1988

446 CORRAVAHAN
OS 21:2:6 (409,497) Hachured OD 300–400
24858, 30943
Rath Raised circular area (int. diam. 36m) enclosed by a substantial earthen bank and a fosse. Earlier descriptions (OPW 1969 and 1970) noted a break in the bank with accompanying causeway at NW which may represent original entrance. Within the internal area are the remains of a possible souterrain (**1231**). Site is situated within a plantation of deciduous trees.
21:19(01) 19-9-1990

447 CORRAVAHAN
OS 21:2:6 (441,503) Hachured OD 200–300
24892, 30950
Rath Raised circular area (int. diam. 35m) enclosed by a low earthen bank and very slight remains of a fosse. Original entrance not recognisable. Site is encircled by a modern field boundary.
21:20 27-9-1990

448 CORRAVEATY
OS 25:7:6 (682,304) Hachured OD 300–400
24179, 30093
Rath Raised circular area (int. dims. 38.2m N–S; 37.3m E–W) enclosed by two earthen banks, the outer one of which is well defined, and an intermediate fosse. Modern trackway accompanied by natural earthen bank replaces outer bank of rath from SSW–WNE. At SE, outer bank and fosse greatly disturbed by modern field boundaries, banks and drains. Original entrance probably at S.
25:31 1-10-1991

449 CORRAWADDY
OS 35:2:4 (271,512) Hachured OD 500–600
27650, 29704
Rath Raised circular area (int. diam. 42m) enclosed by two substantial earthen banks with intermediate wide, deep fosse. Outer bank and fosse largely levelled from ENE–E–SSE. Original entrance at SE.
35:27 15-2-1974

450 CORRAWEELIS (Tullygarvey By.)/ DUNGONNAN
OS 16:15:2 (545,126) Hachured OD 300
24999, 31193
Rath Raised apparently subcircular area (int. dims. *c.* 49m NE–SW; *c.* 39m NW–SE) enclosed by a substantial earthen bank and a wide, deep, partly waterlogged fosse. From E–SE–S, fosse and bank have been modified and incorporated into the field boundary. Bank is absent or very slight from ENE–E–ESE. An earlier report (OPW 1968) noted the presence of a low external earthen bank from SW–W–NW. Break in inner bank with accompanying causeway at SSW represents original entrance. Attached to the site at NE is a small crescent-shaped annex (dims. *c.* 30m NW–SE; *c.* 12.5m NE–SW) bounded by a low earthen bank. Densely overgrown with vegetation.
16:29 10-10-1989

451 CORRAWEELIS (Upper Loughtee By.)
OS 26:7:2 (552,426) Hachured OD 500–600
25015, 30230
Rath Raised circular area (int. dims. 36.5m WNW–ESE; 37m NNE–SSW) enclosed by a substantial earthen bank and a well-defined fosse. Fosse is absent from W–N–NNE and has been infilled and replaced by a pathway from NNE–E. Break in bank with accompanying causeway at ESE probably represents original entrance.
26:19 4-3-1992

452 CORRAWILLIN
OS 26:7:2 (574,423) Hachured OD 300–400
25039, 30226
Rath Raised circular area (int. dims. 41.4m NNW–SSE; 37.5m ENE–WSW) enclosed by a substantial earthen bank and a fosse. Fosse fairly well defined from S–SW–W; elsewhere only faint traces survive. Original entrance probably at E represented by a now blocked-up break in bank.
26:20 19-3-1992

453 CORRAWILLIN
OS 26:5:5 (138,363) Hachured 24579, 30159
Rath Raised circular area (int. dims. 33m E–W; 37.4m N–S) enclosed by a substantial earthen bank and a fosse which is visible from SW–W–N and at NE and SE. Break in bank at SSE may represent original entrance.
26:21 19-3-1992

454 CORRINSHIGO (Clankee By.)
OS 35:2:3 (414,549) Hachured OD 300–400
27800, 29744
Rath Raised circular area (int. diam. *c.* 29m) enclosed by a substantial earthen bank and a wide, deep fosse which has been modified and incorporated into the field drainage system. The bank has been largely levelled from E–S–SW. Original entrance not recognisable.
35:28 20-3-1974

Fig. 14—*A bivallate rath at Corraveaty* (**448**).

455 CORRINSHIGO (Tullygarvey By.)
OS 16:4:5 (781,485) Hachured OD 300–400
25245, 31574

Rath Raised circular area (int. diam. *c.* 24.7m) enclosed by a substantial earthen bank and a wide, shallow, partly waterlogged fosse. Disturbed break in bank at NE probably represents original entrance. Densely overgrown with vegetation.
16:30 21-10-1989

456 CORRONAGH
OS 39:15:2 (593,88) Indicated OD 300–400
26049, 28601

Rath Raised circular area (int. diam. *c.* 39m) enclosed by a largely denuded drystone wall which is well preserved from ESE–SE–S and is fragmentary elsewhere. An earlier report (OPW 1969) suggested that the original entrance may have been at N and noted indications of a small lean-to structure in the form of remains of a bank of earth and stones inside the wall at SSE. The entrance to the lean-to was at NNW.
39:29 1-9-1970

457 CORRYROURKE
OS 40:5:3 (162,429) Hachured OD 500
26566, 28967

Rath Raised circular area (int. diam. 41m E–W) enclosed by a substantial, although partly denuded, earthen bank and a wide, shallow fosse identifiable only from WNW–N–NE. Bank has been modified and incorporated into the field boundary. Original entrance not recognisable. Internal area is divided into two unequal portions by a modern field boundary running NW–SE.
40:19 10-7-1987

458 CORSTRUCE
OS 25:14:5 (348,64) Hachured OD 200–300
23828, 29836

Rath Subcircular area (int. dims. 41m WSW–ESE; 37m NNE–SSW) enclosed by a substantial earthen bank and a partly modernised fosse, both of which have been incorporated into the field boundary from WNW–N. Well-defined break in bank at ESE probably represents original entrance.
25:28 10-9-1991

459 CORTOBER (Clankee By.)
OS 35:6:4 (232,356) Hachured OD 500
27611, 29539
Rath Raised circular area (int. diam. *c.* 34m) enclosed by a low, much-denuded earthen bank. Break in bank at S may represent original entrance.
35:29 15-3-1974

460 CORTOBER (Clankee By.)
OS 35:10:1 (279,298) Hachured OD 400–500
27660, 29478
Rath Raised circular area (int. diam. *c.* 32m) enclosed by a substantial earthen bank and a wide, deep fosse. Remains of a low counterscarp bank at the outer lip of the fosse. At N and W counterscarp bank has been replaced by a modern field boundary. Original entrance at SE.
35:30 13-3-1974

461 CORTOBER (Clankee By.)
OS 35:6:4 (292,349) Hachured OD 500–600
27674, 29532
Rath Raised circular area (int. diam. 40m) enclosed by a low, much-denuded earthen bank and a wide, shallow fosse. At the outer lip of the fosse is a low counterscarp bank. A slight depression running inside the bank from E–S–W possibly represents the remains of an internal fosse. Original entrance not recognisable.
35:31 13-3-1974

462 CORTOBER (Clankee By.)
OS 35:10:1 (300,295) Hachured OD 500–600
27683, 29476
Rath Raised circular area (int. diam. *c.* 35m) enclosed by a substantial earthen bank and a wide, shallow fosse identifiable only at S. From NNW–E–ESE the perimeter has been destroyed as a result of the construction of modern farm buildings. Original entrance not recognisable. Internal area now utilised as a farmyard.
35:32 13-2-1974

463 CORTRASNA OR EDERGOLE
OS 16:11:4 (509,227) Hachured OD 300–400
24960, 31299
Rath Raised subrectangular area (int. dims. *c.* 33m WNW–ESE; *c.* 20m NNW–SSE) enclosed by a low earthen bank and a wide, shallow fosse which is partly waterlogged from NE–E–SE. Original entrance not recognisable.
16:31 28-10-1990

464 CORTRASNA OR EDERGOLE/DUNGONNAN
OS 16:11:5 (549,208) Hachured OD 200–300
25003, 31279
Rath Raised circular area (int. diam. *c.* 23m) enclosed by a low earthen bank and a wide, deep, partly waterlogged fosse. Site is divided into two roughly equal portions by a field boundary running NNE–SSW. Original entrance not recognisable. Internal area is densely overgrown with vegetation.
16:32 28-10-1990

465 CORWEELIS (Tullygarvey By.)
OS 17:5:6 (175,373) Not marked OD 200–300
25945, 31288
Rath (site) Marked 'Fort' on OS 1836 and 1876 eds. Situated on W slope of a low drumlin ridge. Largely levelled. Raised circular area (int. diam. 34m) enclosed by a low scarp from N–E–S. A short segment of earthen bank survives on the upper edge of the scarp at N. Original entrance not recognisable.
17:22 22-9-1989

466 CORWEELIS (Tullygarvey By.)
OS 17:5:3 (182,396) Hachured OD 400–500
25975, 31306
Rath (site) Marked 'Fort' on OS 1836 and 1876 eds. Site has been levelled. Situated on the summit of a high drumlin hill. An earlier report (OPW 1969) describes a raised circular area (int. diam. *c.* 28m) enclosed by a low earthen bank and traces of a possible fosse from S–W–NW. Elsewhere the perimeter had been levelled at that stage. Original entrance was not recognisable. Not visible at ground level.
17:23 22-9-1989

467 COUNTENAN
OS 21:10:6 (452,180) Hachured OD 400–500
24906, 30609
Raths (conjoined) Conjoined raths encircled by a modern field boundary and separated by a fosse. Both raths comprise raised areas enclosed by a bank and fosse. Rath at N is oval in plan (int. dims. 38.5m NE–SW; 29m NW–SE). Break in bank at N probably marks original entrance. Just outside of the entrance the level of the fosse drops accutely from W down to E. The S rath is circular in plan (int. diam. 29.8m). Bank barely discernible over the interior throughout most of its course. Fosse is only identifiable from SE–S–SW and at NE. Wide break in bank at WSW with no visible remains of accompanying causeway probably represents original entrance. Both raths have been planted with trees.
21:21 25-9-1990

468 CREENAGH GLEBE
OS 19:15:5 (555,66) Hachured OD 300–400
23066, 30471
Rath Raised circular area (int. dims. 28.4m NNW–SSE; 27m ENE–WSW) enclosed by a low earthen bank and a wide, deep fosse which has been

much modified for drainage purposes. Outside the fosse from S–W–N is a low earthen bank, almost certainly modern. From ESE–S–SW the perimeter has been levelled. An earlier description (OPW 1968) suggests that the original entrance may have been at SE.

19:12 11-7-1990

469 CREENY (ED Milltown)

OS 14:12:1 (698,300) Hachured OD 300–400
23209, 31360

Rath Raised circular area (int. dims. *c.* 50m NNW–SSE; 49.5m ENE–WSW) enclosed by a substantial earthen bank and a wide, deep fosse. Original entrance may have been either at E or at SW.

14:19 16-7-1989

470 CREEVE OR CORGARVE

OS 21:6:2 (329,428) Hachured OD 300–400
24774, 30870

Rath Raised circular area (int. dims. 43.5m NE–SW; 40m NW–SE) enclosed by a substantial earthen bank and a wide, deep fosse. Break in bank with accompanying causeway at ESE probably represents original entrance.

21:22 11-9-1990

471 CREIGHAN

OS 25:4:1 (752,547) Hachured OD 200–300
24250, 30350

Rath Situated on a low outcrop knoll beside Green Lough. It comprises an irregularly shaped area (int. dims. 57m N–S; 42m E–W) enclosed by a low outer earthen bank, a wide, deep intermediate fosse and much-defaced inner earthen bank. Outer bank identifiable only from SSE–S–WSW. Fosse visible from SE–S–W. Inner bank discernible from SE–S–SW. Site defined by a natural scarp from WNW–NNW. Break in bank at S with accompanying well-preserved causeway represents original entrance.

25:32 13-9-1991

472 CRENARD

OS 25:10:4 (308,171) Hachured OD 314
23785, 29949

Rath Raised circular area (int. dims. 31.7m NNE–SSW; 30.6m WNW–ESE) enclosed by a substantial earthen bank and a wide fosse. Original entrance almost certainly at E.

25:34 5-9-1991

473 CRENARD

OS 25:14:2 (316,136) Hachured OD 200–300
23793, 29912

Rath Raised broad oval area (int. dims. 43.6m N–S; 33.7m E–W) enclosed by the remains of an earthen bank, which is best preserved at NNW. Wide ill-defined break in bank at NNW may represent original entrance.

25:35 5-9-1991

474 CROAGHAN

OS 43:2:6 (397,496) Hachured OD 400–500
25844, 28391

Rath An almost circular raised area (int. dims. 50m N–S; 45.6m E–W) enclosed by a low earthen bank identifiable from SSW–N–NE. The site is divided into two unequal portions by a field boundary running NW–SW. The smaller portion, SE of the field boundary, has been levelled but the outline of the perimeter may still be traced. Original entrance not recognisable. An L-shaped depression at the centre of the internal area probably represents the site of a souterrain (**1232**).

43:9(01) 2-9-1970

475 CROLEY

OS 23:16:6 (911,60) '*Lisnageer Fort*' OD 400–500
27343, 30504

Rath Raised circular area (int. diam. 24.3m) enclosed by a substantial earthen bank and traces of a fosse. From ENE–SSE the bank has been transformed into a field boundary. Original entrance not recognisable.

23:17 30-3-1992

476 CROSS

OS 20:4:6 (873,455) '*Cross Forts*' OD 400–500
24373, 30895

Rath Large raised circular area (int. diam. *c.* 61.1m) enclosed by a substantial earthen bank which has been much modified and incorporated into the field boundary. Modern narrow roadways, bordered by high earthen banks, divide the site into four roughly equal quadrants. Original entrance not recognisable.

20:7 3-8-1990

477 CROSSBANE

OS 40:1:2 (130,540) Hachured OD 400–500
26531, 29083

Rath (site) Almost completely levelled. Situated on a slight natural rise close to a stream. All that survives are faint traces of a low scarp identifiable from SE–S–W enclosing a roughly circular area (diam. *c.* 23m). Otherwise nothing visible at ground level.

40:20 6-7-1987

478 CROSSERLOUGH

OS 38:2:5 (362,519) Indicated OD 400–500
24826, 29045

Rath Raised circular area (int. diam. 27m) enclosed by a substantial earthen bank which has been modified and incorporated into the field boundary. Modern

trenches skirt the exterior of the bank. An earlier report (OPW 1970) suggested that the original entrance may have been at SE.
38:14 14-8-1986

479 CROSSERLOUGH
OS 38:2:5 (379,491) Hachured OD 300–400
24844, 29016
Rath Raised circular area (int. diam. 45m) enclosed by a low earthen bank and suggestions of a wide, shallow fosse. An earlier report (OPW 1970) noted stonework on the exterior of the bank and suggested that the original entrance may have been at SE.
38:15 14-8-1986

480 CROSSERULE
OS 39:1:4 (22,468) Not marked OD 600
25443, 28998
Rath Marked 'Fort' on OS 1836 ed. Not marked on subsequent OS eds. Raised circular area (int. diam. *c.* 36m) defined by a steep scarp and enclosed by a low counterscarp bank and the remains of a fosse. Counterscarp bank identifiable only from SW–NW. Original entrance not recognisable.
39:30 12-9-1986

481 CROVER
OS 38:14:1 (258,142) Hachured OD 200–300
24719, 28647
Rath Raised circular area (int. diam. 31.5m) enclosed by two substantial earthen banks with outer fosses. Traces of a counterscarp bank enclose the outer fosse from S–SW and from NNW–N. An earlier report (OPW 1970) suggested that the original entrance may have been at S.
38:20 12-8-1986

482 CRUBANY
OS 26:7:1 (465,388) Hachured OD 500–600
24924, 30188
Rath Raised circular area (int. dims. 20.8m NW–SE; 20.3m NNE–SSE) enclosed by a low earthen bank and a fosse. An earlier report (OPW 1974) described the fosse as being wide and shallow, and the bank as substantial. Fosse is now only identifiable from W–N–NNE. Elsewhere it has been infilled. Bank has been levelled from NNE–E. Perimeter has been incorporated into the field boundary from SSE–S–SSW. Narrow break in bank at NNW, with slight traces of a possible causeway, represents original entrance.
26:23(01) 18-3-1992

483 CULLABOY UPPER
OS 41:6:2 (314,441) Hachured OD 200–300
23806, 28314
Rath Raised circular area (int. diam. *c.* 42m) enclosed by a low earthen bank and a wide, shallow fosse. Slight traces of a counterscarp bank at the outer lip of the fosse at W. Field boundary runs alongside the outer edge of fosse at N and E. Original entrance not recognisable.
41:9 21-6-1974

484 CULLENTRAGH (Upper Loughtee By.)
OS 21:5:2 (136,438) Hachured OD 300–400
24570, 30878
Rath Raised circular area (int. dims. 33.5m WNW–ESE; 31m NNE–SSW) enclosed by a substantial earthen bank and traces of a fosse. From W–N–SSE bank has been modified and incorporated into the field boundary. From SSE–S–W it has been levelled to only 0.5m above external ground level. Original entrance not recognisable.
21:23 23-9-1990

485 CULLIES (Lower Loughtee By.)
OS 20:12:1 (766,246) Hachured OD 300–400
24262, 30672
Rath Raised circular area (int. diam. *c.* 40m) enclosed by a substantial earthen bank. Situated immediately ESE of St Patrick's College and just S of the summit of a drumlin hill. From W–N–E a modern drain has been dug at the external foot of bank. Original entrance not recognisable. Several modern paths traverse the internal area which has been planted largely with beech and pine.
20:8 3-8-1990

486 CULLIES (Lower Loughtee By.)
OS 20:8:5 (784,306) Hachured OD 300–400
24280, 30736
Rath Raised circular area (int. diam. 29.6m) enclosed by a substantial earthen bank and a wide, deep fosse which survives only from S–WSW. Elsewhere it has been infilled. Wide break in bank with accompanying causeway at NE may represent original entrance.
20:9 3-8-1990

487 CULLIN
OS 22:2:1 (289,605) Not marked OD 200–300
25705, 31065
Rath Raised circular area (int. diam. 55m) enclosed by a substantial earthen bank and a fosse. Site is bisected by a field boundary running SSE–NNE. The area W of this has been almost completely levelled but outline of perimeter may still be distinguished. The enclosing features E of field boundary have also been partially levelled. Original entrance not recognisable.
22:10 14-10-1990

488 CULLOW
OS 32:13:3 (221,111) Hachured OD 400–500
24674, 29254

Rath Raised circular area (int. diam. *c.* 47m NNE–SSW; *c.* 35m ENE–WSW) enclosed by a substantial earthen bank and a wide, shallow fosse. Original entrance not recognisable. Densely overgrown with vegetation.
32:10 3-7-1919

489 CULLYLEENAN
OS 10:14:1 (270,140) Hachured OD 200–300 22752, 31828
Rath Raised circular area (int. dims. 48m NW–SE; 46.1m NE–SW) enclosed by a substantial earthen bank and a wide, shallow fosse. Perimeter has been destroyed from N–NE where a modern dwelling abuts the site. Original entrance not recognisable.
10:11 6-10-1989

490 CURRAGHANOE
OS 15:12:5 (810,170) Hachured OD 200–300 24303, 31232
Rath Raised circular area (int. diam. 28.2m) enclosed by the remains of a low earthen bank and a wide, shallow fosse. A modern field boundary has been built against the external face of bank from NE–SE, and fosse has been infilled. Break in bank at SE represents original entrance.
15:20 21-9-1989

491 CURRAGHGLASS
OS 6:1:1 (52,599) Hachured OD 400–500 20562, 32932
Rath Raised circular area (int. diam. 26.6m) enclosed by a low earthen bank and traces of a fosse. Perimeter has been slightly modified and incorporated into the field boundary. Original entrance not recognisable.
6:5 23-8-1988

492 CURRAGHGLASS
OS 6:9:3 (156,285) Hachured OD 400–500 20674, 32601
Rath Raised circular area (int. diam. 24.7m) enclosed by a substantial earthen bank and remains of a fosse. Stone field boundary has been built against the outer face of the bank at S. Original entrance not recognisable. A small stone enclosure (probably modern) projects from the bank into the interior at N.
6:6 23-8-1988

493 CURRAGHVAH
OS 6:9:3 (191,245) Hachured OD 300 20712, 32559
Rath Raised circular area (int. dims. 26.2 NE–SW; 23.3m NW–SE) enclosed by two earthen banks with a wide, deep, waterlogged intermediate fosse. Although the NW half of the site has been largely levelled, the outline of the perimeter is still identifiable. Original entrance not recognisable. Short stretch of relatively recent drystone walling on internal face of inner bank at E. A small stone-lined subcircular depression at the centre of the interior is believed to be a spring well (OPW 1977). Situated on the floor of an upland valley.
6:7 27-8-1988

494 DAGGAN
OS 20:4:4 (700,469) Hachured OD 300–400 24190, 30907
Rath Raised circular area (int. diam 31.2m) enclosed by two earthen banks with intermediate fosse. Outer bank has been incorporated into the field boundary and has a modern external trench. From W–NNW it is absent and has been replaced by a modern earthen bank which elsewhere runs immediately outside of it. Corresponding breaks in banks at ESE, with accompanying causeway across intermediate fosse, represents original entrance.
20:10 10-8-1990

495 DENN GLEBE
OS 26:13:2 (84,120) Hachured OD 700–800 24524, 29902
Rath Situated on the NE slope of a drumlin hill. An earlier report (OPW 1969) recorded a raised circular area (int. dims. 24.5m NW–SE; 23.8m NE–SW) enclosed by a slight earthen bank and a narrow fosse which is visible only from SE–S–N. At W a breach in the bank gives access to a small square alcove built into the hillside. Narrow break in bank at S may represent original entrance.
26:27 24-10-1992

496 DENNMORE OR LEGGANDENN
OS 26:13:2 (91,95) Hachured OD 500–600 24532, 29875
Rath Raised circular area (int. dims. 40.2m E–W; 44m N–S) enclosed by an earthen bank and a fosse which is well preserved from NW–W–S and much disturbed elsewhere. Outer face of bank modernised from E–SE and incorporated into the field boundary. Original entrance not recognisable.
26:29 24-10-1991

497 DERAMFIELD
OS 19:4:5 (845,480) Hachured OD 200–300 23368, 30912
Rath (site) An earlier description (OPW 1968) described a raised circular area (int. dims. 54m NNE–SSW; 52m ESE–WNW) enclosed by a low bank of earth and stone and a wide, shallow fosse. Original entrance was probably at SSE. Although site has been levelled its outline may still be traced.
19:13 16-7-1990

Plate 7a—*An impressive motte and bailey at Relagh Beg* (**1793**).

Plate 7b—*A three-storey tower house at Tonymore* (**1851**).

Plate 8a—*Looking down through the murder-hole above the main entrance to Tonymore tower house* (**1851**).

Plate 8b— *A beehive-type sweathouse at Legeelan* (**1873**).

498 DEREDIS LOWER
OS 20:3:2 (543,586) Hachured OD 100–200
24023, 31030
Rath Raised D-shaped area (int. dims. 29.6m NE–SW; 18m NW–SE) enclosed by a slight earthen bank and a wide, shallow fosse. The Annalee River skirts the outer foot of the bank from NE–E–S and as a result the fosse runs inside the bank at this point. Wide break in bank with accompanying causeway at NNW represents original entrance.
20:12 16-8-1990

499 DERNAKESH
OS 22:8:2 (836,425) Hachured OD 400–500
26285, 30880
Rath Raised oval area (int. dims. *c.* 38m WNW–ESE; 26.5m NE–SW) enclosed by a substantial earthen bank and a fosse which has been infilled from NNW–N–ESE. Bank has been considerably disturbed by modern digging and modified and incorporated into field boundary from N–NE–E. Original entrance is at SE.
22:11 19-10-1990

500 DERNASKEAGH
OS 17:13:1 (19,84) Hachured OD 200–300
25501, 31133
Rath Situated within a plantation of coniferous trees. Raised circular area (int. diam. *c.* 42m) enclosed by slight traces of an earthen bank. A modern bank with external trench has been built against the lower portion of the scarp. Wide break in scarp at E probably represents original entrance.
17:24 14-3-1969

501 DERRIES LOWER
OS 19:12:5 (788,199) Hachured OD 200–300
23311, 30614
Rath Raised circular area (int. dims. 44m NW–SE; 43.5m NE–SW) enclosed by a low earthen bank and a narrow, deep fosse which has been modified and utilised as a field drain. Original entrance was probably at SE where the bank barely rises above the enclosed area. Modern roadway runs N–S through the site dividing it into two roughly equal portions.
19:15 6-7-1990

502 DERRIES UPPER
OS 19:16:2 (795,100) Indicated OD 200–300
23319, 30510
Rath Raised oval area (int. dims. 55m NNW–SSE; 46m ENE–WSW) enclosed by a low, narrow earthen bank and a narrow, shallow fosse. Both have been much modified and incorporated into the field boundary. Original entrance not recognisable.
19:16 6-7-1990

503 DERRY (Clankee By.)
OS 29:5:1 (30,442) Hachured OD 600–700
27390, 30268
Rath Raised circular area (int. dims. 50m NW–SE; 41m NE–SW) enclosed by a much-denuded, low earthen bank and very slight traces of a fosse. Bank has been modified and incorporated into the field boundary from W–NNW and from SE–S–SW. Original entrance not recognisable.
29:2 23-3-1977

504 DERRYCASSAN
OS 13:12:4 (702,195) Hachured OD 200
22239, 31241
Rath Situated on SSW slope of a high drumlin ridge overlooking Derrycassan Lough *c.* 40m to S. Raised oval area (int. dims. 38.3m E–W; *c.* 28m N–S) enclosed by an earthen bank which is substantial from W–N–E and more poorly defined elsewhere, and a wide, deep fosse. At E the perimeter has been defaced as a result of the erection of a field boundary. An earlier report (OPW 1969) noted that the original entrance was at E.
13:18 15-11-1989

505 DERRYCASSAN
OS 13:12:4 (729,185) Hachured OD 100–200
22267, 31230
Rath Raised circular area (int. diam. 24.8m) enclosed by a low earthen bank. An earlier report (OPW 1969) recorded traces of an outer fosse and suggested that the original entrance may have been at S.
13:19 15-11-1989

506 DERRYCASSAN
OS 13:12:5 (779,220) Hachured OD 100–200
22319, 31267
Rath Marked 'Fort' on OS 1836 and 1876 eds. A slightly raised, formerly oval-shaped area enclosed by a substantial bank and a wide, shallow fosse from NNW–E–SE. Elsewhere, site has been largely levelled. Original entrance not recognisable. Internal area slopes quite steeply from NE–SW.
13:21 15-11-1989

507 DERRYGEERAGHAN
OS 14:8:6 (897,313) Hachured OD 200
23419, 31376
Rath Raised circular area (int. diam. *c.* 40m) enclosed by two substantial earthen banks with wide, deep, intermediate fosse. A modern trench, which was apparently dug on the site of a fosse, encloses the outer bank from NNW–N–NE. Outer bank identifiable only from SSW–N–NE. An earlier report (OPW 1969) recorded that the original entrance was at SE.
14:24 15-8-1989

508 DERRYGLEN
OS 26:13:2 (101,100) Hachured OD 500–600
24542, 29881
Rath Raised circular area (int. diam. 31.5m) enclosed by a substantial earthen bank and a wide, deep, waterlogged fosse. An earlier description (OPW 1974) recorded a low outer bank which is no longer visible. Perimeter levelled from E–S–SSW. Large break in bank (Wth 12.1m) with accompanying causeway at NNW is probably modern. Original entrance not recognisable.
26:30 19-3-1992

509 DERRYGOSS
OS 15:15:4 (466,35) Hachured OD 200–300
23941, 31087
Rath Raised circular area (int. diam. 35.6m) enclosed by a substantial earthen bank and a wide, deep fosse. Break in bank at N with accompanying causeway presumably represents original entrance.
15:21 21-9-1989

510 DERRYHOO (Tullygarvey By.)
OS 11:15:5 (575,73) Hachured OD 100–200
24050, 31768
Rath Raised almost oval area (int. dims. *c.* 30m NW-SE; *c.* 22m NE–SW) enclosed from NW–E–S by a substantial earthen bank and a wide, deep fosse. Elsewhere bordered by Derryhoo Lough. Original entrance not recognisable.
11:14 18-6-1989

511 DERRYHUM
OS 33:3:4 (469,502) Hachured OD 600–700
25908, 29678
Rath Raised circular area (int. diam. *c.* 22m) enclosed by a much-denuded low earthen bank. From S–W–NW a modern field boundary abuts the outer face of the bank. Original entrance not recognisable.
33:22 13-9-1988

512 DERRYLAHAN (Castlerahan By.)
OS 32:11:4 (486,219) Hachured OD 400–500
24954, 29370
Rath Raised circular area (int. dims. 68m N–S; 67m E–W) enclosed by a low earthen bank and fosse. Fosse has been recut and incorporated into the field drainage system from SSW–NW and has been infilled elsewhere. Break in bank at S may represent original entrance.
32:11 25-4-1989

513 DERRYLANE (Tullyhunco By.)
OS 24:7:1 (481,407) Hachured OD 300–400
22990, 30191
Rath Raised circular area (int. diam. 49m) enclosed by two substantial earthen banks with a wide, deep, waterlogged intermediate fosse. Outer bank survives only from N–NNE. Fosse has been infilled from NE–SE. Large break in inner bank at SSE possibly represents original entrance.
24:27 21-8-1991

514 DERRYLEA
OS 38:3:5 (597,482) Hachured OD 200–300
25074, 29009
Rath Raised circular area (int. diam. 36m) enclosed by a low, much-denuded earthen bank and slight traces of a fosse identifiable only from SSW–SW. Bank has been modified and incorporated into the field boundary. Original entrance not recognisable.
38:23 15-8-1986

515 DERRYLEAGUE
OS 15:15:4 (497,56) Hachured OD 200–300
23974, 31110
Rath Raised circular area (int. diam. 28.2m) enclosed by a low earthen bank. An earlier description (OPW 1968) noted traces of an external fosse from NNW–N–NNE and from S–SE. Original entrance not recognisable.
15:23 21-9-1989

516 DERRYVACKNY
OS 20:1:1 (37,556) Not marked OD 200–300
23489, 30993
Rath Marked 'Fort' on OS 1836 and 1876 eds. Raised circular area (int. diam. *c.* 50m) enclosed by a low earthen bank and a shallow fosse. From ESE–S–NW the perimeter has been levelled but is still identifiable. Elsewhere it has been much modified and incorporated into the field boundary. Original entrance not recognisable.
20:22 12-8-1990

517 DEVALLY
OS 16:7:3 (659,429) Hachured OD 200–300
25117, 31514
Rath Raised circular area (int. diam. 25.2m) enclosed by a substantial earthen bank and a wide, shallow fosse. Modern counterscarp bank runs from SW–WNW and from N–NNE. Original entrance not recognisable.
6:33 27-10-1990

518 DILLAGH
OS 31:6:5 (358,366) Hachured OD 300–400
23842, 29515
Rath Raised circular area (int. diam. *c.* 39.7m) enclosed by a substantial earthen bank and a narrow, waterlogged fosse recut from W–NW–N. Bank best preserved from NW–N–NNE. Original entrance not

recognisable.
31:18 5-4-1974

519 DINGIN
OS 35:1:6 (226,503) Hachured OD 500–600
27603, 29695
Rath Raised circular area (int. diam. *c.* 35m) enclosed by a substantial earthen bank and a wide, deep fosse which has been incorporated into the field boundary. Slight indications of a possible counterscarp bank at the outer lip of the fosse. Original entrance at SSE.
35:33 19-3-1974

520 DINGINAVANTY
OS 22:4:1 (700,604) Hachured OD 300–400
26140, 31067
Rath Raised circular area (int. diam. 26.9m) enclosed by two very substantial earthen banks with partly waterlogged intermediate fosse. An earlier report (OPW 1969) noted slight indications of an outer fosse. Corresponding breaks in banks with accompanying causeway at SE represents original entrance.
22:12 8-10-1990

521 DINGINAVANTY
OS 22:4:1 (722,595) Hachured OD 300–400
26163, 31058
Rath Raised circular area (int. diam. 24.6m) enclosed by a substantial earthen bank and a wide, deep, partly waterlogged fosse. The site is encircled by a modern field boundary. Break in bank with accompanying causeway at SE represents original entrance. Possible souterrain within internal area (**1233**).
22:13(01) 17-10-1990

522 DINGINS
OS 30:8:1 (737,397) Hachured OD 336
23268, 29540
Rath Raised circular area (int. diam. 34m) enclosed by two very substantial earthen banks with deep and partly waterlogged outer fosses. Original entrance represented by corresponding breaks in banks with accompanying causeways at SE. An earlier report (OPW 1980) recorded a tradition of a 'tunnel off the fort' which is probably a reference to a souterrain (**1234**).
30:15(01) 8-10-1991

523 DOOCARRICK
OS 17:5:4 (57,345) Hachured OD 300–400
25793, 31372
Rath Raised circular area (int. diam. 30.4m) enclosed by a substantial, although partly denuded, earthen bank and a fosse. Only a short segment of the fosse at SE is now identifiable. Elsewhere it has been infilled and replaced by a modern trackway. An earlier report (OPW 1969) suggested that the original entrance may have been at NNE.
17:26 21-11-1989

524 DOOCARRICK
OS 17:5:1 (71,399) Hachured OD 300–400
25861, 31416
Rath Raised oval area (int. dims. 57.5m WNW–ESE; *c.* 47m NNE–SSW) enclosed by a low earthen bank and a narrow, deep, partly waterlogged fosse which has been replaced by a modern trench from NE–ESE. Break in bank with accompanying causeway at SE represents original entrance.
17:27 21-11-1989

525 DOOCARRICK
OS 17:5:4 (72,362) Not marked OD 400
25826, 31376
Rath Not marked on any OS ed. but known as a 'fort' (local information). Raised circular area (int. diam. *c.* 26m) enclosed by a low earthen bank and a fosse. From SE–S–WSW the perimeter has been much modified and incorporated into the field boundary. Elsewhere it has been levelled but is identifiable as a low scarp. Original entrance not recognisable.
17:28 21-11-1989

526 DOOCARRICK
OS 17:5:5 (135,342) Hachured OD 300–400
25873, 31294
Rath Raised circular area (int. diam. *c.* 41.8m) enclosed by a substantial but partly denuded earthen bank and a wide, deep, partially waterlogged fosse, infilled from ESE–S and enclosed by a low, possibly modern counterscarp bank from S–SW–W. Break in bank at S may represent original entrance.
17:29 21-11-1989

527 DOOCASSAN
OS 21:3:2 (604,592) Hachured OD 300–400
25063, 31046
Rath Raised circular area (int. diam. 30.3m) enclosed by a substantial earthen bank. The site is further encircled by a modern field boundary from SSW–N–E and by a modern roadway from E–S–SSW. A wide ditch which is presumably on the line of an external fosse, occurs outside the bank. Break in bank at E probably represents original entrance.
21:25 25-9-1990

528 DOON (Castlerahan By.)
OS 33:15:6 (676,22) Hachured OD 400–500
26131, 29173
Rath Raised almost circular area (int. diam. *c.* 19m) enclosed by two much-denuded low earthen banks with intermediate fosse. Outer bank and fosse difficult

to identify from N–E–S. Original entrance not recognisable. Davies (ITA Survey 1942) described a stone ditch 'driven across the centre' which 'partly interrupts the bank'. Densely overgrown with vegetation.
33:23 21-9-1988

529 DOON (Castlerahan By.)
OS 39:4:1 (732,584) Hachured OD 300–400
26191, 29127
Rath Raised circular area (int. diam. *c.* 36m) enclosed by a substantial earthen bank and a wide, shallow fosse. Wide break in bank at SSE probably represents original entrance. An earlier report (OPW 1969) recorded possible remains of a souterrain within the internal area (**1235**).
39:41(01) 11-6-1987

530 DREENAN
OS 25:11:2 (606,295) Hachured OD 300
24099, 30083
Rath Raised circular area (int. diam. 49m NE–SW) enclosed by an inner fosse and a substantial earthen bank with external fosse running from E–S–NNW. From NNW–N–E the perimeter is almost completely demolished where modern houses have encroached on the site. Original entrance not recognisable.
25:36 1-10-1991

531 DRESTERNAGH
OS 16:10:4 (256,160) Hachured OD 200–300
24694, 31226
Rath Raised circular area (int. diam. *c.* 30m) enclosed by a substantial earthen bank and a wide, shallow, partly waterlogged fosse which survives only from WSW–NW and from ENE–SSE. Elsewhere it has been infilled. Bank has been modified and incorporated into the field boundary. Original entrance not recognisable.
16:34 27-10-1990

532 DROMORE
OS 33:8:3 (869,438) Hachured OD 400–500
26331, 29614
Rath Raised circular area (int. diam. *c.* 32m) enclosed by a substantial earthen bank and a fosse. Break in bank at E probably represents original entrance.
33:24 21-9-1988

533 DRUMACARROW
OS 34:5:2 (79,415) Hachured OD 500–600
26472, 29591
Rath Marked 'Fort' and indicated as a circular enclosure (int. diam. *c.* 40m) on the OS 1836 and 1876 eds. Site is divided into two unequal portions by a field boundary running NNE–SSW. A raised area enclosed by a substantial earthen bank and traces of a fosse is visible WNW of the boundary. The larger portion ESE of this has been levelled.
34:19 25-4-1974

534 DRUMACARROW
OS 34:5:2 (124,441) Hachured OD 500–600
26520, 29619
Raths (conjoined) Conjoined raths now separated by a laneway which probably overlies a fosse. The NW rath comprises a raised circular area (int. diam. *c.* 37m) enclosed by a substantial earthen bank and traces of a fosse. From NNE–SE bank has been modified and incorporated into field boundary. It is accompanied by a modern narrow external trench. From SE–S–W and from NW–N–NNE fosse has been destroyed and replaced by a laneway. Original entrance not recognisable. The SE rath comprises a raised circular area (int. diam. *c.* 34m) enclosed by a wide, shallow fosse and substantial earthen bank. Original entrance at SE.
34:20 25-3-1974

535 DRUMACHON
OS 16:15:3 (680,105) Hachured OD 300–400
25143, 31172
Rath Raised circular area (int. diam. 32m) enclosed by two substantial earthen banks with intervening wide, deep, waterlogged fosse. Corresponding breaks in banks with accompanying causeway at ESE represents original entrance. Perimeter densely overgrown with vegetation.
16:36 19-10-1990

536 DRUMAD
OS 28:7:2 (591,408) Not marked OD 500–600
27007, 30229
Rath Raised circular area (int. diam. *c.* 23m) defined by a low scarp. Apparently the former enclosing features were a bank and fosse. Original entrance not recognisable. An earlier report (OPW 1977) noted possible traces of a souterrain within the internal area (**1236**).
28:13(01) 14-9-1988

537 DRUMAD
OS 28:7:3 (651,407) Indicated OD 500–600
27071, 30228
Rath Raised circular area (int. diam. *c.* 37m) enclosed by a low, wide earthen bank and slight remains of a fosse. The perimeter has been levelled from NW–N–NE and replaced by a modern roadway. Original entrance not recognisable.
28:14 28-3-1974

538 DRUMAGOLAN
OS 33:14:5 (359,67) Hachured OD 400–500
25797, 29218

Rath Raised circular area (int. diam. *c.* 48m) enclosed by a low earthen bank and a wide, shallow fosse. Bank has been levelled from ESE–SSE and a laneway skirts its external face from SSW–W. Fosse identifiable only from N–ENE. Original entrance probably at SE. A small pile of stones of unknown significance lies inside the bank at SW.
33:25 5-4-1974

539 DRUMAGOLAN
OS 33:14:6 (433,30) Hachured OD 400–500
25875, 29179
Rath Raised circular area (int. diam. *c.* 28m) enclosed by a wide and low earthen bank and a broad but shallow fosse. Original entrance not positively identifiable but may have been at NE. Site has been planted with coniferous trees.
33:26 3-4-1974

540 DRUMAGOLAN
OS 33:15:4 (465,16) Hachured OD 400–500
25909, 29164
Rath Raised oval area (int. dims. *c.* 35m N–S; 25m E-W) enclosed by two earthen banks with intermediate narrow, shallow fosse. Outer bank and fosse not identifiable from SSW–W–NW. Original entrance not recognisable.
33:27 3-4-1974

541 DRUMAGOLAN
OS 33:15:4 (482,1) Hachured OD 400–500
25927, 29148
Rath (site) Marked 'Fort' on OS 1836 and 1876 eds. Situated just S of the summit of a high drumlin hill. An earlier report (OPW 1969) described a roughly circular area enclosed by very slight traces of a fosse and scarp. Original entrance was not recognisable. Site has since been levelled.
33:28/39:42* 27-3-1987

542 DRUMAKEENAN
OS 16:1:1 (30,568) Hachured OD 200–300
24452, 31655
Rath Raised circular area (int. diam. 20.2m) enclosed by a very low earthen bank and a wide, shallow fosse which is only identifiable from NW–N. The site is further enclosed by modern field boundaries from N–S–NW. Original entrance not recognisable.
16:38 22-9-1989

543 DRUMAKEENAN
OS 16:1:4 (58,528) Hachured OD 200–300
24481, 31613
Rath An earlier report (OPW 1968) described a raised oval area (int. dims. *c.* 38m NW–SE; *c.* 28m ENE–WSW) enclosed by a low earthen bank and fosse. Break in bank with accompanying causeway at WSW presumably marked original entrance. Site has since been levelled.
16:39 22-9-1989

544 DRUMAKINNEO
OS 31:11:6 (638,186) Hachured OD 374
24139, 29328
Rath Large almost oval-shaped area (int. dims. *c.* 40m N–S; *c.* 35m E–W) enclosed by a substantial earthen bank and a wide, deep, partially waterlogged fosse. Modern field banks run outside the fosse from E–S–NW and from N–E–SE. Original entrance not recognisable.
31:20 10-4-1974

545 DRUMALURE MORE
OS 15:6:6 (459,328) Indicated OD 200–300
23931, 31396
Rath A much-disturbed, raised circular area (int. dims. 39m E–W; 36m N–S) enclosed by a low earthen bank and the remains of a fosse. The bank has been extensively modified from ENE–E–SE with a modern shed constructed against its external face at NE. Original entrance not recognisable. Internal area is divided into two unequal portions by a roadway aligned NE–SW. The smaller SE portion is now occupied by a modern dwelling-house.
15:26 11-9-1989

546 DRUMAMRY
OS 24:4:4 (726,497) Hachured OD 300–400
23248, 30289
Rath (site) An earlier report (OPW 1968) described a raised almost circular area (int. dims. 59.5m E–W; 53.5m N–S) enclosed by two earthen banks with intermediate fosse. Original entrance was not recognisable. Rath has been largely levelled with modern farm buildings now occupying the greater part of the site.
24:28 21-8-1991

547 DRUMAMRY
OS 24:4:4 (728,525) Hachured OD 300–400
23250, 30318
Rath Raised circular area (int. dims. 27.4m N–S; 26.6m E–W) enclosed by an earthen bank and a fosse which has been modified and incorporated into the field drainage system. Original entrance not recognisable.
24:29 21-8-1991

548 DRUMANESPICK
OS 27:16:5 (787,12) Indicated OD 600
26243, 29803
Rath Raised circular area (int. diam. 31m) enclosed by a substantial earthen bank and a narrow fosse. Bank

much denuded at E. Original entrance not recognisable. Densely overgrown with vegetation.
27:7 19-7-1989

549 DRUMARD (Clanmahon By.)
OS 31:14:3 (427,80) Hachured OD 300 23917, 29214
Rath Raised almost oval area (int. dims. *c.* 29m NW–SE; *c.* 26m NE–SW) enclosed by a low earthen bank and slight remains of a fosse which has been infilled from E–SE–S. Bank modified and incorporated into the field boundary from E–S–WNW. Original entrance not recognisable.
31:21 9-4-1974

550 DRUMARD (Upper Loughtee By.)
OS 20:9:3 (225,287) Hachured OD 200–300 23690, 30711
Rath Raised circular area (int. diam. 39.6m) enclosed by a substantial earthen bank and a wide fosse which has been infilled from SE–S–SSW. Wide break in the bank at ESE may represent original entrance.
20:24 12-8-1990

551 DRUMASLADDY
OS 14:8:1 (755,452) Hachured OD 200–300 23268, 31521
Rath Raised oval area (int. dims. 45.3m NNW–SSE; 40.5m ENE–WSW) enclosed by a low earthen bank. Modern field drains have been dug at the external foot of the bank. An earlier report (OPW 1969) recorded that the original entrance was at S. The site is situated within a plantation of deciduous trees and is extremely overgrown with vegetation.
14:25 15-8-1989

552 DRUMAVADDY (Clanmahon By.)
OS 25:16:6 (848,19) Hachured OD 600–700 24357, 29793
Rath A small raised circular area (int. diam. 25m) enclosed by an inner bank and fosse separated from an outer bank and external fosse by a berm (Wth 9m). Original entrance may have been at ENE where there are corresponding breaks in the banks.
25:37 20-9-1991

553 DRUMAVADDY (Tullygarvey By.)
OS 16:5:4 (36,358) Hachured OD 300–400 24460, 31433
Rath Raised circular area (int. diam. *c.* 38m) enclosed by a well-defined earthen bank and a wide, shallow fosse. Narrow break in bank with accompanying wide causeway at NE represents original entrance. From NE–S–W the site is enclosed by modern field boundaries.
16:42 19-10-1990

554 DRUMAVEIL NORTH
OS 17:11:2 (614,295) Burial Gd., Quaker's Meeting House OD 300–400 26334, 30783
Rath Marked 'Fort' on OS 1836 ed. Raised circular area (int. diam. *c.* 34.7m) enclosed by a low earthen bank. A rectangular stone building representing the remains of a Quakers' Meeting House, marked on all OS eds, stands at the centre of the internal area. Davies (ITA Survey 1946) also noted 'a few graves' within the enclosure. Original entrance may have been at W where there was an old laneway. A wide depression at the external foot of the bank at NW probably represents the remains of another laneway. On the OS 1836 ed. dwelling-houses are depicted skirting the site from ENE–SE.
17:30(01) 14-7-1990

555 DRUMBANNAN
OS 28:14:4 (284,47) Hachured OD 500–600 26687, 29845
Rath Marked 'Fort' on OS 1836 and 1876 eds. Situated close to the summit of a steep drumlin hill within a dense modern plantation of coniferous trees. Not located.
28:15 13-9-1988

556 DRUMBAR (Clanmahon By.)
OS 25:10:4 (263,187) Hachured OD 100–200 23737, 29966
Rath Raised oval area (int. dims. 42.1m NW–SE; 35.3m NE–SW) enclosed by two earthen banks. A modern drain, which may follow the line of a former outer fosse, encloses the outer bank. Original entrance at S represented by a break in bank with accompanying causeway. A stream flows outside the bank at NW.
25:39 24-9-1991

557 DRUMBAR (ED Enniskeen)
OS 35:13:1 (10,137) Indicated OD 575 27378, 29306
Rath Marked 'Fort' on OS 1836 and 1876 eds. Raised circular area (int. diam. *c.* 42m) enclosed by a wide, low earthen bank. The bank is encompassed by a modern roadway from NW–NNE, a laneway from ESE–SSW and a field drain from SSW–NW. Original entrance not recognisable.
35:34 15-3-1974

558 DRUMBAR (Tullyhaw By.)
OS 7:11:5 (564,215) Hachured OD 400–500 22081, 32541
Rath Raised circular area (int. diam. *c.* 50m) enclosed by an earthen bank and the remains of a fosse which is bounded by a stream from W–N. From E–S–W bank has been modified and incorporated into the field boundary. A modern field boundary running NNW–SSE divides the site into two roughly equal

Fig. 15—*Rath at Drumavaddy* (**552**).

portions. Original entrance not recognisable.
7:8 12-3-1992

559 DRUMBAR (Upper Loughtee By.)
OS 20:15:1 (506,129) Hachured OD 200–300
23989, 30547
Rath Raised circular area (int. diam. *c*. 35m) enclosed by three earthen banks with intermediate fosses. From NE–SE the outer bank is low and wide and has a modern external trench. It has been faced with stone in recent times. Corresponding breaks in the intermediate and inner banks at SSW with accompanying causeways across the fosses may represent original entrance. An earlier description (OPW 1968) recorded a circular area (diam. 9m) defined by a very narrow, shallow, channel-like depression inside the bank at NNW. Immediately to the S of this a similar although less well-defined feature was identified.
20:25 7-8-1990

560 DRUMBARTAGH
OS 16:7:4 (533,324) Not marked OD 200–300
24984, 31402
Rath Marked 'Fort' on OS 1836 ed. Not marked on subsequent eds. It apparently comprised a raised circular area (int. diam. *c*. 26.4m) enclosed by a bank and fosse. The site is divided into unequal portions by a field boundary running NNW–SSE. N of this there is no trace of the site visible at ground level. However, S of the field boundary the outline of the perimeter is still identifiable.
16:44 10-10-1990

561 DRUMBEE
OS 32:13:1 (33,76) Hachured OD 400–500
24476, 29215
Rath Raised circular area (int. diam. 30m) enclosed by two substantial earthen banks, each accompanied by an outer fosse. External fosse only visible from E–SE–S. Corresponding breaks in banks at NE may represent original entrance. Site densely overgrown with vegetation.
32:14 30-6-1989

562 DRUMBESS
OS 24:3:5 (610,476) Hachured OD 400
23125, 30265

Rath Raised circular area enclosed by a substantial earthen inner bank, a fosse and possible remains of a levelled outer bank. From ESE–ENE the inner bank has a modern, internal, drystone facing. The fosse is infilled both here and at WNW. Break in bank with accompanying causeway at E probably represents original entrance.
24:30 21-8-1991

563 DRUMBESS

OS 24:3:6 (640,484) Hachured OD 300–400
23157, 30274
Rath Raised circular area (int. diam. 50.5m) enclosed by a substantial earthen bank and a wide, deep, waterlogged fosse. A counterscarp bank, most likely a modern feature, occurs at the outer lip of the fosse. Original entrance not recognisable.
24:33 22-8-1991

564 DRUMBESS
OS 24:7:3 (658,384) Hachured OD 400–500
23177, 30168
Rath The site has been extensively dug by heavy machinery in recent years in an effort to remove badger sets. It comprises a raised circular area (int. diam. 41m) enclosed by two substantial earthen banks with a wide, deep, waterlogged intermediate fosse. From NE–SE the fosse has been modified and the outer bank removed to facilitate a modern roadway. Original entrance not recognisable. Two shallow irregular depressions of unknown significance occur inside the inner bank at SW.
24:34 22-8-1991

565 DRUMBESS
OS 24:3:6 (649,499) Hachured OD 300–400
23166, 30289
Rath Raised circular area (int. diam. 47.9m) enclosed by a substantial earthen bank and a fosse which has been largely infilled. Bank is best preserved at N. Otherwise modernised and incorporated into the field boundary. Original entrance not recognisable.
24:35 22-8-1991

566 DRUMBESS
OS 24:7:3 (666,405) Hachured OD 400–500
23186, 30190
Rath Raised circular area (int. diam. 27m) enclosed by a substantial earthen bank, a wide, deep waterlogged fosse and slight traces of an outer bank which appears modern. Wide break in inner bank at N represents original entrance.
24:36 22-8-1991

567 DRUMBO (Tullygarvey By.)
OS 16:7:1 (525,404) Hachured OD 400–500
24975, 31487
Rath Raised circular area (int. diam. 28.4m) enclosed by a low earthen bank and a wide, deep, partly waterlogged fosse. Break in bank with accompanying causeway at E represents original entrance. The interior is divided into two roughly equal portions by a wide and low earthen bank running NW–SE.
16:45 19-9-1989

568 DRUMBO (Upper Loughtee By.)
OS 20:12:2 (840,281) Hachured OD 300–400
24340, 30710
Rath Raised circular area (int. dims. 34m N–S; 32.5m) enclosed by a substantial earthen bank and a wide, deep fosse which has been partly infilled from NE–S–SW. Original entrance not recognisable.
20:26 22-8-1990

569 DRUMBO (Upper Loughtee By.)
OS 20:8:6 (892,339) Indicated OD 400–500
24395, 30772
Rath Raised circular area (int. diam. 25m) enclosed by a slight earthen bank. External fosse has been infilled but its outline is still identifiable. The rath is encircled by a modern bank from NE–S–WSW which may easily be confused with the original bank. Original entrance not recognisable.
20:27 22-8-1990

570 DRUMBRADE (Tullygarvey By.)
OS 18:14:1 (272,81) Hachured OD 400–500
26662, 31160
Rath Raised circular area (int. diam. 31.5m) enclosed by a substantial earthen bank and a narrow, deep, partly waterlogged fosse which is well preserved from ENE–S–WSW and largely infilled elsewhere. An earlier report (OPW 1969) recorded that the original entrance was at SE.
18:6 15-7-1990

571 DRUMBRAWN
OS 15:8:5 (789,336) Indicated OD 200–300
24280, 31408
Rath Raised circular area (int. diam. 28.9m) enclosed by a low earthen bank which has been extensively modified and incorporated into the field boundary. An earlier report (OPW 1968) noted traces of a wide, shallow external fosse from NE–S–NW and suggested that the original entrance may have been at SE.
15:28 21-9-1989

572 DRUMBROLLISK
OS 16:12:2 (838,289) Hachured OD 300–400
25307, 31367
Rath Raised oval area (int. dims. *c.* 48m NNW–SSE; *c.* 31m ENE–WSW) enclosed by a substantial earthen bank and a wide, shallow fosse. Both have been

greatly modified and incorporated into the field boundary. Fosse is absent from SSE–SSW and from ESE–SSE a modern drain has been cut along its line. Original entrance may be represented by a break in the bank at S.
16:46 18-10-1989

573 DRUMBRUCKLIS (ED Loughdawan)
OS 31:9:4 (8,198) Hachured OD 355
23474, 29334
Rath Raised roughly circular area (int. dims. *c.* 43m NW–SE; *c.* 40m NE–SW) enclosed by a very substantial earthen bank and a wide, deep, partly waterlogged fosse. Traces of a low counterscarp bank at the outer lip of the fosse from E–S–SW and from WNW–NNE are almost certainly relatively modern in date. Break in bank with accompanying causeway at SSE represents original entrance. Internal area very overgrown with vegetation.
31:23 10-6-1992

574 DRUMBRUGHAS (Tullyhaw By.)
OS 7:11:1 (514,261) Hachured OD 300–400
22028, 32589
Rath Raised circular area (int. diam. 31.6m) enclosed by an earthen bank and a wide, deep, waterlogged fosse which is barely discernible from ESE–S–W and almost completely infilled at W. Break in bank with accompanying causeway at NE represents original entrance.
7:9 12-3-1992

575 DRUMCARN
OS 16:10:3 (433,254) Hachured OD 300–400
24880, 31326
Rath Raised circular area (int. diam. 37.4m) enclosed by a substantial earthen bank and a wide, deep fosse. In the fosse at S is a spring well and the surrounding area is very waterlogged. Break in the bank at SE (Wth 4.2m) with accompanying very wide causeway (Wth *c.* 10m) represents original entrance.
16:49 12 10-1989

576 DRUMCHOE
OS 22:5:1 (17,411) Hachured OD 300–400
25420, 30857
Rath Raised circular area (int. diam. 30.7m) enclosed by two substantial earthen banks with wide, deep intervening fosse. Outer bank largely levelled from ENE–W–NW. Fosse poorly preserved from ENE–S. Very wide break in inner bank at ENE probably represents original entrance.
22:14 27-10-1990

577 DRUMCHOE
OS 22:5:1 (66,447) Hachured OD 400–500
25472, 30896
Rath Raised oval area (int. dims. 47m WNW–ESE; *c.* 38m NNW–SSE) enclosed by a low earthen bank, absent from SSE–S, and a wide, shallow fosse identifiable only from SSW–N–ESE. Original entrance not recognisable.
22:15 27-10-1990

578 DRUMCONLESTER
OS 19:11:6 (651,158) Indicated OD 300
23166, 30569
Rath Raised circular area (int. diam. 33.7m) enclosed by a low earthen bank and an apparently modern narrow, shallow trench. An earlier description (OPW 1968) suggested that the original entrance may have been at ENE. (ITA Survey 1942)
19:21 16-7-1990

579 DRUMCONNICK
OS 20:15:1 (506,77) Not marked OD 300–400
23990, 30491
Rath (site) Not marked on any OS ed. Identified as a cropmark from aerial photograph (CUCAP, BGL 87). Circular area (int. diam. *c.* 33.6m) enclosed by a wide, low, ill-defined scarp, presumably the outline of the levelled bank and fosse. Break in scarp at NE may represent original entrance.
20:28 27-8-1990

580 DRUMCONNICK
OS 25:3:4 (515,528) Hachured OD 200–300
24000, 30328
Rath Raised circular area (int. diam. *c.* 35m) enclosed by an earthen bank and a fosse both of which are well preserved from W–N–SSE and ploughed out elsewhere. Original entrance not recognisable.
25:47 17-9-1992

581 DRUMCONRA
OS 16:2:6 (411,457) Hachured OD 400–500
24855, 31541
Rath Raised circular area (int. diam. 18.6m) enclosed by a low earthen bank which survives only from W–N–NE, and a fosse identifiable from NW–N. Elsewhere the internal area is defined by a low scarp. Very wide break in perimeter at NE presumably represents original entrance.
16:50 12-9-1989

582 DRUMCONRA OR LOWFORGE
OS 7:7:1 (463,398) Hachured OD 200–300
21972, 32733
Rath Raised circular area (int. diam. 31.5m) enclosed by a denuded inner earthen bank, a V-shaped fosse, outside of which is a possible berm enclosed by a substantial earthen bank, and a narrow external fosse. Breaks in external bank at SSE and WNW. No

corresponding breaks in inner bank to indicate causewayed entrance. (CUCAP ALQ 19; ALQ 20).
7:10 12-3-1992

583 DRUMCONRA OR LOWFORGE
OS 7:3:4 (518,520) Hachured OD 200
22029, 32862
Rath Raised circular area (int. diam. 33.2m) enclosed by an earthen bank and a wide fosse. NE half of site has been totally levelled (OPW 1988). Original entrance not recognisable.
7:11 14-8-1989

584 DRUMCOR (Clanmahon By.)
OS 31:13:3 (172,121) Hachured OD 300–400
23648, 29255
Rath Raised oval area (int. dims. *c*. 50.7m NW–SE; *c*. 43m ENE–WSW) enclosed by a very substantial earthen bank and a wide, deep, partly waterlogged fosse. Modern laneway at the outer lip of the fosse from S–W. Break in bank at SSE with accompanying causeway represents original entrance. Densely overgrown with vegetation.
31:24 10-6-1992

585 DRUMCOR (Upper Loughtee By.)
OS 20:13:6 (214,24) Indicated OD 200–300
23681, 30433
Rath Raised circular area (int. diam. 25.8m) enclosed by a low earthen bank modified and incorporated into the field boundary, and a fosse which survives from NW–NNE, has been replaced by a drain and trackway from NNE–SSE and infilled elsewhere. Original entrance not recognisable.
20:29 11-8-1990

586 DRUMCRAUVE
OS 20:16:3 (876,80) Indicated OD 300–400
24380, 30499
Rath Unusually large raised oval area (int. dims. 78m NNW–SSW; 53m ENE–WSW) defined by a scarp with a very short segment of denuded earthen bank on its upper edge at NW. From NNW–E–SE scarp is disturbed by the ruins of a late 18th-century dwelling and modern fencing. Wide depression in scarp at SSE probably represents original entrance.
20:31 30-8-1990

587 DRUMCRAUVE/KILLYNEBBER
OS 20:16:2 (840,93) Hachured OD 300–400
24341, 30512
Rath Raised circular area (int. diam. 27.8m) enclosed by a slight earthen bank and a shallow fosse. Site is divided into two roughly equal portions by a field boundary running NE–SW. To SE of this the site has been levelled but the outline is still identifiable. Original entrance not recognisable.
20:30 30-8-1990

588 DRUMCROW (ED Denn)
OS 25:16:5 (770,8) Hachured OD 400
24275, 29782
Rath Raised circular area (int. dims. 35.3m NNW–SSE; 32.4m ENE–WSW) enclosed by an earthen bank and a fosse which is best preserved from NNE–S–SSW. Bank with accompanying causeway at ESE represents original entrance. A stream flows immediately N of the site, and at S there is an infilled well.
25:48 1-9-1991

589 DRUMCROW (ED Drumcarban)
OS 25:13:4 (57,12) Hachured OD 100–200
23522, 29779
Rath Raised subrectangular area (int. dims. 36.3m NW–SE; 27.4m NE–SW) enclosed by fragmentary remains of a low earthen bank with shallow external fosse. From ESE–S–SSW both bank and fosse are absent where the River Erne skirts the site, and have been levelled and replaced by a modern field boundary from NNE–E–SSE. Original entrance not recognisable.
25:49 5-9-1991

590 DRUMCROW (ED Stradone)
OS 21:15:4 (534,75) Hachured OD 300–400
24994, 30499
Rath Raised circular area (int. diam 37.5m) enclosed by a badly denuded earthen bank. No visible remains of an external fosse. Original entrance not recognisable.
21:26 19-9-1990

591 DRUMCROW (Lower Loughtee By.)
OS 15:7:5 (609,359) Indicated OD 200–300
24089, 31430
Rath Marked ‘Fort’ on OS 1836 eds. and known as such in the locality. Raised circular area (int. diam. *c*. 33m) enclosed by a low earthen bank which barely rises above the internal area, and vague traces of a fosse. Original entrance not recognisable.
15:31 22-9-1989

592 DRUMCULLION (Tullyhunco By.)
OS 24:4:4 (713,484) Hachured OD 300–400
23234, 30275
Rath Raised circular area (int. diam. 36.5m) enclosed by a substantial inner earthen bank, a wide, deep, waterlogged fosse and the remains of an outer earthen bank, all of which have been modified in recent times. Original entrance at ENE represented by break in inner bank accompanied by a causeway.
24:38 4-9-1991

593 DRUMEENY
OS 37:16:1 (750,135) Hachured OD 200–300
24264, 28635
Rath Raised circular area (int. diam. 38m) enclosed by a low earthen bank. Original entrance may have been at NW or ESE. An earlier report (OPW 1970) recorded a large stone slab protruding above ground level just inside the bank at NE, a large stone standing on edge on the bank at NW and a third large stone lying on the ground beside it.
37:27 31-7-1986

594 DRUMGART
OS 10:12:4 (732,218) Hachured OD 100–200
23239, 31914
Rath Raised circular area (int. diam. 24m) enclosed by a low, wide earthen bank and a wide, deep fosse. From S–W–WNW fosse has been largely infilled and replaced by a modern laneway. Break in bank at E with accompanying causeway represents original entrance.
10:15 10-10-1988

595 DRUMGERD
OS 19:3:2 Hachured OD 300–400
23125, 30402
Rath Raised circular area (int. diam. 38.5m) enclosed by two substantial earthen banks with wide, deep, partly waterlogged intermediate fosse. Outer bank identifiable from NW–E–SW. From SW–NW a modern earthen bank has been constructed along the base of the fosse. Wide break in bank with accompanying causeway at S represents original entrance.
19:23/24:39* 16-7-1990

596 DRUMGONEY
OS 21:16:3 (884,151) Hachured OD 400–500
25363, 30582
Rath Raised circular area (int. dims. 41.5m ENE–WSW; 39.5m NNW–SSE) enclosed by a substantial earthen bank and a fosse which is well preserved except from NW–NNE where it is shallow and appears modern. Original entrance not recognisable. Internal area densely overgrown with vegetation.
21:28 12-9-1990

597 DRUMGONEY
OS 21:16:3 (887,121) Hachured OD 400–500
25366, 30551
Rath Raised circular area (int. diam. 24.1m) enclosed by an earthen bank modified and incorporated into the field boundary from S–WNW, and the remains of a fosse. A low earthen mound of unknown significance occurs at the centre of the interior.
21:29 12-9-1990

598 DRUMGORA (Castlerahan By.)
OS 39:2:2 (316,592) Hachured OD 400–500
25752, 29132
Rath The site is divided into two unequal portions by a modern field boundary running NNW–SSE, flanked by a modern laneway on its W side. The larger portion, NE of this, has been levelled. The surviving portion is defined by a partially defaced steep scarp from S–NW. Original entrance not recognisable.
39:43 25-3-1987

599 DRUMHARID
OS 15:12:4 (701,223) Hachured OD 300
24188, 31288
Rath Raised subcircular area (int. dims. *c.* 58.5m N–S; *c.* 52m E–W) enclosed by a substantial earthen bank and a wide fosse. From SW–NNW a modern bank of earth and stone has been built at the external lip of the fosse. Original entrance not recognisable. An earlier report (OPW 1968) recorded a scarp inside the bank from N–E–S, indicating that the rath may have originally been bivallate.
15:33 26-9-1989

600 DRUMHARID
OS 15:16:1 (716,120) Hachured OD 200–300
24205, 31179
Rath Raised circular area (int. diam. 64m) enclosed by a wide, low bank. A modern field drain has been dug at the external foot of the bank at SE. Original entrance not recognisable.
15:34 26-9-1989

601 DRUMHAWNAGH
OS 31:13:5 (80,44) Hachured OD 300–400
23551, 29172
Rath Raised circular area (int. diam. *c.* 33m) enclosed by a substantial earthen bank modified and incorporated into the field boundary and a wide, deep, partially waterlogged fosse. Original entrance not recognisable.
31:27 29-3-1974

602 DRUMHAWRAGH
OS 31:9:1 (4,302) Hachured OD 391
23468, 29444
Rath Raised almost circular area (int. dims. 48.8m NW–SE; 44.6m NE–SW) enclosed by a low earthen bank and traces of an infilled fosse. Break in bank with accompanying causeway at W is probably original. Close to the centre of the interior is a shallow rectangular trench which is traditionally believed to be the work of a local schoolteacher searching for a 'tunnel' *c.* 100 years ago. His efforts were unsuccessful (local information).
31:28 10-6-1992

603 DRUMHAWRAGH
OS 31:9:6 (163,227) Hachured OD 300–400
23637, 29366

Rath Raised circular area (int. diam. *c.* 40m) enclosed by a substantial earthen bank modified and incorporated into a field boundary and a fosse which has been infilled and replaced by a modern laneway from NNW–N–NNE. Break in bank at SE with accompanying causeway may represent original entrance. Internal area very overgrown with vegetation.
31:29 10-6-1992

604 DRUMHEEL (Castlerahan By.)
OS 39:16:6 (883,11) Indicated OD 400
26356, 28523

Rath Marked 'Fort' on OS 1836 and 1876 eds. Raised circular area (int. diam. *c.* 34m) enclosed by a low but well-defined bank of earth and stone which has been extensively modified and incorporated into the field boundary. Break in bank at NE may represent original entrance.
39:44 29-5-1987

605 DRUMHILLAGH (Clanmahon By.)
OS 31:15:1 (475,136) Hachured OD 300–400
23968, 29273

Rath Raised subcircular area (int. dims. *c.* 40m N–S; *c.* 35m E–W) enclosed by a substantial earthen bank and a wide, deep, partially waterlogged fosse. A low earthen bank at outer lip of fosse from N–E is almost certainly modern. Break in bank at S with accompanying causeway presumably represents original entrance.
31:30 5-6-1992

606 DRUMHILLAGH (ED Killeshandra)
OS 19:15:2 (584,92) Hachured OD 300–400
23096, 30500

Rath (site) Marked 'Fort' on all OS eds. Situated on the summit of a drumlin hill. Davies (ITA Survey 1942)) described a raised circular area (int. diam. *c.* 28m) enclosed by a low earthen bank. Site has been levelled.
19:24 9-7-1990

Fig. 16—*Rath at Drumcullion* (**592**).

607 DRUMHILLAGH (Tullygarvey By.)
OS 21:3:6 (629,513) Hachured OD 400–500
25090, 30962
Rath Raised circular area (int. diam. 28.9m) enclosed by a bank and fosse. Site is divided into two roughly equal portions by a field boundary aligned NE–SW. In the NW field the fosse has been levelled and the bank is slight; in the SE field the fosse is wide and deep and the bank much more substantial. Perimeter incorporated into field boundary from NW–NE. Break in bank with accompanying causeway at SSE.
21:32 27-9-1990

608 DRUMHILLAGH (Upper Loughtee By.)
OS 26:13:5 (97,18) Hachured OD 400–500
24539, 29794
Rath Raised circular area (int. dims. 27.4m ENE–WSW; 28.3m NNW–SSE) enclosed by a substantial earthen bank and a shallow fosse. Low outer bank noted in an earlier report (OPW 1970) has been almost totally levelled. Original entrance may have been at SSE where there is a narrow break in the inner bank and a causeway across the fosse.
26:31 27-3-1992

609 DRUMHIRK (ED Stradone)
OS 26:6:4 (291,343) Hachured OD 471
24741, 30139
Rath Raised almost circular area (int. diam. *c.* 48.9m) divided into two unequal portions by a roadway running N–S. Enclosed by a scarp with slight remains of an earthen bank on its upper edge, and a wide, shallow fosse which has been levelled in at the E half of circuit. Original entrance not recognisable. Overlooks Beaghy Lough 150m to E.
26:32 23-10-1991

610 DRUMHIRK (Tullygarvey By.)
OS 17:10:5 (316,196) Hachured OD 300–400
25923, 30965
Rath Raised circular area (int. diam. 31.7m) enclosed by a substantial, although much-denuded, earthen bank and a fosse which is wide and deep from WNW–ENE but has been largely infilled from ENE–ESE. Original entrance not recognisable. Modern farm buildings skirt the site from SE–S.
17:31 29-9-1990

611 DRUMHURT
OS 22:2:2 (373,578) Hachured OD 444
25794, 31037
Rath Raised circular area (int. diam. 43.1m) enclosed by an earthen bank and a fosse. Bank only survives in its original form at NE. From NNE–S–SSW the perimeter has been incorporated into the field boundary. Elsewhere it has been levelled but its outline may still be traced. An earlier report (OPW 1969) noted a possible entrance feature at NE. Internal area is largely occupied by a modern water tower.
22:19 27-10-1990

612 DRUMINISCLIN (Castlerahan By.)
OS 32:13:2 (86,145) Hachured OD 400–500
24532, 29288
Rath Large oval-shaped raised area (int. dims. *c.* 58m NW–SE; *c.* 43m NE–SW) enclosed by a low earthen bank. Perimeter modified and incorporated into the field boundary from ESE–SE and from S–W. Modern field boundary at the outer foot of the bank from NNW–E–ESE. Original entrance not recognisable.
32:17 13-7-1989

613 DRUMKEERAN BEG
OS 24:12:2 (772,290) Hachured OD 300–400
23298, 30070
Rath Raised circular area (int. diam. *c.* 37m) enclosed by a substantial earthen bank, which has been removed from SSE–SSW, and a totally infilled wide fosse. Large silage pit within the internal area. Original entrance not recognisable.
24:42 22-8-1991

614 DRUMKEERAN MORE
OS 24:11:3 (681,268) Hachured OD 400
23203, 30046
Rath Raised circular area (int. dims. 32m E–W; 35m N–S) enclosed by a low earthen bank and fosse. Break in bank with accompanying causeway at SSE represents original entrance.
24:44 22-8-1991

615 DRUMKILLY
OS 31:12:2 (771,248) Hachured OD 400
24279, 29395
Rath Raised oval area (int. dims. 38.5m NW–SE; 30.8m NE–SW) enclosed by an earthen bank and fosse, both of which have been modified and incorporated into the field boundary. Original entrance not recognisable.
31:31 5-6-1992

616 DRUMKILROOSK
OS 24:7:5 (565,313) Hachured OD 300–400
23080, 30092
Rath Raised circular area (int. diam. *c.* 36m) enclosed by a very substantial inner earthen bank, a wide, shallow intermediate fosse and fragmentary remains of an outer earthen bank. Original entrance represented by wide break in inner bank at SE. Densely overgrown with vegetation.
24:45 22-8-1991

617 DRUMLANE (Tullygarvey By.)
OS 21:7:3 (624,386) Hachured OD 300–400
25086, 30828
Rath Raised circular area (int. diam. 28.3m) enclosed by a slight earthen bank and a fosse. An earlier description (OPW 1968) suggested that original entrance may have been at ESE. From NW–NE the site is bounded by a river ravine.
21:33 19-9-1990

618 DRUMLARK
OS 20:7:6 (672,313) Hachured OD 300–400
24162, 30743
Rath A much-disturbed, raised circular area (int. diam. *c.* 32m) enclosed by a low earthen bank identifiable only from NNE–S–SSW, and a fosse discernible only at E. A field boundary running N–S divides the site into two unequal portions. The smaller portion W of this is the site of a plantation of mature deciduous trees.
20:37 27-8-1990

619 DRUMLARNEY
OS 24:5:3 (213,416) Hachured OD 200–300
22706, 30198
Rath Raised circular area (int. diam. 50.4m) enclosed by an earthen bank and a fosse which is only visible from WNW–NNE and has been almost totally infilled here. Many breaks in the bank. Original entrance not recognisable.
24:46 27-8-1991

620 DRUMLEAGUE
OS 22:1:6 (205,525) Not marked OD 467
25618, 30980
Rath Raised circular area (int. diam. 33.8m) enclosed by an earthen bank and fosse. From ENE–S–WSW the enclosing features have been much modified and incorporated into the field boundary. Elsewhere they have been levelled but their outline is still identifiable. Original entrance not recognisable.
22:22 21-10-1990

621 DRUMLENY
OS 25:6:3 (416,437) Hachured OD 300–400
23896, 30231
Rath Raised oval area (int. dims. 42m N–S; 34m E–W) enclosed by two substantial earthen banks with outer fosses. Outer fosse absent and outer bank greatly disturbed by modern field boundary built along its inner face from NE–ESE. Corresponding breaks in banks with accompanying causeways at SSE represents original entrance.
25:53 7-9-1991

622 DRUMLIFF (ED Ballyhaise)
OS 15:12:6 (918,223) Hachured OD 200–300
24417, 31289
Rath Raised circular area (int. diam. *c.* 30m) enclosed by a substantial earthen bank and a wide, deep fosse. Fosse is slight at E where a modern farm building has encroached on its outer lip. Break in bank at NE with accompanying causeway represents original entrance.
15:36 15-9-1989

623 DRUMLION (Clanmahon By.)
OS 31:2:3 (456,578) Hachured OD 300–400
23943, 29740
Rath An almost circular raised area (int. diam. 37.6m) enclosed by a substantial earthen bank and a wide, deep fosse. Modern field boundaries at the outer lip of the fosse from NNW–E–S. Break in bank at W with accompanying causeway represents original entrance.
31:32 8-4-1974

624 DRUMLION (Clanmahon By.)
OS 31:2:6 (457,527) Not marked OD 300–400
23944, 29686
Rath (site) Marked 'Fort' on OS 1836 and 1876 eds. Raised circular area (int. diam. *c.* 40.7m) enclosed by the outline of a bank and fosse. Perimeter levelled but outline still identifiable from W–N–S. Elsewhere it has been modified and incorporated into the field boundary.
31:33 4-6-1992

625 DRUMLOMAN
OS 31:8:6 (864,334) Hachured OD 400
24377, 29486
Rath Raised circular area (int. diam. *c.* 46m) enclosed by a very substantial earthen bank and a wide, deep, partially waterlogged fosse. The site is encircled by modern field boundaries. Break in bank at SE with accompanying causeway represents original entrance. Inside the bank at W is an irregularly shaped depression of unknown significance and at NE a second depression which may mark the site of a souterrain (**1238**).
31:34(01) 3-4-1974

626 DRUMLON
OS 28:10:3 (421,228) Hachured OD 600–700
26829, 30037
Rath Raised almost circular area (int. diam. *c.* 25m) enclosed by an earthen bank and wide fosse which has been partially recut and is now waterlogged. Spoil from this excavation forms a modern counterscarp bank at the outer lip of the fosse. Original entrance at E.
28:20 1-4-1993

627 DRUMMANBANE
OS 32:8:2 (829,383) Hachured OD 400–500
25314, 29546

Fig. 17—*Rath at Drumlion* (**623**).

Rath Raised circular area (int. diam. 26m) enclosed by the remains of a substantial earthen bank and a fosse which has been infilled at S and replaced by a modern farm laneway. It has also been recut from WSW–NW and is enclosed by a modern external bank. Break in bank at E with accompanying causeway represents original entrance.
32:19 4-5-1989

628 DRUMMANBANE
OS 32:8:2 (834,435) Hachured OD 500–600
25319, 29601

Rath Raised circular area (int. diam. *c.* 35m) enclosed by two substantial earthen banks with intermediate fosse. Break in inner bank at SE with accompanying causeway represents original entrance. Corresponding break in outer bank has been blocked up. Densely overgrown with vegetation.
32:20 4-5-1989

629 DRUMMANDUFF
OS 33:5:4 (68,368) Hachured OD 400–500
25486, 29533

Rath Raised circular area (int. diam. *c.* 38m) enclosed by the remains of a wide, low earthen bank and a shallow fosse. The site is divided into two roughly equal portions by a roadway aligned NW–SE. From NW–N–NE the bank has been largely levelled and the SE quadrant quarried away. Original entrance not recognisable.
33:30 5-4-1974

630 DRUMMANY (Tullygarvey By.)
OS 11:15:6 (671,70) Hachured OD 200–300
24152, 31766

Rath Raised circular area (int. diam. *c.* 38m) enclosed by a substantial earthen bank and a largely infilled fosse. An earlier report suggested that the original entrance was probably at S. Densely overgrown with vegetation.
11:17 18-6-1989

631 DRUMMANY GLEBE
OS 14:16:2 (840,144) Hachured OD 200–300
23361, 31196

Rath Raised circular area (int. dims. 37.2m) enclosed

by a substantial earthen bank and a wide, shallow fosse. An earlier report (OPW 1969) suggested that the original entrance was probably at NNE. Densely overgrown with vegetation.
14:31 11-8-1989

632 DRUMMOLE
OS 21:8:6 (855,305) Hachured OD 465 25330, 30744
Rath Raised circular area (int. diam. *c*. 38m) enclosed by two substantial earthen banks with outer fosses. From ESE–SE and from SSW–N a modern field boundary encircles the site. Corresponding breaks in banks with causeway across inner fosse at E represents original entrance.
21:34 19-9-1990

633 DRUMMONEY
OS 39:10:1 (300,272) Hachured OD 400–500 25737, 28794
Rath Raised oval area (int. dims. 35m NW–SE; 30m NE–SW) enclosed by a bank, absent from N–E, and a fosse identifiable only from SW–N. Original entrance not recognisable.
39:45 4-9-1970

634 DRUMMORA LITTLE
OS 25:5:2 (106,403) Hachured OD 200–300 23569, 30192
Rath An almost circular raised area (int. dims. 48m WSW–ESE; 52m NNW–SSE) enclosed by a substantial earthen bank and a deep, partly waterlogged fosse. Break in bank at ESE probably represents original entrance.
25:55 5-9-1991

635 DRUMMUCK
OS 26:2:3 (407,587) Hachured OD 600–700 24861, 30398
Rath Raised circular area (int. diam. 29.1m) enclosed by two earthen banks with wide, deep intermediate fosse. The inner bank is very substantial while the outer bank is clearly modern. Break in inner bank with accompanying causeway at SE represents original entrance. Possible souterrain within internal area (**1239**).
26:33(01) 23-10-1991

636 DRUMMUCK
OS 26:11:2 (555,278) Hachured OD 500–600 25020, 30073
Rath Raised almost circular area (int. diam. 30.8m N–S) enclosed by a partly modernised, slight earthen bank and an almost totally infilled fosse. Break in bank at S probably represents original entrance. W of the centre of the internal area is a subrectangular depression (dims. 8m E–W; 3.2m N–S; D 0.3m) of unknown significance.
26:34 23-10-1991

637 DRUMMULLIG
OS 20:3:4 (525,498) Indicated OD 200–300 24005, 30937
Rath Raised circular area (int. diam. 41.1m) enclosed by a substantial earthen bank which has been modified and incorporated into a field boundary, and a wide, shallow fosse, which while infilled throughout most of its course, is nonetheless traceable. Break in bank with accompanying causeway at E may represent original entrance. Modern laneway running NNE–SSW divides the internal area into two roughly equal portions.
20:42 14-8-1990

638 DRUMMULLIG
OS 20:3:1 (538,551) Indicated OD 200–300 24018, 30992
Rath Raised circular area (int. diam. 24.7m) enclosed by a low earthen bank and a wide, shallow, partly waterlogged fosse. From SW–S–SSE fosse has been scarped and faced with drystone masonry. Original entrance not definitely recognisable but was probably either at E or NW.
20:43 14-8-1990

639 DRUMMULLY EAST
OS 19:3:6 (631,477) Hachured OD 200–300 23142, 30907
Rath Raised circular area (int. diam. 57.6m) enclosed by a substantial earthen bank. The outer fosse has been levelled. An earlier report (OPW 1968) described it as being wide and deep. Break in bank at SW may represent original entrance.
19:25 14-7-1990

640 DRUMMURY
OS 17:9:3 (229,264) '*Drummury Fort*' OD 300–400 25897, 31121
Rath (site) Situated a short distance from the summit of a drumlin hill. An earlier report (OPW 1969) described a raised circular area (int. diam. *c*. 34m) enclosed by two substantial earthen banks with wide, deep, waterlogged intervening fosse. Original entrance may have been at NE. Levelled in the early 1960s leaving nothing visible at ground level.
17:33 29-9-1990

641 DRUMMURY
OS 17:10:1 (286,244) Hachured OD 300–400 25938, 31045
Rath Depicted on OS 1836 and 1876 eds. as a large oval-shaped enclosure (int. dims. *c*. 65m NE–SW; *c*. 45m NW–SE), with the designation 'Fort', situated within a tree plantation. The enclosing elements

Fig. 18—*Rath at Drummora Little* (**634**).

comprising a substantial earthen bank and a fosse survive only from N–E. Elsewhere both features have been much modified and incorporated into the boundary of the tree plantation. Original entrance not recognisable. The internal area has been planted with trees and is heavily overgrown with vegetation.
17:34 29-9-1990

642 DRUMNAGAR
OS 22:13:1 (55,127) Hachured OD 500–600
25463, 30558
Rath Raised circular area (int. diam. 31.5m) enclosed by a substantial earthen bank. An earlier report (OPW 1977) recorded slight remains of an external fosse which is no longer visible. From SW–N–NW the bank has been modified and incorporated into the field boundary. Original entrance not recognisable. NE half of internal area has been planted with coniferous trees.
22:23 10-10-1990

643 DRUMNAGRESS
OS 22:3:2 (601,572) Hachured OD 400–500
26035, 31033
Rath Raised circular area (int. diam. 39.6m) enclosed by two earthen banks with intermediate fosse. Outer bank absent from SE–SSW where it is partly replaced by a modern fence. Break in inner bank with accompanying causeway at SSW probably represents original entrance.
22:24 16-10-1990

644 DRUMNALARAGH
OS 31:7:3 (650,447) Hachured OD 400–500
24149, 29604
Rath Raised circular area (int. diam. *c.* 40m) enclosed by a substantial earthen bank and a wide, deep, waterlogged fosse. From SW–N–ESE the perimeter is encircled by a relatively modern earthen field bank. Original entrance not recognisable. Internal area very overgrown with vegetation.
31:35 6-6-1992

645 DRUMPEAK
OS 29:14:6 (400,2) Hachured OD 300–400
27785, 29807
Rath Raised circular area (int. diam. 31m) enclosed

Fig. 19—*Rath at Drummully East* (**639**).

by a substantial earthen bank. An earlier description (OPW 1974) noted the presence of a shallow external fosse from W–N–NE. Original entrance may have been at S.
29:3 9-8-1988

646 DRUMPEAK
OS 35:2:3 (446,554) Hachured OD 400–500
27834, 29750
Rath Raised circular area (int. diam. 32m) enclosed by a wide but much-denuded low earthen bank and a shallow fosse identifiable at W. Original entrance not recognisable.
35:35 11-3-1974

647 DRUMPEAK
OS 35:2:3 (454,560) Hachured OD 400–500
27843, 29757
Rath Raised circular area (int. diam. *c*. 38m) enclosed by two earthen banks with intermediate wide, deep fosse. Outer bank is partly denuded. Inside the inner bank at E is a depression of unknown significance. Original entrance may have been at SE.
35:36 11-3-1974

648 DRUMRAT (Castlerahan By.)
OS 39:12:3 (923,303) Not marked OD 400–500
26395, 28832
Rath (site) Marked 'Fort' on OS 1836 and 1876 eds. Situated on the W shoulder of a ridge of high ground. Not visible at ground level.
39:46/40:24* 11-8-1987

649 DRUMRAT (Castlerahan By.)
OS 40:9:1 (21,260) Hachured OD 400–500
26419, 28787
Rath Raised circular area (int. diam. *c*. 24m) enclosed by a substantial, although partly denuded, earthen bank and the remains of a fosse identifiable only from E–SSE and at N. Wide break in bank at ENE presumably represents original entrance.
40:25 11-8-1987

650 DRUMRATH
OS 31:16:5 (809,64) Hachured OD 300–400
24321, 29200
Rath Raised subcircular area (int. dims. 42.1m NNW–SSE; 38.5m NE–SW) enclosed by a substantial

earthen bank and a wide, deep, partly waterlogged fosse. Partly blocked break in bank with accompanying causeway at SSE probably represents original entrance.
31:36 5-6-1992

651 DRUMROCKADY
OS 24:16:5 (816,69) Hachured OD 300–400
23347, 29837
Rath Raised circular area (int. diam. 44.2m) enclosed by an earthen bank and a wide, deep, partly waterlogged fosse infilled from E–SSE. Original entrance represented by break in bank with accompanying causeway at S. Immediately inside the entrance is a wide, shallow depression of unknown significance.
24:47 29-8-1991

652 DRUMROE
OS 24:11:6 (664,227) Hachured OD 300–400
23185, 30002
Rath Raised oval area (int. dims. 63.5m N–S; 50m E–W) enclosed by an earthen bank and well-defined fosse absent at W only. Original entrance at S represented by a blocked-up break in the bank with accompanying causeway.
24:48 29-8-1991

653 DRUMROOSK (Clanmahon By.)
OS 31:5:1 (74,446) Hachured OD 301
23542, 29597
Rath Raised subcircular area (int. dims. 48.8m N–S; 41.3m E–W) enclosed by a substantial earthen bank and a fosse, largely infilled except from E–S–SW where it is wide and shallow. Break in bank with accompanying causeway at NE probably represents original entrance.
31:37 10-6-1992

654 DRUMROOSK (Tullyhunco By.)
OS 19:11:5 (585,196) Hachured OD 300
23096, 30609
Rath (site) Marked 'Fort' on all OS eds. An earlier description (OPW 1968) described a slightly raised circular area (int. diam. 46m NNE–SSW) enclosed by a low earthen bank and traces of a fosse. Site has been levelled. Not visible at ground level.
19:26 15-7-1990

655 DRUMRORAGH
OS 38:6:2 (343,417) Hachured OD 400–500
24807, 28938
Rath Raised circular area (int. diam. 28m) enclosed by three earthen banks with outer fosses. An earlier report (OPW 1970) interpreted the two outermost banks and fosses as being later additions, possibly dating to the period when the site was transformed into a tree-ring. Break in the inner bank at ENE may represent original entrance.
38:24 14-8-1986

656 DRUMSHEIL
OS 17:9:1 (51,293) Indicated OD 300–400
25737, 31323
Rath Marked 'Fort' on OS 1836 eds. Small raised circular area (int. diam 17.5m N–S) enclosed by a low steep-sided earthen bank. At the external foot of the bank is a narrow shallow ditch which appears to be modern. An earlier report (OPW 1969) suggested that the original entrance may have been at SE and recorded a 'slight artifical-looking depression inside the bank at E'. The internal area has been planted with coniferous trees.
17:35 16-11-1989

657 DRUMSILLAGH (Upper Loughtee By.)
OS 15:15:1 (527,106) Hachured OD 200–300
24005, 31162
Rath Raised oval area (int. dims. 33.5m WNW–ESE; 28m NNE–SSW) enclosed by a substantial, although partly denuded, earthen bank and a wide, shallow fosse modified and incorporated into the field drainage system. An earlier report (OPW 1968) suggested that the original entrance was probably at SE. Densely overgrown with vegetation.
15:42 12-9-1989

658 DRUMSIVNEY
OS 17:11:6 (640,209) Hachured OD 300–400
26278, 30666
Rath Almost completely levelled in 1969. Situated on the summit of a high drumlin hill. An earlier report (OPW 1969), written some months after the destruction, recorded that it had apparently comprised a raised circular area (int. diam. *c.* 28m) enclosed by two substantial earthen banks with intermediate fosse. Original entrance was not recognisable. The outer bank has been much modified and incorporated into the field boundary from E–S–SSW and from N–E.
17:40 27-11-1989

659 DRUMSKEAGH
OS 25:2:1 (279,570) Hachured OD 300–400
23750, 30369
Rath Raised oval area (int. dims. 35m N–S; 29m E–W) enclosed by the remains of an earthen bank and a fosse. At W the perimeter is much denuded. Original entrance not recognisable.
25:56 12-9-1991

660 DRUMSKERRY
OS 29:13:6 (228,32) Hachured OD 558
27604, 29837

Rath Raised circular area (int. diam. 40.5m) enclosed by a well-preserved earthen bank and a wide, deep, waterlogged fosse. Break in bank at SE with partially surviving accompanying causeway presumably represents original entrance.
29:5 24-3-1977

661 DRUMSKERRY
OS 29:14:4 (304,26) Hachured OD 400–500
27684, 29831
Rath Raised circular area (int. diam. 26m) enclosed by a low, wide, inner earthen bank, intermediate shallow fosse and very slight remains of an outer bank. Break in bank at SE may represent original entrance.
29:6 20-3-1974

662 DRUMURY
OS 30:4:6 (916,520) Hachured OD 300–400
23456, 29670
Rath Roughly circular raised area (int. diam. 37m) enclosed by a substantial earthen bank and the remains of a partially waterlogged fosse. Modern roadway divides the site into two almost equal portions with breaks in the bank at NW and SSE. At N a modern trackway has replaced the fosse for a short distance. Original entrance not recognisable.
30:17 9-10-1991

663 DRUMYOUTH
OS 24:11:4 (468,215) Hachured OD 300–400
22978, 29988
Rath Raised circular area (int. diam. *c.* 38m) enclosed by a very substantial inner earthen bank, a wide, deep, waterlogged intermediate fosse and fragmentary remains of an outer bank identifiable only at NE and S. Break in inner bank with accompanying causeway at E represents original entrance.
24:49 30-8-1991

664 DUNAREE
OS 35:6:6 (388,364) Hachured OD 400–500
27774, 29549
Rath Raised circular area (int. diam. *c.* 35m) enclosed by a substantial inner earthen bank, a shallow fosse and a berm and outer earthen bank which have been levelled from W–N–SE. A low stone field wall has been built against the inner face of the berm at W. Fosse has been modified at E and is now utilised as a field drain. Original entrance at SE.
35:39 13-3-1974

665 DUNAREE
OS 35:6:3 (386,398) Hachured OD 544
27773, 29585
Rath Raised circular area (int. diam. *c.* 33m) enclosed by a substantial earthen bank. Outside the bank from S–W is a modern narrow laneway which may represent the remains of an infilled fosse. Original entrance not recognisable.
35:40 12-3-1974

666 DUNCOLLOG
OS 16:7:3 (674,384) Hachured OD 200–300
25133, 31467
Rath Raised oval area (int. dims. *c.* 38m NNE–SSW; *c.* 20m ESE–WNW) enclosed from NE–S–W by a narrow earthen bank and a wide, shallow fosse. The bank, and to a lesser extent the fosse, have been much modified and incorporated into the field boundary. From W–NNW fosse and bank are barely identifiable. Original entrance not recognisable.
16:56 2-11-1989

667 DUNCOLLOG
OS 16:7:6 (678,330) Hachured OD 300
25138, 31410
Rath A largely levelled, raised circular area (int. diam. *c.* 27m) enclosed from SE–S–NW by a very low earthen bank and a wide, shallow fosse. From SE–W the perimeter is incorporated into the field boundary and has been ploughed out elsewhere. Original entrance not recognisable.
16:57 5-11-1989

668 DUNDAVAN
OS 37:9:2 (147,281) Hachured OD 200–300
23626, 28783
Rath Raised circular area (int. diam. *c.* 30m) enclosed by a much-denuded low earthen bank. Original entrance not recognisable.
37:28 12-11-1970

669 DUNDRAGON
OS 34:3:2 (578,590) Hachured OD 700–800
26998, 29781
Rath Raised circular area (int. diam. *c.* 33m) enclosed by a bank and a fosse which is absent from N–SE. Original entrance may have been at SW or NE.
34:23 1-6-1988

670 DUNGONNAN
OS 16:11:5 (561,186) Hachured OD 300–400
25016, 31256
Rath (site) A kink in the field boundary running from SE–S–SW is the only surviving indicator of the site. An earlier report (OPW 1968) described a raised subcircular area (int. dims. *c.* 30m E–W; *c.* 27m N–S) enclosed by a low earthen bank and a modern trench. Original entrance location was not identified. Site has been levelled.
16:59 28-10-1989

671 DUNGONNAN
OS 16:11:5 (563,194) Hachured OD 350
25018, 31265
Rath Raised circular area (int. dims. *c.* 35m) enclosed by a substantial earthen bank and a wide, deep fosse. Break in bank with accompanying causeway at E represents original entrance.
16:60 28-10-1989

672 DUNGUMMIN LOWER
OS 42:3:6 (657,506) Hachured OD 200–300
25143, 28394
Rath (site) An earlier report (OPW 1974) described a small raised circular area (int. diam. *c.* 25m) enclosed by a wide, low earthen bank and vague traces of a fosse. Original entrance may have been at SE. Site has been levelled.
42:15 10-9-1986

673 DUNGUMMIN UPPER
OS 42:7:6 (651,364) Hachured OD 200–300
25138, 28245
Rath Raised circular area (int. diam. 54m) enclosed by a very low earthen bank. Original entrance not recognisable. The site is encircled by modern field boundaries and a farmyard abuts it at E.
42:18 18-6-1974

674 DUNGUMMIN UPPER
OS 42:7:3 (652,436) Indicated OD 200–300
25139, 28321
Rath Raised circular area (int. diam. *c.* 28m) enclosed by a low earthen bank and a shallow fosse identifiable only at E. Exterior of bank has been incorporated into the field boundary and faced with drystone masonry. Narrow break in bank at SE may represent original entrance.
42:19 18-6-1974

675 DUNGUMMIN UPPER
OS 42:8:4 (730,343) Hachured OD 365
25221, 28224
Rath Large raised circular area (int. diam. 60m) enclosed by two low earthen banks with wide, shallow intermediate fosse. Original entrance was probably at SE. Within the internal area are several low mounds and slight hollows of unknown significance.
42:20 18-6-1974

676 DUNGUMMIN UPPER
OS 42:8:1 (727,390) Hachured OD 300–400
25218, 28273
Rath Raised circular area (int. diam. *c.* 26m) enclosed by a low bank of earth and stone and a shallow fosse. A modern field boundary runs alongside the perimeter from NW–N–E. Original entrance not recognisable.
42:21 18-6-1974

677 DUNGUMMIN UPPER
OS 42:8:2 (794,406) Hachured OD 300–400
25289, 28291
Rath (site) Depicted as a circular enclosure with the designation 'Fort' on OS 1836 and 1876 eds. Remains comprise a much-disturbed raised subrectangular area (int. dims. 28.8m NE–SW; 26.6m NW–SE) defined by a scarp (max. H 1m) from SW–N. Elsewhere the site has been levelled. Original entrance not recognisable.
42:22 16-5-1993

678 DUNMURRY
OS 16:8:5 (772,339) Hachured OD 300–400
25236, 31419
Rath Raised oval area (int. dims. *c.* 39m NNW–SSE; *c.* 26m ENE–WSW) enclosed by a substantial earthen bank and a wide, deep, waterlogged fosse. Break in bank at NE with accompanying much-disturbed causeway represents original entrance. Densely overgrown with vegetation.
16:61 11-10-1989

679 DUNRORA
OS 12:13:5 (118,15) Hachured OD 200–300
24544, 31712
Rath Raised circular area (int. diam. 46.2m) enclosed by a low earthen bank and narrow, shallow fosse. Break in bank with accompanying causeway at SW presumably represents original entrance. The site was formerly utilised as a tree plantation.
12:2 28-6-1989

680 EDENBURT
OS 44:5:4 (61,308) Hachured OD 300–400
26466, 28198
Rath Raised circular area (int. diam. *c.* 24m) enclosed by a low bank of earth and stone. A modern field fence has been built against the bank at NW. Original entrance may have been at N.
44:6 21-8-1987

681 EDENBURT
OS 44:9:2 (91,297) Hachured OD 400
26498, 28186
Rath (site) An earlier report (OPW 1969) described a raised circular area enclosed by an earthen bank and the remains of a fosse. Original entrance was not recognisable. Site has been levelled. Not visible at ground level.
44:8 21-8-1987

682 EDENBURT
OS 44:9:2 (120,228) Hachured OD 300–400
26530, 28114
Rath Raised circular area (int. diam. 22m) enclosed by a substantial earthen bank. Large break in bank at

W appears to be modern. Original entrance not recognisable.
44:9 21-8-1987

683 EDENBURT
OS 44:9:6 (171,167) Hachured OD 300–400 26584, 28050
Rath Raised circular area (int. diam. *c.* 25m) enclosed by a low bank of earth and stone. No fosse visible. Original entrance not recognisable. An old graveyard, possibly marking the site of an early church, lies 15m to N (**1651**).
44:10(02) 21-8-1987

684 EDENBURT
OS 44:9:6 (174,223) Hachured OD 300–400 26587, 28109
Rath Raised circular area (int. diam. *c.* 37m) enclosed by a substantial earthen bank and a wide, shallow fosse. The S half of the site was destroyed as a consequence of road widening in recent times. Original entrance not recognisable. Situated a short distance SW of an earthen mound (**1898**).
44:11 21-8-1987

685 EDERGOLE
OS 21:15:6 (625,65) Hachured OD 300–400 25090, 30489
Rath Raised circular area (int. diam. 47m) enclosed by a bank and a fosse which have been modernised and incorporated into the field boundary. Original entrance not recognisable. Internal area has been planted with trees.
21:38 19-9-1990

686 ENAGH (Clanmahon By.)
OS 42:10:2 (339,301) Hachured OD 200–300 24809, 28175
Rath Raised circular area (int. diam. *c.* 30m) enclosed by a low earthen bank and a shallow fosse. At the outer lip of the fosse from SE–N–NE there are slight traces of a low counterscarp bank. The internal area was planted with beech trees in the early decades of this century. The site is encircled by a relatively modern field bank of ha-ha type. A tree-ring lies between the rath and this later field boundary.
42:23 20-6-1974

687 ENAGH (Tullygarvey By.)
OS 16:4:6 (868,484) Indicated OD 300–400 25337, 31574
Rath Situated just S of the summit of a high drumlin hill. Much disturbed. Marked 'Fort' on the OS 1836 and 1876 eds. It would appear to have comprised a raised circular area (int. diam. 32.3m). The enclosing features, presumably an earthen bank and fosse, are completely obscured by a complex of modern field boundaries, banks and drains. Large depressions in the perimeter at WSW and W.
16:62 22-10-1989

688 ENNISKEEN
OS 35:7:4 (467,305) Hachured OD 400–500 27859, 29488
Rath Raised circular area (int. diam. *c.* 36m) enclosed by two substantial earthen banks with wide, waterlogged intermediate fosse. Outer bank and fosse survive only from. W–N–SE. Outer bank has been modified and incorporated into the field boundary. Original entrance not recognisable.
35:41 13-3-1974

689 EONISH
OS 19:8:2 (790,380) Hachured OD 100–200 23310, 30805
Rath (site) An earlier report (OPW 1968) described a slightly raised circular area (int. dims. 54m WNW–ESE; 52m NNE–SSW) enclosed by a much-disturbed low earthen bank and slight traces of a fosse. Original entrance may have been at S. Known as 'The Fort Field'. The outline of the site may still be traced.
19:29 14-7-1990

690 ERRIGAL
OS 17:10:3 (450,250) Hachured OD 300–400 26116, 30893
Rath Raised circular area (int. diam. *c.* 32m) enclosed by a substantial earthen bank and a wide, deep, waterlogged fosse. At the external foot of the fosse is a counterscarp bank with external trench, both of which are probably relatively modern features. Original entrance at SSE. Densely overgrown with vegetation.
17:41 22-11-1990

691 FARNHAM
OS 20:11:1 (472,241) Hachured OD 300–400 23951, 30664
Rath Raised circular area (int. dims. 59m NNW–SSE; 52m ENE–WSW) enclosed by a substantial bank of earth and stone and a wide, deep fosse which has been largely infilled from SW–N–NNE. Well-defined break in bank at NNW probably represents original entrance. The internal area has been planted with deciduous trees.
20:45 31-8-1990

692 FARRANGARVE
OS 30:2:5 (356,519) Indicated OD 300–400 22865, 29666
Rath An earlier report (OPW 1974) described an almost circular raised area (int. diam. *c.* 50m) enclosed by a substantial earthen bank and slight traces of a

fosse. Original entrance position was not identifiable. Site has been levelled. Not visible at ground level.
30:19 3-10-1991

693 FARRANGARVE
OS 30:2:2 (357,569) Hachured OD 300–400
22865, 29720
Rath An earlier report (OPW 1974) described an almost circular raised area (int. diam. *c.* 42m) enclosed by a low earthen embankment. Original entrance position was not identifiable. The field in which the site is located has been planted with coniferous trees. Not visible at ground level.
30:20 3-10-1991

694 FARRANSEER
OS 24:12:3 (874,286) Hachured OD 200–300
23406, 30067
Rath Raised circular area (int. dims. 35.4m NNE–SSW; *c.* 33m WNW–ESE) enclosed by an earthen bank and slight traces of a fosse. Perimeter only identifiable from NE–ESE. From ESE–SSW it has been extensively modified and incorporated into the field boundary. Original entrance not recognisable.
24:51 22-8-1991

695 FARTAGH (Castlerahan By.)
OS 44:5:3 (211,396) Hachured OD 400–500
26624, 28292
Rath Raised circular area (int. diam. *c.* 38m) enclosed by a substantial earthen bank which is considerably denuded at E and a wide, shallow, partly waterlogged fosse. Original entrance not recognisable.
44:13 20-8-1987

696 FINAWAY
OS 38:7:4 (481,359) Hachured OD 300–400
24953, 28877
Rath Raised circular area (int. diam. 35m) enclosed by a substantial earthen bank and vague traces of a fosse identifiable only at SE. From S–W and from N–E there are modern trenches at the external foot of the bank. An earlier description (OPW 1970) suggested that the original entrance may have been at SE.
38:25 14-8-1986

697 FORTHILL
OS 30:2:6 (426,469) Hachured OD 463
22939, 29614
Rath Raised circular area (int. diam. 46.2m) enclosed by a massive earthen bank and a wide, deep, partly waterlogged fosse. Break in bank with accompanying causeway at SE represents original entrance. Small circular platform to NW of centre of interior may represent a house site.
30:21 8-10-1991

698 FORTLAND
OS 38:9:1 (6,288) Hachured OD 389
24452, 28798
Rath Large raised circular area (int. diam. 71m) enclosed by a low earthen bank and a fosse which is identifiable from W–N–E. Original entrance not recognisable. Situated within a former tree plantation. Site is not marked on OS 1836 and 1876 eds.
38:26 6-8-1986

699 FORTLAND
OS 38:9:1 (50,253) Hachured OD 300–400
24499, 28762
Rath Raised circular area (int. diam. 33m) enclosed by two earthen banks with wide, deep intermediate fosse. A modern field boundary merges with the outer face of the counterscarp bank at SE. Breaks in banks with accompanying causeway at SE represents original entrance. (CUCAP ALJ 74)
38:27 6-8-1986

700 FORTLAND
OS 38:9:2 (86,240) Hachured OD 300–400
24537, 28748
Rath Raised circular area (int. diam. *c.* 68m) enclosed by a low earthen bank which is no longer identifiable from NE–SE. Original entrance not recognisable. The rath has been planted with trees.
38:28 6-8-1986

701 FORTLAND
OS 38:9:5 (103,225) Hachured OD 300–400
24555, 28732
Rath Raised circular area (int. diam. 38m) enclosed by a substantial earthen bank and a wide, deep fosse. Break in bank at N may represent original entrance. (CUCAP ALJ 77)
38:29 6-8-1986

702 FORTLAND
OS 38:9:5 (130,172) Hachured OD 200–300
24584, 28676
Rath Raised circular area (int. diam. *c.* 41m) enclosed by a very low earthen bank and a wide, shallow fosse outside of which is an apparently modern low counterscarp bank. An earlier report (OPW 1970) suggested that the original entrance may have been at ENE. (CUCAP ALJ 73)
38:31 6-8-1986

703 FURNACELAND
OS 7:10:3 (423,267) Hachured OD 200–300
21931, 32594
Rath Raised circular area (int. diam. *c.* 26m) enclosed by a slight external earthen bank with a deep internal waterlogged fosse. Inside the bank at N and running

parallel to it is a short segment of earthen bank - possibly the remains of a hut site. Break in bank at NE may represent original entrance. Site is overgrown with vegetation.
7:14 21-9-1988

704 GALBOLIE
OS 34:1:5 (150,526) Hachured OD 500–600
26546, 29709
Rath Raised circular area (int. diam. *c.* 36m) enclosed by a much-denuded low earthen bank. A modern field drain skirts the external foot of the bank from N–ESE. Original entrance not recognisable.
34:26 25-3-1974

705 GALLON GLEBE
OS 26:12:2 (801,264) Hachured OD 500–600
25280, 30061
Rath Raised roughly oval area (int. dims. 44.5m N–S; 39.6m E–W) enclosed by a substantial earthen bank and a fosse, slight traces of which are visible at NE and which has been replaced by a modern trench from ENE–SSE. Break in bank at SSE represents original entrance.
26:35 25-10-1991

706 GALLONNAMBRAHER
OS 39:1:5 (81,506) Indicated OD 500–600
25505, 29039
Rath Indicated as a tree plantation on all OS eds. Raised circular area (int. diam. *c.* 31m) enclosed by a much-disturbed but well-defined low earthen bank. Original entrance not recognisable.
39:53 12-9-1969

707 GALLONNAMBRAHER
OS 39:1:2 (104,555) Hachured OD 500–600
25528, 29090
Rath Raised circular area (int. diam. *c.* 37m) enclosed by a substantial earthen bank and a fosse identifiable from SE–W–NE, outside of which is a slight counterscarp bank identifiable from NNW–NE and at SW. Modern farm buildings encroach on the site at E and the fosse has been infilled here as a consequence. An earlier report (OPW 1969) suggested that a break in bank with accompanying causeway at SE represented original entrance.
39:54 12-9-1986

708 GALLONREAGH (Clankee By.)
OS 23:1:5 (86,486) Hachured OD 438
26467, 30946
Rath Roughly circular raised area (int. diam. 27.1m) enclosed by a substantial earthen bank and a wide, shallow, partly waterlogged fosse. Break in bank at E with accompanying causeway represents original entrance. Within the interior are possible traces of a souterrain (**1240**).
23:20(01) 22-4-1992

709 GARRYMORE
OS 25:14:4 (299,36) Hachured OD 200–300
23777, 29807
Rath Raised circular area (int. dims. 40.9m E–W; 40.3m N–S) enclosed by two substantial earthen banks with outer fosses. Outer bank and intermediate fosse have been ploughed out from SE–WSW but their outline is still clearly identifiable. Large break in inner bank at S may represent original entrance, but there is no accompanying causeway.
25:57 10-9-1991

710 GARRYMORE
OS 31:2:5 (316,528) Indicated OD 300–400
23796, 29686
Rath Marked 'Fort' on OS 1836 and 1876 eds. Raised circular area (int. diam. *c.* 31.5m) enclosed by an earthern bank and a fosse identifiable only from S–WSW. Perimeter has been removed from NE–SSE and replaced by a modern roadway. Original entrance not recognisable.
31:38 28-3-1977

711 GARRYMORE
OS 31:2:3 (392,543) Hachured OD 300–400
23876, 29702
Rath Raised circular area (int. diam. 34.6m) enclosed by a substantial earthen bank and a fosse. Slight suggestions of a second bank at the outer lip of the fosse from NW–N–ENE and from SE–SSW. From SW–NW the perimeter and portion of the internal area has been levelled and replaced by a modern laneway running N–S. Immediately W of this is a modern dwelling. From ENE–SE the perimeter has been modified and incorporated into the field boundary. Original entrance not recognisable.
31:39 6-6-1992

712 GARRYMORE
OS 31:2:6 (415,496) Hachured OD 300–400
23900, 29653
Rath Raised subcircular area (int. dims. 43.6m E–W; 47.1m NNW–SSE) enclosed by the remains of a substantial earthen bank and a wide, deep fosse. Perimeter has been levelled from E–SE–S. There are a number of breaks in the bank, some with accompanying causeways. However all of these are apparently modern. Original entrance not recognisable.
31:40 5-6-1992

713 GARRYSALLAGH (O'Reilly)
OS 38:14:5 (379,67) Hachured OD 200–300
24848, 28569

Fig. 20—*Rath at Gallon Glebe* (**705**).

Rath Raised circular area (int. diam. *c*. 75m) enclosed by a much-denuded low earthen bank and a narrow, shallow fosse. Short segment of low counterscarp bank at SW. Fosse has been largely infilled from WSW–N–SE. An earlier report (OPW 1970) suggested that the original entrance may have been at SE.
38:35 2-9-1986

714 GARRYSALLAGH (O'Reilly)
OS 38:14:6 (422,31) Hachured OD 200–300
24894, 28531
Rath Raised circular area (int. diam. 38m) enclosed by a much-denuded low earthen bank and traces of a shallow fosse. An earlier report (OPW 1970) suggested that the original entrance may have been at W.
38:36 2-9-1986

715 GARRYSALLAGH (O'Reilly)
OS 42:2:3 (415,598) Hachured OD 200–300
24886, 28490
Rath Raised circular area (int. diam. *c*. 29m) enclosed by three earthen banks with wide intermediate fosses. Outer bank best preserved from NNW–N–ENE. The outer fosse is shallow; the inner much deeper. Break in bank with accompanying causeway at E represents original entrance. An earlier report (OPW 1970) noted the foundations of a small stone rectangular structure (int. dims. 7.6m E–W; 6.9m N–S) - possibly a hut site, projecting from the inner face of the inner bank at N.
42:26 3-9-1986

716 GARTINARDRESS
OS 24:8:2 (843,408) Hachured OD 300–400
23372, 30196
Rath Raised circular area (int. dims. 42m N–S; 40.2m E–W) enclosed by a substantial earthen bank and a deep, well-defined fosse replaced by a roadway from SSW–SE. A blocked-up break in the bank at SSE probably represents original entrance. The interior has been planted with coniferous trees.
24:54 22-8-1991

717 GARTINARDRESS
OS 24:8:3 (863,437) Indicated OD 200–300
23393, 30226
Rath Marked on the OS 1836 and 1876 eds. as a tree-

covered enclosure. Remains comprise an oval-shaped raised area (int. dims. 47m N–S; 21.6m E–W) enclosed by a low earthen bank and a shallow fosse. Break in bank accompanied by fragmentary traces of a causeway at N probably represents original entrance.
24:55 22-8-1991

718 GARTYLOUGH
OS 24:14:2 (347,101) Hachured OD 300–400
22851, 29866
Rath Raised circular area (int. diam. 23.8m) enclosed by a slight but well-defined earthen bank and a fosse which is largely infilled with the exception of the N portion. Original entrance not recognisable.
24:56 14-8-1991

719 GARVALT LOWER
OS 6:5:4 (63,356) Hachured OD 400–500
20575, 32675
Rath Raised circular area (int. diam. 22.9m) enclosed by a slight earthen bank and the remains of a fosse. Original entrance not recognisable. Situated in rough mountainous terrain close to the summit of a low hill.
6:10 22-8-1988

720 GLASCARRICK
OS 37:2:4 (271,466) Hachured OD 300–400
23755, 28980
Rath Raised circular area (int. diam. *c.* 34m) enclosed by a substantial earthen bank and some suggestion of a fosse. An earlier report (OPW 1970) proposed that the original entrance may have been at SE.
37:30 9-7-1986

721 GLASDRUMMAN (Tullygarvey By.)
OS 16:5:2 (96,433) Not marked OD 499
24523, 31512
Rath Raised circular area (int. diam. 28.6m) enclosed by an earthen bank and a wide, shallow fosse, best preserved at N and much disturbed by field walls elsewhere. Break in bank with remains of causeway at NE may represent original entrance.
16:63 27-9-1989

Fig. 21—*An impressive trivallate rath at Garrysallagh (O' Reilly)* (**715**).

722 GLASDRUMMAN (Upper Loughtee By.)
OS 26:12:2 (796,232) Hachured OD 400–500
25275, 30027

Rath Marked 'Lisdrummin' on the OS Fair Plan and 'Glassdrumman' on the OS 1836 and 1876 eds. Raised circular area (int. diam. *c.* 25m) enclosed by two earthen banks with intermediate fosse. Outer bank has been modified and incorporated into the field boundary from S–W–N. Elsewhere it has been levelled but its outline may still be traced in places. Fosse survives best from NE–SSE where it is deep and waterlogged. From N–NE it has been replaced by a modern drainage trench. Original entrance not recognisable.
26:36 27-3-1992

723 GLASLECK
OS 28:3:6 (687,498) Hachured OD 400–500
27108, 30325

Rath Raised subcircular area (int. dims. 28m E–W; 31m N–S) enclosed by a low earthen bank. No surviving indication of an external fosse. From NW–N–ENE the perimeter has been incorporated into the field boundary. Original entrance not recognisable. At the centre of the internal area and in the W quadrant the ground level is much disturbed as a consequence of digging. (Ó Ríordáin, Prendergast and Rynne 1962, 156) recorded the upper stone of a quern which was discovered at the site.
28:24 29-3-1974

724 GLASLECK
OS 28:4:4 (752,486) Hachured OD 400–500
27176, 30312

Rath Raised circular area (int. diam. 29m) enclosed by a low bank of earth and stone and the remains of a wide, shallow fosse. Original entrance at E. Two large stones, set on edge, project from the inner face of the bank at E.
28:25 29-3-1974

725 GLASLECK
OS 28:8:2 (792,429) Hachured OD 500
27219, 30253

Rath Raised circular area (int. diam. 27m) enclosed by a low earthen bank and the remains of a narrow fosse from W–S–SE. At NW the curve of the bank has been straightened and drystone walling applied to its outer face. From NE–E–SE the perimeter has been levelled and modern buildings occupy the site. Bank has also been levelled from N–NW. Laneway cuts through perimeter at W and runs through the interior to SE. Internal area has been planted with trees.
28:26 29-3-1974

726 GLENCORRAN
OS 26:2:1 (238,582) Hachured OD 500–600
24683, 30391

Rath Raised circular area (int. diam. 28.1m) enclosed by a substantial earthen bank. An earlier report (OPW 1970) recorded that there was formerly an outer fosse and external bank both of which have been levelled. Wide break in bank accompanied by very slight traces of a causeway at NNE represents original entrance.
26:38 25-10-1991

727 GNEEVE
OS 42:10:6 (435,215) Hachured OD 200–300
24912, 28085

Rath Raised circular area (int. diam. *c.* 62m) enclosed by a wide, low bank from WSW–N. From N–E the site is bounded by a tributary of the Upper Inny River and has been much defaced as a consequence of river drainage works. From E–S–WSW the perimeter has been levelled but its outline is still identifiable. Original entrance not recognisable. Internal area is divided into two unequal portions by a field boundary running ESE–WSW.
42:27 19-6-1974

728 GORTAQUILL
OS 1:12:6 (878,217) Hachured OD 300–400
20450, 33808

Rath Not marked on OS 1836 or 1876 eds. Raised circular area (int. diam. *c.* 28m) enclosed by a substantial earthen bank and slight traces of a fosse. From SW–W–NW the perimeter has been incorporated into the field boundary and is skirted by a modern roadway. Break in bank at SE may represent original entrance.
1:4 3-7-1988

729 GORTEEN OR GORTEENATERRIFF
OS 30:3:5 (601,512) Hachured OD 571
23124, 29660

Rath Raised circular area (int. diam. 28.3m) enclosed by a very substantial earthen bank and a deep, partly waterlogged fosse. Break in bank with accompanying causeway at S represents original entrance.
30:22 4-10-1991

730 GORTEEN OR GORTEENATERRIFF
OS 30:3:5 (606,456) Hachured OD 400
23130, 29602

Rath Raised circular area (int. diam. 32.7m) enclosed by a very substantial earthen bank and a wide, deep fosse best preserved from SE–W–N and infilled elsewhere. Break in bank at SE represents original entrance.
30:23 3-10-1991

731 GORTIN
OS 22:1:2 (151,606) Hachured OD 300–400
25560, 31064

Rath Raised circular area (int. diam. 27.1m) enclosed by a substantial earthen bank best preserved from N–E–SSW and denuded elsewhere, and a wide, partly waterlogged fosse which is deep from S–WNW and otherwise quite shallow. A modern laneway running NNW–SSE divides the rath into two approximately equal portions. Partly blocked break in bank at N may represent original entrance.
22:26 21-10-1990

732 GORTMORE
OS 9:2:3 (450,591) Hachured OD 300–400
21963, 32296
Rath Raised circular area (int. diam. 28.3m) enclosed by a low earthen bank and an infilled fosse, the outline of which is still identifiable. Break in bank at W represents original entrance.
9:10 21-9-1990

733 GORTNACLEIGH
OS 14:16:4 (758,15) Hachured OD 200–300
23274, 31060
Rath Raised circular area (int. dims. 31.2m) enclosed by a substantial earthen bank and a fosse. An earlier report (OPW 1969) recorded slight traces of an external bank at NW, ESE and SE. Break in bank with accompanying causeway at NE probably represents original entrance.
14:37 11-8-1989

734 GORTNAKESH
OS 25:4:5 (774,509) Indicated OD 300–400
24274, 30310
Rath Raised circular area (int. dims. 30.5m ENE–WSW; 28.5m NNW–SSE) enclosed by traces of a substantial earthen bank and a wide, shallow fosse. In the NW quadrant the bank does not rise above the internal area. Original entrance not recognisable. Internal area slopes fairly steeply to NW and NNE.
25:58 13-9-1991

735 GORTNAKILLEW
OS 26:9:4 (30,174) Hachured OD 500–600
24467, 29958
Rath Raised circular area (int. diam. 35.2m) enclosed by a substantial earthen bank and a wide, deep, waterlogged fosse. Wide break in bank with vague traces of accompanying causeway at E may represent original entrance. Possible souterrain within internal area (**1241**).
26:39(01) 20-3-1992

736 GORTNAKILLEW
OS 26:9:4 (52,157) Hachured OD 400–500
24490, 29941
Rath Raised circular area (int. diam. 35.1m) formerly enclosed by an earthen bank and a fosse (OPW 1977). The enclosing features have been levelled. Original entrance not recognisable.
26:40 20-3-1992

737 GORTNALECK
OS 13:8:1 (695,434) Hachured OD 200–300
22229, 31493
Rath Raised circular area (int. diam. 30.6m) enclosed by a substantial earthen bank and a wide, shallow fosse. Break in bank at SE with accompanying causeway represents original entrance. A small portion of the site at WSW has been levelled as a result of the construction of a modern roadway and garden.
13:23 8-6-1989

738 GORTSKEAGH
OS 16:14:6 (424,60) Hachured OD 200–300
24872, 31122
Rath Raised circular area (int. diam. *c.* 26m) enclosed by three earthen banks with intermediate fosses. Outer bank identifiable only for a short stretch on either side of the entrance feature at S. It is accompanied by a berm on its external face. The intermediate bank has been levelled from SE–N–NE and elsewhere incorporated into the field boundary. Outer fosse not identifiable from NE–E–SE. Corresponding breaks in the banks with accompanying causeways at S represents original entrance. Densely overgrown with vegetation.
16:65 19-10-1989

739 GORTSKEAGH
OS 21:3:1 (463,582) Hachured OD 300–400
24914, 31033
Rath Raised circular area (int. dims. 35m N–S; 35.5m E–W) enclosed by a wide, low earthen bank and a fosse which survives only from S–W–N. Bank has been modified and incorporated into the field boundary except from NE–SE where it has been considerably denuded. Original entrance not recognisable.
21:40 15-9-1990

740 GREAGHADOO
OS 33:7:1 (528,444) Hachured OD 500–600
25971, 29617
Rath Raised circular area (int. diam. 32m) enclosed by a substantial earthen bank and a deep fosse partly infilled with field-clearance debris. Break in bank at S probably represents original entrance. Internal area overgrown with trees and bushes.
33:32 16-9-1988

741 GREAGHADOO
OS 33:7:2 (551,402) Not marked OD 400–500
25996, 29573

Fig. 22—*Rath at Gortnakesh* (**734**).

Rath Marked 'Fort' on OS 1836 and 1876 eds. Situated on W shoulder of an area of high ground. A circular area (diam. *c*. 26m) enclosed by the remains of a substantial earthen bank and a narrow, deep, partly waterlogged fosse from SW–W–N, both of which have been modified and incorporated into the field boundary.
33:33 16-9-1988

742 GREAGHADOSSAN
OS 33:7:3 (635,444) Hachured OD 400–500
26084, 29618
Rath Raised circular area (int. diam. *c*. 25m) enclosed by a low earthen bank and a shallow fosse. From NW–N the perimeter is incorporated into the field boundary. Narrow break in bank at E probably represents original entrance.
33:35 2-4-1974

743 GREAGHARUE
OS 34:6:5 (362,356) Hachured OD 500–600
26772, 29532
Rath Raised circular area (int. diam. *c*. 28m) enclosed by an irregular, wide, low earthen bank from SW–N–NE. At the remainder of the site the bank has been incorporated into the field boundary and from SE–S–SW a field drain runs outside of it. Outline of small rectangular house site close to the centre of the internal area.
34:27 22-3-1974

744 GREAGHDUFF
OS 33:8:6 (882,363) Hachured OD 400–500
26345, 29535
Rath Raised circular area (int. diam. *c*. 34m) enclosed by a low earthen bank and slight indications of a fosse, identifiable only from SW–NW. Modern laneway cuts along the bottom of the embankment from NW–ENE. Original entrance not recognisable.
33:36 5-4-1974

745 GREAGHNACUNNIA
OS 33:7:6 (640,330) Not marked OD 400–500
26090, 29497
Rath Raised circular area (int. diam. *c*. 28m) enclosed by a low earthen bank and slight traces of a fosse

identifiable only from WSW–SSW. Deserted farmyard abuts the site from E–S–W and the bank is levelled here as a result. Original entrance not recognisable. Internal area now occupied by a silage pit.
33:37 21-9-1988

746 GREAGHNAMALE
OS 34:10:3 (406,239) Hachured OD 400–500
26820, 29408
Rath Raised circular area (int. diam. *c.* 24m) enclosed by an irregular earthen bank which survives only as a low scarp from SSE–W–NW, and traces of a shallow fosse identifiable from SE–W–NE.
34:30 21-3-1974

747 ISLAND
OS 43:11:6 (673,221) Hachured OD 300–400
26138, 28103
Rath Raised circular area (int. diam. *c.* 37m) enclosed by a substantial earthen bank and traces of a fosse. Break in bank at SE may represent original entrance.
43:14 18-6-1987

748 KEADEW (Cavan Rural And Urban)
OS 20:12:4 (706,209) Hachured OD 300–400
24199, 30633
Rath Raised roughly circular area (int. dims. 32m NNE–SSW; 28.5m WNW–ESE) enclosed by a substantial earthen bank and a wide, shallow, partly waterlogged fosse. From W–N–NE fosse has been adapted for use as a field drain in modern times. Break in bank at N with partly destroyed accompanying causeway may represent original entrance.
20:51 22-8-1990

749 KEADEW (ED Clonervy)
OS 21:1:2 (139,543) Hachured OD 300–400
24573, 30989
Rath Raised circular area (int. diam. 31.1m) enclosed by two substantial earthen banks with wide, deep, waterlogged outer fosses encircled by a relatively modern field bank. Break in inner bank at ESE with accompanying causeway across inner fosse represents original entrance. Outer fosse infilled.
21:41 17-9-1990

750 KEELAGH (Tullygarvey By.)
OS 16:9:3 (219,298) Hachured OD 400
24653, 31371
Rath Raised circular area (int. diam. *c.* 22m) enclosed by a low earthen bank best preserved from W–N–NNE and the remains of a fosse identifiable only from S–W–NW. Original entrance not recognisable. Immediately S of centre is an irregularly shaped shallow depression of unknown significance.
16:66 19-10-1989

751 KEELDERRY
OS 31:15:3 (628,94) Hachured OD 300–400
24130, 29231
Rath Raised circular area (int. diam. *c.* 42m) enclosed by a low earthen bank. From ENE–S–WNW bank has been incorporated into the field boundary and is accompanied by a modern external drain. Deep watering-hole at the outer foot of the scarp at WNW. Original entrance not recognisable.
31:41 13-11-1970

752 KEENAGH (Castlerahan By.)
OS 38:7:1 (504,416) Hachured OD 200–300
24977, 28938
Rath Raised circular area (int. diam. 41m) enclosed by a much-denuded low earthen bank and traces of a shallow fosse identifiable from NW–NNE. Modern trenches skirt the outer lip of fosse from NE–SE and S–W. An earlier report (OPW 1970) suggested that the original entrance may have been at S.
38:37 15-8-1986

753 KEENAGH (Tullyhaw By.)
OS 9:16:5 (785,40) Hachured OD 300–400
22321, 31717
Rath Raised circular area (int. diam. *c.* 47m) enclosed by two substantial earthen banks with intervening wide, deep fosse. Densely overgrown with vegetation rendering inspection impossible.
9:12 12-9-1988

754 KEILAGH
OS 14:14:6 (449,1) Hachured OD 200–300
22949, 31042
Rath Raised oval area (int. dims. 37m NNE–SSW; 32m WNW–ESE) enclosed by two earthen banks with outer fosses. The inner bank and fosse have been largely levelled as have the outer bank and fosse from N–E–SSW. Original entrance was probably at S.
14:38/19:38* 14-11-1969

755 KEVIT LOWER
OS 25:10:2 (321,283) Indicated OD 200–300
23797, 30067
Rath Marked 'Fort' on OS 1836 and 1876 eds. Raised oval area (int. dims. 35.4m N–S; 30.2m E–W) enclosed by a low earthen bank and traces of a fosse identifiable only from NW–NE. Break in bank at S may represent original entrance. Davies (ITA Survey 1942) believed it to be more likely a landscape feature than a rath.
25:60 6-9-1991

756 KEVIT LOWER
OS 25:10:5 (355,213) Hachured OD 200–300
23834, 29993

Fig. 23—*Rath at Kevit Lower* (**756**).

Rath Large raised circular area (int. dims. 56m NNW–SSE; 54m ENE–WSW) enclosed by a substantial earthen bank and a fosse which is absent from SSE–S–NW. Break in bank at S may represent original entrance. E of this gap, bank does not rise above the internal area.
25:61 6-9-1991

757 KEVIT LOWER
OS 25:10:2 (360,260) Hachured OD 300–400
23839, 30044
Rath An almost circular raised area (int. dims. 42m E–W; 37m N–S) enclosed by a substantial earthen bank and a fosse which is exceptionally wide and deep at E. Break in bank at S with accompanying causeway probably represents original entrance. Davies (ITA Survey 1942) notes that 'there is said to be a souterrain in this fort' (**1243**).
25:62(01) 6-9-1991

758 KEVIT UPPER OR CASTLECOSBY
OS 25:10:2 (362,294) Hachured OD 300–400
23840, 30079
Rath (site) A largely ploughed-out, slightly raised circular area (int. dims. 44.6m N–S; 42.5m E–W) enclosed by the remains of an earthen bank and a fosse which is identifiable only at NE. Original entrance may have been at SSE.
25:64 6-9-1991

759 KEVIT UPPER OR CASTLECOSBY
OS 25:10:2 (361,277) Hachured OD 300–400
23840, 30062
Rath Raised circular area (int. dims. 45m NNE–SSW; 44.5m WNW–ESE) enclosed by a substantial earthen bank and a wide, deep fosse. Large break in the bank with accompanying causeway at ESE probably represents original entrance. Interior slopes quite steeply to SE.
25:65 6-9-1991

760 KEVIT UPPER OR CASTLECOSBY
OS 25:10:2 (374,301) Hachured OD 300–400
23853, 30087
Rath (site) This rath has been ploughed out but its outline is clearly visible. It comprises a slightly raised

circular area (int. diam. 34m) enclosed by an earthen bank and a fosse. From W–SSW the perimeter has been destroyed by a long, narrow bank with a trench on either side planted with trees. Original entrance not recognisable.
25:66 6-9-1991

761 KILCLOGHA
OS 23:1:1 (53,541) Hachured OD 300–400
26433, 31004
Rath Raised circular area (int. diam. 26m) enclosed by traces of a substantial earthen bank and a fosse identifiable only from NNW–NNE and at SSE. Break in bank with accompanying causeway across the fosse at S probably represents original entrance. Internal area densely overgrown with vegetation.
23:21 27-5-1992

762 KILCOGY
OS 37:10:1 (285,246) Hachured OD 300–400
23772, 28747
Rath A much-disturbed raised circular area (int. diam. 33m) enclosed by two low earthen banks with intermediate fosse. Outer bank identifiable only from W–NW–N. No remains of fosse or inner bank at S. An earlier report (OPW 1970) recorded that the original entrance was at WNW.
37:35 8-7-1986

763 KILDUFF MIDDLE
OS 5:16:1 (708,397) Not marked OD 200–300
20288, 31877
Rath Slightly raised circular area (int. diam. 31.2m) enclosed by a low scarp and a shallow fosse. The perimeter has been incorporated into the field boundary. Original entrance not recognisable.
5:36 21-8-1988

764 KILL
OS 31:16:4 (747,57) Hachured OD 300–400
24255, 29193
Rath Marked 'Fort' on OS 1836 and 1876 eds. The only surface remains comprise a low earthen bank extending in an arc from NE–S–W. From E–S–W, bank has been modified and incorporated into the field boundary. Original entrance not recognisable.
31:42 28-3-1977

765 KILL
OS 37:4:5 (781,514) Hachured OD 300–400
24293, 29035
Rath Raised circular area (int. diam. *c.* 48m) enclosed by a low earthen bank and a deep, partly waterlogged fosse. An earlier report (OPW 1970) noted a slight counterscarp bank at the outer lip of the fosse from ESE–S. Outer face of bank has been modified and fosse is poorly preserved from S–W–NNE. Original entrance may be at S.
37:33 15-7-1986

766 KILLAGHADUFF
OS 7:11:1 (468,231) Hachured OD 300
21979, 32556
Rath Davies (ITA Survey 1946) described it as a roughly circular area (int. dims. 21m N–S; 19m E–W) enclosed by a slight earthen bank and a poorly preserved fosse. Possible hut site within enclosed area at N. Bordered by a field boundary from W–NNW, and by a graveyard from NNW–N–NNE. Although largely levelled, outline of rath may still be traced.
7:16 12-8-1974

767 KILLALISS
OS 23:14:1 (258,142) Hachured OD 500–600
26653, 30584
Rath Raised circular area (int. diam. 35.8m) enclosed by a very substantial earthen bank faced with apparently modern drystone walling from NW–NE, and a wide, deep, waterlogged fosse which has been largely levelled from SW–NW. A relatively modern bank runs outside the fosse from NNE–SE. Break in bank with accompanying causeway at SE represents original entrance.
23:24 9-4-1992

768 KILLATEE
OS 22:4:6 (854,498) Hachured OD 300–400
26303, 30957
Rath Raised circular area (int. diam. *c.* 41m) enclosed by two substantial earthen banks with intermediate wide, deep, partly waterlogged fosse. Break in inner bank with accompanying causeway at NE represents original entrance. From NE–SE the perimeter and much of the internal area have been greatly disturbed by modern quarrying.
22:27 27-10-1990

769 KILLETER
OS 40:10:2 (357,266) Hachured OD 400–500
26773, 28796
Rath Raised circular area (int. diam. *c.* 32m) enclosed by a substantial, although partly denuded, earthen bank identifiable from S–N–E. It has a modern facing of drystone masonry. Modern buildings abut the site from E–SE–S. Original entrance not recognisable.
40:31 13-7-1987

770 KILLYCANNAN
OS 25:11:3 (660,274) Hachured OD 300–400
24156, 30061
Rath Raised oval area (int. dims. 53m N–S; 41m E–W) enclosed by traces of an earthen bank. A field boundary running NNW–SSE divides the internal area

into two roughly equal portions. Although the portion of the site E of this has been levelled, the perimeter can still be clearly traced. In recent times drystone walling has been applied to the outer face of the embankment from S–SW. There are modern trenches outside of bank from SSE–S and from NW–N. Original entrance not recognisable.
25:67 1-10-1991

771 KILLYCARNEY
OS 1:16:3 (881,98)ʃ Hachured OD 200–300
20454, 33682
Rath Raised circular area (int. diam. *c.* 30m) enclosed by a substantial bank of earth and stone. Break in bank at ENE probably represents original entrance. A modern field boundary running WNW–ESE divides the site into two unequal portions.
1:5 2-7-1988

772 KILLYCARNEY
OS 2:9:4 (50,163) Hachured OD 100–200
20552, 33752
Rath Not marked on OS 1836 or 1876 eds. Raised circular area (int. diam. *c.* 28m) enclosed by traces of a very low bank of earth and stone. From NW–NE the perimeter was destroyed as a result of the construction of the Sligo-Enniskillen railway which has long fallen into disuse and has been replaced by a modern roadway at this location. Original entrance not recognisable.
2:7 19-8-1974

773 KILLYCATRON
OS 30:16:3 (885,95) Indicated OD 200–300
23426, 29222
Rath Depicted as a tree-covered enclosure on OS 1836 and 1876 eds. Raised oval area (int. dims. 49.8m NW–SE; 24.1m NE–SW) enclosed by a substantial earthen bank, the outer face of which has been recently scarped, and slight suggestions of a fosse. A small stone structure formerly situated within the interior and at which burnt bones were discovered (local information), has since been levelled.
30:24 10-10-1991

774 KILLYCLUGGIN
OS 13:4:6 (878,506) Not marked OD 200–300
22422, 31570
Rath Not marked on any OS ed. Raised oval area (int. dims. 35m E–W; 29.2m N–S) divided into two roughly equal portions by the now disused Cavan-Leitrim railway. The portion WNW of this is enclosed by a low much-disturbed bank of earth and stone. Projecting into the internal area from the inner face of the bank at WNW are possible remains of a souterrain (**1244**). The portion ESE of the railway has been largely levelled but its outline is readily identifiable. Original entrance not recognisable.
13:27(01) 4-11-1969

775 KILLYCLUGGIN
OS 13:4:3 (884,554) Hachured OD 300–400
22427, 31621
Rath Raised oval area (int. dims. *c.* 56m NNE–SSW; *c.* 40m WNW–ESE) enclosed by two substantial earthen banks with wide, deep, partly waterlogged intermediate fosse. From E–S–SW the external bank has been modified and incorporated into the field boundary. From NNW–N–NE the inner bank has been removed and replaced by a modern field boundary. An earlier report (OPW 1969) suggested that the original entrance may have been at WSW. Densely overgrown with vegetation.
13:28 22-6-1989

776 KILLYCONNAN
OS 26:2:4 (255,506) Hachured OD 500
24701, 30311
Rath Raised circular area (int. diam. *c.* 38m) enclosed by a substantial earthen bank and a deep, partly waterlogged fosse. Original entrance not recognisable. Densely overgrown with vegetation.
26:41 19-3-1992

777 KILLYCREENY
OS 17:9:3 (169,268) Hachured OD 200–300
25837, 31183
Rath (site) Situated on the NW shoulder of a drumlin hill close to a stream. An earlier report (OPW 1969) described a raised circular area enclosed by a partially surviving bank and fosse. Original entrance may have been at NW. Not visible at ground level.
17:45 27-9-1990

778 KILLYCRONE
OS 21:15:6 (664,58) Hachured OD 300–400
25132, 30483
Rath Raised almost circular area (int. diam. *c.* 21.3m) enclosed by an earthen bank which is quite substantial from SSE–SSW, but denuded elsewhere, and a fosse infilled from SE–W–N and replaced by a modern trench from N–E–SSE. Break in bank at NNW probably represents original entrance.
21:42 21-9-1990

779 KILLYDOON
OS 31:13:6 (173,17) Hachured OD 200–300
23649, 29145
Rath (site) An earlier report (OPW 1974) described a raised circular area (int. diam. *c.* 38m) enclosed by a low earthen bank. Original entrance was not identified. Site has been levelled. Not visible at ground level.
31:44 10-6-1992

780 KILLYDOON
OS 31:13:6 (208,42) Hachured OD 300–400 23687, 29172
Rath Raised circular area (int. diam. 27.9m) enclosed by a much-defaced low earthen bank. Modern roadway runs ENE–WSW through the internal area. Original entrance not recognisable.
31:45 9-6-1992

781 KILLYFASSY
OS 38:9:6 (207,226) Hachured OD 300–400 24665, 28734
Rath (site) Levelled in the 1960s (local information). Situated on the summit of a drumlin ridge. An earlier report (OPW 1963) described the site as a circular platform (diam. 36.5m) enclosed by an earthen bank and fosse. Original entrance was not recognisable. Not visible at ground level.
38:38 12-8-1986

782 KILLYFASSY
OS 38:10:4 (288,177) Hachured OD 300 24751, 28684
Rath Raised circular area (int. diam. *c.* 40m) enclosed by a low earthen bank. The NE half of the site has been destroyed as a result of quarrying. Original entrance not recognisable. Densely overgrown with vegetation.
38:39 12-8-1986

783 KILLYKEEN (ED Ballymachugh)
OS 37:7:5 (556,328) Hachured OD 300–400 24057, 28837
Rath (site) Levelled in the early 1980s (local information). An earlier report (OPW 1970) described a raised circular area (int. diam. *c.* 40m) enclosed by a low earthen bank. Original entrance was not recognisable. Not visible at ground level.
37:38 11-7-1986

784 KILLYMORIARTY
OS 13:7:2 (593,415) Hachured OD 200–300 22122, 31471
Rath Raised oval area (int. dims. 46.2m NNW–SSE; 36.7m ENE–WSW) enclosed by a low earthen bank which has been modified and incorporated into the field boundary. It has been levelled for a stretch at E but its outline is still identifiable. Original entrance not recognisable.
13:29 12-6-1989

785 KILLYMULLIN
OS 16:15:2 (602,76) Hachured OD 200–300 25060, 31140
Rath Raised circular area (int. diam. *c.* 23m) enclosed by a low earthen bank and a wide, deep, partly waterlogged fosse infilled from NE–E. Break in bank with remains of accompanying causeway at E represents original entrance. Densely overgrown with vegetation.
16:70 4-11-1989

786 KILLYMULLIN
OS 16:11:6 (638,154) Hachured OD 200–300 25098, 31223
Rath Raised oval area (int. dims. *c.* 39m E–W; *c.* 29m N–S) enclosed by an earthen bank best preserved from ENE–ESE and at SSW, and a wide, shallow fosse absent from N–NE. Wide break in bank at WSW probably represents original entrance.
16:71 14-11-1989

787 KILLYNEBBER
OS 20:16:5 (779,31) Indicated OD 300–400 24278, 30446
Rath Large raised roughly circular area (int. diam. *c.* 79m) enclosed by a low earthen bank and a wide fosse. Site is divided into two roughly equal portions by a field boundary running NNW–SSE, ENE of which the enclosing features were levelled in the late 1980s. At the remainder of the site the fosse has been infilled but its outline may still be traced. Original entrance not recognisable.
20:54 15-8-1990

788 KILLYNURE (Castlerahan By.)
OS 32:7:4 (499,323) Hachured OD 500 24967, 29480
Rath Raised circular area (int. diam. 29m) enclosed by very slight traces of a fosse and earthen bank. Break in bank at SE may represent original entrance. Remains of possible souterrain within internal area (**1245**).
32:24(01) 1-5-1989

789 KILLYRUE (Clankee By.)
OS 22:4:3 (871,559) Not marked OD 300–400 26321, 31022
Rath (site) Designated 'Fort' on OS 1836 ed. Not marked on subsequent eds. Situated on the SW slope of a drumlin hill. It apparently comprised a slightly raised area (int. diam. *c.* 40m) enclosed by an earthen bank and fosse. From ENE–SE the perimeter has been modified and incorporated into the field boundary. Elsewhere the enclosing features have been levelled. Nonetheless their outline can be traced from WNW–NNW. Original entrance not recognisable.
22:28 12-10-1990

790 KILLYTOGHER
OS 32:10:6 (399,191) Hachured OD 500–600 24862, 29339

Rath Raised circular area (int. diam. 37m) enclosed by a low earthen bank and very slight traces of a fosse identifiable only from SW–W. From E–S bank has been replaced with a modern field boundary. Elsewhere its outer face has been scarped and it has a modern external trench. Original entrance not recognisable.
32:25 5-7-1989

791 KILLYTOGHER
OS 32:15:1 (481,131) Hachured OD 400–500
24949, 29277
Rath Raised circular area (int. diam. 34m) enclosed by two substantial earthen banks with external fosses. An earlier report (OPW 1974) recorded a short segment of low earthen bank at the outer lip of the outer fosse at S. Original entrance not recognisable.
32:26 12-4-1989

792 KILLYVAGHAN
OS 17:4:3 (877,566) Hachured OD 300–400
26872, 30815
Rath Raised circular area (int. diam. 31.4m) enclosed by two earthen banks with intermediate fosse. Outer bank has been modified and incorporated into the field boundary from WSW–N–E, and levelled elsewhere. Fosse survives only in the N half of the site where it is very poorly defined. Much of the S half of the site has been levelled. Original entrance not recognisable. Modern buildings abut the site from NNE–E–S.
17:46 10-11-1989

793 KILLYWILLIN
OS 13:7:2 (603,387) Hachured OD 200–300
22132, 31442
Rath (site) Marked on all OS eds. An earlier report (OPW 1969) recorded a raised circular area (int. dims. 34m NNW–SSE; 33.4m ENE–WSW) enclosed by traces of a low earthen bank. Apart from a curve in the field boundary at WNW there are no visible remains at ground level.
13:33 12-6-1989

794 KILMACNORAN
OS 16:14:3 (389,141) Hachured OD 300–400
24834, 31207
Rath Marked 'Fort' on OS 1836 ed. Raised circular area (int. diam. *c.* 33m) enclosed by a low, narrow earthen bank and a narrow, shallow trench, both of which survive only from WSW–N–ENE. The remainder of the site was removed during road building. Original entrance not recognisable.
16:73 6-11-1989

795 KILMACNORAN
OS 16:14:2 (372,141) Hachured OD 200–300
24816, 31207
Rath Raised circular area (int. diam. *c.* 35m) enclosed by a substantial earthen bank and a wide, deep fosse. Break in bank at N may represent original entrance but there are no remains of an accompanying causeway. Densely overgrown with vegetation.
16:74 6-11-1989

796 KILNACOR
OS 32:2:3 (403,597) Hachured OD 500–600
24862, 29769
Rath Raised circular area (int. diam. 27m) enclosed by a substantial earthen bank and a wide, deep, partially waterlogged fosse recut from NW–N–E. Short segment of low counterscarp bank at the outer lip of fosse at SSE is probably relatively modern. Break in inner bank at SE with accompanying causeway may represent original entrance.
32:27 28-4-1989

797 KILNACOR
OS 32:2:3 (406,568) Hachured OD 400–500
24866, 29737
Rath Raised circular area (int. diam. *c.* 30m) enclosed by a substantial earthen bank and slight remains of a wide, deep fosse accompanied by a low counterscarp bank at its outer lip. Break in bank at SE may represent original entrance. Inside the bank at W is a small approximately circular depression (diam. *c.* 2.8m; D 0.3m) of unknown significance. Site is densely overgrown with vegetation.
32:28 28-4-1989

798 KILNACREEVY (Upper Loughtee By.)
OS 26:6:2 (347,387) Hachured OD 500–600
24799, 30186
Rath Raised circular area (int. diam. 29.8m) enclosed by two earthen banks with intermediate fosse. The outer bank survives only from E–SSE. The fosse has been largely infilled. Inner bank contains a substantial amount of stone. Original entrance not recognisable.
26:43 22-10-1991

799 KILNACROSS (ED Drumcarn)
OS 16:5:3 (187,383) Hachured OD 400–500
24618, 31461
Rath Raised circular area (int. diam. *c.* 40m) enclosed by a slight earthen bank. Break in bank at N represents original entrance. A low drystone wall, enclosing a circular area (diam. 38.4m) and divided into two roughly equal parts by a field boundary aligned NW–SE, within the interior of the rath, appears relatively modern.
16:76 12-9-1989

800 KILNAGARBET
OS 21:11:6 (653,209) Hachured OD 300–400
25119, 30641

Rath Raised circular area (int. diam. *c.* 30m) enclosed by a much-denuded low earthen bank. Original entrance not recognisable. Internal area densely overgrown with vegetation.
21:45 25-9-1990

801 KILNAGLARE LOWER
OS 15:11:6 (618,164) Hachured OD 200–300 24100, 31225
Rath Raised circular area (int. diam. 32.8m) enclosed by a low earthen bank and a wide, deep fosse. Original entrance not recognisable.
15:55 10-9-1989

802 KILNAGLARE UPPER
OS 15:15:5 (591,63) Hachured OD 200–300 24073, 31118
Rath Raised circular area (int. diam. 31.4m) enclosed by a low earthen bank and a wide, deep fosse outside of which is a well-defined counterscarp bank running from SW–NW. Break in bank with accompanying causeway at SE represents original entrance.
15:56 10-9-1989

803 KILNAGUN
OS 40:13:4 (26,13) Hachured OD 300–400 26426, 28526
Rath Raised circular area (int. diam. *c.* 29m) enclosed by a substantial earthen bank destroyed from SSE–S–WSW, modified and incorporated into the field boundary from SW–WNW and faced internally with drystone masonry at N. Original entrance not recognisable.
40:36 14-8-1987

804 KILNAGUN
OS 44:1:2 (80,594) Indicated OD 300–400 26484, 28500
Rath Raised circular area (int. diam. 21m) enclosed by a bank of earth and stone, best preserved at S where drystone walling has been applied to its outer face, and denuded elsewhere. Original entrance not recognisable.
44:15 19-8-1987

805 KILNAHARD
OS 37:16:2 (785,81) Hachured OD 200–300 24301, 28579
Rath (site) Marked 'Fort' on OS 1836 and 1876 eds. All that now survives is a slightly raised area enclosed by a low earthen bank from SSW–W. Otherwise, no visible remains at ground level.
37:39 30-7-1986

806 KILNALECK (Lower Loughtee By.)
OS 15:11:5 (550,200) Hachured OD 200–300 24028, 31262
Rath Raised oval area (int. dims. 69m NW–SE; 53.4m NE–SW) enclosed by a low earthen bank and a wide, deep fosse both of which have been modified and incorporated into the field boundary. An earlier report (OPW 1968) suggested that the original entrance may have been at NNW.
15:58 10-9-1989

807 KILNAVAR
OS 26:8:1 (728,448) Hachured OD 500 25201, 30254
Rath Raised almost circular area (int. dims. 45.1m ENE–WSW; 48.9m NNE–SSW) enclosed by a low earthen bank which has been incorporated into the field boundary, and vague traces of a fosse. Original entrance not recognisable.
26:44 20-3-1992

808 KILNAVARA
OS 25:3:6 (653,518) Indicated OD 200–300 24146, 30319
Rath Raised circular area (int. dims. 43m NE–SW; 44.5m NW–SE) enclosed by an earthen bank and traces of a fosse identifiable only from NW–N–NNE and at S. Perimeter has been ploughed out from NNE–E–SE but its outline can still be traced. Original entrance not recognisable.
25:75 2-10-1991

809 KILSALLAGH (Clanmahon By.)
OS 25:14:2 (370,103) Hachured OD 300 23851, 29877
Rath Raised circular area (int. dims. 56m E–W; 55m N–S) enclosed by two earthen banks with wide, deep intermediate fosse. Although the perimeter has been ploughed out from NW–W–SW, its outline is still clearly identifiable. Original entrance may have been at WSW.
25:76 10-9-1991

810 KILSARAN
OS 30:16:6 (882,2) Hachured OD 300–400 23423, 29123
Rath Raised circular area (int. diam. 43.7m) enclosed by a substantial earthen bank denuded almost to the level of the interior from S–SW–W. Bank is surrounded by a fosse accompanied by external modern trenches. Original entrance not recognisable.
30:25/36:7* 9-10-1991

811 KINNYPOTTLE
OS 20:16:4 (707,62) Hachured OD 300–400 24201, 30478
Rath Raised circular area (int. diam. 38.5m) enclosed by a low earthen bank and a fosse which together with the bank has been incorporated into a field boundary

from SW–WNW and levelled elsewhere. Outline of fosse is nonetheless traceable. Slight break in bank at ESE, with gradual slope to field level probably, represents original entrance.
20:55(01) 21-9-1990

812 KNOCKAKISHTA
OS 25:12:4 (739,218) Hachured OD 400 24239, 30003
Rath Raised circular area (int. dims. 38m E–W; 35.5m N–S) enclosed by an earthen bank outside of which is a modern drainage trench and a spring well. Original entrance not recognisable.
25:77 20-9-1991

813 KNOCKAKISHTA
OS 25:12:1 (762,243) Hachured OD 400 24264, 30029
Rath Raised circular area (int. diam. *c.* 29m) enclosed by a substantial earthen bank and a wide, deep fosse outside of which are traces of a possible counterscarp bank. Original entrance may have been at E. Interior slopes considerably from S–N.
25:78 20-9-1991

814 KNOCKANOARK
OS 26:6:1 (234,425) Hachured OD 300–400 24680, 30225
Rath Raised circular area (int. dims. 33m NNW–SSE; 31.2m ENE–WSW) enclosed by an earthen bank and traces of a fosse. At W an apparently modern section of drystone walling has been built against the outer face of the bank. Original entrance not recognisable.
26:46 17-10-1991

815 KNOCKANOARK
OS 26:2:4 (293,456) Hachured OD 300–400 24742, 30259
Rath Raised circular area (int. dims. 28m N–S; 24.3m E–W) enclosed by a substantial earthen bank and a fosse. Former break in bank at E, now blocked by a modern field boundary, probably represents original entrance.
26:47 17-10-1991

816 KNOCKANOARK
OS 26:7:2 (596,447) Hachured OD 300–400 25061, 30252
Rath Raised oval area (int. dims. 37.5m NW–SE; 24.8m NE–SE) enclosed by a denuded earthen bank disturbed in parts, and an almost completely infilled fosse. Original entrance not recognisable.
26:48 17-10-1991

817 KNOCKATAGGART
OS 27:5:6 (218,349) Hachured OD 600–700 25639, 30154
Rath Raised circular area (int. diam. *c.* 28m) enclosed by a substantial earthen bank and a wide, deep, partly waterlogged fosse. Original entrance not recognisable.
27:8 24-7-1989

818 KNOCKATAGGART
OS 27:6:4 (232,339) Hachured OD 600 25654, 30143
Rath Raised circular area (int. diam. *c.* 27) enclosed by a substantial earthen bank and a deep fosse outside of which are the remains of a low counterscarp bank running from W–N–S. Both fosse and counterscarp bank are absent elsewhere. Original entrance not recognisable.
27:9 24-7-1989

819 KNOCKATEERY
OS. 15:8:1 (720,398) Hachured OD 200–300 24206, 31473
Rath Raised almost circular area (int. dims. 30.5m NW–SE; 27.5m NE–SW) enclosed by a substantial earthen bank and a wide, deep, partly waterlogged fosse outside of which is a poorly defined counterscarp bank running from N–E–SSW. Break in bank with accompanying causeway at SE represents original entrance.
15:59 17-9-1989

820 KNOCKATUDOR
OS 21:12:5 (785,212) Hachured OD 300–400 25258, 30646
Rath Raised circular area (int. dims. 30m NE–SW; 32.6m NW–SE) enclosed by a substantial earthen bank and a wide, deep fosse best preserved from S–W–NNW and infilled or replaced by modern trenches elsewhere. Original entrance may have been at S.
21:47 25-9-1990

821 KNOCKATUDOR
OS 21:12:5 (796,172) Hachured OD 300–400 25270, 30603
Rath Raised circular area (int. diam. *c.* 25.2m) enclosed by an earthen bank scarped in recent times, and a fosse infilled from W–N–NNE. Partially blocked break in bank at E may represent original entrance.
21:48 25-9-1990

822 KNOCKBRIDE
OS 23:13:6 (172,23) Not marked OD 500–600 26563, 30458
Rath (site) Marked 'Fort' on OS 1836 and 1876 eds. This site is very badly disturbed. All that survives are the remains of a curving earthen bank running from NNW–N–E defining a slightly raised area. A hole has been quarried on the inside of the bank from N–NE.

Otherwise no visible remains at ground level.
23:27 21-5-1992

823 KNOCKBRIDE
OS 28:1:3 (166,534) Hachured OD 500–600
26557, 30358
Rath Raised circular area (int. diam. *c.* 40m) enclosed by an earthen bank identifiable only from NW–N–NE and a shallow fosse discernible only from SW–NW. Bank merges with a low field boundary which encloses site from NE–S–NW. Original entrance not recognisable. Within the internal area is a possible souterrain (**1248**). (CUCAP BGL 77)
28:29(01) 1-4-1974

824 KNOCKNAGARTAN
OS 43:3:5 (607,519) Not marked OD 400–500
26065, 28417
Rath Marked 'Fort' on OS 1836 ed. and 'Site of' on 1876 ed. Raised circular area (int. dims. 31.8m NE–SW; 33m NW–SE) enclosed by a very low, much-denuded earthen bank. Original entrance not recognisable.
43:19 17-6-1986

825 LABBINLEE
OS 22:11:2 (599,255) Hachured OD 500–600
26036, 30698
Rath Raised circular area (int. diam. 38.8m) enclosed by a slight earthen bank best preserved from W–N–NE and a wide, shallow fosse identifiable only from SW–NNW and replaced by modern drainage trenches elsewhere. Original entrance not recognisable. From NNW–S–SW the site is encircled by a modern field boundary.
22:30 27-10-1990

826 LAHARD
OS 19:16:4 (704,6) Hachured OD 200–300
23224, 30409
Rath (site) An earlier report (OPW 1969) describes a raised circular area (int. dims. 46m E–W; 45m N–S) enclosed by a low earthen bank. Original entrance was at SSE. Situated on the summit of a drumlin hill. Site has been levelled.
19:39 17-7-1990

827 LAHARD
OS 24:3:3 (644,568) Hachured OD 300–400
23160, 30363
Rath Raised circular area (int. diam. *c.* 32m) enclosed by a substantial earthen bank and a wide, deep fosse. From NW–N–S a modern laneway extends along the fosse. Partially blocked break in bank at SE probably represents original entrance. Spring well at NE. Densely overgrown with vegetation.
24:58 14-8-1991

828 LAHARD
OS 24:3:3 (674,573) Hachured OD 300–400
23192, 30368
Rath Raised circular area (int. diam. *c.* 35.7m) enclosed by a substantial earthen bank, best defined at N, and a wide fosse. Break in bank at SE probably represents original entrance.
24:59 14-8-1991

829 LAHARD
OS 24:4:4 (702,518) Hachured OD 200–300
23222, 30311
Rath Raised circular area (int. dims. 36.3m NNW–SSE; 32.7m ENE–WSW) enclosed by an earthen bank and a fosse of which only slight traces survive from NE–SSE. Well-defined break in bank with faint traces of accompanying causeway at NE probably represents original entrance.
24:60 14-8-1991

830 LARAGH
OS 35:5:4 (59,318) Indicated OD 500–600
27428, 29497
Rath Raised circular area (int. diam. *c.* 35m) enclosed by slight remains of a wide earthen bank bounded by a modern laneway, and a wide, deep, waterlogged fosse which survives only from SW–NW where it has been modified and utilised as a field drain. Elsewhere the bank is bounded by a modern laneway. Modern farm buildings abut the site at NNW. Original entrance not recognisable.
35:44 15-3-1974

831 LARAWEEHAN
OS 23:6:4 (263,354) Hachured OD 300–400
26655, 30808
Rath Raised subcircular area enclosed by slight traces of a low earthen bank and faint traces of a fosse. The site was almost certainly originally circular (original int. diam. *c.* 28.5m). The bank is denuded to the level of the interior from SSW–N–ENE. Elsewhere it has been modified in relatively modern times and incorporated into the field boundary. It is accompanied by a modern external trench. Original entrance not recognisable.
23:29 28-5-1992

832 LARGAN
OS 31:8:2 (845,440) Hachured OD 400–500
24356, 29598
Rath Raised circular area (int. dims. 52.4m NNW–SSE; *c.* 49m E–W) enclosed by a substantial earthen bank which has been modified and incorporated into the field boundary, and a wide, deep fosse. Break in bank at S may represent original entrance. However there is no trace of an accompanying causeway.
31:46 18-6-1992

833 LARGAN
OS 31:4:6 (918,478) Hachured OD 500–600
24432, 29639
Rath (site) An earlier report (OPW 1974) described a raised circular area (int. diam. *c.* 35m) enclosed by a low earthen bank and vague traces of a fosse. From NW–N–NE a portion of the adjacent linear earthwork 'The Worm Ditch or Black Pig's Race' (**180**) was utilised as a rampart and at NNE the fosse had been cut through the earlier earthwork. Original entrance was not recognisable. Site has been levelled. Not visible at ground level.
31:47 18-6-1992

834 LARGY OR FORTHENRY
OS 16:12:6 (859,174) '*Fort Henry*' OD 200–300
25330, 31246
Rath Raised circular area (int. diam. 32.4m) enclosed by two substantial earthen banks with accompanying outer fosses. External fosse may be relatively modern. Outer bank is exceptionally broad (Wth 8m). Break in inner bank with remains of accompanying causeway at ESE may represent original entrance.
16:77(01) 30-11-1989

835 LARGY OR FORTHENRY
OS 16:12:3 (889,257) Hachured OD 200–300
25361, 31334
Rath (site) An earlier report (OPW 1968) described a subrectangular area (int. dims. 47m N–S; 24m E–W) enclosed by an earthen bank from NW–N–SE and elsewhere by a scarp with slight remains of an earthen bank on its upper edge in places. At that time, much of the S half of the site had already been disturbed by field boundaries. Original entrance not recognisable. Not visible at ground level.
16:78 30-10-1989

836 LARGY OR FORTHENRY
OS 16:12:6 (888,164) Hachured OD 200–300
25361, 31236
Rath Raised circular area (int. diam. *c.* 28m) enclosed by a substantial earthen bank, an intermediate narrow, deep, waterlogged fosse and a low counterscarp external bank identifiable only from N–E–SE. Break in bank with accompanying causeway at SSW represents original entrance. Situated on the summit of a low drumlin hill which is surrounded by marsh except from WNW–NW–N.
16:79 30-10-1989

837 LARGY OR FORTHENRY
OS 17:9:1 (6,254) Hachured OD 300
25651, 31325
Rath Raised circular area (int. diam. *c.* 33m) enclosed by a substantial earthen bank, the outer face of which has been incorporated into the field boundary, and a wide, shallow, waterlogged fosse identifiable only from NE–S. Original entrance not recognisable.
17:47 10-11-1989

838 LATTACAPPLE
OS 16:4:4 (710,530) Hachured OD 300–400
25169, 31621
Rath Raised circular area (int. diam. 36.8m) enclosed by an earthen bank and a wide, deep fosse, waterlogged from NNW–E–SSE and broadened to form a watering-hole for cattle at SSE. Bank barely rises above the internal area from ENE–E–S. Break in bank with accompanying causeway at NNE represents original entrance.
16:80 16-10-1989

839 LATTAGLOGHAN
OS 32:3:2 (572,534) Hachured OD 400–500
25041, 29704
Rath Raised circular area (int. diam. 28m) enclosed by a substantial earthen bank and traces of a fosse. An earlier description (OPW 1977) recorded a wide, deep, waterlogged fosse enclosed by a low counterscarp bank at SE. Fosse is now identifiable only from E–SE. Perimeter levelled from NW–N–E. Original entrance not recognisable.
32:30 11-4-1989

840 LATTAGLOGHAN
OS 32:3:2 (608,540) Hachured OD 519
25079, 29711
Rath Raised circular area (int. diam. 49m) enclosed by a very substantial earthen bank with scarped outer face and a wide, shallow, partly waterlogged fosse, infilled from N–E–ESE. Break in bank with accompanying causeway at SSE represents original entrance.
32:31 18-3-1977

841 LATTAGLOGHAN
OS 32:8:1 (700,446) Hachured OD 500–600
25178, 29612
Rath Raised circular area (int. diam. 31m) enclosed by a substantial earthen bank and a wide fosse identifiable only from NW–N–SE. Partially blocked break in bank at E probably represents original entrance.
32:32 11-4-1989

842 LATTERRIFF
OS 28:4:1 (742,588) '*Bloomers Fort*' OD 400–500
27165, 30420
Rath Raised circular area (int. diam. *c.* 32m) enclosed by a low, wide earthen bank and the remains of a fosse which has been recut and incorporated into the field drainage system from NW–N–NE. Original entrance

not recognisable.
28:30 28-3-1974

843 LAVAGH
OS 37:12:6 (864,224) Hachured OD 300–400
24383, 28730

Rath A modern dwelling and garden now occupy most of this site. All that survives of the rath are traces of a fosse and former substantial earthen bank running from NE–E. Otherwise no visible remains at ground level.
37:40 5-8-1986

844 LAVEY
OS 26:7:6 (650,333) Hachured OD 300–400
25120, 30132

Rath Raised circular area (int. dims. 32.2m NNW–SSE; 31.3m ENE–WSW) enclosed by a substantial earthen bank which has been scarped and planted with trees, and a fosse, largely infilled from SSW–W. Break in bank at SSW may represent original entrance.
26:50 18-10-1991

845 LAVEY
OS 26:5:6 (676,21) '*Lavey Fort*' OD 400–500
25151, 29803

Rath Raised circular area (int. dims. 39.2m NNW–SSE; 38.2m ENE–WSW) enclosed by a substantial earthen bank and a wide, deep fosse which has been infilled from E–S–SSW. Wide break in bank at ESE may represent original entrance. Densely overgrown with vegetation.
26:51 18-10-1991

846 LECHARROWNAHONE
OS 14:1:1 (37,600) Hachured OD 300–400
22508, 31670

Rath Raised circular area (int. dims. 36.2m) enclosed by a substantial bank of earth and stone and a wide, deep fosse identifiable only from WNW–E–SSE and modified and incorporated into the field boundary from E–SSE. An earlier report (OPW 1969) recorded traces of an outer bank at the external lip of the fosse. Wide break in bank at SE probably represents original entrance.
14:47 16-7-1989

847 LECHARROWNAHONE
OS 14:1:1 (53,597) Hachured OD 200–300
22524, 31668

Rath Raised oval area (int. dims. 26.8m WNW–ESE; 22m NNE–SSW) enclosed by a substantial bank of earth and stone and the remains of an infilled fosse, the outline of which is identifiable in places. An earlier report (OPW 1969) suggested that the original entrance was probably at E and recorded the stone foundations of a rectangular structure (int. dims. 3.45m N–S; 2.3m E–W), probably a hut site, built against the inner face of the bank at W. Entrance to this structure at S.
14:48 16-7-1989

848 LECKS
OS 23:16:6 (825,23) '*Killastueran Fort & Graveyard*'
OD 400–500 27281, 30465

Rath Raised oval area (int. dims. *c.* 32m NNW–SSE; 30m ENE–WSW) enclosed by a low bank of earth and stone. Original entrance not recognisable. Davies (1948, 116) recorded that the rath is 'believed to be a church site' (**1677**), while there is a local tradition that it marks the site of a children's burial ground (**1740**).
23:30(01) 30-3-1992

849 LECKS
OS 28:4:2 (835,600) '*Lecks Fort*' OD 500–600
27263, 30434

Rath Raised circular area (int. diam. *c.* 29m) enclosed by a very low, irregular earthen bank and the remains of a shallow fosse identifiable only from NNE–SE. Narrow break in bank at E probably represents original entrance. Internal area very overgrown with vegetation.
28:31 28-3-1974

850 LECKS
OS 28:4:3 (862,560) '*Black Fort*' OD 500–600
27293, 30392

Rath Raised circular area (int. diam. *c.* 20m) enclosed by a wide, low earthen bank and a shallow fosse. Slight traces of a low external bank at the outer lip of the fosse at N. Break in bank with accompanying causeway at SE represents original entrance.
28:32 28-3-1974

851 LEGALAND
OS 25:5:5 (123,348) Hachured OD 200–300
23588, 30134

Rath Raised circular area (int. dims. 38.4m NNW–SSE; 37.6m ENE–WSW) enclosed by a substantial earthen bank and a well-defined fosse. Break in bank with accompanying causeway at N probably represents original entrance.
25:79 15-9-1991

852 LEGAWEEL
OS 25:14:4 (260,43) Hachured OD 300–400
23735, 29813

Rath Raised oval area (int. dims. 45.1m NW–SE; 38.2m NE–SW) enclosed by an earthen bank and an infilled fosse. Break in bank at E may represent original entrance. An apparently modern, long, narrow

earthen mound, lies just N of the centre of the internal area.
25:80 10-9-1991

853 LEGAWEEL
OS 31:2:1 (268,596) Hachured OD 300–500
23744, 29758
Rath An almost circular raised area (int. diam. *c.* 48m) enclosed by a substantial earthen bank and a fosse. From WSW–NNW the perimeter has been modified and incorporated into the field boundary. Break in bank at SSE may represent original entrance.
31:48 4-5-1974

854 LEGLAND
OS 27:7:6 (632,325) Hachured OD 500–600
26076, 30133
Rath Raised oval area (int. dims. 47m N–S; 36.5m E–W) enclosed by a substantial earthen bank, badly denuded from S–W–NW, and a wide, shallow, partly waterlogged, infilled fosse. A modern field boundary encroaches on the bank at NW. Original entrance may be represented by break in the bank at N.
27:10 27-7-1989

855 LEGNAGROW
OS 6:5:5 (135,346) Not marked OD 400–500
20651, 32666
Rath Marked 'Fort' on OS 1836 ed. Raised circular area (int. diam. 32.5m) enclosed by the remains of an earthen bank and slight traces of a fosse. The S half of the site has been levelled and the perimeter is identifiable only with difficulty. Original entrance not recognisable. Remains of possible stone structure in the interior at SE.
6:13 22-8-1988

856 LEGWEE
OS 31:14:4 (271,68) Hachured OD 300–400
23753, 29199
Rath Raised circular area (int. diam 42.2m NW–SE) enclosed by a substantial earthen bank and slight remains of a wide fosse. Break in bank at SSE with accompanying causeway probably represents original entrance.
31:49 10-6-1992

857 LEITER (ED Baileborough)
OS 28:13:5 (112,22) Indicated OD 500–600
26505, 29816
Rath Raised circular area (int. diam. *c.* 25m) enclosed by a substantial earthen bank and a narrow fosse. Original entrance represented by a break in the bank with accompanying causeway at SE. Wide, shallow depression of unknown significance inside the bank at NW.
28:33 25-3-1974

858 LEITER (ED Baileborough)
OS 28:13:5 (137,41) Indicated OD 500–600
26532, 29837
Rath An almost circular raised area (int. dims. *c.* 42m WSW–ENE; *c.* 47m NNW–SSE) enclosed by an earthen bank identifiable only from NNW–E–SE, and a shallow fosse traceable from SW–N–NNE. Original entrance not recognisable. Internal area now occupied by a modern bungalow.
28:34 25-3-1974

859 LEITRIM (Castlerahan By.)
OS 44:7:1 (512,421) Hachured OD 400–500
26942, 28322
Rath Raised circular area (int. diam. 27m) enclosed by a substantial earthen bank. No indication of a fosse. Break in bank at E may represent original entrance. Tradition of a 'cave' within the internal area (**1249**).
44:17(01) 19-8-1987

860 LEITRIM (Clankee By.)
OS 34:10:3 (411,298) Hachured OD 500–600
26824, 29470
Rath Raised circular area (int. diam. *c.* 30m) defined by a low scarp and a wide, partly waterlogged fosse. Wide, low outer bank running from SW–W–NNW may be an original feature. Original entrance not recognisable.
34:31 21-3-1974

861 LEITRIM (Clankee By.)
OS 34:6:6 (412,338) Hachured OD 500–600
26825, 29513
Rath Raised circular area (int. diam. *c.* 34m) enclosed by two low earthen banks with intervening wide berm (Wth 10–12m) and a partly waterlogged external fosse. A modern field boundary replaces the fosse from NW–N–ESE. External bank also replaced by field boundary throughout most of its circuit. Inner bank levelled from WNW–N–ESE but outline may still be traced. Original entrance not recognisable.
34:32 22-3-1974

862 LEITRIM (Clankee By.)
OS 34:10:3 (424,294) Hachured OD 500–600
26838, 29466
Rath Raised circular area (int. diam. *c.* 42m) enclosed by a low earthen bank and traces of a shallow fosse. Break in bank at SE probably represents original entrance. Lying inside the bank at W is a low stony mound of unknown significance.
34:34 21-3-1974

863 LEITRIM (Clankee By.)
OS 34:10:3 (427,258) Hachured OD 500–600
26842, 29429

Fig. 24—*Rath at Legaweel* (**853**).

Rath Raised circular area (int. diam. *c.* 26m) enclosed by a low earthen bank, partly faced with stone in recent times and levelled at W, and a shallow fosse identifiable from S–W–NE. Original entrance not recognisable.
34:35 31-5-1988

864 LENANAVRAGH
OS 40:2:1 (296,544) Hachured OD 400–500
26706, 29089

Rath Raised circular area (int. diam. *c.* 33m) enclosed by a low earthen bank running from SE–S–N, and vague traces of a fosse. Perimeter has been destroyed from N–E–SE and the site is bordered by a modern roadway. Original entrance not recognisable.
40:37 7-7-1987

865 LENANAVRAGH
OS 40:2:5 (312,518) Hachured OD 400–500
26723, 29062

Rath Raised circular area (int. diam. *c.* 46m) enclosed by a substantial earthen bank and a fosse identifiable only from SW–NW. From NNW–N–NE outer face of bank has been modified where it is bordered by a modern laneway. An earlier report (OPW 1969) suggested that the original entrance may have been at SW.
40:38 7-7-1987

866 LETTERMORE
OS 16:8:3 (867,400) Hachured OD 300–400
25337, 31485

Rath (site) Although the site has been levelled, the outline of its enclosing features is still identifiable. It formerly comprised a raised oval area (int. dims. *c.* 50m NE–SW; *c.* 43m WNW–ESE) enclosed by a low earthen bank and a wide, deep, waterlogged fosse. When first recorded, the original entrance was not recognisable (OPW 1968). No visible remains at ground level.
16:81 16-10-1989

867 LETTERMORE
OS 16:8:6 (892,365) Hachured OD 300–400
25363, 31449

Rath Raised oval area (int. dims. *c.* 28m NNE–SSW;

c. 35m WNW–ESE) enclosed by a low earthen bank and a wide, deep fosse which is identifiable only from NW–N–S where it has been recently infilled with field-clearance debris. Original entrance may have been at NW or S where there are breaks in the bank with accompanying causeways. Internal area densely overgrown with vegetation.
16:82 16-10-1989

868 LETTERMORE
OS 16:8:6 (904,324) Hachured OD 200–300
25376, 31405
Rath Raised circular area (int. diam. 28.4m) enclosed by a substantial earthen bank best preserved from NW–N–NE, and a wide, deep fosse which has been broadened at SW to form a watering-hole for cattle. Break in bank with remains of accompanying causeway at ENE represents original entrance.
16:83 16-10-1989

869 LISACHUNNY
OS 35:10:3 (448,263) Hachured OD 500–600
27839, 29443
Rath Raised circular area (int. diam. *c.* 40m) enclosed by a wide, low earthen bank incorporated into the field boundary from SSE–S–SSW, and vague traces of a fosse. Break in bank at SSE may represent original entrance.
35:47 13-3-1974

870 LISADERG OR CORWEELIS
OS 18:13:2 (80,93) Hachured OD 400–500
26459, 31171
Rath A largely levelled, raised oval area (int. dims. *c.* 40m NW–SE; *c.* 36m NE–SW) enclosed by a substantial earthen bank from NW–E–SE. Elsewhere the perimeter has been levelled and replaced by modern field boundaries. Original entrance not recognisable. There are indications of a possible souterrain within the internal area (**1250**).
18:8(01) 15-7-1990

871 LISAGOAN
OS 29:5:6 (203,315) Hachured OD 629
27574, 30136
Rath Raised circular area (int. diam. 38m) enclosed by a substantial inner bank, a wide, deep fosse, which is absent from NNW–N–E, and the remains of an outer earthen bank. The outer bank survives from S–W–NNW where it has been modified and incorporated into the field boundary. Break in inner bank with accompanying causeway at SE represents original entrance. Inside the bank at NW is a large subcircular depression of unknown significance.
29:7 23-3-1977

872 LISAGOAN
OS 29:10:1 (244,249) Indicated OD 300–400
27618, 30066
Rath Marked 'Fort' on OS 1836 and 1876 eds. Raised circular area (int. diam. *c.* 39m) enclosed from E–SE–S by a substantial earthen bank with external fosse. The enclosing elements are well preserved from E–SE–S. Elsewhere poorly preserved or absent. Original entrance not identifiable.
29:8 10-8-1988

873 LISAGOAN
OS 29:10:4 (264,193) Indicated OD 400–500
27640, 30008
Rath Marked 'Fort' on OS 1836 ed. and 'Site of' on 1876 ed. Raised circular area (int. diam. *c.* 37m) enclosed by an earthen bank from SW–N–E. The site has been quarried at SW. Original entrance not identifiable.
29:9 10-8-1988

874 LISANALSK
OS 34:6:4 (308,323) Hachured OD 590
26715, 29496
Rath Raised circular area (int. diam. *c.* 28m) enclosed by a substantial earthen bank and a deep fosse outside of which are traces of a low counterscarp bank. Wide break in bank at E may represent original entrance.
34:36 12-5-1988

875 LISANISKY
OS 35:6:6 (424,316) Hachured OD 500–600
27814, 29499
Rath Raised circular area (int. diam. *c.* 38m) enclosed by a substantial earthen bank and a wide, shallow fosse which was largely infilled during the course of land reclamation in the late 1960s (local information). Original entrance at SE.
35:48 13-3-1974

876 LISANNY
OS 30:16:2 (791,90) Hachured OD 300–400
23326, 29216
Rath Raised circular area (int. diam. 34.3m) enclosed by a substantial earthen bank and a wide, deep fosse, waterlogged from SSW–NW. Earthen deposits outside of fosse at NW are modern, relating to the re-cutting of the counterscarp to widen the fosse. Original entrance not recognisable.
30:26 7-10-1991

877 LISANNY
OS 30:16:2 (802,110) Hachured OD 300–400
23338, 29237
Rath Raised circular area (int. diam. *c.* 31m) enclosed by a wide, deep, waterlogged fosse and substantial

earthen bank. Break in bank with accompanying causeway at E represents original entrance.
30:27 7-10-1991

878 LISARNEY
OS 16:8:2 (804,425) Hachured OD 300–400
25270, 31511
Rath Raised subcircular area (int. dims. *c.* 46m N–S *c.* 39m E–W) enclosed by a substantial earthen bank and a wide, deep, waterlogged fosse. Break in bank at E presumably represents original entrance but there are no traces of an accompanying causeway.
16:84 16-10-1989

879 LISARNEY
OS 16:8:2 (844,446) Hachured OD 300–400
25312, 31533
Rath Raised subcircular area (int. dims. *c.* 34.5m N–S; *c.* 26m E–W) enclosed by a substantial earthen bank and a wide, deep, waterlogged fosse. An earlier report (OPW 1968) noted possible traces of an outer bank enclosing the fosse. Wide break in bank with possible evidence of accompanying causeway at SE represents original entrance. Densely overgrown with vegetation.
16:85 16-10-1989

880 LISATAGGART
OS 23:13:4 (67,36) Hachured OD 400–500
26452, 30471
Rath Raised circular area (int. diam. 27m) enclosed by two earthen banks with intermediate fosse. Outer bank is best preserved from SE–S, incorporated into the field boundary from W–NW–N and removed elsewhere. Fosse generally wide and shallow except from S–SW–W. Break in inner bank at SE represents original entrance.
23:44 30-3-1992

881 LISATAWAN
OS 21:11:5 (577,173) Hachured OD 300–400
25039, 30603
Rath Raised circular area (int. diam. 29.5m) enclosed by a slight earthen bank modified and incorporated into the field boundary, and a wide, shallow fosse identifiable only from SSE–S–SW and from N–NNE. Original entrance not identifiable.
21:50 27-9-1990

882 LISATAWAN
OS 21:11:5 (600,208) Hachured OD 300–400
25063, 30640
Raths (conjoined) Conjoined raths encircled by a relatively modern field boundary and separated by a fosse. The SE rath comprises a raised circular area (int. diam. *c.* 38m) enclosed by two earthen banks with outer fosses. Outer bank is very substantial; the inner much less so. Both fosses are wide but shallow. Corresponding breaks in banks at E with accompanying causeway across inner fosse represents original entrance. Break in outer bank is now blocked. The NE rath comprises a raised oval area (int. dims. *c.* 36m NE–SW; *c.* 31m NW–SE) enclosed by two earthen banks with intervening deep, partly waterlogged fosse. Outer bank identifiable only from SSW–NNW. Corresponding breaks in banks at SSE of this rath and NNW of the larger rath, with accompanying causeway, allows access from one to the other.
21:51 25-9-1990

883 LISATOO
OS 21:11:5 (542,178) Hachured OD 300–400
25002, 30608
Rath (site) Situated on the summit of a drumlin hill. Modern farm buildings now occupy the site. A previous account (OPW 1970) described a raised circular area (int. diam. 26.5m) enclosed by a low earthen bank. Original entrance was not identifiable. Site has been levelled.
21:52 25-9-1990

884 LISASTURRIN
OS 35:7:4 (488,358) Not marked OD 400
27880, 29544
Rath Raised circular area (int. diam. *c.* 38m) enclosed by a low earthen bank and a shallow fosse identifiable only at NW. Perimeter has been destroyed at W as a result of the construction of a modern dwelling-house. Original entrance not recognisable.
35:50 12-3-1974

885 LISAWAUM
OS 17:8:4 (735,336) Hachured OD 432
26501, 30709
Rath (site) Situated just SE of the summit of a high drumlin hill. When visited in 1969 (OPW 1969) the site was largely occupied by a reservoir. The outline of the perimeter comprising two substantial earthen banks with intermediate fosse could be traced from W–N–S. The remainder of the site has since been levelled.
17:48 11-11-1989

886 LISBALL
OS 28:14:3 (456,104) Hachured OD 500–600
26868, 29906
Rath Raised circular area (int. diam. *c.* 36m) enclosed by a partly denuded, irregular earthen bank and the remains of a fosse infilled from NW–N–NE. Original entrance not recognisable. Internal area now forms part of a modern farmyard.
28:35 26-3-1974

887 LISBODUFF
OS 16:11:2 (597,300) Hachured OD 300–400
25053, 31377

Rath Raised circular area (int. diam. *c*. 37m) enclosed by a low earthen bank and a shallow fosse identifiable from W–NW–N and largely replaced by modern trenches elsewhere. Original entrance not recognisable.
16:86 21-10-1989

888 LISBODUFF
OS 16:7:5 (610,338) Hachured OD 300–400
25066, 31418

Rath Raised circular area (int. diam. *c*. 39m) enclosed by a substantial earthen bank and a wide fosse. Two massive upright boulders, of which there are apparently another ten (local information) within the rath, lie just W of a modern break in the bank. However, dense growth of vegetation precluded examination of additional uprights. Original entrance not recognisable.
16:87 21-10-1989

889 LISBODUFF
OS 16:7:6 (631,342) Hachured OD 300–400
25088, 31422

Rath Raised circular area (int. diam. *c*. 35m) enclosed by a substantial earthen bank and a wide, deep, waterlogged fosse. Break in bank at NNE with accompanying causeway represents original entrance. Perimeter and internal area have been largely levelled except from NW–N–ENE.
16:88 21-10-1989

890 LISBREE
OS 16:12:5 (780,218) Hachured OD 300–400
25247, 31292

Rath Raised circular area (int. diam. 35.6m) enclosed by two substantial earthen banks with outer fosses. A low counterscarp bank surrounds the external fosse from SE–W–N. Corresponding breaks in banks with accompanying causeway at SW represents original entrance.
16:90 21-10-1989

891 LISCLOGHER
OS 23:2:4 (292,491) Hachured OD 487
26685, 30954

Rath Raised circular area (int. diam. 31.7m) enclosed by two substantial earthen banks with a wide, deep, partly waterlogged intermediate fosse. Exterior of outer bank has been faced with earth and stone in modern times. Corresponding breaks in banks with accompanying causeway at SSW represents original entrance. Possible souterrain within internal area (**1251**).
23:31(01) 26-5-1992

892 LISCLONE
OS 21:11:2 (599,263) Hachured OD 300–400
25061, 30698

Rath Raised circular area (int. diam. 30m) enclosed by a substantial earthen bank and a deep, partly waterlogged fosse. Modern farm buildings have encroached on perimeter of site from ESE–S–NNE. Original entrance not recognisable. Internal area has been planted with trees.
21:53 25-9-1990

893 LISDARAN
OS 20:11:6 (630,200) Not marked OD 300–400
24119, 30622

Rath Marked 'Fort' on OS 1836 and 1876 eds. Situated just S of the summit of a drumlin hill. Remains comprise a circular area (diam. 27.1m) raised to between 0.5m and 0.9m above external ground level. Enclosing elements have been levelled. Original entrance not recognisable.
20:57 16-8-1990

894 LISDARAN
OS 20:11:6 (665,194) Hachured OD 200–300
24156, 30617

Rath Raised almost circular area (int. diam. 26.8m) enclosed by two earthen banks with intervening fosse. Outer bank identifiable only from NNE–E–S. Original entrance may have been at ENE.
20:58 16-8-1990

895 LISDEEGIN
OS 21:2:5 (350,511) Indicated OD 300–400
24796, 30958

Rath (site) Marked 'Fort' on OS 1836 and 1876 eds. Situated just S of the summit of a high drumlin ridge in pasture-land. A much-disturbed, slightly raised, formerly circular area (int. diam. 29.9m) enclosed by a very slight earthen bank from S–SSW. Elsewhere the plan of the site has been much distorted by the erection of modern field boundaries.
21:54 10-9-1990

896 LISDOAGH
OS 23:5:2 (110,451) Hachured OD 400
26494, 30909

Rath Raised circular area (int. diam. 29.9m) enclosed by two earthen banks with wide, deep, partly waterlogged intermediate fosse. Outer bank survives from SSE–W–NW. Break in inner bank with remains of accompanying causeway at SE represents original entrance. Within the internal area are the remains of a possible souterrain (**1252**).
23:32(01) 20-5-1992

897 LISDONAN
OS 23:13:5 (112,32) Indicated OD 500–600
26499, 30467

Fig. 25—*A heavily overgrown bivallate rath at Lisbree* (**890**).

Rath Marked 'Fort' on the OS 1836 and 1876 eds. Raised oval area enclosed by a low, narrow earthen bank and a narrow trench incorporated into a field boundary. Site is divided into two unequal portions by a field boundary running NE–SW, NW of which there is nothing visible at ground level. Original entrance not recognisable.
23:33 21-5-1992

898 LISDONAN
OS 28:1:2 (114,560) Hachured OD 500–600
26503, 30385
Rath Raised circular area (int. dims. *c.* 32.3m N–S; *c.* 39.4m E–W) enclosed by a much-denuded earthen bank, the outer face of which has been scarped and incorporated into the field boundary, and surrounded in turn by slight traces of a recut fosse. Original entrance not recognisable.
28:37 26-3-1974

899 LISDONNISH
OS 32:15:1 (516,120) Hachured OD 400–500
24986, 29266
Rath Raised circular area (int. diam. *c.* 27m) enclosed by three earthen banks with wide, deep, partly waterlogged intermediate fosses. While the middle bank is very substantial, the outer one has been replaced by a modern field boundary. Original entrance represented by corresponding breaks in the middle and inner banks with accompanying causeways.
32:33 3-5-1989

900 LISDRUMFAD
OS 23:12:6 (876,180) Hachured OD 400–500
27305, 30631
Rath Raised circular area (int. diam. *c.* 33m) enclosed by a substantial earthen bank and traces of a fosse. Break in bank with remains of accompanying causeway at S probably represents original entrance. Adjoining the inside of the bank at SE is a rectangular house site represented by a slight bank (int. dims. 4.8m NE–SW; 3.3m NW–SE). Entrance to house site at SW corner indicated by break in bank. A possible souterrain also lies within the internal area (**1253**).
23:34(01) 30-3-1992

901 LISDRUMSKEA
OS 23:16:3 (856,109) Hachured OD 400–500
27284, 30556

Rath Raised circular area (int. diam. 28.7m) enclosed by two earthen banks with wide, shallow, intermediate fosse. Outer bank which is enclosed by a modern trench, has been scarped and faced externally with stone, in modern times. Break in inner bank with accompanying causeway at ESE probably represents original entrance. However there is no corresponding break in the outer bank.
23:36 30-3-1992

902 LISDUFF (Castlerahan By.)
OS 43:8:3 (915,390) Hachured OD 300–400
26392, 28284
Rath Raised circular area (int. diam. *c.* 45m) enclosed by a substantial, although partly denuded, earthen bank. An earlier report (OPW 1969) noted vague traces of a wide, shallow fosse and that a modern drystone facade had been applied to the external face of the bank. Break in bank at SE probably represents original entrance. Internal area has been planted with deciduous trees and is overgrown with vegetation.
43:27 7-8-1987

903 LISDUFF (Clanmahon By.)
OS 38:5:4 (52,326) Hachured OD 300–400
24500, 28839
Rath Raised circular area (int. diam. 32m) enclosed by two earthen banks with wide, deep intermediate fosse. Corresponding breaks in the banks with accompanying causeway at SE represents original entrance. (CUCAP AHM 90/91)
38:41 8-8-1986

904 LISDUFF (Clanmahon By.)
OS 38:9:2 (116,296) Hachured OD 300–400
24568, 28807
Rath Raised circular area (int. diam. 38m) enclosed by a substantial earthen bank and traces of a wide, shallow fosse. Break in bank at SE, with accompanying gradual slope to external ground level, represents original entrance.
38:42 7-8-1986

905 LISDUFF (Upper Loughtee By.)
OS 25:7:2 (579,381) Hachured OD 200–300
24069, 30174
Rath Raised oval area (int. dims. 51m NNE–SSW; 43.5m WNW–ESE) enclosed by two substantial earthen banks with a deep intermediate fosse. Fosse and outer bank are partly destroyed at E. Corresponding breaks in banks with accompanying causeway at ESE represents original entrance. Slight depression in the centre of the internal area.
25:81 19-9-1991

906 LISDUNVIS GLEBE
OS 21:1:6 (182,490) Hachured OD 200–300
24618, 30933
Rath (site) Modern farm buildings now occupy the site. An earlier description (OPW 1970) recorded a raised almost circular area (int. dims. 44m E–W; 41.5m N–S) enclosed by a substantial earthen bank and a wide, deep fosse, outside of which is an apparently recent low counterscarp bank. Original entrance was at SE. Not visible at ground level.
21:55 19-9-1991

907 LISEGNY
OS 21:11:3 (679,272) Hachured OD 300–400
25145, 30709
Rath Raised oval area (int. dims. 37.5m E–W; 24.5m N–S) enclosed by a low earthen bank and a fosse. Bank absent from W–NW and from NNE–NE. Fosse best preserved from NNE–S–W and largely infilled elsewhere. Break in bank at SE, with traces of accompanying causeway, probably represents original entrance.
21:56 27-9-1990

908 LISEGNY
OS 21:12:1 (711,238) Hachured OD 300–400
25179, 30672
Rath Raised circular area (int. diam. 48.2m) enclosed by a substantial earthen bank and a wide, shallow fosse best preserved from E–S–SW, and largely levelled elsewhere. Fosse is encompassed by an apparently modern, low counterscarp bank. Break in bank with accompanying causeway at E represents original entrance.
21:57 27-9-1990

909 LISGANNON
OS 21:8:2 (782,445) Hachured OD 300–400
25252, 30891
Rath (site) An earlier description (OPW 1968) described a raised oval area (int. dims. *c.* 47m NNW–SSE; *c.* 40m ENE–WSW) enclosed by a substantial earthen bank and a wide, deep, partly waterlogged fosse. Original entrance may have been at SE. Site has been levelled.
21:58 19-9-1990

910 LISGANNON
OS 21:4:5 (795,458) Hachured OD 300
25266, 30906
Rath Raised circular area (int. diam. *c.* 28m) enclosed by a substantial earthen bank with wide, deep external fosse. Bank has been levelled from NE–E–SE. Fosse has been infilled from S–W–N. Original entrance not recognisable.
21:59 27-9-1990

911 LISGANNON
OS 21:4:2 (802,531) Hachured OD 370
25273, 30982

Rath (site) Although the site has been levelled, the outline of its enclosing features may still be distinguished. An earlier report (OPW 1968) described it as a raised subcircular area (int. dims. *c.* 40m N–W; *c.* 35m E–W) enclosed by two massive earthen banks with outer fosses. Original entrance not recognisable. Davies (1948, 118–9) believed Capt. Hugh O'Reilly transformed the rath into a 'bawn of sods' in 1601 (**1831**). He speculated that it 'was originally single-ringed but was reconstructed with a second ring separated from the fosse by a wide berm'. Not visible at ground level.
21:60(01) 27-9-1990

912 LISGAR
OS 28:10:5 (366,180) Not marked OD 500–600
26772, 29986
Rath Marked 'Fort' on the OS 1836 ed. and 'Site of' on the 1876 ed. Partially levelled. Raised circular area (int. diam. *c.* 38m) enclosed by an earthen bank and a wide fosse, both well preserved from NW–N–NE and elsewhere either levelled or replaced by field boundaries. Original entrance not recognisable.
28:38 23-3-1977

913 LISHENRY
OS 32:11:3 (678,238) Hachured OD 457
25156, 29392
Rath Raised circular area (int. diam. 32m) enclosed by a substantial earthen bank and a wide, deep, partly waterlogged fosse. Low counterscarp bank at outer lip of fosse. Corresponding breaks in banks at E with accompanying causeway probably represents original entrance.
32:34 20-4-1989

914 LISLEA (Castlerahan By.)
OS 39:16:3 (872,99) Indicated OD 300–400
26344, 28616
Rath (site) Marked 'Fort' on OS 1836 and 1876 eds. An earlier report (OPW 1970) described it as a raised circular area (int. dims. 32m ENE–WSW; 31.5m NNW–SSE) enclosed by a substantial earthen bank which by that time had been partly replaced by a modern stone wall. Original entrance was at SE. Site has since been levelled.
39:58 23-3-1987

915 LISLEA (ED Cootehill Rural)
OS 17:11:2 (589,258) Hachured OD 300–400
26271, 30767
Rath Marked 'Fort' on OS 1836 ed. and 'Site of' on 1876 ed. Raised oval area (int. dims. *c.* 43m NE–SW; *c.* 35m NW–SE) enclosed by an earthen bank which has been much modified and incorporated into the field boundary from ENE–S–WNW and survives elsewhere as a low scarp. From SSW–WNW a laneway runs outside it, possibly on the site of an external fosse. Original entrance not recognisable.
17:50 28-9-1989

916 LISLEA (ED Drung)
OS 21:7:4 (494,338) Hachured OD 400
24950, 30776
Rath Raised circular area (int. diam. 33.4m) enclosed by a slight earthen bank and a fosse which is wide and deep from SW–S–SSE and largely levelled elsewhere. Partially blocked-up wide break in bank at NE, probably represents original entrance.
21:62 22-9-1990

917 LISLEA (Upper Loughtee By.)
OS 32:3:4 (494,461) Hachured OD 400–500
24960, 29626
Rath Raised circular area (int. diam. 31m) enclosed by a substantial earthen bank and the remains of a narrow fosse. Break in bank at ESE with accompanying causeway represents original entrance.
32:35 25-4-1989

918 LISLEA (Upper Loughtee By.)
OS 32:7:1 (509,406) Hachured OD 300–400
24977, 29568
Rath Raised circular area (int. diam. 34m) enclosed by two substantial earthen banks with external fosses. Outer fosse identifiable only from NE–E–S. Corresponding breaks in banks at E may indicate original entrance although there is no evidence of accompanying causeway.
32:36 25-4-1989

919 LISLIN (ED Castlerahan By.)
OS 40:15:1 (533,101) Hachured OD 400–500
26961, 28624
Rath Raised circular area (int. diam. *c.* 41m) enclosed by a much-denuded, low earthen bank which has been modified and incorporated into the field boundary, and the remains of a fosse. Original entrance not recognisable.
40:41 14-7-1987

920 LISLIN (Tullygarvey By.)
OS 16:14:3 (442,98) Hachured OD 100–200
24891, 31162
Rath Raised subtriangular area (int. dims. 35.4m ENE–WSW; 23.2m NNW–SSE) defined by the River Annalee from SSE–S–WSW and elsewhere enclosed by a low earthen bank with wide, shallow external fosse which has been partially destroyed as a result of flooding. Original entrance not recognisable.
16:91 8-10-1989

921 LISMACANIGAN LOWER
OS 38:15:6 (666,5) Hachured OD 200–300
25152, 28506
Rath Raised circular area (int. diam. *c.* 30m) enclosed by two substantial earthen banks with wide, deep, intermediate fosse. Outer bank has been partly modified and incorporated into the field boundary. Original entrance not recognisable.
38:44 21-8-1986

922 LISMAGIRIL
OS 33:4:4 (710,475) Hachured OD 400–500
26163, 29652
Rath Raised circular area (int. diam *c.* 26m) enclosed by a low earthen bank, levelled from N–NE–E, and very slight remains of a fosse. Original entrance not recognisable.
33:40 2-4-1974

923 LISMAGRATTY
OS 21:5:1 (18,380) Hachured OD 400–500
24447, 30815
Rath Raised circular area (int. dims. 31.5m NNE–SSW; 33.5m WNW–ESE) enclosed by two substantial earthen banks with outer fosses. Original entrance at E represented by corresponding breaks in the banks with accompanying causeways. Internal area overgrown with vegetation.
21:63 11-9-1990

924 LISMEEN (Castlerahan By.)
OS 32:8:4 (697,362) Hachured OD 400–500
25175, 29523
Rath Raised circular area (int. diam. 33.9m) enclosed by a substantial earthen bank and a wide, deep, partly waterlogged fosse. Break in bank at S with traces of accompanying causeway may represent original entrance. A break occurs in the bank (Wth 2.7m) at ENE. Projecting from this into the interior are possible remains of a souterrain (**1254**).
32:37(01) 12-5-1993

925 LISMEEN (Castlerahan By.)
OS 32:16:6 (893,35) Hachured OD 400–500
25385, 29179
Rath Raised circular area (int. diam. 32m) enclosed by a substantial earthen bank and a wide, deep, waterlogged fosse. Original entrance may have been at SE. Site densely overgrown with vegetation.
32:38 17-4-1989

926 LISMORE DEMESNE
OS 25:9:6 (170,221) Hachured OD 200–300
23638, 30000
Rath Raised circular area enclosed by a substantial earthen bank and a well-defined fosse. Break in bank at SE probably represents original entrance. Site lies within a modern plantation of coniferous trees and is overgrown with vegetation precluding closer examination.
25:82 24-9-1991

927 LISMORE DEMESNE
OS 25:9:3 (188,257) '*Lismore*' OD 200–300
23657, 30039
Rath Raised circular area (int. diam. 34.6m) enclosed by the remains of an outer earthen bank, a wide deep intermediate fosse and substantial inner earthen bank. Corresponding breaks in banks with accompanying causeway at E probably represents original entrance. A second apparently original entrance occurs at SE.
25:83 23-9-1991

928 LISMORE DEMESNE
OS 25:9:6 (212,205) Hachured OD 200–300
23683, 29984
Rath Raised circular area (int. diam. 43.6m) enclosed by slight remains of an outer earthen bank, an intermediate fosse into which a deep drain has been dug in recent times, and a substantial inner earthen bank. Original entrance at E.
25:85 24-9-1991

929 LISMORE DEMESNE
OS 25:10:1 (239,244) Hachured OD 200–300
23711, 30026
Rath Probably originally a rath later transformed into a tree-ring. Raised oval area (int. dims. 37.2m N–S; 23.1m E–W) enclosed by a low earthen bank and slight remains of a fosse. Modern entrance at N. A low earthen bank aligned N–S divides the higher E segment from the W segment of the site. Internal area has been planted with beech trees.
25:87 24-9-1991

930 LISMORE DEMESNE
OS 25:10:1 (243,232) Hachured OD 200–300
23716, 30012
Rath Probably originally a rath later transformed into a tree-ring. A circular raised area (int. dims. 22.4m NW–SE; 23.7m NE–SW) enclosed by an apparently modern trench and low earthen bank. A low earthen embankment running E–W divides the higher northern segment from the southern segment of the site. Break in bank at ENE is probably modern. Internal area has been planted with deciduous trees.
25:88 24-9-1991

931 LISNABANTRY (ED Crossbane)
OS 39:4:4 (750,476) Hachured OD 400–500
26211, 29013
Rath Raised circular area (int. diam. *c.* 33m) enclosed

by two earthen banks. No visible evidence of a fosse. The distance between the banks is *c.* 2m. External bank is low and survives only for a short stretch at ESE. From WNW–NNW the inner bank has been modified and incorporated into the field boundary. Original entrance was probably at ENE. An earlier report (OPW 1969) noted a wide, very shallow depression of unknown significance inside the inner bank running from SSW–N–ENE.
39:60 12-6-1987

932 LISNABANTRY (ED Killinkere)
OS 39:3:6 (678,455) Hachured OD 400–500
26135, 28990
Rath Raised circular area (int. diam. *c.* 38m) enclosed by two substantial earthen banks with a wide, deep, intermediate fosse. Outer bank has been replaced by modern field boundaries and faced externally with drystone masonry from SSE–W–NE and likewise internally at ESE. Corresponding breaks in banks with accompanying causeway represents original entrance. Remains of possible souterrain within the internal area (**1255**).
39:61(01) 30-3-1987

933 LISNABRINNIA
OS 42:3:1 (469,552) Hachured OD 200–300
24944, 28442
Rath Raised almost oval area (int. dims. *c.* 30m NE–SW; *c.* 21m NW–SE) enclosed by a low earthen bank identifiable only from S–W–N and a shallow fosse distinguishable from E–S–W. Original entrance not recognisable.
42:30 17-6-1974

934 LISNACARK
OS 21:1:3 (189,559) Hachured OD 300
24625, 31006
Rath Raised almost oval area (int. dims. 43.5m NE–SW; 55m NW–SE) enclosed by very slight traces of an earthen bank running from SW–W–N. The site is divided into two approximately equal portions by a field boundary running NW–SE the area SE of which has been levelled. Nonetheless its outline may still be traced. Earlier reports (OPW 1969; 1970) suggested that the original entrance may have been at SE.
21:64 21-9-1990

935 LISNACLEA (ED Kingscourt)
OS 29:15:4 (500,1) Hachured OD 355
27890, 29807
Rath Raised circular area (int. diam. *c.* 31m) enclosed by a substantial earthen bank and a fosse. Original entrance not recognisable. An earlier report (OPW 1974) noted a substantial outer earthen bank from NE–S–SW. Original entrance not recognisable. Site overgrown with vegetation.
29:10/35:52* 10-8-1988

936 LISNACLEA (ED Kingscourt)
OS 35:3:1 (483,582) Hachured OD 300–400
27873, 29780
Rath Raised circular area (int. diam. *c.* 27m) enclosed by a substantial earthen bank. Original entrance not recognisable. Internal area has been planted with coniferous trees.
35:51 24-6-1988

937 LISNACLEA (ED Kingscourt)
OS 35:3:1 (520,592) Hachured OD 300–400
27911, 29791
Rath Raised circular area (int. diam. *c.* 26m) enclosed by two substantial earthen banks with wide, deep, intermediate fosse. Original entrance not recognisable. Internal area very overgrown with vegetation.
35:53 24-6-1988

938 LISNACLEA (ED Knappagh)
OS 18:14:5 (349,24) Hachured OD 400–500
26744, 31101
Rath Raised circular area (int. diam. *c.* 30m) enclosed by a substantial earthen bank the outer face of which has been modified and incorporated into the field boundary. There is a modern field drain at its foot. Original entrance was probably at NNW. Possible souterrain within internal area (**1256**).
18:10(01) 15-7-1989

939 LISNACLEA (ED Knappagh)
OS 23:2:1 (300,605) Hachured OD 400
26693, 31074
Rath Raised oval area (int. dims. 31.5m E–W; 27.4m N–S) enclosed by a low earthen bank and a fosse, traces of which are identifiable only from ESE–S–WSW. Break in bank with accompanying causeway at ESE probably represents original entrance.
23:37 22-5-1992

940 LISNACLEA (ED Knappagh)
OS 23:2:2 (351,578) Hachured OD 400–500
26746, 31046
Rath Raised circular area (int. diam. *c.* 30m) enclosed by a substantial earthen bank scarped externally from SE–S–W, and a wide, deep, partly waterlogged fosse recently recut from NNW–N–NE to accommodate a field drain and removed from SE–S–W. Break in bank with faint remains of accompanying causeway at E probably represents original entrance. Internal area densely overgrown with vegetation.
23:38 22-5-1992

941 LISNADARRAGH (Clankee By.)
OS 23:15:6 (638,31) Hachured OD 400–500
27055, 30471

Rath Raised oval area (int. dims. 32.5m E–W; 25m N–S) enclosed by a very substantial earthen bank and a wide, deep, partly waterlogged fosse which has been removed from N–E–SW. A roughly circular depression of unknown significance occurs in the interior and extends into the breach of the bank at WSW. Original entrance represented by break in bank with accompanying causeway at E.
23:40 9-4-1992

942 LISNADARRAGH (Clankee By.)
OS 23:15:6 (670,40) Indicated OD 400–500
27088, 30480
Rath Raised oval area (int. dims. 27.9m E–W; 25.1m N–S) enclosed by a well-defined earthen bank, the outer face of which has been modified and incorporated into the field boundary from N–S–W, and vague traces of a fosse. Break in bank at S may represent original entrance.
23:41 9-4-1992

943 LISNADARRAGH (Clanmahon By.)
OS 41:6:2 (352,445) Hachured OD 300–400
23847, 28318
Rath Raised circular area (int. diam. *c*. 26m) enclosed by a low earthen bank and a narrow, shallow fosse. Narrow break in bank at N may represent original entrance.
41:12 21-6-1974

944 LISNAFANA
OS 39:2:1 (268,585) Hachured OD 400–500
25701, 29123
Rath Raised circular area (int. diam. *c*. 30m) enclosed by two substantial earthen banks with wide, deep, intermediate fosse. An earlier report (OPW 1969) suggested that the original entrance was at E. At the centre of the enclosed area is a small subrectangular area (int. dims. 4m E–W; 2m N–S) enclosed by a low bank of earth and stones which presumably represents a hut site. Extending WNW from the NW corner of the hut site are possible remains of a souterrain (**1257**).
39:62(01) 25-3-1987

945 LISNAFANA
OS 39:2:1 (302,570) Hachured OD 400
25737, 29108
Rath Raised circular area (int. diam. *c*. 31m) enclosed by two earthen banks with wide, deep, partly waterlogged intermediate fosse. Outer bank identifiable only from E–S–SW and fosse visible only from N–S–WSW. Original entrance at E.
39:64 25-3-1987

946 LISNAGEER (ED Ashfield)
OS 16:8:6 (921,357) Hachured OD 300–400
25394, 31440
Rath Raised circular area (int. diam. *c*. 35m) enclosed by a substantial earthen bank and a wide, deep, partly waterlogged fosse outside of which is a broad, low counterscarp bank running from SW–W–NW. Break in bank at SE with accompanying causeway represents original entrance. Densely overgrown with vegetation.
16:94 30-10-1989

947 LISNAGEER (ED Cootehill Rural)
OS 17:16:2 (834,104) Hachured OD 300–400
26381, 30369
Rath Raised oval area (int. dims. *c*. 36m N–S; *c*. 30m E–W) enclosed by a substantial earthen bank, poorly preserved from ENE–NNE, and a wide, deep fosse running from W–N–S. An earlier description (OPW 1969) noted that the original entrance was at ENE and recorded a roughly circular shallow depression inside the bank at W. Overgrown with vegetation.
17:52 19-11-1989

948 LISNAGEER (ED Cootehill Rural)
OS 17:16:5 (846,56) Hachured OD 300
26349, 30306
Rath Raised circular area (int. diam. *c*. 30m) enclosed by a substantial earthen bank and a wide, deep fosse. Break in bank at SE with accompanying causeway represents original entrance. The greater part of the site is encircled by a modern field boundary.
17:53 19-11-1989

949 LISNAGLEA
OS 26:7:3 (640,444) Hachured OD 400–500
25109, 30249
Rath Raised circular area (int. diam. *c*. 39m) enclosed by a substantial earthen bank and slight remains of a fosse. The site is divided into two roughly equal portions by a field boundary aligned ENE–WSW. Southern half of site has been levelled. Original entrance not recognisable.
26:53 22-10-1991

950 LISNAGLEA
OS 26:3:4 (504,461) Hachured OD 400–500
24965, 30266
Rath Raised circular area (int. diam. 38.3m) enclosed by a bank and fosse which has been removed at NE and incorporated into the field boundary from SE–W–NNW. Original entrance not recognisable.
26:54 22-10-1991

951 LISNAGOON
OS 23:1:3 (226,566) Hachured OD 300–400
26615, 31032
Rath Raised oval area (int. dims. 34.8m N–S; 27.3m E–W) enclosed by two substantial earthen banks with intermediate fosse. Outer bank is not concentric with

the inner bank due to a lunate area at WSW which forms an annex between it and the fosse. An earlier description (OPW 1969) noted slight remains of an external fosse outside the outer bank here and the remains of a counterscarp bank along the ENE side of the annex. Corresponding breaks in banks with accompanying causeway at N represents original entrance.
23:42 22-5-1992

952 LISNAGOON
OS 23:2:1 (234,597) Hachured OD 400–500
26623, 31064
Rath Raised circular area (int. dims. 30.8m NNW–SSE; 32.7m NE–SW) enclosed by two substantial earthen banks with a wide, deep, intermediate fosse. Outer bank may date to the time when the rath was planted with deciduous trees. Break in inner bank with accompanying causeway at ENE may represent original entrance.
23:43 22-5-1992

953 LISNAGOWAN
OS 16:9:5 (126,167) Hachured OD 200–300
24557, 31232
Rath Raised circular area (int. diam. *c.* 30m) enclosed by three substantial earthen banks each accompanied by wide, deep outer fosses. Corresponding breaks in banks and causeways at SSW represents original entrance. Situated within a plantation of deciduous trees. Densely overgrown with vegetation.
16:95 21-9-1989

954 LISNAGOWAN
OS 16:9:5 (147,190) Hachured OD 300–400
24578, 31257
Rath Raised circular area (int. diam. *c.* 24m) enclosed by a low earthen bank and a poorly preserved shallow fosse. Original entrance not recognisable. Situated within a plantation of deciduous trees. Densely overgrown with vegetation.
16:96 21-9-1989

955 LISNAHEDERNA (Castlerahan By.)
OS 39:4:3 (901,600) Hachured OD 500–600
26370, 29145
Rath Raised circular area (int. diam. *c.* 35m) enclosed by a much-denuded, low earthen bank modified and incorporated into the field boundary from NNW–N–E, and vague traces of a fosse identifiable only at SE. An unexplained V-shaped depression, defined by slight earthen banks on either side, extends out from the centre of the interior to the perimeter at W.
39:65 10-6-1987

956 LISNALEA
OS 34:2:4 (278,456) Indicated OD 500–600
26682, 29636
Rath Raised circular area (int. diam. 23m) enclosed by a narrow, low earthen bank modified and incorporated into the field boundary, and a shallow fosse. A low stony platform, roughly rectangular in plan, which extends from the inside of the bank at E to the centre of the interior, may represent a house site.
34:37 27-3-1974

957 LISNALEA
OS 34:6:5 (322,352) Indicated OD 500–600
26730, 29527
Rath Not marked on OS 1836 ed. Indicated on 1876 ed. Raised oval area (int. dims. *c.* 24m NE–SW; *c.* 19m NW–SE) enclosed by a low earthen bank and a very shallow fosse encircled from NW–N–NNE by traces of a low outer bank. Modern entrances at W, NE and SE. Original entrance not recognisable.
34:38 27-3-1974

958 LISNAMAINE OR SYCAMORE FIELDS
OS 14:4:6 (886,476) Hachured OD 263
23405, 31548
Rath Raised oval area (int. dims. 45.3m NNE–SSW; 35m WNW–ESE) enclosed by two very substantial earthen banks with wide, deep, intermediate fosse. Corresponding breaks in banks with accompanying causeway at S represents original entrance. A subrectangular hollow with some visible remains of loose masonry occurs in the interior and may represent the remains of a castle built within the rath in the early 17th century (**1836**). In addition, a stone-lined well was constructed at the outer edge of the fosse.
14:49(01) 15-8-1989

959 LISNAMANDRA
OS 25:6:2 (319,407) Hachured OD 200–300
23794, 30198
Rath Raised oval area (int. dims. 48.8m N–S; 32.7m E–W) enclosed by three earthen banks with intermediate fosses. The inner and middle banks are very substantial and separated from each other by a wide, deep, partly waterlogged fosse. The outer fosse is absent at W and its enclosing outer bank identifiable only at SE. Corresponding breaks in banks with accompanying causeways at ESE represents original entrance.
25:90 17-9-1991

960 LISNANANAGH (Clanmahon By.)
OS 31:11:5 (595,218) Hachured OD 300
24093, 29361
Rath An almost circular raised area (int. diam. *c.* 40.5m) enclosed by two earthen banks with wide intermediate fosse. Outer bank has been much modified and incorporated into the field boundary. Original entrance not recognisable.
31:50 10-4-1974

961 LISNANANAGH (Upper Loughtee By.)
OS 26:7:3 (640,444) Hachured OD 300–400
25109, 30249
Rath Raised oval area (int. dims. 35m NNW–SSE; 30m ENE–WSW) enclosed by two substantial earthen banks with intermediate fosse. A modern trench surrounds the outer bank. Original entrance was probably at S.
26:55 23-3-1992

962 LISNASARAN
OS 17:12:1 (713,296) Hachured OD 400–500
26439, 30688
Rath Raised circular area (int. diam. 30.4m) enclosed by a substantial earthen bank and a wide, deep, partly waterlogged fosse encompassed by a modern counterscarp bank. Break in bank at NE with accompanying causeway represents original entrance.
17:54 19-11-1989

963 LISNASASSONAGH
OS 35:5:6 (203,343) Hachured OD 500–600
27579, 29525
Rath Raised circular area (int. diam. *c*. 35m) enclosed by a low earthen bank and slight traces of a fosse. Original entrance may have been at S.
35:55 15-3-1974

964 LISNASHANNA
OS 16:13:5 (152,31) Hachured OD 200–300
24585, 31089
Rath Raised circular area (int. diam. 28.4m) enclosed by a low earthen bank and a deep, narrow, partly waterlogged fosse which has been partly modernised and utilised as a field drain. An apparently modern counterscarp bank surrounds the fosse. A field boundary running NNW–SSE divides the rath into two unequal portions, NE of which the site has been levelled. Nonetheless its outline is still identifiable.
16:97 25-9-1989

965 LISNATINNY
OS 37:9:3 (183,268) Hachured OD 200–300
23664, 28770
Rath Raised circular area (int. diam. *c*. 35m) enclosed by a substantial earthen bank and a wide, deep, partly waterlogged fosse, poorly preserved from NNW–N–NE and infilled and replaced by a modern laneway from W–NNW. Break in bank at NE may represent original entrance.
37:45 8-7-1986

966 LISNATINNY
OS 37:9:3 (200,241) Hachured OD 200–300
23682, 28742
Rath Raised circular area (int. diam. 28m) enclosed by a substantial earthen bank and the remains of a wide, shallow fosse. An earlier report (OPW 1970) suggested that the original entrance may have been at SE.
37:46 8-7-1986

967 LISSACAPPLE
OS 33:10:2 (315,275) Hachured OD 500–600
25747, 29436
Rath Raised oval area (int. dims. *c*. 30m N–S; 25m E–W) enclosed by a substantial earthen bank and a fosse identifiable only from N–E–S and replaced elsewhere by a modern field drain. Break in bank at NE probably represents original entrance.
33:41 3-4-1974

968 LISSANNYMORE
OS 33:15:1 (480,104) Hachured OD 300–400
25923, 29258
Rath Raised circular area (int. diam. 26m) enclosed by a low earthen bank. Site is situated on the NE shoulder of a slight natural ridge and was constructed by scarping the ridge. Depression in bank at E may represent original entrance.
33:42 9-9-1988

969 LISSANNYMORE
OS 33:11:4 (486,164) Hachured OD 400–500
25930, 29321
Rath Raised circular area (int. diam. *c*. 40m) enclosed by a substantial earthen bank with a wide, shallow external fosse. Bank identifiable only from NNW–N–NE. From SSW–W–NNW there are slight traces of an internal fosse. The perimeter has been levelled from E–S–SSW. Original entrance not recognisable.
33:43 4-4-1974

970 LISSANNYMORE
OS 33:11:4 (491,193) Hachured OD 482
25935, 29352
Rath Raised circular area (int. diam. *c*. 29m) enclosed by a low earthen bank, faced externally with drystone masonry from NNW–N–SE. Original entrance not recognisable.
33:44 4-4-1974

971 LISSANOVER
OS 13:4:5 (804,519) Hachured OD 200–300
22343, 31584
Rath (possible) Marked 'Fort' on OS 1836 and 1876 eds. Raised circular area (int. dims. 39.4m NNE–SSW; 37m WNW–ESE) enclosed by a low earthen bank and a narrow, shallow trench, both of which in their present form must be regarded as relatively modern. Original entrance not recognisable. The site was at one time

utilised as a tree-ring.
13:45 27-10-1969

972 LISTIERNAN
OS 14:11:1 (510,252) Hachured OD 300–400
23010, 31308
Rath Raised circular area (int. dims. 45.2m NNW–SSE; *c.* 44m ENE–WSW) enclosed by three earthen banks with outer fosses. From SE–S–SSW the outer fosse and bank and the intermediate fosse have been levelled but their outline is still identifiable. An earlier report (OPW 1969) suggested that the original entrance was probably at SE. Densely overgrown with vegetation.
14:50 15-8-1989

973 LOCH GOWNA
OS 30:15:1 (530,112) Hachured OD 400
23050, 29238
Rath Raised circular area (int. diam. 44.1m) enclosed by a very substantial earthen bank and a wide, deep, partially waterlogged fosse, both best preserved from S–W–NW. Break in bank at SE with accompanying causeway represents original entrance.
30:28 10-10-1991

974 LONG
OS 17:14:3 (418,124) Hachured OD 378
25962, 30791
Rath Raised oval area (int. dims. 38.6m NNW–SSE; 28.8m ENE–WSW) enclosed by a low earthen bank and a wide, shallow fosse identifiable only from NNW–N. Both bank and fosse have been removed from E–S–WSW and a modern laneway now borders the site. Original entrance not recognisable.
17:55 28-4-1993

975 LONNOGS
OS 32:2:5 (341,492) Hachured OD 400–500
24798, 29657
Rath Raised circular area (int. diam. 35m) enclosed by two earthen banks with intermediate fosse. External bank best preserved at N, and absent from NE–E. Break in inner bank with accompanying causeway at ENE presumably represents the original entrance. Inside the inner bank at SSE is a shallow circular depression (diam. 5.4m) of unknown significance, with a short 'tail' extending NNW from it.
32:39 26-4-1989

976 LOORTAN
OS 17:9:5 (131,168) Not marked OD 300–400
25701, 31115
Rath (site) Marked 'Fort' on OS 1836 and 1876 eds. Raised, almost circular area (int. diam. *c.* 26m) the enclosing elements of which have been incorporated into the field boundary from S–W–WNW. Elsewhere it has been levelled and the delimiting feature is a much-defaced scarp. Original entrance not recognisable.
17:56 22-5-1993

977 LOSSET
OS 24:16:1 (765,106) Hachured OD 400–500
23292, 29875
Rath Raised circular area (int. diam. 34m) enclosed by a low but clearly defined earthen bank. Site has been partly destroyed. Original entrance not recognisable.
24:61 29-8-1991

978 LOUGHACONNICK
OS 25:7:4 (534,372) Hachured OD 300–400
24022, 30163
Rath (site) An earlier report (OPW 1970) described a raised circular area (int. dims. 50.5m N–S; 47m E–W) enclosed by a low earthen bank and traces of a fosse. An unusual feature of the site was the presence of a wide, shallow fosse inside the bank. Original entrance was probably at NNW. Site has since been levelled with only the outline of the perimeter now identifiable.
25:92 19-9-1991

979 LURGANAVEELE
OS 34:14:1 (235,76) Hachured OD 500–600
26641, 29235
Rath Raised circular area (int. diam. *c.* 31m) enclosed by a substantial earthen bank. From SSE–WSW the site is bordered by a modern roadway. A field drain which lies between the bank and the roadway may follow the line of the former fosse. Original entrance may have been at NE or SE.
34:39 12-5-1988

980 LURGANBANE/RAKEEVAN
OS 34:6:3 (458,396) Hachured OD 600–700
26873, 29575
Rath Raised circular area (int. diam. *c.* 33m) enclosed by a substantial earthen bank and a fosse. Break in the bank at W may represent original entrance. Within the internal area there are the remains of a possible souterrain (**1258**).
34:40(01) 22-3-1974

981 LURGANBOY (Clankee By.)
OS 23:1:2 (131,556) Hachured OD 300–400
26515, 31020
Rath Raised oval area (int. dims. 28.5m NNE–SSW; 24.5m WNW–ESE) enclosed by an earthen bank and slight traces of a fosse identifiable only from SW–N–NE. Original entrance not recognisable. Within the internal area is a possible collapsed souterrain (**1259**).
23:45(01) 26-5-1992

982 MAGHERABOY LOWER
OS 41:3:2 (584,587) Hachured OD 200–300
24089, 28470

Rath Raised oval area (int. dims. *c.* 67m E–W; *c.* 49m N–S) enclosed by a low earthen bank, partly faced with stone externally and incorporated into the field boundary, and a shallow fosse running from NE–S–NNW. Original entrance not recognisable.
41:15 25-6-1974

983 MAGHERABOY LOWER/MAGHERABOY UPPER
OS 41:3:2 (608,573) Indicated OD 200–300
24115, 28456

Rath Marked 'Fort' on OS 1836 ed. and 'Site of' on 1876 ed. Raised oval area (int. dims. 63.2m WNW–ESE; 51.2m NNE–SSW) enclosed by a substantial earthen bank which has been recently modified and incorporated into the field boundary from N–NNE–E and from SSE–S–W. In addition, a wide cutting has been dug through the perimeter at SW. Original entrance not recognisable. Field-clearance boulders lie at the external foot of the bank at NW.
41:16 17-5-1993

984 MARAHILL (Clankee By.)
OS 35:2:6 (421,500) Hachured OD 400–500
27808, 29693

Rath Raised circular area (int. diam. *c.* 30m) enclosed by a substantial, although partly denuded, earthen bank and a shallow fosse identifiable only from WNW–NNW. Site is divided into two unequal portions by a field boundary running NNW–SSE, ENE of which there are no visible remains at ground level.
35:56 11-3-1974

985 MARAHILL (Clanmahon By.)
OS 31:2:5 (334,492) Hachured OD 300–400
23815, 29648

Rath Large raised circular area (int. diam. *c.* 66m) enclosed by a low earthen bank, modified and incorporated into the field boundary, and a wide, shallow fosse. Modern farm buildings have encroached on the site at NNE and ENE. Part of the bank and fosse has been removed at W. Original entrance not recognisable.
31:51 5-4-1974

986 MARAHILL (Upper Loughtee By.)
OS 25:1:4 (33,482) Not marked OD 100–200
23492, 30274

Rath On a broad rocky ridge in otherwise low-lying wet marshy land. Davies (ITA Survey 1940) describes it as a roughly circular area (diam. *c.* 22.85m) enclosed by a semicircular portion of bank composed mainly of small chips of stone with a less extensive fosse. He speculated that this was a waterside type rath, one side of which is bounded by bog probably representing an extinct lake. Not located.
25:94 24-9-1991

987 MEENASLIEVE
OS 3:15:5 (594,17) Hachured OD 200–300
20157, 32953

Rath Raised circular area (int. diam. 30.1m) enclosed by a low earthen bank and a wide, shallow fosse which has been modified and incorporated into the field boundary. Original entrance may have been at E.
3:20 2-8-1988

988 MIDDLETOWN
OS 30:12:6 (864,173) Hachured OD 300–400
23404, 29304

Rath Raised almost circular area (int. diam. 44.1m) enclosed by a substantial earthen bank, best preserved from NW–E–S and a wide, deep, partially waterlogged fosse, largely infilled throughout most of its circuit. Break in bank with accompanying causeway at N may represent original entrance.
30:29 8-10-1991

989 MOHERLOOB
OS 9:3:1 (511,565) Hachured OD 400–500
22027, 32270

Rath Raised subcircular area (int dims 42.7m NE–SW; 38m NW–SE) enclosed by two substantial earthen banks with intervening wide, deep fosse. Outer bank survives only from SW–W–NNW and has been replaced elsewhere by field boundaries. Stone-lined break in internal bank with accompanying causeway at NE represents original entrance.
9:15 19-9-1988

990 MOHERLOOB
OS 9:3:4 (531,530) Indicated OD 400–500
22049, 32232

Rath Raised oval area (int. dims. 47.3m NE–SW; 28.4m NW–SE) enclosed by a substantially modified earthen bank incorporated into the field boundary, and a fosse best preserved from E–S–W. Narrow break in bank at S with accompanying causeway may represent original entrance.
9:16 19-9-1988

991 MONAGHANOOSE
OS 33:4:5 (845,510) Hachured OD 500–600
26305, 29690

Rath Raised circular area (int. diam. *c.* 23m) enclosed by a low earthen bank and a shallow fosse identifiable from WSW–W–N. Break in bank at SE may represent original entrance.
33:45 20-9-1988

992 MONAGHANOOSE
OS 33:4:6 (890,519) Hachured OD 400–500
26353, 29700

Rath Raised circular area (int. diam. 29m) enclosed by a low earthen bank. Original entrance not recognisable.
33:46 5-4-1974

993 MONEENSAURAN
OS 6:1:5 (139,525) Hachured OD 400–500
20654, 32855

Rath Raised circular area (int. diam. 22.1m) enclosed by two substantial earthen banks with intervening deep, wide, partly waterlogged fosse. Corresponding breaks in banks with accompanying causeway at NE represents original entrance.
6:15 27-8-1988

994 MONEENSAURAN
OS 6:1:3 (215,564) Not marked OD 500–600
20734, 32897

Rath (site) Not marked on any OS ed. Raised circular area (int. diam. *c.* 40m) enclosed by a very wide but low earthen bank and the remains of a fosse, best preserved at NW. N portion of site destroyed as a result of road building in the early decades of this century and further divided by a field bank running NE–SW. Original entrance not recognisable.
6:16 27-8-1988

995 MONEENSAURAN
OS 6:9:6 (202,189) Hachured OD 500–600
20723, 32500

Rath Raised circular area (int. dims. 24.9m) enclosed by an earthen bank and fosse, best preserved at NW. Original entrance not recognisable.
6:18 27-8-1988

996 MONEENTERRIFF
OS 5:13:3 (210,450) Indicated OD 500–600
19763, 31817

Rath Raised circular area (int. diam. 22.1m) enclosed by a low earthen bank and a wide, shallow fosse. The fosse has been largely infilled but its outline is nonetheless identifiable. Original entrance at NE.
5:37 12-8-1988

997 MONNERY UPPER
OS 25:5:3 (182,437) Hachured OD 200–300
23649, 30229

Rath Raised circular area (int. diam. 54m) enclosed by the remains of a low earthen bank and traces of a fosse running from E–S–NW. Original entrance not recognisable.
25:96 24-9-1991

998 MOODOGE
OS 38:4:4 (735,463) Hachured OD 400–500
25220, 28990

Rath Raised circular area (int. diam. *c.* 40m) enclosed by a substantial earthen bank which has been modified and incorporated into the field boundary. An earlier report (OPW 1970) noted slight traces of an external fosse and also suggested that the original entrance may have been at ESE.
38:48 26-8-1986

999 MOUNTPALLAS
OS 42:3:1 (505,550) Hachured OD 200–300
24982, 28440

Rath (site) An earlier report (OPW 1974) described a raised circular area (int. diam. *c.* 36m) enclosed by a fosse. Original entrance was not recognisable. Situated on the summit of a drumlin ridge. Site has been levelled.
42:32 10-9-1986

1000 MOUNTPALLAS
OS 42:3:2 (550,552) Hachured OD 200–300
25029, 28442

Rath Raised circular area (int. diam. *c.* 53m) enclosed by two low, wide earthen banks with a wide, shallow intermediate fosse. Outer bank has been defaced at E. Original entrance not recognisable.
42:33 17-6-1974

1001 MOUNTPALLAS
OS 42:3:2 (570,559) Hachured OD 200–300
25050, 28450

Rath Raised oval area (int. dims. *c.* 41m E–W; *c.* 33m N–S) enclosed by a low, wide earthen bank and a wide, shallow fosse. Original entrance not recognisable.
42:34 17-6-1974

1002 MOUNTPROSPECT
OS 38:16:1 (724,88) Hachured OD 300–400
25212, 28594

Rath Raised circular area (int. diam. *c.* 33m) enclosed by a low earthen bank and a wide, shallow fosse. An earlier report (OPW 1970) noted an external bank with traces of an outer fosse and suggested that the original entrance may have been at ESE.
38:52 29-8-1986

1003 MOYDRISTAN
OS 37:15:6 (676,2) *'Tony Fort'* OD 300–400
24187, 28494

Rath Raised circular area (int. diam. *c.* 46m) enclosed by a low earthen bank, recently faced with stone from W–NW–N, and a wide, deep, waterlogged fosse,

infilled at NE and poorly preserved from E–S–W. Break in bank at SE with slight remains of accompanying causeway probably represents original entrance.
37:50 30-7-1986

1004 MOYNAGH LOWER
OS 37:14:3 (444,104) Hachured OD 300–400
23941, 28599
Rath A much-disturbed raised circular area (int. diam. *c.* 41m) enclosed by a low earthen bank and a wide, deep fosse. Remains of low counterscarp bank identifiable at the outer lip of the fosse from S–WSW–SW. The enclosing elements have been levelled from WSW–N–ESE and replaced by modern field boundaries. Original entrance not recognisable.
37:51 29-7-1986

1005 MOYNAGH LOWER
OS 37:15:1 (522,90) Hachured OD 300–400
24023, 28585
Rath Raised circular area (int. diam. *c.* 42m) enclosed by a low earthen bank, best preserved from ENE–ESE and elsewhere surviving only as a modified scarp or incorporated into the field boundary. Original entrance not recognisable.
37:52 29-7-1986

1006 MOYNAGH UPPER
OS 37:14:6 (430,28) Indicated OD 300–400
23927, 28518
Rath Raised circular area (int. diam. *c.* 58m) enclosed by an earthen bank modified and incorporated into the field boundary and removed from ESE–S–SSW. Modern farmyard abuts the site from ESE–SE–S. Original entrance not recognisable.
37:53 29-7-1986

1007 MOYNAGH UPPER
OS 37:15:4 (498,52) Hachured OD 300–400
23998, 28545
Rath Raised circular area (int. diam. *c.* 43m) enclosed by two earthen banks with intermediate fosse. From NW–N the outer bank has been modified and incorporated into the field boundary and has been levelled from NE–E–SE. Fosse identifiable only from NW–N and at NE. Original entrance not recognisable.
37:54 29-7-1986

1008 MULLACROGHERY
OS 16:6:5 (360,320) Hachured OD 300–400
24802, 31396
Rath Raised circular area (int. diam. *c.* 35m) enclosed by a low earthen bank surmounted by a modern field bank from SW–N–E, and a wide, shallow fosse. Original entrance not recognisable.
16:100 9-10-1989

1009 MULLAGH
OS 40:14:3 (420,106) Hachured OD 300–400
26841, 28627
Rath Raised circular area (int. diam. *c.* 45m) enclosed by two substantial earthen banks with outer fosses. Intermediate fosse is wide and deep while outer fosse is absent from NNW–N–ENE. Corresponding breaks in banks at ENE, with causeway across intermediate fosse, represents original entrance.
40:46 16-7-1987

1010 MULLAGH
OS 40:15:4 (529,9) Hachured OD 300–400
26958, 28526
Rath (site) Marked 'Fort' on OS 1836 and 1876 eds. Situated on relatively level ground just N of Mullagh village. An earlier report (OPW 1969) recorded a slightly raised circular area defined by a low scarp. Site has been levelled.
40:48 16-7-1987

1011 MULLAGHAHY
OS 1:12:3 (895,236) Indicated OD 300–400
20467, 33828
Rath Raised circular area (int. diam. 26.4m) enclosed by a low earthen bank, largely replaced by a low stone wall particularly in the S half of the site, and slight traces of a fosse. A modern laneway encircles the external foot of the wall from SSE–S–SW. Break in perimeter (Wth 2.25m) at E may represent original entrance.
1:7 19-5-1993

1012 MULLAGHBOY (ED Ballymachugh)
OS 37:15:3 (636,138) Hachured OD 400–500
24144, 28637
Rath Raised circular area (int. diam. *c.* 33m) enclosed by a low earthen bank and a fosse identifiable throughout most of its circuit except from NE–E and from ESE–S–SW. An earlier report (OPW 1970) suggested that the original entrance may have been at ESE.
37:55 29-7-1986

1013 MULLAGHBOY (Tullygarvey By.)
OS 16:16:2 (843,131) Hachured OD 200–300
25314, 31201
Rath Raised circular area (int. diam. 40.6m) enclosed by two substantial earthen banks with outer fosses. Inner bank absent from NE–E–SW and only fragmentary remains of outer fosse visible from ENE–E–SE. Outer bank also absent from ENE–E–SE with accompanying outer fosse identifiable only from NNW–N–NE. Corresponding breaks in bank at SW with accompanying causeway represents original entrance.
16:101 15-9-1989

1014 MULLAGHORAN
OS 37:5:3 (220,447) Hachured OD 300–400
23701, 28959
Rath Raised circular area (int. diam. *c.* 42m) enclosed by an earthen bank, best preserved from SE–S–NNW and denuded elsewhere, and a fosse infilled from N–NE–E. An apparently modern counterscarp bank borders the fosse at S. An earlier report (OPW 1970) suggested that the original entrance may have been at W.
37:57 8-7-1986

1015 MULLAGHORAN
OS 37:6:1 (239,425) Hachured OD 200–300
23721, 28937
Rath Raised circular area (int. diam. 33m) enclosed by a much-denuded low earthen bank. An earlier report (OPW 1970) noted traces of an external fosse, suggested that the original entrance may have been at SE, and also observed possible remains of a souterrain within the internal area (**1261**).
37:58(01) 28-7-1986

1016 MULLAGHORAN
OS 37:6:4 (250,378) Hachured OD 300–400
23733, 28886
Rath Raised circular area (int. diam. *c.* 28m) enclosed by a substantial earthen bank and a wide, deep, partly waterlogged fosse infilled from WSW–W–WNW. Original entrance not recognisable.
37:59 9-7-1986

1017 MULLAGHORAN
OS 37:10:1 (270,298) Hachured OD 300–400
23755, 28803
Rath Raised circular area (int. diam. *c.* 27m) enclosed by a substantial earthen bank and a wide, deep, partly waterlogged fosse. An apparently modern, low counterscarp bank is identifiable outside the fosse from S–SW–W. An earlier description (OPW 1970) suggested that the original entrance was probably at E.
37:61 8-7-1986

1018 MULLALOUGHER
OS 16:5:3 (223,388) Hachured OD 476
24656, 31467
Rath A much-disturbed raised circular area (int. diam. 23.6m) defined from SW–W–N and from E–SE–S by a low scarp. From N–NNE–E this has been replaced by a modern stone wall which also extends along the upper edge of the scarp from N–W–SW. Original entrance not recognisable. Internal area very uneven.
16:102 12-10-1989

1019 MULLANACRE LOWER
OS 10:9:4 (72,172) Hachured OD 200–300
22543, 31859
Rath Raised circular area (int. dims. 29.2m E–W; 27.5m N–S) enclosed by a low earthen bank and a largely infilled fosse abutted by a modern field boundary from E–S–NW. Break in bank at E probably represents original entrance.
10:19 28-9-1989

1020 MULLANACROSS
OS 35:9:3 (202,244) Hachured OD 500–600
27580, 29421
Rath Raised circular area (int. diam. *c.* 34m) enclosed by a substantial, although partly denuded, earthen bank. Break in bank at SE may represent original entrance.
35:59 7-6-1988

1021 MULLANACROSS
OS 35:10:1 (244,280) Hachured OD 500–600
27624, 29459
Rath Raised circular area (int. diam. *c.* 60m) enclosed by a wide, low earthen bank modified and incorporated into the field boundary from S–W–NE and a wide, shallow fosse. Original entrance not recognisable.
35:60 14-3-1974

1022 MULLANAVARNOGE
OS 15:4:6 (914,528) Not marked OD 200–300
24410, 31612
Rath Marked 'Fort' on OS 1836 ed. Raised circular area (int. diam. 35m) enclosed by a low earthen bank and a wide, shallow, poorly preserved fosse. From NE–S–WNW the perimeter has been modified and incorporated into the field boundary. Elsewhere it has been largely levelled but its outline is still clearly identifiable. Original entrance not recognisable.
15:61 12-9-1989

1023 MULLYBRACK
OS 23:11:2 (552,301) Hachured OD 300–400
26962, 30755
Rath Raised oval area (int. dims. 28.3m WNW–ESE; 22.5m NNE–SSW) enclosed by an earth and stone bank with modern stone facing, and slight remains of a fosse. Entrance break at SE, the NE side of which is flanked by two large stones which also form part of the bank's external facing.
23:48 4-4-1992

1024 MULLYBRACK
OS 23:11:2 (586,293) Hachured OD 400–500
26998, 30747
Rath Raised oval area (int. dims. 55m NW–SE; 35.5m NE–SW) enclosed by a substantial earthen bank incorporated into the field boundary at SE and elsewhere recently scarped externally. Original entrance not recognisable.
23:49 4-4-1992

1025 MULLY LOWER
OS 6:9:3 (222,240) Hachured OD 400–500
20744, 32554
Rath Raised circular area (int. diam. 27.7m) enclosed by a well-defined earthen bank best preserved at NW, and a partly waterlogged fosse encircled by a modern earth and stone bank from NW–N–E. Break in bank with remains of accompanying causeway at SE represents original entrance.
6:19 26-8-1988

1026 MULLYMAGOWAN
OS 26:3:1 (462,547) Hachured OD 600–700
24920, 30356
Rath Raised circular area (int. diam. 28.1m) enclosed by two substantial earthen banks with intermediate fosse. From E–S–SSW outer bank and fosse have been replaced by a modern field boundary. From NNE–E both banks have been levelled. Original entrance not recognisable. Circular platform at centre presumably represents house site. Extending E from this is a possible collapsed souterrain (**1262**).
26:58(01) 23-10-1991

1027 MUNLOUGH NORTH
OS 9:16:2 (802,122) Hachured OD 200–300
22339, 31805
Rath Raised circular area (int. dims. 38.7m NW–SE; 36.9m NE–SW) enclosed by the remains of a substantial earthen bank and a wide, deep fosse. Bank has been reduced down to level of interior, and fosse infilled from SW–W–N. Original entrance not recognisable.
9:18 22-9-1988

1028 MUNLOUGH SOUTH
OS 9:16:2 (827,82) Not marked OD 300–400
22366, 31762
Rath Marked 'Fort' on OS 1836 ed. Not marked on subsequent eds. Site has been largely levelled leaving only an arc of low bank visible, running from NW–NNE. Situated on the slope of a low hill.
9:19 22-9-1990

1029 MURMOD
OS 39:3:5 (584,508) Hachured OD 400–500
26036, 29045
Rath (site) An earlier report (OPW 1969) described the site as a large raised oval area enclosed by a low earthen bank and vague traces of a fosse. Original entrance was not recognisable. Site has been levelled.
39:68 30-3-1987

1030 NAHEELIS
OS 15:13:5 (98,17) Hachured OD 200–300
23553, 31064
Rath Raised oval area (int. dims. *c.* 68m N–S; 54m E–W) enclosed by fragmentary remains of a once substantial earthen bank and traces of a fosse, both of which have been incorporated into the field boundary. Break in bank at NW with accompanying causeway may represent original entrance.
15:62 10-9-1989

1031 NEDDAIAGH
OS 16:7:4 (471,371) Hachured OD 300–500
24918, 31451
Rath Large raised subrectangular area (int. dims. *c.* 130m NE–SW; *c.* 80m E–W) divided into two unequal portions by a field boundary running ENE–WSW, the area SSW of which has been levelled. NNE of the field boundary the perimeter is much disturbed and difficult to interpret. Nonetheless the evidence suggests an external earthen bank, internal fosse and two scarps with low earthen banks on the upper edge of each. Between the intermediate and innermost bank is a wide angular space. Original entrance not recognisable.
16:103 9-11-1989

1032 NEWTOWN (Clanmahon By.)
OS 25:9:6 (221,171) Hachured OD 200–300
23693, 29948
Rath Raised circular area (int. diam 37.5m) enclosed by a substantial earthen bank and a fosse which is well-defined from S–N–NE and infilled or replaced by modern trenches elsewhere. Original entrance not recognisable.
25:99 24-9-1991

1033 NOLAGH
OS 28:7:5 (548,331) '*Cooneys Fort*' OD 500–600
26963, 30146
Rath Raised circular area (int. diam. *c.* 28m) enclosed by a low earthen bank and a wide, deep fosse. Outer earthen bank identifiable from ENE–SE–SSW appears to be the result of modern excavation of the fosse which now forms part of the field drainage system. Narrow break in bank with accompanying causeway at E represents original entrance.
28:39 1-4-1974

1034 OMARD
OS 37:4:4 (732,513) Hachured OD 300–400
24241, 29034
Rath Raised circular area (int. diam. 44m) enclosed by a substantial earthen bank and a wide, deep, partly waterlogged fosse which has been infilled from NNW–N. An earlier report (OPW 1970) suggested that the original entrance may have been at E.
37:62 15-7-1986

1035 OMARD
OS 37:8:2 (812,441) Hachured OD 300–400
24326, 28958

Rath An earlier report (OPW 1970) described the site as a raised circular area (int. diam *c.* 38m) enclosed by a wide, deep, partly waterlogged fosse and low earthen bank. Original entrance may have been at SE. Site is densely overgrown with vegetation. Modern tree-lined avenue runs from the NNE of the site to Omard Lough *c.* 350m NE.
37:68 17-7-1986

1036 OMARD
OS 37:8:2 (769,400) Not marked OD 300–400
24282, 28915
Rath Marked 'Fort' on OS 1836 and 1876 eds. Remains comprise a raised almost circular platform (dims. 49.3m N–S; 46.8m E–W) defined by a scarp (max. H 0.7m) and enclosed by slight traces of an earthen bank. Original entrance not recognisable.
37:64 27-5-1993

1037 OWNGALLEES
OS 9:14:6 (396,2) Hachured OD 200–300
21911, 31674
Rath Raised circular area (int. diam. 27.5m) enclosed by a substantial earthen bank, which has been removed from SSE–S–SW, and a wide, deep fosse. Break in bank with accompanying causeway at SE represents original entrance.
9:20/13:48* 19-9-1988

1038 PADDOCK
OS 20:14:3 (427,113) Hachured OD 300–400
23905, 30529
Rath (site) Marked 'Fort' on OS 1836 and 1876 eds. Situated on the summit of a long, narrow drumlin ridge. Although site has been levelled, the outline of a bank and fosse is still identifiable enclosing a slightly raised circular area (int. diam. *c.* 32m). Earlier reports (OPW 1968 and 1969) suggested that the original entrance may have been at ESE.
20:63 19-8-1990

1039 PADDOCK
OS 20:14:3 (450,116) Hachured OD 300–400
23930, 30533
Rath (site) Marked 'Fort' on all OS eds. Situated on the S slope of a long drumlin ridge. Although levelled, the outline of an earthen bank and a fosse may still be identified defining a circular area (int. diam. *c.* 28m). Earlier reports (OPW 1968 and 1969) suggested that the original entrance was probably at E.
20:64 19-8-1990

1040 PLUSH
OS 15:11:6 (668,182) Not marked OD 200–300
24153, 31244
Rath Not marked on any OS ed. Raised circular area (int. diam. *c.* 32m) enclosed by fragmentary remains of a low earthen bank and vague traces of a fosse. The site is divided into two roughly equal portions by a field boundary running NW–SE, the NE portion of which has been levelled leaving only the outline identifiable. Original entrance not recognisable. Densely overgrown with vegetation.
15:63 15-9-1989

1041 POLES
OS 21:13:6 (195,44) Hachured OD 300–400
24636, 30463
Rath Raised circular area (int. dims. 35.5m WNW–ESE; 34m NNE–SSW) enclosed by a slight earthen bank and a partly waterlogged fosse, well-defined from NNE–E–SW and very faint elsewhere. A modern field boundary also encroaches on the fosse from SSE–S–SW. Break in bank at ENE with remains of accompanying causeway represents original entrance.
21:66 14-9-1990

1042 POLES
OS 21:14:4 (294,54) Hachured OD 400–500
24741, 30474
Rath Raised circular area (int. dims. 28m N–S; 29.5m E–W) enclosed by a well-preserved earthen bank from SE–S–SW. Wide break in bank at ESE may represent original entrance.
21:67 21-9-1990

1043 POLLAFREE
OS 32:7:6 (630,361) Hachured OD 400–500
25105, 29522
Rath Raised circular area (int. diam. 24m) enclosed by a low earthen bank and traces of a fosse. Site is divided into two roughly equal portions by a roadway running NW–SE. Break in bank at SSW may represent original entrance.
32:43 14-4-1989

1044 POLLAKEEL (Upper Loughtee By.)
OS 26:13:3 (183,112) Hachured OD 700
24629, 29894
Rath Raised circular area (int. diam. 27.7m) enclosed by a low earthen bank with external fosse infilled from S–W–NW. From NW–N–NE fosse is absent where a stream skirts the outer foot of the bank. Break in bank at NNW may represent original entrance.
26:60 4-4-1992

1045 POLLAMORE NEAR
OS 25:4:3 (850,539) Hachured OD 418
24353, 30343
Rath Raised oval area (int. diam. 34.2m) enclosed by an earthen bank and the remains of a fosse. Original

entrance represented by break in bank with accompanying causeway at E.
25:101 13-9-1991

1046 POLLAMORE NEAR
OS 25:4:3 (866,548) Not marked OD 300–400 24370,30353
Rath Not marked on any OS ed. Slightly raised circular area (diam. 32.8m) enclosed by a low embankment. Site is divided into unequal portions by a field boundary running ESE–WNW with only a very faint outline of the rath identifiable N of this. Original entrance not recognisable. A standing stone (**89**) is situated immediately SSW of the site.
25:124 13-9-1991

1047 POLLAREAGH (Castlerahan By.)
OS 31:8:6 (911,332) Hachured OD 400–500 24426, 29485
Rath Subcircular raised area (int. dims. *c*. 40.5m ENE–WSW; *c*. 32m NNW–SSE) enclosed by a low earthen bank modified and incorporated into the field boundary from NW–N–NNE, and vague traces of a fosse. Wide break in bank at S may represent original entrance.
31:53 4-4-1974

1048 POLLAREAGH (Clanmahon By.)
OS 38:15:1 (530,123) Hachured OD 200–300 25007, 28629
Rath Raised circular area (int. diam. *c*. 50m) enclosed by a substantial earthen bank and a wide, deep, waterlogged fosse. Original entrance not recognisable.
38:53 1-9-1986

1049 POLLINTEMPLE
OS 43:4:2 (830,540) Hachured OD 300–400 26301, 28441
Rath Raised circular area (int. diam. 21m) enclosed by a low earthen bank. An earlier report (OPW 1969) suggested that the original entrance was probably at ESE.
43:32 6-8-1986

1050 PORT (ED Bawnboy)
OS 9:16:4 (700,22) Hachured OD 200–300 22233, 31697
Rath Raised circular area (int. diam. 20.2m) enclosed by a low earthen bank and the remains of a fosse which has been deepened and incorporated into the field boundary from E–SE–S. Narrow break in bank at NW may represent original entrance.
9:22 27-9-1988

1051 PORT (ED Bawnboy)
OS 9:16:4 (720,62) Hachured OD 200–300 22252, 31740
Rath Raised oval area (int. dims. *c*. 43m ENE–WSW; *c*. 32m NNW–SSE) enclosed by a substantial earthen bank and a wide, deep fosse. Break in bank at S with accompanying causeway represents original entrance.
9:23 25-9-1988

1052 PORTACLOGHAN
OS 15:10:1 (241,278) Hachured OD 100–200 23701, 31342
Rath Raised oval area (int. dims. 48m ENE–WSW; 43.5m NNW–SSE) enclosed by fragmentary remains of a low earthen bank and a wide, shallow fosse no longer identifiable from SSW–WNW where the site is now skirted by a field boundary. An earlier report (OPW 1968) suggested that the original entrance may have been at SE.
15:65 10-11-1989

1053 PORTANURE
OS 36:4:4 (749,495) Hachured OD 200–300 23284, 29006
Rath Lakeside rath on a promontory jutting into Lough Gowna. Semicircular raised area (int. dims. *c*. 40m NNW–SSE; 28m NE–SW) enclosed by a substantial earthen bank and a partially infilled, deep and wide, waterlogged fosse. The open E side faces the lake and a modern field boundary now extends across it. A small circular area enclosed by a substantial earthen bank, representing a hut site, occurs in the SSW of the interior of the rath. Original entrance not recognisable.
36:12 15-10-1991

1054 POTTLE EAST
OS 16:12:1 (715,290) Hachured OD 300–400 25177, 31367
Rath Raised circular area (int. diam. 23.4m) enclosed by a low earthen bank and a shallow fosse, both of which have been levelled from NNE–E–SE and replaced by a modern linear field boundary. Partly blocked break in bank at SE marks original entrance.
16:104 14-11-1989

1055 POTTLE WEST
OS 16:14:3 (443,134) Hachured OD 200–300 24891, 31200
Rath Raised circular area (int. diam. 33m) enclosed by a low earthen bank, both faces of which have been modified, and a fosse which is shallow and wide from SW–W and ill-defined elsewhere. Original entrance not recognisable but may have been at SW.
16:106 15-10-1989

1056 POTTLE WEST
OS 16:11:4 (465,167) Hachured OD 200–300 24914, 31235

Rath Raised circular area (int. diam. *c.* 44m) enclosed by a much-denuded low earthen bank and slight remains of a fosse identifiable only from NW–E–S. Both bank and fosse have been modified and incorporated into the field boundary. Partly blocked break in bank at E probably represents original entrance.
16:107 15-10-1989

1057 QUIVVY (Tullyhunco By.)
OS 24:12:1 (711,292) Hachured OD 400
23234, 30071
Rath Raised circular area (int. diam. 35m) enclosed by two substantial earthen banks with very wide, deep intermediate fosse. From SSW–W–NNW outer bank has been incorporated into the field boundary. Corresponding breaks in banks with accompanying causeway at SSE represents original entrance.
24:65 4-9-1991

1058 RACLAGHY
OS 42:7:6 (632,366) Hachured OD 200–300
25118, 28246
Rath Raised circular area (int. diam. *c.* 35m) enclosed by two low, wide banks of earth and stone with a wide and shallow intermediate fosse. Only the outline of the outer bank and fosse is discernible at E. From NNW–N–NE a modern field boundary cuts through the enclosing elements. However, the fosse is distinguishable outside this boundary. Original entrance at E.
42:35 25-6-1974

1059 RACLAGHY
OS 42:11:3 (661,296) Hachured OD 200–300
25150, 28173
Rath Raised circular area (int. diam. *c.* 30m) enclosed by a low but wide inner bank, a wide, deep fosse and a substantial outer bank. Original entrance not recognisable.
42:36 19-6-1974

1060 RAFFONY
OS 39:8:5 (829,368) Hachured OD 400–500
26296, 28899
Rath Raised circular area (int. diam. *c.* 24m) enclosed by a much-denuded low earthen bank which has been modified and incorporated into the field boundary from SSE–S–WSW. Original entrance not recognisable.
39:72 9-6-1987

1061 RAGASKIN
OS 20:4:5 (804,473) Hachured OD 400–500
24300, 30912
Rath Raised oval area (int. dims. 28.5m E–W; 21.5m N–S) enclosed by a low earthen bank and infilled external fosse, the outline of which (Wth 2.3m) is still nonetheless identifiable. Site is divided into two unequal portions by a modern field boundary running NW–SE. Original entrance may have been at SE.
20:65 10-8-1990

1062 RAGASKIN
OS 20:4:5 (845,469) Hachured OD 400–500
24343, 30909
Rath Raised almost circular area (int. diam. 32.2m) enclosed by a substantial earthen bank and a wide, shallow fosse best preserved from W–NNW and infilled elsewhere. Wide depression in bank at SE with suggestions of accompanying causeway may represent original entrance.
20:66 10-9-1990

1063 RAHAGHAN
OS 14:3:6 (690,490) Hachured OD 200–300
23198, 31561
Rath Raised circular area (int. diam. 58.5m) enclosed by two substantial earthen banks with wide, deep intermediate fosse. Outer bank identifiable only from N–E–SSE. An earlier report (OPW 1969) suggested that the original entrance may have been at S.
14:53 29-7-1989

1064 RAHEELAGH
OS 21:15:4 (467,13) Hachured OD 300–400
24924, 30433
Rath Raised circular area (int. diam. 24.6m) enclosed by a substantial earthen bank. Break in bank at E probably represents original entrance. The site was formerly situated within a dense forestry plantation, shown on all OS eds., which has since been removed.
21:68 19-9-1990

1065 RAHEELAGH
OS 26:16:2 (775,118) '*Black Fort*' OD 300–400
25254, 29907
Rath Raised circular area (int. dims. 32m NNW–SSE; 29.5m ENE–WSW) enclosed by three low and much-denuded earthen banks with accompanying fosses, the outermost one of which may be modern. Breaks in the two inner banks with traces of a possible blocked-up break in the outer bank almost certainly represents original entrance. Site has been planted with trees.
26:61 19-3-1992

1066 RAHEELAN
OS 11:9:2 (142,234) Hachured OD 200–300
23591, 31934
Rath Raised circular area (int. diam. 31.4m) enclosed by a low earthen bank and a wide, deep fosse distinguishable from NE–S–W. A laneway skirts the

perimeter of the site from NW–N–NE. Original entrance not recognisable.
11:24 10-6-1989

1067 RAHEEVER
OS 42:11:2 (606,242) Hachured OD 200–300
25092, 28115
Rath Raised circular area (int. diam. *c.* 33m) enclosed by two low earthen banks with wide, deep intermediate fosse. Outer bank best preserved at S. On top of the inner bank from E–S–W are traces of what appear to be foundations of a stone wall. Corresponding breaks in banks at E with accompanying causeway represents original entrance.
42:40 9-9-1986

1068 RAHEG
OS 21:1:1 (41,577) Hachured OD 382
24469, 31024
Rath An almost rectangular raised area (int. dims. 26m E–W; 26m N–S) enclosed by an earthen bank. The unusual plan of the site is probably due to its incorporation into the field boundary. The bank is very slight from N–NE–ENE. Original entrance not recognisable.
21:69 19-9-1990

1069 RAHULTAN
OS 20:3:5 (589,479) Indicated OD 200–300
24073, 30917
Rath Raised circular area (int. diam. 34.9m) enclosed by an earthen bank modified and incorporated into the field boundary, and a modern external trench. Partly blocked break in bank at E may represent original entrance. Internal area has been planted with apple trees.
20:67 6-8-1990

1070 RAKANE
OS 17:14:6 (395,13) Indicated OD 300–400
25830, 30696
Rath Marked 'Fort' on OS 1836 eds. Raised circular area (int. diam. 31.4m) enclosed by a substantial earthen bank and a wide, deep fosse infilled from WSW–N–SE. Break in bank at S with accompanying causeway represents original entrance.
17:58 17-11-1989

1071 RAKANE
OS 17:15:4 (476,33) Hachured OD 200–300
25934, 30639
Rath Marked 'Fort' on OS 1836 and 1876 eds. Raised circular area (int. diam. *c.* 35m) enclosed by the remains of a substantial earthen bank and slight traces of a fosse identifiable only at WNW. Both enclosing elements have been levelled from NW–E–S. Original entrance not recognisable.
17:59 17-11-1989

1072 RAKEEVAN
OS 34:2:6 (416,482) Hachured OD 500–600
26828, 29665
Rath Raised circular area (int. diam. 33m) enclosed by a substantial earthen bank and a narrow, shallow fosse, both of which have been incorporated into the field boundary from SW–W–NW. Narrow break in bank at SE may represent original entrance.
34:42 22-3-1974

1073 RAKEEVAN
OS 34:3:4 (482,471) Hachured OD 600–700
26897, 29654
Rath Large raised circular area (int. diam. *c.* 58m) enclosed by a wide, low earthen bank and slight traces of a fosse. Original entrance not recognisable.
34:43 22-3-1974

1074 RAKEEVAN
OS 34:7:2 (558,402) Hachured OD 500–600
26979, 29582
Rath Raised circular area (int. diam. *c.* 26m) enclosed by three earthen banks with intermediate fosses. Outer bank and fosse survive only from WSW–N–NE. Outer fosse has been recut and incorporated into the field boundary. Inner fosse is wide and deep. Break in bank at NE may represent original entrance.
34:44 26-3-1974

1075 RALAGHAN (ED Corraneary)
OS 22:8:6 (899,321) Hachured OD 400–500
26353, 30770
Rath Site is almost completely obscured by vegetation. An earlier report (OPW 1969) described it as a raised circular area (int. diam. *c.* 28m) enclosed by an earthen bank and a fosse which is clearly defined from N–S–WSW and poorly preserved elsewhere. Bank also poorly preserved from WSW–W–N. Break in bank at ENE probably represents original entrance. Indications of a possible souterrain in the internal area (**1264**).
22:31(01) 18-10-1990

1076 RALAGHAN (ED Taghart)
OS 28:8:1 (742,402) Hachured OD 600–700
27167, 30224
Rath Raised circular area (int. diam. *c.* 35m) enclosed by a substantial inner earthen bank, a wide, deep fosse and traces of an outer bank. Both fosse and outer bank are now only identifiable from NNE–SE. Narrow entrance at E may be original.
28:42 29-3-1974

1077 RALUDAN
OS 17:10:4 (258,176) Hachured OD 300–400
25844, 31000
Rath Raised circular area (int. diam. *c*. 33m) enclosed by a substantial earthen bank and an infilled fosse (Wth 3.2m) the outline of which is nonetheless distinguishable. An earlier report (OPW 1969) noted that the original entrance was at E.
17:62 19-9-1990

1078 RAMONAN
OS 38:3:6 (679,527) Hachured OD 400–500
25160, 29057
Rath Raised circular area (int. diam. *c*. 40m) enclosed by a substantial earthen bank and a wide, deep, waterlogged fosse, poorly preserved from NNE–E–SW. Break in bank with accompanying causeway at ENE represents original entrance. Internal area densely overgrown with vegetation.
38:56 15-8-1986

1079 RANRENAGH
OS 32:3:6 (618,484) Hachured OD 500
25090, 29651
Rath Raised circular area (int. diam. 30m) enclosed by a substantial earthen bank and a wide, deep, partly waterlogged fosse. Break in bank at E with accompanying causeway probably represents original entrance.
32:45 27-4-1989

1080 RANRENAGH
OS 32:7:3 (626,412) Hachured OD 400–500
25099, 29575
Rath Raised circular area (int. diam. 33m) enclosed by an earthen bank and a shallow fosse overgrown with scrub, which survives only from S–SW–W. Break in bank at SE may represent original entrance.
32:46 27-4-1989

1081 RARAGH
OS 29:14:5 (340,10) Hachured OD 400–500
27722, 29815
Rath Raised circular area (int. diam. *c*. 32m) enclosed by a substantial earthen bank and a fosse, both of which are best preserved at W. Break in bank with traces of accompanying causeway at NE may represent original entrance.
29:11 8-8-1988

1082 RARAGH
OS 29:14:5 (340,31) Hachured OD 400–500
27721, 29837
Rath Raised circular area (int. diam. *c*. 30m) enclosed by a substantial earthen bank and a fosse best preserved from ESE–S–SW where it is partly waterlogged and otherwise infilled. Break in bank at SE may represent original entrance. Internal area densely overgrown with vegetation.
29:12 8-8-1988

1083 RARAGH
OS 29:14:5 (360,51) Indicated OD 400–500
27743, 29858
Rath Raised circular area (int. diam. *c*. 38m) enclosed by a substantial earthen bank and a fosse identifiable from ENE–SE–SSW. Original entrance not recognisable.
29:13 8-8-1988

1084 RASKILL
OS 21:10:5 (371,176) Hachured OD 400–500
24820, 30604
Rath (site) Although levelled in 1952, the outline of the enclosing elements can be distinguished for a short stretch at SW. From earlier descriptions (OPW 1968 and 1970) it would appear that the site comprised a slightly raised oval area (int. dims *c*. 32m NNW–SSE; 24.5m ENE–WSW) enclosed by a slight earthen bank and a fosse. Original entrance may have been at SSE.
21:70 14-9-1990

1085 RASKILL
OS 21:10:5 (376,168) Hachured OD 400–500
24826, 30596
Rath (site) Levelled in 1952. Earlier reports (OPW 1969 and 1970) recorded that it comprised a raised circular area (int. diam. 33.6m) enclosed by a substantial earthen bank and a fosse. During levelling operations, very large stones were found in the outer face of the bank (local information). Original entrance was not recognisable. Not visible at ground level.
21:71 19-9-1990

1086 RASSAN
OS 32:15:4 (520,27) Hachured OD 300–400
24991, 29167
Rath Raised circular area (int. diam. 36m) enclosed by a substantial earthen bank and a wide, deep, partly waterlogged fosse running from SE–W–NE. Elsewhere the enclosing features have been replaced with a modern field bank and drain. Original entrance not recognisable. Internal area densely overgrown with vegetation.
32:47 19-4-1989

1087 RASSAN
OS 32:15:5 (559,21) Hachured OD 300–400
25033, 29162
Rath Raised circular area (int. diam. 35m) enclosed by a substantial earthen bank and the remains of a

largely infilled fosse. Break in bank at E may represent original entrance.
32:48 19-4-1989

1088 RASSAN
OS 38:3:1 (539,596) Hachured OD 200–300
25011, 29128
Rath Raised circular area (int. diam. *c.* 29m) enclosed by a substantial earthen bank and traces of a fosse. Both fosse and bank have been levelled from NE–E–SSE. Original entrance not recognisable.
38:57 28-3-1977

1089 RASUDDAN
OS 38:8:6 (875,334) Hachured OD 400–500
25369, 28855
Rath Raised circular area (int. diam. *c.* 34m) enclosed by a substantial earthen bank and vague traces of a fosse. Break in bank at ENE with accompanying causeway represents original entrance.
38:58 27-8-1986

1090 RATHCORICK
OS 25:8:3 (851,405) Hachured OD 500
24356, 30202
Rath Raised circular area (int. diam. 45m) enclosed by two very substantial earthen banks with a deep intermediate fosse. Original entrance at ESE represented by corresponding breaks in the banks with accompanying causeway. Eight years ago during the course of tree planting, the landowner discovered a wooden post, roughly 1m high, inside the inner bank, which he speculated was probably part of a palisade. (CUCAP, ALJ 83/85).
25:103 15-9-1991

1091 RAY
OS 13:3:6 (653,502) Hachured OD 200–300
22184, 31565
Rath Not marked on OS 1836 eds. Raised circular area (int. diam. 39.1m) enclosed by a low earthen bank and a wide, shallow fosse. The site is divided into three unequal portions by field boundaries. Original entrance not recognisable.
13:52 27-6-1989

1092 REASK
OS 25:4:6 (923,507) Indicated OD 400–500
24432, 30310
Rath Marked 'Fort' on OS 1836 and 1876 eds. Raised circular area (int. diam. 37.3m) enclosed by an earthen bank and a fosse, both of which have been modified and incorporated into the field boundary from SSW–W–NNW. From NNW–N a field boundary runs immediately outside of the site. Here the fosse has been levelled in and the bank is slight. Break in bank at SE with remains of accompanying causeway may represent original entrance.
25:105/26:62* 29-4-1993

1093 RELAGH MORE
OS 34:14:3 (419,76) Hachured OD 500–600
26835, 29237
Rath Raised circular area (int. diam. *c.* 36m) enclosed by two earthen banks with outer fosses. Both the external bank and the outer fosse, which is waterlogged and infilled from ESE–S–SW, have been largely incorporated into the field boundary. Original entrance not recognisable.
34:47 21-3-1974

1094 ROEBUCK
OS 42:7:1 (519,414) Indicated OD 200–300
24998, 28296
Rath Marked 'Fort' on OS 1836 and 1876 eds. Raised circular area (int. diam. *c.* 35m) enclosed by a low earthen bank faced externally with drystone masonry and incorporated into the field boundary, and vague traces of a shallow fosse identifiable only from N–E–S. A low counterscarp bank surrounds the fosse. Original entrance not recognisable.
42:43 20-6-1974

1095 RONARD
OS 16:3:5 (610,479) Not marked OD 300–400
25065, 31566
Rath Marked 'Fort' on OS 1836 ed. and 'Site of' on 1876 ed. Raised circular area (int. diam. 24.8m) enclosed by a low earthen bank and possible remains of a fosse. The bank has been incorporated into the field boundary from WNW–NNW, and from NNE–N–E it survives only as a low scarp. Original entrance not recognisable. Very overgrown with vegetation.
16:109 26-10-1989

1096 ROOSKY
OS 23:13:4 (20,24) Hachured OD 500–600
26403, 30458
Rath Raised circular area (int. diam. *c.* 28.6m) enclosed by a substantial earthen bank and a wide, deep, waterlogged fosse. An earlier report (OPW 1977) noted the remains of a low outer bank from S–W–NW. From NNW–N–NE fosse has been deepened and widened and is now used as a watering-hole for cattle. Original entrance not recognisable.
23:50 21-5-1992

1097 ROSEHILL (Tullyhaw By.)
OS 13:3:6 (676,480) Hachured OD 300–400
22208, 31541
Rath Raised circular area (int. diam. 31.2m) enclosed

Fig. 26—A bivallate rath at Rathcorick (**1090**)
(Reproduced courtesy of Cambridge University Committee for Aerial Photography).

by a substantial earthen bank and a wide, deep, waterlogged fosse. An earlier report (OPW 1969) noted an entrance feature at E.
13:53 15-6-1989

1098 ROSSCOLGAN
OS 25:4:4 (718,526) Hachured OD 300–400 24214, 30327
Rath Raised circular area (int. dims. 43m NW–SE; 41.5m NE–SW) enclosed by a substantial earthen bank which has been incorporated into the field boundary from WNW–N. A deep external trench surrounding the bank may have been dug on the site of a fosse. Original entrance not recognisable.
25:106 13-9-1991

1099 ROSSKEERAGH
OS 15:2:4 (290,507) Hachured OD 200–300 23751, 31584
Rath Raised circular area (int. diam. 21.6m) enclosed by a low much-denuded earthen bank and vague traces of a fosse. The site is divided into equal portions by a field boundary running WNW–ESE. Although site has been levelled to SSW, its outline is still identifiable. Original entrance not recognisable. A possible hut site lies *c*. 20m NW of rath (**1271**).
15:69(01) 12-9-1989

1100 SALLAGHAN (ED Scrabby)
OS 30:11:6 (666,222) Hachured OD 300–400 23193, 29354
Rath Raised circular area (int. diam. 41.1m) enclosed a very wide, deep, waterlogged fosse and substantial earthen bank. Fragmentary traces of a low counterscarp bank identifiable at the outer lip of the fosse from S–SW–N. Fosse absent from N–NNE. Original entrance at SE.
30:34 9-10-1991

1101 SALLAGHILL
OS 32:13:2 (138,130) Hachured OD 300–400 24588, 29273
Rath Marked 'Fort' on OS 1836 and 1876 eds. Located at the confluence of two streams in level, low-lying ground. Site is densely overgrown with vegetation rendering inspection impossible.
32:49 28-6-1989

1102 SEEHARAN
OS 40:2:4 (232,503) Hachured OD 400–500 26640, 29045
Rath Raised circular area (int. diam. *c*. 35m) enclosed by a partly denuded, low earthen bank which has been modified and incorporated into the field boundary from N–E–SSE. Another more recent boundary has been built against its outer face from NNW–N. Original entrance not recognisable.
40:49 8-7-1987

1103 SEEHARAN
OS 40:6:1 (286,395) Hachured OD 400 26697, 28932
Rath Raised circular area (int. diam. *c*. 34m) enclosed by a substantial earthen bank and a fosse identifiable from S–W–E. An apparently modern, low counterscarp bank encircles the fosse. Break in bank at ESE probably represents original entrance. Projecting from the inner face of the bank at NW is a rectangular area (int. dims. 7m N–S; 3.5m E–W) enclosed by a low earthen bank which presumably represents a hut site. Break in bank at E represents original entrance to the structure.
40:50 8-7-1987

1104 SHANCOR (Clanmahon By.)
OS 31:3:4 (535,501) Hachured OD 400–500 24027, 29660
Rath Raised circular area (int. diam. *c*. 33m) enclosed by two substantial earthen banks with outer fosses. External fosse best preserved at SE and largely infilled elsewhere. From SE–W–NE a modern field boundary surmounts the outer bank. Corresponding breaks in banks with accompanying causeway across inner fosse represents original entrance.
31:55 8-6-1992

1105 SHANNOW LOWER
OS 31:7:5 (591,351) Hachured OD 400–500 24088, 29502

Rath Raised circular area (int. diam. *c.* 37m) enclosed by two substantial earthen banks with intermediate fosse. Outer face of external bank has been scarped in relatively modern times and a trench cut on its outer side. Original entrance not recognisable. Internal area very overgrown with vegetation.
31:56 5-6-1992

1106 SHANTEMON
OS 21:5:6 (206,312) Hachured OD 718
24645, 30746
Rath D-shaped raised area (int. dims. *c.* 36m ENE–WSW; 40m NNW–SSE) enclosed by a low bank of earth and stone which has been removed from WNW–N–NE. Original entrance not recognisable. Internal ground level uneven. Situated on the summit of a hill affording magnificent views over the surrounding countryside.
21:72 27-9-1990

1107 SHANTULLY
OS 25:10:1 (268,243) Indicated OD 200–300
23742, 30025
Rath (possible) May originally have been a rath later transformed into a tree-ring. Raised circular area (int. dims. 27.2m N–S; 24.7m E–W) enclosed by an earthen bank and traces of a fosse or trench identifiable only from SW–W–N. Original entrance not recognisable. Interior planted with coniferous trees.
25:107 5-9-1991

1108 SHINAN
OS 23:16:4 (731,73) Hachured OD 400–500
27153, 30516
Rath Raised circular area (int. diam. 24.3m) enclosed by a low earthen bank. Slight break in bank at E may represent original entrance. Inside the bank at W is a shallow, roughly parallel-sided depression extending from E–W.
23:51 4-4-1992

1109 SKEAGH (Clankee By.)
OS 28:9:3 (220,293) 'Lisgrania Fort' OD 600–700
26616, 30103
Rath (possible) Raised circular area (int. diam. *c.* 24m) enclosed by two earthen banks with outer fosses. External fosse has been recut and is now utilised as a field drain. Original entrance not recognisable.
28:44 25-8-1988

1110 SLIEVEBRICKAN
OS 14:2:1 (232,565) Hachured OD 200–300
22714, 31635
Rath Raised circular area (int. diam. 25.8m) enclosed by a low earthen bank. An earlier report (OPW 1969) suggested that the original entrance may have been at SSW.
14:54 19-7-1989

1111 SNUGBOROUGH
OS 10:9:6 (158,197) Hachured OD 200–300
22634, 31886
Rath Raised circular area (int. dims. 34.8m NE–SW; 32.7m NW–SE) enclosed by a substantial earthen bank and a wide, shallow fosse, both of which have been destroyed at N as a consequence of quarrying. Break in bank at E with traces of accompanying causeway represents original entrance.
10:20 20-9-1989

1112 SNUGBOROUGH
OS 10:9:3 (159,248) Hachured OD 200–300
22634, 31940
Rath Crescent-shaped raised area (int. dims. 45.5m NW–SE; *c.* 35m NE–SW) enclosed from NW–N–SE by a substantial earthen bank and a wide, shallow fosse. Elsewhere the site is defined by a sheer cliff-face. Break in bank at NW with accompanying causeway represents original entrance.
10:21 20-9-1989

1113 SNUGBOROUGH
OS 10:9:6 (204,217) Hachured OD 200–300
22682, 31908
Rath Raised D-shaped area (int. dims. *c.* 34m N–S; *c.* 24m E–W) enclosed by a substantial earthen bank and a fosse surrounded by traces of a low counterscarp bank. Original entrance not recognisable.
10:22 20-9-1989

1114 STRAMAQUERTY
OS 33:15:4 (539,8) Hachured OD 400–500 25987, 29157
Rath Raised circular area (int. diam. *c.* 33m) enclosed by two low earthen banks with intermediate shallow fosse. Outer bank has been levelled and farm buildings run along the outer edge of the fosse from NE–E–SSE. Original entrance not recognisable.
33:47 3-4-1974

1115 STRAMAQUERTY
OS 33:15:5 (556,36) Hachured OD 400–500
26005, 29187
Rath Raised circular area (int. diam. *c.* 35m) enclosed by a wide, low earthen bank, stone-faced in part externally, and a fosse which has been infilled from SE–S and recut and incorporated into the field boundary from S–W–N. Original entrance not recognisable.
33:48 3-4-1974

1116 STRANADARRAGH
OS 13:2:2 (320,575) Hachured OD 200–300
21831, 31638
Rath Raised oval area (int. dims. 37.3m N–S; 31.1m) enclosed by a substantial earthen bank and a wide, deep, partly waterlogged fosse. An earlier report (OPW 1969) suggested that the original entrance was probably at SE.
13:56 3-7-1989

1117 STRANADARRAGH
OS 13:2:2 (356,549) Hachured OD 207
21870, 31611
Rath Raised circular area (int. diam. 32.4m) enclosed by a substantial earthen bank and a shallow fosse identifiable only from SSE–S–W. Both bank and fosse have been destroyed from NNW–N–NE as a consequence of road construction. A stream flows through a narrow channel at the external foot of the bank from ENE–E–SSE and a modern pump-house has been erected at E. An earlier report (OPW 1969) suggested that the original entrance was probably at E.
13:57 3-7-1989

1118 STRANAGAP
OS 5:14:2 (323,594) Hachured OD 100–200
19883, 31666
Rath Situated immediately N of the Owenmore River. Raised almost circular area (int. diam. 24.4m) enclosed by two substantial earthen banks with intermediate fosse. Outer bank and fosse identifiable only from ESE–S–SW. Fosse is flooded by the waters of the river for most of the year (local information). A modern laneway skirts the external foot of the bank from NNW–N–NE. Original entrance not recognisable.
5:38 12-8-1988

1119 SWELLAN LOWER
OS 20:15:5 (570,75) '*Drumgoon Fort*' OD 300–400
24057, 30490
Rath Raised oval area (int. dims. 41.5m NNE–SSW; 36m WNW–ESE) enclosed by two earthen banks with outer fosses. Modern field boundaries skirt the exterior of the outer fosse from S–W–NNW and from NW–N. Corresponding breaks in banks at E probably represent original entrance, although there are no accompanying causeways.
20:70 22-8-1990

1120 SWELLAN LOWER
OS 20:15:5 (581,52) Hachured OD 300–400
24069, 30465
Rath Raised roughly circular area (int. dims. *c.* 38m NE–SW; 32m NW–SE) enclosed by a low earthen bank and a wide, shallow fosse identifiable only from W–N–NE and from SE–S–SSW. Original entrance not recognisable.
20:71 22-8-1990

1121 SWELLAN UPPER
OS 20:15:3 (620,116) '*Swellan Fort*' OD 300–400
24109, 30534
Rath Large oval area (int. dims. 49m N–S; 42.5m E–W) enclosed by a substantial earthen bank with an external fosse and low counterscarp bank best preserved from NW–N–NE. A level area (Wth 2.4m) lies outside of this again and is encircled by a third bank which is planted with trees and may be a later landscape feature. It is accompanied by an external fosse. The counterscarp bank is best preserved from NW–N–NE. Corresponding breaks in all three banks at S may represent original entrance, although there are no accompanying causeways.
20:72 22-9-1990

1122 TANDERAGEE
OS 34:6:2 (364,415) Hachured OD 500–600
26774, 29594
Rath Raised circular area (int. diam. 27m) enclosed by a wide, low earthen bank and traces of a shallow fosse. Site is divided into two apparently equal portions by a field boundary running NNW–SSE. Although the site has been levelled to ENE, its outline is still distinguishable. Original entrance not recognisable.
34:50 22-3-1974

1123 TAWLAGHT (Clanmahon By.)
OS 37:11:6 (621,168) Indicated OD 300–400
24127, 28668
Rath Raised circular area (int. diam. 41m) enclosed by a low earthen bank and a narrow, shallow fosse with traces of an apparently modern counterscarp bank outside of it at N. An earlier report (OPW 1970) suggested that the original entrance may have been at NE.
37:70 29-7-1986

1124 TEDEEHAN UPPER
OS 31:15:2 (578,95) Hachured OD 300–400
24076, 29231
Rath Raised circular area (int. diam. *c.* 38.5m) enclosed by a substantial earthen bank which has been modified and incorporated into the field boundary and is now surrounded by a modern drain. The bank has also been levelled from WSW–W–N and a modern laneway, delimited by an earthen bank on its W side, is built on its site and encroaches on the interior of the rath. Original entrance not recognisable.
31:57 10-4-1974

1125 TEEBOY
OS 9:13:3 (204,136) Indicated OD 300–400
21707, 31813
Rath Raised circular area (int. diam. 24.9m) enclosed by an earthen bank and a fosse identifiable only from

S–WSW and infilled elsewhere. Site has been destroyed by road building from NE–E–SE. Break in bank at W may represent original entrance.
9:25 10-9-1988

1126 TERMON (Upper Loughtee By.)
OS 33:6:6 (444,349) Hachured OD 400–500
25883, 29516
Rath Raised circular area (int. diam. *c*. 29m) enclosed by a low earthen bank and very slight traces of a fosse identifiable only from NW–E–SE and replaced by modern field drains. Original entrance not recognisable.
33:50 4-4-1974

1127 TERMON (Upper Loughtee By.)
OS 33:11:1 (510,258) Hachured OD 400–500
25954, 29420
Rath Raised circular area (int. diam. *c*. 28m) enclosed by a low earthen bank. Original entrance may have been at SE.
33:51 14-9-1988

1128 THOMASCOURT OR DRUMROOSK
OS 25:8:4 (703,309) Hachured OD 300–400
24200, 30099
Rath Raised almost circular area (int. dims 49m NNW–SSE; 53m ENE–WSW) enclosed by an earthen bank and slight traces of a fosse running from ESE–SSE. Original entrance not recognisable. A well is situated outside the bank at NNW.
25:111 1-10-1991

1129 TICOSKER
OS 24:13:3 (160,87) Hachured OD 300–400
22654, 29850
Rath Raised circular area (int. diam. 45.6m) enclosed by a substantial earthen bank and a shallow, narrow, partly waterlogged fosse. Break in bank with accompanying causeway at SE represents original entrance.
24:66 20-8-1991

1130 TIEVENAMAN
OS 33:6:1 (286,380) Hachured OD 500
25716, 29547
Rath Raised circular area (int. diam *c*. 24m) enclosed by a substantial earthen bank faced externally with intermittent drystone masonry, and a fosse which has been recut and is now surrounded by a bank of modern spoil. Original entrance not recognisable. Internal area divided into two roughly equal portions by a field boundary running NW–SE.
33:52 5-4-1974

1131 TIRCULLEN
OS 25:6:6 (395,352) Hachured OD 200–300
23875, 30141
Rath Raised oval area (int. dims. 42m N–S; 37m E–W) enclosed by two substantial earthen banks with wide, deep intermediate fosse. Outer bank absent from NE–E–SSW and replaced by a field boundary from NE–E–ESE. Original entrance may possibly have been at E.
25:114 14-9-1991

1132 TIRLAHODE UPPER
OS 27:9:4 (27,219) Hachured OD 600–700
25439, 30014
Rath Raised circular area (int. diam. 35.5m) enclosed by a low, broad earthen bank and a fosse which has been recut to accomodate a drain from SSW–N–NNE and is shallow and partly waterlogged elsewhere. Original entrance not recognisable.
27:11 18-3-1977

1133 TIRLAHODE UPPER
OS 27:13:5 (82,73) Hachured OD 500–600
25498, 29861
Rath Raised roughly circular area (int. diam. 27.8m) enclosed by a substantial earthen bank and a fosse which been infilled and partly modified and incorporated into the field drainage system. Site is divided into two unequal portions by a modern roadway which cuts through both bank and fosse at NW and ESE. Original entrance not recognisable.
27:12 18-3-1977

1134 TOBERLYAN DUFFIN
OS 13:8:2 (837,427) Hachured OD 200–300
22379, 31487
Rath Raised circular area (int. diam. 38.4m) enclosed by a substantial earthen bank and a wide, deep, partly waterlogged fosse. Field boundaries skirt the site from SW–N–NNE. Original entrance was probably at NE.
13:62 10-6-1989

1135 TOGHER OR DANESFORT DEMESNE
OS 20:14:4 (247,57) Indicated OD 200–300
23716, 30468
Rath Raised circular area (int. dims. *c*. 53m ENE–WSW; *c*. 38m NNW–SSE) enclosed by a substantial earthen bank surmounted by a modern wall, and a wide, deep fosse infilled and paved with a pathway from SW–N–E. The internal area is used as an orchard. Original entrance not recognisable.
20:75 10-9-1993

1136 TOGHERNAROSS
OS 37:14:4 (294,72) Not marked OD 300–400
23783, 28564

Rath Marked 'Fort' on OS 1836 ed. and 'Site of' on 1876 ed. Raised circular area (int. diam. *c.* 30m) enclosed by a low earthen bank. Original entrance not recognisable.
37:73 7-7-1986

1137 TONAGH (Clanmahon By.)
OS 42:6:1 (281,451) Hachured OD 200–300
24747, 28333
Rath Raised circular area (int. diam. *c.* 25m) enclosed by a low, partly denuded earthen bank and faint traces of a fosse identifiable only at E and at S. Original entrance not recognisable.
42:44 20-6-1974

1138 TONAGH (Clanmahon By.)
OS 42:6:2 (311,412) Hachured OD 200–300
24778, 28292
Rath (site) Although this rath has been largely levelled and incorporated into the field boundary from SSW–W, the outline of the bank and fosse is still identifiable enclosing a circular area (diam. *c.* 40m).
42:45 20-6-1974

1139 TONAGHBANE
OS 17:5:6 (209,340) Hachured OD 300–400
25949, 31220
Rath Raised circular area (int. diam. *c.* 37m) enclosed by a substantial, although partly denuded, earthen bank and faint traces of a fosse identifiable only from SW–N–NE. Elsewhere, fosse has been infilled and replaced by a modern trackway. Partly blocked break in bank at S may represent original entrance.
17:64 12-11-1989

1140 TONAGHBANE
OS 17:6:4 (233,342) Indicated OD 300–400
25977, 31200
Rath Marked 'Fort' on OS 1836 ed. Raised circular area (int. diam. *c.* 27m) enclosed by an earthen bank, which been much modified and incorporated into the field boundary from S–W–NNW, and traces of a shallow fosse. Both bank and fosse have been levelled from NNW–E–S. Original entrance not recognisable.
17:65 12-11-1989

1141 TONAGHBANE
OS 17:6:4 (257,343) Hachured OD 300–400
26003, 31177
Rath Raised circular area (int. diam. 31.7m) enclosed by a substantial earthen bank and a wide, deep fosse encompassed by a low but well-defined counterscarp bank from SSW–NW. An earlier report (OPW 1969) recorded that the original entrance may have been at ENE.
17:66 12-11-1989

1142 TONYHALLAGH
OS 13:4:3 (849,569) Hachured OD 200–300
22390, 31637
Rath Raised circular area (int. diam. 38.4m) enclosed by two low earthen banks with poorly defined shallow outer fosses. External fosse and bank are absent from WNW–N–ENE. Corresponding breaks in banks at WSW represent original entrance.
13:64 22-10-1969

1143 TONYHULL
OS 22:11:3 (689,251) Hachured OD 500–600
26131, 30695
Rath Raised circular area (int. diam. 38.4m) enclosed by a bank which has been replaced by a modern field boundary from W–NW–N, and a fosse. The E half of the site has been levelled although the outline of the enclosing features is still identifiable. Original entrance not recognisable. The site is encircled by a modern field boundary from SE–S–WSW. Indications of a possible souterrain (**1265**) in the internal area.
22:33(01) 27-10-1990

1144 TONYIN
OS 22:3:1 (507,587) Hachured OD 400–500
25936, 31048
Rath Raised circular area (int. diam 45.6m) with a small subrectangular annexe at NE, enclosed by a substantial earthen bank modernised at NE and SE, and a fosse identifiable from SE–W–N. Bank has been removed from NNE–E. Original entrance not recognisable.
22:34 15-10-1990

1145 TRINITY ISLAND
OS 20:13:4 (13,12) Hachured OD 100–200
23469, 30418
Rath (site) Marked 'Fort' on OS 1836 and 1876 eds. and depicted as a semicircular enclosure extending from SW–N–NE, bordered by a linear field boundary from NE–S–SW. Davies (ITA Survey 1942) described the site as being roughly triangular (dims. 37.8m x 22.6m), enclosed by a low earthen bank and traces of a fosse. Davies also noted that 'two pieces of iron slag were found in the fort'. Trinity Island is now occupied by a huge plantation of coniferous trees. The site was levelled prior to tree planting (local information).
20:76 19-11-92

1146 TULLANIERIN
OS 5:14:2 (344,555) Indicated OD 300–400
19906, 31707
Rath Raised circular area (int. diam. 28.6m) enclosed by a low earthen bank and a narrow, shallow, infilled fosse surrounded by a low counterscarp bank at SW. A series of largely grassed-over boulders are visible in the bank at N and a low field-clearance cairn of stones

lies within the internal area. Original entrance not recognisable.
5:43 19-8-1988

1147 TULLAVALLY
OS 16:16:1 (752,128) Hachured OD 300–400
25218, 31196
Rath Raised circular area (int. diam. 26m) enclosed by a substantial earthen bank and a fosse which is wide, shallow and waterlogged and identifiable only from SW–W–NE. From ESE–SSW the bank has been modified and is surmounted by a modern field boundary. Wide break in bank at NNW probably represents original entrance.
16:111 12-11-1989

1148 TULLAVALLY
OS 16:16:2 (774,108) Indicated OD 200–300
25242, 31175
Rath Raised circular area (int. diam. 32m) enclosed by a steep scarp surmounted by a low modern bank incorporated into the field boundary, and an infilled fosse. Depression in scarp at S may represent original entrance.
16:112 12-11-1989

1149 TULLY (Tullyhunco By.)
OS 24:3:2 (599,602) Hachured OD 300–400
23113, 30398
Rath (site) An earlier report (OPW 1970) described an almost circular area (int. diam. *c.* 32m) enclosed by the remains of an earthen bank which has been levelled except where incorporated into the field boundary at S. Original entrance may have been at S. Site has been levelled. (ITA Survey 1946)
24:68 7-9-1991

1150 TULLY (Tullyhunco By.)
OS 24:3:2 (602,568) Hachured OD 300–400
23116, 30362
Rath (site) An earlier report (OPW 1970) described a raised circular area (int. diam. 39m) enclosed by a bank which has been levelled, except at E where it is incorporated into the field boundary, and an external fosse. Original entrance not recognisable.
24:69 7-9-1991

1151 TULLYAGAN
OS 38:15:5 (558,16) Hachured OD 200–300
25037, 28516
Rath Raised circular area (int. diam. *c.* 28m) enclosed by a substantial earthen bank which has been scarped and incorporated into the field boundary. An earlier report (OPW 1970) noted slight traces of an external fosse and suggested that the original entrance may have been at E.
38:59 2-9-1986

1152 TULLYBRICK (ED Cootehill Rural)
OS 18:5:4 (56,351) Hachured OD 400–500
26431, 31444
Rath Raised oval area (int. dims. *c.* 40m NE–SW; 34m NW–SE) enclosed by a substantial earthen bank and a fosse identifiable only from SSW–W–N and infilled elsewhere. An earlier report (OPW 1969) recorded that the original entrance was at SE.
18:13 15-7-1990

1153 TULLYCOE (Tullygarvey By.)
OS 21:8:5 (780,344) Hachured OD 300–400
25251, 30785
Rath Raised circular area (int. diam. 26.8m) enclosed by two earthen banks with wide, deep, intermediate fosse. Outer bank, identifiable only from SW–W–NW and from NE–S–SSW, has been much modified and incorporated into the field boundary. An earlier report (OPW 1968) recorded that the original entrance was at SW.
21:74 21-9-1990

1154 TULLYGULLIN
OS 41:1:2 (151,567) Hachured OD 300–400
23632, 28445
Rath Raised circular area (int. diam. *c.* 28m) enclosed by a low earthen bank and a wide, shallow fosse. Original entrance not recognisable.
41:21 21-6-1974

1155 TULLYNACROSS (Tullyhaw By.)
OS 6:5:2 (117,447) Hachured OD 400–500
20632, 32772
Rath Raised circular area (int. diam. 21.9m) enclosed by a well-defined, low but steep-sided bank, and a fosse which is largely infilled. Original entrance not recognisable.
6:20 28-8-1988

1156 TULLYNAMOYLE
OS 5:15:3 (644,587) Hachured OD 283 20223, 31676
Rath Raised circular area (int. diam. 30.5m) enclosed by a very low earthen bank and a wide, shallow fosse which has been infilled from NNE–S–SSW. Original entrance was probably at W. Internal area is divided into three unequal portions by field boundaries.
5:45 21-8-1988

1157 TULLYNASKEAGH
OS 34:10:3 (458,230) Hachured OD 500
26875, 29399
Rath Large raised circular area (int. diam. 52m) enclosed by a low earthen bank and a shallow, irregular fosse, both of which are identifiable only from SW–W–N. Elsewhere the defining feature is a

low scarp. Original entrance not recognisable.
34:51 29-3-1974

1158 TULLYUNSHIN (ED Larah North)
OS 27:1:6 (173,516) Hachured OD 600–700
25589, 30330
Rath Raised circular area (int. diam. *c.* 36m) enclosed by two earthen banks with wide, deep intermediate fosse. Outer bank may be relatively modern. Break in bank at SSW with traces of a possible accompanying causeway probably represents original entrance. Low raised circular platform at centre of internal area (diam. 9m) may represent a house site.
27:14 27-7-1989

1159 TULLYVIN
OS 17:13:3 (155,134) Indicated OD 300–400
25694, 31055
Rath Depicted as a tree-ring on OS 1836 and 1876 eds. Raised circular area (int. diam. 36.4m) enclosed by a low earthen bank identifiable only from SSE–S and from W–NW–N. A modern field boundary has been built against the scarp from N–E–S. An earlier report (OPW 1969) suggested that the original entrance may have been at NW.
17:70 24-9-1990

1160 TULLYVIN
OS 17:13:3 (163,124) Hachured OD 200–300
25693, 31037
Rath (site) Marked 'Fort' on OS 1836 and 1876 eds. Situated on the NE shoulder of a drumlin hill adjacent to a stream. An earlier report (OPW 1969) described the much-disturbed remains of a raised circular area (int. diam. *c.* 43m) enclosed by a wide, low earthen bank. Original entrance was not recognisable. Not visible at ground level.
17:71 24-9-1990

1161 TULLYVIN
OS 17:13:3 (189,122) Indicated OD 300
25718, 31010
Rath Marked 'Fort' on OS 1836 and 1876 eds. Raised circular area (int. diam. 27.1m) enclosed by a low, narrow earthen bank and the remains of an infilled fosse, the outline of which (Wth 3.2m) is nonetheless identifiable. Wide break in bank at N with accompanying causeway represents original entrance.
17:72 24-9-1990

1162 TULLYVIN
OS 17:13:3 (205,134) '*Gallows Hill*' OD 300
25746, 31008
Rath Depicted as a tree-ring on OS 1836 and 1876 eds. Raised circular area (int. diam. 28.6m) enclosed by slight traces of a low earthen bank. The site has been modified as a tree-ring and a relatively modern earthen bank with an external trench constructed outside the bank of the rath. Original entrance not recognisable.
17:73 24-9-1990

1163 TURE (Tullyhaw By.)
OS 2:9:6 (230,159) Not Marked OD 200–300
20742, 33749
Rath (site) Marked 'Fort' on OS 1836 and 1876 eds. Almost completely levelled. Raised circular area (int. diam. *c.* 36m) enclosed by a low earthen bank identifiable only from E–S–SSW. Original entrance not recognisable.
2:26 19-8-1974

1164 TURIN
OS 38:9:2 (130,280) Hachured OD 300–400
24583, 28791
Rath Raised circular area (int. diam. *c.* 58m) enclosed by a much-denuded low earthen bank with some remains of a fosse identifiable from E–SE–S. Original entrance not recognisable.
38:60 7-8-1986

1165 TURIN
OS 38:9:5 (141,220) Hachured OD 319
24595, 28728
Rath Raised circular area (int. diam. 33m) enclosed by two earthen banks with a wide, deep, partly waterlogged, intermediate fosse and vague traces of an external fosse. An earlier report (OPW 1970) noted that the intermediate fosse had been considerably modified and furthermore suggested that this fosse together with the outer bank and fosse are more recent features attributed to the later development of the site as a tree-ring. Break in bank with accompanying causeway at SE represents original entrance.
38:61 6-8-1986

1166 TURIN
OS 38:9:2 (144,292) Hachured OD 300–400
24598, 28804
Rath Raised circular area (int. diam. 33m) enclosed by a low, much-denuded earthen bank. Two earthen banks extend outside the scarp from ESE–N–NNE. These are later features probably dating to the period in which the site was transformed into a tree-ring. A modern field boundary extends outside the scarp from NNE–E–ESE. Original entrance not recognisable. Possible remains of a souterrain (**1266**) in the internal area.
38:62(01) 7-8-1986

1167 TURIN
OS 38:9:6 (177,227) Hachured OD 300–400
24633, 28735

Rath (site) An earlier report (OPW 1970) described a large raised circular area (int. diam. *c.* 52m) enclosed by a substantial earthen bank. Original entrance was probably at NE. All that remains to indicate the presence of the site is an irregular mound of earth and stone. Otherwise nothing visible at ground level.
38:64 7-8-1986

1168 URAGH (Lower Loughtee By.)
OS 14:8:3 (852,395) Indicated OD 100–200
23370, 31462
Rath Marked 'Fort' on 1836 and 1876 eds. Raised circular area (int. diam. 29.7m) enclosed by a low, narrow earthen bank and suggestions of a fosse. Original entrance not recognisable.
14:55 15-8-1989

1169 URCHER
OS 34:2:4 (246,457) Not marked OD 500–600
26649, 29637
Rath (site) Marked 'Urcher Fort' on OS Fair Plan and 'Fort' on 1836 and 1876 eds. Slightly raised circular area (int. diam. *c.* 22m) defined by a scarp. Original entrance not recognisable. Situated on the NE shoulder of a drumlin ridge. Site has been almost totally levelled.
34:53 11-5-1988

1170 URNEY (Clanmahon By.)
OS 31:3:1 (515,566) Hachured OD 300–400
24006, 29728
Rath Raised circular area (int. diam. *c.* 43m) enclosed by two substantial earthen banks, each accompanied by wide, deep, partly waterlogged outer fosses. Corresponding breaks in banks at S with accompanying causeway across inner fosse represents original entrance.
31:58 9-4-1974

1171 URNEY (Clanmahon By.)
OS 31:3:2 (539,600) Hachured OD 400–500
24030, 29764
Rath Raised subcircular area (int. dims. *c.* 47m NNW–SSE; *c.* 42m ENE–WSW) enclosed by a very substantial earthen bank and a wide, deep, partly waterlogged fosse skirted by modern field boundaries. Wide break in bank at S presumably represents original entrance. However there is no accompanying causeway. Densely overgrown with vegetation.
31:59 9-4-1974

1172 YEWER GLEBE
OS 19:11:2 (546,246) Hachured OD 200–300
23055, 30661
Rath Raised circular area (int. diam. 44.2m) enclosed by a substantial earthen bank levelled from NE–S–SSE, and a wide, shallow fosse largely infilled from NNW–N–SSE. A field fence has been erected against the outer face of the bank from NNW–N–NNE. Original entrance may be at E.
19:44 10-7-1990

CASHELS

1173 BARRAN
OS 3:4:2 (780,598) Indicated OD 341
20349, 33569
Cashel Not marked on OS 1836 or 1876 eds. Raised circular area (int. diam. 28.3m) enclosed by the base of a stone rampart. The upper courses of the wall have been removed and the stone apparently utilised as building material for field boundaries in the vicinity. Original entrance not recognisable.
3:1 31-3-1977

1174 BARRAN
OS 3:4:2 (798,556) Indicated OD 300–400
20369, 33525
Cashel Indicated on OS 1836 and 1876 eds. Raised circular area (int. diam. *c.* 28m) enclosed by the moss-covered base of a stone rampart. The upper courses of the wall have been removed and the stones apparently utilised as building material for nearby field boundaries. Original entrance not recognisable.
3:2 31-3-1977

1175 BARRAN
OS 3:4:2 (825,579) Indicated OD 300–400
20397, 33550
Cashel Marked 'Fort' on OS 1836 and 1876 eds. Roughly circular raised area (int. diam. 25m) enclosed by a collapsed stone wall. Original entrance not recognisable. A possible souterrain is situated in the internal area (**1223**).
3:3(01) 31-3-1977

1176 BEHERNAGH
OS 43:3:6 (657,478) Indicated OD 300–400
26118, 28375
Cashel Raised circular area (int. diam. *c.* 41m) enclosed by a substantial wall of drystone masonry which has been removed from N–E–S. Original entrance may have been at WSW. Internal area overgrown with vegetation.
43:3 31-8-1970

1177 CARRICK (Clanmahon By.)
OS 43:2:1 (302,538) Indicated OD 400–500
25743, 28434
Cashel Raised oval area (int. dims. 35.4m ENE–WSW; 30.5m NNW–SSE) enclosed by a well-preserved substantial drystone wall. Wide gap at

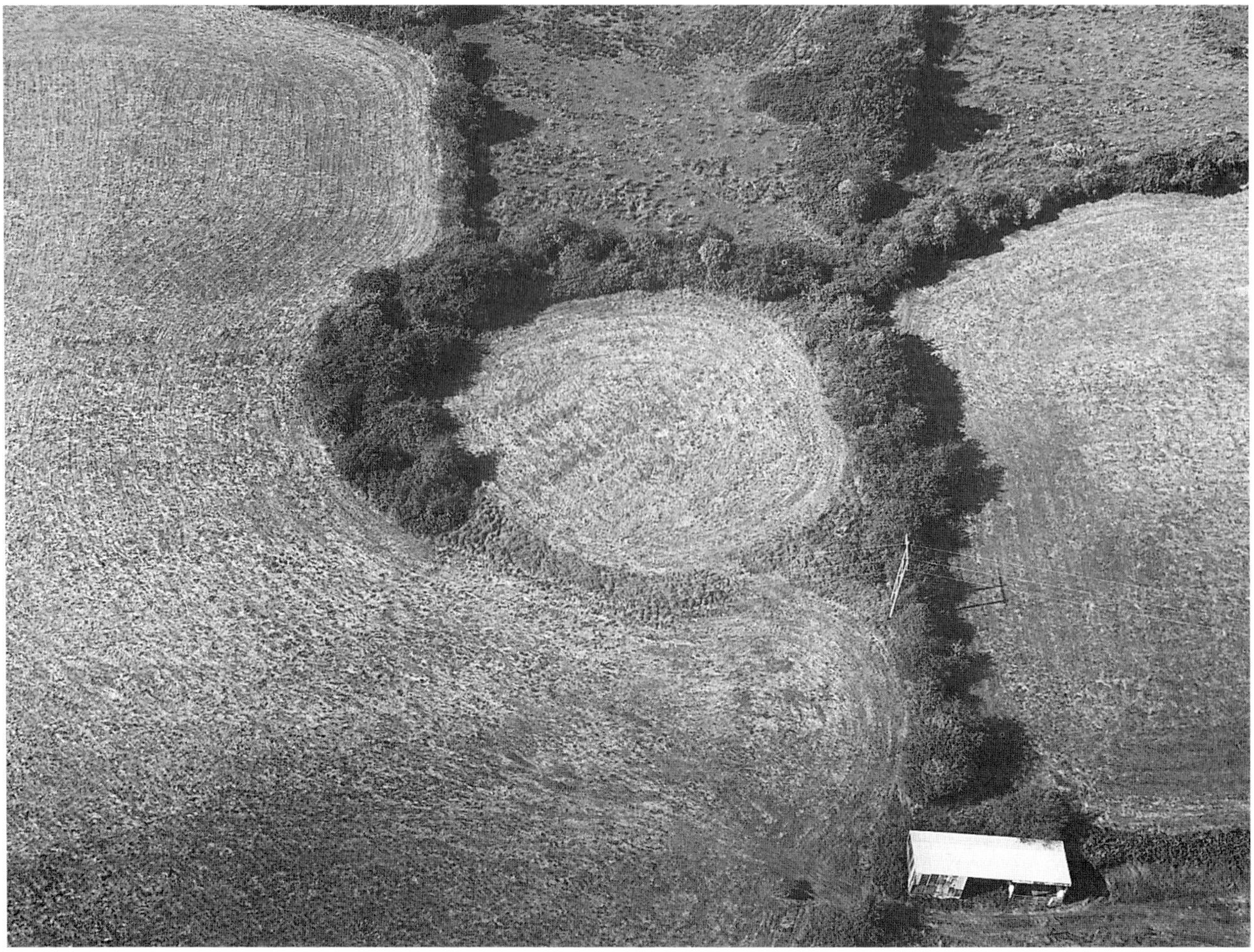

Fig. 27—*Rath at Yewer Glebe* (**1172**).

WNW probably represents original entrance.
43:6 3-9-1970

1178 CARRICKBRANNAN
OS 5:15:1 (471,503) Not marked OD 200–300
20038, 31763

Cashel Marked 'Fort' on OS 1836 and 1876 eds. Situated on the NE shoulder of a low hill in rough mountainous terrain. A roughly circular area (int. diam. *c*. 21.7m) enclosed by the almost completely denuded remains of a drystone wall. Original entrance not recognisable.
5:3 19-5-1993

1179 CASHEL (Tullyhaw By.)
OS 5:14:3 (457,509) Hachured OD 200–300
20024, 31757

Cashel Raised circular area (int. diam. 25.2m) enclosed by a much-denuded drystone wall. Original entrance not recognisable. Projecting from the inner face of the wall at NE into the internal area is a rectangular structure (H 1.2m; int dims. 2.2m NE–SW; 1.25m NW–SE), the side walls of which are composed of large stone slabs. It is roofed by a massive irregularly shaped flat slab (L 2.6m; 1.4m x 0.3m). The SW of the structure is now open. Interpreted by Richardson (1940, 170–71) as the remains of a megalithic tomb.
5:4 12-8-1988

1180 CASHELBANE
OS 5:14:3 (444,557) Indicated OD 200–300
20011, 31706

Cashel Marked 'Fort' on OS 1836 and 1876 eds. Raised circular area (int. diam. 22.7m) enclosed by an almost completely denuded drystone wall. The site is divided into four roughly equal portions by a field boundary running NW–SE and a laneway aligned NE–SW. The enclosing wall is best preserved from NE–E–SE (Wth 3.2m; H 1.1m). From SE–S–SW a series of large upright boulders define its outline. Elsewhere only faint traces survive. Original entrance not recognisable.
5:5 19-8-1988

1181 CASHELBANE
OS 5:14:3 (392,508) Hachured OD 100–200
19955, 31757

Cashel Raised circular area (int. diam. 25.3m) enclosed by a much-denuded drystone wall. Original entrance was probably at SW. Built against the internal face of the perimeter at NW are the remains of a small circular stone structure (int. diam. 1.8m H 0.6m) — probably the remains of a small hut site of beehive-type construction. The roof has collapsed. The lintelled entrance to the structure (H 0.6m) is at SE.
5:7 19-8-1988

1182 CORCASHEL (Tullygarvey By.)
OS 15:8:6 (859,356) Indicated OD 200–300
24353, 31430
Cashel Raised circular area (int. diam. *c.* 32m) enclosed by a partly collapsed drystone wall. Both faces of the wall have been partially refurbished in modern times. Original entrance not recognisable. Internal area densely overgrown with vegetation.
15:15 15-9-1989

1183 CORNAGEE (Tullyhaw By.)
OS 2:13:5 (96,48) Indicated OD 300–400
20601, 33631
Cashel Not marked on OS 1836 or 1876 eds. Raised oval area (int. dims. *c.* 33m NE–SW; *c.* 23m NW–SE) enclosed by a narrow, much-collapsed drystone wall. Original entrance not recognisable. Densely overgrown with vegetation.
2:1 19-8-1974

1184 CORNAGEE (Tullyhaw By.)
OS 2:13:2 (131,77) Indicated OD 300–400
20638, 33662
Cashel Marked 'Fort' on OS 1836 and 1876 eds. Roughly circular raised area (int. diam. *c.* 26.5m) enclosed by a substantial drystone wall faced internally and externally with large stones. Original entrance not recognisable.
2:2 30-5-1977

1185 CORNASHESK
OS 39:12:5 (820,214) Indicated OD 400–500
26288, 28737
Cashel (possible) Marked 'Fort' on OS 1836 eds. Circular area (int. diam. 26.5m) enclosed by a partly collapsed drystone wall. Original entrance not recognisable. A ring of beech trees skirts the internal face of the wall.
39:24 23-3-1987

1186 CORNEENFLYNN
OS 6:3:6 (688,465) Indicated OD 400–500
21234, 32796
Cashel Raised circular area (int. diam. 23.4m) enclosed by a largely collapsed stone wall (Wth 1.9m; H 0.3m). Original entrance not recognisable. Projecting out from the wall at NE is a small square drystone-built structure (int. diam. 1.8m) the perimeter of which has been incorporated into the field boundary.
6:4 26-8-1988

1187 CORRONAGH
OS 39:15:5 (582,003) Indicated OD 300–400
25992, 28681
Cashel Depicted as a circular enclosure with the designation 'Fort' on OS 1836 ed. Raised circular area (int. dims. 39.6m NW–SE; 39.4m NW–SE) enclosed by a largely collapsed drystone wall. Original entrance at N. An earlier report (OPW 1969) recorded a possible lean-to structure inside the cashel wall at SSE. This feature is no longer identifiable.
43:8/39:28* 10-9-1994

1188 CULLION
OS 7:15:5 (568,48) Indicated OD 500
22087, 32364
Cashel (possible) Circular area (int. diam. 46m) enclosed by the remains of a drystone wall (Wth 3.5m). Site is divided into two unequal portions by a field boundary running NW–SE. Remains of outer wall at NW and SE. Original entrance not recognisable. Known locally as a 'fort'.
7:7 3-9-1988

1189 DOWRA
OS 5:15:2 (606,413) Indicated OD 300
20181, 31860
Cashel Marked 'Fort' on OS 1836 and 1876 eds. Raised circular area (int. diam. 28.2m) enclosed by a much-denuded, low drystone wall which has been modified and incorporated into the field boundary. At NE the perimeter has been destroyed and replaced by a more substantial modern stone field wall. Original entrance not recognisable.
5:30 15-8-1988

1190 DOWRA
OS 5:15:2 (587,380) Indicated OD 200–300
20160, 31894
Cashel Not marked on OS 1836 or 1876 eds. Raised circular area (int. diam. 28.6m) enclosed by a low, much-denuded drystone wall. Original entrance may have been at NW.
5:31 15-8-1988

1191 DRUMCALPIN (Lower Loughtee By.)
OS 15:14:3 (408,151) Indicated OD 100–200
23880, 31209
Cashel Marked 'Fort' on 1836 and 1876 eds. Raised circular area (int. diam. *c.* 40m) enclosed by a largely collapsed drystone wall. Original entrance not recognisable. Densely overgrown with vegetation.
15:29 15-9-1989

1192 DRUMHURRIN
OS 3:16:6 (912,13) Indicated OD 300–400 20493, 32953
Cashel Not marked on OS 1836 or 1876 ed. Raised circular area (int. diam. 31.7m) enclosed by the base of a stone rampart. The upper courses of the wall have been removed and the stone apparently utilised as building material for field boundaries in the vicinity. Original entrance not recognisable.
3:15 17-8-1988

1193 FARTAGH (Castlerahan By.)
OS 44:6:1 (233,396) Hachured OD 300–400 26648, 28292
Cashel Marked 'Fort' on OS 1836 and 1876 eds. Small raised circular area (int. diam *c.* 17m E–W) enclosed by a poorly preserved low drystone wall. Original entrance not recognisable.
44:14 20-8-1987

1194 GARVALT LOWER
OS 6:5:1 (69,390) Indicated OD 400–500 20581, 32712
Cashel Raised circular area (int. diam. 21.9m) enclosed by a largely collapsed drystone wall. Original entrance not recognisable. Situated in rough mountainous terrain close to the summit of a low hill.
6:11 22-8-1988

1195 GLASDRUMMAN (Tullygarvey By.)
OS 16:5:2 (98,415), Not marked OD 400–500 24524, 31494
Cashel Marked 'Fort' on OS 1836 ed. and 'Site of' on 1876 ed. The site apparently comprised a roughly circular area (int. diam. *c.* 39m) enclosed by a drystone wall. The site is divided into two apparently roughly equal portions by a field boundary running ENE–WSW, S of which there are no visible remains. From NNE–ENE the wall is quite substantial. From W–NW–NNE its outline may be identified as a low rise.
16:64 27-9-1989

1196 GORTAQUILL
OS 1:12:6 (865,189) Indicated OD 300 20437, 33778
Cashel Marked 'Fort' on OS 1836 and 1876 eds. Circular area (int. diam. *c.* 25m) enclosed by a narrow drystone wall. Original entrance was probably at S. Part of the enclosed area is at a lower level than the external ground level. Along the internal face of the wall at W there are two large stones which may represent the remains of a house site.
1:3 3-7-1988

1197 KILLYBANDRICK
OS 15:4:4 (767,488) Indicated OD 200–300 24255, 31568
Cashel (possible) Indicated on all OS eds. Known as a 'fort' (local information). Raised circular area (int. diam. *c.* 40m) enclosed by a largely grass-covered, much-denuded low drystone wall. Original entrance not recognisable. On OS 1836 ed. a rectangular building is shown adjoining the site at NE. Within the enclosed area at NE are the foundations of a rectangular stone building (int. dims. 8.3m x 3.7m) with an internal dividing wall. Site is densely overgrown with vegetation. The OS 1836 ed. depicts a rectangular building adjoining the site at NE which has since been levelled.
15:51 18-9-1989

1198 KILLYCARNEY
OS 2:13:1 (32,149) Indicated OD 200–300 20533, 33737
Cashel An almost circular raised area (int. diam. 20.1m N–S) enclosed by a largely collapsed drystone wall (H 1m; Wth 5.25m). A possible house platform (dims. 7.4m NE–SW; 6.4m NW–SE) is situated in the NE sector of the interior. Possible outer enclosure attached to the site from E–S–W defined by an irregular bank of earth and stone which incorporates bedrock.
2:6 28-4-1993

1199 KILLYMEEHAN
OS 26:2:4 (256,494) Not marked OD 300–400 24702, 30299
Cashel Marked 'Fort' on the OS 1836 and 1876 eds. Raised circular area (int. diam. 31.5m) enclosed by a drystone wall which has been largely levelled. Even where best preserved at S, it barely rises above the enclosed area. Original entrance not recognisable.
26:42 22-10-1991

1200 KNOCKARAHEEN
OS 43:7:4 (471,341) Hachured OD 400–500 25924, 28228
Cashel Raised circular area (int. diam. *c.* 48m) enclosed by a largely collapsed drystone wall. Original entrance not recognisable. A rectangular hut site (int. dims. 6m E–W; 5m N–S) enclosed by a low stone wall, accompanied by an L-shaped depression which may represent a souterrain (**1246**) or possibly a second hut site, occur within the internal area. Traces of an internal dividing wall running N–S are visible at N.
43:15(01) 18-6-1987

1201 KNOCKATEMPLE
OS 43:3:1 (495,536) Indicated OD 400–500 25947, 28434
Cashel Raised circular area (int. diam. *c.* 45m) enclosed by a substantial well-preserved drystone wall. Original entrance may have been at SE.
43:17 16-6-1987

1202 KNOCKNAGARTAN
OS 43:3:2 (611,563) Indicated OD 400–500
26070, 28464
Cashel Raised circular area (int. diam. *c*. 35m) enclosed by a substantial although partly collapsed drystone wall which has been modified and incorporated into the field boundary. Gap at E may represent original entrance.
43:20 17-6-1987

1203 LURGANBOY (Castlerahan By.)
OS 43:2:6 (401,468) Indicated OD 400–500
25849, 28360
Cashel Raised circular area (int. dims. 50m NE–SW; 49m NW–SE) enclosed by a substantial drystone wall. Gap in wall at S probably represents original entrance. From WNW–NW the wall is absent where a rectangular stone building was erected, the foundations of which are still visible. This is believed to have been built as a refuge by tenants evicted from a nearby house in the last century.
43:29 3-9-1970

1204 MANRAGH UPPER
OS 4:6:1 (294,442) Indicated OD 500–600
20813, 33408
Cashel Marked 'Fort' on OS 1836 and 1876 eds. Raised circular area (int. diam. 28.4m) enclosed by the base of a stone rampart (original Wth 2.2m) which has been modernised and incorporated into the field boundary. Original entrance not recognisable. The site is divided into two unequal portions by a field boundary running NW–SE. The smaller portion ENE of this has been levelled but the outline of the perimeter may still be traced as a low mound of earth and stone.
4:14 10-8-1988

1205 MONEYGASHEL
OS 4:5:1 (67,392) Indicated OD 500–600
20573, 33353
Cashel Not marked on OS 1836 or 1876 eds. Raised circular area (int. diam. 23.2m) enclosed by the base of a substantial stone rampart (original Wth 3.9m) which has been partly modernised and incorporated into the field boundary. Richardson (1938, 20) recorded an entrance feature (Wth 0.9m) at S. At the centre of the internal area is a roughly circular area (diam. 4.6m) paved with cobblestones. Richardson (*ibid.*) suggested that this 'may be the recent foundation for a haystack'. Also within the internal area at S is a sweathouse (**1877**).
4:15(01) 10-8-1988

1206 MONEYGASHEL
OS 4:5:2 (87,427) Indicated OD 500–600
20593, 33391
Cashel Raised circular area (int. diam. 24.7m) enclosed by a massive stone wall. Within the thickness of the wall there is an external stairway at S comprising seven steps, and two internal stairways at NW and NE, both of which have been blocked up. A souterrain (**1260**) entrance is visible in the external face of the wall at S. A largely blocked-up water conduit, which it is believed (Richardson 1938, 20, and local information) carried water to the site from a stream higher up on the hill, is visible in the internal face of the wall at S. (Milligan 1890–1, 580–2; Lowry-Corry and Richardson 1937, 163–4; Richardson and Lowry-Corry 1938, 21)
4:16(01) 10-10-1992

1207 MONEYGASHEL
OS 4:1:5 (120,478) Indicated OD 700–800
20628, 33446
Cashel Raised circular area (int. diam. 30.9m) enclosed by the base of a stone rampart (original Wth 4.3m) which has been largely modernised and incorporated into the field boundary. A rectangular area (int. dims. 6.35m NE–SW; 3m NW–SE) enclosed by a drystone wall adjoins the cashel wall at SW and is accompanied by an indentation in the cashel wall itself at this point. Richardson (1938, 19) suggested that the original entrance was at S 'where one of the facing stones of the jamb survives'.
4:18 10-8-1988

1208 MOYDRISTAN
OS 37:15:6 (636,26) Indicated OD 300–400
24145, 28519
Cashel Raised circular area (int. diam. *c*. 43m) enclosed by a low partly destroyed drystone wall. Original entrance not recognisable. Some 10m in from the cashel wall the internal area is level but rises to a height of *c*. 1.5m above that of the wall at the centre of the interior.
37:47 30-7-1986

1209 MULLAGHAHY
OS 1:12:6 (904,191) Indicated OD 300–400
20478, 33780
Cashel Not marked on OS 1836 or 1876 eds. Raised circular area (int. dims. *c*. 25m N–S; 23.4m E–W) enclosed by a low drystone wall (Wth 3.6m). Original entrance not recognisable. On the OS 1911 ed. a field boundary is shown skirting the site from NE–E–SE. This has been removed. However, there is a semicircular enclosure projecting from the cashel wall between these points. The structure of its enclosing wall is similar to that of the cashel.
1:9 10-7-1988

1210 MULNANARRAGH
OS 12:13:3 (200,77) Indicated OD 100–200
24629, 31777

Cashel Roughly oval-shaped raised area (int. dims. 25.6m N–S; 21.6m E–W) enclosed by a substantial, rough drystone wall. Original entrance was probably at SE.
12:4 28-6-1989

1211 PORT (ED Esky)
OS 1:12:2 (797,243) Indicated OD 200–300
20364, 33834
Cashel Indicated on all OS eds. Raised circular area (diam. *c.* 36m) enclosed by a substantial drystone wall. Original entrance not recognisable. Densely overgrown with vegetation.
1:13 3-7-1988

1212 PORT (ED Esky)
OS 1:12:5 (809,225) Indicated OD 300–400
20377, 33815
Cashel Indicated on all OS eds. Raised circular area (int. diam. 32.9m). enclosed by the grassed-over lower portion of a drystone wall. Original entrance not recognisable.
1:14 19-5-1993

1213 PORT (ED Esky)
OS 1:12:5 (816,207) *'Giant's Grave'* OD 300–400
20385, 33796
Cashel Depicted as an almost oval-shaped enclosure (dims. *c.* 38m N–S; *c.* 33m E–W) on OS 1911 ed. Only the outline of the cashel wall described by Lowry-Corry and Richardson (1937, 157–9) is now identifiable. Well-defined entrance at SE. (de Valera and Ó Nualláin 1972, 137, No. 1)
1:15(01) 3-7-1988

1214 TERMON (Tullyhaw By.)
OS 2:13:1 (55,92) Indicated OD 300
20558, 33677
Cashel Not marked on OS 1836 or 1876 eds. Known locally as a 'fort'. Raised oval area (int. dims. 32.3m ENE–WSW; 18m NNW–SSE) enclosed by a substantial although largely collapsed drystone wall. Original entrance not recognisable. Densely overgrown with vegetation.
2:16 27-8-1988

1215 TUAM
OS 2:9:2 (150,285) Hachured OD 100–200
20656, 33882
Cashel Situated on the shore of Lough MacNean Upper. Raised oval area (int. dims. 41.6m N–S; 31.4m E–W) enclosed by a substantial although largely collapsed drystone wall which has been denuded at SW, N and SE. Original entrance not recognisable. Internal area has been planted with trees and supports scrub.
2:21 11-7-1988

1216 TUAM
OS 2:9:3 (210,256) Hachured OD 100–200
20719, 33852
Cashel Raised circular area (int. diam. *c.* 28m) enclosed by a largely collapsed drystone wall. Original entrance not recognisable.
2:22 21-8-1974

1217 TULLAGHYRORY
OS 5:15:1 (512,444) Indicated OD 200–300
20082, 31827
Cashel Raised circular area (int. diam. 26.4m) enclosed by a partly denuded low drystone wall. Stones were drawn from this in the 1940s for the construction of field boundaries (local information). Original entrance not recognisable. A possible house site comprising an oval-shaped raised area (int. dims. 15.5m E–W; 5.2m N–S), is situated in the interior.
5:40 17-8-1988

1218 TULLANTEEN
OS 5:14:3 (419,587) Indicated OD 200–300
19985, 31674
Cashel (site) Marked 'Fort' on OS 1836 ed. Situated on the SW shoulder of a hill in rough mountainous terrain. All that survives of the site is a short stretch of low drystone wall at N which is incorporated into the field boundary. Otherwise site has been levelled.
5:44 21-8-1988

1219 UNSHOGAGH
OS 2:13:4 (25,5) Indicated OD 400–500
20526, 33585
Cashel Raised circular area (int. diam. 27.3m) enclosed by a substantial although largely collapsed drystone wall with some very large stones in its composition. From SE–S–SW the perimeter has been incorporated into the field boundary. Original entrance not recognisable.
2:29 14-7-1988

Souterrains

The term *souterrain* derives from the French *sous terre* meaning below ground. A souterrain can be defined as an artificially constructed subterranean chamber. In many cases there are two or more chambers linked by low narrow passages or creepways. In almost all examples the entrance is through a narrow opening at ground level. Most are constructed of drystone masonry, but rock-cut, clay-cut and timber-built examples have also been recorded. While most are situated within or close to ringforts or early church sites, some isolated examples are also known. The results of research and excavation indicate that, like ringforts and early church sites, souterrains can generally be dated to the Early Christian Period. A number of suggestions have been put forward as to their function. On the basis of morphological evidence it is likely that the majority were places of refuge. Other suggestions for their use have included storage places and temporary dwelling places during inclement weather (Ó Ríordáin 1979, 70–1).

1220 AGHACONNY
OS 31:3:6 (624,526) Not marked OD 400–500
24120, 29687
Souterrain (site, possible) Local tradition refers to a tunnel within the interior of Aghaconny rath site (**189**). An earlier report (OPW 1974) recorded a depression to W of centre which may have marked the site of a souterrain. Not visible at ground level.
31:2(02) 8-6-1992

1221 AGHALATTAFRAAL/DERRYLURGAN
OS 32:15:3 (656,96) Not marked OD 450
25134, 29242
Souterrain (possible) At Aghalattafraal/Derrylurgan rath (**196**). Two depressions in the interior probably mark the site of a souterrain. The first is at N. It is almost V-shaped in plan (dims. 7m NNW–SSE; 6.6m ENE–WSW). The second is at NE and is somewhat similar in plan (dims. 9.5m NE–SW; 5.8m NW–SE).
32:1(02) 18-5-1977

1222 ALTBEAGH
OS 26:8:3 (896,416) Not marked OD 400–500
25379, 30222
Souterrain (possible) At Altbeagh rath (**214**). A Y-shaped depression inside the N sector of the bank probably represents the remains of a collapsed souterrain.
26:3(02) 22-10-1991

1223 BARRAN
OS 3:4:2 (825,579) Not marked OD 300–400
20397, 33550
Souterrain (possible) At Barran cashel (**1175**). A wide, shallow, subrectangular depression (L 7.8m; Wth 3m) extending N from the centre of the internal area may represent a collapsed souterrain.
3:3(02) 31-3-1977

1224 BRACKLAGH (Tullygarvey By.)
OS 16:7:2 (549,424) Not marked OD 200–300
25000, 31508
Souterrain (possible) Not marked on any OS ed. Davies (ITA Survey 1945) recorded a 'rather rough souterrain' at this location. He described it as being 'walled with boulders' and the roof constructed of rough slabs. The site is now inaccessible. Locally it is believed that the 'cave' was used as a hiding place for the Catholic clergy during Penal times. Situated on the summit of a steep hill in rough terrain. A Mass Rock lies *c.* 90m to SE.
16:9 17-9-1989

1225 CASHEL (Clankee By.)
OS 23:2:1 (267,540) Not marked OD 400–500
26658, 31005
Souterrain (possible) At Cashel rath (**313**). Two long, low mounds of earth and stone at the centre of the interior may mark the site of a souterrain.
23:5(02) 26-5-1992

1226 CLONBOCKOGE
OS 42:3:5 (611,496) Not marked OD 200–300
25094, 28384
Souterrain (possible) Local tradition refers to a passage under Clonbockoge rath (**335**). A high, circular, apparently natural mound (H 2m) surmounted by two large stones —an upright boulder (H 1.5m) and a flat slab (dims. 2m x 1m), may indicate the site of a souterrain in the interior of the rath.
42:5(02) 10-4-1986

1227 CLONCOSE (ED Killashandra)
OS 14:16:4 (735,66) Not marked OD 200–300
23250, 31113
Souterrain (site, possible) At Cloncose rath (**336**). The entrance to the rath is at NE. Running W from this to the centre of the internal area is a long, shallow depression (L 28.3m; Wth 2.4m; D 0.3m) which may represent the remains of a collapsed souterrain.
14:12(02) 17-7-1989

1228 CLONEARY
OS 13:3:3 (685,536) Not marked OD 200–300
22218, 31600
Souterrain (possible) Situated *c.* 3m E of the centre of

the internal area of Cloneary rath (**339**). An earlier report (OPW 1969) recorded a partially buried slab (L 0.9m; dims. 0.67m x 0.29m) which was interpreted as a possible souterrain lintel. Not indentified in the course of the last site visit.
13:9(02) 8-6-1989

1229 CLONOOSE BIG
OS 37:7:1 (472,390) Not marked OD 300–400 23967, 28902
Souterrain (possible) At 'Muckram Fort' (**345**). An elongated depression (L 6.8m; Wth 4.4m) in the WNW of the interior of the rath may represent the site of a souterrain.
37:25(02) 11-7-1986

1230 CORLISBANNAN
OS 5:14:1 (304,495) Not marked OD 300–400 19863, 31771
Souterrain (possible) At Corlisbannan rath (**397**). Extending from the centre of the internal area to the inner face of the bank at NW is a wide, shallow depression (L 14m; Wth 3m) which may represent the remains of a collapsed souterrain.
5:21(02) 24-8-1988

1231 CORRAVAHAN
OS 21:2:6 (409,497) Not marked OD 300–400 24858, 30943
Souterrain (possible) At Corravahan rath (**446**). An earlier report (OPW 1970) recorded a long, shallow, slightly curving depression, orientated NE–SW, 2m NNE of the centre of the rath's interior. This may represent the remains of a souterrain.
21:19(02) 19-9-1990

1232 CROAGHAN
OS 43:2:6 (379,496) Not marked OD 400–500 25844, 28391
Souterrain (possible) Within Croaghan rath (**474**). An L-shaped depression, the longer leg (L 8m; Wth 3.4m; D 1m) aligned NW–SE and the other (L 6m; Wth 3.5m; D 0.6m) running NE–SW at the centre of the interior, probably represents the site of a souterrain.
43:9(02) 2-9-1970

1233 DINGINAVANTY
OS 22:4:1 (722,595) Not marked OD 300–400 26163, 31058
Souterrain (possible) At Dinginavanty rath (**521**). Extending into the internal area from a break in the bank at SW is a long, shallow, rectangular depression, presumably representing the site of a souterrain.
22:13(02) 17-10-1990

1234 DINGINS
OS 30:8:1 (737,397) Not marked OD 336 23268, 29540
Souterrain (site, tradition) Local tradition refers to a tunnel running off Dingins rath (**522**), which suggests a souterrain site.
30:15(02) 8-10-1991

1235 DOON (Castlerahan By.)
OS 39:4:1 (732,584) Not marked OD 300–400 26191, 29127
Souterrain (possible) Situated within Doon rath (**529**), at the internal foot of bank at N. An earlier report (OPW 1969) recorded a shallow, subrectangular depression aligned WNW–ESE (L *c.* 6m; Wth *c.* 4m; D 0.7m) possibly marking the site of a souterrain.
39:41(02) 11-6-1987

1236 DRUMAD
OS 28:7:2 (598,408) Not marked OD 500–600 27007, 30229
Souterrain (possible) An earlier report (OPW 1977) recorded that much of the W half of Drumad rath (**536**) is occupied by three connected depressions which probably represent the remains of a souterrain.
28:13(02) 14-9-1988

1237 DRUMELTAN
OS 22:6:3 (451,414) '*Giant's Grave* (Site of)' OD 600–700 25879, 30865
Souterrain (possible, site) Marked 'Giant's Grave' on OS 1836 and 1876 eds. Shown situated within a tree plantation on OS 1913 ed. An earlier report (de Valera and Ó Nualláin 1972, 139, No. 11) recorded that the site was then represented by a trench (L 8m; Wth 3m; D 1m) which has since been infilled. The nature of the site is uncertain, but local information would suggest it may have been a souterrain. Not visible at ground level.
22:16(01) 22-10-1990

1238 DRUMLOMAN
OS 31:8:6 (864,334) Not marked OD 400–500 24377, 29486
Souterrain (possible) At Drumloman rath (**625**). A roughly rectangular, partially waterlogged depression (L 8.5m; Wth 4.9m; D 0.35m) inside the bank at NE, may mark the site of a souterrain.
31:34(02) 3-4-1974

1239 DRUMMUCK
OS 26:2:3 (407,587) Not marked OD 600–700 24861, 30398
Souterrain (possible) At Drummuck rath (**635**). Inside the bank at S is a Y-shaped depression which

probably marks the site of a souterrain. Local tradition of a tunnel here.
26:33(02) 23-10-1991

1240 GALLONREAGH (Clankee By.)
OS 23:1:5 (86,486) Not marked OD 438 26467, 30946
Souterrain (possible) At Gallonreagh rath (**708**). An L-shaped depression, the longer leg (L 6m; Wth 1.5m; D 0.45m) running NW–SE and the other (L 3m; Wth 1.2m; D 0.45m) aligned NE–SW, cutting through the bank at W, may mark the site of a timber souterrain.
23:20(02) 22-4-1992

1241 GORTNAKILLEW
OS 26:9:4 (30,174) Not marked OD 500–600 24467, 29958
Souterrain (possible) Situated within Gortnakillew rath (**735**). According to local information a timber-lined tunnel, presumably a souterrain, was uncovered in the interior some years ago. It has since been infilled.
26:39(02) 20-3-1992

1242 INCH ISLAND
OS 19 NPL Not marked OD 100–300
Souterrain (possible) Davies (ITA Survey 1942) noted a local tradition of a cave somewhere on the island which is now planted with coniferous trees. Not located.
19:46

1243 KEVIT LOWER
OS 25:10:2 (360,260) Not marked OD 300–400 23839, 30044
Souterrain (possible) Davies (ITA Survey 1942) recorded the former presence of a souterrain within Kevit Lower rath (**757**). Not visible at ground level.
25:62(02) 6-9-1991

1244 KILLYCLUGGIN
OS 13:4:6 (878,506) Not marked OD 200–300 22422, 31570
Souterrain (site, possible) Situated within Killycluggin rath (**774**). A long, deep depression (L 7.7m; Wth 1.8m; D 1m) projecting into the interior from the inner face of the bank of the rath at WNW, may represent a collapsed souterrain.
13:27(02) 4-11-1969

1245 KILLYNURE (Castlerahan By.)
OS 32:7:4 (499,323) Not marked OD 500 24967, 29480
Souterrain (possible) At Killynure rath (**788**). Inside the bank at W is a long, subrectangular, waterlogged depression (L 8.9m; Wth 2.6m; D 0.3m) which may mark the site of a souterrain.
32:24(02) 1-5-1989

1246 KNOCKARAHEEN
OS 43:7:4 (471,341) Not marked OD 400–500 25924, 28228
Souterrain (possible) At Knockaraheen cashel (**1200**). An L-shaped depression, the longer leg (L 14m; Wth 4m) aligned E–W and the other (L 6m; Wth 2m) running N–S within the interior, may indicate the site of a souterrain.
43:15(02) 18-6-1987

1247 KNOCKBRIDE
OS 23 NPL Not marked
Souterrain An earlier record, (NMI 1937) described a souterrain with 'beautiful masonry'. Discovered in 1850 on or near the summit of the hill on the E side of Corraneary Lough. Not located.
23:53/28:46*

1248 KNOCKBRIDE
OS 28:1:3 (166,534) Not marked OD 500–600 26557, 30358
Souterrain (possible) Situated within the interior of Knockbride rath (**823**). Likely remains of a souterrain comprise a depression with a rectangular opening, partially lined with drystone walling at its E end.
28:29(02) 1-4-1974

1249 LEITRIM (Castlerahan By.)
OS 44:7:1 (512,421) Not marked OD 400–500 26942, 28322
Souterrain (site, tradition) Tradition of a 'cave' within the interior of Leitrim rath (**859**) which is possibly a reference to a souterrain.
44:17(02) 19-8-1987

1250 LISADERG OR CORWEELIS
OS 18:13:2 (80,93) Not marked OD 400–500 26459, 31171
Souterrain (possible) At Lisderg or Corweelis rath (**870**). An L-shaped depression within the interior and close to the perimeter at W may represent the site of a souterrain.
18:8(02) 15-7-1990

1251 LISCLOGHER
OS 23:2:4 (292,491) Not marked OD 487 26685, 30954
Souterrain (possible) Situated within Lisclogher rath (**891**). A large L-shaped depression with the longer leg (L 13m; Wth 2.3m) aligned NNE–SSW and the other (L 5.5m; Wth 2.2m) running NNW–SSE occurs inside

the bank at WSW and may indicate the site of a souterrain.
23:31(02) 26-5-1992

1252 LISDOAGH
OS 23:5:2 (110,451) Not marked OD 400 26494, 30909
Souterrain (possible) Situated inside the bank of Lisdoagh rath (**896**) at SW. An L-shaped depression, the longer leg (L 6.9m) aligned NE–SW and the shorter one (L 3m) running NW–SE, probably represents the site of a souterrain.
23:32(02) 20-5-1992

1253 LISDRUMFAD
OS 23:12:6 (876,180) Not marked OD 400–500 27305, 30631
Souterrain (possible) Situated inside a break in the bank of Lisdrumfad rath (**900**) at WSW. Two narrow, shallow depressions meeting at an angle, the longer leg (L 9.7m) aligned NE–SW and the other (L 4.8m) running NNW–SSE, probably indicates the site of a souterrain.
23:34(02) 30-3-1992

1254 LISMEEN (Castlerahan By.)
OS 32:8:4 (697,362) Not marked OD 400–500 25175, 29523
Souterrain (possible) Situated within Lismeen rath (**924**). A well-defined rectangular trench (L 11.6m; Wth 2.9m; D 0.75m) projecting into the interior from a break in the bank at ENE (Wth 2.7m), may represent a collapsed souterrain.
32:37(02) 12-5-1993

1255 LISNABANTRY (ED Killinkere)
OS 39:3:6 (678,455) Not marked OD 400–500 26135, 28990
Souterrain (possible) Situated within the interior of Lisnabantry rath (**932**) at SE. A subrectangular depression (L 8m NW–SE; Wth 4m NE–SW) with stone wall-footings at its SE end may represent the site of a collapsed souterrain.
39:61(02) 30-3-1987

1256 LISNACLEA (ED Knappagh)
OS 18:14:5 (349,24) Not marked OD 400–500 26744, 31101
Souterrain (possible) Situated near the inner face of the bank of Lisnaclea rath at N (**938**). A small Y-shaped depression, comprising short vertical leg (L 2m; Wth 1.9m; D 0.3m), a branch aligned NW–SE (L 3.4m; Wth 1.8m; D 0.35m) and a longer branch running NE–SW (L 5m; Wth 1.65m; D 1.1m), may represent the site of a souterrain.
18:10(02) 15-7-1989

1257 LISNAFANA
OS 39:2:1 (268,585) Not marked OD 400–500 25701, 29123
Souterrain (possible) Situated within the interior of Lisnafana rath (**944**). A wide, shallow, rectangular depression (L 11m; Wth 3m; D 0.25m) projecting out from the NW corner of a hut site and running due NW to adjoin a break in the bank of the rath, may mark the site of a souterrain.
39:62(02) 25-3-1987

1258 LURGANBANE/RAKEEVAN
OS 34:14:1 (235,76) Not marked OD 500–600 26641, 29235
Souterrain (possible) Situated within a rath (**980**). A narrow rectangular trench accompanied by a low stony mound, projecting into the interior from a break in the bank at W, possibly represents the site of a souterrain.
34:40(02) 12-5-1988

1259 LURGANBOY (Clankee By.)
OS 23:1:2 (131,556) Not marked OD 300–400 26515, 31020
Souterrain (possible) Situated inside the bank of Lurganboy rath (**981**) at NW. An L-shaped depression, the longer leg (L 6.2m; Wth 2.7m) aligned NW–SE and the shorter one (L 3.5m; Wth 3.2m) running NE–SW, possibly represents the remains of a collapsed wooden souterrain.
23:45(02) 26-5-1992

1260 MONEYGASHEL
OS 4:5:2 (87,427) Not marked OD 500–600 20593, 33391
Souterrain At Moneygashel cashel (**1206**). Built into the external face of the wall at S is a blocked-up souterrain entrance. Richardson (1938, 20) recorded that 'the souterrain ran radially under the cashel, where its roofstones were discovered at one time'.
4:16(03) 10-10-1992

1261 MULLAGHORAN
OS 37:6:1 (239,425) Not marked OD 200–300 23721, 28937
Souterrain (possible) At Mullaghoran rath (**1015**). An earlier report (OPW 1970) recorded a large, shallow, irregularly shaped depression (max. dim. 9.3m; D 1m) just W of the centre of the interior which may mark the site of a souterrain.
37:58(02) 28-7-1986

1262 MULLYMAGOWAN
OS 26:3:1 (426,547) Hachured OD 600–700 24920, 30356
Souterrain Situated within Mullymagowan rath (**1026**). A well-defined, long rectangular depression

extending SW from the house site in the interior of the rath, with a second depression opening off its SE side at a right angle. Most likely the site of a souterrain.
26:58(02) 23-10-1991

1263 RAFFONY
OS 39:8:2 (816,393) Not marked OD 400–500
26282, 28926

Souterrain Two depressions which probably represent a collapsed souterrain. The first is rectangular (dims 4m N–S; 2.5m E–W), the second sub-rectangular (dims. 4.5m NW–SE; 1.5m NE–SW). Situated *c.* 17m from the wall enclosing Raffony graveyard (**1695**). Both depressions partially cut the bank which formed part of the original perimeter of the earlier ecclesiastical foundation.
39:71(02) 9-6-1987

1264 RALAGHAN (ED Corraneary)
OS 22:8:6 (899,321) Hachured OD 400–500
26353, 30770

Souterrain (possible) Projecting into the interior of Ralaghan rath (**1075**) from the bank at W. A long, shallow depression (L 10.5m; Wth 1.9m; D 0.7m) with a second depression (L 2.4m; Wth 1.8m; D 0.7m) adjoining its N side, probably represent the site of a souterrain.
22:31(02) 18-10-1990

1265 TONYHULL
OS 22:11:3 (689,251) Hachured OD 500–600
26131, 30695

Souterrain (possible) At Tonyhull rath (**1143**). A wide, shallow depression (L 8.7m; Wth 3m; D 1.05m) extending into the interior from the bank at WNW may mark the site of a souterrain.
22:33(02) 27-10-1990

1266 TURIN
OS 38:9:2 (144,292) Hachured OD 300–400
24598, 28804

Souterrain (possible) At Turin rath (**1166**). A subrectangular depression (dims. *c.* 9m NW–SE; *c.* 2m NE–SW) within the interior may indicate the site of a souterrain.
38:62(02) 7-8-1986

Hut Sites

Hut sites are generally identifiable as relatively small circular, oval, or rectangular platforms, often defined either by low earthen banks or by the foundations of drystone walls. Hut sites have been identified at a number of ringforts in County Cavan. This chapter is concerned with isolated examples. Hut sites span the period from the Neolithic to modern times. In general, it is almost impossible to determine the date of an individual hut site on the basis of its upstanding remains. Three of the County Cavan examples (**1268, 1269, 1270**) are situated at the summit of Cuilcagh Mountain close to a large apparently prehistoric cairn (**123**) which may be Bronze Age in date. It is possible that they represent the remains of temporary shelters erected by the prehistoric cairn-builders. However, on the basis of surface evidence they could equally represent the remains of relatively modern booley huts which functioned as temporary summer dwellings. The Rosskeeragh hut site (**1271**) which is located in close proximity to a ringfort may be associated with it, while there are no known monuments in the immediate vicinity of the Burnew example (**1267**).

1267 BURNEW
OS 39:3:3 (657,546) Hachured OD 300–400
26112, 29086
Hut site Small almost circular raised area (int. diam. *c.* 16.2m) partially dug into the natural SW–NE inclining slope of a hillside. Enclosed from WNW–E–SSE by a low bank of earth and stone and elsewhere by its scarped remains. Original entrance not recognisable. Densely overgrown with vegetation.
39:16 16-10-1969

1268 COMMAS
OS 6:3:6 (688,465) Not marked OD 2100–2200
21234, 32797
Hut site Small circular area (int. diam. 1.8m) enclosed by the remains of a crude drystone wall (H 0.4m). Situated 3m SE of a substantial cairn in rough terrain close to the summit of Cuilcagh Mountain and the border between counties Cavan and Fermanagh (**123**). Two similar hut sites are situated nearby (**1269, 1270**).
6:3(01) 23-9-1989

1269 COMMAS
OS 6:3:6 (688,465) Not marked OD 2100–2200
21234, 32796
Hut site Circular area (int. diam. 3.2m) enclosed by the remains of a crude drystone wall (H. 0.6m) with entrance feature (Wth 0.8m) at SE. Situated *c.* 100m SE of a substantial cairn (**123**) in rough terrain close to the summit of Cuilcagh Mountain. Two similar hut sites are situated nearby (**1268, 1270**).
6:3(02) 23-8-1989

1270 COMMAS
OS 6:3:6 (688,465) Not marked OD 2100–2200
21234, 32796
Hut site Situated 110m SE of a substantial cairn (**123**) in rough terrain close to the summit of Cuilcagh Mountain. Roughly circular area (int. diam. 4.5m) enclosed by the remains of a crude drystone wall. At NW, SW and SE its foundation stones can be seen protruding from the heather. Two similar hut sites are close by (**1268, 1269**).
6:3(03) 23-8-1989

1271 ROSSKEERAGH
OS 15:2:4 (290,507) Not marked OD 200–300
23751, 31584
Hut site Situated *c.* 20m NW of a rath (**1099**), close to the summit of a steep drumlin hill. Low, circular, flat-topped earthen mound (diam. 13.2m; H 0.5m).
15:69(02) 12-9-1989

Enclosures

This chapter describes circular, oval or irregularly shaped enclosures which cannot be categorised with any degree of confidence on the basis of surface remains and other available evidence. Also included are levelled or destroyed sites, either marked as antiquities on Ordnance Survey and other maps, or pointed out to the archaeologists in the course of fieldwork.

1272 AGHOUTEREERY
OS 38:5:3 (193,409) Hachured OD 400–500
24648, 28928
Enclosure (possible) Depicted as a tree-ring on OS 1836 and 1876 eds. Raised circular area (int. diam. 34m) enclosed by a much-denuded, narrow, low earthen bank and vague traces of a fosse. Wide break in bank at NE may represent original entrance. Internal area has been planted with conifers. Most likely a rath later planted with trees.
38:1 11-8-1986

1273 ANNAGHARD
OS 17:16:5 (783,44) Indicated OD 200–300
26269, 30354
Enclosure (site, tradition) Depicted on OS 1836 and 1876 eds. as a small subtriangular field. Situated on the summit of a drumlin hill. Slightly raised circular area (diam. 26.8m). All that survives of the perimeter is a kink in the field boundary from N–E–S. Believed to be the site of a 'fort' (local information).
17:3 19-11-1989

1274 ARDKILL MORE
OS 31:4:6 (879,521) Not marked OD 800–900
24388, 29683
Enclosure Shown as a faintly delineated circle on the 1836 ed. A circular area (diam. 25m) enclosed by a much defaced, heather-grown bank, situated on the flat-topped summit of a hill. The site commands an extensive outlook.
31:60 15-6-1993

1275 ARDLOW
OS 39:4:6 (852,467) Not marked OD 400–500
26319, 29004
Enclosure (site) Marked 'Fort' on OS 1836 and 1876 eds. Situated on a slight natural rise in otherwise relatively level ground. Not visible at ground level.
39:5 10-6-1987

1276 ASHGROVE
OS 15:10:1 (253,236) Not marked OD 100–200
23714, 31298
Enclosure (site) Depicted as a small circular enclosure on OS 1876 ed. Not marked on OS 1836 ed. Situated in wet low-lying ground falling WNW to a stream. Not visible at ground level.
15:4 12-8-1989

1277 BALLAGHANEA
OS 39:12:4 (706,191) Not marked OD 300
26168, 28712
Enclosure (site) Marked 'Fort' on OS 1836 and 1876 eds. Situated on the SE slope of a drumlin ridge. Not visible at ground level.
39:9 5-6-1987

1278 BALLINLOUGH
OS 15:2:5 (376,517) *'Friar's Fort'* (Site of)
OD 100–200 23842, 31595
Enclosure (site) Marked on OS 1836 and 1876 eds. Situated on a low peninsula jutting into Common's Lough. Not visible at ground level.
15:8 19-8-1989

1279 BEAGH GLEBE
OS 33:12:4 (729,221) Not marked OD 537
26185, 29384
Enclosure (site) Marked 'Fort' on OS 1836 ed and 'Site of' on 1876 ed. Situated on the summit of a high drumlin hill. Almost completely levelled. The site is now occupied by a small rectangular field. All that survives is a low earthen bank running alongside the field boundary from ESE–S–SSW.
33:3 2-5-1974

1280 BEAGH GLEBE
OS 33:16:1 (748,145) Not marked OD 400–500
26206, 29303
Enclosure (site) Marked 'Fort' on OS 1836 ed. and 'Site of' on 1876 ed. Situated on a low rise. Not visible at ground level. Probably the site of a rath.
33:5 2-5-1974

1281 BEAGH GLEBE
OS 33:12:4 (766,213) Not marked OD 400–500
26225, 29375
Enclosure (site, possible) Marked 'Fort' on OS 1836 ed. and 'Site of' on 1876 ed. Situated on the E slope of rising ground. Not visible at ground level. Probably the site of a rath.
33:8 19-9-1988

1282 BEHERNAGH
OS 43:3:5 (606,458) Not marked OD 500–600
26065, 28352
Enclosure (site) Marked 'Fort' on OS 1836 and 1876 eds. Situated on the SE shoulder of a drumlin ridge.

Not visible at ground level.
43:1 16-6-1987

1283 BRACKLAGH (Tullygarvey By.)
OS 16:3:5 (548,455) Not marked OD 300–400
24999, 31541
Enclosure (site) Not marked on any OS ed. Davies (ITA Survey 1945) recorded a local tradition of a 'fort' at this location. He identified a 'small scarp' which he believed may have represented the remains of an enclosure which has since been levelled. Situated on a drumlin hilltop. Not visible at ground level.
16:8 17-9-1989

1284 BURREN (ED Tuam)
OS 4:1:6 (218,495) Indicated OD 800–900
20731, 33464
Enclosure Not marked on OS 1836 or 1876 eds. Oval enclosure (dims. *c.* 40m E–W; *c.* 30m N–S) marked on OS 1911 ed. The entire townland is the site of a dense modern plantation of coniferous trees. Not located.
4:2 16-6-1987

1285 CARN (Castlerahan By.)
OS 38:4:6 (850,474) Indicated OD 700–800
25341, 29002
Enclosure Marked 'Carn' on OS 1836 and 1876 eds. Circular area (int. diam. *c.* 30m) enclosed by a low earthen bank, skirted by a modern drain from SW–W–NW. Original entrance not recognisable. Internal area slopes steeply from E–W.
38:5 27-8-1986

1286 CAROLINA
OS 17:4:6 (849,509) Not marked OD 300
26788, 30781
Enclosure (site) Davies (ITA Survey 1946) recorded the site of a rath at this location. Not marked on any OS ed. Situated on a low mound overlooking a valley and a stretch of marshland. Not visible at ground level.
17:10 14-11-1990

1287 CAROLINA
OS 17:4:6 (855,480) Not marked OD 200–300
26767, 30745
Enclosure (site, possible) Depicted as a circular tree-ring (diam. *c.* 45m) on OS 1836 ed. Not marked on subsequent eds. Situated within the demesne of Bellamont House on the SW slope of a drumlin hill. It was possibly a rath that was later adapted for use as a landscape feature. Not visible at ground level.
17:11 14-11-1990

1288 CARRAKEELTY BEG
OS 43:4:3 (848,582) Not marked OD 300–400
26319, 28486
Enclosure (site) Marked 'Fort' on OS 1876 ed. Not marked on OS 1836 ed. Situated on a natural rise overlooking a stream. Not visible at ground level.
43:4 6-8-1987

1289 CARRICKCREENY
OS 23:11:3 (688,241) Not marked OD 400–500
27105, 30693
Enclosure (site) Marked 'Fort' on OS 1836 ed. and 'Site of' on 1876 ed. Situated on the summit of a drumlin hill overlooking Sillan Lough 200m to SW. Not visible at ground level.
23:3 4-4-1992

1290 CARRICKMORE
OS 16:9:4 (40,186) Hachured OD 300–400
24465, 31251
Enclosure Slightly raised oval area (int. dims. 53m NNW–SSE; 41.4m WSW–ENE) enclosed by a low, narrow, steep-sided earthen bank and a deep, narrow fosse. The site may be a tree-ring.
16:13 21-9-1989

1291 CARRICKNAVEAGH
OS 33:12:6 (848,194) Indicated OD 500–600
26311, 29356
Enclosure (possible) Raised circular area (int. diam. 28m) enclosed by a narrow, low bank of earth and stone. Original entrance not recognisable. Known locally as a 'Fort' but not marked as same on any OS ed. It may in fact be a landscape feature.
33:11 13-9-1988

1292 CARRIGABURSE
OS 44:1:1 (36,599) Not marked OD 300–400
26437, 28505
Enclosure (site) Marked 'Fort' on OS 1836 and 1876 eds. Situated on the N slope of a low drumlin ridge. Not visible at ground level.
44:1 19-8-1987

1293 CASTLEPOLES
OS 30:3:1 (504,585) Hachured OD 500–600
23021, 29737
Enclosure (site) Marked 'Fort' on OS 1836 and 1876 eds. Situated on a small natural spur on the NW slope of a steep rocky hill. Overlooked by higher ground to the E, S and SW. Not visible at ground level.
30:3 4-10-1991

1294 CASTLESAUNDERSON DEMESNE
OS 11:12:4 (734,176) Not marked OD 200–300
24218, 31879
Enclosure (site) Depicted as a large oval enclosure on OS 1836 and 1876 eds. Situated on the SW slope of a

drumlin hill in a heavily wooded area. Not visible at ground level.
11:5 16-6-1989

1295 CASTLESAUNDERSON DEMESNE
OS 11:12:5 (770,176) Indicated OD 200
24255, 31879
Enclosure (site) Depicted as a small oval enclosure on OS 1836 and 1876 eds. Destroyed from SE–S–NNW as a result of road building. Elsewhere site outline is still clearly identifiable despite having been levelled.
11:7 16-6-1989

1296 CLOGGY
OS 24:16:3 (914,150) Indicated OD 200–300
23449, 29923
Enclosure Not marked on OS 1836 or 1876 eds. Raised oval area (int. dims. 42.2m NNW–SSE; 36.3m ENE–WSW) defined by a scarp with a low earthen bank on its upper edge. From S–W–WNW the perimeter has been modified and incorporated into the field boundary. Original entrance not recognisable. Internal area slopes steeply from ENE–WSW.
24:14 7-5-1993

1297 CLOGHBALLYBEG
OS 40:14:4 (279,55) Indicated OD 400–500
26693, 28573
Enclosure (possible) Depicted as a tree-ring on OS 1836 ed. Raised circular area (int. diam. *c.* 57m N–S) enclosed by a low bank of earth and stone. Break in bank at S may represent original entrance.
40:4 13-8-1987

1298 CLOGHBALLY UPPER
OS 44:2:5 (340,528) Not marked OD 400–500
26759, 28432
Enclosure (site) Marked 'Fort' on OS 1836 and 1876 eds. Situated on the W shoulder of a high drumlin ridge. A slight scarp traceable from W–NW–N is the only surviving surface indication of the site.
44:5 20-8-1987

1299 CLOGHERGOOLE
OS 39:12:6 (922,191) Not marked OD 300–400
26395, 28714
Enclosure (site) Marked 'Fort' on OS 1836 ed. and 'Site of' on 1876 ed. Situated on the E slope of a drumlin ridge. Not visible at ground level.
39:20 5-6-1987

1300 CLONERVY
OS 21:6:4 (244,307) Not marked OD 400 24685, 30741
Enclosure (site, possible) Depicted as a large circular tree-covered enclosure on OS 1836 ed. Not marked on subsequent eds. Situated on a drumlin hilltop. Not visible at ground level.
21:7 22-9-1990

1301 CLONERVY
OS 21:6:4 (262,303) Not marked OD 400–500
24705, 30737
Enclosure (site) Marked 'Fort' on OS 1836 ed. and 'Site of' on 1876 ed. Situated on the summit of a low hill. Not visible at ground level.
21:8 22-9-1990

1302 CLONLOSKAN
OS 25:9:1 (63,264) Not marked OD 100–200
23525, 30045
Enclosure Not marked on any edition of OS. Possible remains of a rath represented by an irregular-shaped earthen mound (H 0.3m; dims. 31.9m N–S x 17.8m E–W) bordered by a drain on E side.
25:122 5-9-1991

1303 COPPANAGH (Clankee By.)
OS 34:12:6 (877,179) Not marked OD 500–600
27318, 29349
Enclosure (site) Marked 'Fort' on OS 1836 and 1876 eds. Situated on the summit of a drumlin hill. Not visible at ground level.
34:17 15-3-1974

1304 CORCLOGHAN (Clankee By.)
OS 23:7:1 (471,385) Not marked OD 300–400
26875, 30843
Enclosure (site) Marked 'Fort' on OS 1836 ed. and 'Site of' on 1876 ed. Situated in low-lying ground adjacent to Lough Tacker. Not visible at ground level.
23:9 22-5-1992

1305 CORFAD (Castlerahan By.)
OS 39:12:2 (846,289) Not marked OD 300–400
26314, 28817
Enclosure (site) Marked 'Fort' on OS 1836 ed. and 'Site of' on 1876 ed. Situated on a ridge of high ground within a valley. Not visible at ground level.
39:21 8-6-1987

1306 CORGLASS (ED Baileborough)
OS 28:10:4 (297,186) Not marked OD 500–600
26699, 29991
Enclosure (site) Marked 'Fort' on OS Fair Plan and 1836 ed. Not marked on subsequent eds. Probably the site of a rath. Situated on the NE slope of a drumlin hill. Not visible at ground level.
28:4 24-8-1988

1307 CORMEEN (Tullyhunco By.)
OS 14:1:5 (140,518) Not marked OD 100–200
22617, 31585

Enclosure (site) Marked 'Fort' on OS 1836 ed. and shown as occupying a small area of low-lying ground between the Woodford River and a stream. The stream was diverted in 1847 (local information) at which time the site was presumably levelled. The outline of a small circular enclosure (diam. *c.* 23.3m) may still be traced.
14:44 18-7-1989

1308 CORNABASTE
OS 16:16:5 (777,23) Not marked OD 300–400
25245, 31086

Enclosure (site) Marked 'Fort' on OS 1836 ed. and 'Site of' on 1876 ed. Situated on the summit of a drumlin hill. Not visible at ground level.
16:25 29-10-1989

1309 CORNAGLARE OR PALMIRA
OS 40:10:5 (338,209) Not marked OD 400–500
26754, 28736

Enclosure (possible) Marked 'Fort (Site of)' on OS 1876 ed. Not marked on previous or subsequent eds. Situated on the S shoulder of a ridge of high ground in marshland. The possible remains of an enclosure represented by a raised oval-shaped mound which has been damaged by quarrying.
40:12 10-7-1987

1310 CORNALARA
OS 29:1:4 (51,518) Not marked OD 600–700
27412, 30349

Enclosure (site) Marked 'Fort' on OS 1836 and 1876 eds. No remains visible at the location indicated. However, a partly grassed-over conical mound of stones (H 1m) with some large stones visible at its base, lies a short distance to NW. This is believed to be the remains of a 'Fort' (local information).
29:1 15-8-1988

1311 CORNANAFF
OS 28:13:1 (25,83) Hachured OD 600
26413, 29880

Enclosure Raised oval area (int. dims. *c.* 21m E–W; *c.* 18m N–S) enclosed by a shallow fosse and low scarp with remains of a low bank of earth and stone on its upper edge. There is also a subcircular outer enclosing element consisting of a bank set on a scarp with shallow external fosse. From NE–SE four linear banks of earth and stone connect the inner and outer enclosing elements.
28:6 25-3-1974

1312 CORPORATION LANDS
OS 15:2:5 (331,516) Not marked OD 100–200
23794, 31593

Enclosure (site, possible) Marked 'Fort' on OS 1836 ed. and 'Site of' on 1876 ed. The site is divided into two unequal portions by a very deep modern drain running ENE–WSW. The much larger SSE portion has been levelled and there are no surface remains. To NNW is a low circular mound (dims. 15m ENE–WSW; 7m N–S ; H *c.* 1m) which Davies (ITA Survey 1942) believed to be a natural feature.
15:18 10-9-1989

1313 CORR (Tullyhunco By.)
OS 24:8:6 (848,329) Hachured OD 200
23378, 30112

Enclosure (site) Marked 'Fort' on OS 1836 and 1876 eds. An earlier report (OPW 1977) recorded that the site had been levelled in 1976. Outline of perimeter, enclosing a circular area (int. diam. *c.* 3m) can still be traced. Otherwise not visible at ground level.
24:19(01) 21-8-1991

1314 CORRAGLOON
OS 40:5:1 (40,403) Not marked OD 400–500
26437, 28938

Enclosure (site) Marked 'Fort' on OS 1836 ed. and 'Site of' on 1876 ed. Situated on a natural rise on the E shoulder of an area of high ground. All that survives is a slight depression at NE and traces of a low scarp at W and N. Otherwise, nothing visible at ground level.
40:18 10-8-1987

1315 CORRATOBER UPPER
OS 5:14:2 (312,541) Indicated OD200–300
19872, 31722

Enclosure (site) Marked 'Fort' on OS 1836 and 1876 eds. Situated at the base of a valley adjacent to a stream. An earlier report (OPW 1977) described a slightly raised, small circular area (int. diam. *c.* 19m) enclosed by a narrow earthen bank and very slight traces of a fosse. Site has been levelled largely as a result of the construction of a field boundary running N–S. Nonetheless its outline may still be traced.
5:26 16-8-1988

1316 CORRONAGH
OS 39:15:2 (574,80) Indicated OD 300–400
26030, 28593

Enclosure Slightly raised circular area (int. diam. 55m) enclosed by a low bank of earth and stone from NE–S–W and elsewhere by modern stone walls. Original entrance not recognisable. Although the site is marked 'Fort' on OS 1836 and 1876 eds., it may in fact be a landscape feature.
39:27 28-5-1987

1317 CORWEELIS (Clankee By.)
OS 28:6:4 (267,309) Indicated OD 500–600
26666, 30121

Enclosure (site) Marked 'Fort' on OS 1836 and 1876 eds. Situated on the E shoulder of a high drumlin hill. Not visible at ground level.
28:7 29-8-1988

1318 CRAN
OS 22:4:5 (796,464) Not marked OD 400–500
26242, 30921
Enclosure (possible) Marked 'Fort' on OS 1836 and 1876 eds. Inspection not possible due to heavy growth of vegetation in vicinity of site. Situated on a drumlin hilltop.
22:9 15-10-1990

1319 CROVER
OS 38:9:6 (189,164) Hachured OD 200–300
24646, 28669
Enclosure (site, possible) Depicted as a tree-ring on OS 1836 and 1876 eds. Site is now largely occupied by a modern dwelling. All that survives is a very short stretch of earthen bank at SE. Otherwise nothing visible at ground level. The site may have been merely a landscape feature.
38:17 12-8-1986

1320 CULLIAGH
OS 9:13:6 (203,9) Hachured OD 200–300
21708, 31679
Enclosure Subcircular slightly raised area (int. dims. 74m NE–SW; 53m NW–SE) enclosed by an earthen bank which has been modified and incorporated into the field boundary from SSW–W–N, and a fosse well preserved from SW–W–NW and replaced by field drains elsewhere. Both bank and fosse have been levelled from N–NNE–NE. Original entrance not recognisable.
9:9 19-9-1988

1321 CULLOW
OS 32:13:3 (211,97) Indicated OD 500
24664, 29239
Enclosure (possible) Small almost oval-shaped enclosure with its long axis aligned N–S, marked on the OS 1913 ed. but not on previous eds. Site is densely overgrown with vegetation rendering inspection impossible.
32:8 3-7-1989

1322 CULLOW
OS 32:13:3 (216,85) Hachured OD 500–600
24670, 29226
Enclosure (possible) Raised circular area (int. dims. 29.8m E–W; 29m N–S) enclosed by a narrow earthen bank faced externally with drystone masonry and incorporated into the field boundary from W–NW–N. Original entrance not recognisable.
32:9 10-4-1974

1323 DERNASKEAGH
OS 17 NPL Not marked
Enclosure (site, tradition) Davies (ITA Survey 1946) recorded a tradition of a 'fort', long since levelled, on the summit of a drumlin hill in this townland. Not located.
17:25

1324 DERRY (Clankee By.)
OS 28:4:6 (893,501) Not marked OD 500–600
27326, 30329
Enclosure (site) Marked 'Fort' on OS 1836 ed. and 'Site of' on 1876 ed. Situated on the W shoulder of a drumlin hill. All that survives today are faint traces of a low scarp curving from N–E. Otherwise nothing visible at ground level.
28:11 31-8-1988

1325 DERRYHEEN
OS 20:2:3 (446,534) Indicated OD 100–200
23921, 30973
Enclosure (site) Marked 'Fort' on OS 1836 and 1876 eds. Raised almost circular area (diam. *c.* 30m) which has been planted with trees. Situated in low-lying wet marshy ground.
20:18 21-8-1990

1326 DERRYLINA
OS 15:14:3 (390,111) Not marked OD 200–300
23860, 31167
Enclosure (site) Marked 'Fort' on OS 1836 and 1876 eds. Situated on the summit of a low drumlin hill. Davies (ITA Survey 1942) speculated that this may be the remains of a ruined cashel. Not visible at ground level.
15:24 21-9-1989

1327 DILLAGH
OS 31:6:2 (367,412) Not marked OD 300–400
23851, 29564
Enclosure (site) Marked 'Fort' on OS 1836 ed. and 'Site of' on 1876 ed. Situated on the summit of a drumlin hill. Levelled *c.* 25 years ago (local information) and modern farm buildings erected on its site. Not visible at ground level.
31:19 3-6-1992

1328 DRUMAD
OS 28:7:2 (547,395) Not marked OD 500–600
26962, 30214
Enclosure (possible) Marked 'Fort' on OS 1836 and 1876 eds. Largely levelled. It apparently comprised a raised circular area (int. diam. *c.* 40m) enclosed by an earthen bank which is still identifiable from SE–W–NW and discernible as a low scarp from N–NE. A modern drain lies outside the bank at W and

a modern laneway skirts the perimeter from SE–S. Original entrance not recognisable. A barrow (**108**) is situated inside the bank at NW.
28:12(01) 14-9-1988

1329 DRUMAUNA
OS 16:15:6 (667,16) Not marked OD 400–500
25129, 31078
Enclosure (site) Marked 'Fort' on OS 1836 and 1876 eds. All that survives today is a short stretch of low earthen bank running from NNE–E, defining a much-levelled slightly raised area. From WSW–N–NNE the outline of the perimeter can be traced. Situated on the summit of a drumlin hill.
16:41 21-9-1989

1330 DRUMAVADDY (Clanmahon By.)
OS 25:16:6 (864,42) Indicated OD 600–700
24373, 29818
Enclosure Unusually small enclosure known locally as a 'fort'. It comprises a raised circular area (int. diam. 18.4m NNW–SSE) enclosed by a low earthen bank and a narrow, partly waterlogged fosse, both of which appear to have been modified in relatively recent times. Original entrance not recognisable.
25:38 20-9-1991

1331 DRUMBANNAN
OS 34:2:2 (326,552) Not marked OD 600–700
26732, 29738
Enclosure (site) Marked 'Fort' on OS 1836 and 1876 eds. Situated on the SW shoulder of a drumlin hill. Not visible at ground level.
34:21 19-5-1988

1332 DRUMCROW (ED Denn)
OS 31:4:2 (792,570) Hachured OD 500–600
24297, 29735
Enclosure Marked 'Fort' on OS 1836 and 1876 eds. Raised circular area (int. diam. 15.5m) enclosed by a narrow, steep-sided earthen bank and a trench, both of which look relatively modern in date. No break in bank but there is a narrow causeway crossing the trench at N. Internal area densely overgrown with vegetation.
31:25 18-6-1992

Fig. 28—*A small enclosure at Drumavaddy* (**1330**), *locally known as a 'fort'.*

1333 DRUMELIS
OS 20:11:5 (571,190) Not marked OD 200–300
24057, 30611
Enclosure (site) Marked 'Fort' on OS 1836 ed. and 'Site of' on 1876 ed. Situated on the summit of a drumlin hill. Site has been levelled and the only surface indication of its former presence is a kink in the field boundary at SSW.
20:32 15-8-1990

1334 DRUMERDANNAN
OS 19:4:5 (775,485) Hachured OD 200–300
23294, 30916
Enclosure (site, possible) Not marked on OS 1836 or 1876 eds. Situated on the summit of a low drumlin hill. Although the site was levelled in the early 1950s, the outline of the perimeter may still be traced.
19:22 15-7-1990

1335 DRUMGALLON
OS 21:4:4 (699,481) Hachured OD 300–400
25165, 30929
Enclosure (site) Situated on the summit of a high drumlin hill. Site has been levelled and apart from a kink in the field boundary at SE there are no surface remains.
21:27 21-9-1990

1336 DRUMGESH
OS 14:12:2 (790,229) Not marked OD 200
23306, 31286
Enclosure (site, tradition) Not marked on any OS ed. The site apparently comprised a 'half circle' (diam. *c.* 30m) enclosed by a low earthen bank and a shallow fosse and was levelled in the 1940s or 1950s (local information). Not visible at ground level.
14:26 17-8-1989

1337 DRUMGESH
OS 14:12:2 (800,242) Hachured OD 200–300
23316, 31300
Enclosure (site) Levelled in the late 1940s. Marked 'Fort' on OS 1836 and 1876 eds. An earlier report (OPW 1969) recorded the outline of the site as being circular (int. diam. *c.* 20m E–W). Not visible at ground level.
14:27 17-9-1989

1338 DRUMHALLAGH (Tullygarvey By.)
OS 21:12:4 (722,219) Not marked OD 200–300
25191, 30653
Enclosure (site) Marked 'Fort' on OS 1836 ed. and 'Site of' on 1876 ed. Situated on a steep drumlin hillside in average pasture adjacent to a stream. Site has been levelled.
21:30 8-9-1992

1339 DRUMHALLAGH (Tullygarvey By.)
OS 21:12:1 (748,237) Indicated OD 200–300
25218, 30672
Enclosure (site, possible) Not marked on any OS ed. Site is divided into two unequal portions by a field boundary running NE–SW. The larger portion SE of the boundary has been levelled. On the NW side of the boundary it survives as an earthen platform (dims. 42.3m NE–SW; 9m NW–SE). No indication of an external fosse. Original entrance not recognisable.
21:31 8-9-1990

1340 DRUMHART
OS 24:6:2 (321,409) Hachured OD 300–400
22821, 30191
Enclosure (site) Marked 'Fort' on OS 1836 and 1876 eds. Situated at the S of a high drumlin ridge. Site has been levelled and apart from a kink in the field boundary at SW, there is nothing visible at ground level.
24:41 22-8-1991

1341 DRUMHECKNAGH
OS 25:7:4 (506,354) Indicated OD 200–300
23992, 30144
Enclosure (site, possible) Not marked on OS 1836 or 1876 eds. Known as the 'fort field' (local information). Subrectangular area (int. dims. 37m E–W; 32.2m N–S) enclosed by a low modern-looking earthen bank with the exception of E quadrant where it is bounded by a deep trench which is coterminous with the townland boundary. Situated close to the base of a drumlin ridge overlooked by rising ground. Probably the site of a rath.
25:50 19-9-1991

1342 DRUMHIRK (ED Denn)
OS 32:5:4 (68,373) Hachured OD 300–400 24511, 29528
Enclosure (site) Marked 'Fort' on OS 1836 and 1876 eds. Situated in fairly level low-lying ground to the N of a stream. Not visible at ground level.
32:16 3-7-1989

1343 DRUMINNICK
OS 23:15:1 (505,123) Not marked OD 400–500
26914, 30567
Enclosure (site) Marked 'Fort' on OS 1836 ed. Not marked on subsequent eds. Situated on the SE slope of a drumlin hill. Although levelled, very faint traces of the perimeter are still identifiable. It was apparently circular in plan (diam. *c.* 32m).
23:19 4-4-1992

1344 DRUMKEERAN BLACK
OS 24:7:6 (624,340) Indicated OD 400–500
23142, 30122

Enclosure (possible) Marked on OS 1836 and 1876 eds. as a tree-covered enclosure. Oval area (int. dims. 42m E–W; 34m N–S) enclosed by an earthen bank with modern external trench. Both have been incorporated into the field boundary. Original entrance not recognisable.
24:43 22-8-1991

1345 DRUMLARK
OS 20:11:3 (656,254) Hachured OD 200–300
24146, 30680
Enclosure (site) The only indication of the presence of a site here is a kink in the field boundary from NNW–N–SE. Not marked on OS 1836 or 1876 eds. and not known locally as an antiquity. Site has been levelled.
20:36 27-8-1990

1346 DRUMMALLAGHT
OS 32:12:3 (917,260) Indicated OD 400–500
25409, 29418
Enclosure (site) Marked 'Fort' on the OS 1836 and 1876 eds. Situated on SW shoulder of a drumlin hill. Site has been levelled.
32:18 10-4-1989

1347 DRUMMANY (Pleydell)
OS 15:9:3 (199,231) Indicated OD 200–300
23657, 31291
Enclosure (site, possible) Not marked on OS 1836 or 1876 eds. Situated on a drumlin hilltop. Davies (ITA Survey 1941) described an oval area (dims. 72m N–S; 24.4m. E–W) enclosed by a low earthen bank and speculated that it may have been a house enclosure. Site has been levelled.
15:41 10-11-1989

1348 DRUMMORA GREAT
OS 25:5:5 (97,344) Indicated OD 100–200
23561, 30130
Enclosure (site) Although site has been levelled, the outline of the perimeter is still identifiable enclosing a circular area (diam. *c.* 43m). From NW–NNW the perimeter has been extensively modified and incorporated into field boundary.
25:54 5-9-1991

1349 DRUMPEAK
OS 29:14:6 (406,56) Hachured OD 300–400
27791, 29864
Enclosure (site) Marked 'Fort' on OS 1836 and 1876 eds. Situated in flat low-lying ground on the S bank of a river which forms part of the border between counties Cavan and Monaghan. The site is now occupied by a quarry.
29:4 9-8-1992

1350 DRUMRANE
OS 16:16:4 (708,5) Not marked OD 400–500
25172, 31067
Enclosure (site) Marked 'Fort' on OS 1836 ed. and 'Site of' on 1876 ed. Situated on the summit of a drumlin hill. The site is now occupied by a dwelling. Not visible at ground level.
16:55 12–10-1989

1351 DRUMRANE
OS 21:4:1 (708,556) Indicated OD 400
25173, 31008
Enclosure Marked 'Fort' on OS 1836 and 1876 eds. An irregular earthen mound, possibly representing the remains of a rath, situated on the summit of a drumlin hill.
21:35 22-9-1990

1352 DRUMRAT (Tullygarvey By.)
OS 21:16:5 (837,65) Not marked OD 400–500
25314, 30491
Enclosure (site) Marked 'Fort' on OS 1836 ed. and 'Site of' on the 1876 ed. Situated on the summit of a drumlin hill. The only surface indication of the site is a curve in the field boundary at W.
21:36 9-9-1990

1353 DRUMSALLAGH
OS 35:2:1 (292,563) Hachured OD 400–500
27671, 29758
Enclosure (site) Marked 'Fort' on OS 1836 and 1876 eds. Situated on the summit of a high drumlin hill. Not visible at ground level.
35:37 19-3-1974

1354 DRUMSHEIL
OS 17:9:1 (73,280) Indicated OD 300–400
25747, 31288
Enclosure (site, possible) Depicted as a tree-ring on OS 1836 and 1876 eds. Situated on the summit of a drumlin hill. An earlier report (OPW 1969) described a raised circular area (int. diam. *c.* 21m) enclosed by a low, narrow but steep-sided earthen bank and a narrow shallow fosse. Original entrance was not recognisable. Site has been levelled.
17:36 16-11-1989

1355 DRUMSHINNY
OS 30:2:3 (413,577) Hachured OD 400–500
22925, 29728
Enclosure (site) Outline of perimeter of an enclosure may be traced, albeit with difficulty, defining an almost oval-shaped area (int. dims. *c.* 38m NW–SE; *c.* 33m NE–SW). Original position of entrance not recognisable.
30:18 4-10-1991

1356 DUNCOLLOG
OS 16:7:6 (682,350) Hachured OD 300–400
25142, 31430
Enclosure (site) An earlier report (OPW 1968) noted a small circular area (int. diam. 26.3m) defined by a very low scarp, presumably representing the perimeter. Situated just SSW of the summit of a high drumlin hill. Site has been levelled.
16:58 5-11-1989

1357 DUNGUMMIN LOWER
OS 42:3:3 (649,580) Not marked OD 300–400
25134, 28473
Enclosure (site, tradition) Not marked on any OS ed. Known as 'The Fort Field' (local information). Situated on the W shoulder of a drumlin ridge. Not visible at ground level.
42:14 10-9-1986

1358 EIGHTER
OS 43:1:6 (205,501) Not marked OD 300–400
25641, 28394
Enclosure (site) Marked 'Fort' on OS 1836 ed. Not marked on subsequent eds. Situated on the NE slope of a drumlin ridge. Davies (1948, 115) recorded a tradition that the site was a rath and was known to have contained graves. Not visible at ground level.
43:11 25-5-1987

1359 ENAGH (Clanmahon By.)
OS 42:10:2 (376,275) Not marked OD 200–300
24849, 28148
Enclosure (site) Marked 'Fort' on OS 1836 and 1876 eds. Situated within a densely wooded area on a natural ridge of high ground close to a river. Not visible at ground level.
42:24 5-9-1986

1360 ENAGH (ED Castlerahan)
OS 39:10:4 (246,223) Hachured OD 400–500
25681, 28741
Enclosure (site) Not marked on OS 1836 and 1876 eds. Situated on the W shoulder of a ridge of high ground. The perimeter has been modified and incorporated into the field boundary from WSW-W-N. Otherwise nothing visible at ground level.
39:47 25-5-1987

1361 ENNISKEEN
OS 35:11:2 (542,261) Not marked OD 200–300
27939, 29442
Enclosure (site) Marked 'Fort' on OS 1836 and 1876 eds. Situated on a slight rise in otherwise low-lying ground. Not visible at ground level.
35:43 26-8-1988

1362 FARTADREEN
OS 34:13:2 (119,83) Not marked OD 500–600
26518, 29241
Enclosure (site) Marked 'Fort' on OS 1836 and 1876 eds. Situated on the SE shoulder of a high knoll. Not visible at ground level.
34:24 26-6-1988

1363 FARTADREEN
OS 34:13:6 (168,16) Not marked OD 400–500
26570, 29171
Enclosure (site) Marked 'Fort' on OS 1836 ed. and 'Site of' on 1876 ed. Remains comprise a slightly raised area (int. diam. *c.* 22m) defined by a low scarp. Original entrance not recognisable.
34:25 26-6-1988

1364 FEUGH (Maxwell)
OS 15:5:5 (119,370) Indicated OD 200–300
23572, 31438
Enclosure Not marked on OS 1836 or 1876 eds. Small subtriangular area (int. dims. 14m N–S; 9.9m E–W) enclosed by a low, narrow bank of earth and stone and a shallow fosse both of which have been incorporated into the field boundary. Original entrance may have been at SE.
15:43 15-9-1989

1365 FORTLAND/LISDUFF (Clanmahon By.)/TURIN
OS 38:9:2 (115,234) *'Four Half Moons'* OD 300–400 24567, 28743
Enclosure Large circular area (int. diam. 102m N–S) enclosed by a low earthen bank and vague traces of a fosse identifiable only in SE quadrant. A modern drain occurs at the external foot of bank in NE quadrant. The site is divided into four roughly equal portions by a crossroads. The NW and SW quadrants have been levelled and no surface remains are now identifiable. Original entrance not recognisable. The site was formerly utilised as a tree-ring. (CUCAP ALJ 77)
38:30 6-8-1986

1366 FREEDUFF
OS 41:2:2 (328,594) Hachured OD 300–400
23820, 28475
Enclosure (site) Marked 'Fort' on OS 1836 and 1876 eds. Situated on the W shoulder of a drumlin ridge. Not visible at ground level.
41:10 2-7-1986

1367 GARRYSALLAGH (D'arcy)
OS 38:14:5 (314,8) Not marked OD 200–300
24779, 28506
Enclosure (site) Marked 'Fort' on OS 1836 ed. and 'Site of' on 1876 ed. Situated on the N slope of a

drumlin ridge. Not visible at ground level.
38:33 3-9-1986

1368 GARRYSALLAGH (D'arcy)/TONAGH (Clanmahon By.)
OS 42:2:2 (353,548) Not marked OD 200–300
24821, 28436
Enclosure (site) Depicted on OS 1836 and 1876 eds. as a large circular enclosure with the designation 'Fort' divided into two unequal portions by a roadway running NNW–ESE. Situated in relatively level pasture-land. Not visible at ground level.
42:25 3-9-1986

1369 GARRYSALLAGH (O'Reilly)
OS 38:14:5 (363,46) Not marked OD 200–300
24832, 28547
Enclosure (site) Marked 'Fort' on OS 1836 and 1876 eds. Situated on a ridge of high ground overlooking a stream. All that survives to indicate the presence of the site is a low roughly circular flat-topped earthen mound (diam. *c.* 24m E–W).
38:34 2-9-1986

1370 GARTYLOUGH
OS 24:14:5 (360,26) Hachured OD 200–300
22866, 29787
Enclosure Large subcircular raised area (int. dims. 83m N–S; 68m E–W) enclosed by an earthen bank best preserved from SW–N–NNE, and a fosse well-defined from NW–N–SSW only. Both bank and fosse have been disturbed by quarrying. Depression in bank with accompanying causeway at ESE may represent original entrance. Within the interior at S is a short segment of earthen bank extending 5m N from the enclosing bank. Situated at the foot of a high drumlin hill.
24:57 14-8-1991

1371 GARVALT LOWER
OS 6:5:4 (44,320) Indicated OD 400–500
20555, 32637
Enclosure Not marked on OS 1836 or 1876 ed. Situated 25m SW of a stream. A subtriangular-shaped area (int. dims. 12.9m NE–SW; 11.3m NW–SE) enclosed by a drystone wall (Wth 0.6m; H. 0.8m) with a breach at NW possibly representing original entrance. The interior contains a number of features including a low circular cairn of stones, a stone wall (L. 5.3m) aligned NE–SW and the remains of a small rectangular unroofed stone building (int. dims. 4m NE–SW; 3.3m NW–SE) with an entrance in its NW wall.
6:9 22-8-1988

1372 GARVALT LOWER
OS 6:1:4 (7,523) Not marked OD 653
20515, 32851
Enclosure (tradition) Tradition of large stone 'fort' at the summit of a hill (local information). Situated within a dense modern plantation of coniferous trees. Not located.
6:8 16-8-1988

1373 GLENCORRAN
OS 26:9:2 (107,274) Not marked OD 500–600
24547, 30065
Enclosure (site) Marked 'Fort' on the OS 1836 and 1876 eds. Remains comprise a raised circular area (int. diam. *c.* 31.5m). The enclosing features have been levelled. The site was formerly utilised as a garden serving the now disused dwelling to SW of the site.
26:37 25-10-1991

1374 GORTNALECK
OS 13:4:4 (695,474) Not marked OD 200–300
22229, 31535
Enclosure (site) Marked 'Fort' on 1836 and 1876 eds. Situated on a low knoll adjacent to Gortnaleck Lough. Not visible at ground level.
13:25 18-6-1989

1375 GORTOORLAN
OS 10:9:3 (225,262) Not marked OD 200–300
22703, 31956
Enclosure (site) Marked 'Fort' on OS 1836 and 1876 eds. Situated close to the foot of a mountain. Not visible at ground level.
10:16 6-10-1989

1376 GREAGHADOSSAN
OS 33:7:6 (640,354) Not marked OD 400–500
26090, 29523
Enclosure (site) Not marked on OS 1836 or 1876 eds. Much disturbed. A roughly circular area (int. diam. *c.* 26m) enclosed by a low earthen bank and traces of a narrow, shallow fosse identifiable only from W–NNW. A modern field boundary both abuts and overlies the bank from N–E–S and a very deep drain has also been cut into the site in this area. Original entrance not recognisable. No trace of 'Greaghadossan Cross' noted at the site on the OS 1913 ed. (Davies 1948, 98–9)
33:34(01) 9-9-1988

1377 GREAGHCLOGH
OS 34:14:4 (242,32) Hachured OD 400–500
26649, 29188
Enclosure (site) Marked 'Fort' on OS 1836 and 1876 eds. and depicted as a circular enclosure. On the current OS ed. it is depicted as a hachured semi-circular arc extending from N–E–SSW. Situated on the SE slope of rising ground. Not visible at ground level.
34:28 31-5-1988

1378 GREAGHCLOGH
OS 40:1:3 (171,531) Not marked OD 500–600
26575, 29074
Enclosure (site) Marked 'Fort' on OS 1836 ed. and 'Site of' on 1876 ed. Situated on the S shoulder of an area of high ground. All that survives to indicate the presence of the site is a slight but perceptible kink in the field boundary at W. Otherwise nothing visible at ground level.
40:26 8-7-1987

1379 GREAGHNAMALE
OS 34:10:2 (332,244) Not marked OD 500–600
26742, 29413
Enclosure (site) Marked 'Fort' on OS 1836 ed. Not marked on subsequent eds. Situated on the SW shoulder of a drumlin ridge. Not visible at ground level.
34:29 13-5-1988

1380 INCH ISLAND
OS 19:12:5 (844,200) Indicated OD 200–300
23369, 30616
Enclosure Marked 'Fort' on OS 1836 and 1876 eds. Inch Island is now the site of a dense plantation of coniferous trees. Davies (ITA Survey 1942) described a raised oval area (int. dims. *c.* 9.7m x 7.8m) enclosed by a low earthen bank and a fosse. Not located.
19:36 (01)

1381 INISHMORE
OS 20:2:2 (345,549) 'Cornabrassan Fort' OD 200
23814, 30989
Enclosure Raised almost circular area (int. diam. *c.* 118.5m) enclosed by a substantial earthen bank from WSW–N–E and a wide, deep fosse. A scarp which appears to be natural in part runs from S–WSW. Bank is breached at SSE and NW and one of these breaks probably represents the original entrance. The site is situated in low-lying ground, bounded by a swamp from SE–S–WSW, and overlooked by higher ground.
20:48 19-8-1990

1382 INISHMORE
OS 20:2:3 (386,603) '*Granshagh or Riverview Fort* (Site of)' OD 200–300 23857, 31046
Enclosure Marked as 'Granshagh or Riverview Fort' on OS 1836 and 1876 eds. Situated just S of the top of a high drumlin ridge. Although levelled, the outline of what was apparently an earthen bank and fosse may still be identified enclosing a large approximately circular area (int. diam. *c.* 70m).
20:49 19-8-1990

1383 ISLAND
OS 43:11:3 (617,296) Hachured OD 400–500
26078, 28182
Enclosure (site) Marked 'Fort' on OS 1836 and 1876 eds. The site is now occupied by a small circular, apparently natural earthen mound (diam. *c.* 23m). However, the field in which the site is situated, is locally known as 'The Fort Field' which may imply the former presence of an antiquity here.
43:13 18-6-1987

1384 KIFFAGH
OS 32:14:6 (444,10) Not marked OD 300–400
24911, 29149
Enclosure (site) Depicted as a large circular enclosure on OS 1836 ed. Not marked on subsequent eds. Situated on the S slope of a low hill.
32:23 26-4-198

1385 KILL
OS 37:4:1 (741,531) Not marked OD 300–400
24251, 29053
Enclosure Marked 'Fort' on OS 1836 and 1876 eds. A circular area (int. diam. *c.* 28m) defined by a scarp from NE–S–W. Original entrance not recognisable.
37:31 15-7-1986

1386 KILLARAH
OS 14:5:2 (87,434) Not marked OD 300–400
22562, 31496
Enclosure Depicted as a circular enclosure on OS 1836 and 1876 eds. Situated within a dense plantation of coniferous trees, close to the summit of Ballyheady Mountain. Not located.
14:42 18-7-1989

1387 KILDUFF (Tullygarvey By.)
OS 16:9:1 (46,270) Not marked OD 300–400
24471, 31340
Enclosure (site) Marked 'Fort' on OS 1836 ed. and 'Site of' on 1876 ed. It is believed (local information) that during the War of Independence (1919–21) the site was used as a hiding place for the insurgents. Situated on the summit of a drumlin hill. Not visible at ground level.
16:68 21-9-1989

1388 KILDUFF LOWER
OS 5:16:2 (773,370) Not marked OD 100–200
20356, 31907
Enclosure (site) Marked 'Fort' on OS 1836 and 1876 eds. Situated on the NW shoulder of a hillside in wet, precipitous mountainous terrain. Not visible at ground level.
5:35 21-8-1988

1389 KILLETER
OS 40:10:6 (436,183) Not marked OD 500
26858, 28710

Enclosure (site) Marked 'Fort' on OS 1836 ed. and 'Site of' on 1876 ed. Situated on the S shoulder of a steep hill. The site is now occupied by a silage pit. Not visible at ground level.
40:34 14-9-1987

1390 KILLETER
OS 40:10:6 (452,164) Not marked OD 400–500
26875, 28689
Enclosure (site, possible) Not marked on any OS ed. Known locally as the site of a 'fairy fort' (local information). All that survives to indicate the possible presence of an enclosure here is a raised circular platform (diam. *c*. 25m) demarcated by the curve of a now disused laneway from SE–S–NW. The inner face of the laneway is bordered by a low narrow bank of earth and stone.
40:35 14-9-1987

1391 KILLYBANDRICK
OS 15:4:5 (792,504) Not marked OD 200–300
24281, 31585
Enclosure (site, possible) Not marked on any OS ed. Known as the site of a rath (local information). Situated on the summit of a high drumlin hill. Not visible at ground level.
15:52 18-9-1989

1392 KILLYGARRY (ED Ballyhaise)
OS 21:2:1 (268,579) Indicated OD 200–300
24708, 31028
Enclosure (site) Marked 'Fort' on OS 1836 and 1876 eds. Situated on the summit of a drumlin hill. Apart from a kink in the field boundary at N there are no visible remains at ground level.
21:44 27-9-1990

1393 KILMACNORAN
OS 16:14:2 (320,104) Hachured OD 200–300
24762, 31168
Enclosure (possible) Marked 'Fort' on OS 1836 and 1876 eds. Raised circular area (int. diam. 32.4m) enclosed by a low, narrow earthen bank and a narrow, shallow trench. Original entrance not recognisable. Internal area has been planted with trees. The site may be a landscape feature.
16:72 6-11-1989

1394 KILNAGARBET
OS 21:11:6 (685,168) Hachured OD 300–400
25152, 30599
Enclosure Raised oval area (int. dims. 73m N–S; 67m E–W) enclosed by vague traces of a fosse, and a scarp with slight traces of an earthen bank on its upper edge. Modern trench replaces fosse from W–NW–N. Poorly defined break in bank at S may represent original entrance. Known in the locality as a 'fort'.
21:46 25-9-1990

1395 KILNAVARA
OS 25:3:3 (651,573) Indicated OD 200–300
24143, 30377
Enclosure Large almost circular raised area (int. dims. 95m E–W; 89m N–S) enclosed by an earthen bank with an external fosse which has been partially replaced by a modern drain. Both bank and fosse have been levelled from E–S–SSW but their outline is still traceable. Original entrance may have been at ESE.
25:74 2-10-1991

1396 KINNABO
OS 2:13:3 (166,113) Indicated OD 300–400
20675, 33700
Enclosure Not marked on OS 1836 or 1876 eds. Depicted on OS 1911 ed. as a large roughly oval enclosure (dims. *c*. 59m N–S; *c*. 50m E–W). Densely overgrown with vegetation rendering inspection impossible.
2:8 8-7-1988

1397 KINNABO
OS 2:13:3 (167,92) Indicated OD 300–400
20676, 33678
Enclosure Not marked on OS 1836 or 1876 eds. Small circular area (int. diam. 12.7m) enclosed by a drystone wall. Original entrance not recognisable. Densely overgrown with vegetation.
2:9 8-7-1988

1398 KINNABO
OS 2:13:3 (197,111) Indicated OD 300–400
20707, 33698
Enclosure Not marked on OS 1836 or 1876 eds. Known locally as a 'fort'. Raised circular area (int. diam. *c*. 30.7m) enclosed by the remains of a drystone rampart. Original entrance not recognisable. Densely overgrown with vegetation.
2:10 8-7-1988

1399 KNOCKARAHEEN
OS 43:7:1 (472,395) Not marked OD 500–600
25925, 28285
Enclosure (site) Marked 'Fort' on OS 1836 and 1876 eds. Situated on the S shoulder of a drumlin ridge. Not visible at ground level.
43:16 18-6-1987

1400 LANLISS
OS 2:14:1 (298,135) Indicated OD 300–400
20814, 33725
Enclosure Not marked on OS 1836 or 1876 eds.

Raised circular area (int. diam. 27.2m) enclosed by a substantial but partly collapsed drystone wall. Original entrance not recognisable. A curving stone wall connects the W sector of this site to the NE of a small subrectangular raised area (int. dims. 16.4m NW–NE; 8.7m NE–SE). This is enclosed by a rampart similar in morphology to the circular enclosure. Again original entrance not recognisable. Densely overgrown with vegetation.
2:11(01) 12-7-1988

1401 LARAGH
OS 35:5:5 (103,345) Not marked OD 500–600
27474, 29526
Enclosure (site) Marked 'Fort' on OS 1836 ed. and 'Site of' on 1876 ed. Situated on the NE slope of a drumlin ridge. Not visible at ground level.
35:45 15-6-1988

1402 LATNADRONAGH
OS 32:10:1 (275,230) Hachured OD 500–600
24731, 29379
Enclosure (site) Marked 'Fort' on OS 1836 and 1876 eds. Situated on the summit of a drumlin ridge. Not visible at ground level. Possibly the site of a rath.
32:29 20-6-1989

1403 LATT
OS 20:8:4 (756,332) Indicated OD 200–300
24251, 30763
Enclosure (site) Marked 'Fort' on OS 1836 and 1876 eds. Davies (ITA Survey 1942) recorded a subcircular area (int. diam. 23.7m) bounded by a low earthen bank and a shallow fosse at W and NW and elsewhere by a steep scarp. He described a break in the bank and fosse at W which he speculated was probably the original entrance. Situated adjacent to a stream in wet infertile ground. Not visible at ground level.
20:56 16-8-1990

1404 LAVAGH
OS 37:12:6 (909,210) Hachured OD 300–400
24431, 28716
Enclosure (site) Marked 'Fort' on OS 1836 and 1876 eds. Situated on the S shoulder of a drumlin ridge. Site has been levelled. Not visible at ground level.
37:43 5-8-1986

1405 LEGGYKELLY
OS 11:16:5 (778,74) Indicated OD 200–300
24265, 31771
Enclosure (possible) Not marked on OS 1836 or 1876 eds. but known locally as a 'fort'. Raised circular area (int. diam. *c.* 32m NW–SE) enclosed by a narrow, shallow trench and low, narrow earthen bank, both of which are similar in morphology to field boundaries in the vicinity. Original entrance not recognisable.
11:23 16-6-1989

1406 LEGNAGROW
OS 6:5:1 (69,390) Not marked OD 359
20581, 32712
Enclosure Raised circular area (int. diam. 8m) enclosed by a low, narrow earthen bank accompanied by an apparently modern external trench. Site is divided into two roughly equal portions by a field bank running NW–SE, the area SW of which has been levelled. Entrance feature (Wth 3m) at N. Known locally as a 'fort'.
6:12 27-2-1991

1407 LEITRIM (Clankee By.)
OS 34:6:6 (419,307) Not marked OD 500–600
26833, 29480
Enclosure (site) Marked 'Fort' on OS 1836 and 1876 eds. Situated on the W shoulder of a drumlin ridge. No visible remains at ground level.
34:33 31-5-1988

1408 LISADERG OR CORWEELIS
OS 18:13:2 (119,133) Indicated OD 500–600
26501, 31214
Enclosure (site) Almost completely levelled. Marked 'Fort' on OS 1836 and 1876 eds. and known as same within the locality. Situated on the summit of a drumlin hill. All that survives is a much-denuded raised area (H 1.5m) defined by a low scarp from S–SW.
18:9 15-7-1990

1409 LISANISKY
OS 35:6:6 (458,324) Indicated OD 400–500
27849, 29507
Enclosure (site) Marked 'Fort' on OS 1836 and 1876 eds. Situated on the E shoulder of a drumlin ridge. Not visible at ground level.
35:49 21-6-1988

1410 LISGREA
OS 39:2:6 (436,512) Not marked OD 400–500
25879, 29048
Enclosure (site) Marked 'Fort' on OS 1836 and 1876 eds. Situated on the SW shoulder of a drumlin hill. Not visible at ground level.
39:57 26-3-1987

1411 LISLEA (Castlerahan By.)
OS 39:16:3 (887,83) Not marked OD 300–400
26360, 28599
Enclosure (site) Marked 'Fort' on OS 1836 and 1876 eds. Situated on the S shoulder of a low drumlin hill. All that survives to indicate the presence of the site is a

curve in the field boundary from ENE–E–SSE. Otherwise nothing visible at ground level.
39:59 23-3-1987

1412 LISLEA (Castlerahan By.)
OS 40:13:1 (30,92) Not marked OD 300–400
26429, 28610
Enclosure (site) Marked 'Fort' on OS 1836 ed. and 'Site of' on 1876 ed. Situated on the SW shoulder of an area of high ground. The field in which the site was located is still known as 'The Fort Field' (local information). Not visible at ground level.
40:39 14-8-1987

1413 LISLIN (ED Castlerahan By.)
OS 40:15:1 (505,132) Indicated OD 300–400
26931, 28656
Enclosure (possible) Not marked on OS 1836 or 1876 eds. Raised almost circular platform (int. diam. *c.* 27m) enclosed by a well-defined narrow fosse from S–W–SE which has been infilled and replaced by a laneway from SE–S. Original entrance not recognisable. Possibly the remains of a rath.
40:40 14-7-1987

1414 LISLIN (Tullygarvey By.)
OS 16:15:1 (503,121) Not marked OD 300
24955, 31187
Enclosure (site) Site was levelled in the early 1960s during land reclamation. Outline of perimeter may still be traced enclosing a circular area (diam. int. 41m). Situated on the SE slope of a drumlin hill, close to the summit.
16:93 18-10-1989

1415 LISMACANIGAN LOWER
OS 38:15:6 (616,3) Not marked OD 200–300
25099, 28503
Enclosure (site) Marked 'Fort' on OS 1836 ed. Not marked on subsequent eds. Situated on SW slope of a drumlin ridge. Not visible at ground level.
38:43/42:28* 29-8-1986

1416 LISNABRINNIA
OS 42:3:1 (476,576) Not marked OD 200–300
24952, 28467
Enclosure (site) Marked 'Fort' on OS 1836 ed. and 'Site of' on 1876 ed. Situated on the summit of a natural knoll in otherwise level pasture-land. Not visible at ground level.
42:31 10-9-1986

1417 LISNADARRAGH (Clanmahon By.)
OS 41:2:5 (370,527) Not marked OD 200–300
23864, 28406
Enclosure (site) Marked 'Fort' on OS 1836 ed. and 'Site of' on 1876 ed. Situated on a natural knoll in low-lying ground. Not visible at ground level.
41:13 1-7-1986

1418 LISNAFANA
OS 39:2:1 (283,591) Not marked OD 300–400
25717, 29130
Enclosure (site, possible) Tradition of a 'Fort' at this location. Situated on the N slope of a drumlin hill. Not visible at ground level.
39:63 25-3-1987

1419 LISNAGEER (ED Ashfield)
OS 17:5:4 (26,377) Not marked OD 200–300
25791, 31436
Enclosure (site) Marked 'Fort' on OS 1836 and 1876 eds. Situated in low-lying ground close to a stream. Not visible at ground level.
17:51 23-11-1989

1420 LOUGHAN
OS 2:9:4 (39,224) Indicated OD 300–400
20540, 33816
Enclosure Not marked on OS 1836 or 1876 eds. Situated within a forestry plantation *c.* 90m from Lough MacNean Upper. Depicted on the OS current ed. as a small oval enclosure (dims. *c.* 25m N–S; *c.* 20m E–W). Not located.
2:13 14-7-1988

1421 LURGANBOY (Castlerahan By.)
OS 43:2:6 (389,456) Not marked OD 500–600
25836, 28348
Enclosure (site) Tradition of a 'Fort' at this location. Not marked on any OS ed. Situated on the SW shoulder of a drumlin ridge. Not visible at ground level.
43:28 16-6-1987

1422 MAGHERABOY UPPER
OS 41:3:6 (675,493) Hachured OD 200–300
24187, 28372
Enclosure (site) Marked 'Fort' on OS 1836 and 1876 eds. Situated in wet low-lying ground adjacent to Lough Sheelin. Not visible at ground level.
41:17 25-6-1974

1423 MANRAGH UPPER
OS 4:6:1 (277,424) Indicated OD 500–600
20794, 33390
Enclosure (site) Marked 'Fort' on OS 1836 and 1876 eds. Situated on the SE shoulder of a hillside in rough mountainous terrain. Levelled in the early 1980s, the site is now partly occupied by a modern dwelling-

house. It was known locally as a 'stone fort'.
4:12 10-8-1988

1424 MARAHILL (Clankee By.)
OS 35:2:6 (450,496) Indicated OD 300–400
27839, 29689
Enclosure (site) Marked 'Fort' on OS 1836 and 1876 eds. Situated on the E shoulder of a drumlin ridge. Site is now occupied by a modern dwelling-house and garden. Not visible at ground level.
35:57 9-6-1988

1425 MIDDLETOWN
OS 30:12:6 (918,166) Indicated OD 300–400
23460, 29296
Enclosure Depicted as a tree-covered enclosure on the OS 1836 and 1876 eds. Raised oval area (int. dims. 50.2m N–S; 26m E–W) enclosed by an earthen bank and traces of an outer fosse which has been modified and incorporated into the field drainage system. Break in bank with accompanying causeway at S is probably modern. Known in the locality as a 'Fort'.
30:32 10-10-1991

1426 MIDDLETOWN
OS 30:16:3 (921,146) Indicated OD 300–400
23463, 29275
Enclosure Depicted on OS 1836 and 1876 eds. as a tree-covered enclosure. Raised oval area (int. dims. 49.7m NW–SE; 25.9m NE–SW) enclosed by an earthen bank and traces of an outer fosse which has been modified and incorporated into the field boundary. Breaks in bank at N and S. Internal area presently utilised as a garden. Known in the locality as a 'fort'.
30:33 10-10-1991

1427 MOYDUFF
OS 23:3:4 (534,530) Indicated OD 400–500
26941, 30997
Enclosure Marked 'Fort' on the OS 1836 and 1876 eds. and known locally as same. It comprises what appears to be a natural outcrop hillock encircled by a grass-covered bank of earth and stone. The enclosed area is approximately circular (int. diam. *c.* 31.7m). Original entrance not recognisable.
23:46 22-5-1992

1428 MULLAGH
OS 40:14:3 (415,136) Not marked OD 300–400
26836, 28660
Enclosure (site) Marked 'Fort' on OS 1836 and 1876 eds. Situated on a natural knoll in otherwise relatively flat ground within a modern plantation of coniferous trees. Not visible at ground level.
40:45 16-7-1987

1429 MULNANARRAGH
OS 12:13:6 (164,26) Not marked OD 200
24593, 31723
Enclosure (site) Marked 'Fort' on OS 1836 ed. Not marked on subsequent eds. Situated close to the base of a low drumlin hill. The site is occupied by a now disused dwelling-house and farm buildings. Not visible at ground level.
12:3 28-6-1989

1430 OGGAL
OS 1:16:6 (888,31) Indicated OD 300–400
20463, 33612
Enclosure Depicted as a subcircular enclosure on all OS eds. Large approximately circular area (int. diam. *c.* 52m) enclosed by a low earthen bank which has been levelled from NE–E–SE. Original entrance not recognisable. Known locally as a 'fort'.
1:10 2-7-1988

1431 OGGAL
OS 1:16:6 (908,21) Indicated OD 400–500
20484, 33601
Enclosure Depicted as a subcircular enclosure on all OS eds. Raised oval area (int. dims. *c.* 30m N–S; *c.* 26m E–W) enclosed by the remains of a drystone wall. Original entrance not recognisable.
1:11 16-8-1974

1432 OGHILL
OS 31:5:6 (179,340) Indicated OD 300
23653, 29487
Enclosure Known locally as a 'fort'. Irregular eglongated area (int. dims. 46.3m NNW–SSE; 18.5m ENE–WSW) enclosed by a narrow earthen bank with an external trench and traces of an internal trench.
31:52 10-6-1992

1433 RACRAVEEN
OS 38:14:3 (419,113) Not marked OD 200–300
24890, 28617
Enclosure (site) Marked 'Fort' on OS 1836 ed. and 'Site of' on 1876 ed. Situated on W shoulder of a low drumlin ridge. Not visible at ground level.
38:54 13-8-1986

1434 RAHARDRUM
OS 39:11:2 (614,299) Not marked OD 300–400
26070, 28825
Enclosure (site) Marked 'Fort' on OS 1836 ed. and 'Site of' on 1876 ed. Situated in relatively flat pasture-land. Not visible at ground level.
39:74 1-4-1987

1435 RAHARDRUM
OS 39:11:6 (659,266) Not marked OD 300–400
26117, 28747

Enclosure (site) Marked 'Fort' on OS 1836 ed. and 'Site of' on 1876 ed. The site is now occupied by the back gardens of a small terrace of houses. Not visible at ground level.
39:76 1-4-1987

1436 RAHEEVER
OS 42:11:2 (600,280) Not marked OD 200–300
25085, 28156
Enclosures (conjoined, site) Depicted on OS 1836 ed. as two conjoined oval enclosures with the designation 'Forts'. Marked 'Forts (Site of)' on 1876 ed. Situated on a natural knoll in rolling pasture-land. Not visible at ground level.
42:39 9-9-1986

1437 RAHEEVER
OS 42:11:2 (581,262) Not marked OD 200–300
25066, 28137
Enclosure (site) Depicted on OS 1836 ed. as a small circular enclosure. Not marked on subsequent eds. The site is occupied by a natural knoll, roughly circular in plan (diam. *c.* 25m E–W). Not visible at ground level.
42:38 9-9-1986

1438 RAHEEVER
OS 42:11:3 (661,277) Hachured OD 300–400
25149, 28153
Enclosure (site) Marked 'Fort' on OS 1836 ed. and 'Site of' on 1876 ed. Situated on the S shoulder of a drumlin ridge. Not visible at ground level.
42:42 9-9-1986

1439 RALAGHAN (ED Taghart)
OS 28:7:6 (692,310) '*Black Fort* (Site of)' OD 700–800 27115, 30126
Enclosure (site) Marked 'Black Fort' on OS 1836 ed. and 'Site of' on 1876 ed. Site has been levelled.
28:41 23-7-1977

1440 RATHCORICK
OS 25:8:6 (852,372) Not marked OD 400–500
24357, 30167
Enclosure (site) Marked 'Fort' on OS 1836 and 1876 eds. and known in the locality as same (local information). Raised circular area (int. diam. 24m). The site is divided into two unequal segments by a laneway running ENE–WSW. The larger SE segment survives as a very low earthen mound. At NW the perimeter has been incorporated into the field boundary.
25:104 15-9-1991

1441 RATRUSSAN
OS 22:10:5 (309,185) Not marked OD 700–800
25731, 30622
Enclosure (site) Marked 'Fort' on OS 1836 and 1876 eds. Situated on the summit of a drumlin hill. Not visible at ground level.
22:32 19-10-1990

1442 ROO
OS 1:16:4 (733,64) Hachured OD 200–300
20298, 33645
Enclosure Marked 'Fort' on OS 1836 and 1876 eds. This site has been largely levelled. Raised circular area (int. diam. *c.* 24m NE–SW) formerly enclosed by a stone wall of which the outline only is now discernible. Original entrance not recognisable. Overgrown with scrub.
1:16 14-8-1974

1443 ROO
OS 1:16:4 (736,62) Indicated OD 200–300
20301, 33642
Enclosure Depicted as a tree-ring on OS 1836 and 1876 eds. Site has been largely levelled. Raised circular area (int. diam. *c.* 34m) enclosed by a low bank of earth and stone which probably represents the base of a stone rampart. Original entrance not recognisable.
1:17 14-8-1988

1444 SHANTULLY
OS 25:10:4 (277,210) Indicated OD 200–300
23752, 29989
Enclosure (site) Marked 'Fort' on OS 1836 and 1876 eds. Situated at the SSE end of a long, broad drumlin ridge orientated NNW–SSE. Site has been levelled.
25:108 5-9-1991

1445 SRAHAN
OS 34:15:4 (512,39) Indicated OD 600–700
26934, 29198
Enclosure Marked 'Fort' on OS 1836 and 1876 eds. Raised circular area (int. diam. *c.* 23m) enclosed from S–W–N by a narrow, low bank of earth and stone and elsewhere by a stone wall. A farmyard abuts the site at W at which point the enclosing bank is identifiable only as a low scarp. A modern roadway curves around the site from WNW–N. Original entrance not recognisable.
34:48 23-5-1988

1446 SRUHAGH
OS 13:11:6 (631,166) Not marked OD 100–200
22164, 31209
Enclosure (site) Marked 'Fort' on OS 1836 ed. Not marked on subsequent eds. Situated in very wet low-lying ground adjacent to the point where the Woodford River enters Ballymagauran Lough. The site is marked by a line of vegetation curving from NW–N–SE. Not

visible at ground level.
13:55 16-5-1993

1447 TAWLAGHT (Clanmahon By.)
OS 37:11:5 (606,195) Not marked OD 300–400
24112, 28697

Enclosure Marked 'Fort' on OS 1836 and 1876 eds. Situated on the N slope of a drumlin ridge. All that remains to indicate the presence of the site is a low almost circular mound (diam. *c.* 37m). Otherwise nothing visible at ground level.
37:69 27-7-1986

1448 TAWLAGHT (Lower Loughtee By.)
OS 15:5:2 (119,414) Hachured OD 200–300
23575, 31484

Enclosure Marked 'Fort' on OS 1836 ed. Raised subrectangular area (int. dims. 37.6m NW–SE; 20.7m NE–SW) enclosed by a low, narrow earthen bank and narrow fosse. The bank and fosse resemble other field boundaries in the vicinity casting some doubt on its antiquity. Original entrance not recognisable.
15:71 12-8-1989

1449 TERMON (Tullyhaw By.)
OS 2:9:5 (95,198) Not marked OD 100–200
20598, 33790

Enclosure Not marked on any OS ed. Known locally as 'St. Brigid's House' and 'The Queen's Bed'. Approximately circular area (int. diam. *c.* 12m) enclosed by a low drystone wall. The interior has been lowered below that of the surrounding ground level. Just inside the wall at S are two opposed slabs. Both Davies (1939, 98) and Richardson (Richardson and Lowry-Corry 1940, 170) were of the opinion that the site represented the remains of a megalithic tomb but there is no evidence to suggest that this is in fact the case. Thickly overgrown with vegetation.
2:19 10-7-1988

1450 TOGHERNAROSS
OS 37:14:1 (242,80) Hachured OD 200–300
23728, 28572

Enclosure (site) Marked 'Fort' on OS 1836 and 1876 eds. Situated on the W slope of a drumlin ridge. Almost completely levelled. All that now remains to indicate the presence of the site is a kink in the field boundary from W–NW–N. Otherwise nothing visible at ground level.
37:72 7-7-1986

1451 TONAGHBANE
OS 17:9:3 (187,303) Hachured OD 300–400
25890, 31203

Enclosure (site) Marked 'Fort' on OS 1836 and 1876 eds. Situated on a prominent hillock. Not visible at ground level.
17:63 12-11-1989

1452 TULLYGULLIN
OS 41:1:5 (136,524) Hachured OD 300
23617, 28399

Enclosure Marked 'Fort' on OS 1836 and 1876 eds. Large almost circular natural rock-outcrop mound (diam. at base *c.* 27m; H *c.* 4m) encircled from NW–N–SE by a low earthen bank with partially infilled external fosse. Bank has been levelled from SE–S–SW and is identifiable only as a low scarp.
41:20 2-7-1986

1453 TULLYLORCAN
OS 27:4:3 (874,566) Hachured OD 400–500
26329, 30389

Enclosure Raised circular area (int. diam. 24.5m) enclosed by a narrow steep-sided earthen bank, badly denuded from NE–E–SW, and slight remains of a fosse. Original entrance not recognisable.
27:13 18-3-1977

1454 TULLYVIN
OS 17:13:3 (210,120) Not marked OD 300
25738, 30987

Enclosure (possible) Tradition of 'Fort', said to predate the modern burial ground at this location (local information). Not visible at ground level.
17:75(01) 22-5-1993

1455 TURE (Tullyhaw By.)
OS 2:13:3 (227,128) Indicated OD 400–500
20739, 33716

Enclosure (site) Not marked on OS 1836 or 1876 eds. Levelled in the early 1980s. It formerly comprised a circular area (int. diam. *c.* 15m) enclosed by a substantial drystone wall (local information). Outline of perimeter may still be traced.
2:25 11-7-1988

1456 UNSHOGAGH
OS 2:13:4 (14,40) Indicated OD 400–500
20515, 33621

Enclosure Not marked on OS 1836 or 1876 eds. Depicted on OS current ed. as a subcircular enclosure (diam. *c.* 15m) with a rectangular enclosure (dims. *c.* 30m NW–SW; *c.* 20m NE–SW) adjoining it at SE. Situated in rough mountainous terrain within a modern plantation of coniferous trees. Not located.
2:28(01) 14-7-1988

1457 VIRGINIA
OS 39:7:4 (516,361) Not marked OD 300–400
25965, 28889

Enclosure (site) Marked 'Fort' on OS 1836 ed. and 'Site of' on 1876 ed. Situated on a slight natural knoll in gently sloping pasture-land. Not visible at ground level.
39:78 2-4-1987

1458 YEWER GLEBE
OS 19:11:2 (568,269) Not marked OD 200
23078, 30686

Enclosure (site) Marked on the OS 1836 and 1876 eds. as a large tree-covered circular enclosure. All that remains to indicate the existence of the site is a kink in the field boundary from S–SSW–SW.
19:45 10-7-1990

Hilltop Enclosures

A hilltop enclosure can be defined as an enclosed area on the summit of a hill. In general the area enclosed is much larger than that defined by ringforts, many of which in County Cavan also have hilltop sitings. While some hilltop enclosures from other parts of the country are strongly defended, a distinguishing feature of the County Cavan examples is that their enclosing elements are much less substantial. Hilltop enclosures are too large to be considered habitation sites, but on the other hand their ramparts are usually too insignificant to allow for their interpretation as military strongholds. They are likely to date to the Iron Age and the Early Christian period.

1459 ARDAMAGH
OS 16:9:6 (213,216) Indicated OD 409
24648, 31285
Hilltop enclosure (possible) A very large heart-shaped area (int. dims. *c.* 150m NE–SW; *c.* 85m NW–SE) on the summit of a hill, enclosed by a low, narrow bank and a shallow ditch similar in morphology to field boundaries in the vicinity. On the OS 1836 and 1876 eds. a break is indicated in the perimeter from SSW–W–NW, while the OS 1912 ed. shows the same area fully enclosed. Within the past decade the enclosing elements have been levelled from SSW–W–NW (local information). Known locally as a 'fort'.
16:3 19-9-1989

1460 BELLAHEADY OR ROSSBRESSAL
OS 13:8:3 (892,410) Indicated OD 200–300
22437, 31469
Hilltop enclosure (possible) Not marked as an antiquity on any OS ed. but known locally as a 'fort'. Oval area (int. dims. *c.* 160m NE–SW; 100m NW–SE) enclosed by a low earthen bank and a wide, shallow fosse, both of which have been modified and incorporated into the field boundary, the area NE of which has been levelled leaving nothing visible at ground level. The site is divided into two roughly equal portions by a field boundary running NW–SE. Original entrance not recognisable.
13:3 7-8-1989

1461 DERRYRAGH
OS 13:7:6 (654,373) *'Derryragh Fort'* OD 382
22186, 31428
Hilltop enclosure Large oval area (int. dims. 104m N–S; 58.8m E–W) enclosed by a low earthen bank, the outer face of which has been modified and incorporated into the field boundary. An earlier report

Fig. 29—*Hilltop enclosure at Derryragh* (**1461**), *traditionally associated with the pagan idol Crom Cruaich.*

(OPW 1969) noted a shallow depression at the internal foot of the bank from SSW–N–SSE which may indicate the presence of an internal fosse. Original entrance not recognisable. The site is traditionally associated with the pagan idol Crom Cruaich (local information). (Dalton 1921, 23–67)
13:22 19-6-1989

1462 DRUMACLEESKIN
OS 16:2:3 (429,540) Hachured OD 400–500
24873, 31629

Hilltop enclosure Large raised oval area (int. dims. *c.* 110m NW–SE; 90m NE–SW) enclosed by a low earthen bank and a wide, shallow fosse identifiable from SSE–S–SSW. The bank has been scarped and surmounted by a modern low bank of earth and stone. Break in bank with accompanying causeway at SSW apparently marks the original entrance. Just outside the fosse at E is a holy well (**1759**).
16:37(01) 25-9-1989

1463 MAGHERINTEMPLE
OS 16:3:3 (649,555) 'Grave Yard' OD 300–500
25105, 31646

Hilltop enclosure Marked 'Fort' on OS 1836 ed. Large oval area on the summit of a high drumlin hill enclosed by field boundaries. The outline of the enclosing elements, which have been levelled from NNE–ENE and SSE–S–SSW, is still traceable. Davies (1948, 95) speculated that the site is 'almost certainly a neolithic monument of the type of Lyle's Hill and others in Ulster'. He noted that it is approached by several old roads, and was important as a fair ground in the sixteenth century. A church site (**1685**) lies within the enclosure (CUCAP AVR 32)
16:99(01) 16-10-1989

Crannógs

Crannógs are habitation sites constructed on natural or artificial islands in lakes, marshy areas or very occasionally in rivers or seas. The term is also sometimes applied to lakeside habitation sites. Crannóg-builders generally sited their dwellings in shallow water close to the shore and undoubtedly they would have been attracted to the extensive lakeland systems which characterise County Cavan. The method of construction was to lay down a platform of timbers upon the core of a natural island or shoal, augmented by a bed of brushwood, peat, stone and other debris. The horizontal timbers were held in place by vertical wooden piles or stakes. An enclosing palisade of one or more rows of piles or split-planking was then erected. Excavation has revealed that the area thus enclosed would have contained house sites and outbuildings normally similar in morphology, dating and function to those found in ringforts. In essence therefore the majority should be regarded as being of Early Christian date — the aquatic equivalent of the ringforts, albeit with a greater defensive emphasis. However, there are crannógs known from the Late Bronze Age while some of the County Fermanagh examples are thought to be of late 15th/early 16th-century date, so the monument type has a long dating span. Today crannógs often appear as small tree-covered islands in lakes, or as mounds of earth and stone in marshland where formerly there were lakes. A large number of the crannógs listed in this chapter were not visited. Most of the information derives from cartographic sources, Davies' ITA and NMI surveys conducted between 1940 and 1946, and publications by Wood-Martin (1886), Wakeman (1878), Milligan (1885), Hall (1907) and Davies (1942 and 1948).

1464 AGHABANE/DERRINDREHID
OS 19:6:6 (422,364) Indicated OD 164
22923, 30785

Crannóg (possible) Small circular island (diam. *c.* 12m) in Disert Lough, *c.* 100m from the shoreline. Very overgrown with vegetation.
19:2 8-7-1990

1465 AGHAVADRIN
OS 19:11:1 (496,239) Indicated OD 171
23002, 30654

Crannóg (possible) Marked on all OS eds. Small island in Dumb Lough, *c.* 55m from the shoreline and *c.* 250m NW of a second possible crannóg (**1466**). The lake has been drained and the water-level lowered considerably. The site is now joined to the mainland. From the shore it appears as a low, roughly circular, vegetation-covered mound (diam. *c.* 16m) among the reeds. (ITA Survey 1942)
19:3 19-7-1990

1466 AGHAVADRIN
OS 19:11:4 (514,221) Indicated OD 171
23020, 30635

Crannóg (possible) Marked on all OS eds. Small island in Dumb Lough, *c.* 55m from the shoreline and *c.* 250m SW of a second possible crannóg (**1465**). The lake has been drained and the water-level lowered considerably. The site is now joined to the mainland. From the shore it appears as a low roughly circular, vegetation-covered mound (diam. *c.* 12m) among the rushes. Davies (ITA Survey 1942) noted 'one probable pile projecting at the edge'.
19:4 19-7-1990

1467 AGHAVOHER
OS 14:2:6 (418,511) Indicated OD 171
22911, 31580

Crannóg Small circular island (diam. *c.* 20m) in Aghavoher Lough, *c.* 1 km from the shoreline marked on all OS eds. Davies recorded that it was apparently a log platform and detailed finds from the site including several animal bones and shells, hones, two pieces of quern, a block of iron, a jug handle and *c.* twenty sherds of unglazed crannóg pottery from which seven pots were identified. He noted the former presence of a 19th-century stone cottage on the island and contemporary glazed sherds and pieces of an iron cauldron. It was suggested that the crannóg was occupied principally in the 16th century.
14:4

1468 ANNAGH (Lower Loughtee By.)
OS 15:11:4 (485,208) Indicated OD 175
23960, 31270

Crannóg (possible) Small irregular-shaped island (max. dim. *c.* 26m NE–SW) in Annagh Lough, *c.* 40m from the shoreline. When water-levels are low during the summer months the island is in fact joined to the mainland. Davies (NMI Survey 1941) recorded a rectangular house foundation (int. dims. 6.7m x 8.8m; H 3.8m) comprising large upright blocks with apparently a good depth of earth inside.
15:2

1469 ANNAGH (Tullyhaw By.)
OS 10:10:6 (448,205) Indicated OD 156
22939, 31898

Crannóg (possible) Small irregular-shaped island (max. dim. *c.* 30m) in Annagh Lough, *c.* 75m from the shoreline. Marked on all OS eds.
10:2

1470 ANNAGHARNET
OS 33:16:4 (711,73) Indicated OD 371
26168, 29227

Crannóg (possible) Small apparently circular island (diam. *c*. 18m) in Corratinner Lough, *c*. 40m from the shoreline.
33:2

1471 ARDRA
OS 24:8:6 (915,354) Indicated OD 200–300
23449, 30139
Crannóg An almost circular island (diam. *c*. 15m) in Ardra Lough, *c*. 100m from the shoreline. According to Davies (ITA Survey 1942) it is flat-topped with a kerb of stones and rises 1.4m above the water-level. There were formerly piles around the edge and the discovery of some charcoal is also recorded.
24:5 21-8-1991

1472 ARDRA
OS 24:11:1 (491,253) Indicated OD 200–300
23002, 30028
Crannóg Davies (ITA Survey 1942) recorded an approximately circular island (diam. *c*. 2.1m) rising 0.4m above the water-level of the lake. On the landward side he identified a horizontal beam, at least one pile and a layer of charcoal.
24:6 21-8-1991

1473 ASHGROVE
OS 15:10:2 (330,250) Indicated OD 100–200
23796, 31313
Crannóg Small roughly circular island (diam. *c*. 25m) in the Erne River, *c*. 25m from the shoreline. Marked on all OS eds. Davies (1942, 19; NMI Survey 1941) described a flat-topped mound (dims. of summit 8.8m x 6m; H 2.4m) composed of whitish clay and stones, surrounded by a few piles. Some charcoal, scraps of burnt bone and old bricks were noted on the summit of the mound.
15:7

1474 BARNAGROW
OS 23:10:1 (301,252) Indicated OD 316
26697, 30701
Crannóg Circular island (diam *c*. 12m) in Barnagrow Lough, *c*. 100m from the shoreline and 70m SW of a second larger crannóg (**1475**). Hall (1910, 361–2) noted that the site had only become visible as a consequence of the lowering of water-levels in the lake at the turn of this century. The perimeter of the island was protected by a large number of outwardly projecting pointed stakes. He recorded that 'the smaller island could scarcely ever have been made use of, seeing that heretofore it had been almost completely beneath the water. To it also there was one landing place, where there were no stakes; this was on the side towards the larger island'.
23:1 28-5-1992

1475 BARNAGROW/CULLIES (Clankee By.)
OS 23:10:2 (308,254) 'Small Island' OD 136
26705, 30703
Crannóg In Barnagrow Lough, *c*. 150m from the shoreline and *c*. 70m NE of a second smaller crannóg (**1474**). Hall (1910, 361–2) noted that the site had only become properly visible following the lowering of water-levels at the turn of this century. He recorded an almost perfectly circular crannóg (diam *c*. 20m) with a raised centre and protected by a large number of outwardly projecting stakes. Possible foundations of a small house, a broad hearth stone, four quernstones, none of which matched, were discovered on the summit.
23:2 28-5-1992

1476 BRANKILL (Lanesborough)
OS 11:13:2 (98,107) Not marked OD 163
23547, 31800
Crannóg Not marked on any OS ed. Small roughly circular island in Tom's or Kilconny Lough, *c*. 20m from the shoreline. Davies (NMI Survey 1942) recorded many close-set piles protruding from the mud at the water's edge. At N he noted 'some radially set beams'. He also described a black layer 0.15m below ground level containing some bones and sherds. Other finds from the site include animal bones, teeth and millstones.
11:1

1477 CAPPAGH
OS 19:10:5 (371,204) Indicated OD 166
22870, 30615
Crannóg (possible) Small island in Derreskit Lough, *c*. 70m from the shoreline. From the shore it appears as a low, roughly circular mound (int. diam. *c*. 14m) densely overgrown with trees and bushes.
19:7 8-7-1990

1478 CARRICK (Clanmahon By.)
OS 41:7:5 (615,366) 'Watty's Rock' OD 212
24125, 28238
Crannóg (possible) Small roughly circular island (diam. *c*. 25m) in Lough Sheelin, *c*. 100m from the shoreline. Marked on all OS eds.
41:5

1479 CARRICK (Clanmahon By.)
OS 41:7:3 (622,385) Indicated OD 212
24132, 28258
Crannóg (possible) Not marked on OS 1836 or 1876 eds. Small oval-shaped island (dims. *c*. 28m E–W; *c*. 12m N–S) in Lough Sheelin, *c*. 100m from the shoreline. Marked on OS current ed.
41:6

1480 CLONAGONNELL
OS 25:3:4 (495,493) Not marked OD 200–300
23979, 30291

Crannóg Small circular mound (dims. 17.2m NE–SW; max. H 0.37m) composed largely of earth and stones with burnt stone and timbers protruding from its sides. Situated in low-lying marshy land in what was once Tonymore Lough. (Wood-Martin 1886, 197–9; Davies 1942, 19)
25:13

1481 CLONAGONNELL
OS 25:3:4 (516,499) Not marked OD 200–300
24001, 30298

Crannóg (site) Situated in low-lying, marshy ground in what was once Tonymore Lough. It is said to have been *c.* 22m in diameter and to have risen to about 0.7m. It was almost entirely destroyed as a result of the construction of a railway line. (Wood-Martin 1886, 197–9; Davies 1942, 19)
25:17

1482 CLONAGONNELL
OS 25:0:0 Not marked OD 200–300

Crannóg Roughly circular mound (H 0.45m; dims 12.1m NW–SE; 3.2 NE–SW) composed of earth and small stones. Apparent break in the embankment 3.1m wide at NE. Scattered about the mound are numerous small stones. According to local information the site had been investigated previously and some ashes were uncovered. (Wood-Martin 1886, 197–9; Davies 1942, 20)
25:128 17-9-1991

1483 CLONAMULLIG
OS 14:3:3 (620,532) Indicated OD 167
23124, 31604

Crannóg Irregular-shaped island (dims. *c.* 50m E–W; *c.* 35m N–S) in Clonamullig Lough, *c.* 100m from the shoreline. Davies (NMI Survey 1942) recorded that on the shore of the island, horizontal cross beams were identified at many locations. Other finds from the shoreline include some iron slag, many unburnt bones and part of a rotary quern, but none datable.
14:10

Fig. 30—*A possible crannóg in Derreskit Lough at Cappagh* (**1477**).

1484 CLONTYGRIGNY
OS 14:10:1 (280,276) Not marked OD 181
22768, 31331
Crannóg (possible) Small circular island (diam. *c.* 20m) marked on OS 1836 and 1876 eds. In Greenville Lough, *c.* 60m from the shoreline.
14:13

1485 CLOONE
OS 30:15:4 (472,17) Indicated OD 200–300
22990, 29137
Crannóg (possible) Subcircular island (diam. *c.* 28m) in Lough Gowna, *c.* 15m from the shoreline. Densely overgrown with vegetation.
30:6

1486 CLOONE
OS 36 NPL Not marked OD 214
Crannóg Not marked on any OS ed. Small subrectangular tree-and-bush-covered crannóg-cairn in Lough Gowna, *c.* 50m from the shoreline.
36:15

1487 CLOWNINNY
OS 11:5:6 (200,324) Indicated OD 100–200
23651, 32030
Crannóg Situated in Lough Tee. Davies (NMI Survey 1946) described the site as a 'low marshy flat, connected to the shore in dry weather'. He recorded charcoal and burnt bones, but no visible wooden structure.
11:10

1488 CONLEEN
OS 38:14:4 (262,20) Not marked OD 212
24725, 28518
Crannóg (possible) Small roughly circular island (diam. *c.* 28m) called 'Currant Island'. Marked on OS 1836 and 1976 eds. In Lough Sheelin, *c.* 60m from the shoreline. On the 1913 ed. the island is shown as being part of the mainland, probably the result of a substantial drop in water-levels in the lake.
38:11

1489 COOLOGE
OS 13:12:2 (835,280) Indicated OD 174
22378, 31332
Crannóg (possible) Not marked on OS 1836 or 1876 eds. Small, oval, tree-covered island (dims. *c.* 25m NNE–SSW; *c.* 12m WNW–ESE) in Coologe Lough, *c.* 100m from the shoreline.
13:10

1490 CORAGH (Lower Loughtee By.)
OS 11:9:2 (98,296) Indicated OD 152
23544, 31999
Crannóg Situated in Corraback or Teemore Lough, *c.* 60m from the shoreline. Small oval island (dims. 15m by 13m). Davies (NMI Survey 1946) recorded finds of charcoal, burnt and unburnt bones and iron slag but no visible wooden structure.
11:11

1491 CORCLARE
OS 23:12:4 (748,171) 'Bush Island' OD 311
27170, 30620
Crannóg (possible) An almost circular tree-and-grass-covered island (diam. *c.* 16m) in Lough Tacker, *c.* 160m from the shoreline. Known in the locality as an antiquity.
23:11 4-4-1992

1492 CORDALEA
OS 19:8:4 (767,372) Indicated OD 161
23287, 30796
Crannóg Large island in Lough Oughter, *c.* 100m from the shoreline. Davies (ITA Survey 1942) described it as a crannóg-cairn composed of small stones with piles and logs around it forming a log platform. Cairn, circular in plan (diam. *c.* 32m) and rising to between 1.5m and 2.1m in height. He also noted several radial beams of fir and oak at N. (Davies 1942, 17)
19:9 12-7-1990

1493 CORFREE
OS 30:10:6 (409,196) Indicated OD 200–300
22923, 29325
Crannóg (possible) Subcircular island (diam. *c.* 20m) in Lough Gowna, *c.* 125m from the shoreline. Davies (ITA Survey 1941, 17) recorded a crannóg-cairn on the island composed of medium-sized stones (diam. *c.* 10m). (Davies 1942, 17)
30:9

1494 CORFREE
OS 30 NPL Not marked OD 200–300
Crannóg (possible) Not marked on any OS ed. Located in Lough Gowna. Large, low, circular cairn of small to medium-sized stones. Largely overgrown with vegetation. Only a few meters away to S is a second crannóg (**1495**) while directly N on the shore is a lakeside rath (**381**).
30:36

1495 CORFREE
OS 30 NPL Not marked OD 200–300
Crannóg Not marked on any OS ed. Located in Lough Gowna. Small, high, circular cairn of small to medium-sized stones surmounted by a tree. A few meters away to N is a second crannóg (**1494**) and beyond this on the shore, a lakeside rath (**381**).
30:37

1496 CORGLASS (Clanmahon By.)
OS 31:16:1 (706,94) Indicated OD 200–300 24212, 292310
Crannóg (possible) Small almost circular island (diam. *c.* 23m) in Corglass Lough, *c.* 100m from the shoreline, marked on all OS eds.
31:13

1497 CORGLASS (Lower Loughtee By.)
OS 19:4:3 (866,533) Indicated OD 161 23389, 30968
Crannóg (possible) Small island in Deralk Lough, *c.* 70m from the shoreline. From the shore it appears as a roughly circular vegetation-covered mound (diam. *c.* 15m). Davies (ITA Survey 1942) noted a stone kerb at the perimeter of the island and a few piles and a good deal of horizontal timbers on the S shore.
19:10

1498 CORNAGALL
OS 21:7:1 (467,443) Not marked OD 200–300 24920, 30887
Crannóg (possible) In Cornagall Lough, *c.* 45m from the shoreline. First identified in 1878 and then described as an artificial island almost perfectly circular in form, and measuring about thirty yards in diameter. Upon the island were rows of oaken stakes. Portion of a dug-out canoe, two adzes, a hammer, a chisel, a wooden handle and a thin knife-like piece of iron, a whet stone and an oak implement were discovered at the site.
21:14

1499 CORNAGARROW
OS 16:11:6 (689,156) Not marked OD 100–200 25151, 312260
Crannóg (possible) Large subcircular island (dims. *c.* 35m NW–SE; *c.* 28m WSW–ENE) in Cormuttog Lough, *c.* 110m from the shoreline. Marked on OS 1836 and 1876 eds. This lake has been drained and is now marshland. The site is no longer identifiable.
16:27 29-10-1989

1500 CORNAGRAN (Tullyhunco By.)
OS 36:3:1 (538,603) Not marked OD 214 23060, 29119
Crannóg (possible) In Lough Gowna, *c.* 70m from the shoreline. Davies (ITA Survey 1941) recorded that a crannóg-cairn occupies the SW side and centre of the island. He recorded piles and radial logs around the cairn, additional oak piles located on the W and NW shores, finds of teeth of ox, sheep and horse, and fragments of burnt bones.
36:2

1501 CORNAGRAN (Tullyhunco By.)
OS 36:3:2 (583,552) Indicated OD 214 23108, 29065
Crannóg (possible) Small oval-shaped island (dims. *c.* 25m NE–SW; *c.* 12m NW–SE) in Lough Gowna, *c.* 40m from the shoreline.
36:4

1502 CORNAGRAN (Tullyhunco By.)
OS 36 NPL Not marked OD 214
Crannóg (possible) Not marked on any OS ed. Small almost circular island in Lough Gowna, *c.* 60m from the shoreline. The island appears to be composed of earth and stone.
36:16

1503 CORNASEER
OS 25:15:3 (660,111) Not marked OD 392 24157, 29889
Crannóg (possible) In Cornaseer Lough. A small number of large boulders are visible from the shoreline. Davies (ITA Survey 1942) noted a couple of timbers protruding above the water-level. Situated *c.* 80m from the shoreline. (Milligan 1885,148–9)
25:24 1-10-1991

1504 CORPORATION LANDS
OS 15:6:2 (316,434) Indicated OD 161 23780, 31506
Crannóg (possible) Not marked on OS 1836 or 1876 eds. Very small circular island (diam. *c.* 15m) in Bun Lough, *c.* 25m from the shoreline. Densely overgrown with vegetation. Davies (NMI Survey 1941) recorded a log platform 'with criss-cross beams laid out, piles to hold the whole structure in place, and stones laid on top of these'. He also found animal remains and a lead musket bullet. (Davies 1942, 19)
15:17

1505 CORRAGHO
OS 26:8:6 (924,340) Indicated OD 338 25409, 30143
Crannóg (possible) Oval-shaped island (dims. *c.* 40m NNW–SSE; *c.* 20m ENE–W–SW) in Lavey Lough, *c.* 40m from the shoreline. Known as an ancient habitation site (local information). Very overgrown with vegetation. Habitation material was found on a large island *c.* 220m to ESE (**1506**).
26:17

1506 CORRAGHO/KNOCKANOARK/LAVEY
OS 26:8:6 (415,562) Indicated OD 338 25355, 30320
Crannóg (possible) In Lavey Lough, *c.* 60m from the shoreline. Davies (ITA Survey 1942) described it as a seemingly natural 'fairly large island... covered with small stones'. He recorded several close-set piles on the SW shore and a few inches of humus containing scraps of burnt bone. A smaller island, also reputedly a

Fig. 31—*A possible crannóg in Lavey Lough at Corragho* (**1505**).

crannóg (**1505**), lies 220m to WNW.
26:18

1507 CORRAN (Tullyhunco By.)
OS 24:10:3 (452,298) Not marked OD 200–300
22960, 30075
Crannóg (possible) Marked on the OS 1836 and 1876 eds. as a small circular island in Ardra Lough, *c.* 20m from the shoreline. The water-levels in the lake have been significantly lowered and today the site adjoins the shoreline. It comprises a low irregularly shaped mound of earth and stone (H 0.4m; dims. 6.4m NE–SW; 5.6m NW–SE).
24:23 21-8-1991

1508 CORRANEARY (ED Corraneary)
OS 23:13:2 (106,96) Indicated OD 351
26492, 30534
Crannógs In Corraneary Lough, *c.* 230m from the shoreline. There are at least four and possibly five crannógs in the lake visible from the shore. The largest and furthermost to NE was excavated by Barron in 1937 and 1938. Two periods of occupation were discerned; one relatively early and the second was attributed to the 16th or 17th century. Remains then comprised an irregularly shaped artificial platform (dims. 10.6m x 9m) of horizontal beams and twigs, with possible traces of a stockade. Finds included six pots, five crucibles, two pieces of a mould and an iron cannon ball. The cannon ball may be connected with the tradition that Knockbride old church (**1672**), which lies on the shoreline, was attacked by Cromwell's troops. A stone trough now at the house on the shoreline is believed to have come from one of the other crannógs in the lake. (Davies 1942, 25–8; ITA Survey 1946)
23:13(01) 21-5-1992

1509 CORRAROD
OS 15:3:3 (678,585) Indicated OD 160
24160, 31670
Crannóg (possible) Not marked on OS 1836 or 1876 eds. Very small circular island (diam. *c.* 18m) in Drumgorry Lough, *c.* 80m from the shoreline.
15:19

1510 CORRATINNER
OS 33:16:1 (703,109) Not marked OD 371 26159, 29265
Crannóg (possible) Small roughly circular island (diam. *c.* 18m) in Corratinner Lough, *c.* 20m from the shoreline. Marked on OS 1836 and 1876 eds.
33:20

1511 CORRONAGH
OS 39:11:5 (540,164) 'Stony Islands' OD 277 25992, 28681
Crannóg (possible) Long narrow island (dims. *c.* 60m WNW–ESE; *c.* 12m NNW–SSW) in Lough Ramor, *c.* 120m from the shoreline and 20m WNW of a second island (**1529**).
39:26

1512 CORRONAGH
OS 39:15:1 (534, 89) 'Porter's Islands' OD 277 25987, 28602
Crannógs (possible) Two islands *c.* 50m apart situated in a shallow bay in Lough Ramor. The larger NE island is roughly oval in plan (dims. *c.* 80m NNE–SSW; *c.* 45m WNW–ESE). The SW island is subrectangular in plan (dims. *c.* 70m NNW–SSE; *c.* 30m E–W). Davies (ITA Survey 1942) described both islands as 'fairly open', with central mounds rising to *c.* 3m above the water-level of the lake.
39:84

1513 CORRONAGH
OS 39:15:1 (519, 87) 'Cock Island' OD 277 25971, 28600
Crannóg Irregularly shaped island (dims. *c.* 70m NW–SE; *c.* 65m NE–SW) in Lough Ramor. Davies (ITA Survey 1940) recorded foundations of a rectangular hut site on a mound, *c.* 3m above the water-level of the lake.
39:85

1514 CORRONAGH
OS 39:15:1 (518, 120) 'Corlea Island North' OD 277 25969, 28635
Crannóg (possible) Subtriangular-shaped island (dims. *c.* 100m NW–SE; *c.* 60m NE–SW) in Lough Ramor. Davies (ITA Survey 1942) noted that the island contained a small mound.
39:86

1515 CRANAGHAN
OS 10 NPL Not marked OD 168
Crannóg (site, possible) Not marked on any OS ed. Mitchell (1941, 30) found sherds of pottery, representing three pots, all of coarse black ware, at this location, on the shore of Killywilly Lough. Davies suggested that this was probably the site of a crannóg. Not located.
10:24

1516 CREIGHAN/TIRQUIN
OS 25:4:1 (568,754) Not marked OD 244 24256, 30373
Crannóg In Green Lough. Davies (ITA Survey 1946) described an almost circular mound (diam. *c.* 15m) surrounded by a stone kerb with large logs arranged in criss-cross fashion around the side, the gaps being infilled with gravel, sand and peat. Situated *c.* 30m from the shoreline. Not visited.
25:33 13-9-1991

1517 CROSSAFEHIN
OS 39:14:2 (382,109) Indicated OD 277 25827, 28622
Crannóg (possible) Small circular island in Lough Ramor, *c.* 480m from the shoreline. Marked on all OS eds.
39:66

1518 CROSSAFEHIN
OS 39:14:5 (355, 68) 'Crossafehin Islands' OD 277 25798,28578
Crannógs (possible) Two islands 60m apart, situated in a shallow sheltered bay, close to the SW shoreline of Lough Ramor. The larger NW island is subrectangular in plan (dims. *c.* 100m WNW-ESE; 60m NNE–SSW). The SE island is roughly circular (diam. *c.* 40m). Davies (ITA Survey 1940) recorded a mound at the centre of one of these islands *c.* 2m high but did not specify its location or whether the mound was natural or artificial.
39:81

1519 CROVER
OS 38:14:1 (240,104) Indicated OD 212 24701, 28606
Crannóg (possible) Not marked on OS 1836 and 1876 eds. Depicted on OS 1913 ed. Subrectangular island (dims. *c.* 26m ENE–WSW; *c.* 12m WNW–ESE) in Lough Sheelin, *c.* 50m from the shoreline.
38:18

1520 CROVER
OS 38:14:4 (260,58) Indicated OD 212 24723, 28558
Crannóg (possible) Not marked on OS 1836 or 1876 eds. Depicted on OS 1913 ed. Small subrectangular-shaped island (dims. *c.* 25m NW–SE; *c.* 18m NE–SW) in Lough Sheelin, *c.* 30m from the shoreline. Not visited.
38:21(01)

1521 CROVER
OS 38:14:4 (260,58) Indicated OD 212 24723, 28558
Crannóg (possible) Not marked on OS 1836 or 1876

eds. Depicted on OS 1913 ed. Small subrectangular-shaped island (dims. *c*. 60m N–S; *c*. 16m E–W) in Lough Sheelin, *c*. 40m from the shoreline.
38:21(02)

1522 CROVER
OS 38:14:4 (284,46) Not marked OD 212
24748, 28546
Crannóg (possible) Small oval island (dims. *c*. 40m NW–SW; *c*. 20m NE–SW) with the designation 'Crab Island' on OS 1836 and 1876 eds. Situated in Lough Sheelin, *c*. 20m from the shoreline. On the 1913 ed. the island is shown incorporated into the mainland, probably the result of a substantial drop in the level of the lake.
38:22

1523 CROVER
OS 38:14:1 (240,93) Indicated OD 212
24700, 28594
Crannóg (possible) Not marked on OS 1836 or 1876 eds. Small irregular-shaped island (max. dim. *c*. 30m) in Lough Sheelin, *c*. 150m from the shoreline. A second island (**1524**) lies *c*. 30m to E.
38:46(01)

1524 CROVER
OS 38:14:1 (240,93) Indicated OD 212
24700, 28594
Crannóg (possible) Not marked on OS 1836 or 1876 eds. Small irregular-shaped island in Lough Sheelin, *c*. 170m from the shoreline. A second island lies *c*. 30m to W (**1523**).
38:46(02)

1525 CUILCAGH
OS 39:8:3 (913,403) Indicated OD 433
26384, 28937
Crannóg (possible) Small roughly circular island (diam. *c*. 20m) in Cuilcagh Lough, *c*. 65m from the shoreline. Not marked on OS 1836 and 1876 eds.
39:32

1526 DEERPARK
OS 39:10:5 (381,194) Not marked OD 277
25824, 28712
Crannóg (possible) Small roughly circular island (diam *c*. 17m) with the designation 'Stones' marked on OS 1836 and 1876 eds. Situated in Lough Ramor, *c*. 90m from the shoreline.
39:34

1527 DEERPARK
OS 39:10:6 (401,187) Indicated OD 277
25846, 28704
Crannóg (possible) Small roughly circular island (diam. *c*. 23m) in Lough Ramor, *c*. 65m from the shoreline. Marked on all OS eds. On the OS 1836 ed. the site has the designation 'Stones'.
39:35

1528 DEERPARK
OS 39:10:6 (418,161) Indicated OD 277
25864, 28677
Crannóg (possible) Small oval island in Lough Ramor (dims. *c*. 30m WSW–ENE; *c*. 20m NNW–SSE), *c*. 200m from the shoreline. Marked on all OS eds. On the OS 1836 ed. the site has the designation 'Stones'.
39:36

1529 DEERPARK
OS 39:11:4 (534,169) 'Stony Islands' OD 277
25986, 28686
Crannóg (possible) Long, narrow island (dims. *c*. 60m NNW–SSE; c. 15m ENE–WSW) in Lough Ramor, *c*. 350 from the shoreline. A second island (**1511**) lies 20m to ESE. The two islands have the collective designation 'Stony Islands' on all OS eds.
39:39

1530 DEREDIS UPPER
OS 20:6:3 (407,381) Indicated OD 163
23882, 30811
Crannóg Davies (1942, 30) recorded a circular habitation area (diam. 7m; H 0.2m) defined by a few oak piles and branches capped by earth and stones, on an island in Lough Inchin, *c*. 40m from the shoreline. An occupation layer of greyish sand (D *c*. 0.3m) containing charcoal and burnt bone, was found at the centre of this deposit, with yet another layer below this comprising a patchwork floor of twigs and small boughs of oak.
20:13 16-8-1990

1531 DEREDIS UPPER/DERRYGID (Upper Loughtee By.)
OS 20:7:4 (463,362) Indicated OD 162
23941, 30792
Crannóg Small circular island in Farnham Lough, *c*. 150m from the shoreline. Davies (ITA Survey 1946) recorded that the island has a stone facing from which piles protrude. He also noted a wooden platform on which habitation material is piled at the centre of the island and suggested a 17th-century date on the basis of finds of bellarmine at the site. (Davies 1942, 19).
20:14 16-8-1919

1532 DERINISH MORE
OS 20:9:1 (47,291) 'Stony Island' OD 161
23502, 30713

Crannóg Small roughly circular island (diam. *c.* 30m) situated in Lough Oughter in a strait between the townlands of Derinish More and Eonish, in shallow water, *c.* 80m from the shoreline. Davies (ITA Survey 1942) described a cairn (diam. *c.* 5.4m; H *c.* 2.4m) encircled with piles situated on the central part of the island. A pot which Davies dated to the Late Bronze Age was found at the site. (Milligan 1885, 151)
20:15

1533 DERINISH MORE
OS 20:9:2 (98,276) Not marked OD 161
23557, 30698
Crannóg (possible) Not marked on any OS ed. Small circular island (diam. *c.* 22m) situated in Lough Oughter, in shallow water, *c.* 50m from the shoreline. Some stone is visible, possibly representing the remains of a low platform. Water-levels in Lough Oughter were lowered considerably during the middle decades of this century. Hitherto the site was not visible (local information).
20:16

1534 DERRIES UPPER
OS 19:16:2 (810,98) Indicated OD 161
23334, 30508
Crannóg Two small islands in Lough Oughter, *c.* 25m and *c.* 60m from the shoreline respectively. Davies (ITA Survey 1942) noted that both islands are now connected to the mainland and described them as comprising rock outcrop strewn with boulders. The outer island rises 0.45m above the old lake level. Here Davies discovered a roughly circular cairn (diam. *c.* 12m; H *c.* 0.9m) containing a thin layer of settlement refuse (Davies 1942, 17).
19:18(01)

1535 DERRYBRICK
OS 14:16:6 (895,56) Indicated OD 162
23419, 31104
Crannóg (site, possible) Davies (ITA Survey 1946) noted the discovery of fragments of burnt bone, an ox tooth, a piece of iron slag and possible traces of furnace-lining on the peaty shore of Drumlane Lough.
14:23

1536 DERRYCASSAN
OS 13:12:4 (748,195) Indicated OD 173
22287, 31241
Crannóg (possible) Not marked on OS 1836 or 1876 eds. Small oval island (dims. *c.* 30m WNW–ESE; *c.* 20m NNE–SSW) in Ballymaguaran Lough, *c.* 200m from the shoreline.
13:20

1537 DERRYCASSAN
OS 13 NPL Not marked OD 100–200
Crannóg (possible) Situated in a reed-and-scrub-covered area on what is presently the N shore of a channel linking Derrycassan and Coologe Loughs. During the cleaning of a drain in 1992, a number of vertical timbers were revealed some of which were pointed, while others had possible mortices. Nearby there were horizontal timbers and deposits of stone and peat. It is believed (OPW 1992) that the remains represent the edge of a circular crannóg (diam. 25m–30m).
13:70 14-5-1993

1538 DERRYHEEN
OS 20:2:5 (382,520) Not marked OD 100–200
23854, 30959
Crannóg (possible) Circular island (diam. *c.* 40m) marked on OS 1836 and 1876 eds. in Lough Oughter, *c.* 65m from the shoreline. Water-levels in the lake were lowered considerably during the middle decades of this century. As a consequence, the site is now joined to the mainland by a stretch of treacherous marshland.
20:17

1539 DERRYHOO (Lower Loughtee By.)
OS 15:9:3 (166,244) Not marked OD 160
23622, 31305
Crannóg (possible) Small island, roughly square in plan, in Drummany Lough, *c.* 10m from the shoreline. Marked on OS 1836 and 1876 eds. The level of the lake has fallen considerably with the result that the area of the island has become marshland.
15:22

1540 DERRYNA
OS 20:1:6 (156,465) Not marked OD 161
23616, 30898
Crannóg (possible) Not marked on any OS ed. Small, low, subcircular island (diam. *c.* 20m) in Lough Oughter, *c.* 50m from the shoreline. The level of the lake was lowered considerably during the middle decades of this century. Hitherto the site was not visible (local information).
20:19

1541 DERRYNA
OS 20:5:2 (141,381) Indicated OD 161
23600, 30809
Crannóg (possible) Marked on all OS eds. Small, low, subcircular island (diam. *c.* 26m) in Lough Oughter, *c.* 100m from the shoreline.
20:61 14-8-1990

1542 DERRYNAGAN
OS 20:6:2 (328,432) Not marked OD 161
23798, 30865

Crannóg Davies (1942, 20) recorded a packwork crannóg with morticed cross-beams at this location. He (ITA Survey 1942) added that there were formerly both uprights and horizontal beams, but all had been removed. Two of these could be seen together with a dugout canoe on the opposite shore of the lake, at that time.
20:20

1543 DERRYVACKNY
OS 20:1:1 (25,543) Indicated OD 161
23477, 30979
Crannóg Davies (ITA Survey 1942) described the site as being of log-platform type composed of horizontal beams set radially and accompanied by a small cairn presumably representing the floor of a hut.
20:21 12-8-1990

1544 DERRYVEHIL
OS 15:13:1 (12,135) Indicated OD 161
23461, 31188
Crannóg Large roughly circular island (diam. *c.* 25m) in Derryvehil Lough, *c.* 75m from the shoreline. Davies (NMI Survey 1941) recorded a few piles around the shore and noted that these formerly extended about the circumference of the island. On the E side of the island he identified a circular mound (diam. *c.* 10m) rising 1.22m over the main part of the island. (Davies 1942, 21)
15:25

1545 DILLAGH
OS 31:6:5 (355,339) Not marked OD 300–400
23839, 29486
Crannóg Situated *c.* 10m from the old shoreline of Dillagh Lough. The crannóg was revealed following drainage of the lake in 1982. It comprises an almost circular platform (diam. *c.* 20m) composed of brushwood and horizontal beams held in position by vertical piles or stakes. Finds included two barrel-staves, a wooden weaving spindle, leather, and pottery of the 13th–15th century.
31:17 17-9-1982

1546 DOON (Castlerahan By.)
OS 39:3:3 (690,544) Indicated OD 300–400
26148, 29084
Crannóg (possible) Small circular island (diam. *c.* 25m) marked on all OS eds. in Doon Lough, *c.* 30m from the shoreline. The lake has been drained and the area which the crannóg occupied is now treacherous marshland. The site is no longer identifiable.
39:40 31-3-1987

1547 DRUMACHON
OS 16:15:3 (674,136) Not marked OD 100–200
25136, 31205
Crannóg (possible) Small roughly circular island (diam. *c.* 15m) marked on OS 1836 and 1876 eds. in Cormuttog Lough, *c.* 25m from the shoreline. This lake has been drained and the site is now inaccessible.
16:35

1548 DRUMCALPIN (Lower Loughtee By.)/ 0HACKELTY
OS 15:10:6 (459,164) Indicated OD 175
23933, 31223
Crannóg In Annagh Lough, *c.* 60m from the shoreline. Trial-excavation carried out at this site by Davies in 1941. He discovered that the core of the island is a natural morainic ridge, with a mound comprising three distinct habitation layers at its N extent. Finds included medieval pottery in the lowest and middle layers, a large shaped beam of oak, a piece of copper and portion of a shoe. Also found on the island were scraps of burnt bone, ox-teeth, a weathered sherd of pottery and a worked triangular flake of chert. Not visited. (Davies 1942, 21–5)
15:30

1549 DRUMCARBAN
OS 25:13:2 (110,136) Indicated OD 174
23576, 29911
Crannóg (possible) In White Lough, *c.* 80m from the shoreline. Recorded by Davies (1942, 19; ITA Survey 1946). Circular crannóg (diam. *c.* 25m) consisting of a log platform with stone kerb around the edge. A small arc of juxtaposed logs are exposed on one side. Tradition of stone causeway but depth of lake makes this unlikely.
25:40 4-9-1991

1550 DRUMEAGUE
OS 28:2:1 (242,544) Indicated OD 400–500
26637, 30369
Crannóg (possible) Not marked on OS 1836 or 1876 eds. Small almost oval-shaped island (dims. *c.* 30m NW–SE; *c.* 20m NE–SW) in Drumeague Lough Lower, *c.* 25m from the shoreline.
28:16

1551 DRUMERSNAW
OS 36:4:2 (786,603) Not marked OD 214
23322, 29121
Crannóg (possible) Oval-shaped island (dims. *c.* 45m E–W; 25m N–S) marked on OS 1836 and 1876 eds. The water-level in the lake has dropped considerably and the site is now visible only as a clump of trees and bushes rising above the reeds and rushes.
36:5

1552 DRUMHEEL (Lower Loughtee By.)
OS 20:1:6 (184,469) Indicated OD 161
23646, 30903

Crannóg (possible) Situated in Lough Oughter. Small grass-covered platform of loose stones (diam. *c.* 15m; H *c.* 1.2m) connected to the shoreline by a long, narrow causeway of small and medium-sized stones (L *c.* 23m). The level of the lake was lowered considerably during the middle decades of this century. Hitherto the site was barely identifiable (local information).
20:33 29-8-1990

1553 DRUMHEEL (Lower Loughtee By.)
OS 20:1:6 (193,472) Indicated OD 161
23655, 30906
Crannóg Small, almost circular tree-covered island (diam. *c.* 26m) in Lough Oughter, *c.* 35m from the shoreline. Stone kerb visible at perimeter.
20:34 29-8-1990

1554 DRUMHEEL (Lower Loughtee By.)
OS 20:1:6 (156,497) Indicated OD 161
23615, 30932
Crannóg (possible) Not marked on OS 1836 and 1876 eds. Small, low, subcircular island (diam. *c.* 19m) in Lough Oughter, *c.* 100m from the shoreline.
20:62 14-8-1990

1555 DRUMKEERY
OS 28:9:6 NPL Not marked OD 451
Crannóg In Drumkerry Lough. Wood-Martin (1886, 200–1) recorded how the lowering of the water-levels in the lake in 1863 had converted an oval-shaped island (dims. *c.* 40m N–S; *c.* 25m E–W), situated close to the SE shore of the lake, into a peninsula. The island was enclosed by a stockade of birch and oak piles. A layer of gravelly clay and large stones added height to the summit. At N burnt bones and charcoal, which Wood-Martin interpreted as a kitchen midden, were discovered. The entrance to the crannóg was apparently at S with a landing-place identified at NE. He also noted a dugout canoe shaped from an oak trunk embedded in the bottom of the lake, close to a second landing-place.
28:47

1556 DRUMLANE (Lower Loughtee By.)
OS 14:16:3 (881,142) Indicated OD 162
23403, 31195
Crannóg Not marked on OS 1836 or 1876 eds. Small subrectangular island (dims. *c.* 22m NNW–SSE; *c.* 15m WNW–ESE) in Drumlane Lough, *c.* 50m from the shoreline. Davies (NMI Survey 1942) recorded a row of piles around the edge of the island and some large horizontal logs near its centre. He also noted several stones and a few animal bones on the island. Milligan (1885, 149–50) recorded a very fine iron cauldron found here by a farmer the previous summer 'when cutting turf about two and a-half feet below the surface of bog, which was formerly the bottom of the lake'.
14:29

1557 DRUMLOUGHER (Lower Loughtee By.)
OS 15:13:1 (55,88) Indicated OD 161
23507, 31139
Crannóg Small triangular-shaped island (*c.* 28m ENE–WSW; *c.* 22m NW–SE) in shallow water, in Derrybrick Lough, *c.* 35m from the shoreline. Davies (NMI Survey 1941) recorded the foundations of a small roughly circular hut consisting of loose rough stones one course high, which apparently had a small rough porch, on the inshore point of the island. Within the hut he found (Davies 1942, 16) a bronze axe with low hammered flanges and a cross-inscribed slab which he speculated may have been taken from Drumlane *c.* 500m to WNW (**1647**). Stakes were also observed between the island and the mainland.
15:38

1558 DRUMMANY (Pleydell)
OS 15:5:6 (178,314) Indicated OD 162
23635, 31378
Crannóg Large irregularly shaped island (dims. *c.* 75m NNE–SSW; *c.* 50m WNW–ESE) in deep water, in Black Lough, *c.* 80m from the shoreline. Davies (NMI Survey 1941) described the island as being a gravel flat surrounded by reeds with many piles on the W shore.
15:74

1559 DRUMMANY RAHAN
OS 20:5:2 (116,410) Indicated OD 161
23574, 30840
Crannóg (possible) Small almost circular tree-and-bush-covered island (diam. *c.* 25m) in Lough Oughter *c.* 15m from the shoreline. The island appears slightly convex in profile possibly indicating a low cairn.
20:40 15-8-1990

1560 DRUMMANY RAHAN
OS 20:5:2 (125,411) Indicated OD 161
23583, 30840
Crannóg (possible) Small roughly circular tree-and-bush-covered island (diam. *c.* 23m) in Lough Oughter, *c.* 80m from the shoreline.
20:41 15-8-1990

1561 DRUMSHEIL
OS 17:9:5 (82,211) Indicated OD 215
25691, 31206
Crannóg (possible) Small circular island (diam. *c.* 20m) in White Lough, *c.* 50m from the shoreline, marked on all OS eds. Densely overgrown with vegetation.
17:37 16-11-1989

1562 FARRANSEER
OS 24:12:6 (910,211) Not marked OD 100–200
23445, 29988
Crannóg (site) In Cornafean Lough. Davies (ITA Survey, 1942) described it as being 'a fairly regular pile of logs about 15 yards across; no upright posts'. Situated *c.* 20 yards from the shore. Not located.
24:53 22-8-1991

1563 GARFINY
OS 15:13:4 (54,8) Not marked OD 161
23507, 31054
Crannóg (possible) Davies (NMI Survey 1941) described a small island (diam. 12.8m) in Garfiny Lough, *c.* 27.4m from the shoreline with a low cairn and some horizontal oak trunks visible on it. He also found a quern at the site. (Davies 1942, 17)
15:44

1564 GARFINY
OS 15:13:4 (58,1) Not marked OD 161
23511, 31047
Crannóg Situated in Garfiny Lough. Davies (NMI Survey 1941) described a roughly triangular cairn (H 1m; dims. 13.7m x 9m) located at the end of a morainic ridge, now adjoining the land. Black clay containing fragments of burnt bone were identified on the cairn and three piles projecting from the water on its W side.
15:45

1565 GARTNANOUL
OS 19:12:2 (780,260) Indicated OD 161
23301, 30679
Crannóg (possible) One of two small islands marked on the OS current ed., situated in a narrow inlet of Lough Oughter between the townlands of Gartnanoul and Derries Lower. The level of the lake has been lowered and both islands are now joined to the shore by a marshy stretch of land. The more northerly of the two islands appears to be entirely natural. Davies (ITA Survey 1942) described an oval cairn of small stones (dims. 19.8m x 11.2m) rising to 2m above water-level on the S island. He described the cairn as a habitation site and noted that some animal bones were found on the shore *c.* 100m ENE.
19:33

1566 GLASLECK
OS 28:3:3 (674,549) 'Green Island' OD 366
27094, 30378
Crannóg (possible) Marked on all OS eds. An almost circular island (diam. *c.* 30m) in Milltown Lough, *c.* 110m from the shoreline. Densely overgrown with vegetation.
28:23

1567 GORTNASHANGAN UPPER or HERMITAGE/KEVIT UPPER or CASTLECOSBY/LISNAMANDRA
OS 25:6:5 (332,337) Not marked OD 200
23808, 30124
Crannóg Situated in Castlecosby Lough. Davies (1942, 20; ITA Survey 1942) described a mound *c.* 1.5m above the water-level with 0.9m of this depth comprising habitation refuse, stones and packwork. He also noted that it contained a superimposed cobbled floor and sherds of what appeared to be medieval pottery. Not located.
25:59 6-9-1991

1568 GRILLY
OS 11:14:2 (378,133) Not marked OD 156
23842, 31830
Crannóg (possible) Not marked on any OS ed. Situated in Grilly Lough, *c.* 80m from the shoreline. A few large stones protruding above the water-level of the lake presumably represent a crannóg cairn. Known locally as a crannóg.
11:19

1569 INISHCONNELL
OS 20:9:2 (114,262) 'Buck Island' OD 161
23573, 30684
Crannóg (possible) Large circular tree-and-bush-covered island (diam. *c.* 40m) in Lough Oughter, *c.* 140m from the shoreline. Davies (ITA Survey 1946) recorded some evidence of habitation here.
20:46 14-8-1990

1570 INISHMUCK
OS 15:13:6 (191,5) Indicated OD 160
23651, 31053
Crannóg (possible) An apparently natural island in Inishmuck Lough, 60m from the shoreline. On it Davies (NMI Survey 1941) found a rough quern. Otherwise no habitation evidence.
15:47

1571 KEELAGH (Tullygarvey By.)/ MULLACROGHERY
OS 16:10:1 (262,287) Not marked OD 276
24699, 31360
Crannóg (possible) Small subcircular island marked on OS 1836 and 1876 eds. Situated in Coppony Lough, *c.* 45m from the shoreline.
16:67

1572 KEENAGHAN/MULLANAFFRIN
OS 10:16:4 (735,57) Indicated OD 182
23245, 31744
Crannóg (possible) Small circular island (diam. *c.* 20m) in Long Lough, *c.* 40m from the shoreline,

marked on OS 1836 and 1876 eds.
10:17

1573 KILLYBANDRICK
OS 15:4:2 (788,553) Indicated OD 169
24277, 31637
Crannóg Marked on all OS eds. Small circular island (diam. *c.* 15m) in Killybandrick Lough, *c.* 85m from the shoreline. Davies (NMI Survey 1941) recorded that the island was surrounded by a rough kerb of stones. He found a pile on the beach, a few horizontal logs, pottery, burnt bones and teeth.
15:53

1574 KILLYBANDRICK
OS 15:4:2 (845,592) Not marked OD 169
24336, 31679
Crannóg (possible) Not marked on any OS ed. Small circular tree-and-bush-covered island (diam. *c.* 18m) in Killybandrick Lough, *c.* 35m from the shoreline.
15:54

1575 KILLYVAHAN
OS 18:1:1 (50,549) Indicated OD 262
26423, 31653
Crannóg (possible) Not marked on OS 1836 or 1876 eds. Small subtriangular island (dims. *c.* 22m NNW–SSE; *c.* 18m ENE–WSW) in Killyvaghan Lough, *c.* 90m from the shoreline. Marked on OS 1912 ed.
18:7 15-7-1990

1576 KILLYVALLY (Upper Loughtee By.)
OS 25:1:2 (98,576) Indicated OD 100–200
23559, 30374
Crannóg Situated in Lough Oughter, 180m from the shoreline. Recorded by Davies (ITA Survey 1942). Surrounded by a very soft peaty foreshore, the island is large and comprises a low ridge of granite. At its N end it rises about 1.2m above water-level at which point there is a cairn (diam. 27.4m; H 1.2m). There are two rings of close-set piles on the peaty foreshore, the outer piles being *c.* 0.9m apart and between 13.7m and 18.2m from the edge of the rock. Additional horizontal piles, which may be fallen trees, lie around these. Ox teeth and bones were found on the beach. Tradition that the island was used as a fishing station by the monks of Trinity Island (**1711**).
25:68

1577 KILLYWILLIN
OS 13:7:2 (553,424) Indicated OD 183
22078, 31481
Crannóg (possible) Small subcircular island (diam. *c.* 20m) in Killywillan Lough, *c.* 25m from the shoreline. Marked on all OS eds.
13:32

1578 KILNAVAR
OS 26:8:1 (752,411) Indicated OD 400–500
25226, 30216
Crannóg Circular island (diam. *c.* 15m) in Gortnakillew Lough, *c.* 20m from the shoreline. Covered with vegetation. Davies (ITA Survey 1942) noted that 'from its edge there projects several horizontal beams, and at one place in the upper part of the bank there appears brown earth with a little charcoal'. Situated *c.* 20m from the shoreline.
26:45 20-3-1992

1579 KNOCKATEMPLE
OS 39:15:4 (480,70) Not marked OD 277
25930, 28581
Crannóg (possible) Marked on OS 1836 and 1876 eds. Very small circular island (diam. *c.* 16m) in Lough Ramor, just 20m NNW of 'Knockatemple Island' and 130m from the shoreline.
39:56

1580 KNOCKATEMPLE
OS 39:14:3 (444,93) 'Crane Island' OD 277
25891,28605
Crannóg (possible) Subrectangular island (dims. *c.* 90m NNW–SSE; *c.* 40m WNW–ESE) in Lough Ramor, *c.* 37m from the shoreline. Davies (ITA Survey 1940) described the island perimeter as a rock-strewn beach with the central mound rising about 3m above the water-level of the lake.
39:82

1581 KNOCKATEMPLE
OS 39:15:4 (472,64) 'Cow Island' OD 277
25921,28575
Crannóg (possible) Large irregularly shaped island (dims. *c.* 70m NW–SE; *c.* 50m NW–SW) in Lough Ramor, *c.* 70m from the shoreline. Davies (ITA Survey 1940) recorded foundations of a rectangular hut on the central mound which is *c.* 3.5m above the water-level of the lake.
39:83

1582 KNOCKNAGARTAN
OS 43:3:3 (667,596) 'Knocknagartan North' OD 277
26128, 28499
Crannóg (possible) Small oval-shaped island (dims *c.* 30m N–S; *c.* 18m E–W) in Lough Ramor, *c.* 50m from the shoreline. Depicted on all OS eds.
43:24

1583 KNOCKNAGARTAN
OS 43:4:4 (706,523) 'Knocknagartan South' OD 277 26170, 28422
Crannóg (possible) Small oval-shaped island (dims *c.* 20m N–S; *c.* 12m E–W) in Lough Ramor, *c.* 30m from

the shoreline. Depicted on all OS eds.
43:25

1584 LAKEFIELD
OS 9:15:1 (488,139) Indicated OD 183
22007, 31819
Crannóg (possible) Small, oval, tree-covered island (dims. *c.* 20m NW–SE; *c.* 15m NE–SW) in Larkfield Lough, *c.* 50m from the shoreline.
9:13

1585 MULLYNAGOLMAN
OS 14:6:1 (283,423) Indicated OD 171
22769, 3148
Crannóg (possible) Small roughly circular island (dims. *c.* 18m) adjacent to the SW shore of Togher Lough, marked on OS 1836 and 1876 eds.
14:51

1586 OWNGALLEES
OS 9:14:3 (453,136) Indicated OD 183
21970, 31816
Crannóg (possible) Small, circular, tree-covered island (diam. *c.* 12m) situated in Larkfield Lough, *c.* 100m from the shoreline.
9:21

1587 PORT (ED Bawnboy)
OS 13:3:3 (616,586) Indicated OD 182
22144, 31652
Crannóg (possible) Small circular island (diam. *c.* 17m) marked on all OS eds., *c.* 25m N of St Mogue's island on which is situated an early ecclesiastical site (**1692**), and 170m from the shoreline. Davies (1948, 116) described it as probably being a crannóg. (CUCAP BGQ 69)
13:50

1588 PORTALIFF OR TOWNPARKS
OS 19:11:6 (646,193) Indicated OD 19
23161, 30607
Crannóg (possible) Small subcircular island (diam. *c.* 22m) in Mill Lough, *c.* 70m from the shoreline. Very overgrown with vegetation.
19:42

1589 PORTAN
OS 32:9:2 (147,254) Indicated OD 332
24595, 29404
Crannóg (possible) Small, circular, tree-covered island (diam. *c.* 15m) in Groddum Lough, *c.* 80m from the shoreline.
32:44 4-7-1989

1590 PORTANURE
OS 36:4:4 (762,485) Indicated OD 214
23297, 28996
Crannóg (possible) Small almost circular island (diam. *c.* 14m) in Lough Gowna, *c.* 80m from the shoreline where there is a lakeside rath (**1053**).
36:9

1591 PORTANURE
OS 36:4:1 (768,598) Not marked OD 214
23302, 29115
Crannóg (possible) Small circular island (diam. *c.* 30m) in Lough Gowna, *c.* 30m from the shoreline. Marked on OS 1836 and 1876 eds. The water-levels in the lake have been lowered and the site is now identifiable only as a clump of trees and bushes rising above the reeds.
36:13(01)

1592 PORTANURE
OS 36:4:1 (768,598) Not marked OD 214
23302, 29115
Crannóg (possible) Small circular island (diam. *c.* 30m) in Lough Gowna, *c.* 50m from the shoreline. The water-levels in the lake have been lowered and the site is identifiable only as a clump of trees and bushes rising above the reeds.
36:13(02)

1593 PORTANURE
OS 36:4:2 (777,600) Not marked OD 214
23312, 29118
Crannóg (possible) Small oval-shaped island (dims. *c.* 30m ENE–WSW; *c.* 18m NNW–SSE) marked on OS 1836 and 1876 eds., *c.* 45m from the shoreline. Water-levels in the lake have dropped considerably and the site is now identifiable only as a clump of vegetation protruding above the reeds.
36:14

1594 PROSPECT
OS 9:6:3 (420,401) 'Baron's Island' OD 209
21933, 32095
Crannóg (possible) Small almost circular tree-covered island (diam *c.* 20m) in Brackley Lough, *c.* 320m from the shoreline. Modern landing place at NE of island.
9:24

1595 RAHARDRUM
OS 39:11:6 (650,176) Indicated OD 277
26109, 28696
Crannóg (possible) Small heavily wooded, oval-shaped island (dims. *c.* 25m N–S; 12m E–W) in an inlet in Lough Ramor, *c.* 20m from the shoreline. Not marked on OS 1836 or 1876 eds.
39:75

1596 REDHILL DEMESNE
OS 12:13:5 (107,9) Indicated OD 100–200
24532, 31705
Crannóg (possible) Small circular island (diam. *c.* 20m) in Dunrora Lough, *c.* 20m from the shoreline. Davies (1942, 17) described this site as a crannóg-folly, built in the eighteenth century as support for a summerhouse.
12:6

1597 RINN
OS 20:5:1 (50,446) Indicated OD 161
23504, 30877
Crannóg (possible) Small oval-shaped island, (dims. *c.* 30m N–S; *c.* 28m E–W), in Corglass Lough, *c.* 100m from the shoreline. Densely overgrown with trees and bushes.
20:68

1598 RINN
OS 20:5:2 (95,386) Indicated OD 161
23552, 30814
Crannóg (possible) Small almost circular tree-and-bush-covered island (diam. *c.* 27m) in Lough Oughter, *c.* 35m from the shoreline.
20:69 2-8-1990

1599 RIVORY
OS 15:14:4 (282,33) Indicated OD 160
23747, 31083
Crannóg Situated in deep water in Carrafin Lough, *c.* 45m from the shoreline. Excavated by Davies in 1938. He found (Davies 1942, 28–9) that the core of the island was a natural gravel ridge running N–S which was considerably extended E and W with logs and stones. On the exposed W side of the island Davies found a well-preserved stone kerb and at E three visible layers of radial logs with cross-logs between, and on top of this structure a criss-cross log-floor with some stones. Finds from the crannóg included burnt animal bone, teeth, hazelnuts, decorated sherds of pottery, querns, a stone axe, a single-bladed iron axe with socket-hole, a hollowed pebble, a 'fairly recent' brass spur and two ring-headed pins. Local tradition maintains that this was the first stronghold of Owen Roe O'Neill, which he later abandoned for Clogh Oughter Castle (**1796**).
15:60

1600 ROSSKEERAGH
OS 15:1:6 (230,466) Indicated OD 164
23688, 31540
Crannóg Marked on all OS eds. Small circular island in Putigan Lough, *c.* 45m from the shoreline. Davies (NMI Survey 1941) recorded a mound (diam *c.* 18.2m; H *c.* 1.5m) with the remains of a horizontal log platform and a few piles on the island.
15:67

1601 RYEFIELD
OS 43:1:2 (118,653) 'Ryfield Stony Island' OD 277
25547, 28553
Crannóg (possible) Subrectangular island (dims. *c.* 25m NE–SW; *c.* 20m NW–SE) in Lough Ramor, *c.* 80m from the shoreline. Depicted on all OS eds.
43:35

1602 SRUHAGH
OS 13:11:5 (598,178) Indicated OD 173
22129, 31221
Crannóg (possible) Small oval island (dims. *c.* 30m WNW–ESE; *c.* 20m NNW–SSE) in Ballymaguaran Lough, *c.* 190m from the shoreline. Not marked on OS 1836 or 1876 eds.
13:54

1603 TERMON (Tullyhaw By.)
OS 2 NPL Not marked OD 174
Crannóg (possible) Not marked on any OS ed. Situated in shallow water in Lough Macnean, *c.* 130m from the shoreline from where it is clearly visible. Flat-topped circular cairn of small and medium-sized stones (diam. *c.* 15m) rising *c.* 1m above the current water-level.
2:32 18-5-1993

1604 TOGHER OR DANESFORT DEMESNE
OS 20:13:6 (204,75) Indicated OD 164
23670, 30487
Crannóg Situated in marshy ground in Lough Atrain, *c.* 15m from the shoreline. Davies (1942, 19) described the site as a roughly circular mound (diam. *c.* 29m) of sterile puddled clay, resting on a raft of branches which comprised logs running radially, with a set of cross-wise logs superimposed on the radial members. The pressure of the peat had caused the radial logs to become tilted upwards.
20:74 10-8-1990

1605 TOMASSAN
OS 10:15:2 (574,129) Indicated OD 164
23073, 31818
Crannóg Small circular island in Cuillaghan Lough, *c.* 150m from the shoreline. Marked on all OS eds. Hall recorded digging into a mound at the centre of the island and finding a substantial bed of ashes and debris incorporating coarse black sherds of pottery, fragments of quernstones, large quantities of broken bones and a grooved stone. An oak dugout canoe was discovered at that time on the SE shore.
10:23

1606 TOMKINROAD
OS 10 NPL Not marked OD 168
Crannóg (possible) Not marked on any OS ed.

Davies (NMI Survey 1942) described an apparently artificial promontory rising about 0.3m above the water-level and jutting into Holy Lough in the Tomkin Road area. He noted that at W the promontory was composed entirely of peat. At E he identified a grey sandy clay at about 0.15m below water-level, and slight traces of a habitation layer at water-level containing charcoal and burnt and unburnt bones. Not located.
10:25

1607 TONYIN
OS 17:14:6 (459,4) Indicated OD 243
25889, 30624

Crannóg (possible) Marked on all OS eds. Small, tree-covered, circular island (diam. *c.* 25m) in White Lough, *c.* 50m from the shoreline.
17:69

Ecclesiastical Remains

The ecclesiastical remains in the county include a variety of site types spanning a period of over 1,000 years. The earliest known sites are the Early Christian monastic foundations of Drumlane (**1647**) and Mullynagolman (**1689**), reputedly founded in the 6th century by St Maedoc and St Brecin respectively. Drumlane contains the only upstanding round tower in the county, while traces of that at Mullynagolman were still visible when recorded by Davies in 1948. Local tradition accounts for the site of a possible early anchorite cell dedicated to St Felimy in the townland of Tonymore (**1710**). Eight bullaun stones from a diversity of contexts also feature in the Early Christian corpus. They include examples at Carnagh Lower (**1615**) and Toberlyan Duffin (**1707**), both associated with holy wells, a multiple bullaun stone at Termon (**1703**) grouped with two large boulders collectively known as cursing stones, two isolated examples from Derrintiny (**1637, 1638**) and one from Derrycassan (**1639**), and another at Knockbride (**1672**) which may originally have been located in the nearby church. The only bullaun situated within an ecclesiastical site is that at Clonosey (**1627**) which is housed within the enclosure which surrounds the site of a friary. The inscribed stone at Killymacaran, on the site of a possible early church (**1663**), and the Crilea (**1613**) and Tullynamoyle examples (**1715**) in addition to the cross-slab (**1618**) from Carrickaboy Glebe church and graveyard, may also be attributed to the Early Christian Period.

Romanesque ecclesiastical architecture is represented in the county by the very fine mid-12th-century decorative doorway incorporated into the 19th-century cathedral at Kilmore (**1668**) and believed to be originally from Trinity island, having arrived at its present location via Slandore and the earlier cathedral at Kilmore.

The most numerous site type in this chapter is the medieval parish church with or without a graveyard. One of the more unusual churches, displaying strong Jacobean architectural influences, was built by Lord Southwell at Portaliff or Townparks (**1694**) in 1688.

A cathedral was erected at Kilmore (**1666**), probably in the late medieval period, reputedly on the site of a late 9th-century foundation and was still in use in 1646. It is accompanied by an episcopal residence (**1669**) which was largely restored together with the cathedral in the late 17th century.

There are also a small number of religious foundations, among them the Augustinian abbey of Drumlane (**1647**) founded in the mid-12th century, the Premonstratensian priory of Trinity Island (**1711**) established in 1237 and a Franciscan friary at Tullymongan Lower (**1714**) founded in the early 14th century. There are no upstanding structural remains of the friary at Clonosey (**1626**). On the basis of an architectural fragment recorded by Davies at the site in 1948, it may be dated to the 15th century.

Miscellaneous ecclesiastical remains include six stone heads from church site contexts, two of which are believed to have come from Trinity Island together with a stone mortar (**1681**) now at Lisnamandra. A sheela-na-gig (**1676**) found at the site of Lavey church and a peculiar exhibitionist figure (**1641**) at Doon, which may originally have been incorporated into the doorway of a church, are also included.

1608 AGHNASKEAGH
OS 42:2:2 (366,533) Not marked OD 200–300
24835, 28420

Church (site, tradition) Tradition of an ancient church site at this location (local information). Davies (1948, 96–7) speculated that it may have been used for Catholic workship after the Reformation and noted only two surviving stones of the former church. Today there is nothing of it visible at ground level. Apparently an architectural fragment from the church was incorporated into a grotto beside an early 19th-century church in Mountnugent. A stone cross (**1718**) is situated at the W end of the field in which the church is said to have been located.
42:1(01) 3-9-1985

1609 ANNAGELLIFF
OS 20:16:6 (857,26) '*Graveyard, Church* (Site of)'
OD 300–400 24360, 30442

Church and graveyard (site) Situated on the summit of a drumlin hill within an approximately square graveyard containing modern grave-markers. Davies (1948, 77) noted that 'under Charles I it was recommended that the church be moved to Gortnakesh, as more convenient to the manor-house of Monyehall (**1839**) but it does not seem that this was done.' Not visible at ground level.
20:1(01) 9-8-1990

1610 ANNAGH (Lower Loughtee By.)
OS 15:11:4 (468,220) '*Church (in Ruins), Grave Yd.*'
OD 200–300 23941, 31283

Church and graveyard Undivided nave and chancel church (int. dims. 16.7m E–W; 7.1m N–S) built of roughly coursed limestone. Chancel lit by single-light E window with pointed head, cusped tracery and external beaded hood-moulding. Doorway was probably in W end of S wall. Davies (1948, 78) recorded 'a rectangular ope with internal jambs of rough ashlar' at the E end of N wall. Within the graveyard are several architectural fragments now utilised as grave-markers.
15:1(01) 11-9-1989

1611 AUGHRIM
OS 10 NPL *'Church Hill'* OD 600–700
Church (site, possible) Davies (1948, 73–7) noted the place-name Church Hill in this townland and in documents of the late 16th and early 17th centuries but could discover no tradition or remains of a church on it.
10:26 10-7-1988

1612 BALLINTEMPLE
OS 31:7:1 (496,447) *'G. Yard'* OD 300–400 23986, 29602
Church and graveyard (site) Formerly situated within an irregularly shaped graveyard, on a cliff above the River Erne and probably originally beside a ford. According to Davies (1948,80) the church was unroofed in the early 17th century and a new one built on the opposite side of the road in 1821. He noted a few blocks of dressed ashlar in the old graveyard. No visible remains at ground level.
31:7(01) 4-6-1992

1613 BRACKLAGH (Clanmahon By.)
OS 41:2:6 (421,471) *'Church, graveyard'* OD 300–400 23919, 28347
Church and graveyard (site) Church of Ireland chapel built in 1739 situated at the E end of a roughly rectangular contemporary graveyard. Davies (1948, 95) claimed that the site is ancient and 'marked on the Baronial map'. Nothing visible at ground level at this location.
41:2(01) 30-6-1986

1614 CABRA
OS 35 NPL Not marked
Church (possible) Noted by Davies (1948, 73–7) under 'Parish of Enniskeen' in his catalogue of church sites mentioned in documents of the late 16th and early 17th centuries. Not located.
35:61

1615 CARNAGH LOWER
OS 37:1:4 (71,482) Not indicated OD 200–300 23543, 28994
Bullaun stone Situated at NW edge of 'St Patrick's Well' (**1746**). Small irregularly shaped boulder (max. dim. 0.3m) with a shallow bullaun (Wth 0.15m) at its centre.
37:17(02) 10-7-1986

1616 CARRICK (Clanmahon By.)
OS 41:3:4 (493,509) Not marked OD 300–400 23994, 28388
Church (site, possible) Not marked on any OS ed. Tradition of an old church site at this location (local information). Not visible at ground level.
41:3 1-7-1986

1617 CARRICKABOY GLEBE
OS 26:13:4 (10,30) 'Church (in ruins), Graveyard' OD 600–700 24447, 29806
Church (site) Davies (ITA Survey 1940; Davies 1948, 81) noted the foundations of a small church at the SE end of a rectangular graveyard. He also recorded a cross-slab (**1618**) in the graveyard and suggested that the decorated pillar stone at the Denn Glebe Church of Ireland chapel (**1636**), 1200m to NE, originated from here. Outside the perimeter at SW are two holy wells (**1747**). Densely overgrown with vegetation.
26:14(01) 24-10-1991

1618 CARRICKABOY GLEBE
OS 26:13:4 (10,30) Not indicated OD 600–700 24447, 29806
Church Davies (1948, 81–2) recorded a broken slab decorated with a ringed cross in low relief (Wth 0.65m), within the graveyard of Carrickaboy Glebe church (**1617**). Graveyard is presently overgrown with vegetation. Not located.
26:14(03) 24-10-1991

1619 CASHEL (Clanmahon By.)
OS 25 NPL Not marked OD 297
Church (site, tradition) Tradition of a chapel close to Cashel crossroads on land now occupied by a quarry. (ITA Survey 1942).
25:127

1620 CASTLERAHAN
OS 38:16:3 (860,127) Not marked OD 400–500 25355, 28636
Church (site, possible) Davies (1948, 80) recorded a local tradition that the original Castlerahan church stood '50 yds. to the east' of the present church (**1621**). Not visible at ground level. Possible remains of a ringwork castle (**1787**) *c.* 100m to W.
38:8(03) 28-8-1986

1621 CASTLERAHAN
OS 38:16:3 (860,127) *'Church (in ruins), Grave Yd.'* OD 400–500 25355, 28636
Church and graveyard Church situated at NW corner of a subrectangular graveyard. Rectangular building of stone and mortar construction (dims. 16m E–W; 7m N–S). Features include a collapsed doorway in W wall, an intact doorway in S wall and one window in the N, E and S walls respectively. Some gravestones and trees within the church. Davies (1948, 80) recorded that the church was erected in the 18th century and was abandoned in 1834. He noted the local tradition that the original Castlerahan church stood '50 yds. to the east' of the present church (**1620**). (CUCAP AYS 34, AYS 35, AYS 36)
38:8(02) 28-8-1986

1622 CASTLETERRA
OS 21:6:1 (242,422) Not marked OD 400–500
24683, 30863

Stone head Built into the wall above the N doorway of the modern Catholic church at Castleterra. Apparently a male head with bulging eyes, squat nose and plain unsmiling mouth. Arm comes from behind the head on the left-hand side. Four fingers are used to open the mouth. The thumb is turned upwards. The head may have come from the early church site *c.* 25m to W (**1623**). Davies (1948, 80) described it as a 'grotesque of the 15th or 16th century'.
21:6(04) 24-9-1990

1623 CASTLETERRA
OS 21:6:1 (242,422) '*Grave Yard*' Hachured
OD 400–500 24683, 30863

Church (site) and graveyard A church formerly stood within an oval-shaped rath (**316**) just E of the summit of a high drumlin hill. No visible remains of church at ground level. However, a stone head (**1622**) probably originally from the site is now built into the wall of the modern Catholic church *c.* 25m E of the graveyard. Also, two stoups of late medieval date are housed there. Graveyard is a raised area defined by a scarp faced with drystone walling, outside of which there is a modern trench running from N–NE–E and from S–SW. Oldest headstone inscription dates to 1740. Original entrance, now marked by a modern gate and pillars, was at ESE. (Davies 1948,80).
21:6(02) 24-8-1990

1624 CLIFFERNA
OS 26:8:6 (922,341) Not marked OD 400–500
25407, 30143

Church (site) Davies (1948, 111) recorded that there was an early church here, apparently a short distance to the NE of the present church. Not visible at ground level.
26:15/25:5*/27:5* 22-10-1991

1625 CLONOSEY
OS 15:2:3 (422,544) OD 100–200 23889, 31634

Ecclesiastical enclosure A raised circular area (int. diam. *c.* 40m) enclosed by a much-denuded, low, narrow earthen bank and the remains of an infilled fosse, the outline of which is still distinguishable. The

Fig. 32—*A medieval head in the N wall of the RC church at Castleterra* (**1622**).

remains of a friary (**1626**) and a bullaun stone (**1627**) lie within the interior. Davies (1948, 78) suggested that it may have been a 'fort'.
15:10(01) 10-9-1989

1626 CLONOSEY
OS 15:2:3 (422,544) '*Friary* (Site of)' OD 100–200 23889, 31634
Friary (site) Davies (1948, 78–9) noted some banks which possibly marked the foundations of the friary. He also recorded portion of a 15th-century cusped ogee window and a piece of flanged gable-coping at the site. In addition, he noted the tradition of an 'unassuming Mass-house' which was in existence as late as 1800 and lay within the enclosure (**1625**) which surrounds the site of the friary.
15:10(02) 10-9-1989

1627 CLONOSEY
OS OS 15:2:3 (422,544) Not indicated OD 100–200 23889, 31634
Bullaun stone Within Clonosey ecclesiastical enclosure (**1625**). Large irregularly shaped boulder (H 1.1m; dims. 0.95m x 0.6m) containing a bullaun (Wth 0.28m; D 0.12m).
15:10(02) 10-9-1989

1628 CLOONE
OS 30:15:4 (531,17) *Church, Grave Yd* OD 253 23052, 29138
Church and graveyard Marked 'Fort', with a 'Church' indicated within it, on the OS Fair Plan and OS 1836 ed. Today it comprises a raised approximately circular area (int. diam. *c.* 47.4m) enclosed by an earthen bank and a much modified external fosse. Bank denuded to internal ground level except at E. At NE the track of the original bank can be traced following a different angle to that of the modernised bank indicating that the original enclosed area may have been somewhat smaller. Modern roadway encloses site at N. Recently renovated early 19th-century Church of Ireland chapel and a few late 19th and 20th-century burials within the enclosed area. Davies (1948, 115) recorded that 'there were formerly two chapels, perhaps side by side'. He also noted part of an ashlar coping and a round-headed window arch, perhaps Romanesque or later in date, within the graveyard.
30:7(02) 10-10-1991

1629 CORRANEA GLEBE
OS 24:15:1 (496,146) '*Grave Yard*' OD 200–300 23009, 29915
Church (site, possible) Davies (1948, 98) speculated that 'a piece of glebe called Corranea' probably marks the site of a church. A Mass-rock — a naturally occurring knoll of rock outcrop, lies within the graveyard. There is no trace of an early church visible at ground level and no tradition of same (local information).
24:24(01) 22-8-1991

1630 CORRAWILLIN
OS 26:7:1 (465,387) Not marked OD 300–400 24924, 30188
Stone heads Architectural fragments from St Dabnet's church (**1631**) have been erected in its vicinity and serve as stations. Included are two stone heads recorded by Davies (1948, 111–2). The first is quite eroded and may originally have functioned as a window finial projecting 0.15m from the wall. It now lies on its side embedded in concrete and is used as a kneeling stone. The second head was formerly the finial of a gable-coping. It is very worn, but nose, eyes and a solid mass of hair are still distinguishable. Davies (*ibid.*) suggested a 15th-century date for both heads.
26:22(02) 18-10-1991

1631 CORRAWILLIN
OS 26:7:1 (465,387) '*St Dabnet's Chapel* (Site of)' OD 300–400 24924, 30187
Church (site) Only the foundations of the church survive, aligned N–S (int. dims. 13.2m N–S; 7.4m E–W). Within it is a low irregular-shaped cairn of large and small stones which is said to represent the 'Saint's Grave' (local information) and according to Davies (1948, 111–2) was formerly enclosed by upright slabs, only two of which were still *in situ* at that time. He also noted an altar in the S corner which appeared to him to be of recent construction, and some small slabs set on edge and buried in turf outside the N wall of the church. A total of nine architectural fragments, including two stone heads, originally from the church, have been erected in its vicinity and serve as stations. A holy well (**1753**) is situated in the bed of the river immediately below the church. Davies (1948, 111–2) commented that the church is 'apparently pre-Reformation; but it is not shown on any early map, nor did the townland belong to the church, so it may have been a private oratory'.
26:22(01) 18-10-1991

1632 CRILEA
OS 23:10:6 (449,192) Not marked OD 300–400 26854, 30640
Inscribed stone (site) Davies recorded a well at this location which was known to have housed a cross-inscribed stone. No visible remains at ground level.
23:16 21-4-1992

1633 CROSSBANE
OS 40:1:5 (143,472) '*Burial Ground*' OD 500–600 26545, 29012

Church and graveyard (site) Marked 'Fort' and 'Old Burial Ground' on OS 1836 and 1876 eds. Large pear-shaped area (int. dims. *c.* 85m N–S; *c.* 72m E–W) enclosed by a substantial, although partly denuded, earthen bank. The NE quadrant is separated from the remainder of the site by portion of a dividing wall comprising a single row of boulders laid end to end. Davies (1948, 115) records that 'The area thus enclosed, hardly a quarter of the rath, is believed to be a graveyard and the site of a church'. Also within the enclosure is the site of a well (**1754**) which has been infilled (local information).
40:21(01) 6-7-1987

1634 CROSSERLOUGH
OS 32:13:6 (219,60) '*Grave Yard*' OD 400–500
24673, 29199

Church and graveyard Foundations of a church (int. dims. 16.9m NW–SE x 6.3m NE–SW) situated close to the centre of an almost circular graveyard (int. diam *c.* 48m E–W). Site enclosed by a bank of earth and stone except from WSW–N–NNE where it has been replaced by a modern wall due to new road at this point. Graveyard contains many 18th and 19th-century gravestones. Densely overgrown with vegetation.
32:7 7-7-1989

1635 CULLIN
OS 22 NPL Not marked

Church (possible) Noted by Davies (1948, 73–7) under 'Parish of Kildrumsherdan' in his catalogue of church sites mentioned in documents of the late 16th and early 17th centuries. Not located.
22:35

1636 DENN GLEBE
OS 26:13:2 (84,120) Not marked OD 300–400
24524, 29902

Pillar stone Situated within the modern Church of Ireland graveyard. A weathered rectangular stone pillar (dims. *c.* 0.4m x *c.* 0.31m) decorated with interlace, the remains of three figures, and pairs of rampant winged horses. Davies (1948, 81) suggested that it was originally located at Carrickaboy Glebe church.
26:26(02) 18-10-1991

1637 DERRINTINNY
OS 14:16:6 (884,5) Not marked OD 200–300
23407, 31050

Bullaun stone Marked 'Lackmogue' on OS 1836 and 1876 eds. The root, lack, is an anglicization of *leac*— a flagstone. St. Mogue was a local saint. Davies (1948, 94) described a rough boulder of sandstone, with about thirty-seven cup-marks on the flat upper surface, the largest not more than 0.75m in depth and 0.07m across. Not located.
14:20(01) 15-8-1989

1638 DERRINTINNY
OS 14:16:6 (890,13) Not marked OD 200–300
23414, 31059

Bullaun stone Not marked on any OS ed. Large rough block of sandstone (H 0.38m; max. dim. 0.55m) with a bell-shaped bullaun (D 0.45m; Wth 0.45m) in its upper surface.
14:21 15-8-1989

1639 DERRYCASSAN
OS 13:12:4 (747,219) Not marked OD 100–200
22285, 31266

Bullaun stone Irregularly shaped earthfast stone (max. dims. 0.85m x 0.75m) with a circular bullaun (diam. 0.23m; D 0.18m) in its upper surface at one end, accompanied by three shallow depressions (dims. 0.05–0.06m) roughly arranged in an arc. Tradition that it was a cure for warts (local information).
13:71 14-5-1993

1640 DERRYWINNY
OS 20 NPL Not marked

Church (possible) Noted by Davies (1948, 73–7) under 'Parish of Kilmore' in his catalogue of church sites mentioned in documents of the late 16th and early 17th centuries. Not located.
20:82

1641 DOON (ED Ballyconnell)
OS 10:9:6 (225,193) Not marked OD 200–300
22704, 31883

Exhibitionist figure Situated in the grounds of the Church of Ireland chapel in Ballyconnell village. Large sandstone architectural fragment (H 0.2m; max Wth 0.33; D 0.3m) — possibly the apex of a doorway or tympanum, decorated with what appears to be an exhibitionist figure of unusual form. Figure comprises a long, oval, bearded face with staring eyes and high-set ears, no body, but wide splaying arms and legs, buttocks and possible representations of testicles. The left hand holds a small purse in the form of a human face, the right, a horseshoe-shaped object. Davies (1948, 116–7) believed that it originally surmounted the doorway of Mullynagolman round tower (**1689**) — a theory refuted by Barrow (1979, 58) who claimed it more likely came from the church at that site as the round tower doorway would have been too narrow to accomodate the large figure.
10:12(02) 6-10-1989

1642 DRUMCOR (Upper Loughtee By.)
OS 20 NPL Not marked

Church (possible) Noted by Davies (1948, 73–7) under 'Parish of Kilmore' in his catalogue of church sites mentioned in documents of the late 16th and early 17th centuries. Not located.
20:83

Fig. 33—*Bullaun stone at Derrintinny* (**1638**).

1643 DRUMEDERGLASS
OS 33:6:2 (320,386) Not marked OD 400–500
25752, 29554

Church (site, possible) Davies (1948, 98) records the tradition of a monastery at this location. Situated on the NW slope of a drumlin hill and SW of a stream. Not visible at ground level.
33:29 23-9-1988

1644 DRUMERKILLEW
OS 22 NPL Not marked

Church (possible) Noted by Davies (1948, 73–7) under 'Parish of Kildrumsherdan' in his catalogue of church sites mentioned in documents of the late 16th and early 17th centuries. Not located.
22:36

1645 DRUMGOON (Clankee By.)
OS 22:4:2 (775,568) *'Drumgoon Grave Yard'*
OD 400–500 26219, 31031

Church (site, possible) and graveyard A large, apparently modern, heart-shaped graveyard on the summit of a high drumlin hill, within which may have been a church, which according to Davies (1948, 73–7) was possibly located in a depression in the S part of the site. He also suggested that the graveyard enclosure may originally have been 'a large hilltop rath'. However, there is no surface evidence to support this suggestion.
22:18(01) 27-10-1990

1646 DRUMHURT
OS 22:2:3 (405,531) *'Grave Yard'* OD 300–400
25829, 30988

Church (site, possible) and graveyard O'Connell (1927, 124–9) recorded that this is the site of 'Disert Fincheallor Teallachgarneach' parish church which is mentioned in 14th-century documents. The site comprises a large graveyard, oval in plan, (present int. dims. *c.* 86m NW–SE; *c.* 60m ENE–WSW) defined by a low earthen bank from SW–N–ENE. From ENE–S–SW the site is defined by a stone wall where a roadway skirts the site. The burials are concentrated at the centre of the enclosed area and here there is also a low tree-covered earthen mound which may represent the last vestiges of the chapel. (1948, 97)
22:20(01) 19-10-1990

1647 DRUMLANE (Lower Loughtee By.)
OS 14:12:6 (897,168) '*Round Tower, Church* (in Ruins) *Abbey* (in Ruins)' OD 200–300
23420, 31222

Monastic complex Reputedly founded by St Maedoc, Bishop of Ferns, at the close of the 6th century. St Mary's priory for Augustinian canons established here in mid-12th century. Remains comprise a round tower, church and graveyard, fragment of a cross-inscribed stone, and the site of an abbey. Round tower (int. diam 2.92m) built with finely executed blocks of stone for first 6.7m and rough rubble masonry for remaining 4.9m. Plain round-headed doorway just above first floor level at S. Badly weathered carvings of birds on external face of wall at N, *c.* 2.2m above ground level. Fragment of cross-inscribed stone (dims. 0.32m x 0.27m; Wth 0.15m) decorated with a small cross (0.18m x 0.17m across arms) with expanded terminals, incorporated into masonry of N gate-pier at entrance to graveyard. Top right and bottom left corners of stone have been shattered. Church (int. dims. 32.7m E–W; 7.46m N–S) is aligned E–W and situated at the centre of a rectangular graveyard. It is constructed of roughly coursed rubble, the N and S walls of which have been buttressed. Late medieval doorway in W wall with bishop's head on keystone of arch. Additional doorways in N and S walls of nave. Fenestration includes very fine traceried E window, with three sculpted human heads on external face of arch; window with hood-moulding in N wall; and remains of three traceried windows in S wall. Also remains of probable screen wall situated 10.6m from E end of church, which formerly divided chancel from nave. Two tomb niches in S wall, late medieval graveslab leaning up against internal face of N wall and several architectural fragments stored within church. Attendant graveyard contains predominantly 18th-century headstones. Approximately 150m S of church there are a series of earthworks with the designation 'Abbey (in Ruins)' on all OS eds, and the remains of a building comprising portion of the S wall (L 6.7m; H *c.* 3.5m), foundations of E gable (max. L 15.5m) and part of foundations of N wall (max. L 23.4m). Additional foundations of walls running E–W on the E side of the site may represent the remains of the domestic range. (Davies 1948, 83–94; Barrow, 1979, 56–8; CUCAP ALU 40; ASV 46; AVR 35; AVR 36)
14:28 23-7-1993

Fig. 34—*Aerial view of Drumlane monastic complex* (**1647**).

Fig. 35—*Traceried E window of the Augustinian abbey church at Drumlane* (**1647**).

1648 DRUMNAGRESS
OS 22 NPL Not marked
Church (possible) Noted by Davies (1948, 73–7) in his catalogue of church sites mentioned in documents of the late 16th and early 17th centuries. Not located.
22:37

1649 DRUMSKEAGH
OS 25 NPL Not marked
Church (possible) Noted by Davies (1948, 73–77) under 'Parish of Kilmore' in his catalogue of church sites mentioned in documents of the late 16th and early 17th centuries. Not located.
25:118

1650 DRUNG
OS 21:3:1 (525,538) '*Church* (in ruins), *Grave Yard*' OD 478 24980, 30987
Church and graveyard Site lies just below the summit of a hill. Remains comprise a rectangular ivy-clad church of randomly coursed masonry (dims. *c.* 20m E–W; 8m N–S) situated at the N end of an irregularly shaped graveyard. Blocked window with wide, flat arch in S wall and remains of former doorway in W wall. According to Davies (1948,95) the church is no earlier than the 17th century.
21:37 22-9-1990

1651 EDENBURT
OS 44:9:6 (172,167) '*Grave Yard*' OD 300–400 26585, 28050
Church (site, possible) Noted by Davies (1948, 73–7). The most likely location for the church is a large, disused, oval-shaped graveyard marked on all OS eds. No visible remains at ground level. A rath (**683**) lies 15m to S.
44:10 (01) 21-8-1987

1652 ENNISKEEN
OS 35:11:1 (530,248) '*Church* (Site of) *Graveyard*' OD 200–300 27925, 29427
Church (site) and graveyard Enniskeen Church apparently lay within the now disused large rectangular graveyard. It was abandoned in the 17th century. No visible remains of church at ground level. Davies (1948, 95–6) recorded some 15th-century

Fig. 36—*Medieval graveslab at Drumlane* (**1647**).

architectural fragments built into the graveyard wall which are now in the National Museum. He also recorded a socketed dressed stone, probably the girdle of a memorial cross, inscribed on all four faces, cemented to a large boulder and located within a small enclosure W of the graveyard.
35:42(01) 22-6-1988

1653 GALLON
OS 33:11:5 (579,170) '*Church* (in Ruins), *Graveyard*' OD 400–500 26028, 29328
Church and graveyard Ruined rectangular church (int. dims. *c.* 16m E–W; 6m N–S), situated near the centre of an oval-shaped graveyard (int. dims. *c.* 50m E–W; *c.* 40m N–S) which is enclosed by a stone wall. Remains of church comprise foundations of E, S and W walls and a small rectangular window at the centre of W gable (H *c.* 4m). According to Davies, (1948, 98) W gable formerly adjoined a barrel vault 'nine feet wide running across the church, which may have supported a gallery'. He also noted that the church is first mentioned in 1406.
33:31 22-9-1988

1654 GALLONREAGH (Clanmahon By.)
OS 38:10:6 (450,170) '*Grave Yd.*' OD 238` 24921, 28678
Church (site) Disused roughly circular graveyard containing a large number of 18th, 19th and 20th-century inscribed gravestones, the earliest dating to 1720. In addition there are a number of uninscribed crude stone crosses and grave-markers. Davies (1948, 96) recorded this as the location of 'the old parish church in Gallonreagh' and noted that a field *c.* 160m to W is known as 'Church Field' (**1655**). No visible remains of church at ground level.
38:32 13-8-1986

1655 GALLONREAGH (Clanmahon By.)
OS 38 NPL Not marked OD 200–300
Church (site, tradition) Davies (1948, 96) recorded that 'the second field to the west' of Gallonreagh parish church (**1654**) is called 'Church Field'. No visible remains of a church here.
38:67 13-8-1986

1656 KEADEW (Cavan Rural and Urban)
OS 20:12:1 (694,229) Not marked OD 100–200 24186, 30654
Church (site, possible) At the site of a holy well (**1766**). Davies (1948, 118) speculated that this place may have been a refuge for a band of friars after the Dissolution. He further suggested that although the townland was not church land, it is possible that there had been an early establishment here. No visible remains of a church at ground level.
20:50(02) 22-8-1990

1657 KILL
OS 37:4:2 (820,562) '*Church* (in Ruins) *Graveyard*' OD 300–400 24334, 29086
Church and graveyard Large semicircular graveyard (int. dims. 70m NE–SW) enclosed by an earthen bank and stone wall. This is the site of an early foundation which O'Connell (1965, 455) identified with the church of SS Patrick, Carthach and Brigid, noted in historical documents in 1422 and 1425. There are no visible remains of this early church. In the NW quadrant of the graveyard are the remains of a ruined 16th-century rectangular church (dims. 18m E–W; 10m N–S) containing a doorway in the S wall and the remains of two damaged windows. The N wall is featureless and only the foundations of the W wall survive. Davies recorded the remains of a window in the E wall describing it as 'a pointed cusped lintel arch, 8 ins wide, unglazed and with slightly concave chamfer on outer edge' which most likely surmounted a lancet and was reused from the earlier church. Within the graveyard is a small crude cross of unknown date and a graveslab with an inscription dating to 1688.
37:34 16-7-1986

1658 KILLAGHADUFF
OS 7:11:1 (472,236) '*Church* (in ruins) *Grave Yard,* ' OD 300–400 21984, 32562
Church and graveyard Ruined remains of a church comprising ivy-clad E gable (L *c.* 7.5m) with base batter. Situated within a roughly rectangular graveyard (dims. 54m E–W x 52m N–S). E gable contains a square-framed, double-cusped window with hood-moulding and upturned stops. Above it is a second window with similar jambs, set off centre. (Davies 1948,110)
7:17 12-3-1992

1659 KILLAN
OS 28:6:3 (460,401) '*Church* (in ruins), *Grave Yard*' OD 473 26870, 30220
Church and graveyard Ruins of a church (int. dims. *c.* 16m E–W; *c.* 7m N–S) situated on a naturally occuring mound at the centre of an almost circular (int. dims. *c.* 62m E–N; *c.* 58m N–S) graveyard. Remains comprise foundations of N and S walls, W gable, and E gable standing to its full height (*c.* 5m). Large pointed window, the top of which was repaired in 1950s, in E gable and a small rectangular window in W gable. W end of church is occupied by the burial vault of the Cosby family. Graveyard contains 19th and 20th-century gravestones and is enclosed by a low earthen and stone bank except from S–WSW where it has been replaced by a modern wall.
28:27(01) 30-8-1988

1660 KILLOUGHTER
OS 16:1:5 (96,473) '*Old Church* (Site of) *Grave Yard*' OD 300–400 24521, 31555
Church (site) and graveyard No surviving remains of church visible at ground level. It formerly stood in an oval-shaped graveyard (int. dims. 31.6m N–S; 48.6m E–W). Davies (1948, 99) identified two *c.* 15th-century cut-stone architectural fragments which were reused as headstones.
16:69(01) 12-9-1989

1661 KILLYCRONE
OS 21:15:3 (678,94) G. Yd., Ch OD 300–400 25146, 30520
Church (site) and graveyard Davies (1948, 111) recorded that the graveyard at Killycrone marks the site of an early church. No visible remains of a church here.
21:43(01) 19-9-1990

1662 KILLYFINLA
OS 38 NPL Not marked
Church and graveyard (site, possible) Davies (1948, 80) recorded a tradition of a graveyard 'on a hilltop at Killyfinla' which may mark the site of the church and also noted references to it in documents of the late 16th and early 17th centuries. Not located.
38:68

1663 KILLYMACARAN
OS 23:10:6 (454,187) Not marked OD 300–400 26860, 30634
Inscribed stone Fragment of a decorated stone discovered in a small hollow beside the River Annalee and on the site of a possible early church (**1664**). According to Barron (1942, 120–1) it was clearly portion of a longer slab, formerly decorated with groups of six-petalled rosettes enclosed in circles, of which only one complete and one half rosette is visible on the surviving fragment. Now in the National Museum.
23:25(02) 22-4-1992

1664 KILLYMACARAN
OS 23:10:6 (454,187) Not marked OD 300–400 26860, 30634
Church (site) Possible early church site situated in a

small hollow beside Annalee River. Recorded by Barron (1942, 120–1) who found 'a stone with incised arcs' at the site (**1663**). Not visible at ground level.
23:25(01) 22-4-1992

1665 KILMACNORAN
OS 16:14:3 (395,118) Hachured OD 200–300 24841, 31183
Church (site, possible) and graveyard Slightly raised circular area (int. diam. *c.* 75m) enclosed from SW–W–N by a steep-sided waterlogged fosse and from N–E–SE by a barely perceptible scarp. Davies (1948, 95) recorded that the site 'is locally known as 'the Caldragh', and the townland name suggests the former existence of a church'.
16:75 6-11-1989

1666 KILMORE UPPER
OS 25:2:2 (366,565) Indicated OD 306 23842, 30366
Cathedral Possibly erected on the site of an earlier foundation reputedly established here in 885 AD and of which there is now no trace. Episcopal seat of the Diocese of Kilmore in 1454. Present church dates to Late Medieval period and comprises the remains of a rectangular structure (dims. *c.* 26m E–W; *c.* 8m N–S) built of roughly coursed limestone, with batter at base of E gable and dressed quoinstones at SE angle. Described as having a roof of wood and sods in 1646. Entrance in S wall was formerly adorned by the Romanesque doorway which is now housed in the modern cathedral (**1668**). Cathedral appears to have been restored, together with the Bishop's Palace (**1669**) which adjoins its NNW wall, in the period following the Williamite wars. (Davies 1948, 99)
25:70(04) 16-5-1993

1667 KILMORE UPPER
OS 25 NPL Not marked
Church (site) Davies (1948, 99) claimed that the earliest reference to a church here dated from 885AD and that until 1454 it was no more than a parish church. In that year it became an episcopal seat perhaps translated from Slandore.
25:131

1668 KILMORE UPPER
OS 25:2:2 (369,556) '*Cathedral*' OD 200–300 23846, 30356
Romanesque doorway A late Romanesque doorway in four orders with beaded hood-moulding, decorated with animal, geometric and foliage motifs. Set into the vestry entrance on N side of the modern Church of Ireland cathedral during its construction in *c.* 1860. Doorway is believed to have originated from Trinity Island (**1711**), was subsequently moved to Slandore (**1701**) and from there to its present location. (Davies 1948, 101–9; Killanin and Duignan, 102)
25:71(02) 16-5-1993

1669 KILMORE UPPER
OS 25:10:2 (343,237) Not marked 26759, 28766
Bishop's palace An early 17th-century episcopal residence constructed at a right angle to WSW end of NNW wall of the old cathedral (**1666**). Largely restored in the period after the Williamite wars. Described in 1739 as 'long, lofty and capacious, about a hundred feet in length, and forty in width; it has two fronts; the entrance is by the E side. The front is a large square court, the south side of which is formed by the church, the west by the house, the north by a wall'd enclosure ... from the east side, which seems open, there is descent by several steps into a spacious gravelled terrace'.
25:73 16-5-1993

1670 KILNAVERT
OS 13:4:5 (787,468) 'St. Mogue's R.C. Church' OD 267 22325, 31530
Church (site, possible) and graveyard Modern Catholic church within a circular graveyard (diam. *c.* 60m). The graveyard is enclosed by a much-disturbed low bank of earth and stone which must in its present condition be regarded as relatively modern. Davies (1948, 116) suggested that it was of considerable antiquity.
13:39 19-6-1989

1671 KNOCKATEMPLE
OS 43:3:1 (517,557) '*Church, Graveyard*' OD 400–500 25970, 28456
Church (site) and graveyard Graveyard situated on a high open hill marked as circular in plan on OS 1835 ed. No visible remains of a church at ground level.
43:18(01) 16-6-1987

1672 KNOCKBRIDE
OS 23:13:5 (134,74) '*Church* (in ruins), *Grave Yard*' OD 400–500 26522, 30512
Church and graveyard Simple rectangular church (int. dims. 12.3m NW–SE; 6.3m NE–SW) built with large and small split slabs, situated roughly at the centre of an irregularly shaped graveyard. All of the church windows have been blocked up and access is by a lintelled rectangular doorway in the NW wall. Davies (1948, 110–1) noted that the rectangular windows do not look older than the 17th century though tradition says that the E wall is pre-Reformation. The foundation of the N wall, however, cannot have been made for the present church. The walls contain a few punch-dressed stones, and above the NW door are stones from a two-light window with

Fig. 37—*Detail of the arch orders of the Romanesque doorway at Kilmore Upper* (**1668**).

plain chamfer, probably of the 15th or 16th century.
23:26 21-5-1992

1673 KNOCKBRIDE
OS 23:13:5 (134,70) Not marked OD 200–300
26523, 30508
Bullaun stone Small irregularly shaped boulder (H 0.2m; dims. 0.67m x 0.6m) containing a well-defined, basin-shaped depression (diam. 0.19m; D 0.07m). Tradition that the bullaun was used as a 'font' during Penal times (local information). On the surface of the stone are a number of carvings which presumably date to this period. Situated in a farmyard *c.* 175m E of Knockbride church (**1672**).
23:54 23-7-1993

1674 LAVAGH
OS 37:12:6 'St. Paul's Ch.' OD 200–300
24408, 28665
Church and graveyard (site) Noted by Davies (1948,73–7) in his catalogue of church sites mentioned in documents of the late 16th and early 17th centuries. No visible remains at ground level.
37:41 5-8-1986

1675 LAVEY
OS 26:3:4 (504,461) '*Church* (Site of)' OD 355
24965, 30266
Church (site) Davies (1948,111) recorded an early church site at this location and Guest (1936,109) recorded a sheela-na-gig from the site (**1676**). No visible remains of a church at ground level.
26:52(01)

1676 LAVEY
OS 26:3:4 (504,461) '*Church* (Site of)' OD 355
24965, 30266
Sheela-na-gig Found at the site of Lavey church (**1675**). Described by Guest (1936,109) as having arms flexed in front of splayed thighs and hands directed towards the lower abdomen. Now in the National Museum.
26:52(02) 17-10-1991

1677 LECKS
OS 23:16:6 (852,23) '*Killastueran Fort & Grave Yard*'
OD 400–500 27281, 30465
Church and graveyard (site, possible) Davies (1948,116) suggested that the rath (**848**) at this location

contained a church site. Raised oval area (int. dims. *c.* 32m NNW–SSE; 30m WSW–ENE) enclosed by a bank of earth and stone. Traditionally believed to be the site of a children's burial ground (**1740**).
23:30(02) 30-3-1992

1678 LISEGNY
OS 21 NPL Not marked
Church (possible) Noted by Davies (1948,73–7) under the 'Parish of Larah' in his catalogue of church sites mentioned in documents of the late 16th and early 17th centuries. Not located.
21:76

1679 LISNALEA
OS 34 NPL Not marked
Church (possible) Noted by Davies (1948,73–7) under the 'Parish of Knockbride' in his catalogue of church sites mentioned in documents of the late 16th and early 17th centuries. Not located.
34:54

1680 LISNAMANDRA
OS 25:6:2 (317,390) Not marked OD 200–300
23792, 30181
Stone head This apparently late medieval head is believed to have been taken from Trinity Island (**1711**) (local information) and is now lying up against the NW wall of a modern dwelling-house. It has slightly bulging eyes, prominent ears, a partly chipped nose and smiling mouth. The chin has been broken off. The head is crowned with a plain band with foliate tips.
25:89(03) 17-9-1991

1681 LISNAMANDRA
OS 25:6:2 (317,390) Not indicated OD 200–300
23792, 30181
Mortar Lying against the NW wall of a modern dwelling-house and now utilised as a flowerpot. Small, flat-based, roughly executed sandstone mortar (H 0.26m; dims. 0.3m x 0.28m; int. diam. 0.2m) equipped with corner lugs. It is accompanied by a stone head (**1680**), both items having been reputedly taken from Trinity Island (**1711**) (local information).
25:89(02) 17-9-1991

Fig. 38—*Sheela-na-gig originally from Lavey* (**1676**), *now housed in the National Museum (Reproduced courtesy of National Museum of Ireland).*

Fig. 39—*Medieval stone head reputedly from Trinity Island and now at Lisnamandra* (**1680**).

1682 LISSANNYMORE
OS 33 NPL Not marked

Church (possible) Noted by Davies (1948, 73–7) under the 'Parish of Killinkere' in his catalogue of church sites mentioned in documents of the late 16th and early 17th centuries. Not located.
33:53

1683 LURGAN
OS 39:6:1 (235,452) '*Church* (in Ruins), *Graveyard*' OD 400–500 25668, 28983

Church and graveyard A rectangular church (dims. 16m E–W; 8m N–S) of which only the S and W walls have survived, situated within a circular graveyard. When recorded by Davies (1948, 112–3), the only surviving architectural feature of the church was 'a piece of door-jamb in the graveyard'. A barrel-vaulted structure (int. dims. 7.2m N–S; 4.3m E–W) projects out from the external face of W wall and apparently was built upon when the church was already ruined. Its S wall contains a damaged ope. Davies also recorded that the church was abandoned in 1818 'when most of it was carried away to build the church at Virginia'.
39:67 24-3-1987

1684 MAGHERANURE
OS 17:7:5 (586,315) '*Church* (Site of) *G. Yd.*' OD 300–400 26323, 30830

Church (site) and graveyard Marked 'Church (in ruins)' on OS 1836 and 1876 eds. O'Connell (1937, 157–9) claimed that the disused cemetery in Cootehill marks the site of a 14th-century church. He recorded that 'the walls have long since been demolished' but that 'near the entrance gate some traces of the old church may be detected'. Davies (1948, 83) found nothing surviving of the church. Not visible at ground level.
17:57(01) 15-8-1989

1685 MAGHERINTEMPLE
OS 16:3:3 (649,555) '*Grave Yard*' OD 300–500 25105, 31646

Church (site) and graveyard Situated at the centre of Magherintemple hilltop enclosure (**1463**). Davies (1948, 95) recorded that the church was a chapel-of-ease and not the centre of a parish and that it is shown with a tower on the 'Escheated Counties Map.' On the ground he noted some masonry among which was a cut-stone fragment possibly from an early window. No visible remains of church at ground level. (CUCAP AVR 32)
16:99(02) 16-10-1989

1686 MARAHILL (Upper Loughtee By.)
OS 25:5:1 (19,431) '*Caldragh*' OD 200–300 23477, 30221

Church (site, possible) Davies (1948, 110) speculated that this children's burial ground (**1741**) is probably an early church site. No visible remains of a church at ground level.
25:93(02) 24-4-1991

1687 MONNERY LOWER/MONNERY UPPER
OS 25 NPL Not marked

Church (possible) Noted by Davies (1948, 73–77) under the 'Parish of Kilmore' in a catalogue of church sites mentioned in documents of the late 16th and early 17th centuries. He did not specify whether the townland in question is Monnery Lower or Monnery Upper. Not located.
25:119

1688 MULLAGH
OS 40:14:6 (405,26) '*Templekelly* (in Ruins)' OD 400–500 26826, 28543

Church and graveyard A small rectangular building (int. dims. *c.* 9m E–W; *c.* 6m N–S) locally known as 'Teampaill Ceallaigh' and associated with St Killian. Situated on a raised mound within an early 19th-century graveyard. Remaining features of building include outline of a much-ruined window in E wall, a blocked-up doorway at the centre of S wall and a chimney and narrow fireplace built into W wall. Davies (1948, 115) was of the opinion that this is not an ecclesiastical building and if it is, it must be post-Reformation. Original location of Mullagh ogham

Fig. 40—*St Mogue's church at Port* (**1692**), *Templeport Lough (Reproduced courtesy of Cambridge University Committee for Aerial Photography).*

stone (**182**). (CUCAP BGQ 72)
40:44 16-7-1987

1689 MULLYNAGOLMAN

OS 14:6:2 (309,409) Not marked OD 100–300
22796, 31471

Monastic complex (site) Locally known as 'Church Meadow', this site is traditionally believed to be St Brecin's monastic settlement which formerly comprised a round tower, church and cemetery. According to Davies (1948, 116–7) traces of both church and round tower were evident as late as 1948, in addition to a number of cut stones, querns, and a large lump of iron slag which may have been a furnace bottom. The 'Tomregan Stone' (**1641**) situated at the Church of Ireland chapel in Ballyconnell village is traditionally believed to have originated from here. No trace of monastic site at ground level. (Barrow 1979, 58).
14:52 19-8-1989

1690 NOLAGH

OS 28:12:4 (713,182) Not marked OD 600–700
27139, 29991

Church (site, possible) Davies (1948, 116) recorded a tradition of a 'chapel site' at this location. No visible remains at ground level.
28:40 1-9-1988

1691 POLLINTEMPLE

OS 43:4:2 (777,565) Not marked OD 200–300
26245, 28467

Church (site, possible) O'Connell (1937, 91–2) quoting historical sources stated that there was an early ecclesiastical foundation established by SS Brandubh and Colum on Woodward's Island in Lough Ramor, *c.* 60m from the shoreline. He believed that the site was destroyed in the early 18th century as a result of the building of a mansion on the island by the Woodward family. (Davies 1948, 113)
43:30 6-8-1987

1692 PORT (ED Bawnboy)
OS 13:3:2 (615,577) '*St Mogue's Church* (in Ruins), *Grave yd.*' OD 100–200 22143, 31643
Church (site) and graveyard Situated on a natural island in Templeport Lough. Davies (1948, 116) noted documentary evidence for a church here in 1496. Patterson and Davies (1940, 154–6) described foundations of a rectangular drystone-built church (int. dims. 12m ENE–WSW; 5.3m NNW–SSE). They recorded that E wall then stood to a height of 0.9m and that S wall had been destroyed at W corner and another wall of rough ashlar standing about 6m high had been built across it. The W wall according to their observations contains a large rectangular window which they suggested was 'a type unusual in ecclesiastical buildings, in this position'. Within the graveyard they found several querns and architectural fragments indicative of the late 15th or early 16th century. Not visited. (CUCAP BGQ 69)
13:49

1693 PORT (ED Bawnboy)
OS 13:3:3 (636,597) '*Templeport Church, Grave Yd.*' OD 200 22165, 31664
Church (site) and graveyard Davies (1948, 116) recorded that 'the modern church occupies a pre-Reformation site which is marked on the Baronial Map as Aghavanme. There are no ancient remains'.
13:51 27-6-1989

1694 PORTALIFF OR TOWNPARKS
OS 19:7:5 (568,338) '*Church in Ruins, Graveyard*' OD 100–200 23077, 30759
Church Church with nave (int. dims. *c.* 20m E–W; *c.* 8m N–S) and large south transept (dims. *c.* 9m E–W; *c.* 9m N–S) situated within a former embanked enclosure. Hachured arc marked on current OS indicates an enclosure running from SSW–W–NNE which is no longer visible at ground level. Graveyard extends beyond line of enclosure. According to Davies' (1948, 97–8) reading of papal registers, there may have been a church on this site as early as 1433. A heraldic plaque on S gable of transept indicates that present structure was built by Lord Southwell in 1688. Davies described nave as having a W door, two N windows and an E window now blocked. All windows in church are round-headed with two rounded lights surmounted by a circular ope. He also noted 'the fine Jacobean door in S transept

Fig. 41—*Wayside crosses at Relagh Beg* (**1698**).

Fig. 42—*Detail of an ecclesiastic on the shaft of a wayside cross at Relagh Beg* (**1698**).

leading down to a font with elaborate Jacobean canopy and hence into the nave, or upwards to a gallery beneath the brick vaulting of the transept'. The E portion of transept was walled off and probably used as a vestry. Ornamental terminals on gable-coping.
19:40(01) 10-7-1990

1695 RAFFONY
OS 39:8:2 (816,393) '*Graveyard*' OD 400–500
26282, 28926
Church and graveyard Foundations of a rectangular drystone-built church (int. dims. 13m E–W; 6.5m N–S) situated within a subrectangular graveyard (int. dims. *c.* 53m NW–SE; *c.* 37m NE–SW) enclosed by a stone wall. Davies (1948,115) speculated that a separate chamber (L 3m) at the W end of the church foundations may have been 'part of a vault supporting a gallery'. He also noted some blocks of sandstone built into the gateposts which he suggested were possibly the jambs of 'primitive widely splaying windows, with small chamfer on outer edge'. Examination of the fields around the existing graveyard revealed that the original enclosure was circular (diam. *c.* 60m) and considerably larger than the area now defined by the graveyard. From SE–S–SW the original perimeter survives as a low earthen bank with a shallow but clearly defined external depression, presumably the remains of a fosse. From W–NW and at E the perimeter is identifiable only as a scarp. Two depressions which probably represent a collapsed souterrain (**1263**) occur *c.* 16m S of the graveyard wall.
39:71(01) 9-6-1987

1696 RAKANE
OS 17 NPL Not marked
Church (possible) Noted by Davies (1948, 73–7) under the 'Parish of Kildrumsherdan' in his catalogue of church sites mentioned in documents of the late 16th and early 17th centuries.
17:76

1697 RANTAVAN
OS 44:3:1 (498,563) Not marked OD 300–400
26925, 28472

Church (site) Not marked on any OS ed. According to Davies (1948, 115) a chapel is mentioned as having existed at the corner of two fields and the road in this area in 1608. He also noted that some flags in the kitchen of Rantavan House are thought to have come from here and that there may have been a stoup at the site. Tradition that ogham stone at Mullagh (**182**) originated from this church site (local information).
44:18(01) 18-8-1987

1698 RELAGH BEG
OS 34:15:4 (488,30) 'Church (in Ruins) Graveyard'
OD 600–700 26908, 29189
Church and graveyard Gwynn and Hadcock (1970, 354) state that this site is associated with St Fintan of Moy bolc and that in addition to the ecclesiastical structures, there was a hospital or hospice here. Davies (1948, 113–4) recorded that 'the Baronial map shows the church unroofed, with a round tower beside it'. The late medieval church, constructed of roughly coursed limestone rubble, was formerly accompanied by a S transept or priest's residence. All that survives of the church is the featureless nave portion of the N wall (L 18.5m). The transept or priest's residence (int. dims. 6m N–S; 4.8m E–W) was originally attached to the S side of the chancel. It is two storeys high and has windows in the S and E walls at both levels. Those in the E wall are blocked up. That at first-floor level in the S wall has a flat head accompanied by a hood-moulding. The building is otherwise featureless. Embedded in concrete beside the N wall of the nave are a cross-slab and three cross-heads, with three shafts constituting the remains of three former wayside crosses. Each of the cross-heads depict the crucifixion and two bear inscriptions, one dating to 1684, the other to 1686. A font lies nearby, while a holed stone (diam. of hole *c.* 0.18m) and a graveslab depicting a cleric in medieval garb, are situated E of remains of Church. (King 1987, 303–5)
34:46 27-7-1994

1699 ROSSCOLGAN
OS 25 NPL Not marked
Church (possible) Noted by Davies (1948, 73–77) under the 'Parish of Urney' in his catalogue of church sites mentioned in documents of the late 16th and early 17th centuries. Not located.
25:129

1700 ROSSCOLGAN
OS 25 NPL Not marked
Church (possible) Church in this area noted by Davies (1948, 73–7) under the 'Parish of Urney' in his catalogue of church sites mentioned in documents of the late 16th and early 17th centuries. Not located.
25:132

Fig. 43—*Triple-light E window at Termon medieval parish church* (**1702**).

1701 SLANDORE
OS 25:1:4 (17,524) '*Abbey Field*' OD 100–200
23474, 30319
Church (site) and graveyard (possible) Davies (1948, 109) suggested that this was an early church site, and reputedly the seat of a bishop until the 15th century. Tradition holds that the Romanesque door at Kilmore Cathedral (**1668**) came from Trinity Island (**1711**) via Slandore. Site today comprises a rectangular raised area (int. dims. 45m NNE–SSW; 50m WNW–ESE) enclosed by a shallow fosse and low earthen bank, except at NNE where both bank and fosse have been incorporated into a field boundary. This area may define the site of a graveyard. It contains a poorly defined rectangular platform at W which may represent the remains of a church, and two stray pieces of dressed stone lying within the enclosed area at E. Traditionally known as 'The Abbey Field' (local information).
25:109 17-9-1991

1702 TERMON (Tullyhaw By.)
OS 2:9:5 (90,193) '*Church* (in Ruins), *Grave Yard*'
OD 100–200 20593, 33784
Church and graveyard Rectangular church (int. dims. 20.8m E–W; 5.8m N–S) constructed of roughly coursed limestone blocks and rubble. Beam-holes in N and S walls at W end of church are almost certainly for carrying a loft. Large blocks of masonry in W wall possibly belong to an earlier church. Remaining

features include a three-light round-headed window with glazing-bar holes, in E gable, small plain flat-headed windows in N and S walls of nave, and small round-headed windows in N and S walls of chancel. No evidence of W doorway or window. (Davies 1939, 98–102; Lowry-Corry 1939, 102–4; Davies 1948, 98)
2:18 28-4-1993

1703 TERMON (Tullyhaw By.)
OS 2:9:5 (95,207) *'Bullans stone'* OD 100–200 20598, 33799
Bullaun stone Not marked on OS 1836 or 1876 eds. Three large irregularly shaped boulders set close together. The largest of these contains eleven bullauns, some of which are apparently natural depressions, while the other two boulders contain one and four basins respectively. Rounded stones have been placed into each bullaun, probably in relatively recent times. These are known locally as 'St Brigid's Stones' and were formerly used as cursing stones (local information). (Wakeman 1875, 460; Lowry-Corry 1939, 103–4; Richardson and Lowry-Corry 1940, 170; Price 1959, 166; Killanin & Duignan 1989, 78; Harbison 1991, 226–7)
2:20 10-7-1988

1704 TERMON (Upper Loughtee By.)
OS 33:6:2 (313,416) 'Clanaphilip R.C. Church' OD 400–500 25744, 29585
Church (site) and graveyard Davies (1948, 98) claimed that an O'Reilly of Mullagh founded a chapel at this site. Mentioned as early as 1608, it may have stood within the graveyard on a gentle slope and a little below the 19th-century Catholic church marked on all OS eds. A late medieval head (**1705**), now incorporated into a grotto at the site, and half a cusped-ogee window-head of the same period were also noted by Davies.
33:49(01) 14-9-1988

1705 TERMON (Upper Loughtee By.)
OS 33:6:2 (313,416) Not marked OD 400–500 25744, 29585
Stone head Davies (1948, 98) recorded that this medieval stone head together with a number of medieval architectural fragments had been built into the sacristy wall of the 19th-century Catholic church at Clanaphilip (**1704**). This church was removed in the 1980s and its site is today partly occupied by a modern grotto in honour of Our Lady into which a stone head has been incorporated. Traditionally the head is believed to represent the *Cailleach Geargain* destroyed by St Patrick in the vicinty of the old church at Moybolgue (**1698**). It has bulging eyes and a prominent nose, and hair represented by a profusion of deep grooves covering the top of the head and cheeks. The lips are shaped, suggestive of the *Cailleach* blowing her breath.
33: 49(02) 14-9-1988

1706 TIRLAHODE LOWER/TIRLAHODE UPPER
OS 26 NPL Not marked
Church (site, possible) According to Davies (1948, 73–77) there was a church site here. However, he does not specify whether the townland in question is Tirlahode Lower or Upper, in the Parish of Larah. It is apparently mentioned in documents of the late 16th and early 17th centuries.
26:64/27:15*

1707 TOBERLYAN DUFFIN
OS 13:8:6 (881,366) Not marked OD 100–200 22426, 31423
Bullaun stone Circular, shallow bullaun (diam. 0.23m; D 0.14m) in a boulder (H 0.15m; dims. 0.72m x 0.22m) which was formerly one of a series of boulders which surrounded a holy well (**1779**) and served as penitential stations (local information). Bullaun stone is now situated close to a boundary *c.* 60m SSW of original location.
13:63(02) 10-6-1989

1708 TONYMORE
OS 20 NPL Not marked
Church (site, possible) Martyrology of Donegal refer to a monastery of 'Donaghmore' apparently founded by St Columcille and later associated with both St Feidhlimidh and St Colman (O'Connell 1937, 23–38). O'Connell equates, 'Donaghmore' with Tonymore in Kilmore parish. Not located. No local tradition.
20:78

1709 TONYMORE
OS 25 NPL Not marked
Church (possible) Noted by Davies (1948, 73–77) under the 'Parish of Kilmore' in his catalogue of church sites mentioned in documents of the late 16th and early 17th centuries. Not located.
25:120*

1710 TONYMORE
OS 20 NPL Not marked
Cell Tradition of the site of 'St Felimy's Cell — possibly an anchorite's cell or small early oratory in this townland. Not located. (O'Connell, 1937, 35)
20:80

1711 TRINITY ISLAND
OS 20:13:4 (68,16) 'Trinity Abbey' (in Ruins) OD 100–200 23527, 30423
Priory The priory of Holy Trinity, Lough Oughter, founded by grant of Cathal O'Reilly in 1237, was a daughterhouse of the Premontratensian abbey of Trinity Island, Loughkey, Co. Roscommon (Gwynn & Hadcock 1970, 206). Situated at the centre of a now

Fig. 44—*Stone head* (**1712**) *reputedly from Holy Trinity Abbey, Trinity Island, Lough Oughter (Reproduced courtesy of National Museum of Ireland).*

disused, roughly oval-shaped graveyard (dims. 56m N–S; 40m E–W). Remains comprise ivy-clad W gable and portions of N and S walls of a rectangular church (int. dims. *c.* 16m E–W; *c.* 5m N–S) with a transept on S side (int. dims. *c.* 6m N–S; *c.* 5m E–W) which appears to have been added during restoration of the priory in the 17th century. Walls of main body of church have a pronounced base batter. Main entrance in W gable, which it is believed, may have been originally adorned by the celebrated Romanesque doorway (**1668**) now at the modern cathedral of Kilmore. Additional blocked entrance with masonry arch at W end of S wall. Fenestration includes large pointed window with chamfered ashlar jambs directly above W gable entrance and stray fragments of window spandrels, tracery and mullions of 15th-century date, scattered about the graveyard. W gable may have been surmounted by a small belfry. A bevelled cross-base with square socket and possible ringed cross-head, and a grotesque head (**1712**) which is now in the National Museum, were noted at the site in 1948. (O'Connell 1937, 242–289; Davies 1948, 99–109)
20:77(01) 19-11-92

1712 TRINITY ISLAND
OS 20:13:4 (68,16) Not marked OD 100–200
23527, 30423

Stone head Davies (1948, 100) recorded a grotesque male head (now in National Museum) which is believed to have come from Trinity Abbey (**1711**). The head has bulging eyes, one of which appears to be closed, a long prominent nose, wrinkles on both cheeks and hair on top.
20:77(02)

1713 TULLY (Lower Loughtee By.)
OS 20 NPL Not marked

Church (possible) Noted by Davies (1948, 73–7) under the 'Parish of Kilmore' in his catalogue of church sites mentioned in documents of the late 16th and early 17th centuries. Not located.
20:84

1714 TULLYMONGAN LOWER
OS 20:16:4 (704,65) Indicated OD 200–300
24199, 30480

Friary Franciscan friary founded between 1300 and 1330 by Gilla-Isu Roe O'Reilly. Burnt in 1405, again in 1451 through the carelessness of an inebriated friar, by the English in 1468, and finally by an enraged woman of the O'Reilly family in 1576. Depicted on Netherclift's plan of Cavan town (*c.* 1593). It was demolished in 1815 and all that now remains is a three-storey square tower (ext. dims. 4.3m x 4.3m; H *c.* 16.7m) with 18th-century moulded opes in E and W walls and similar openings in all four walls at third-floor level. (O'Connell 1937, 335; Gwynn and Hadcock 1970, 245)
20:55(02) 19-11-1992

1715 TULLYNAMOYLE
OS 5:15:3 (625,572) Not marked OD 200–300 20202, 31692

Inscribed stone A partially split boulder (now in the National Museum) decorated with an incised ring (diam. 0.63m). Formerly located in a field wall. (Richardson, 1940, 173–4).
5:46 21-8-1988

1716 URNEY (Clanmahon By.)
OS 25:14:6 (457,17) '*Caldragh* (Site of)' 23943, 29788

Church (site, possible) Davies (1948, 110) believed that the children's burial ground in this townland (**1745**) was probably the site of an early church.
25:115(02) 21-9-1993

1717 URNEY (Upper Loughtee By.)
OS 15:14:6 (410,75) '*Urney Church* (in Ruins), *Grave Yd.*' OD 100–200 23882, 31128

Church and graveyard Undivided nave and chancel church (int. dims. 13.2m E–W; 5.8m N–S) built of uncoursed rubble masonry. Single-light lancet E window. Two-centred chamfered arch over W doorway. Remains of plain window in E end of S wall with stone dressing indicative of late 16th-century date. An annexe, possibly a priest's quarters, adjoins church on W side and is accessed via a stairwell constructed against the inside of W gable.
15:73 12-5-1993

Crosses

This chapter records stone crosses which are located in apparent isolation from any related ecclesiastical monument. There are three upstanding wayside crosses of late 16th or 17th-century date, and both map evidence and local tradition regarding the sites of two other crosses in the county.

Fig. 45—*A 17th-century wayside cross at Aghnaskeagh* (**1718**).

1718 AGHNASKEAGH
OS 42:2:2 (366,533) Not marked OD 200–300
24835, 28421

Cross Situated at W end of field close to boundary with roadway. Field is reputedly site of an ancient church (**1608**). Badly weathered wayside cross (H *c.* 1m) with right arm broken off. Davies (1948, 97) described it as 'an unperforated ringed cross', 0.83m across the arms, the shaft being 0.33m x 0.20m. Furthermore he noted that it was inscribed in raised letters with the name Newell and the date 1626.
42:1(02) 3-9-1986

1719 CORRATINNER
OS 33:11:6 (664,183) Not marked 26117, 29343

Cross Moved from a rath in Caragagh (**286**) to present location in the 1940s (1948, 98). Designated 'Remarkable Stone' on OS Fair Plan and 'Cargagh Cross' on subsequent OS ed. Plain 16th or 17th-century wayside cross comprising pyramidal base and short rectangular shaft with chamfered corners and a broken collar piece. Shaft inscribed on S face with now illegible dedication in English.
33:18 4-5-1974

1720 OMARD
OS 37:8:5 (805,353) '*Cross*' OD 300–400
24319, 28866

Cross Standing against a stone wall on E side of road and obscured by dense growth of vegetation. Locally known as the 'Cat's Cross'. A plain wayside cross (H *c.* 0.5m) with imperforate ring (diam *c.* 0.4m) set in socketed base slab. Left arm (L 0.15m) intact and right arm broken off. (Davies 1948, 80)
37:66 17-7-1986

1721 RAHEEVER
OS 42:11:2 (579,243) '*Stone Cross*' OD 200–300
25063, 28116

Cross (original location) Marked on all OS eds. Situated in flat rolling pasture-land. It is believed that it was removed in the 1930s and buried near a field boundary N of field in which it was originally located. According to local tradition, mass was formerly celebrated at the cross.

42:37 9-9-1986

1722 TOWNPARKS (Cavan Urban District)

OS 20:16:4 (693,49) Not marked OD 200–300
24187, 30463

Cross (site) Netherclift's plan of Cavan Town, (*c.* 1593) depicts a Latin cross mounted on a stepped base. Original location was at the junction of Main Street and Bridge Street. No visible remains at ground level. (Bradley and Dunne 1989, 40; O'Connell 1937, 300–1)

20:55(03) 19-11-1992

Caldraghs and Miscellaneous Burial Grounds

In County Cavan the term *caldragh* is applied to a burial place for those who could not be buried in consecrated ground, namely unbaptized babies, but also in some instances suicide cases, famine victims and foreigners or 'strangers' whose religion was not known at the time of their death. Elsewhere in Ireland they are known variously as *ceallúnach*, *calluragh*, *cillín* and *children's burial grounds*. Often they were sited within abandoned church sites or ringforts but in other instances they were unenclosed and in such cases the surface remains are usually scant. Individual burials were sometimes marked by low upright stones or low mounds of earth and stone. The practice dates back at least as far as early medieval times. It largely died out in the late 19th century but there are instances of their use as late as the 1960s.

Also included in this chapter are miscellaneous burial grounds and a burial mound at Aghnaskeagh (**1723**) which may date to the Early Christian period. None of the burial grounds, with the exception of Kilmore (**1738**), are within close proximity to known early church sites. Some, such as Lavey (**1739**) and Omard (**1743**) have been included solely on the basis of local tradition. It is likely that the Derryvony site (**1732**) was used as a burial place for those slain at a nearby battle in 1689. Drumcarn (**1734**) may have been a private burial ground. In the absence of archaeological excavation however, the majority must remain enigmatic in terms of precise dating and interpretation.

1723 AGHNASKEAGH
OS 42:2:5 (362,479) Not marked OD 200–300
24832, 28363

Burial mound An irregularly shaped mound of earth and stone within which large quantities of human skeletal remains were uncovered in 1992 during land reclamation works. The site was investigated by the National Museum and was tentatively dated to the Early Christian period (E. Kelly pers. comm.). Lying by the field boundary to the SW of the mound is a large boulder bearing a crude Latin cross.
42:46 21-3-1994

1724 CALDRAGH
OS 11:9:5 (121,184) Indicated OD 100–200
23569, 31881

Children's burial ground (possible) Known as 'The Relic Field' (local information) this is traditionally believed to be the site of an ancient burial ground. A number of bones are said to have been found at the Rag River, 210m W of the reputed burial ground. (ITA Survey 1941; Davies 1948, 94)
11:2 10-6-1989

1725 CARRICKATOBER
OS 32:2:6 (431,511) Not marked OD 400–500
24892, 29678

Graveyard (site) Tradition of a graveyard and holy well on the hill of Carrickatober which moved to the other side of the hill owing to the 'impiety' of the owner. A rock bearing two depressions, said to be the track of St Patrick's knees is believed to mark the site of the burial ground. Not visible at ground level. (Davies 1948, 81-2)
32:5(01) 14-4-1989

1726 CLONKEIFFY
OS 42:4:6 (911,529) Not marked OD 300–400
25411, 28422

Children's burial ground (site) Tradition of a children's burial ground at this location (local information). Situated on level pasture-land close to a stream. No visible remains at ground level. (Davies 1948, 80)
42:8 15-6-1987

1727 CORCASHEL (Tullygarvey By.)
OS 15:8:3 (847,381) Not marked OD 200–300
24341, 31456

Children's burial ground (site) Not marked on any OS ed. Situated in a hollow in rough stony ground surrounded by a number of low hillocks. Believed to be the site of a children's burial ground (local information). No visible remains at ground level.
15:14 15-9-1989

1728 CORNAKILL (Castlerahan By.)
OS 40:10:4 (234,223) Hachured OD 400–500
26644, 28750

Children's burial ground (site) Not marked on OS 1836 or 1876 eds. Situated on the SW shoulder of an area of high ground. Known locally as 'The Caldragh', this is believed to be the site of a children's burial ground (local information). No visible remains at ground level.
40:15 15-7-1987

1729 CORRARD
OS 5:2:3 (510,560) 'G. Yard' OD 214
20080, 31703

Graveyard According to Davies (1948, 98) this is an ancient graveyard, although nothing is known of its history. The enclosing wall appears to be relatively modern. Nonetheless there are many small stones protruding above the surface of the graveyard which presumably represent early grave-markers. Otherwise no visible remains.
5:24 16-8-1988

Plate 5a—*The abbey church, round tower and graveyard at Drumlane* (**1647**).

Plate 5b—*A multiple bullaun stone at Termon* (**1703**) *containing St Brigid's cursing stones.*

Plate 6—*A Romanesque doorway at Kilmore Upper* (**1668**), *originally from Trinity Island, Lough Oughter.*

1730 DAGGAN
OS 20:8:1 (745,422) Not marked OD 300–400
24238, 30858
Children's burial ground (site, possible) Known as 'The Caldragh Field' (local information). It is believed to be the site of a burial ground predating the graveyard at Cullies, 700m to SE. Situated adjacent to a large enclosure locally known as 'Shane's Fort' (**1731**). No visible remains at ground level.
20:81 10-8-1990

1731 DAGGAN
OS 20:8:1 (742,422) Indicated OD 400
24235, 30858
Burial ground (possible) A slightly raised, crescent-shaped area (int. dims. *c.* 71.6m NW–SE; *c.* 31m NE–SW) enclosed by a trench and low earthen bank which form part of the field boundary. Original entrance not recognisable. The site is known as 'Shane's Fort' and is believed to be the burial place of Shane O'Neill (local information). An earlier report (OPW 1969) speculated that the site may be a relatively modern landscape feature but noted that the field bordering the site from SE–S–WNW is known as 'The Caldragh' (**1730**).
20:11 10-8-1990

1732 DERRYVONY
OS 11:2:2 (367,575) '*Galloon Burial Ground*'
OD 100–200 23826, 32296
Burial ground Not marked on OS 1836 eds. Oval area (int. dims. 18m NW–SE; 8.4m NE–SW) enclosed by a narrow, shallow trench from SE–S–NW and elsewhere by a hedge. Apart from a number of small low stones protruding above the surface of the site, there are no visible remains. Known locally as 'Callaghan's Burial Ground' and is believed to have had a connection with the site of the Battle of Bloody Pass, *c.* 70m to NW (**1888**). Davies (1948, 94) suggested that it was more likely an early ecclesiastical site, the name of which has been forgotten.
11:16 11-6-1989

1733 DRUMBESS
OS 24:8:4 (712,360) '*Grave Yard* (disused)'
OD 400–500 23235, 30143
Graveyard (possible) Circular area (int. diam. 54m) enclosed by a well-built drystone wall which appears to have been erected on an earlier rampart. Original entrance not recognisable. A blocked-up holy well occurs inside the wall at NE (**1761**). Believed locally to be a famine graveyard. (Davies 1948, 98)
24:37(01) 22-8-1991

1734 DRUMCARN
OS 16:10:3 (388,279) Not marked OD 260–300
24832, 31352
Burial ground (site, possible) Marked on the OS 1912 ed. as a small subrectangular enclosure (dims. *c.* 22m NW–SE; *c.* 16m ENE–WSW). Known as the burial ground for Ballyhaise Castle (local information). However, given that Ballyhaise is situated almost 4km NE of Drumcarn House, this association of castle with burial ground seems unlikely. Site has been levelled.
16:47 27-10-1989

1735 EIGHTER
OS 43:1:3 (222,562) Not marked OD 400–500
25659, 28458
Children's burial ground (site, possible) Davies (1948, 115) recorded that this site is known as the 'Caldragh Field'. Situated in rolling pasture-land. No visible remains.
43:12 25-5-1987

1736 EONISH
OS 19:8:3 (880,398) Not marked OD 100–300
23406, 30825
Graveyard (possible) Large, slightly raised, roughly circular area (int. diam. *c.* 70.5m) enclosed by vague traces of a fosse and a much-levelled low earthen bank. Original entrance not recognisable. Not marked on any OS ed. Known locally as 'The Graveyard Field'. A holy well lies *c.* 30m to NE (**1763**).
19:30 14-7-1990

1737 KILDALLAN
OS 14:10:3 (452,254) '*The Relic Grave Yard*'
OD 300–400 22949, 31309
Graveyard Marked on all OS eds. Circular graveyard (int. dims. 35m NNW–SSE; 30.4m ENE–WSW) enclosed by a bank of earth and stone with modern external trench. The outer face of the bank has been modified and incorporated into the field boundary. Entrance at ESE through iron gate held on 18th-century octagonal stone gateposts, with stone walling on either side. The earliest identifiable gravestone dates to 1763. A cross-inscribed stone recorded by Davies (1948, 97) and reused as a headstone, may have originally functioned as the lintel of a doorway. (Patterson, Gaffikin and Davies, 1938, 146)
14:39 27-7-1989

1738 KILMORE UPPER
OS 25:2:2 (366,565) 'Grave Yd.' OD 306
23842, 30366
Graveyard Situated SSE of the old Cathedral (**1666**). Its chief pride is the tomb of William Bedell, the Protestant Bishop of Kilmore from 1629 to 1642, compiler of an Irish grammar and (in collaboration with three others) first translator of the Old Testament into the Irish language. There are, in addition, a considerable number of late 17th-century and 18th-century tombs and gravestones. (O'Connell 1937,

400–3, 428–9; Davies 1948, 99; Killanin and Duignan 1989, 102)
25:70(01) 16-5-1993

1739 LAVEY
OS 26:6:6 (456,346) Not marked OD 300–400
24915, 30144
Burial ground (possible) Traditionally known as an ancient graveyard associated with St Dabnet's Chapel (**1631**), 450m to NNE (local information). Situated in low-lying ground close to a stream. No visible remains at ground level.
26:65 18-3-1991

1740 LECKS
OS 23:16:6 (853,24) '*Killastueran Fort & Grave Yard*'
27282, 30465
Children's burial ground A rath (**848**) which appears to have been utilised as a burial ground. A number of low upright stones which are believed to mark the graves of unbaptized children (local information) occur on the bank and within the internal area.
23:30(03) 28-5-1992

1741 MARAHILL (Upper Loughtee By.)
OS 25:5:1 (19,431) '*Caldragh*' OD 200–300
23477, 30221
Children's burial ground Rectangular area (int. dims. 28m NNW–SSE; 15m WSW–ENE) enclosed by a slight bank of earth and stone except at NNW where it is bounded by a field bank with a modern external trench. A number of large boulders lie along the perimeter of the enclosure on three sides. Recorded by Davies (1948, 110).
25:93(01) 24-9-1991

1742 MOHER (ED Waterloo)
OS 32:4:2 (814,583) '*Grave Yard* (disused)'
OD 600–700 25297, 29758
Graveyard (site) Rectangular area (int. dims. 27m N–S; 28m E–W) enclosed by a bank of earth and stone and a stone wall. Within this are the foundations of two small buildings, neither likely to have been the site of a church. Davies (1948, 111) recorded that a coin dated 1573 was found in or near it.
32:40(01) 2-5-1989

1743 OMARD
OS 37:8:4 (762,317) Not marked OD 200–300
24275, 28828
Burial ground (site, possible) Large approximately oval-shaped raised area (dims. *c.* 60m E–W; *c.* 40m N–S) surrounded by marshland. Believed to be the site of an ancient burial ground (local information). Not visible at ground level.
37:63 18-7-1986

1744 TULLAGHYRORY
OS 5:15:2 (546,398) Indicated OD 100–200
20117, 31876
Burial ground (possible) Indicated on all OS eds. Situated on a low hill in rough mountainous terrain. At the location indicated, there is an approximately circular area (int. diam. *c.* 18m) defined by a series of boulders, which appears to be an entirely natural feature. However, there is a tradition of an ancient burial ground on the hill (local information).
5:39 17-8-1988

1745 URNEY (Clanmahon By.)
OS 25:14:6 (457,17) '*Caldragh* (Site of)'
OD 300–400 23943, 29788
Children's burial ground (site) Although this site has been levelled, the outline of the enclosing features are still visible from E–S–N, encompassing an almost circular area (diam *c.* 57.2m) which has been bisected by a field boundary running NE–SW. Davies (1948, 110) believed that it was probably the site of an old church (**1716**).
25:115(01) 21-9-1991

Holy Wells

The tradition of the veneration of spring wells has a long history in Ireland. Evans (1988, 298) has written that 'the attributes of purification, healing and fertility are natural concomitants of the magic swelling of spring water, but besides possessing supernatural powers of this kind the holy wells are regarded as having had miraculous origins'. The veneration of the holy wells at Knocknagartan (**1771**) may be a tradition dating from pre-Christian times. Most holy wells are dedicated to an individual saint, and annual *patterns* or *rounds* in his or her honour are held at some to this day. A number are located within or in close proximity to early church sites, such as Drumbess (**1761**), but most of the County Cavan examples are found in isolation. Bullaun stones have been found in association with a number of holy wells, such as that at Toberlyan Duffin (**1779**).

1746 CARNAGH LOWER
OS 37:1:4 (71,482) '*St Patrick's Well*' OD 200–300
23543, 28994
Holy well Small circular spring well (int. diam. *c.* 1m) enclosed from N–E–S by a much-disturbed drystone wall. An overflow channel occurs at W. A small bullaun stone (**1615**) is situated at the NW edge of the well. Patterns are still held annually here on March 17th (local information).
37:17(01) 10-7-1986

1747 CARRICKABOY GLEBE
OS 26:13:4 (10,30) 'Holy Wells' OD 600–700
24447, 29806
Holy wells Situated a short distance SW of Carrickaboy Glebe church (**1617**). Two holy wells marked on all OS eds. Davies (ITA Survey 1940) described them as two open springs on a hillside with 'a little walling at the back'. In recent years the wells have been amalgamated and are now used as a large watering-hole for cattle.
26:14(05) 24-10-1991

1748 CARRICKATOBER
OS 32:2:6 (431,511) 'St Patrick's Well' OD 400–500 24892, 29678
Holy well (site) Situated on the W slope of a steep rocky hill a short distance N of the site of a possible graveyard (**1725**). Well has been infilled and there are no remains visible at ground level. (Davies 1948, 81–2).
32:5(02) 14-4-1989

1749 CLOGHBALLYBEG
OS 40:13:6 (221,44) Indicated OD 300–400
26632, 28560
Holy well Indicated on all OS eds. but not acknowledged as an antiquity. Dedicated to St Killian (local information). The well is sited within a subrectangular enclosure defined by a stone and concrete wall which is rounded at E and open at W. A small stone cross inscribed with the date 1927 is set into the wall behind the well.
40:2 13-8-1987

1750 CORNASEER
OS 25:12:4 (700,179) Indicated OD 300–400
24198, 29961
Holy well (site) Known as the site of a holy well (local information). Davies (ITA Survey 1942) described 'a spring among rocks' at this location. This has since been covered with concrete.
25:26 1-11-1991

1751 CORRAN (Tullyhaw By.)
OS 13:4:5 (812,463) '*Tober Patrick*' OD 200–300
22352, 31525
Holy well Marked on all OS eds. Rectangular water-filled trench (L 6m; Wth 2.1m) aligned NW–SE (D 0.3m – 1.1m). There are a number of boulders and large stones in the vicinity of the well which function as stations (local information). Patterns are held here annually at the end of July (local information).
13:15 19-6-1989

1752 CORRATINNER
OS 33:15:3 (631,127) '*Tober Ultan*' OD 300–400
26083, 29284
Holy well (site) Small apparently circular well now grassed over. The 'Ultan' to whom the well is dedicated may be the 7th-century St Ultan of Ardbraccan, Co. Meath (O'Connell 1937, 39).
33:16 20-9-1988

1753 CORRAWILLIN
OS 26:7:1 (465,387) Indicated OD 300–400
24924, 30188
Holy well Situated in the bed of the river, adjacent to St Dabnet's chapel (**1631**). Deep oval-shaped hole (dims. 0.22m x 0.18m) which according to local tradition was formed by a horse's hoof (local information). One of the stations of the pilgrimage of St Dabnet.
26:22(03) 18-10-1991

1754 CROSSBANE
OS 40:1:5 (143,472) Not marked OD 500–600
26545, 29012
Holy well (site, possible) At Crossbane church and graveyard site (**1633**). Within the enclosure is the site

of an infilled well (local information). Possibly the site of a holy well.
40:21(02) 6-7-1987

1755 CURRAGHMORE
OS 39:2:4 (240,481) '*Toberpatrick*' OD 400–500
25672, 29014
Holy well Marked on all OS eds. Rectangular well (dims. 2m x 1m) enclosed by a stone wall. Stone steps lead down to the well from the adjacent roadway at S. Patterns are held here annually on March 17th (local information).
39:33 24-3-1987

1756 DEERPARK
OS 39:10:3 (457,264) '*Toberpatrick*' OD 300–400
25904, 28786
Holy well Marked on all OS eds. Roughly circular well (diam. *c.* 1m) enclosed by a stone wall and roofed by a single flat slab. The enclosing wall is absent at W. Patterns were formerly held annually at the well on March 17th (local information).
39:37 25-5-1987

1757 DERRINTINNY
OS 14:16:6 (898,26) '*Tobermogue*' OD 200–300
23422, 31073
Holy well (site) Marked on all OS eds. It has been infilled and there are no surface remains at ground level. Davies (1948, 95) recorded that 'it's name given on the OS has been locally forgotten'.
14:22 15-8-1989

1758 DERRYNALESTER
OS 3:14:6 (415,13) '*Tobermurvy*' OD 300–400
19969, 32948
Holy well Marked on all OS eds. Small subrectangular well (int. dims. 3.6m NE–SW; 2.8m NW–SE) of drystone masonry construction. Lintelled entrance at SW (H 1.1m; Wth 0.8m). At SE a series of stone steps lead down to the well. Patterns are held here annually on August 13th.
3:13 17-8-1988

1759 DRUMACLEESKIN
OS 16:2:3 (429,540) Not marked OD 400–500
24873, 31629

Fig. 46—*Tobermurvy holy well at Derrynalester* (**1758**).

Holy well At Drumacleeskin hilltop enclosure (**1462**). Just outside the fosse at E is a small circular unlined well dedicated to St Patrick (local information).
16:37(02) 25-9-1989

1760 DRUMBESS
OS 24:7:3 (617,421) *'Holy Well'* OD 300–400 23133, 30206
Holy well Spring well on the NW slope of a hill overgrown with furze and bracken. No artificial lining visible.
24:31 14-3-1977

1761 DRUMBESS
OS 24:8:4 (713,360) *'Holy Well'* OD 400–500 23235, 30143
Holy well (site) At Drumbess graveyard. Inside the perimeter at NE is a small circular area (int. diam. 1.2m) enclosed by a low drystone wall (H 0.2m). This represents the site of the well which has been blocked up.
24:37(03) 22-8-1991

1762 DRUMBO (Tullyhunco By.)
OS 19:3:2 (567,562) *'Tober Patrick'* OD 200 23073, 30995
Holy well Marked on all OS eds. Dense growth of vegetation precluded investigation of the site. Situated in low-lying ground adjacent to a stream.
19:20 15-7-1990

1763 EONISH
OS 19:8:3 (884,406) Not marked OD 200–300 23410, 30833
Holy well (site) Not marked on any OS ed. Known locally as 'St Patrick's Well' (local information). It has been levelled in. Situated in low-lying marshy ground on the shore of Lough Oughter. A large enclosure known as 'The Graveyard Field' is situated *c.* 30m SW of well (**1736**).
19:31 14-7-1990

1764 GALLONNAMBRAHER
OS 39:1:1 (18,541) *'Holy Well'* OD 500–600 25437, 29074
Holy well A small roughly circular spring well with remains of drystone facing. Situated at the foot of a hillock. A second holy well (**1765**) lies 80m to NNE.
39:51 17-10-1969

1765 GALLONNAMBRAHER
OS 39:1:1 (18,550) 'Holy Well (Site of)' OD 500–600 25437, 29084
Holy well (site) Marked 'Holy Well' on OS 1836 and 1876 eds. Situated at the foot of a hillock, *c.* 80m SSW of another holy well which survives intact (**1764**). Davies (1948, 113) noted that the site was known as the 'Friars's Well' and adjoining it the 'Friar's Orchard'.
39:52 17-10-1969

1766 KEADEW (Cavan Rural and Urban)
OS 20:12:1 (694,229) *'Friars Well'* OD 100–200 24186, 30654
Holy well Site has been infilled. An earlier report (OPW 1968) described a small stagnant pool of water, irregular in plan. Two large stones were identified in the water to one side. Davies (1948, 118) speculated that this place may have afforded refuge for a band of friars following the Dissolution (**1656**).
20:50(01) 22-8-1990

1767 KILLAN
OS 28:7:1 (494,420) *'St Anne's Well* (Site of)' OD 400–500 26906, 30240
Holy well (site) Marked on all OS eds. Situated in low-lying ground near a stream. No visible remains at ground level. Killan church lies 400m to SW (**1659**).
28:28 30-8-1988

1768 KILLETER
OS 40:10:6 (434,167) Not marked OD 400–500 26856, 28692
Holy well Circular well (diam. *c.* 1m) enclosed by a stone wall except at SW where there is an overflow channel. Known as 'St Patrick's Well', patterns were held here up until the mid-1970s (local information).
40:33 14-7-1987

1769 KILMORE UPPER
OS 25:2:2 (371,546) *'St Felimys Well'* OD 200–300 23848, 30345
Holy well Situated in the side of a hillslope, S of the modern Church of Ireland cathedral. Dedicated to St Feidhlimidh. The well is circular and is covered by an L-shaped stone structure. Three stone steps lead down to it. Davies (ITA Survey 1942) speculated that it may be 17th or 18th century in date. (O'Connell 1937, 35; Killanin and Duignan 1989, 102)
25:72 12-9-1991

1770 KILNACROSS (Tullyhunco By.)
OS 14:7:5 (562,315) *'Tobermogue'* OD 300–400 23065, 31375
Holy well Marked on all OS eds. Situated in wet low-lying ground. Large irregular pool now used as a watering-hole for cattle.
14:46 24-7-1989

Fig. 47—*Holy well dedicated to St Feidhlimidh at Kilmore Upper* (**1769**).

1771 KNOCKNAGARTAN
OS 43:3:3 (630,571) '*St Patrick's Wells*' OD 300–400 26090, 28472

Holy wells Marked on all OS eds. The NW well is a small subrectangular spring well, open at SE and lined on three sides with stone and on the fourth with natural rock. A second well lies 10m to SE. This is a large, shallow pool faced with drystone masonry and natural rock. A nearby outcrop called Carraig Crom may refer to the mythological pre-Christian idol Crom Cruaich (local information).
43:23(01) 19-6-1987

1772 KNOCKNASHAMMER
OS 22:15:2 (580,92) '*Holy Well*' OD 500–600 26018, 30526

Holy well Marked on all OS eds. It has been concreted over and a manhole cover placed on top. It was circular (diam *c.* 4m) and was lined with a drystone wall (local information).
22:29 25-10-1990

1773 MULLAGHLEA
OS 9:6:3 (444,444) '*Toberpatrick*' OD 200–300 21958, 32141

Holy well Marked on all OS eds. Small circular well (int. diam. 0.9m) on the N shore of Lakefield Lough. Used as a place of pilgrimage up until the 1890s (local information).
9:17 19-9-1988

1774 MURMOD
OS 39:7:2 (606,435) '*Toberfin*' OD 600–700 26059, 28968

Holy well (site) Marked on all OS eds. Situated on the NE slope of a steep hill. The well has been infilled and there are no visible remains at ground level.
39:70 16-10-1969

1775 RAFFONY
OS 39:8:2 (816,394) Indicated OD 400–500 26282, 28927

Holy well Situated *c.* 55m ENE of the foundations of Raffony church and outside of the original perimeter of the ecclesiastical establishment (**1695**). The well is semicircular and is enclosed by a drystone wall and roofed by two flat slabs. Entrance is at S where there is a semicircular stone-built area which appears to be some sort of forecourt. Three apparently modern cross-inscribed stones lie on the roof.
39:71(03) 9-6-1987

1776 RAHEEVER
OS 42:11:3 (645,234) *'St Patrick's Well'* OD 200–300 25133, 28108

Holy well Small semicircular stone-built well (diam. *c.* 1m) partially covered by a large flat slab. Patterns were formerly held here annually on March 17th but the practice has died out (local information). (Davies 1948, 97)
42:41 9-9-1986

1777 ROGARY
OS 15:9:4 (56,169) *'Holy Well'* OD 100–200 23507, 31225

Holy well Marked on all OS eds. This now infilled well, dedicated to St Mogue, apparently comprised a roughly circular unlined spring (diam. 2m). A largely grassed-over, horseshoe-shaped mound of loose stones is situated nearby.
15:66 15-9-1989

1778 TERMON (Tullyhaw By.)
OS 2:9:4 (75,188) *'Toberbride'* OD 100–200 20578, 33779

Holy well Marked on all OS eds. Circular well (diam. *c.* 4m) enclosed by a low drystone wall which has been infilled. Situated *c.* 110m WSW of Killinagh church (**1702**).
2:17 10-7-1988

1779 TOBERLYAN DUFFIN
OS 13:8:6 (881,366) 'Toberlyan' OD 100–200 22426, 31423

Holy well Marked on all OS eds. A wall was erected around the well in the early 1980s. Prior to this, it was surrounded by a number of boulders which served as penitential stations. Six of these are visible close to the field boundary, *c.* 60m to SSW (**1707**).
13:63(01) 10-6-1989

Moated Sites

Moated sites are a form of medieval settlement commonly found in those areas once controlled by the Normans and Anglo-Normans in north-western Europe, including Britain and parts of the south and east of Ireland. Essentially, they were isolated, well-defended farmsteads. A typical moated site comprises a rectangular area enclosed by a wide, water-filled moat or fosse with internal bank. The main defensive element was the moat, but in addition, a wooden palisade would have been constructed on the bank. Six of the estimated 750 moated sites identified to date in Ireland have been excavated and all six have yielded evidence for 13th and 14th-century habitation.

1780 CARRICKABANE (ED Kilgolagh)
OS 41:2:6 (441,487) Hachured OD 413
23940, 28364

Moated site Raised subrectangular area (int. dims. *c.* 65m NW–SE; *c.* 40m NE–SW) enclosed by a substantial inner bank, a wide, deep, partly waterlogged intermediate fosse and a partially surviving outer bank. Outer fosse is best preserved at S but its outline may be traced throughout its course. An earlier report (OPW 1974) noted that the NE and SE corners of the outer bank and the NW and SW corners of the inner bank are raised. Break in inner bank (but without any trace of accompanying causeway) midway along the W side probably represents original entrance.
41:7 30-6-1986

1781 INISHMORE
OS 15:14:5 (346,4) Not marked OD 100–200
23815, 31054

Moated site (site, possible) Marked 'Fort' and depicted as a rectangular enclosure on OS 1836 and 1876 eds. Situated on the shore of Carrafin Lough. Although site has been levelled, its outline may still be traced (int. dims. 48.3m E-W; 43.3m N–S). The perimeter has been incorporated into the field boundary at N. Elsewhere it is identifiable as a wide, shallow depression, best preserved at S (Wth 7.6m; D 0.2m).
15:46 28-4-1993

1782 LISNADARRAGH (Clanmahon By.)
OS 41:2:6 (411,485) Not marked OD 300–400
23908, 28361

Moated site (site, possible) Depicted as a rectangular enclosure with the designation 'Fort' on OS 1836 and 1876 eds. Site has been levelled. Its rectangular outline (ext. dims. 32m x 26.5m) was just about traceable when recorded by Davies (1948, 109). There are now no visible remains at ground level.
41:14 30-6-1986

1783 SWELLAN LOWER
OS 25:3:3 (626,553) Indicated OD 200–300
24117, 30355

Moated site Marked 'Fort' on the OS 1836 and 1876 eds. Raised rectangular area (int. dims. 44.9m N–S; 24.9m E–W) enclosed by a well-preserved inner earthen bank, a wide, deep fosse and a low external earthen bank. Outer bank and fosse absent on E side. Outer bank levelled at NNW but its outline is still clearly identifiable. Break in banks with accompanying causeway at N probably represents original entrance.
25:110 2-10-1991

Rectangular Enclosures

This chapter accounts for sites which are rectangular in plan, but which lack the necessary evidence to be classified as moated sites. The Monnery Upper site (**1786**) is almost certainly an antiquity but the remaining sites may be of relatively recent origin.

1784 FARTAN LOWER
OS 21:5:1 (59,406) Hachured OD 300–400
24489, 30843
Rectangular enclosure Situated on a natural terrace on the slope of a high hill. The ground falls steeply to a stream 20m to W. Trapezium-shaped area (int. dims. *c.* 28m N–S x 27.5m across its broader S side) enclosed by the remains of a bank and fosse on its W side and elsewhere by a low earthen bank and a well-defined, partly waterlogged fosse. Original entrance not recognisable.
21:39 19-9-1992

1785 GLASLECK
OS 28:3:3 (664,540) Indicated OD 300–400
27083, 30369
Rectangular enclosure Marked on all OS eds. Situated in the centre of a promontory jutting into Milltown Lough, *c.* 30m SE of a possible promontory fort (**185**). An approximately rectangular area (int. dims. 72m NW–SE; 24m NE–SW) enclosed by a low earthen bank. Outside the bank at NW is a slight depression which may represent the site of a fosse.
28:22 2-9-1988

1786 MONNERY UPPER
OS 25:5:3 (201,422) Indicated OD 200–300
23669, 30213
Rectangular enclosure Marked 'Fort' on OS 1836 and 1876 eds. A raised, approximately rectangular area (int. dims. 18.1m NW–SE; 18.3m SW–SE) enclosed by a much-denuded earthen bank, which only rises above the interior at NW, and a fosse. NW corner is ill-defined. Original entrance not recognisable.
25:97 24-9-1991

Medieval Earthwork Castles

Prior to the Anglo-Norman invasion of Ireland in the late 12th century, just seven 'castles' are recorded in contemporary literature, none of which have survived. One of the reasons for the success of the Anglo-Norman campaign was that they speedily erected formidable fortresses at strategic locations in order to consolidate the lands that they had conquered.

Early earthen fortresses assumed two basic forms — the motte and the ringwork castle.

A motte is a generally circular, high, steep-sided, flat-topped earthen mound. A wooden tower would have been constructed on the summit and defended by a wooden stockade. A bailey often accompanies the motte, separated from it by a fosse or moat. A typical bailey comprises a low, usually rectangular, earthen platform upon which stood dwellings for the knight's retinue and shelters for animals. The bailey too would have been protected by a stockade. Motte and bailey were usually encircled by a moat or fosse. Stockades, towers, dwellings and outhouses were timber-built structures and consequently have not survived above ground level.

In essence a ringwork castle comprises a raised, often circular area enclosed by a bank of earth and stone, upon which a substantial palisade would have been constructed, and an external ditch. Entrance to the area thus enclosed would have been through a strong gate-tower. A strong wooden tower would have stood within the enclosure. As the tower, gate-tower and palisade were timber-built they do not survive above ground level. Ringwork castles are difficult to identify as their surface remains are often similar to those of raised ringforts.

Both the motte and ringwork castle gradually became obsolete from the early decades of the 13th century.

Fig. 48—*Ringwork at Castlerahan* (**1787**) *(Reproduced courtesy of Cambridge University Committee for Aerial Photography).*

1787 CASTLERAHAN
OS 38:16:3 (860,127) Hachured OD 484
25355, 28636

Ringwork Situated on the summit of a high drumlin hill. Adjacent to the site at SW are the remains of an 18th-century church, thought to have been built on or close to the site of a medieval church (**1620, 1621**). Raised subrectangular platform (H *c.* 4m; int. dims. *c.* 42m NE–SW; *c.* 24m N–S) enclosed by two very substantial banks of earth and stone with wide, deep intermediate fosse. Foundations of a rectangular building (int. dims. *c.* 11m NE–SW; *c.* 7m NW–SE) lie within the enclosed area in SW quadrant and those of a circular structure (int. diam. *c.* 6.5m) which Davies (1947, 88) postulated was a gatehouse, occur at NE. At SW he identified the foundations of a second approximately circular structure (diam. *c.* 11m) which he interpreted as the remains of a tower. (CUCAP AYS 34, AYS 35, AYS 36)
38:8(01) 20-5-1993

1788 KILMORE UPPER
OS 25:2:2 (354,554) Hachured OD 278
23830, 30354

Motte and bailey Built by de Lacy in 1211 and dismantled in 1224–6 by Cathal O'Reilly. A very substantial motte with exceptionally well-preserved bailey enclosed by a well-defined fosse and substantial earthen bank. Both have been levelled from NE–ENE–E. Motte consists of a high (H *c.* 8m), steep-sided, flat-topped subcircular mound (dims. at base *c.* 48m NNW–SSE; *c.* 45m WNW–ESE). The summit is oval in plan (dims *c.* 26m NE–SW; *c.* 18m NW–SE). A wide, deep fosse runs between the motte and bailey at NNW. Bailey is crescentic in plan. Site has been planted with deciduous trees and a number of relatively modern garden demesne features have been incorporated into its fabric. These include an icehouse built into the N of the bailey, a stone passageway built through the outer bank of the bailey at NNW, a low concave stone wall built into the base of the motte at SE and a demesne wall set against the outer bank at S. (Henry 1987, 9; Davies 1947, 79–81)
25:69 12-9-1991

1789 KNOCKATEMPLE
OS 39:14:6 (403,63) '*Castle* (in Ruins) *Moat*'
OD 200–300 25848, 28573

Motte and bailey Situated on a small promontory jutting into Lough Ramor and cut off from the mainland by a substantial external bank and wide, deep fosse curving from NE–E–SE. The motte is situated in the SE of the enclosed area. It comprises a high, steep-sided flat-topped circular earthen mound (diam. at base *c.* 28m; H 4–5m). The summit of the mound is also circular (diam. *c.* 12m N–S). A shallow fosse to the NE of the motte separates it from the bailey which itself comprises two courts separated by a low stone wall. The outer court adjoins a rectangular depression which may have been a slipway for boats. No trace of any buildings within bailey. (Davies, 1947,78)
39:55 27-5-1987

1790 LAVAGH
OS 37:16:3 (903,126) Hachured OD 300–400
24426, 28627

Motte Situated within a tree plantation. Motte is a high, very steep-sided, circular mound (diam. at base *c.* 28m; H *c.* 3.5m) with a flat-topped summit (diam. *c.* 22m N-S). It is enclosed by a fosse which is wide and deep from NW–N–ENE and identifiable only as slight traces from ENE–E–ESE. Site is skirted by a modern laneway from SSE–S–W. An earlier report (OPW 1970) described a segment of mortared masonry built against the counterscarp at NW which may have formed part of a bridge connecting the site with 'Holywell House' *c.* 25m to ENE.
37:42 1-8-1986

1791 MOAT
OS 41:4:1 (745,560) Hachured OD 200–300
24260, 28443

Motte (possible) Circular mound (diam. at base *c.* 28m) enclosed by a fosse. Mound is high (H 3–4m), steep-sided and flat-topped (diam. of summit 19.7m N–S). Fosse is best preserved from N–E–SE. Original entrance not recognisable. On the summit at SE there is an approximately circular round-bottomed depression (diam. 6.2m; D 0.3m) of unknown significance.
41:18 30-7-1986

1792 RACRAVEEN
OS 38:15:1 (470,142) Hachured OD 200–300
24944, 28648

Motte and bailey Situated at a bend in a wide river which encircles the NE half of the site. Elsewhere enclosed by a wide, shallow fosse now identifiable only from SE–S–WNW. The motte comprises a high, steep-sided, flat-topped oval earthen mound (H 3m – 5.75m; dims. at base *c.* 38m NW–SE; *c.* 27m NE–SW), the summit of which (int. dims. 32.4m NW–SE; 23.3m NE–SW) is enclosed by the remains of a low earthen bank. Foundations of a rectangular stone building (int. dims. *c.* 8m E–W; *c.* 6m N–S) occur on the summit. Break in bank with accompanying causeway at SW represents original entrance. Traces of possible rectangular bailey to SW. Davies (1947, 87) speculated that this may be the location of a Nugent castle noted in historical documents.
38:55 19-5-1993

1793 RELAGH BEG
OS 34:15:4 (480,40) '*Moat*' OD 667
26900, 29199

Motte and bailey Motte comprises a roughly circular (diam. at base *c.* 30m), high (H *c.* 5m), very steep-sided mound, the W portion of which has been quarried away. The summit of the mound was originally flat-topped (diam *c.* 12m). A fosse which runs between the motte and bailey at E is almost completely infilled. Bailey is approximately rectangular in plan (int. dims. *c.* 35m N–S; *c.* 20m E–W) and is enclosed by a substantial earthen bank with external fosse which has been infilled at N. A low counterscarp bank skirts the outer lip of the fosse. Moybolgue Church is situated 100m to SE (**1698**).
34:45 28-5-1994

1794 STRAHEGLIN
OS 11:13:5 (148,3) '*Castle & Fort* (Site of)' OD 100–200 23600, 31690

Motte and bailey Strategically situated on Turbet Island, an important fording point on the River Erne, close to the boundary between the medieval kingdoms of East Breifne and Fermanagh. Constructed in 1210/11 by John Grey, King John's Justiciar. It was one of seven fortifications erected to isolate Ulster (in native Irish control) from Connacht. The campaign was short-lived as the Irish under Aedh O'Neill threw back the invaders. Davies (1947, 82) believed that the Turbet Island motte and bailey had probably been abandoned by 1213. Motte comprises a high, steep-sided earthen mound, oval in plan (dims. at base 47.5m WNW–ESE; 34m ENE–WSW) and basically conoid in profile (H 5.5m). At its highest point, at ESE, there are foundations of a small, subcircular, mortared stone structure (int. dims. 2.05m x 2.9m). Davies (*ibid.*, 81) interpreted this as the remains of a tower and speculated that it may be 16th-century in date. At the centre of the summit of the mound there is a deep, precipitous depression (Wth 9m; D 3.6m) aligned NNE–SSW which separates the highest ESE part of the motte from a crescent-shaped area (max. dims. 8.4m NW–SE; 6.2m NE–SW) set at a lower level at WNW. A narrow fosse separates motte from bailey at SSW. Bailey is a raised subrectangular area (dims. 38.8m NNE–SSW; 38m WNW–ESE) covering some 1278 square meters and enclosed by an earthen bank, traces of which are identifiable at SSW. Three low earthen mounds (dims. 1.2m, 2m and 3.2m respectively) of unknown significance also occur at SSW, close to the perimeter of the bailey. A wide, deep fosse running from NNW–W–ENE effectively isolates motte and bailey from the island. Shoreline of island has been scarped at ESE and WNW.
11:13(02) 16-7-1989

1795 TANDERAGEE
OS 34:6:2 (356,437) Hachured OD 500–600 26765, 29617

Motte A substantial motte enclosed by a wide, deep, partly waterlogged fosse. Motte comprises a roughly circular, high and steep-sided mound (diam. at base *c.* 23m) divided into two unequal portions by a field boundary running NNW–SSE. The roughly circular summit (diam *c.* 10m N–S) is uneven, containing a number of large depressions.
34:49 4-5-1988

Fig. 49—*Motte at Tanderagee* (**1795**).

Medieval Stone Fortresses

The earliest Anglo-Norman stone castles in Ireland date from the late 12th century. Clogh Oughter castle in Lough Oughter is the only definite example from County Cavan. This circular keep, which was excavated by Conleth Manning for the Office of Public Works in 1987, was constructed in the early 13th century and continued in use at least until the 17th century. The ruined remains of the castle on Port Island (**1850**) has some features in common with Clogh Oughter, such as its island location and circular plan. In 1947 Davies observed possible evidence for a first-floor doorway entrance to Port Castle, a feature which is considered characteristic of early castles. On this basis, Port has been included here as a possible early stone castle of the Medieval period.

Fig. 50—*Clogh Oughter Castle* (**1796**), *an Anglo-Norman fortress in Lough Oughter (Reproduced courtesy of Cambridge University Committee for Aerial Photography).*

1796 INISHCONNELL
OS 20:5:5 (121, 357) '*Clogh Oughter Castle*' (in Ruins) OD 161 23580, 30784

Anglo-Norman castle The remains of a circular tower (int. diam 10.55m; H 18.35m; wall T 2.5m) standing on a rocky man-made island in a locally shallow spot in Lough Oughter, 120m from the S shore at Inishconnell. Probably built by the de Lacys in the early 13th century but fell into the hands of the O'Reillys soon after. Made a royal castle as part of the Plantation of Ulster 1608–9 and recaptured by the O'Reillys in 1641. Almost one third of the tower on the S side is missing from top to base as a result of slighting with explosives after the Cromwellian siege of 1653. There are two thirteenth-century embrasures with narrow loops at ground-floor level and the remains of a later doorway. The beam sockets from the original wooden first floor are visible and there is evidence for three doors at first floor level, the main entrance and access to a wall-walk on the curtain wall and an attached turret. There were also at least two windows at this level. The upper part of the tower has just two surviving windows, both of 17th-century date. Excavation in 1987 revealed a mortar surface on the ground floor and the remains of a late cross-wall with a fireplace and connecting doorway at this level. (Manning 1989–90)
20:60

1850 PORT (ED Esky)
OS 1:8:4 (764,309) 'Port Island' OD 100–200 20329, 33904

Early castle Situated on a small rocky island in Lough Macnean, *c.* 500m from the Co. Cavan shoreline and close to the border between counties Cavan and Fermanagh. Possibly the castle of 'Inis-Ochta' where Melaghlin Mac Rannall was imprisoned by Con O'Rourke in 1499 (*AFM*). Davies (1947, 83) recorded the foundations of a circular tower (int. diam. 6.8m) comprising a wall of ashlar and mortar (Wth 1.37m) surviving to a height of 1.8m and having a marked batter. He noted 'three deep recesses with loopholes' and speculated that the doorway must have been on the first floor. He also recorded a number of small rectangular stone structures of uncertain age on the island including one on the W side of the tower which was not bonded into the masonry of the main structure. Island is densely overgrown with vegetation rendering inspection impossible. Not visited.
1:6

Sites of Castles and Bawns

This chapter describes the sites of castles and bawns identified from maps and historical sources and noted in local tradition, and of which there are now little or no extant remains.

1797 AGHABANE
OS 19:6:3 (408,410) Not marked OD 200–300
22907, 30833
Castle (site, possible) Davies (1948, 124) recorded a tradition of a castle formerly situated on the lawn of Aghabane House on the downward slope to Aghabane lake. Not visible at ground level.
19:1 6-7-1990

1798 ANNAGH (Tullyhaw By.)
OS 10:10:4 (265,176) 'Ballyconnell House' OD 100–200 22746, 31865
Castle (site) Captain Culme and Walter Talbot were granted 1500 acres in this area during the reign of James I. According to Pynnar's survey of 1619 there was a strong three-storey castle and a bawn with two flanking towers here. This castle was entirely destroyed by accidental fire and a house built on its site by G. Mountgomery Esq, in 1764. (Lewis 1837,vol. 1, 130)
10:1 6-10-1988

1799 ASHGROVE
OS 15:10:1 (285,265) 'Ashgrove' OD 200–250
23748, 31328
Castle (possible) The current house at Ashgrove is an 18th-century structure. However, Davies (1948, 113) recorded that this house stands on massive foundations and vaults, which he believed, belonged to an earlier 17th-century castle. In addition, he identified portion of what may have been the former bawn wall at S (T *c.* 0.6m), 'built with a row of arched recesses flanked by engaged masonry-columns', W of house.
15:6 12-8-1989

1800 BALLAGHANEA
OS 39:16:1 (700,122) Not marked OD 277
26162, 28639
Castle (site, possible) An island stronghold in Lough Ramor is mentioned in the annals as early as 846 AD. Local tradition identifies this with Ballaghanea Island which can be reached from the land by a ford. No evidence for a later castle. The walls and quays presently identifiable on the island suggest an occupation no earlier than the 19th century. (Davies 1947, 76)
39:8 5–6-1987

1801 BAWN (Tullyhunco By.)
OS 19:11:1 (482,284) Not marked OD 200–300
22986, 30701
Castle (site) A turreted house and bawn, possibly in Scottish baronial style, was supposedly built here in the post-Plantation period by Sir Claude Hamilton. No visible remains at ground level. (Davies 1948, 123–24)
19:6 10-7-1990

1802 BELLANACARGY
OS 16:14:5 (344,46) Not marked OD 100–200
24788, 31107
Castle (site) An O'Reilly castle built in the 16th century, reoccupied in the 17th century and according to legend finally destroyed by Cromwell (ITA Survey 1942). Also known as Castle Carrick, it was formerly situated on a low plateau of rock on S bank of Annalee River. A keep once stood here on a mound (H 1.8m) and was surrounded by a roughly rectangular bawn (53m x 32m) with projecting towers at SE and SW corners on landward side. Rock-cut fosses featured on its E (Wth *c.* 4.2m) and W (Wth *c.* 5.1m) sides and a narrower and more shallow fosse on S side, where entrance is likely to have been. Bawn rose *c.* 1.6m above fosses and level of river. No visible remains at ground level. (Davies 1947, 99–100)
16:6 17-9-1989

1803 BELLVILLE
OS 25:10:5 (376,193) Not marked OD 200–300
23857, 29973
Bawn (site) Possible plantation bawn on Fleming's estate. Remains comprise a low, subrectangular, earthen platform (dims. *c.* 53m NW–SW; 38m NE–SW) with apparently rounded corners, extending W from the present early 18th-century house. The site has been levelled and the surface remains are difficult to distinguish. (ITA Survey 1941; Davies 1948, 94)
25:6(01) 19-9-1991

1804 BOAGH
OS 18:13:5 (89,16) Not marked OD 300–400
26470, 31090
Castle (site, possible) Marked 'Bell Green' and depicted as a large estate house on OS 1836 ed. Davies (1948, 117) recorded ruins known as 'Bruncott's Castle' here and suggested that this may be the site of a plantation castle built by James Archibald. No visible remains at ground level.
18:2 15-7-1990

1805 CABRA
OS 35:3:1 (515,535) '*Castle* (in ruins)' OD 200–300
27907, 29731
Castle (site) Extant remains comprise the ruins of portion of a four-storey house of late 18th or early

19th-century date, incorporating 17th-century stonework in NE angle, especially in lower courses. This may have been the site of a castle built by Captain Gerald Fleming in 1607 and lost during the Williamite wars. Depicted on Petty's Down Survey (*c.* 1656) as a large castle accompanied by a small building, perhaps a mill, on the bank of the river. No visible remains of mill building.
35:11 20-5-1993

1806 CASTLEPOLES
OS 30:3:2 (542,554) Not marked 23062, 29705
Castle (site) A bawn wall of the Plantation period, constructed of stone and clay, was according to Davies, (1948, 124–5) situated on an old road a little below the summit of Castlepoles hill. However, local tradition identifies the site of the castle as being *c.* 110m WSW of this (local information). No visible remains at either location.
30:4 4-10-1991

1807 CASTLESAUNDERSON DEMESNE
OS 11:12:1 (706,284) 'Castle Saunderson' OD 200–300 24187, 31992
Castle (site) Captain Alexander Saunderson reputedly built a house of lime and stone and a bawn accompanied by two flankers, at this site. It was destroyed during the Williamite wars. The present 'Castle Saunderson' is a composite structure dating to the late 18th, 19th and early 20th centuries. (Hill 1872, 54–9; Saunderson 1936, 11–12).
11:4 16-6-1989

1808 CLOGHBALLYBEG
OS 40:14:5 (327,51) '*Castle* (Site of)' OD 398 26744, 28569
Castle (site) Situated on a slight rise on W shore of Mullagh Lough. An O'Reilly castle built in 1485, granted to King James in 1605 and subsequently repaired as the manor house of Sir William Taaffe's plantation estate. It was abandoned during the Cromwellian period. No visible remains at ground level. (Davies 1947, 98–9)
40:5 13-8-1987

1809 CLOONE
OS 36:3:1 (494,601) Indicated OD 200–300 23013, 29116
Castle (site, possible) Marked 'Cloone House' on OS 1836 and 1876 eds. A late 18th/early 19th-century house which is believed to have been built on the site of a castle (local information). No visible remains of this earlier structure.
36:1 15-5-1993

1810 CORDOAGH (ED Enniskeen)
OS 35:5:2 (104,411) '*Castle* (Site of)' OD 400–500 27475, 29596
Castle (site) Erected by Conor O'Reilly in the 15th century. Apparently abandoned after the Plantation. Although there are now no convincing visible remains at ground level, an earlier account (Davies 1947, 100) described what may have been the remains of three walls of a bawn enclosing an irregular rectangle 58m by 43.8m. The wall on NW side, which is likely to have housed the entrance, may have been removed during road construction. Local tradition associates this site with the 'Fair Green' at Muff (**1894**).
35:16 10-6-1988

1811 CORGREAGH (Lower Loughtee By.)
OS 10:12:6 (920,218) '*Castle Bagshaw* (Site of)' OD 200–300 23438, 31916
Castle (site) Built by Sir Hugh Wirrall in 1618, subsequently occupied by Edward Bagshaw and thereafter by Thomas Richardson. An earlier account (Davies 1948, 114) noted the survival of just one corner of a building which appeared to have been constructed within a hilltop rath (**390**) as evidenced on the various OS eds. However this location is at variance with local tradition which places the site of the castle *c.* 40m ENE of the rath. No visible remains at ground level.
10:8 10-10-1988

1812 CORLAT
OS 40:11:1 (472,253) Not marked OD 300–400 26895, 28784
Castle (site) Marked 'Site of Old Castle' on OS 1836 ed. Not marked on subsequent eds. Situated on a slight natural rise close to a river which forms part of the Cavan/Meath border. Davies (1948, 105–6) speculated that the castle probably belonged to Sir John Elliott who was assigned the estate of Kilcronehan under the Plantation. No visible remains at ground level.
40:9 9-7-1987

1813 CORRANEARY (ED Corraneary)
OS 23:13:2 (95,144) Not marked OD 400–500 26480, 30585
Castle (site) John Hamilton was granted this estate in 1613 and on it built a castle and bawn and a nearby enclosure. Also known as 'Hansborough'. No visible remains at ground level. (Davies 1948, 107–8)
23:12 21-5-1992

1814 CROCKNAHATTIN
OS 28:13:6 (218,25) 'Bailieborough Castle' OD 400–500 26617, 29821
Castle (site, possible) A castle and bawn was apparently erected in the mid-17th century by William Baillie, a Cromwellian planter, on or near the site of

Crocknahattin House, about a mile from the town of Bailieborough. Crocknahattin House is not marked on any OS ed. and was not located. An earlier account recorded the site as being situated at the end of a promontory formed by a loop of the Bailieborough River. (Davies 1948, 108)
28:9 14–9–1988

1815 DOON (ED Ballyconnell)
OS 10:9:6 (225,193) Not marked OD 200–300
22704, 31883
Castle (site, possible) Henry (1987, 23) writing in 1739 recorded a redoubt at Ballyconnell, the location of which has been tentatively identified with that of the Church of Ireland chapel in the village (Davies 1948, 96). The present church (erected *c.* 1800) is situated on a mound (diam *c.* 36.5m) which Davies (*ibid.*) suggested was artificial. He described it as being quite steep at N and W (H 3.9m) where the ground falls away to a stream. He noted a slight re-entrant at SW and claimed that a fosse was traceable as far as E wall of graveyard. However, his interpretation of the mound as artificial is questionable as there are a number of natural mounds of similar appearance in the immediate locality.
10:12(01) 6-10-1989

1816 DRUMCARN
OS 16:10:3 (402,285) Not marked OD 200–300
24846, 31359
Castle (site) Marked on Petty's Down Survey map of 1685 and recorded as being part of the lands of one Hugh Brady at that time. Foundations of a house, reputedly built by the Saundcrsons, marked on 1836 ed. Described (ITA Survey 1945) as comprising 'fragments of mortared walls' situated in a hollow. Site now largely covered by modern farmyard, leaving no visible remains at ground level. (Davies 1948, 120)
16:48 27-10-1989

1817 DRUMCROW (ED Ballyhaise)
OS 16:13:2 (77,98) Not marked OD 100–200
24506, 31159
Castle (site, possible) A castle was apparently erected by John Taylor at Ballyhaise *c.* 1610, on the instruction of the Lord Deputy. Although there are now no visible remains of this structure, an earlier report (Davies 1948, 111–12) described it as a 'timber house' probably built on the site of the present Ballyhaise House, which itself was partly constructed in 1705. It is situated on a gentle slope commanding a view of the Annalee River and a ford upon which a bridge was built in the early 18th century.
16:52 15–10–1989

1818 DRUMHOME
OS 16:13:1 (22,111) Not marked OD 100–200
24447, 31171
Castle (site) Possibly an O'Reilly castle which was destroyed before the second half of the 16th century (1947, 91). An earlier account (*ibid.*) described the remains of an enclosure (diam. *c.* 50.2m) comprising traces of a semicircular bank (H 1.5m) accompanied externally by a platform, perhaps representing the site of a fosse and outer bank. A modern field boundary and laneway cut through the site making identification of its features very difficult.
16:53 15-10-1989

1819 DRUMMAN
OS 17:11:4 (532,209) Not marked OD 200–300
26164, 30770
Castle (site, possible) Marked as a tower on Petty's Down Survey map of 1654. Reputedly built by Coote, it apparently stood on an artificial platform beside a stream. No visible remains at ground level. (Davies 1948, 118-9)
17:32 22-9-1990

1820 DRUMSHEIL
OS 17:9:2 (97,252) Not marked OD 300
25746, 31236
Bawn (site, possible) A bawn of clay and stones was apparently erected here during the Plantation period. The hill upon which it was situated is called 'Castle Hill', and a nearby field 'Piers Field' reputedly derives its name from massive walls with stone gateposts which formerly surrounded it. No visible remains at ground level. (Davies 1948, 116–7)
17:38 16-11-1989

1821 DRUMSHEIL
OS 17:9:2 (109,244) Not marked OD 200–300
25751, 31216
Bawn (site, possible) A bawn of sods was possibly erected at this location during the Plantation period. Water was apparently drawn from the nearby White Lough to fill its fosses. No visible remains at ground level. (Davies 1948, 116–7)
17:39 16-11-1989

1822 DUFFCASTLE
OS 32:14:2 (308,93) Not marked OD 400–500
24767, 29235
Bawn (site, possible) Marked 'Bawn' on OS Fair Plan and 'Fort' on OS 1836 and 1876 eds. Situated on E shoulder of a natural scarp. No visible remains at ground level.
32:22 13-7-1989

1823 DUNDAVAN
OS 37:9:6 (170,216) Not marked OD 200–300
23650, 28715
Castle (site, possible) Site of a 16th-century O'Reilly

Plate 7a—*An impressive motte and bailey at Relagh Beg* (**1793**).

Plate 7b—*A three-storey tower house at Tonymore* (**1851**).

Plate 8a—*Looking down through the murder-hole above the main entrance to Tonymore tower house* (**1851**).

Plate 8b— *A beehive-type sweathouse at Legeelan* (**1873**).

castle (NMI 1946). No visible remains at ground level. A large ruined house and outbuildings of late 18th/early 19th-century date now occupy the site.
37:29 4-6-1987

1824 FARNHAM
OS 20:10:6 (461,179) Not marked OD 200–300
23941, 30599
Castle (site) A castle comprising a stone house and a bawn of sods with four flankers was erected here in the second decade of the 17th century. Parts of this appear to have been incorporated into a modern house which now occupies the site. An earlier account (Davies 1948, 112) described what must have been a flanker at the SE corner of the bawn — a two-storey strong structure with cross-vaulting over the upper floor. A tunnel (dims. 1.8m x 1.2m) roofed with slabs apparently ran outside the bawn enclosure in a northerly direction.
20:44 31-8-1990

1825 GRILLY
OS 11:14:2 (368,98) '*Grilly Castle* (Site of)'
OD 200–300 23831, 31792
Castle (site) Marked Grilly Castle (in Ruins) on OS 1836 ed. and (Site of) on 1876 ed. Situated on W slope of a drumlin hill adjacent to an old road to Belturbet. Possibly an O'Reilly stronghold. Although there are now no visible remains of this site at ground level, an earlier account (Davies 1947, 91) noted some grassed-over mounds possibly marking the outline of a small building. During land clearance in the vicinity of the site in the early 1980s red brick and rubble were uncovered (local information).
11:18 15-6-1989

1826 KEELAGH (Tullyhunco By.)
OS 19:11:3 (669,298) 'Home Farm' OD 254
23184, 30718
Castle (site) Castle site situated S of a late 19th/early 20th-century house which itself was constructed from the castle material (local information). Davies (1948, 123) recorded what he believed to be a standing portion of the castle. However, this is unlikely as the later house is at least 100 years old.
19:37(01) 17-5-1993

1827 KEVIT UPPER OR CASTLECOSBY
OS 25:6:5 (340,326) 'Castle Cosby' OD 200–300
23818, 30112
Castle (site) Reputedly the site of 'Bunraskeen Castle', a 16th-century structure with two flanking towers formerly positioned at the corners of the yard of 'Castle Cosby' house (1947, 97). All that survives is the S portion of the SW tower (int. diam. *c.* 2.2m) built of roughly coursed limestone masonry. Late medieval stone head in modern dwelling-house nearby (**1892**).
25:63(01) 16-5-1993

1828 KILLYFANA
OS 11:16:4 (739,29) Not marked OD 200–300
24224, 31724
Bawn (site) The remains of what may have been a bawn possibly built by Richard Tyrell of Killyfana in the 17th century were noted by Davies (1948, 95) at this location. He described some curious banks enclosing a rectangular area *c.* 21m wide, of which there are now no visible remains at ground level.
11:22 16-6-1989

1829 KNOCKNAVEAGH
OS 43:11:1 (517,297) Not marked OD 300–400
25973, 28181
Castle (site) Depicted as a rectangular building with the designation 'Site of Old Castle' on OS 1836 and 1876 eds. Situated on S slope of a drumlin ridge. No visible remains at ground level. (1947, 98).
43:26 18-6-1987

1830 LISDRUMSKEA
OS 23:16:2 (787,131) Not marked OD 300–400
27211, 30578
Castle (site) Sir Henry Piers apparently built a bawn, castle and town at Shercock in the early 17th century. The present Catholic chapel in the town is believed to have been built on the site of the castle. No visible remains at ground level.
23:35(02) 9-4-1992

1831 LISGANNON
OS 21:4:2 (802,531) Hachured OD 370
25273, 30982
Bawn (site, possible) In 1601 Captain Hugh O'Reilly erected a 'bawn of sods' at this location. It has been suggested (1948, 118–9) that Lisgannon rath (**911**) may have been modified to accommodate this bawn, a second bank and wide berm having been added to the pre-existing bank and fosse of the rath. No visible remains at ground level.
21:60(02) 27-9-1990

1832 LISLEA (ED Cootehill Rural)
OS 17:11:2 (568,239) Not marked OD 300–400
26231, 30767
Castle (site, possible) Not marked on any OS ed. Situated near the summit of a high drumlin hill. Known as 'Castle Saunders' and thereby believed to be the site of a Saunderson stronghold (local information). No visible remains at ground level.
17:49 28-9-1989

1833 LISLIN (Tullygarvey By.)
OS 16:15:1 (488,108) Not marked OD 200
24939, 31173
Castle (site) A castle is marked within this townland

on Petty's map of 1685. Site has been largely levelled. Remains comprise a raised circular area (diam *c.* 49m E–W) bounded by the Annalee River from SE–S–SSW and elsewhere by a much-disturbed scarp. Lislin House which borders the site from NNE–E–SE was inspected by Davies (1948, 120) and he concluded that despite its thick walls and marked batter, it did not appear to be of early 17th-century date. He also recorded that five horse skulls, most likely some form of foundation offering, were found beneath the drawing-room floor.
16:92 8-10-1989

1834 LISMACANIGAN UPPER
OS 38:15:2 (596,118) Not marked OD 200–300
25077, 28624
Castle (site, possible) Possibly built during the period of the Cromwellian Settlement by Thomas Burton. A castle is marked in Lismacanigan Td on Petty's map of 1685 and was then in the ownership of Sir Richard and Christopher Nugent. Local tradition recalls that it was located on a low mound. No visible remains at ground level. (Davies 1948, 106)
38:45 1-9-1986

1835 LISMORE DEMESNE
OS 25:9:3 (205,268) '*Lismore Castle*' (in Ruins) OD 100–200 23675, 30051
Castle (site) Marked 'Castle' on OS 1836 ed. and 'Site of' on 1876 ed. No visible remains at ground level. (ITA Survey 1946; Davies 1947, 97)
25:84 24-9-1991

1836 LISNAMAINE OR SYCAMORE FIELDS
OS 14:4:6 (886,476) Hachured OD 263
23405, 31548
Castle (site) Between 1611 and 1613, John Fishe apparently built a castle of brick and lime in a rath (**958**) in this Td. A subrectangular hollow (dims 18.4m NE–SW; 1.4m NW–SE) containing some loose masonry is visible in the interior of the rath and an earlier account (Davies 1948, 113) suggested that this may mark the cellars of a house. The site was abandoned in 1719. (O'Reilly 1985, 263–6, 275)
14:49(02) 15-8-1989

1837 LISSANOVER
OS 13:4:2 (807,602) Not marked OD 300–400
22345, 31671
Castle Depicted on OS 1836 and 1876 eds. as a large L-shaped building (long axis aligned NE–SW). An earlier account (Davies 1947, 95) claimed that the ruins were largely removed in 1909 leaving a somewhat confused complex of grass-covered banks. Today the only standing portion of the former castle is a block of masonry at the NE angle which is surmounted by a tree.
13:46 22-6-1989

1838 LURGANBOY (Upper Loughtee By.)
OS 20:15:6 NPL Not marked OD 200–300
Castle (site) A castle was built by Walter, Patrick and Thomas Brady in this townland sometime before its destruction by Phillip O'Reilly (*CSPI* 1592–6, 541–2) in 1596. A representation of same on Netherclift's plan of Cavan (*c.* 1593) suggests that it was a tower house. Rebuilt (*CSPI* 1600, 420) and referred to in 1601 as the castle of Walter and Thomas Brady (Hunter 1971, 68). No visible remains at ground level. (Davies 1948, 101; Bradley and Dunne 1989, 41–42)
20:55(06)

1839 MOYNEHALL
OS 25:8:1 (750,431) 'Moynehall' OD 300–400
24250, 30228
Castle (site) Davies (1948, 115) recorded the site of a plantation 'house and bawn' at this location. All that survives is a large moulded stone at the SW corner of the yard which may possibly be the base of a 17th-century turret. Otherwise no visible remains at ground level.
25:98 16-8-1992

1840 POTTLE EAST
OS 16:12:1 (750,302) Not marked OD 200–300
25214, 31381
Bawn Marked 'Fort' on OS 1836 and 1876 eds. Raised rectangular area (int. dims. 42m NW–SW; 40m NW–SE). Perimeter has been levelled or incorporated into the field boundary but outline of site is clearly visible. Davies (1948, 120) speculated that it was probably a bawn with a large circular flanker (diam 8.9m) at its NE corner.
16:105 16-5-1993

1841 RAHARDRUM
OS 39:16:1 (714,142) '*Rahardrum*' OD 277
26177, 28660
Castle (site) Small oval-shaped island (dims. *c.* 50m NE–SW; *c.* 36m NW–SE) in Lough Ramor, separated from the mainland by a deep and narrow fosse. Davies (1947, 97–8) suggested that this may have been the site of a late 16th-century O'Reilly castle which possibly superseded an earlier 15th-century fortification. No visible remains at ground level.
39:77 4-6-1987

1842 SKEAGH (Clankee By.)
OS 28:5:6 (189,340) Not marked OD 500–600
26584, 30152
Castle (site) According to Davies (1948, 108) a plantation castle with a bawn and two flankers was built by William Hamilton on a low hill W of Skeagh Lough Lower and immediately SE of a 19th-century house and farmyard. No visible remains at ground level.
28:43 25-8-1988

1843 TOWNPARKS /LURGANBOY (Upper Loughtee By.)
OS 20 NPL Not marked OD 200–300

Castle (site) A late 16th-century account (*CSPI* 1592–6) noted two castles at Cavan Town. The first was in all probability at Tullymongan (**1844**). The second was not located. (Bradley and Dunne 1989, 42)
20:55(05)

1844 TULLYMONGAN UPPER
OS 20:16:4 (720,40) Not marked OD 300–400
24216, 30454

Castle (site) Marked 'Fort' on OS 1836 ed. and 'Site of' on 1876 ed. Formerly situated at the N end of a long drumlin ridge to SE of Cavan Town. Site is now occupied by a fair green. Probably an O'Reilly castle of late 14th-century date, first mentioned in 1427 when it was destroyed by the English. It was apparently rebuilt, as a castle stood here as late as the early 17th century. A map of 1591 depicts it as a large square building with a door in its W wall, an extramural staircase at S, corner turrets at NW and SE, rising above the roofline, and a bawn enclosing several outbuildings. Lewis (1837, vol. 1, 318) recorded vaults and parts of the foundations surviving in the 19th century. However by the time of Davies' visit in 1946 there were only low banks (H 0.75m) remaining, indicating the former line of a roughly square bawn (dims. *c.* 29m x 29m). There are now no visible remains of castle at ground level.
20:55(04) 21-8-1990

1845 TULLYVIN
OS 17:13:3 (200,96) '*Castle* (Site of)' OD 200–300
25704, 30971

Castle (site) Formerly situated on a low, isolated, rocky hillock overlooking a tributary of the Annalee River. Apparently an O'Reilly castle built *c.* 1450, which became the most important stronghold in Tullygarvey barony in the late 16th century. Following the Plantation, it became the centre of the Moore Manor. No visible remains at ground level.
17:74 24-9-1990

Tower Houses and Bawns

In 1429, in a move designed to ensure the defence of the Pale, King Henry VI announced that a subsidy of £10 would be granted to each 'liege man of our Lord the King' who would build a fortified castle or tower to particular minimum specifications in counties Dublin, Kildare, Louth and Meath. In the following 150 years many tower houses were constructed throughout Ireland both by Gaelic and Old English families. In general they comprise rectangular, or more infrequently circular towers, of between three and five storeys. Battlements protected a wall-walk at roof level. Other defensive features include machicolations located above the entrance, or bartizans at the angles, murder-holes, loops for archery and guns, and narrow slit windows. A barrel or pointed vault was normally constructed at ground or first-floor level. A large number of rural tower houses were partially enclosed by a bawn. There are two bawns included in this chapter (**1847**, **1848**) which may formerly have been attached to tower houses. However, of the upstanding tower houses in the County none have surface evidence of a bawn. In general, tower houses can be interpreted as the strongly defended residences of the contemporary landowning classes.

Fig. 51—*Remains of tower house at Ballymagauran* (**1846**).

1846 BALLYMAGAURAN
OS 13:11:2 (582,283) Indicated OD 100–200
22110, 31332

Tower house Remains of rectangular building (int. dims. 9.5m E–W; 5.9m N–S) of rough, uncoursed limestone masonry. Plain splayed window in W end of S wall. Fireplace and chimney in E end of S wall. The structure was apparently two stories in height. Lying on the ground is half of the doorway arch. Dressed stone indicates a late 16th or early 17th-century date. Remains of a largely destroyed stone head at NW angle. Davies (1947, 94–5) recorded that this 'although barbarously mutilated in recent years, looks from the grooves under the chin to have been a grotesque of a type not likely to have been made after 1600'.
13:2 15-5-1993

1847 BAWN (Clanmahon By.)
OS 41:1:3 (196,559) Hachured OD 405
23680, 28438

Bawn Raised subrectangular area (*c.* 75m N–S; *c.*

Fig. 52—*Interior of Tonymore tower house* (**1851**).

60m E–W) enclosed by two low, wide earthen banks with intermediate fosse. Outer bank identifiable only at N and E sides. At S and W it has been replaced with modern field boundaries. Break in inner bank midway along the W side, with accompanying causeway, represents original entrance.
41:1 2-7-1986

1848 BAWNBOY
OS 9:11:2 (611,276) 'Bawnboy House' OD 200–300 22135, 31965
Bawn Davies (1948, 121) described the castle as having comprised 'a small bawn and house'. All that survives are the remains of a featureless D-shaped or open-backed tower (int. diam. 5m N–S) built of uncoursed rubble masonry with modern building attached. Possibly late medieval in date.
9:3 10-5-1993

1849 CROVER
OS 38:14:4 (252,38) '*Crover Old Castle* (in Ruins)' OD 212 24714, 28536
Tower house Situated on a small rocky island, *c.* 300m from the W shore of Lough Sheelin. Constructed in the late 14th century by Thomas McMahon O'Reilly. Davies described it as a two-storey rectangular tower with base batter, a barrel vault over the ground floor and remains of a doorway in S wall. Intramural staircases occur in E wall leading to first floor, and in N wall leading to roof level. Site is densely overgrown with vegetation.
38:19 3-9-1986

1850 See PORT (ED Esky) p. 203

1851 TONYMORE
OS 25:3:4 (484,515) '*Castle* (in Ruins)' OD 200–300 23968, 30314
Tower house A three-storey tower house constructed of roughly coursed limestone blocks, with pronounced base batter rising to a height of *c.* 3m. Remains comprise the E and S walls and featureless N wall. W wall is largely destroyed. Entrance with remains of masonry arch at centre of E wall above which is a well-preserved cut-stone loop. A large opening at ground-floor level flanks doorway on its N side. Fenestration in S wall includes two loops, one placed directly above the other lighting the staircase, a narrow ope with large embrasure at ground-floor level and the remains of a large window-opening at first-floor level. Inside entrance is a short hallway, with murder-hole over head, leading W to the main ground floor area. A small rectangular chamber leads off this to N and a stairwell to S. A pointed doorway leads W from the hall to an inner room containing two wall cupboards. On first floor another dressed, pointed doorway leads from the staircase to a room at W which contains large recesses, and beam slots in its S wall.
25:113 10-6-1993

Fortified Houses

From the early 15th century, up until the closing decades of the 16th century, the principal form of defended dwelling among the landowning classes, both Planters and native Irish, was the tower house. Houses constructed immediately after this period are characterised by a generally larger plan facilitating a greater number of commodious private rooms. They also tend to have more and larger windows than their poorly lit predecessors and retain limited defensive features. Many fortified houses were destroyed or abandoned during or in the aftermath of the 1641 rebellion as was probably the case with the house at Inishconnell (**1852**). The Redhills Demesne example (**1853**) is a large strongly fortified house apparently of 18th-century date.

1852 INISHCONNELL
OS 20:5:5 (132,341) '*Castle Offices* (Site of)'
OD 100–200 23591, 30767

Fortified house (site) Built by the Culme family in the early decades of the 17th century. Under the terms of the Plantation the family also rented Clough Oughter castle (**1796**) *c*. 200m to NW, and its associated lands. On OS 1836 ed. the house is designated 'Ruin of Offices belonging to Clough Oughter Castle', and depicted as an L-shaped structure with the long axis aligned NE–SW. Culme had apparently begun to build a strong fort between Lough Oughter and a nearby area of woodland in 1642, in order to defend his house. It appears that the site was abandoned after the Cromwellian wars of the early 1640s. Manning (1990, 17) speculated that it was probably levelled prior to the 1909 OS ed. Davies (1948, 99) noted black earth containing mortar and bones deposited along the top of the shore-bank and recorded that a number of possible sockets for doorposts had been found in the vicinity. No visible remains of house at ground level.
20:47 17-8-1990

1853 REDHILL DEMESNE
OS 12:13:4 (47,5) '*Castle* (in Ruins)' OD 200–300
24468, 31700

Fortified house Large almost square building (int. dims. 16.7m NW–SE; 16.45m NE–SW) built of roughly coursed limestone and rubble, divided internally by a wall running NE–SW. Remains of doorway with bolt-hole in SE wall. Fragments of windows survive in SW and NE walls. N wall has been partially reconstructed. Probably of mid-18th-century date.
12:5 15-5-1993

Miscellaneous Towers

This chapter describes the sites of two towers identified from map sources, and a small tower at Coolnashinny or Croaghan (**1855**) which may have been constructed as a memorial monument.

1854 CLOWNEY
OS 14:3:3 (654,576) Not marked OD 200–300
23159, 31652

Tower (site) Depicted as a circular structure with the designation 'Tower in Ruins' on OS 1836 ed. Not marked on subsequent eds. Situated on the summit of a low drumlin hill. No visible remains at ground level.
14:15 29-7-1989

1855 COOLNASHINNY OR CROAGHAN
OS 19:7:1 (507,425) Not marked OD 200–300
23012, 30851

Tower Circular, free-standing, two-storey tower (int. diam. 2.8m) constructed of rubble masonry. Possibly the SW corner tower of the bawn of the former Croaghan Castle. Second storey corbelled internally. Fenestration comprises simple rectangular slits. Doorway positioned in NE face. A 19th-century graveslab commemorating the Rev. George Carson and his wife Mary was formerly housed in the tower and has since been removed to 'Croghan House' *c.* 100m to N. (Davies 1948, 124)
19:8(01) 10-5-1993

1856 RANTAVAN
OS 44:3:1 (530,568) Not marked OD 300–400
26960, 28477

Tower (site) Situated on a valley floor to the W of a stream. A 'tower' is indicated at this location on Petty's Down Survey map of 1654. Davies (ITA Survey 1942) recorded 'walls of mortar and rubble' enclosing a rectangular area. However, there are now no visible remains of this structure at ground level. (Davies 1947, 99)
44:21 18-8-1987

Star-Shaped Forts

A star-shaped fort comprises a rectangular embanked enclosure with angled bastions at each corner to facilitate flanking gunfire. In most cases there is a fosse or moat at the foot of the bank. Although they appeared in Continental Europe as early as the 16th century, in Ireland they were a 17th-century innovation designed in response to the increased use of artillery in this war-torn period.

1857 CORPORATION LANDS
OS 11:13:6 (190,15) 'Deanery Banks' OD 200–300
23644, 31703
Star-shaped fort Davies (1948, 100) recorded that this site was constructed by Col. Wolseley in 1689. Bradley and Dunne (OPW 1989, 27) were of the opinion that the site was probably 'originally square with triangular platform bastions set inside each of the four corners'. Only the WSW side survives. This comprises a large earthen rampart with external fosse. The NNW rampart has been substantially altered and incorporated into the field boundary. Wide break in centre of WSW rampart, with accompanying causeway, may represent original entrance.
11:13(01) 20-5-1993

1858 CORPORATION LANDS
OS 15:1:3 (178,600) Hachured 23632, 31681
Star-shaped fort Davies (1948, 100) recorded that this site was constructed by Col. Wolseley in 1689. It is now largely occupied by a modern Church of Ireland chapel and graveyard. Bradley and Dunne (OPW 1989, 25–6) were of the opinion that 'it had been originally square with salient angled bastions at each corner'. Only the S side has survived. This comprises a substantial linear earthen rampart with external fosse and bastions at each end. Very slight traces of the NW bastion are also identifiable. The W and E ramparts and the NE bastion have been destroyed as a result of grave-digging. The graveyard wall and the modern roadway at its external foot are built on the site of the N rampart.
15:16/11:3* 20-5-1993

Sweathouses and Duck House

Sweathouses are a feature of the archaeology of the mountainous western portion of County Cavan. They are all remarkably similar in morphology, being circular, low, drystone-built corbelled structures. Entrance was through a low lintelled doorway usually measuring under 0.5m in height. The majority of the County Cavan examples also have roughly built chimney flues. A fire was lit within the structure and left burning for a few days. When it had reached a sufficient heat the 'patients' would enter and perspire profusely for a period of between a half an hour and five hours in the manner of the modern sauna-user. Entrance and chimney flue would have been blocked up with sods and other debris to ensure concentrated heat. This process was believed to be a cure for an astonishing number of ailments including lameness, sciatica, sore eyes, gout, skin disorders, psychiatric disorders and even impotence and infertility! However, it is likely that rheumatic complaints accounted for the majority usage. After 'treatment' the usual practice was to bathe in a nearby stream. Weir (1989, 10-13) has recorded that 'although their present distribution is mainly in remote and depopulated parts of counties Leitrim and Cavan, with several examples in neighbouring parts of Roscommon, Fermanagh, Sligo and Donegal, they were almost certainly to be found the length and breadth of Ireland'. The earliest record of an Irish sweathouse is from the late 18th century although the tradition is undoubtedly older than this. It appears that they fell into general disuse after 1851 when the first dispensaries were established. However, according to local tradition, in the more remote mountainous regions including the western portion of County Cavan, sweathouses were regularly used up until the early decades of this century.

Also included in this chapter is an unusual structure known in the locality as a duck house. Its function is self-explanatory but the nature of its morphology makes it impossible to assign it to any particular period.

1859 COPPANAGHBANE
OS 5:8:2 (105,433) *'Sweat Ho.'* OD 500–600
19652, 31834

Sweathouse Not marked on OS 1836 or 1876 eds. Situated on a riverbank. Partly built into a hillside. Small beehive-shaped, circular (int. diam. 1.7m; H *c.* 2m), drystone-built structure roofed internally with small flat slabs. Low lintelled entrance at NE (H 0.65m; Wth 0.45m). Richardson (1939, 33–4) recorded 'two flues on the left of the door'.
5:8 27-8-1988

1860 CORCASHEL (Tullyhaw By.)
OS 5:7:4 (393,397) *'Sweat Ho.'* OD 300–400
19956, 31875

Sweathouse (site) Not marked on OS 1836 or 1876 eds. Situated within a dense modern plantation of coniferous trees adjacent to a stream. Described as 'almost completely ruined' in 1939 (1939, 34), it is now largely destroyed. A small beehive-shaped drystone-built structure (int. diam. 1.65m). The roof-stones and the wall at NW have collapsed.
5:13 19-5-1993

1861 CORCASHEL (Tullyhaw By.)
OS 5 NPL Not marked OD 400–500

Sweathouse Not marked on any OS ed. Situated at the foot of a high hill adjacent to a stream, within a dense plantation of coniferous trees. Described by Richardson (1939, 34) as a circular structure (int. diam. *c.* 2.5m) with collapsed roof. Not visited.
5:47

1862 CORRADEVERRID
OS 5:2:7 (567,494) *'Sweat Ho.'* OD 200–300
20140, 31774

Sweathouse Indicated on OS 1836 and 1876 eds. Situated on the ESE shoulder of a low mountainous hill. A small beehive-shaped, drystone-built structure, roofed internally by four small flat slabs. Low lintelled entrance at NW (H 1.25m; Wth 0.6m). (Richardson 1939, 34)
5:23 17-8-1988

1863 CORRAKEELDRUM
OS 3:14:3 (435,98) Not marked OD 400–500
19989, 33037

Sweathouse Marked on OS 1836 and 1876 eds. Situated adjacent to a stream. Described by Richardson (1939, 34) as a small, circular, beehive-shaped, drystone-built structure (int. diam. *c.* 1.8m; H *c.* 1.8m) roofed internally by three narrow slabs. Entrance roofed by two lintels and chimney at back of structure on W side. Not visited.
3:8

1864 CORRAQUIGLEY
OS 3:15:1 (529,91) *'Sweat Ho.'* OD 300–400
20089, 33032

Sweathouse Not marked on OS 1836 or 1876 eds. Situated 85m E of a stream. Small circular drystone-built structure (int. diam. 2.4m; H 1.8m) of beehive-type construction roofed internally by three large flat slabs. Outer facing of wall is of cut stone, set alternately in headers and stretchers (Richardson 1939, 34). Low lintelled entrance at E (H 0.6m; Wth 0.5m).
3:9 15-7-1988

1865 CORRATAWY
OS 3:16:6 (908,53) Not marked OD 300–400
20489, 32995

Sweathouse (site) Marked on OS 1836 and 1876 eds.

Situated 180m NE of Drumhurrin Lough. In the early decades of this century it was dismantled and the stones utilised as building material for field boundaries in the vicinity (local information). No visible remains at ground level.
3:11 18-7-1988

1866 CORRATOBER LOWER
OS 5:3:6 (241,506) '*Sweat Ho.*' OD 200–300
19796, 31758
Sweathouse Marked on all OS eds. Situated adjacent to a stream. Small oval drystone-built structure (H 1.6m; int. dims. 2.4m NW–SE; 1.5m NE–SW) of beehive-type construction, roofed internally by a flat slab. Partly built into a hillside at SE. Lintelled entrance at NE (H 0.7m; Wth 0.5m). Richardson (1939, 34) recorded 'a flue on each side of it'.
5:25 16-8-1988

1867 DOWRA
OS 5:6:1 (648,411) '*Sweat Ho.*' OD 200–300
20225, 31863
Sweathouse Not marked on OS 1836 or 1876 eds. Situated on a rough mountainous hillside a short distance from a stream. Small circular drystone-built structure (int. diam. 1.65m) of beehive-type construction, roofed internally by a flat slab. Low lintelled entrance at E (H 0.8m; Wth 0.65m). Richardson (1939, 34) noted a chimney near it.
5:28 15-8-1988

1868 DOWRA
OS 5:6:1 (626,439) '*Sweat Ho.*' OD 200–300
20201, 31833
Sweathouse Not marked on OS 1836 or 1876 eds. Situated on a steep hillside in rough mountainous terrain. Small circular drystone-built structure (int. diam. 1.6m) of beehive-type construction, roofed internally by a number of flat slabs. Richardson (1939, 34) recorded that two of the closing slabs had fallen. Low lintelled entrance at W (H 0.4m; Wth 0.5m).
5:29 15-8-1988

1869 DRUMLION (Upper Loughtee By.)
OS 20:14:6 (408,28) '*Sweat Ho.*' OD 200–300
23886, 30439
Sweathouse (site) Not marked on 1836 or 1876 eds. Situated in a small valley, 30m SW of a stream. The site has been quarried away. Davies (ITA Survey 1942) recorded that the site was once occupied by an extensive brickworks within which was a small vaulted building. He described the building as being of 18th or early 19th-century style. No visible remains at ground level.
20:38 15-1-1991

1870 GOWLAT
OS 5:4:6 (22,506) Not marked OD 300–400
19565, 31756
Sweathouse (site) Marked on OS 1836 ed. Not marked on subsequent eds. Situated in rough mountainous terrain adjacent to a stream and waterfall. No visible remains at ground level.
5:34 27-8-1988

1871 GUBAVEENY
OS 3:11:3 (648,289) '*Sweat Ho.*' OD 400–500
20212, 33242
Sweathouse Not marked on OS 1836 or 1876 eds. Situated in rough, wet, mountainous terrain. Small circular drystone-built structure (int. diam. 1.5m; H 1.65m) of beehive-type construction, roofed internally by two large flat slabs. Low entrance at SW (H 0.47m; Wth 0.6m) roofed by two lintels (the upper now broken). Richardson (1939, 34) noted a 'chimney on either side'.
3:18 19-7-1988

1872 GUBAVEENY
OS 3:12:4 (705,202) '*Sweat Ho.*' OD 200–300
20273, 33151
Sweathouse Not marked on OS 1836 or 1876 eds. Small circular drystone-built structure (int. diam. 2m) of beehive-type construction (H *c.* 1.6m). Richardson (1939, 35) noted a 'facade of semi-ashlar' and walls compactly mortared with sandy clay. The roof (since collapsed) was corbelled to two summits and there was no chimney in evidence. Low lintelled entrance (H 0.7m; Wth 0.7m) at SE.
3:19 19-7-1988

1873 LEGEELAN
OS 4:5:3 (156,433) '*Sweat Ho.*' OD 600–700
20667, 33398
Sweathouse Small circular drystone-built structure (int. diam. 1.7m; H 1.4m) of beehive-type construction, roofed internally by a single slab. Low lintelled entrance at SW (H 0.45m; Wth 0.5m). Richardson (1939, 34) recorded a 'small chimney just above it'. (Weir 1989, 10)
4:11 12-8-1988

1874 LEGNAGROW
OS 6:1:4 (58,523) '*Sweat Ho.*' OD 700–800
20568, 32852
Sweathouse Marked on all OS eds. An earlier description (1939, 34–5) noted that it had an internal diameter of *c.* 1.7m, a max height of *c.* 1.5m and that the walls were *c.* 0.8m thick. A large slab which formed the roof had been removed some thirty years previously. Not visited.
6:14

1875 MEENASLIEVE
OS 3:15:3 (642,84) '*Sweat Ho.*' OD 200–300
20207, 33025

Sweathouse Not marked on OS 1836 or 1876 eds. Situated adjacent to the Black River within a dense modern plantation of coniferous trees. Described by Richardson (1941, 35) as a small circular drystone-built structure (int. diam. *c.* 1.8m; H *c.* 1.2m) of beehive- type construction, roofed internally by two slabs which had collapsed. It had a low entrance (H *c.* 0.9m; Wth *c.* 0.4m) the lintel of which had been raised at one time. The structure had no chimney. Not visited.
3:21

1876 MONEEN
OS 3:14:2 (339,105) '*Sweat Ho.*' OD 500–600
19887, 33045

Sweathouse Marked on all OS eds. Described by Richardson (1939, 35) as a small circular drystone-built structure (ext. H *c.* 2.1m) of beehive-type construction. The roof had collapsed and the low entrance (Wth *c.* 0.6m) was already partially demolished. Not visited.
3:22

1877 MONEYGASHEL
OS 4:5:1 (67,392) '*Sweat Ho.*' OD 500–600
20573, 33353

Sweathouse Not marked on OS 1836 or 1876 eds. Situated within a cashel (**1205**). Small circular drystone-built structure (int. diam. 1.4m; H 1.4m) of beehive-type construction, roofed internally by two large slabs. Richardson (1939, 35) recorded a chimney at SW, *c.* 0.9m above floor level.
4:15(02) 10-8-1988

1878 PORT (ED Esky)
OS 1:12:2 (784,257) '*Sweat Ho.*' OD 200–300
20350, 33849

Sweathouse Small circular drystone-built structure (int. diam. 1.3m; H 1.9m) of beehive-type construction, roofed internally by two flat slabs. Low lintelled entrance at N (H 0.55m; Wth 0.5m). Richardson (1939, 35) recorded a chimney on S side.
1:12 2-7-1988

1879 TERMON (Tullyhaw By.)
OS 2:13:1 (40,81) '*Sweat Ho.*' OD 300
20541, 33666

Fig. 53—*A drystone-built sweathouse at Moneygashel* (**1877**).

Sweathouse Not marked on OS 1836 or 1876 eds. Largely destroyed. Only the foundations are identifiable today. Described by Richardson (1939, 35) as a small subcircular drystone-built structure (int. dims. *c*. 1.9m x *c*. 1.5m). The corbelled roof was closed by a single slab and at a height of *c* 0.8m and set within the walls there were a series of aperatures which were presumably flues for the smoke. The doorway was *c*. 0.5m high and *c*. 0.7m wide. A circular well (diam. 3m), enclosed by a low drystone wall, lies 12m to SW. Site is densely overgrown with vegetation.
2:14(01) 27-8-1988

1880 TULLAGHYRORY
OS 5:15:1 (502,433) Not marked OD 100–200
20071, 31838

Sweathouse Marked 'Sweat House' on OS 1836 and 1876 eds. Situated in wet low-lying ground, *c*. 50m SSW of the River Shannon. Largely collapsed. Small circular drystone-built structure (int. diam. 1.7m) of bee-hive type construction. The upper portion of the wall has collapsed and has been partly rebuilt by the landowner (local information). The roof has also collapsed. Original entrance was probably at N.
5:41 17-8-1988

1881 TULLAGHYRORY
OS 5:14:3 (452,444) '*Sweat Ho.*' OD 200
20018, 31825

Sweathouse Marked on all OS eds. Situated in low-lying wet terrain adjacent to a stream. Almost completely destroyed. The foundations of a small circular drystone-built structure (int. diam. 1.8m) can be distinguished except at N where it is likely that the original entrance was located. Richardson (1939, 35) noted that it was *c*. 1.5m in height, had an internal diameter. of *c*. 1m and that the doorway (H *c*. 0.5m; Wth *c*. 0.4m; D *c*. 0.3m) was roofed by a single lintel.
5:42 17-8-1988

1882 TULLYNAFREAVE
OS 3:16:4 (706,45) '*Sweat Ho.*' OD 200–300
20276, 32984

Sweathouse Not marked on OS 1836 or 1876 eds. Situated *c*. 45m NW of the Black River. Partly built into a hillside at NW. Small circular drystone-built structure (int. diam. 1.3m; H 1.1m) of beehive-type construction, roofed internally by two flat slabs. Low lintelled entrance at SE (H 0.6m; Wth 0.4m). (Richardson 1939, 35)
3:29 15-8-1988

Fig. 54—*A duck house at Moneensauran* (**1884**).

1883 TULLYNAMOYLE
OS 3 NPL Not marked OD 300–400
Sweathouse (site) Not marked on any OS ed. Situated in rough mountainous terrain. Richardson (1939, 35) recorded that it was demolished a few years ago. Not visited.
3:30

1884 MONEENSAURAN
OS 6:9:3 (192,230) Not marked OD 400–500
20712, 32544
Duck house Known locally as a 'duck house'. Remains comprise a subrectangular stone structure (int. dims. 5.3m NE–SW; 1.7m NW–SE) enclosed by a thick drystone wall. Roof is apparently comprised of flat slabs. Entrance feature in NE wall (Wth 0.4m; H 0.6m) capped with three substantial lintels.
6:17 27-8-1988

Miscellaneous Monuments

This chapter provides accounts of monuments which by virtue of their scarcity or anomalous character do not warrant separate chapters in this volume. Monuments as diverse as an unusual earthwork at Dungummin Upper (**1890**) and a folly at Bellville (**1886**) are included.

Fig. 55—*Fleming's Folly at Bellville* (**1886**).

1885 ABBEY LANDS/LURGANBOY (Upper Loughtee By.)/ TOWNPARKS (Cavan Rural District)
OS 20:16:4 (694,49) Indicated OD 200–300
24188, 30464
Bridge (site) Depicted as early as *c.* 1593 on Netherclift's plan of Cavan Town, crossing Bridge Street in the same location as the present-day bridge. (O'Connell 1937, 301; Bradley and Dunne 1989, 45)
20:55(08) 19-7-1993

1886 BELLVILLE
OS 25:10:6 (440,197) '*Fleming's Folly*' OD 562
23924, 29978
Folly A two-storey square tower (int. dims. 7.15m x 7.15m; max H *c.* 6.2m) with thick mortared walls of rough unworked stones, situated on rock outcrop. Doorways in W and S walls. Intramural stairs runs from doorway in S wall through E wall to viewing point. Beam slots and two recesses (dims. 2.75m x 1.15m) in S wall and round-headed fireplace in N wall.
25:9 18-9-91

1887 COOLNAGOR OR RICEHILL
OS 25:2:5 (335,466) Indicated OD 200–300
23811, 30261
Schools Two schoolhouses associated with William Beddell, Church of Ireland Bishop of Kilmore from 1629–42. The E school, now a modernised dwelling-house, is thick-walled, vaulted and apparently 17th century in date, while the W school dates to the early 19th century.
25:22 21-5-1993

1888 DERRYVONY
OS 11:2:2 (367,585) '*Bloody Pass*' OD 100–200
23825, 32307

Ford Marked on all OS eds. An ancient fording point on the River Erne which itself forms the boundary between counties Cavan and Fermanagh. The name 'Bloody Pass' commemorates an engagement between a small party of Enniskilleners and a detachment of King James' army, in the summer of 1689, in which the King's force was routed and many drowned while attempting the pass. The dead from the battle are said to have been buried in Galloon burial ground (**1733**) *c.* 70m to SE. A modern bridge now spans the River Erne at this location. (Davies 1948, 95; Henry 1987, 25)
11:15 11-6-1989

1889 DRUMARAW/DRUMCROW (ED Ballyhaise)
OS 16:13:2 (97,99) Indicated OD 187
24528, 31158

Bridge An eight-span limestone bridge repointed in more recent times, crossing the Annalee River, 650m NE of Ballyhaise village. Parapets are capped with large dressed coping stones. An almost illegible inscription on the S parapet gives the date 1705 for its erection. The bridge was rebuilt following its collapse in the early 19th century (local information) and a second inscription with the date 1822 refers to this rebuilding.
16:40 22-9-1989

1890 DUNGUMMIN UPPER
OS 42:3:6 (647,485) Hachured OD 200–300
25133, 28373

Earthwork (unclassified) Depicted as a circular enclosure with the designation 'Fort' on OS 1837 ed. A rectangular structure aligned NW–SE is shown within the W portion of the enclosed area. The site comprises a large, oval-shaped, natural earthen mound with scarped sides and flattened summit (dims. of summit *c.* 39.5m NE–SW; *c.* 28m NW–SW). In the SW quadrant there is a low, narrow, stone-built circular tower standing on a larger rounded stone structure which appears to be a folly probably of late 18th or early 19th-century construction. The site is densely overgrown with vegetation rendering inspection difficult. Davies (1947, 86) described this as a 14th or 15th-century castle 'of keep and bawn type'. However there is no documentary or archaeological evidence to validate this claim.
42:17(01) 11-9-1986

1891 KEELAGH (Tullyhunco By.)
OS 19:11:3 (669,298) 'Home Farm' OD 200–300
23184, 30718

Courtyard An early 17th-century courtyard much altered in late 18th century as evidenced by brickwork around windows. Features include an entrance gateway with rounded pedimented arch, the N pier inscribed with date of 1610 while the S pier carries the date 1789; two early 17th-century cut-stone doorways in N range; and a plaque bearing the Hamilton coat of arms set in wall of S range.
19:37(03) 17-5-1993

1892 KEVIT UPPER OR CASTLECOSBY
OS 25:10:2 (340,326) Not marked OD 200–300
23818, 30112

Stone head Built into the wall of a modern dwelling-house, *c.* 30m SSE of the remains of a 16th-century castle (**1827**). The head has a pointed chin, a flattened nose and slightly bulging eyes and is late medieval in date.
25:63(02) 16-5-1993

1893 MONESK
OS 3:6:3 (439,395) 'Boulder' OD 1300–1400
19991, 33352

Boundary stone Not marked on OS 1836 or 1876 eds. Massive irregularly shaped boulder marking the border between counties Cavan and Leitrim at this point. A small pile of loose stones has been placed on top of the boulder.
3:23 12-9-1989

1894 MUFF (Clankee By.)
OS 35:5:2 (133,408) 'Fair Green' OD 500–600
27505, 29592

Fair green Marked on all OS eds. Large subrectangular level area (dims. *c.* 150m x *c.* 80m) situated on a rocky eminence on the NW shoulder of a drumlin ridge. A gravel pit is marked on the OS 1836 ed. at N. There has been more recent quarrying at W and SW. The site may have been associated with Cordoagh Castle (**1810**), *c.* 250m to WNW.
35:58 17-6-1988

1895 TULLYMONGAN LOWER
OS 20:16:4 (704,65) Not marked OD 200–300
24199, 30480

School (site) In the early 17th century the Plantation commissioners decreed that Tullymongan Friary (**1714**) be converted into a parish church and school. The nearby castle (**1844**) was also to be used as a source of stone for these new buildings The first schoolmaster was apparently appointed *c.* 1623 (Davies 1948, 101). It is possible that this is the same school as that mentioned in the *Calendar Patent Rolls James I* for 1622 (**1900**). No visible remains at ground level. (Bradley and Dunne 1989, 42)
20:55(07) 19-11-1992

Addenda

1896 CLOGHBALLY UPPER
OS 44:6:1 (253,449) Not marked OD 300–400 26356, 28524

Horizontal mill (site) Three cut, shaped and morticed wooden beams discovered in the bed of a stream during the course of drainage works in 1984. Stream flows NW–SE and forms the boundary between the townlands of Cloghbally Upper and Fartagh. The location of these timbers on the downhill path of a fast-flowing stream suggests that they were components of a horizontal mill. Additional timbers were noted by the landowner at the same find-spot. Local tradition points to the site of an 'old road' aligned E–W, crossing the stream to S of mill site.
44:2 22-3-1985

1897 DERRYLAHAN (Tullyhaw By.)
OS 3:12:6 (906,181 Hachured OD 400–500 20485,33130

Mound Not marked on OS 1836 or 1876 eds. A small, circular, steep-sided earthen mound (diam. at base *c.* 4.2m; H 1.3m) tapering to a point. Significance unknown.
3:12 18-7-1988

1898 EDENBURT
OS 44:9:3 (183,228) Not marked OD 300–400 26596, 28115

Mound A roughly circular round-topped, grass-covered earthen mound (H at NW 0.2m), scarped about base of perimeter. Situated a short distance NE of a partially destroyed rath (**684**).
44:12 21-8-1987

1899 KILGOLAGH
OS 41:11:1 (519,278) Indicated OD 225–300 24024,28144

Bridge Three arches of the old medieval bridge of Finnea survive on either side of the modern single-span bridge which fords the drained River Inny. Those on the north side lie within Co. Cavan, while the corresponding southern arches are in Co. Westmeath. The bridge in its original state was a nine-span structure, three of the central spans having been since replaced with a modern single span. At some point the medieval bridge was added to on its E side. The surviving medieval arches are round headed (Wth 4.5m) and bear the remains of wicker centering together with some of the projecting corbels which formerly supported the centering (pers. comm. Conleth Manning). An ancient armorial plaque is incorporated into the east parapet of the modern span. In his memoirs, the Earl of Castlehaven refers to a skirmish at this bridge in 1644 and to the fact that it was built of stone and had a castle at its southern end (Castlehaven 1815, 70).
41:22 19-7-1995

1900 KINNYPOTTLE/LURGANBOY (Upper Loughtee By.)/ SWELLAN UPPER/TOWNPARKS (Cavan Urban District)/ TULLYMONGAN LOWER
OS 20 NPL Not marked OD 200–300

School (possible, site) In 1622, by a grant of James I, John Stern was appointed schoolmaster of the public school in Cavan. He was to hold it 'during good behaviour in as beneficial and ample a form' as his predecessor Alexander Julius (*Calender Patent Rolls, James I,* 528). While this public school may possibly be one and the same as that decreed at Tullymongan by the Plantation commissioners (**1895**), the above reference indicates that there was a school already in existence within Cavan Town prior to 1622.
20:55

1901 SHANCROAGHAN
OS 19:7:2 (595,397) Not marked OD 100–200 23105, 30821

Crannóg (possible) Not marked on OS 1836 or 1876 eds. A small peninsula locally known as 'the island', projecting into Town Lough on NE side. Timber piles noted here (local information).
19:46

1902 SHANCROAGHAN
OS 19:7:2 (572,398) Not marked OD 200–300 23081, 30822

Enclosure (site, possible) Not marked on OS 1836 or 1876 eds. Local tradition of a 'fort' in this townland, overlooking Town Lough to S. A field called the 'fort field' is pointed out as the location of the site. Not visible at ground level.
19:47 25-7-1994

BIBLIOGRAPHY

Abbreviations

BAR	British Archaeological Reports
CUCAP	Cambridge University Collection of Aerial Photographs
ITA	Irish Tourist Association Survey
NMI	National Museum Topographical Files
OPW	Office of Public Works
AFM	*Annals of the Four Masters*
Breifne	*Cumann Seanchais Bhreifne*
CSPI	*Calendar of State Papers relating to Ireland*
JRSAI	*Journal of the Royal Society of Antiquaries of Ireland*
PRIA	*Proceedings of the Royal Irish Academy*
UJA	*Ulster Journal of Archaeology*

ALDRIDGE, R. B. (1969) 'Notes on children's burial grounds in Mayo', *JRSAI* **99**, 83–7.

BAILLIE, M.G.L. (1988) 'The dating of timbers from Navan Fort and the Dorsey, Co. Armagh', *Emania*, 37–40.

BARROW, G. L. (1979) *The round towers of Ireland.* The Academy Press, Dublin.

BORLASE, W.C. (1897) *The dolmens of Ireland*, vol. 1. Chapman and Hall, London.

BRADLEY, J. and DUNNE, N. (1989) *Urban archaeological survey, part xxvi, County Cavan.* OPW, Dublin.

BREWER, J. S. and BULLEN, W. (eds.) (1873) *Calendar of State Papers Carew, 1603–24.* London.

BURL, A. (1987) 'The sun, the moon, and megaliths', *UJA* **50**, 7–21.

CASTLEHAVEN, EARL OF (1815) *The Earl of Castlehaven's memories; or, his review of the Civil Wars in Ireland.* Dublin.

CHANNING, J. (1993) 'Aughrim wedge tomb, Co. Cavan' in Bennett, I. (ed.) *Excavations 1992: summary accounts of archaeological excavations in Ireland*, 4. Wordwell, Wicklow.

DALTON, J. P. (1921–4) 'Cromm Cruaich of Magh Sleacht', *PRIA* **36**C, 23–67.

DAVIES, O. (1939) 'Killinagh church and Crom Cruaich', *UJA* **2**, 98–102.

— (1942) 'Contributions to the study of crannógs in south Ulster', *UJA* **5**, 14–30.

— (1947) 'Types of rath in southern Ulster', *UJA* **10**, 1–14.

— (1947) 'The castles of County Cavan', part 1', *UJA* **11**, 74–100.

— (1948) 'The castles of County Cavan', part 2', *UJA* **11**, 80–126.

— (1948) 'The churches of County Cavan', *JRSAI* **78**, 73–118.

DE VALERA, R. and Ó NUALLÁIN, S. (1972) *Survey of the megalithic tombs of Ireland,* vol. 3. Stationery Office, Dublin.

DE VISMES KANE, W. F. (1908–9) 'The Black Pig's Dyke: The ancient boundary fortification of Uladh', *PRIA* **28**C, 301–28.

— (1916–17) 'Additional researches on the Black Pig's Dyke', *PRIA* **34**C, 539–63.

EVANS, E. E. (1988) *Irish folk ways.*

FERGUSON, S. (1875 'On an Ogham inscription at Mullagh, Co. Cavan' *PRIA* **1**C, 303.

FLANAGAN, L. (1992) *A dictionary of Irish archaeology.* Gill and Macmillan, Dublin.

GLANGELVIN ICA (1983) *The Kingdom of Glan, Cavan.*

GUEST, E. M. (1936) 'Irish sheela-na-gigs in 1935', *JRSAI* **66**, 107–29.

GWYNN, A. and HADCOCK, R. N. (1988) *Medieval religious houses, Ireland.* Academic Press, Dublin.

HALL, T. (1907) 'Crannog near Belturbet', *JRSAI* **37**, 240–41.

— (1910) 'Barnagrow Lake and crannogs, County Cavan', *JRSAI* **40**, 361–2.

HARBISON, P. (1988) *Pre-Christian Ireland: from the first Settlers to the early Celts.* Thames and Hudson, London.

— (1991) *Pilgrimage in Ireland: the monuments and the people.* London.

HENRY, W. (1987) *Upper Lough Erne in 1739.*

HERITY, M. and EOGAN, G. (1977) *Ireland in Prehistory.* Routledge and Kegan Paul, London.

HILL, REV. G. (1872) *An historical account of the Plantation of Ulster at the commencement of the seventeenth century, 1608–20.* Belfast.

HUNTER, R. J. (1971) 'Towns in the Ulster Plantation', *Studia Hibernica,* 28–60.

KILBRIDE-JONES, H. E. (1951) 'Double horned cairn at Cohaw, County Cavan', *PRIA* **54**C, 75–88.

KILLANIN, LORD and DUIGNAN, M.V. (1989) *The Shell Guide to Ireland.* Gill and Macmillan, Dublin.

KING, H. A. (1987) 'Seventeenth century effigial sculpture in the north Meath area', in Rynne, E. (ed.), *Figures from the past: studies on figurative art in Christian Ireland in honour of Helen M. Roe,* 283–307. Glendale Press, Dun Laoighre.

KIRKER, S. K. (1890–91) 'Cloughoughter Castle, County Cavan', *JRSAI* **21**, 294–7.

LEWIS, S. (1837) *A topographical dictionary of Ireland*, 2 vols. S. Lewis and Co., London.

LOWRY-CORRY, D. (1939) 'Notes on the traditions and early history of the Parish of Killinagh', *UJA* **2**, 102–4.

LOWRY-CORRY, D. and RICHARDSON, P. (1937) 'Megalithic monuments in the Parish of Killinagh, Co. Cavan, *JRSAI* **67**, 155–75.

— (1940) 'Some further megalithic discoveries in the counties of Cavan and Leitrim', *JRSAI* **70**, 169–81.

LYNCH, A. (1981) *Man and environment in SW Ireland,* BAR British series 85. Oxford.

MACALISTER, R.A.S. (1916–17) 'Notes on certain Irish inscriptions', *PRIA* **33**C, 81–92.

— (1922) 'On a stone with La Tène decoration recently discovered in Co. Cavan', *JRSAI* **52**, 113–16.

MANNING, C. (1989–90) 'Clough Oughter Castle, Cavan', *Breifne* **8**, no. 1, 20–61.

MILLIGAN, S. F. (1885) 'Crannogs in County Cavan', *JRSAI* **17**, 148–52.

— (1890–91) 'Ancient forts in County Sligo', *JRSAI* **21**, 574-82.

O'CONNELL, P. (1937) *The Diocese of Kilmore: its history and antiquities.* Dublin.

— (1965) 'The Kildrumfertan epitaphs', *Breifne* **2**, no. 8, 455–9.

O'DONOVAN, P. (1991–2) 'Turbet Island motte and bailey, Belturbet, Co. Cavan', *UJA* **54–5**, 129–33.

O'KELLY, M. J. (1954) 'Excavations and experiments in ancient Irish cooking-places', *JRSAI* **84**, 105–55.

Ó NUALLÁIN, S. (1975) 'The stone circle complex of Cork and Kerry', *JRSAI* **105**, 83–131.

O'REILLY, REV. H. (1985) 'Lisnamaine Castle', *Breifne* **6**, no. 23, 236–76.

O'REILLY, J. (1988) 'An unrecorded Tomregan megalith', *Breifne* **7**, 575–8.

Ó'RÍORDÁIN, B. (1957) 'Bronze Age burials at Termon, near Blacklion, Co. Cavan', *JRSAI* **87**, 53–9.

— (1967) 'A prehistoric burial site at Gortnacargy, Co. Cavan', *JRSAI* **97**, 61–73.

Ó'RÍORDÁIN, B. PRENDERGAST, E. M. and RYNNE, E. (1962) 'National Museum of Ireland archaeological acquisitions in the year 1960', *JRSAI* **62**, 139–72.

Ó'RÍORDÁIN, S. P. (1933) 'Discovery of an ancient burial in a cairn near Ballyconnell, Co. Cavan', *JRSAI* **63**, 167–71.

— (1952) 'Fragment of the Killycluggin Stone', *JRSAI* **82**, 68.

— (1942) (5th ed. 1979) *Antiquities of the Irish countryside.* Methuen, London.

PATERSON, T.G.F. and DAVIES, O. (1940) 'Ecclesiastical remains in Co. Cavan', *UJA* **3**, 154–6.

PATERSON, T.G.F. GAFFIKIN, M. and DAVIES, O. (1938) 'Dean Richardson's further account of Com. Cavan', *UJA* **1**, 142–54.

POWER, D. BYRNE, E. EGAN, U. LANE, S. and SLEEMAN M. (1994) *Archaeological Inventory of County Cork vol. 2: East and South Cork.* Stationery Office, Dublin.

PRICE, L. (1959) 'Rock-basins or "bullauns", at Glendalough and elsewhere', *JRSAI* **89**, 161–88.

RAFTERY, B. (1978) 'Excavations at Killycluggin, County Cavan', *UJA* **41**, 49–54.

RAFTERY, J. (1942) 'Finds from three Ulster counties', *UJA* **5**, 120–31.

— (1944) 'The Turoe Stone and the Rath of Feerwore', *JRSAI* **74**, 23–52.

RICHARDSON, P. (1939) 'Sweathouses between Blacklion and Dowra, County Cavan', *UJA* **2**, 32–5.

RICHARDSON, P. and LOWRY-CORRY, D. (1938) 'The cashels of Moneygashel, County Cavan', *UJA* **1**, 19–21.

— (1940) 'Some further megalithic discoveries in the Counties of Cavan and Leitrim', *JRSAI* **70**, 169–81.

SAUNDERSON, CAPT. A. (1936) *The Saundersons of Castle Saunderson.* Privately published, London.

WADDELL, J. (1990) *The Bronze Age burials of Ireland.* Galway University Press.

WAKEMAN, W. F. (1875) 'On certain markings on rocks, pillar-stones, and other monuments, observed chiefly in the County Fermanagh', *JRSAI* **13**, 445–74.

— (1878) 'On certain lines of stones, and other antiquities, at Cavancarragh, Co. Fermanagh', *JRSAI* **14**, 499–512.

— (1879) 'On some recent antiquarian discoveries at Toam and Killicarney, near Blacklion, in the County of Cavan', *JRSAI* **15**, 183–200.

WALSH, A. (1987) 'Excavating the Black Pig's Dyke', *Emania* **3**, 5–11.

WEIR, A. (1989) 'Sweathouses: puzzling and disappearing', *Archaeology Ireland*, vol. 3. no. 1, 10–13. Wordwell, Dublin.

WILDE, R.W. (1861–4) 'Description of a crannog in the County of Cavan', *PRIA* **8**, 274–8.

WOOD-MARTIN, W.G. (1886) (Reprint 1983) *The lake dwellings of Ireland: or ancient lacustrine habitations of Erin, commonly called crannogs.* Hodges, Figgis and Co., Dublin.

Townland Name Index

Inventory numbers follow the site classifications in this index and refer the reader to the relevant entries in the text.

Location Maps

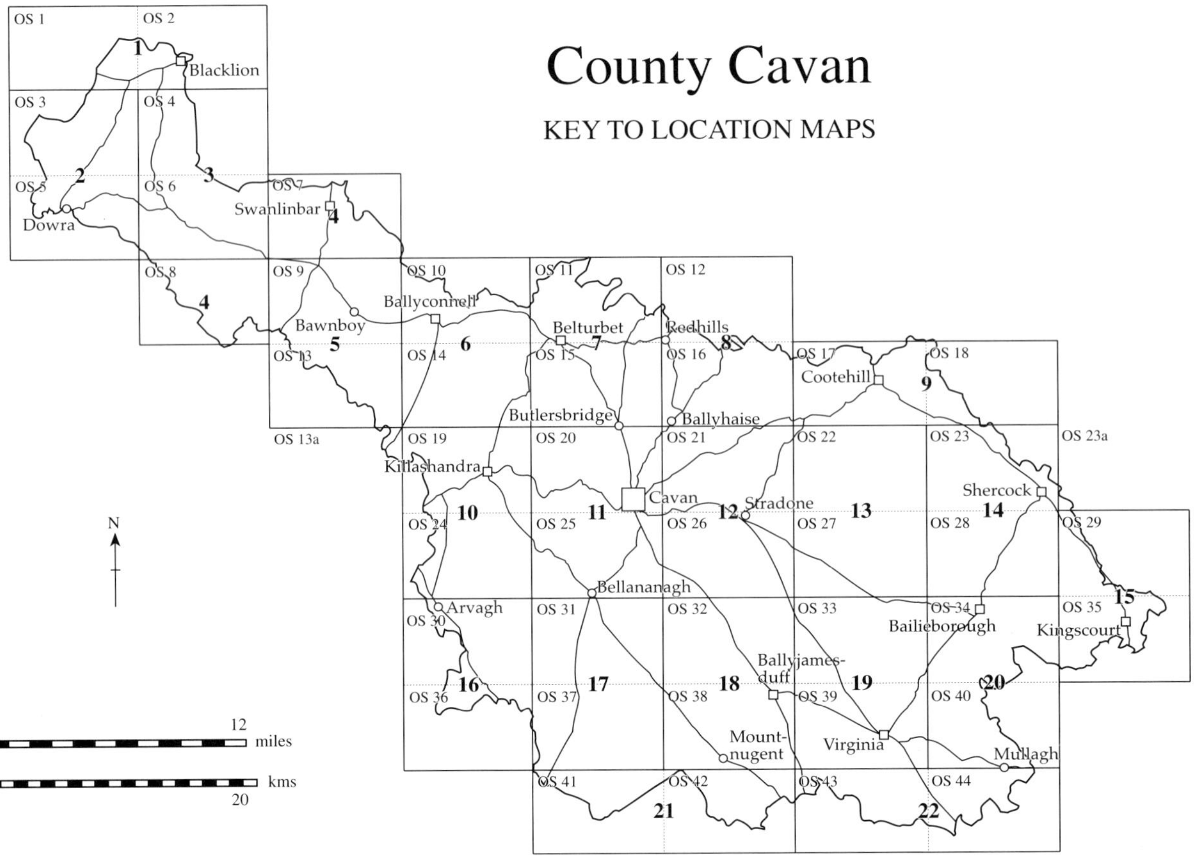

County Cavan—key to location maps

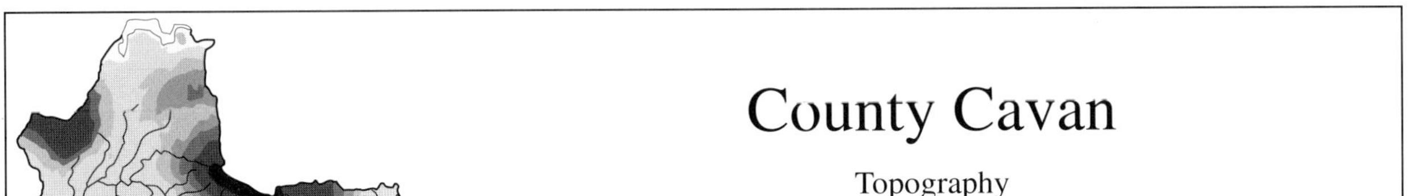

County Cavan—topography

MAP 1

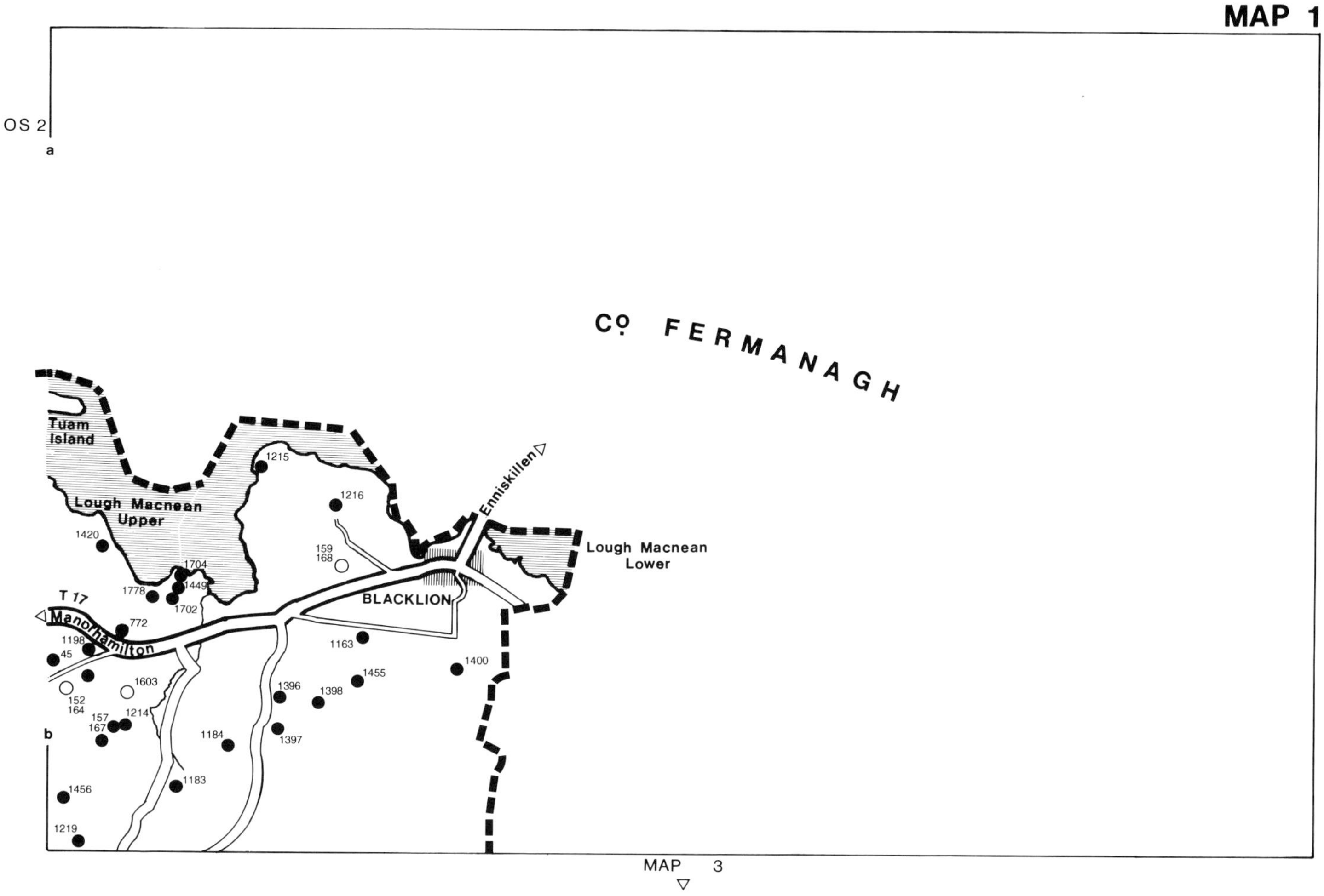
OS 2
a
b
Cº FERMANAGH
Tuam Island
Lough Macnean Upper
Lough Macnean Lower
Enniskillen
BLACKLION
T 17
Manorhamilton
1215
1216
1420
159
168
1704
1449
1778
1702
772
1198
45
1163
1400
1603
1455
1396
1398
152
164
157
167
1214
1184
1397
1183
1456
1219
MAP 3

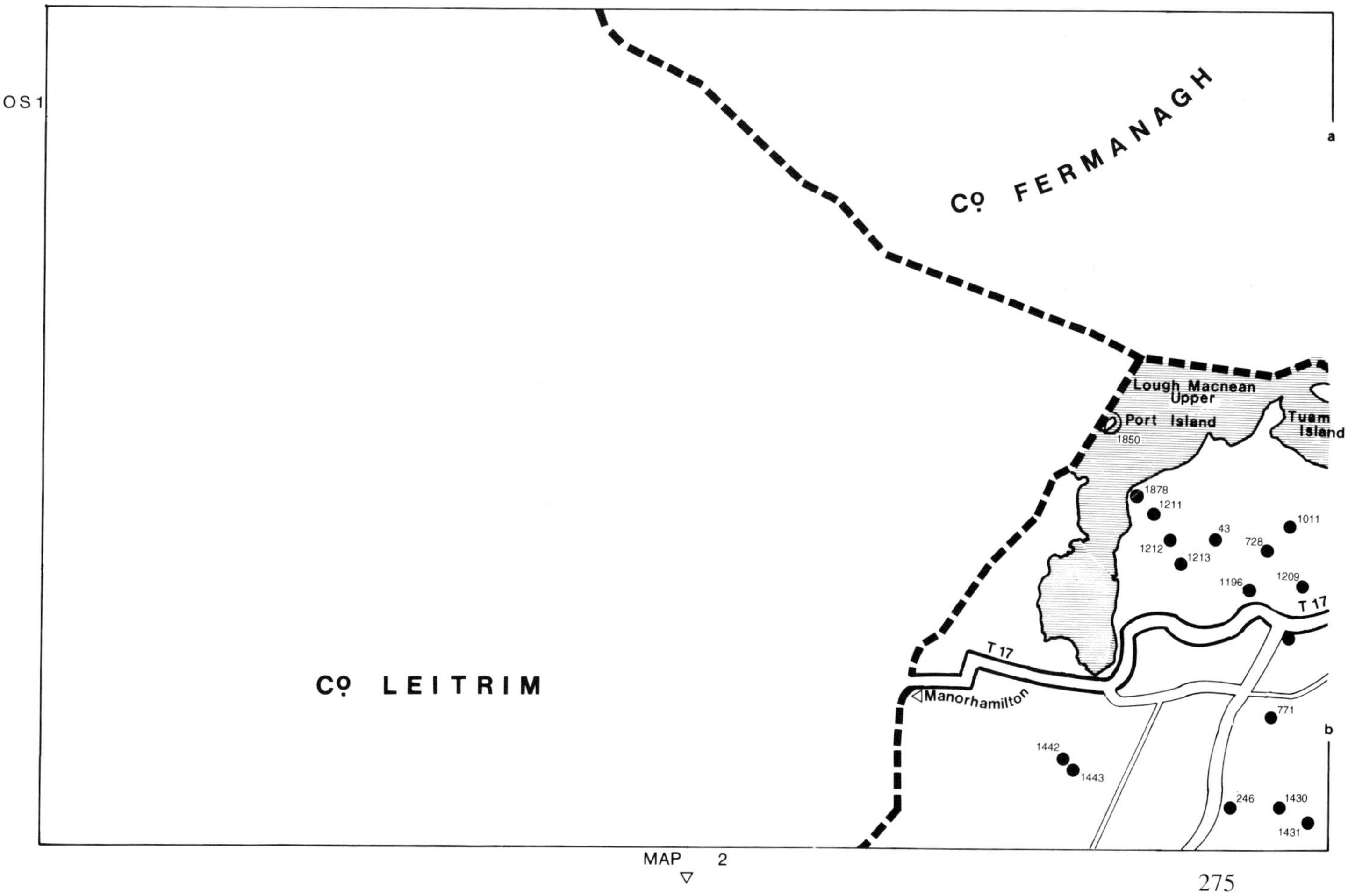
OS 1
a
b
Cº FERMANAGH
Cº LEITRIM
Lough Macnean Upper
Port Island
Tuam Island
1850
1878
1211
43
1011
1212
1213
728
1196
1209
T 17
T 17
Manorhamilton
771
1442
1443
246
1430
1431
MAP 2

MAP 2

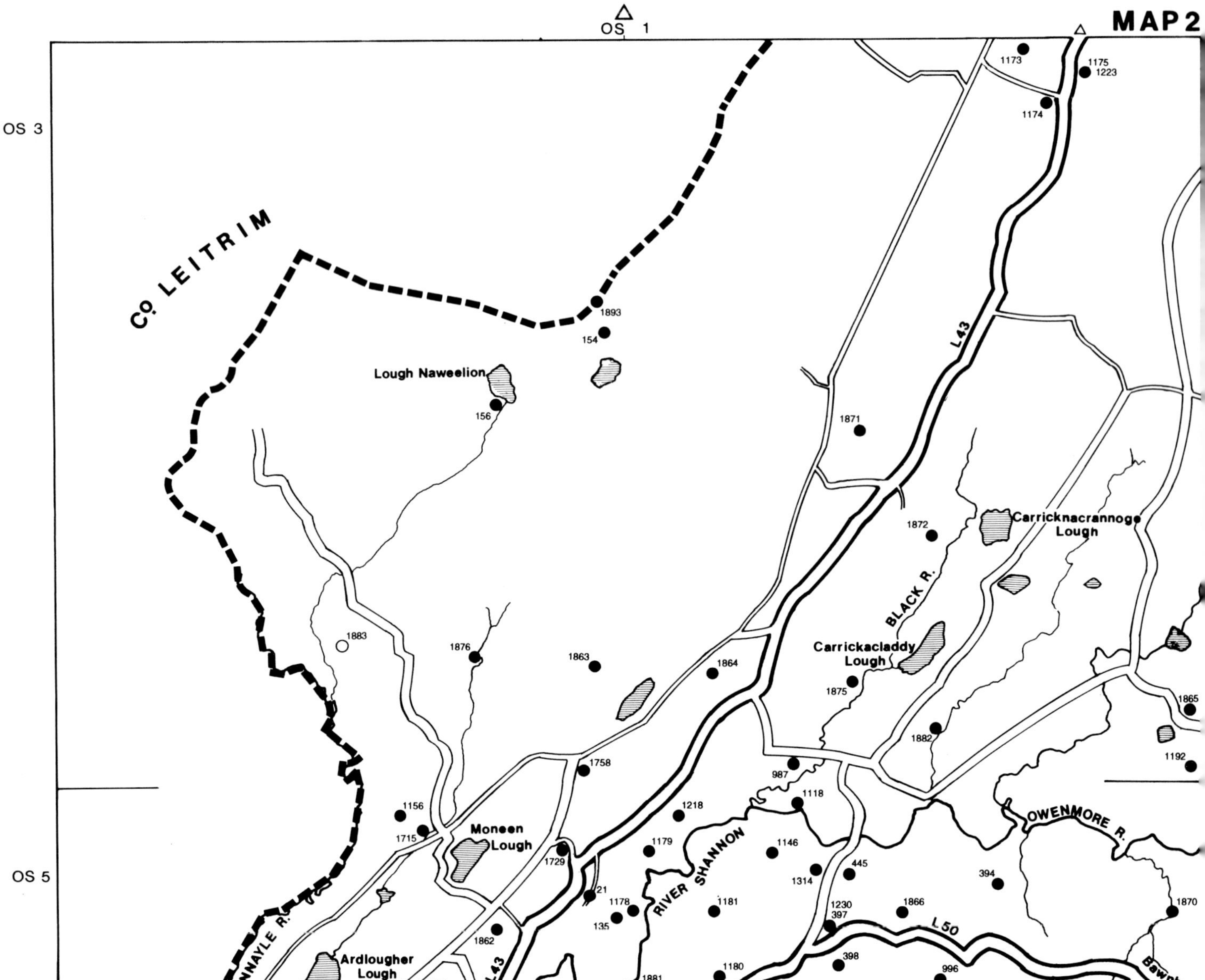

OS 1
OS 3
OS 5
Cº LEITRIM
Lough Naweelion
Carricknacrannoge Lough
Carrickacladdy Lough
BLACK R.
Moneen Lough
Ardlougher Lough
OWENNAYLE R.
RIVER SHANNON
OWENMORE R.
DOWRA
L43
L 50
Bawnboy
Cº LEITRIM
1173
1175
1223
1174
1893
154
156
1871
1872
1883
1876
1863
1864
1875
1882
1865
1192
1758
987
1118
1218
1156
1715
1179
1146
1729
1314
445
394
21
1178
135
1181
1230
397
1866
1870
1862
398
996
1180
1881
1868
1217
1880
1859
1867
1189
370
1861
763
1744
1860
371
372
1387
181
1190
147
141
142
143
139
140
137
138

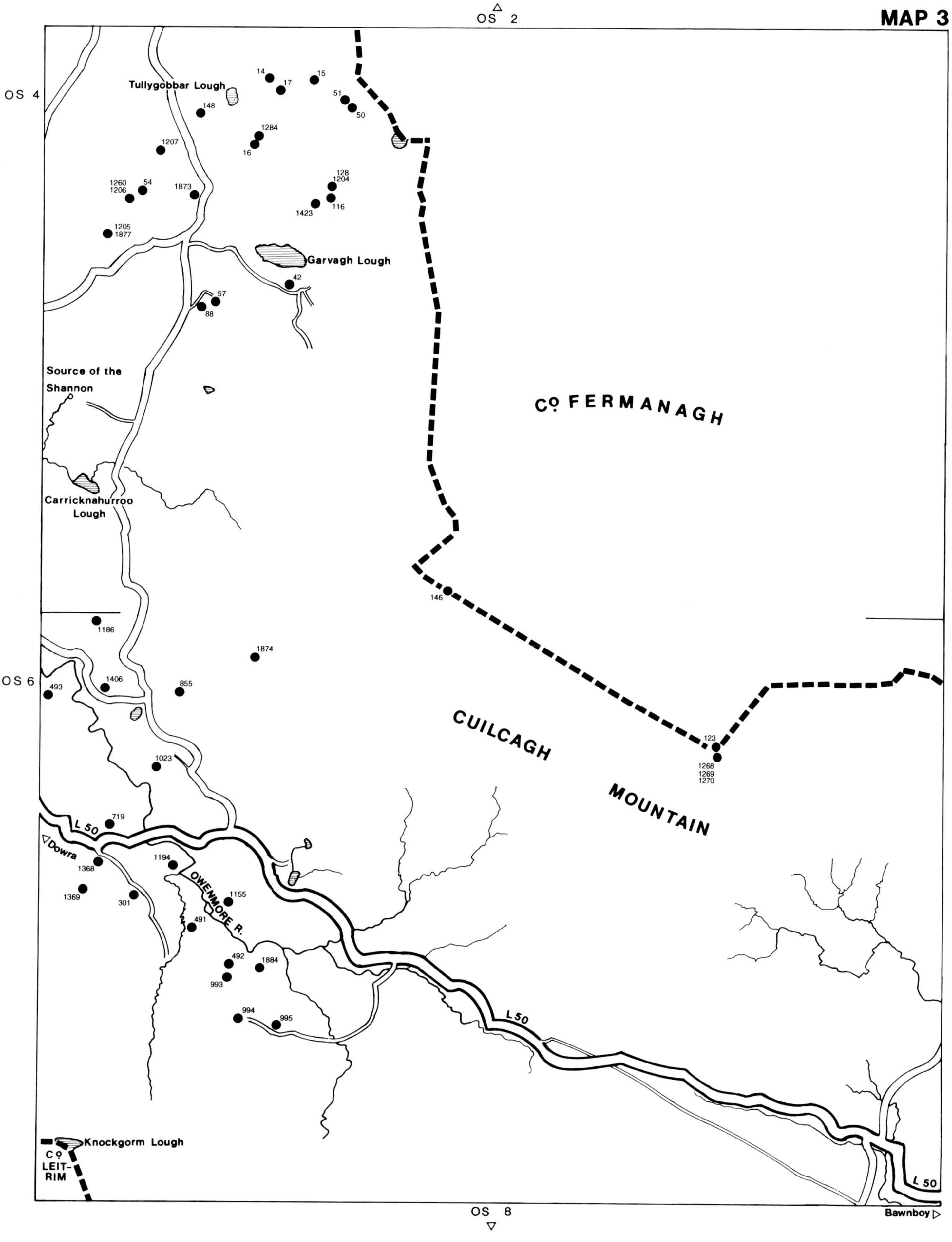
MAP 3
OS 2
OS 4
OS 6
OS 8
Tullygobbar Lough
Garvagh Lough
Source of the Shannon
Carricknahurroo Lough
Co FERMANAGH
CUILCAGH MOUNTAIN
L 50
Dowra
OWENMORE R.
Knockgorm Lough
Co LEIT-RIM
Bawnboy
14
15
17
51
50
148
1284
16
1207
128
1204
1260
1206
54
1873
1423
116
1205
1877
42
57
88
146
1186
1874
1406
493
855
123
1268
1269
1270
1023
719
1194
1368
1369
301
1155
491
492
1884
993
994
995

OS 7

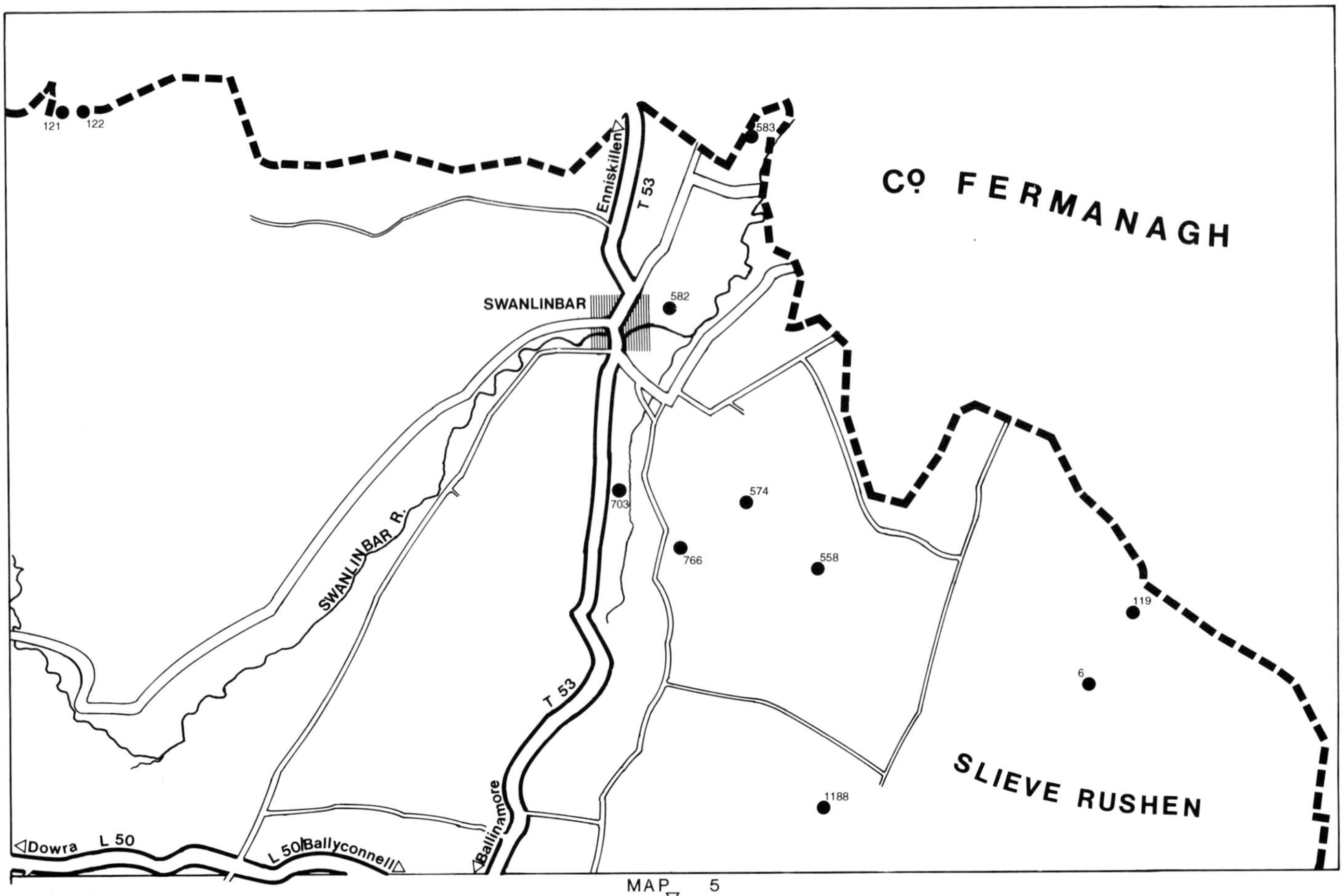

MAP 5

MAP 3

OS 8

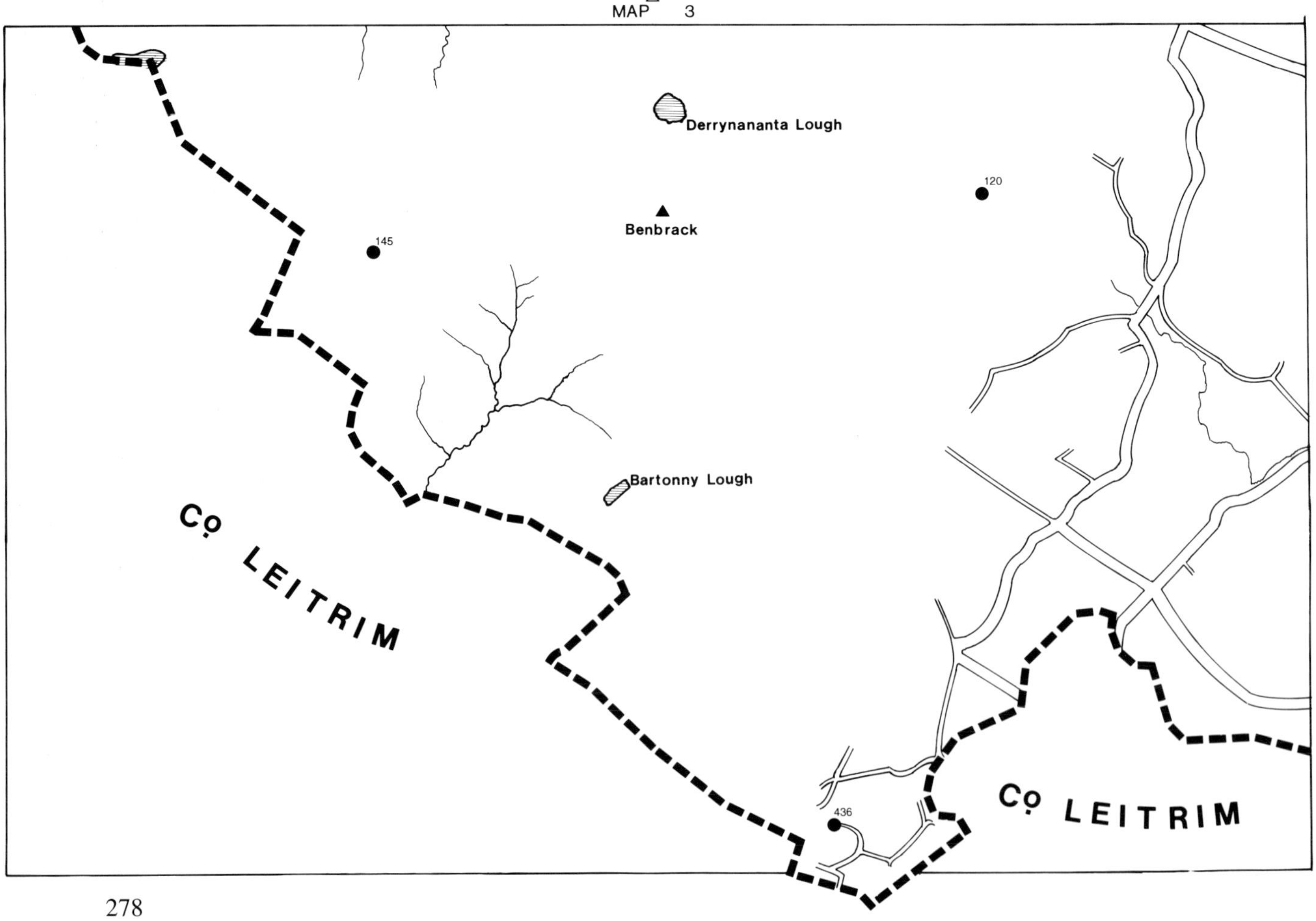

MAP 5

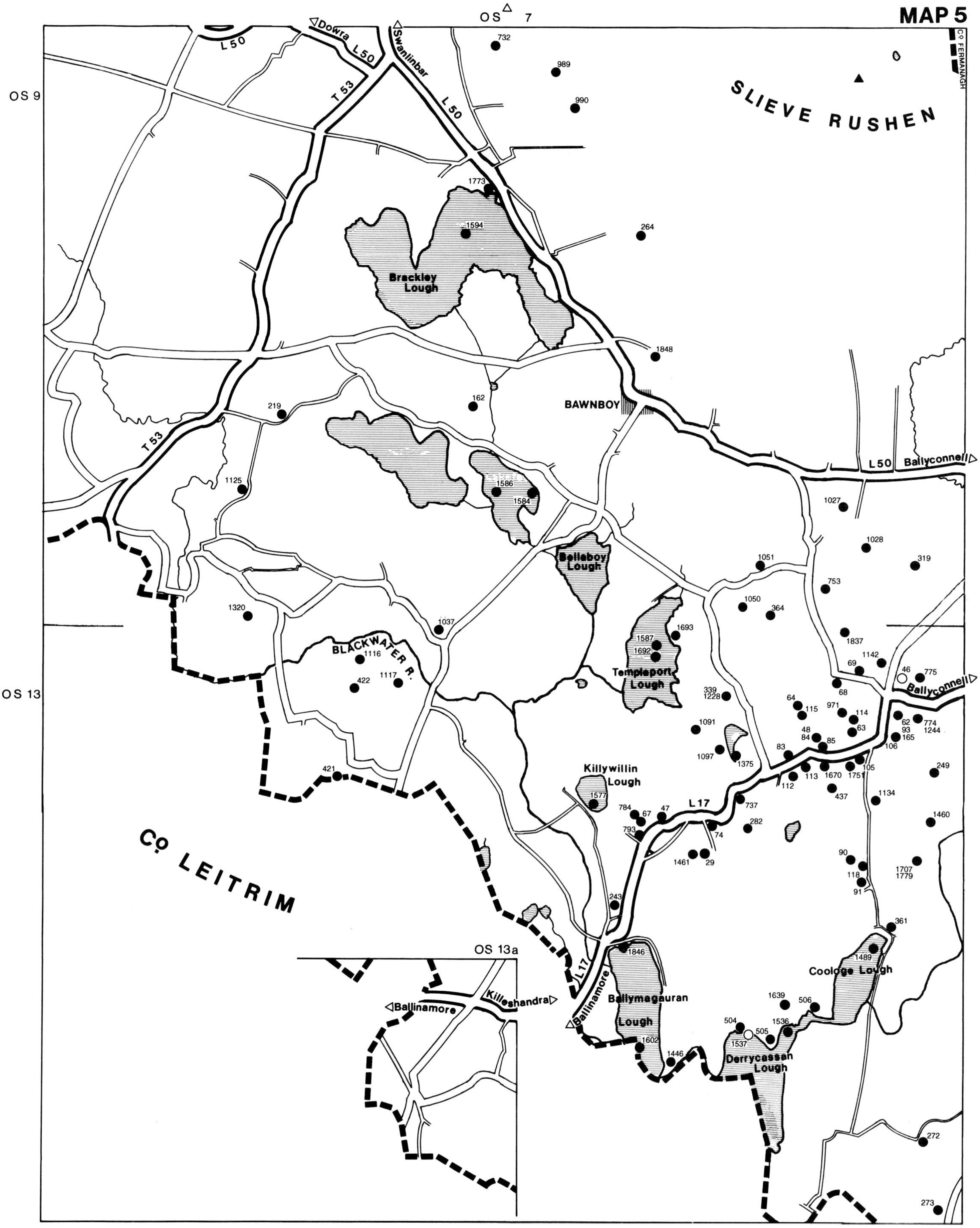
OS 7
OS 9
OS 13
OS 13a
Co FERMANAGH
Co LEITRIM
SLIEVE RUSHEN
Dowra
Swanlinbar
L 50
T 53
L 17
Ballyconnell
Ballinamore
Killeshandra
BAWNBOY
Brackley Lough
Bellaboy Lough
Templeport Lough
Killywillin Lough
Ballymagauran Lough
Derrycassan Lough
Coologe Lough
BLACKWATER R.
732
989
990
1773
1594
264
1848
162
219
1125
1586
1584
1027
1028
319
1051
753
1050
364
1320
1037
1693
1587
1692
1837
1142
69
46
775
1116
422
1117
339
1228
68
64
115
971
114
62
774
1244
93
165
1091
63
48
84
85
106
1097
1375
83
249
421
112
113
1670
1751
105
437
1134
1577
784
67
47
737
282
1460
793
74
1461
29
90
118
91
1707
1779
243
361
1846
1489
1639
506
504
505
1536
1537
1602
1446
272
273

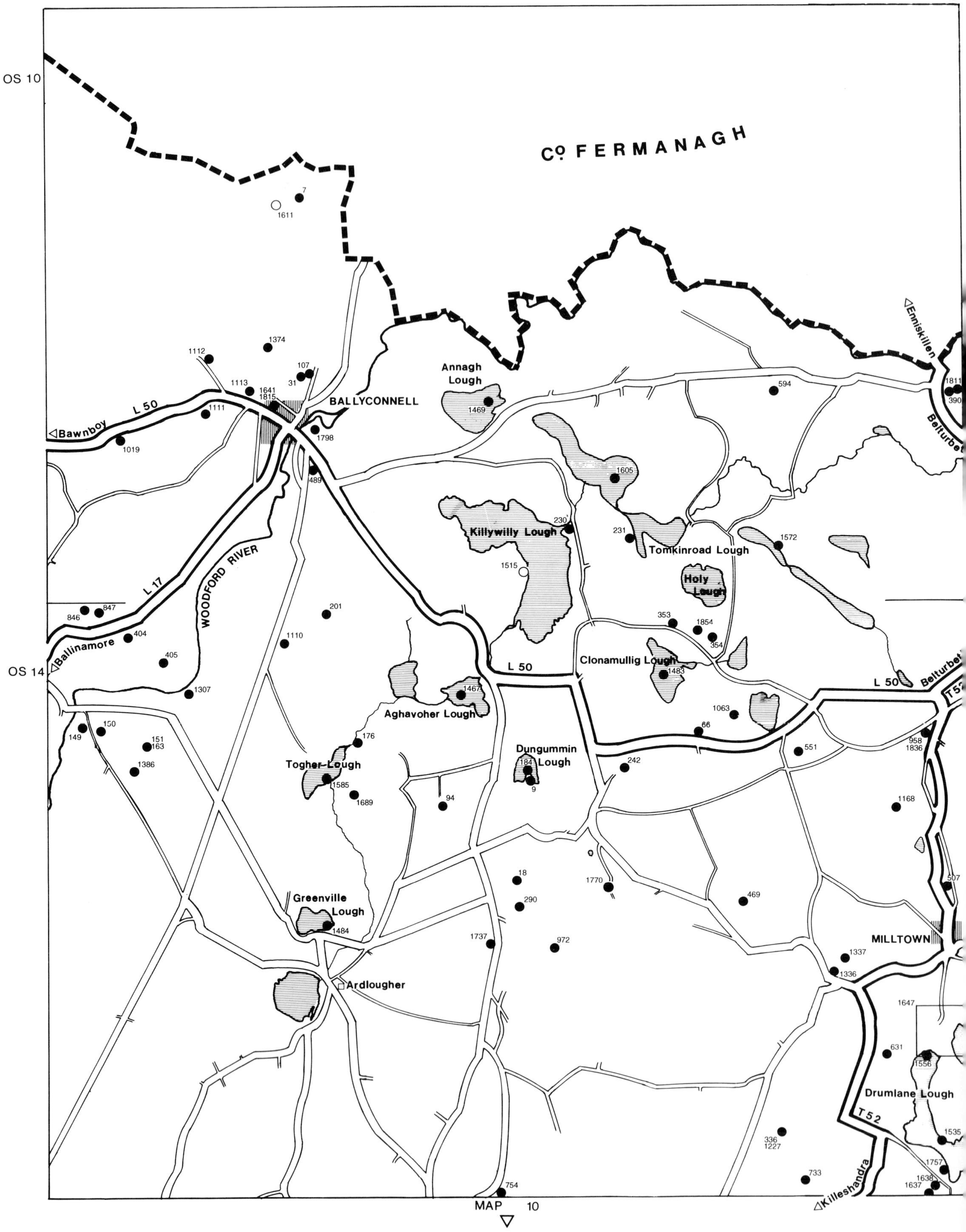
OS 10
OS 14
Cº FERMANAGH
BALLYCONNELL
L 50
◁Bawnboy
L 17
WOODFORD RIVER
◁Ballinamore
Annagh Lough
Killywilly Lough
Tomkinroad Lough
Holy Lough
Clonamullig Lough
Aghavoher Lough
Togher Lough
Dungummin Lough
Greenville Lough
Ardlougher
MILLTOWN
Drumlane Lough
T52
◁Enniskillen
Belturbet
L 50 Belturbet
◁Killeshandra
MAP 10

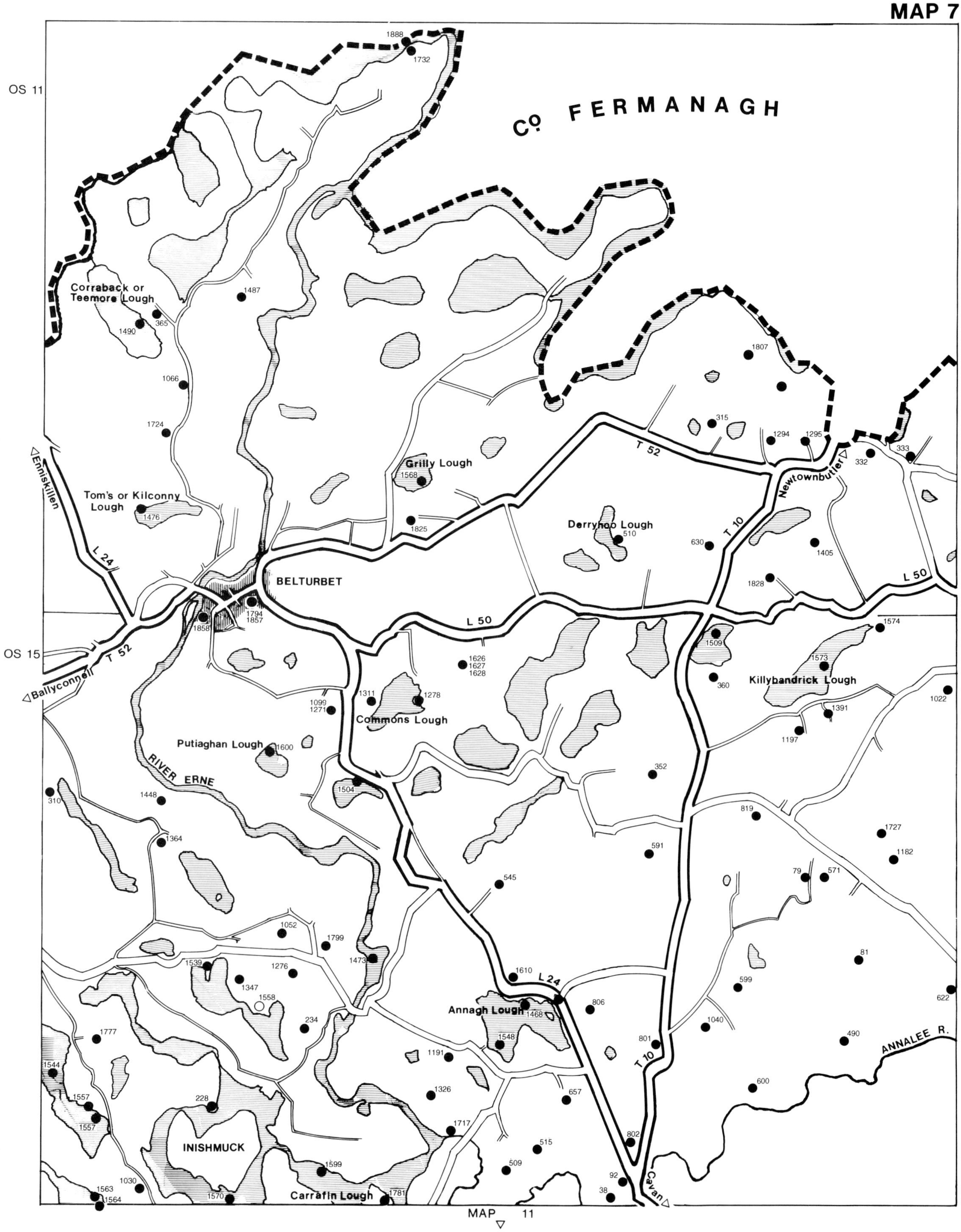

OS 11
OS 15
Co FERMANAGH
Corraback or Teemore Lough
Tom's or Kilconny Lough
Grilly Lough
Derryhoo Lough
BELTURBET
Commons Lough
Putiaghan Lough
Killybandrick Lough
RIVER ERNE
Annagh Lough
INISHMUCK
Carrafin Lough
ANNALEE R.
Enniskillen
Ballyconnell
Newtownbutler
Cavan
L 24
T 52
L 50
T 10
MAP 11
1888
1732
1487
365
1490
1066
1724
1476
1568
1825
1794
1857
1858
315
1807
1294
1295
332
333
510
630
1405
1828
1574
1509
1573
360
1022
1391
1197
1626
1627
1628
1311
1278
1099
1271
1600
1504
310
1448
1364
352
819
1727
1182
591
79
571
545
1052
1799
1473
1539
1276
1347
1558
234
1610
806
1468
599
81
622
1040
490
1777
1544
1548
1191
801
600
1557
228
1326
657
1717
802
515
509
1599
92
38
1563
1564
1030
1570
1781

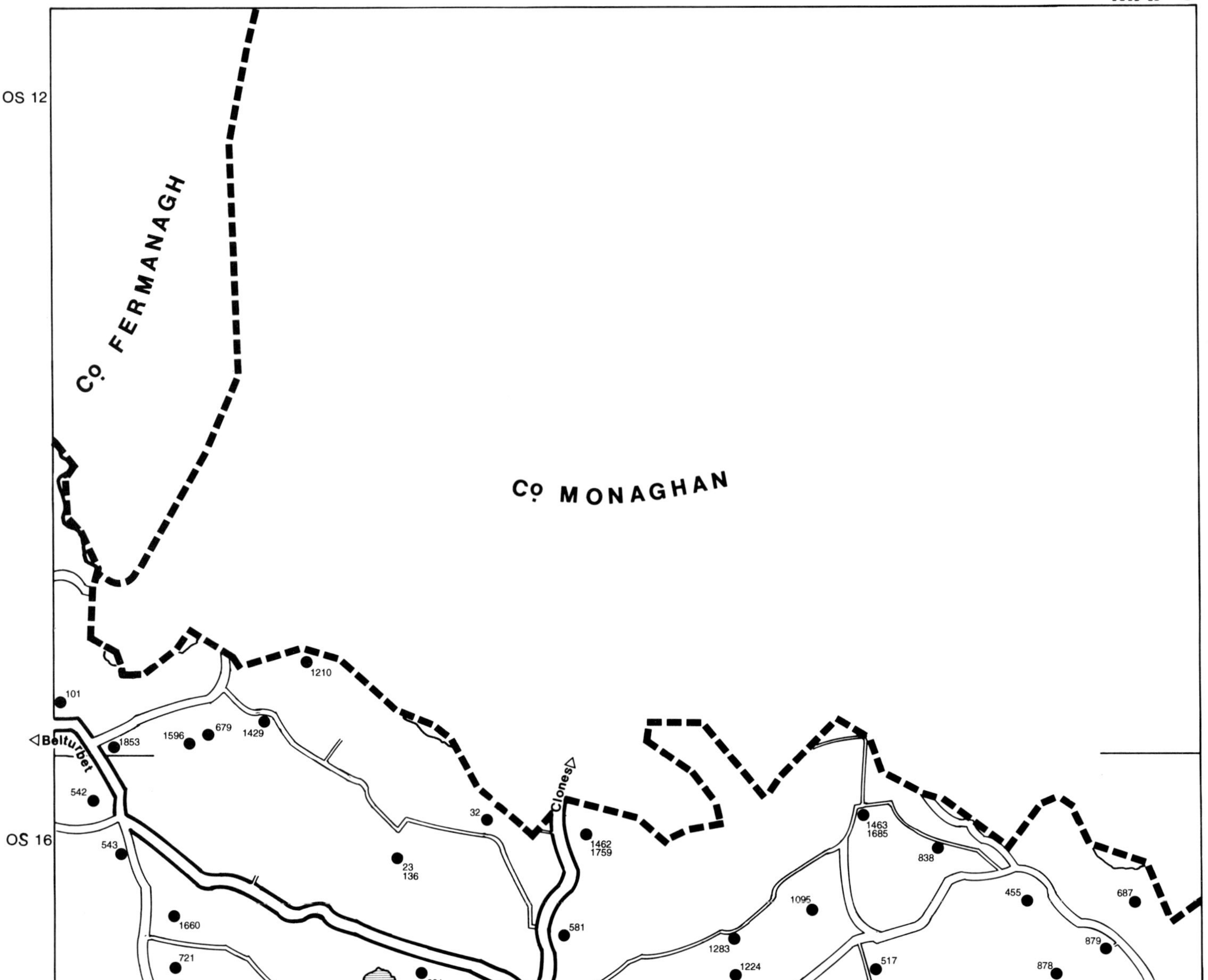
OS 12
OS 16
Co FERMANAGH
Co MONAGHAN
Belturbet
Clones
Cootehill
Annaghoash Lough
Coppony Lough
ANNALEE R.
BALLYHAISE
Cavan
Cavan
Cootehill
MAP 12

MAP 9

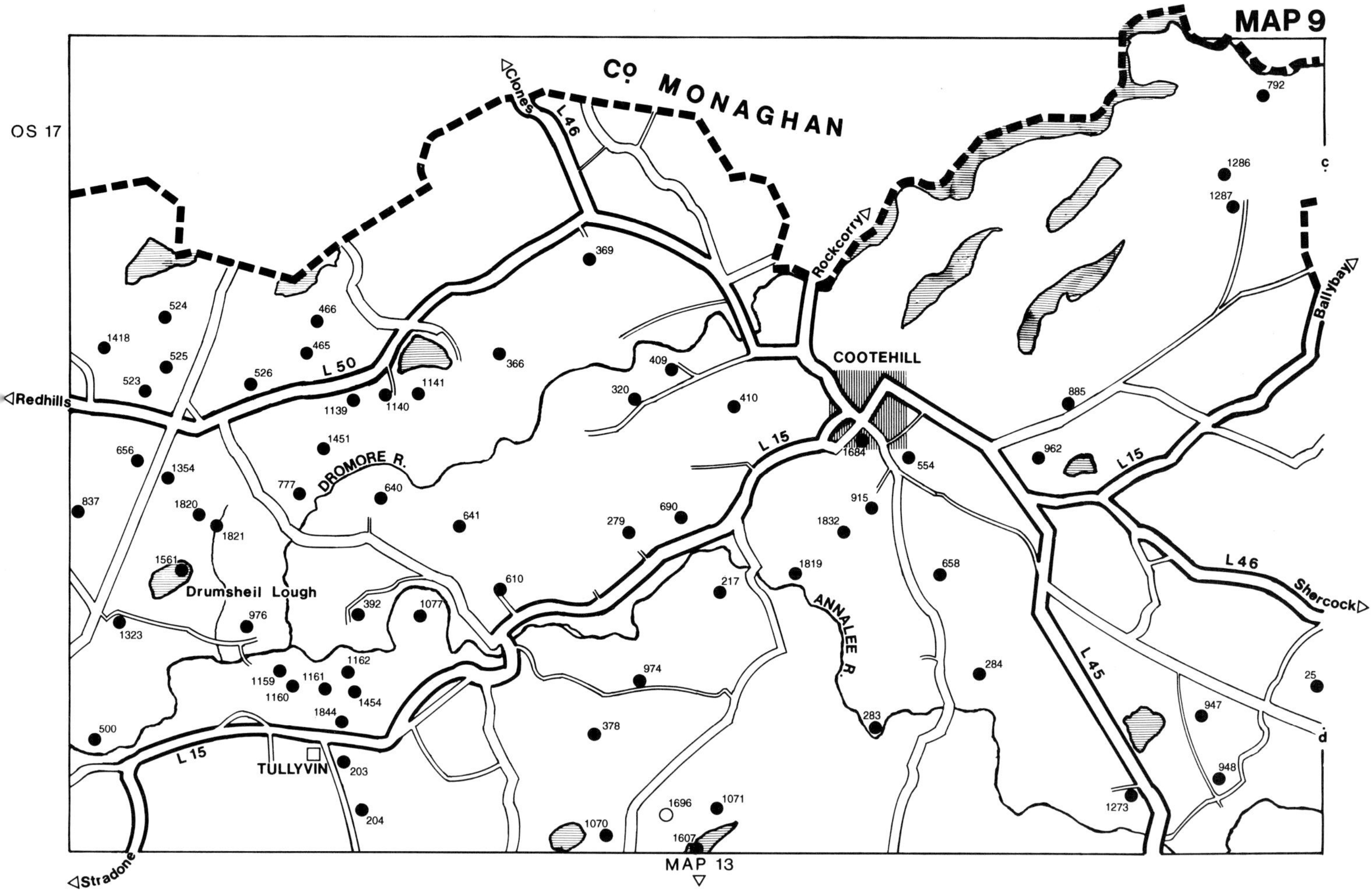

OS 17
Co. MONAGHAN
Clones
L 46
Rockcorry
Ballybay
COOTEHILL
Redhills
L 50
L 15
L 45
DROMORE R.
ANNALEE R.
Drumsheil Lough
TULLYVIN
Shercock
Stradone
MAP 13
792
1286
1287
369
524
1418
525
523
526
466
465
1139
1140
1141
366
409
320
410
885
962
1451
656
1354
837
777
640
1820
1821
641
279
690
1684
554
915
1832
1561
1819
658
217
610
392
1077
976
1323
1162
1159
1161
1160
1454
1844
974
284
25
947
500
378
283
948
203
204
1273
1696
1071
1070
1607

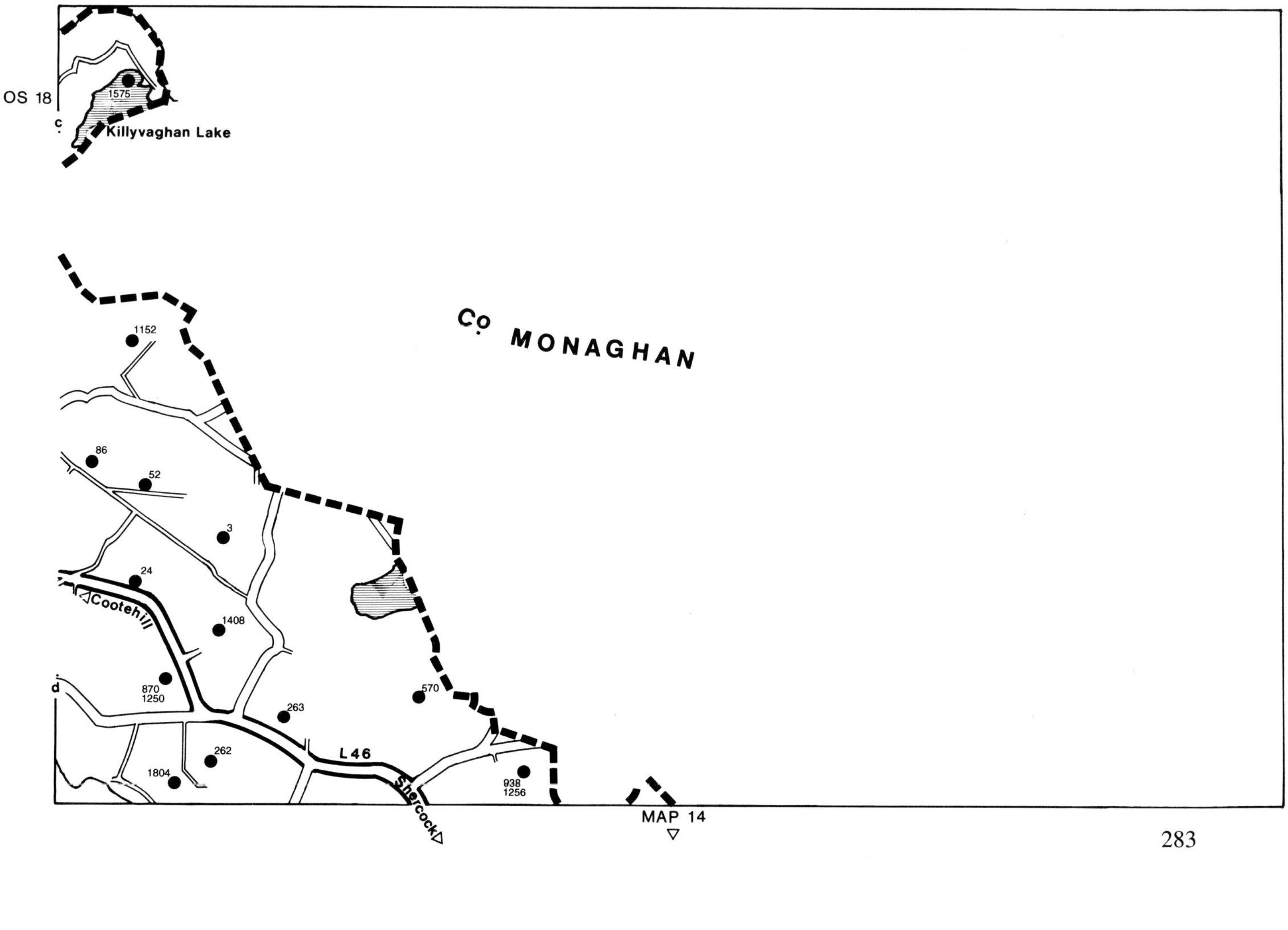

OS 18
1575
Killyvaghan Lake
Co. MONAGHAN
1152
86
52
3
24
Cootehill
1408
870
1250
570
263
262
1804
L 46
Shercock
938
1256
MAP 14

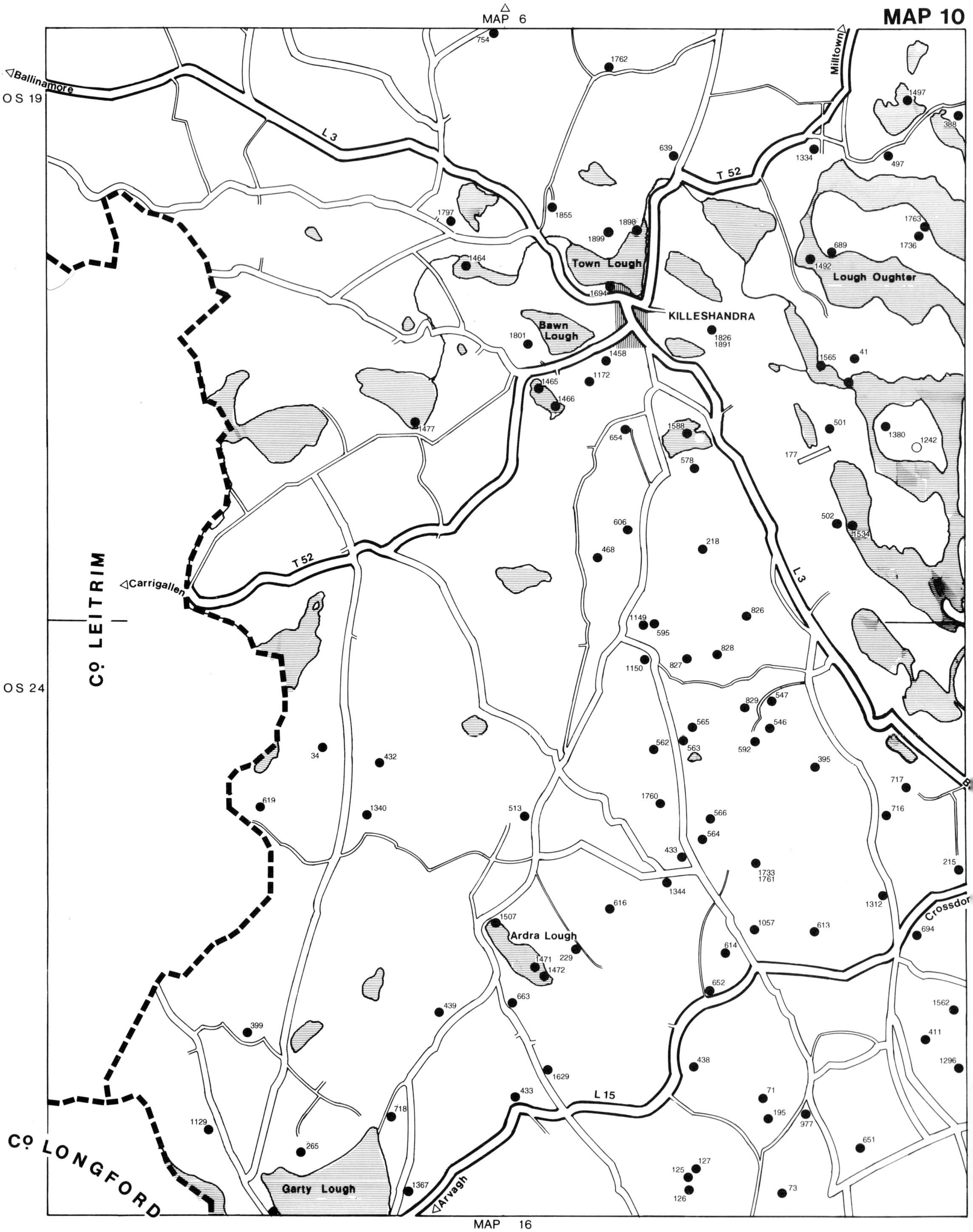
MAP 6
MAP 16
OS 19
OS 24
Ballinamore
Milltown
Carrigallen
Arvagh
Crossdor
L 3
T 52
L 15
Co. LEITRIM
Co. LONGFORD
KILLESHANDRA
Town Lough
Bawn Lough
Lough Oughter
Ardra Lough
Garty Lough
754
1762
1497
388
639
1334
497
1855
1797
1898
1899
1763
1736
689
1492
1464
1694
1826
1891
1801
1458
1565
41
1172
1465
1466
1477
1588
654
501
1380
1242
177
578
502
1534
606
218
468
826
1149
595
828
1150
827
829
547
565
546
562
563
592
34
432
395
717
619
1340
513
1760
566
716
564
433
215
1733
1761
1344
1312
616
1507
1057
613
694
229
614
1471
1472
652
663
439
1562
399
411
438
1296
1629
71
433
L 15
718
195
977
1129
651
265
127
125
126
1367
73

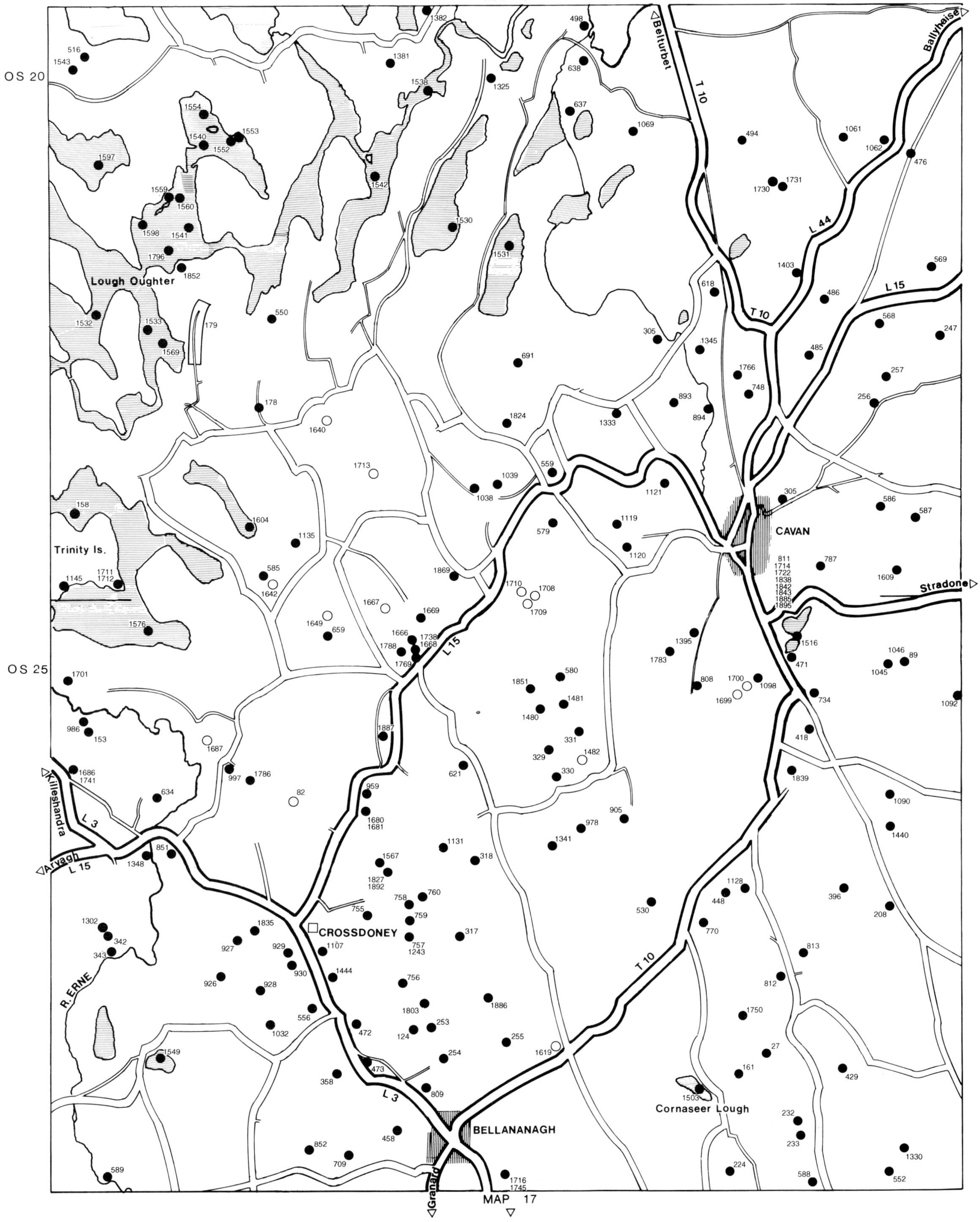
MAP 7
OS 20
OS 25
Lough Oughter
Trinity Is.
Belturbet
Ballyhaise
T 10
L 44
L 15
CAVAN
Stradone
Killeshandra
Arvagh
L 3
R. ERNE
CROSSDONEY
Cornaseer Lough
BELLANANAGH
Granard
MAP 17

MAP 12

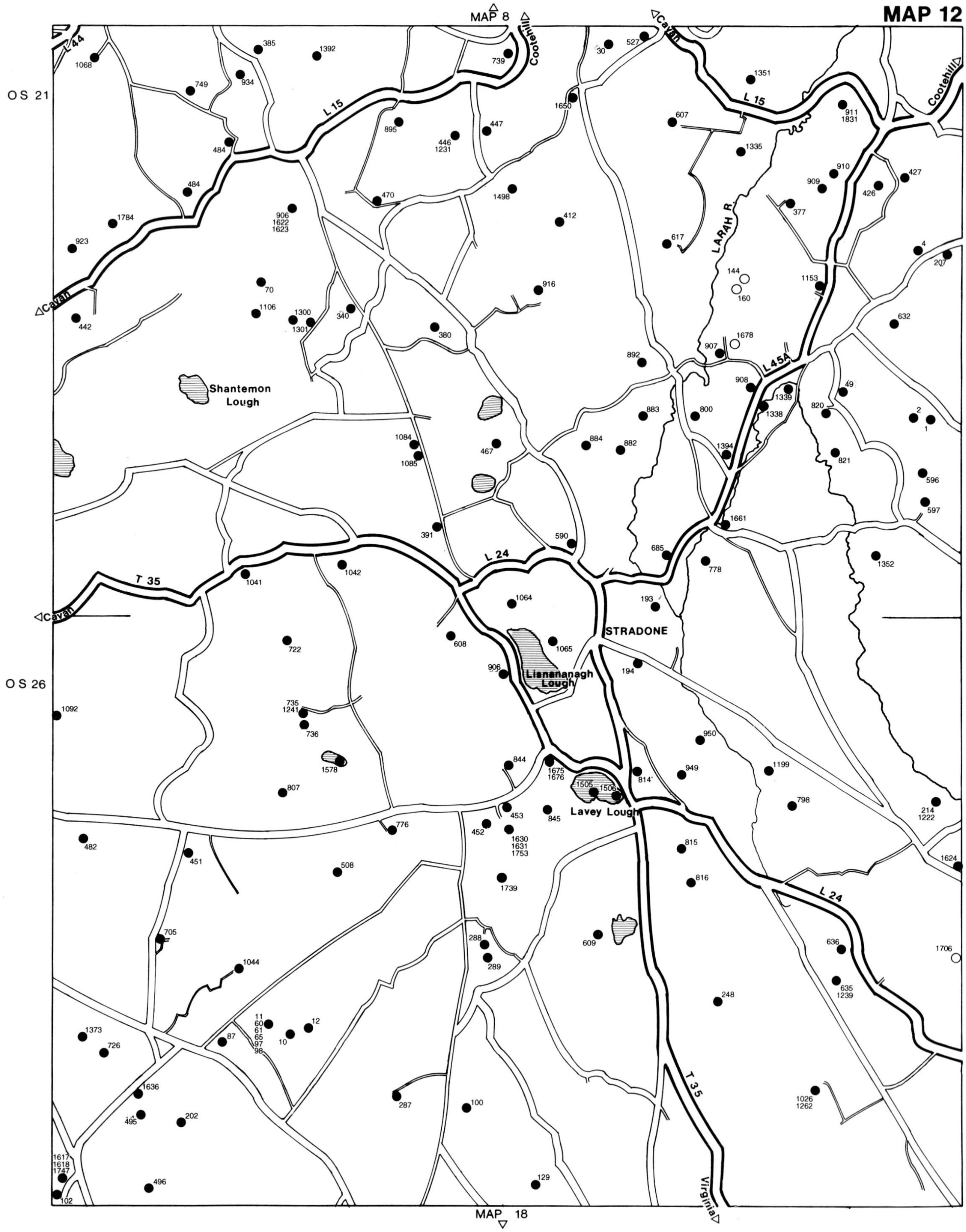

MAP 8
MAP 18
OS 21
OS 26
Cootehill
Cavan
Virginia
L 44
L 15
L 24
L 45A
T 35
LARAH R.
Shantemon Lough
Lisnananagh Lough
Lavey Lough
STRADONE
1068
385
1392
749
934
739
30
527
1351
1650
607
911
1831
895
446
1231
447
484
1335
910
909
427
426
377
470
1498
906
1622
1623
1784
412
617
923
4
207
144
160
1153
916
70
1106
1300
1301
340
442
380
632
892
907
1678
908
1339
1338
49
820
2
1
883
800
1394
884
882
467
1084
1085
821
596
597
391
590
1661
685
778
1352
1042
1041
1064
193
608
722
1065
906
194
1092
735
1241
736
950
1578
844
1675
1676
949
1199
814
807
1505
1506
798
214
1222
453
845
776
452
1630
1631
1753
482
451
508
815
1624
1739
816
705
609
288
289
636
1706
1044
635
1239
248
11
60
61
65
97
98
12
10
87
1373
726
1636
287
100
1026
1262
495
202
1617
1618
1747
102
496
129

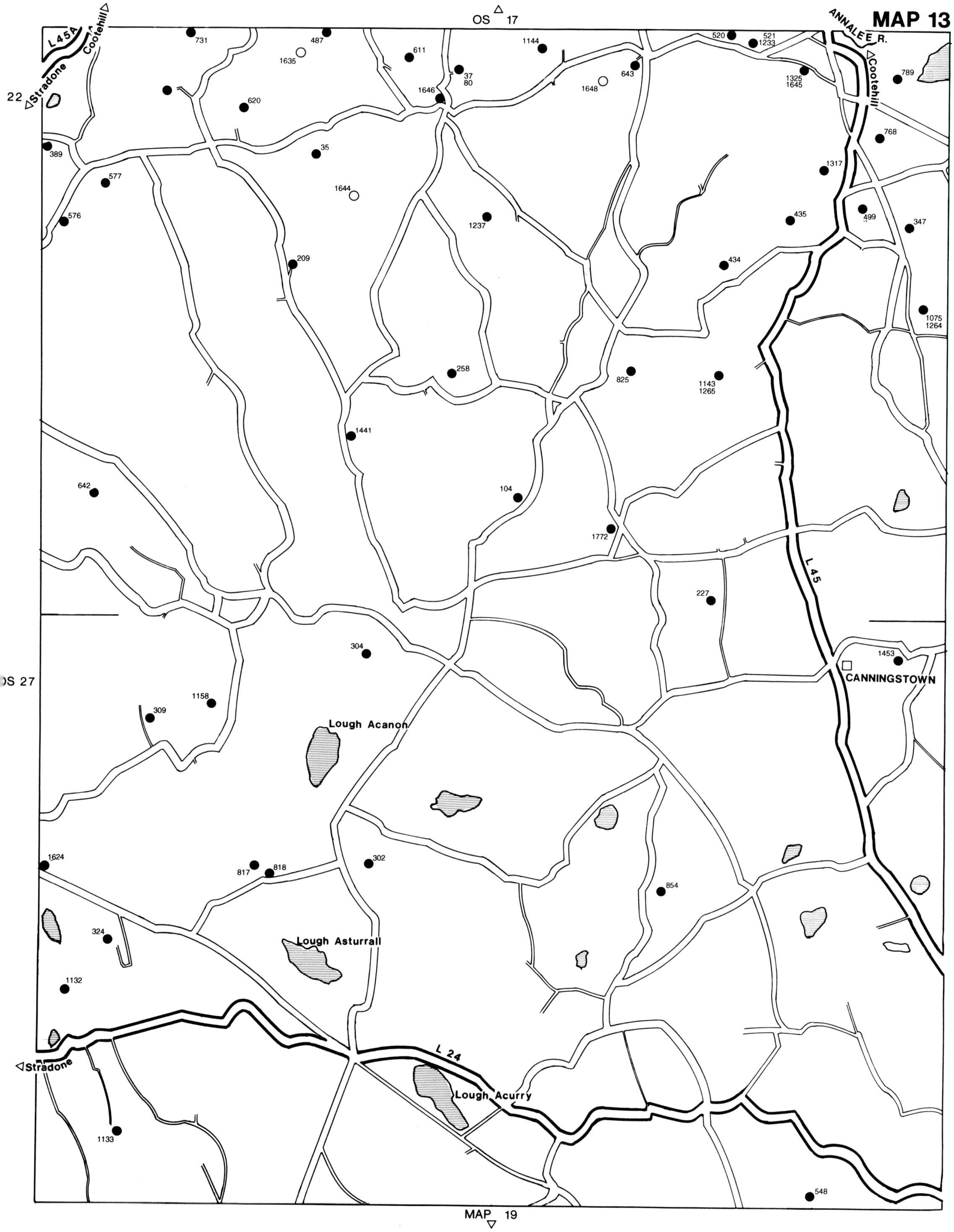
MAP 13
OS 17
L45A
Stradone
Cootehill
22
ANNALEE R.
Cootehill
OS 27
CANNINGSTOWN
L 45
Lough Acanon
Lough Asturrall
Lough Acurry
L 24
Stradone
MAP 19
731
487
1635
611
1144
520
521
1233
37
80
1646
1648
643
1325
1645
789
620
389
35
768
577
1644
1317
576
1237
435
499
347
209
434
1075
1264
258
825
1143
1265
1441
642
104
1772
227
304
1453
1158
309
1624
817
818
302
854
324
1132
1133
548

MAP 14

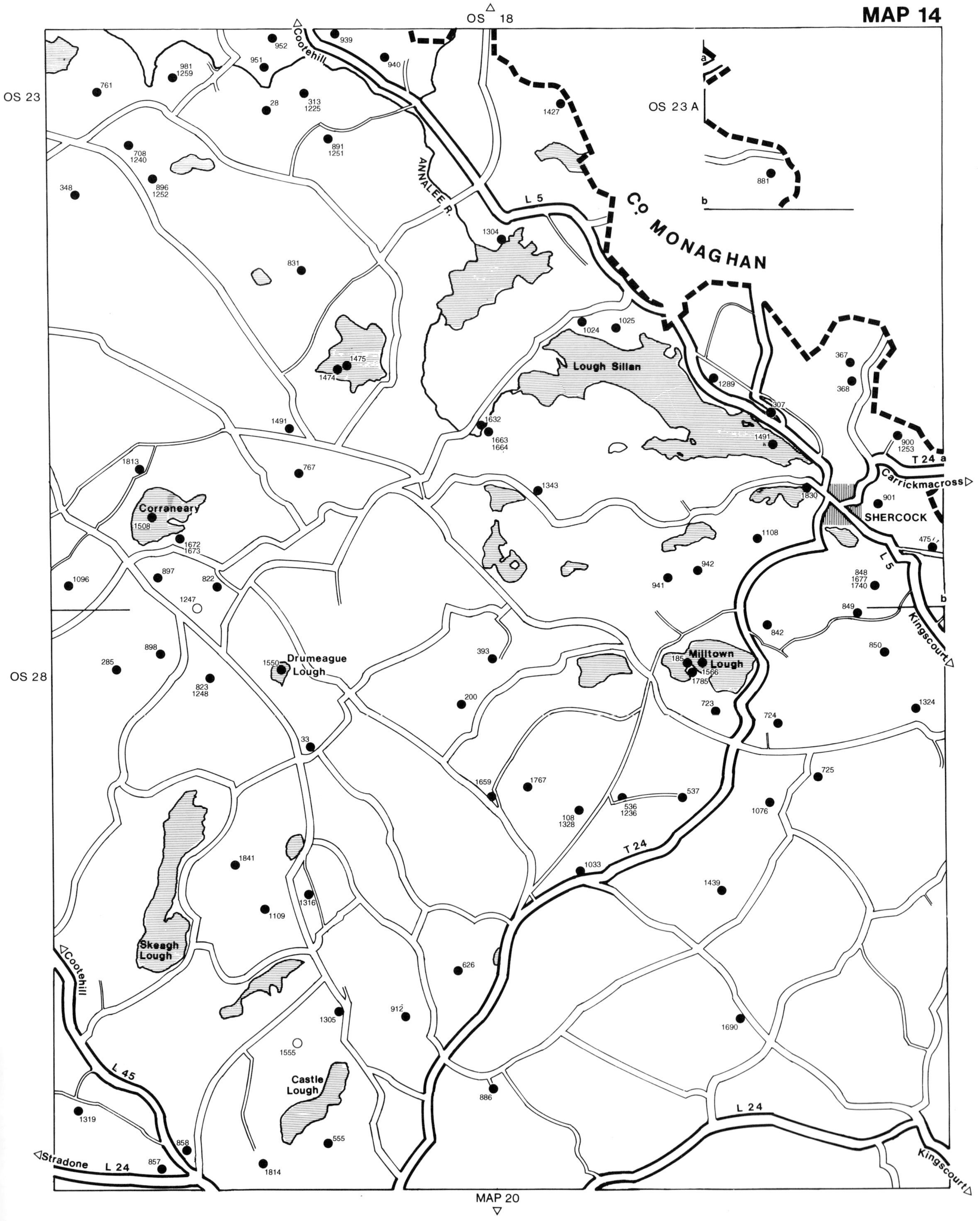

OS 18
OS 23
OS 23 A
OS 28
Cootehill
ANNALEE R.
L 5
Co. MONAGHAN
Lough Sillan
Corraneary
Drumeague Lough
Milltown Lough
Skeagh Lough
Castle Lough
SHERCOCK
T 24
Carrickmacross
Kingscourt
T 24
L 24
L 45
Stradone
MAP 20
939
952
951
981
1259
940
761
28
313
1225
1427
708
1240
891
1251
348
896
1252
881
1304
831
1024
1025
1475
1474
367
368
1289
1307
1491
1632
1663
1664
900
1253
1813
767
1343
1830
901
1508
1672
1673
1108
475
1096
897
822
941
942
848
1677
1740
1247
849
842
898
285
1550
823
1248
393
185
1566
1785
850
200
723
724
1324
33
1659
1767
537
536
1236
108
1328
725
1076
1841
1033
1439
1316
1109
626
912
1305
1690
1555
886
1319
858
857
555
1814

MAP 15

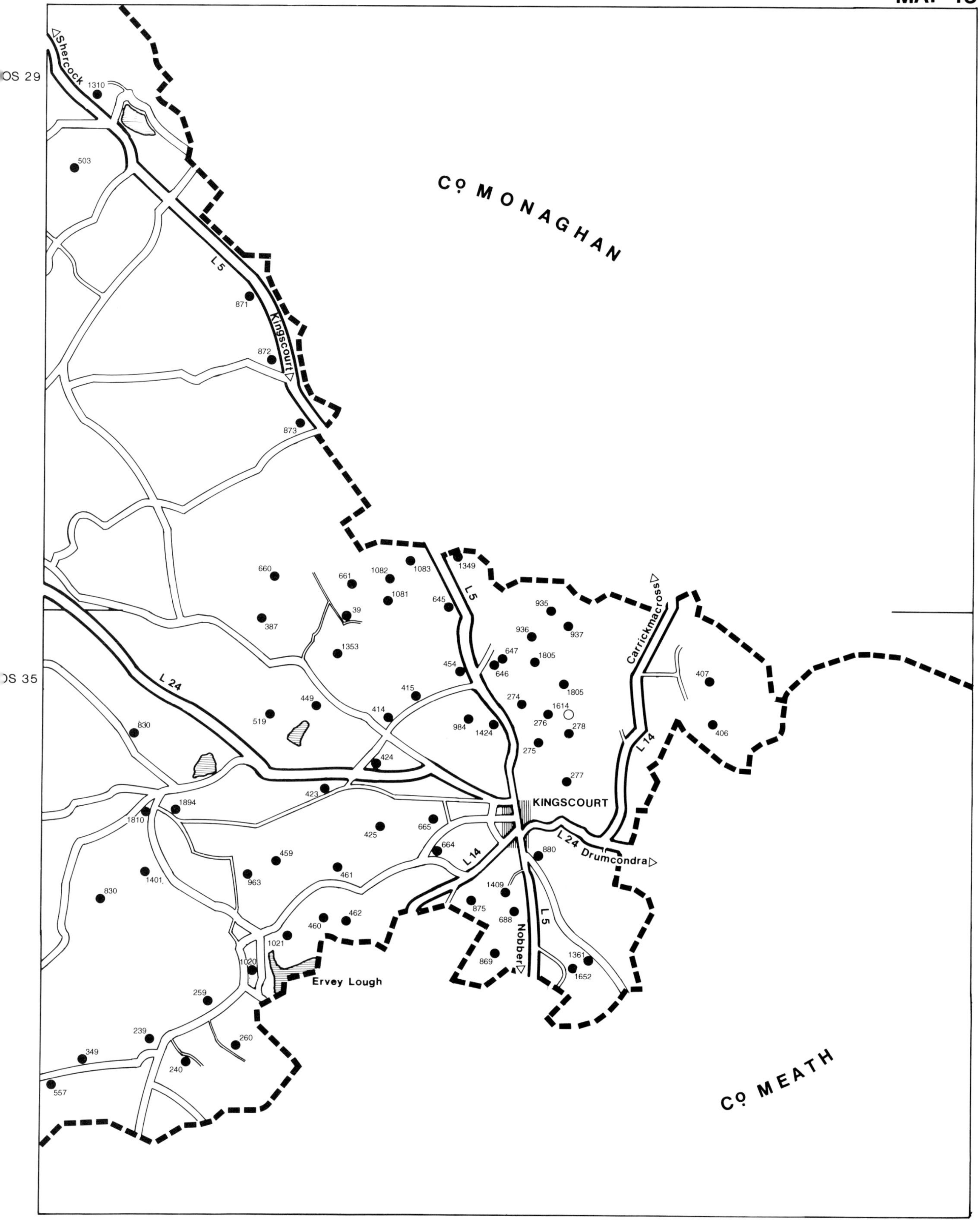
OS 29
OS 35
Shercock
Kingscourt
L 5
L 24
L 14
Co MONAGHAN
Co MEATH
KINGSCOURT
Carrickmacross
Drumcondra
Nobber
Ervey Lough
1310
503
871
872
873
660
661
1082
1083
1349
1081
645
39
387
1353
935
936
937
647
1805
454
646
415
1805
274
449
414
1614
519
984
1424
276
278
830
275
424
277
407
406
423
1894
1810
425
665
664
459
880
461
963
1401
1409
830
875
688
462
460
1021
869
1361
1652
1020
259
239
260
349
240
557

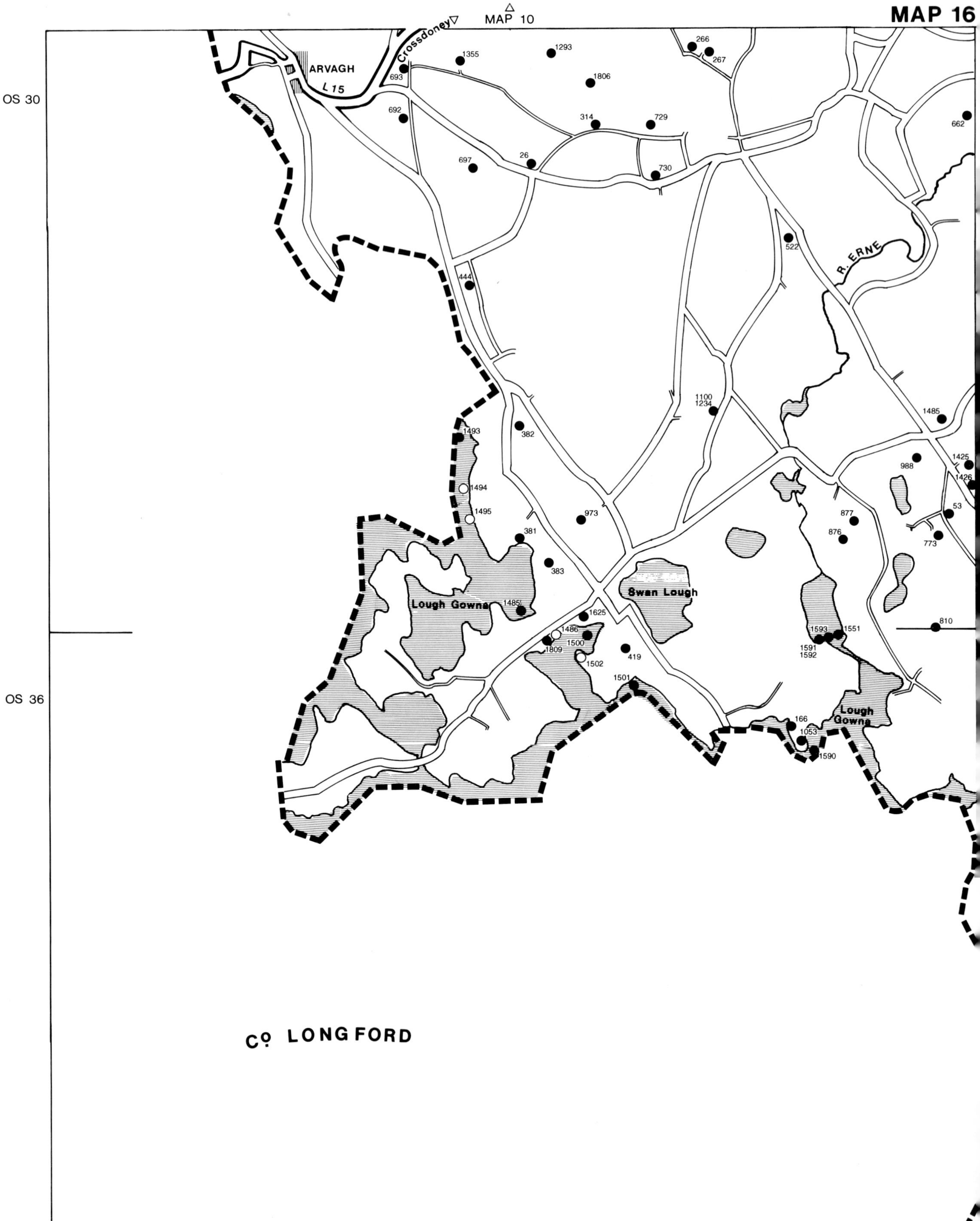
MAP 10
Crossdoney
ARVAGH
L 15
OS 30
OS 36
R. ERNE
Lough Gowna
Swan Lough
Lough Gowna
Co LONGFORD
1355
1293
266
267
693
1806
692
314
729
662
697
26
730
522
444
1100
1234
1485
382
1493
988
1425
1426
1494
1495
973
877
53
876
381
773
383
1485
1625
810
1486
1500
1593
1551
1809
1591
1592
419
1502
1501
166
1053
1590

MAP 17

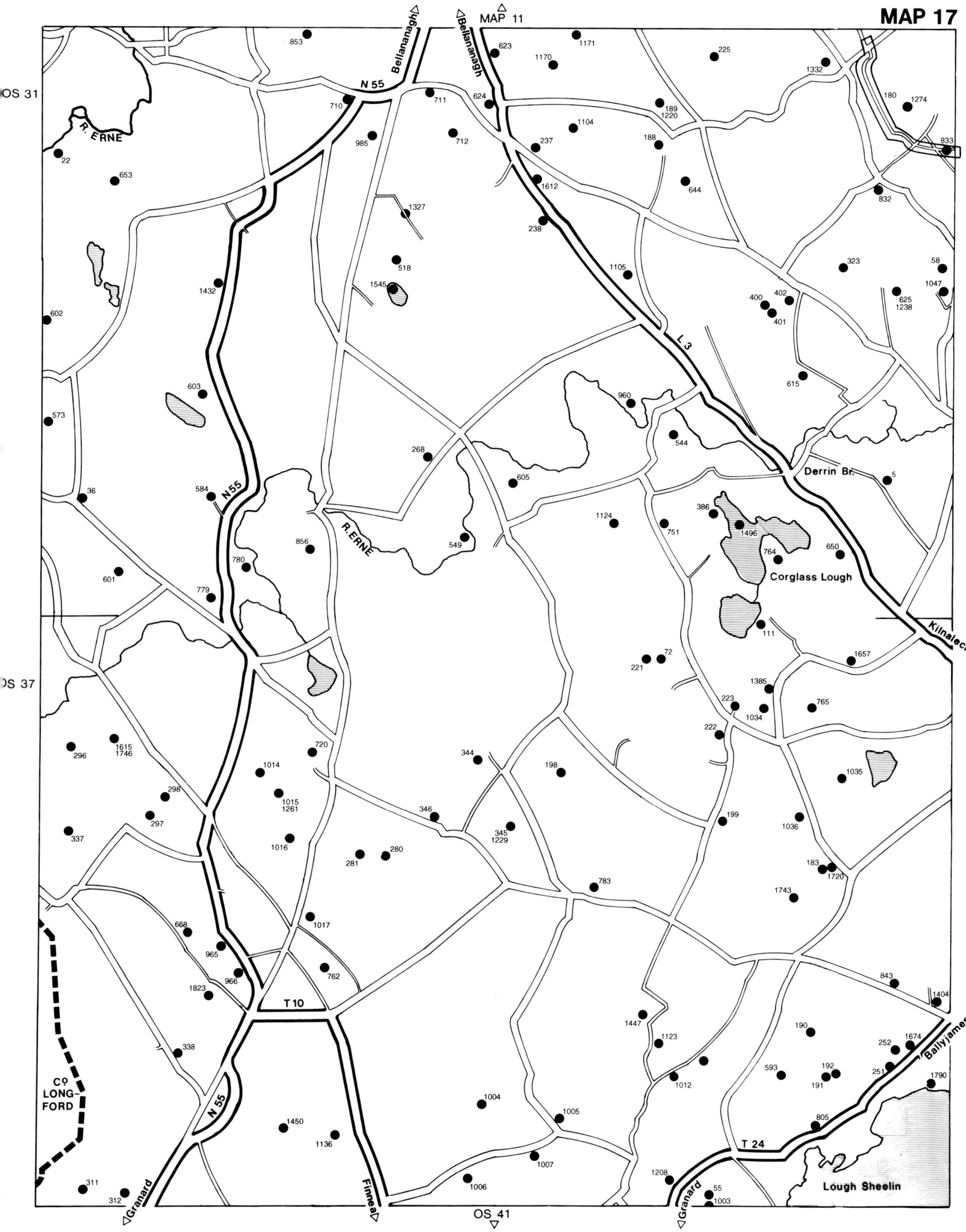
MAP 11
OS 31
OS 37
OS 41
Bellananagh
Bellananagh
N 55
N55
N 55
R. ERNE
R. ERNE
L 3
Derrin Br.
Corglass Lough
Kilnaleck
T 10
T 24
Ballyjamesduff
Granard
Granard
Finnea
Lough Sheelin
Cº LONG-FORD
853
623
1171
1170
225
1332
710
711
624
189
1220
180
1274
22
985
712
1104
237
188
833
653
1612
644
832
1327
238
518
1105
323
58
1545
1432
402
400
401
1047
625
1238
602
615
603
960
573
544
268
605
5
584
36
1124
386
751
1496
856
549
764
650
780
601
779
111
1657
221
72
1385
223
1034
765
222
720
344
198
1035
296
1615
1746
1014
1015
1261
298
297
346
345
1229
199
1036
337
1016
281
280
183
1720
783
1743
1017
668
965
966
762
843
1404
1823
1447
190
1123
252
1674
338
593
192
191
251
1012
1790
1004
1450
1136
1005
805
1007
1208
311
312
1006
55
1003

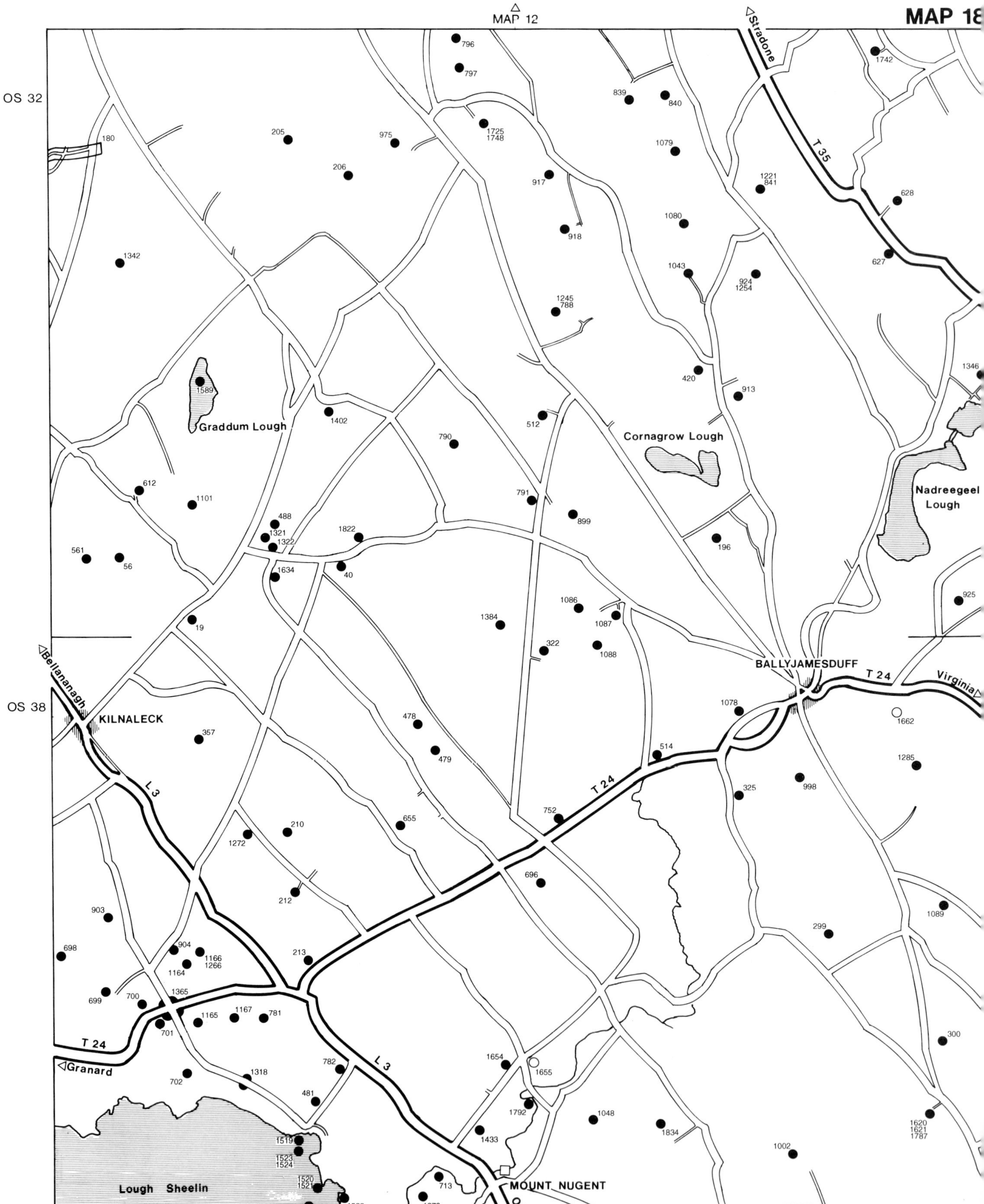
MAP 12
OS 32
OS 38
OS 42
Stradone
T 35
Bellananagh
KILNALECK
L 3
T 24
Granard
Graddum Lough
Cornagrow Lough
Nadreegeel Lough
BALLYJAMESDUFF
Virginia
Lough Sheelin
MOUNT NUGENT
Oldcastle
796
797
839
840
1742
180
205
975
1725
1748
1079
206
917
1221
841
628
1080
918
1342
1043
627
924
1254
1245
788
1346
420
913
1589
1402
512
790
612
1101
791
899
488
1321
1322
1822
561
56
40
1634
196
1086
925
1384
1087
19
322
1088
1078
1662
357
478
479
514
1285
998
325
210
1272
655
752
696
212
903
1089
299
698
904
1166
1266
1164
213
699
700
1365
1167
781
1165
701
300
1654
1655
702
1318
782
481
1792
1048
1834
1620
1621
1787
1519
1523
1524
1433
1002
1520
1521
713
1522
1372
1849
714
1151
1488
1370
1415
921

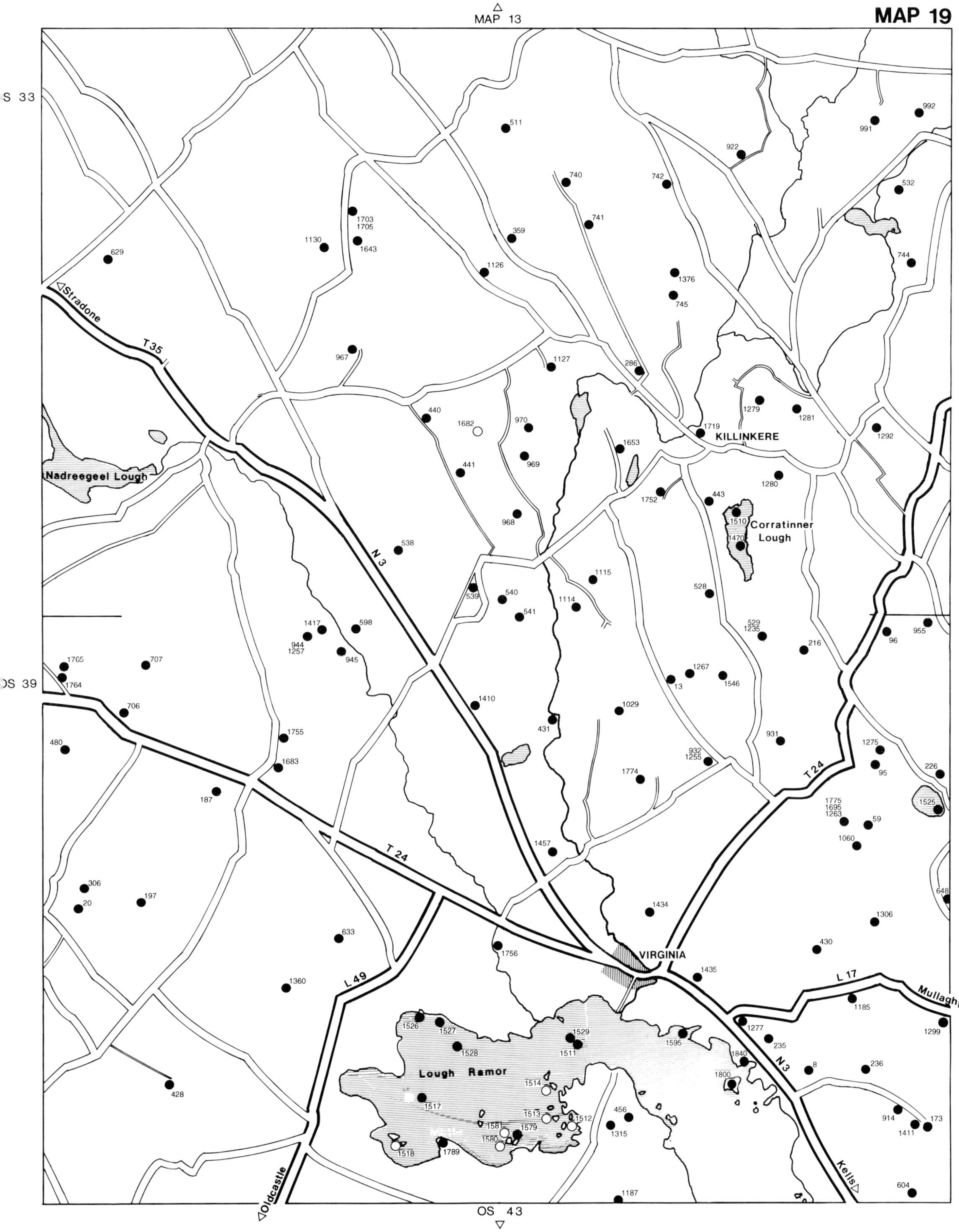
MAP 13
OS 33
OS 39
OS 43
Stradone
T 35
Nadreegeel Lough
N 3
KILLINKERE
Corratinner Lough
T 24
L 49
L 17
VIRGINIA
Lough Ramor
Mullagh
Kells
Oldcastle

MAP 20

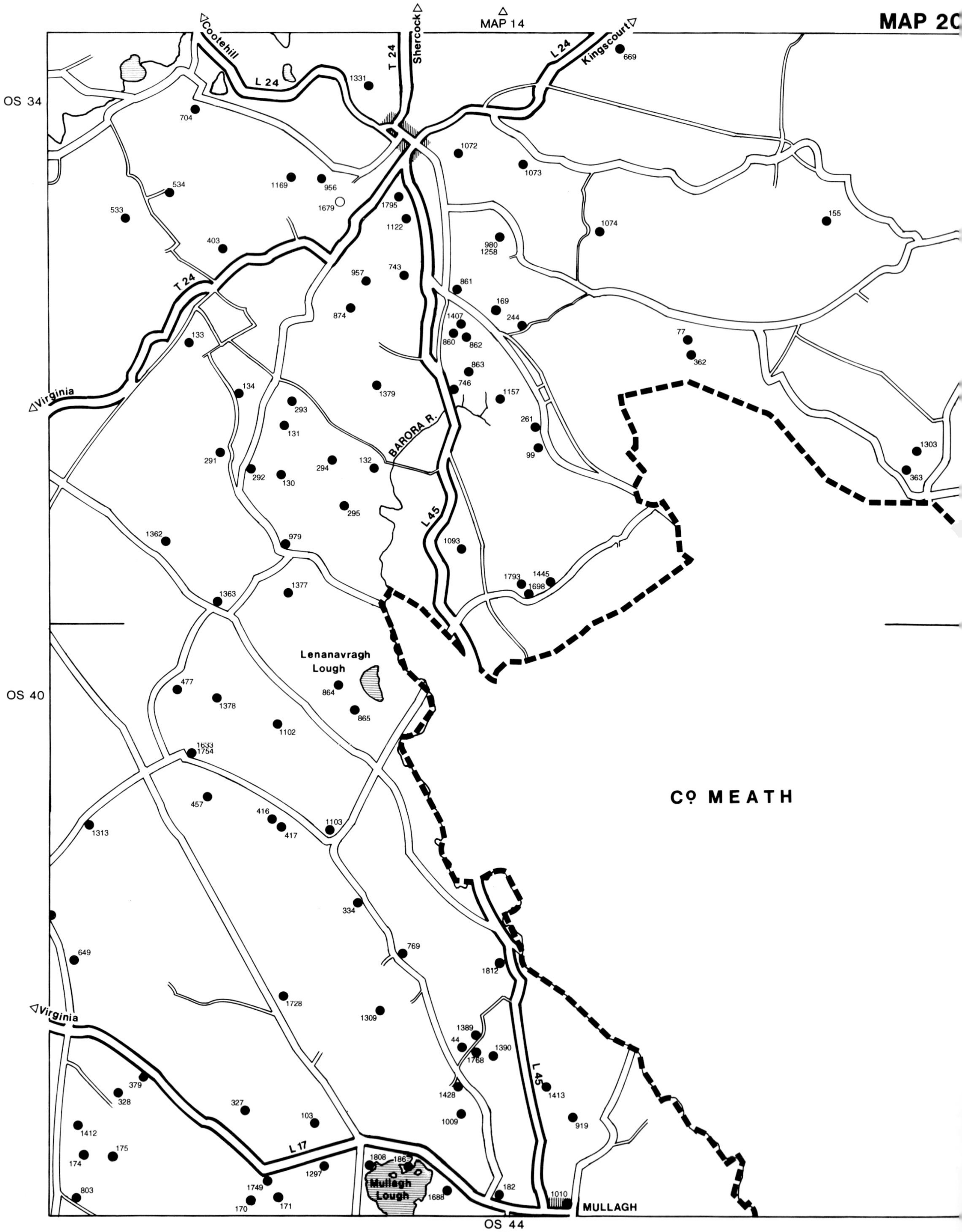
MAP 14
Cootehill
Shercock
Kingscourt
T 24
L 24
OS 34
OS 40
OS 44
Virginia
Virginia
BARORA R.
L 45
L 17
Lenanavragh Lough
Mullagh Lough
MULLAGH
Cº MEATH
669
1331
704
1072
1073
534
1169
956
1679
1795
533
1122
155
1074
403
980
1258
957
743
861
169
874
244
1407
860
862
77
362
133
863
746
1157
134
1379
293
261
131
1303
99
291
294
132
363
292
130
295
1362
979
1093
1793
1445
1698
1363
1377
477
864
1378
865
1102
1633
1754
457
416
1103
1313
417
334
769
649
1812
1728
1309
1389
44
1768
1390
379
1413
328
1428
327
103
1009
919
1412
175
174
1808
186
1297
1749
182
803
1688
1010
170
171

MAP 21

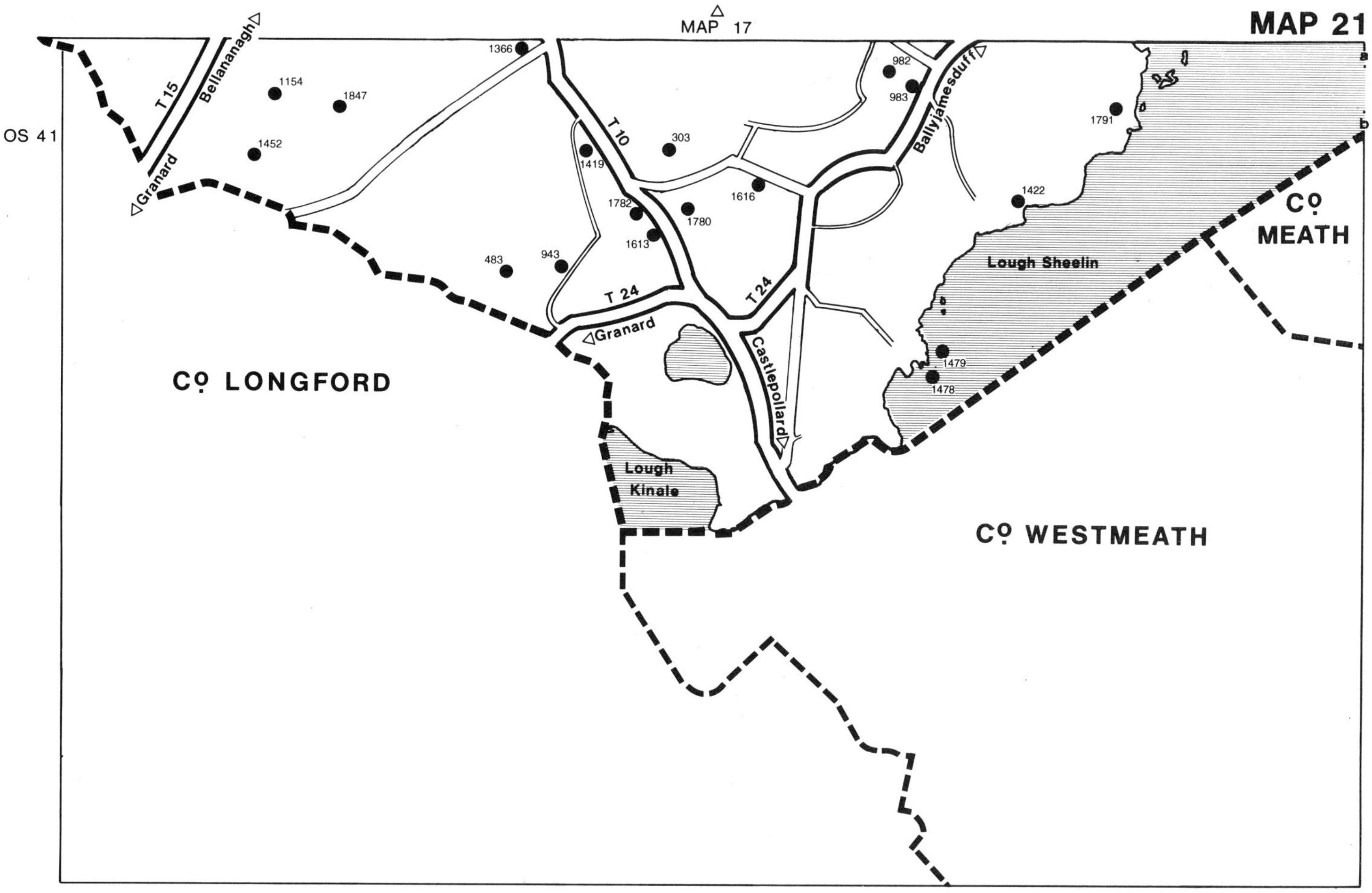
MAP 17
OS 41
T 15
Bellananagh
Granard
T 10
T 24
Granard
T 24
Castlepollard
Ballyjamesduff
Lough Sheelin
Lough Kinale
Cº LONGFORD
Cº WESTMEATH
Cº MEATH
a
b
1366
1154
1847
1452
1419
303
1616
1782
1780
1613
483
943
982
983
1791
1422
1479
1478

MAP 18
OS 42
Kilnaleck
L 3
Oldcastle
Lough Sheelin
UPPER INNY R.
Cº WESTMEATH
Cº MEATH
a
b
715
211
1416
933
999
1000
1001
1415
1357
76
75
1726
1371
1608
1718
1723
672
335
1226
109
1890
245
1137
1138
674
1094
676
677
1058
673
675
350
351
1059
686
1359
1436
1437
1438
1067
1721
1776
727

MAP 22

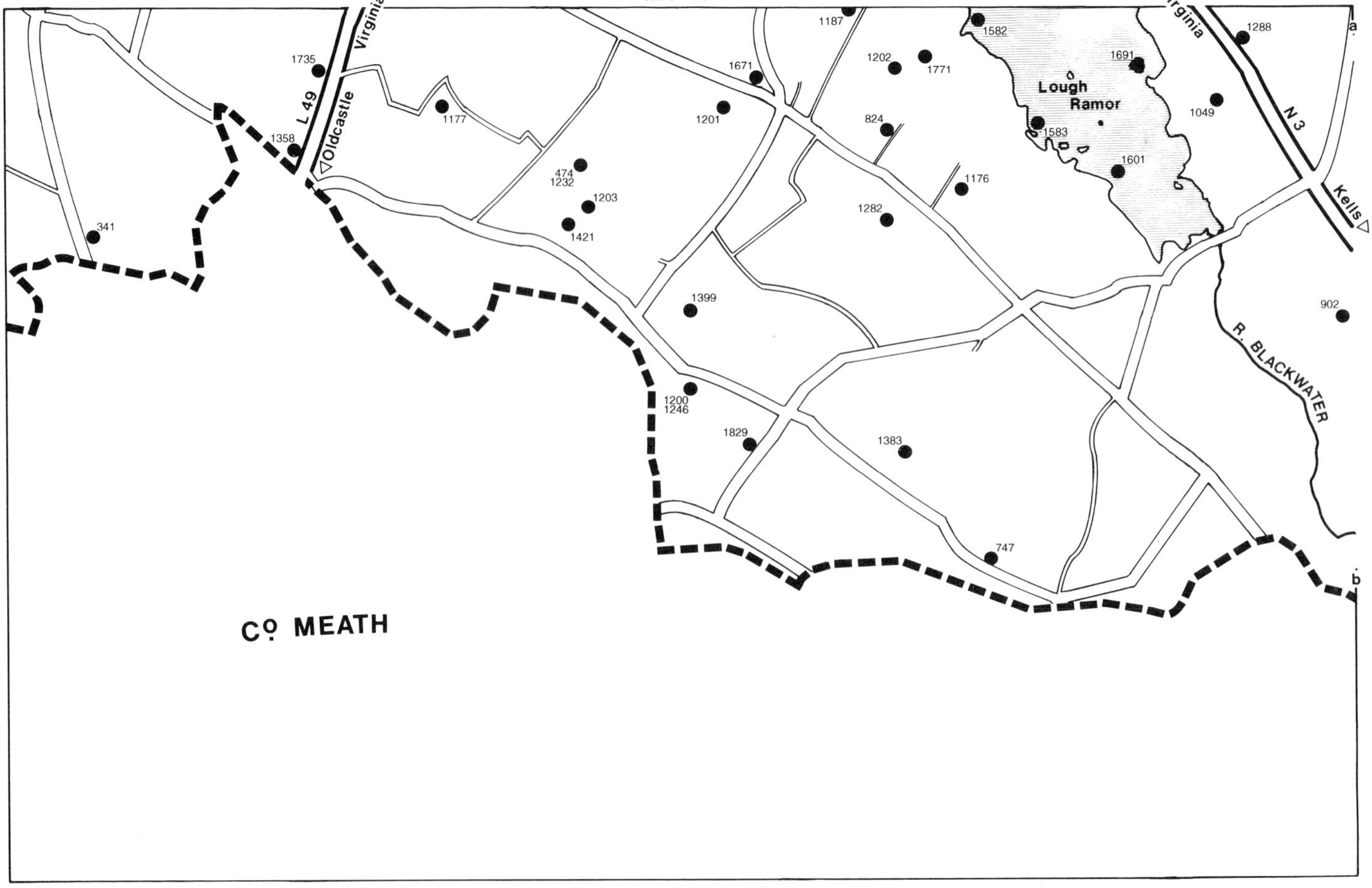
MAP 19
OS 43
Virginia
Oldcastle
L 49
Lough Ramor
N 3
Kells
R. BLACKWATER
CO MEATH
1735
1358
341
1177
474
1232
1203
1421
1187
1671
1201
1202
1771
824
1176
1282
1582
1583
1691
1601
1288
1049
902
1399
1200
1246
1829
1383
747
a
b

MAP 20
OS 44
MULLAGH
L 17
Moynalty
Virginia
N 3
Kells
R. BLACKWATER
CO MEATH
a
b
1290
804
172
326
1298
1856
1697
1896
695
1193
859
1249
110
680
681
682
684
1897
683
1651

NOTES